Commercial and Business Organisations Law in Papua New Guinea

Business and commerce form the twin engine that propels the economy of a modern nation. They ensure steady economic growth and development. In an age of globalisation, they assume even greater importance than at any time in human history. A nation risks being marginalised or left behind in the race for a share of the world economic market unless it ensures the stability of its business and commercial sector. Trade regulation, good governance and democratic institutions go hand in hand in guaranteeing political and social equilibrium. Thus, laws designed to facilitate trade and commerce are a vital component of the political and social equation.

In a developing economy such as that of Papua New Guinea, the place of commercial and business law cannot be underrated. This text, *Commercial and Business Organisations Law in Papua New Guinea*, is therefore a timely and apposite treatise in Papua New Guinea's economic environment, given the nation's vast and mostly untapped natural resources and therefore its potential for participation in the global market. The book covers business organisations law and various aspects of commercial law in Papua New Guinea.

This is a valuable book for law students, legal practitioners, accountants and business executives, not only within Papua New Guinea but also in Australia and throughout the South Pacific.

Associate Professor John T Mugambwa teaches law at Murdoch University and is a former senior lecturer and Head of Department in the Faculty of Law at the University of Papua New Guinea. **Associate Professor Harrison A Amankwah** has taught law in several law schools in Africa, United States and recently retired from James Cook University. He is also a former senior lecturer and Dean of Law at the University of Papua New Guinea. The late **Dr C E P (Val) Haynes** taught law in Africa and the University of Tasmania. He was also senior lecturer and former Dean of Law at the University of Papua New Guinea. All three authors have extensive publications on various aspects of Papua New Guinean law.

Commercial and Business Organisations Law in Papua New Guinea

John T Mugambwa,
Harrison A Amankwah,
C E P (Val) Haynes

Routledge·Cavendish
Taylor & Francis Group
LONDON AND NEW YORK

First published 2007 by Cavendish Publishing

Transferred to digital printing 2008
by Routledge-Cavendish
2 Park Square, Milton Park, Abingdon, Oxon, OX14 4RN

Simultaneously published in the USA and Canada
by Routledge-Cavendish
270 Madison Avenue, New York, NY 10016

Routledge-Cavendish is an imprint of the Taylor & Francis Group, an informa business

Typeset in Sabon by Exeter Premedia Services Pvt Ltd

British Library Cataloguing in Publication Data
A catalogue record for this book is available from the British Library

Library of Congress Cataloging in Publication Data
A catalog record for this book has been requested

ISBN 10: 1-84568-048-0 (pbk)
ISBN 10: 0-415-42532-8 (hbk)

ISBN 13: 978-1-84568-048-0 (pbk)
ISBN 13: 978-0-415-42532-2 (hbk)

To Val, Our Intellectual Colleague and Friend.
Rest in Peace.

Contents

Foreword ix
Acknowledgements xi
Table of cases xiii
Table of Papua New Guinean Statutes xliii
Table of Statutes from Other Jurisdictions xlix

PART I
Sale of Goods (John Mugambwa) 1

1 Introduction to the Law of Sale of Goods in Papua New Guinea 3
2 Terms of the Contract of Sale of Goods 13
3 Effects of the Contract of Sale of Goods 34
4 Performance of the Contract of Sale of Goods and the Remedies 55

PART II
Law of Agency (Alex Amankwah) 85

5 Agency Law in Papua New Guinea 87

PART III
Law of Banking (Alex Amankwah) 121

6 Law of Banking in Papua New Guinea 123

PART IV
Company Law (Val Haynes) 171

7 Introduction to Company Law in Papua New Guinea 173
8 Capacity and Structure of Companies 226
9 Directors' Duties 273
10 Shareholder Remedies 341
11 Corporate Liability 379
12 Shares and Company Financing 474
13 Receivership 528
14 Liquidation 562

PART V
Law of Other Business Organisations 633

15 Partnerships Law in Papua New Guinea (Alex Amankwah) 635
16 Law of Co-operatives (John Mugambwa) 683
17 Business Group Incorporation (John Mugambwa) 705

Index 721

Foreword

This work is an important addition to the growing volume of texts on Papua New Guinea law. It is also very timely because it deals comprehensively and most competently with the many laws that govern and regulate the conduct of commerce and business organisations in Papua New Guinea.

Our private sector is today growing more rapidly and widely than it has at any time since Independence. Sound fiscal management in recent years and strong GDP growth as well as government policies conducive to investment and private sector growth have combined to create a sound investment and business climate in Papua New Guinea presently.

Commercial and Business Organisations Law in Papua New Guinea will be a valuable guide to our own expanding private sector, overseas investors and to the overall sound development of our private sector.

This work has been written by academics who themselves have contributed enormously to the training of members of our own growing legal profession and the development of our key legal institutions. It therefore benefits greatly from the years of practical experience the authors have had, and their individual contribution to our evolving legal system.

Sadly, as the manuscript went to press, one of the authors, Dr C E P Haynes passed away. Dr Haynes was not only a former Dean of the UPNG Faculty of Law but also the very effective Project Leader of Access to PNG Law program initiated by AusAID and completed in 2000. That project has led to the publication of a number of text books on Papua New Guinea and I want to use this opportunity to pay warm and genuine tribute to the late Dr Haynes for his contribution to the development of our law. This publication will be a worthy and lasting memorial to his contribution, and that of his fellow contributors.

This work will, of course, directly benefit students in our legal faculties, but I believe it will be of real benefit to the legal and other professions, and importantly, business executives and leaders of our private sector generally. In a rapidly growing economy in which growth is, and must continue to be driven by the private sector, it could not be more timely.

I congratulate the authors on the commitment and professionalism that has resulted in a work of the highest quality. It will have wide use and value in Papua New Guinea today and in the future.

Rt Hon Sir Rabbie Namaliu, CSM, KCMG, MP
Parliament House,
Port Moresby, Papua New Guinea

Acknowledgements

We (Alex Amankwah and John Mugambwa) wish to express our deepest gratitude to Mieneke Haynes for her support and encouragement of Val, which enabled him to complete his share of the project in very difficult times. We are also grateful to Mieneke for keeping us posted of Val's health and progress and promptly responding to our emails when Val was too sick to do so. In addition, we wish to thank NiuMedia Pacific Pty Ltd for allowing us access to their collection of Papua New Guinean legislation and judgments on generous terms. No doubt, there are people whose assistance Val might have liked to acknowledge. On Val's behalf, we thank all those people. We wish also to thank the publishers, especially Sonny Leong, for their patience and understanding.

Alex Amankwah wishes to thank his former colleagues, Professors Paul Fairall, Stephen Graw and Wolfgang Fisher for their intellectual and moral support during the course of writing of this work. John Mugambwa wishes to thank Mr Eruel Passinganloi, Registrar of Cooperative Societies in Papua New Guinea, for providing him information about the co-operative movement in PNG and the government plans to revamp it; Sarah Costa and Yvette Maker (former law students, Murdoch University) for proofreading some of the chapters; and the Division of Art, Murdoch University, for financial assistance. We thank our respective spouses: Gwen Amankwah and Juliet Mugambwa, for their encouragement and support, which sometimes we take for granted. Finally, Alex Amankwah wishes to express special thanks and appreciation to his daughter, Alexandra Anika, for her devotion and love and for demonstrating an incredible sense of tolerance rarely seen in children of her age group.

While every care has been taken to trace and acknowledge copyright, the publishers tender their apologies for any accidental infringement where copyright has proven unascertainable. They would be pleased to come to a suitable accommodation with the rightful owners in each case.

Table of cases

195 Crown Street Pty Ltd v Hoare 400

Abbott and Co v Wolsey 6
Aberdeen Railway Co Ltd v Blaikie Bros 304
Ace Guard Dog Security Services Ltd and Yama Security Services Ltd v Telikom PNG Ltd 605
Advance Bank Australia Ltd v Fleetwood Star Pty Ltd 459
Advance Bank of Australia Ltd v FAI Insurances Australia Ltd 314
Aes v Benham 665
AGC (Pacific) Ltd v Woo International Pty Ltd 99, 226, 232, 256,261, 379, 380, 383, 394, 395, 399, 412, 418, 425–426, 433, 438, 444, 447, 449,455
AGK Pacific (NG) Ltd v Anderson 364
AIDC Ltd v ANZ Banking Group New Zealand Ltd 376
Airlines Airspares Ltd v Handley Page Ltd 541
Airpeak Pty Ltd v Jetstream Aircraft Ltd 363
Alan Arthur Morris v PNG Associated Industries Ltd 303, 324
Albert Areng v Gregory Babia 267
Alberta Ltd v Pocklington 326
Alfex Doors & Windows Ltd v Alutech Windows & Doors Ltd 600
Allam v Europa Poster Services 107
Allied Mills Ltd v Gwydir Valley Oilseed Pty Ltd 42
Aluminium Industrie Vaassen BV v Romalpa Aluminium Ltd 523
AM Bisley Ltd v Gore Engineering & Retail Sales Ltd 523
American Dairy (Qld) Pty Ltd v Blue Rio 316
Amos Bai v Morobe Provincial Government [1992] 548
Andrew Wag v Mount Hagen Town Authority 397
Anglian Sales Ltd v South Pacific Manufacturing Co Ltd 597
ANZ Banking Group Ltd v Richardson 662
ANZ Banking Group Ltd v Westpac Banking Group 161
Apple Fields Ltd v Damesh Holdings Ltd 545
AR Wright & Son Ltd v Romford Borough Council 399

Arab Bank v Ross 155, 156
Arabicas Pty Ltd v Coffee Industry Corporation Pty Ltd 214
Arcos Ltd v Ronaasen and Sons Ltd 18
Arctic Shipping Co Ltd v Mobilia AB (The Tatra) 425
Arden v Bank of New South Wales 162
Armagas Ltd v Mundogas SA (The Ocean Frost) 384, 434, 435
Armour v Thyssen Edelstahlwerke AG 523
Armstrong v Stokes 114
Armstrong v Strain 115
Arnold v Cheque Bank 165
Ashbury Railway Carriage and Iron Co v Riche 103, 396, 469
Ashford v Thomas Cook & Sons (Bankers) Ltd 139
Ashington Piggeries Ltd v Christopher Hill Ltd 17, 19, 20, 21, 22, 25
ASIC v Austimber Pty Ltd 574
ASIC v Rich 332
Astley Industrial Trust Ltd v Miller (Oakes) 47
Attorney General v L D Nathan and Co Ltd 9
Auravale Industries Ltd v Shalimar Knitwear Ltd 598
Austin v Austin 147
Austral Mining Construction Pty Ltd v NZI Capital Corporation Ltd 500
Australia and New Zealand Banking Group (PNG) Ltd v Kila Wari 545
Australia Independent Distributors Ltd v Winter 127
Australian Capital Television Pty Ltd v Minister for Transport and Communications 410, 451, 452
Australian Growth Resources Corporation Pty Ltd v Van Reesema 326
Australian Knitting Mills v Grant 24
Australian Metropolitan Life Assurance Co Ltd v Ure 313, 314
Australian Mutual Provident Society v George Myers & Co Ltd (in liq) 539
Australian Securities Commission v AS Nominees Ltd 574, 582
Australian Securities Commission v Lucas 350
Automatic Self-Cleansing Filter Syndicate Co Ltd v Cunninghame 296, 411
Automobile Association (Canterbury) Inc v Australasian Secured Deposits Ltd 519
Avoney v Ausitianus 131

B Liggett (Liverpool) Ltd v Barclay's Bank Ltd 442
B S Brown & Son Ltd v Craiks Ltd 23, 24
Badeley v Consolidated Bank 643, 644
Baden Delvaux and Lecuit v Societe Generale pour Favoriser le Developpement du Commerce et de L'Industrie en France SA 461
Bagel v MillenMiller 653, 654

Bailee v Goodwin 90
Bailey v Bank of Australia 163
Baines v National Provincial Bank 143, 157
Baker v ANZ Banking Group Ltd 163, 165
Bamford v Bamford 296, 302, 344
Bangor Punta Operations Inc v Bangor & Aroostook R Co 241
Bank of Australiasia v Breillat 651
Bank of Baroda v Punjab National Bank 136, 167
Bank of Chettinad v CIT Colombo 127
Bank of Credit and Commerce International SA v BRS Kumar Bros Ltd 531
Bank of England v Vagliano Bros Ltd 127, 136, 635
Bank of Hawaii v PNG Banking Corporation and Others 159
Bank of Montreal v Young 147
Bank of New South Wales v Milvain 163
Bank of New Zealand v Fiberi Pty Ltd 409, 447, 451, 453, 460, 461, 462
Bank of NSW v Laing 142, 143, 163
Bank of NSW v The Commonwealth 127
Bank of Papua New Guinea v Resources and Investment Finance Ltd 365
Bank of PNG v Muteng Basa 548, 549, 550
Banking Group (PNG) Ltd v Kila Wari 545
Barclays Bank Ltd v Okenarhe 130
Barclays Bank Ltd v WJ Simms Sons & Cooke (Southern) Ltd 160
Barclays Bank v Bluff 678
Barclays Finance Holdings Ltd v Sturgess 451
Barnett, Hoares & Co v South London Tramways Co 291
Bartlett v Sidney Marcus Ltd 22
Baxter v West 672
Bayclay Brothers (PNG) Ltd v Independent State of Papua New Guinea 93
BB Shipping (NZ) Limited 594
Beale v Taylor 16
Beavan v Webb 653
Beckingham v Port Jackson & Manly Steamship Company 643
Behrend v Produce Brokers Co 60
Bell v Balls 107
Bell v Capital and Counties Bank 163
Belven Enterprises Pty Ltd v Lydham Ply Ltd 452
Belvoir Finance Co Ltd v Harold (G) Cole & Co Ltd 46
Bennetts v Board of Fire Commissioners of NSW 280, 319
Bentley Poultry Farm Ltd v Canterbury Poultry Farmers Co-operative Ltd (No 2) 253
Bermuda Cablevision Ltd v Colica Trust Co Ltd 272

Bernard Nuri v Kaipel Du 397, 433, 449
Bertram Armstrong & Co v Godrey 106
Besser Industries (NT) Pty Ltd v Steelcon Constructions Pty Ltd 597
Bevan v Webb 91, 663
Bexandale v Bennet 153
Bhullar v Bhullar 306
Biddle v Bond 108
Biggerstaff v Rowan's Wharf Ltd 416, 417
Birch v Cropper 477
Bird v Brown 104
Birtchnell v Equity Trustees, Executors and Agency Co Ltd 665
Bishop Shipping Services Pty Ltd v The MV "Pedro" 604, 605, 606
Bishop v Chung Bros 655
Bishopsgate Motor Finance Corporation Ltd v Transport Brakes Ltd 43, 54
Bishopsgate Investment Management Ltd (in liq) v Maxwell 313
Bissell & Co v Fox Bros & Co 167
Bistead v Buck 105
Black White & Grey Cabs Ltd v Fox 297
Blades v Free 117
Blaustein v Maltz, Mitchell & Co 108
Blisset v Daniel 666
Bloomenthal v Ford 425
Boardman v Phipps 303
Bolton Partners v Lambert 103, 104
Bond Brewing Holdings Ltd v National Australia Bank Ltd 531, 534
Bond v Hale 666
Boorne v Wicker 677
Borden (UK) Ltd v Scottish Timber Products Ltd 514
Borland's Trustee v Steel Bros & Co Ltd 475, 476
Boston Deep Sea Fishing & Ice Co v Ansell 305
Boulas v Angelopoulos 101
Bowden v Macdonald 620
BP Refinery Pty Ltd v Hastings Shire Council 13
Bray v Ford 303
Breen Holdings Pty Ltd v Thiess Contractors Pty Ltd 595
Bricar Nominees Pty Ltd v Rowella Pty Ltd 673
Brick and Pipe Industries Ltd v Occidental Life Nominees Pty Ltd 409, 413, 417, 420, 451, 456, 460, 464, 465
Brien v Dwyer 152
Briggs v James Hardie & Co Pty Ltd 240, 244
Brinks Incorporated and Brinks Air Courier Australia Pty Ltd v Brinks Pty Ltd 207, 208, 214, 217, 521

British Bank of the Middle East v Sun Life Assurance Co of Canada (UK) Ltd 431
British Movietonews v London & District Cinemas Ltd 117
Broken Hill Proprietary Co Pty Ltd v Bell Resources Ltd 363
Bromley and Manton Pty Ltd v Eremas Andrew 380, 386, 388
Brook v Hook 103, 162
Brunninghausen v Glavanics 322
BTH v Federated European Bank 418
Budberg v Jerwood & Ward 46
Bullen v Tourcorp Developments Ltd 531
Bunge Corporation v Tradax Corporation 59, 63
Burchell v Wilde 677
Burdick v Sewell 140
Burland v Earle 344
Burnett v Westminster Bank Ltd 142, 148
Bute v Barclays Bank 168
Butterworth v Kingsway Motors Ltd 30
Buttomley v Harrison 90
BW Broughton v Longview Products Ltd 356
Byrne v Reid 662

C M L Life Assurance Society Ltd v Producers and Citizens Co-operative Assurance Co of Australia Ltd 89
CAC (NSW) v Walker 531
Calder v Dobell 113
Cameron v Murdoch 636, 678
Cammell Laird & Co v Manganese Bronze & Brass Co 21
Campbell v Ridgeway 131
Canadian Aero Service Ltd v O'Malley 306, 307
Canbook Distribution Corporation v Borins 326
Canisius Karingu v Papua New Guinea Law Society 657
Canny Gabriel Castle Jackson Advertising Pty Ltd v Volume Sales (Finance) Pty Ltd 182, 638, 645
Capital and Counties Bank v Gordon 166
Capper's Pty Ltd v L & M Newman Pty Ltd 416
Car and Universal Finance v Caldwell 49
Carlos Federspiel & Co v Charles Twigg & Co Ltd and another 40, 41
Carpenters' Co v British Mutual Banking Co 168
Carpet Mill Products (Wellington) Ltd v Williams 219
Carter Bros v Renouf 658
Cary v Rural Bank of NSW 168
Cave v Cave 524
Cayron v Russell 672, 673

CBC v George Hudson Pty Ltd (in liq) 514
CBS Inc v Ranu Investments Pty Ltd 214, 242, 256, 259
Cehave NV v Bremer Handelsgesellschaft (The Hansa Nord) 15
Central Newbury Car Auctions Ltd v Unity Finance Ltd 45
Central Province Forest Industries Pty Ltd (Provincial Liquidator Appointed) v Rainbow Holding Pty Ltd 68, 69, 79, 80
Champagne Perrier-Jouet SA v HH Finch Ltd 544
Chan v Zacharia 303, 638, 657, 665
Chapleo v Brunswick Permanent Benefit Building Society 433, 443
Charles Rickards Ltd v Oppenheim 59, 60
Charlton v Baber 377
Charter v Sullivan 70
Charton v Douglas 676, 677
Cheeseman v Price 672
Chen v Butterfield 245
Chen v Karandonis 333
Chow Yoong Hong v Choong Fah Rubber Manufactory 138
Christie v Permewan, Wright and Co Ltd 91
CIC Insurance Ltd (prov liq apptd) v Hannan & Co Pty Ltd 572
City Bank v Australian Joint Stock Bank 157
Clarke v London County Bank Ltd 130
Clarkson Booker v Andjel 113
Clay Hill Brick Co v Rawlings 417, 418
Clayton Robard Management Ltd v Siu 421
Clode v Barnes 655
Club Flotilla (Pacific Palms) Ltd v Isherwood 419
Cocks v Masterman 161
Codelfa Construction Pty Ltd v State Rly Authority of New South Wales 117
Cohen v Kittell 106
Coleman v Myers 321, 322, 330
Colland v Lloyd 131
Colley v Overseas Exporters Ltd 66, 67
Commercial Bank of Australia Ltd v Hulls 143
Commercial Bank of Australia Ltd v Younis 160
Commercial Banking Co (Sydney) Ltd v Mann 167
Commercial Banking Co (Sydney) v RH Brown & Co 146
Commercial Banking Co of Sydney Ltd v Jalsard Pty Ltd 144
Commercial Trading Bank of Australia v Sydney Wide Stores Pty Ltd 148
Commissioner for Corporate Affairs v Harvey 575
Commissioner of Inland Revenue v Chester Trustee Services Ltd 596, 599
Commissioner of Inland Revenue v Lebus 644

Commissioner of Taxation v English Scottish and Australian Bank Ltd 168
Commissioners of State Savings Bank of Victoria v Permewan Wright & Co Ltd 167
Commissioners of Tax v English Scottish and Australian Bank 129
Commissioners of the State Savings Bank of Victoria v Permewart Writh & Co Ltd 127
Commissions of Inland Revenue v Williamson 645
Commonwealth Bank of Australia v Friedrich 320, 336, 616
Commonwealth Trading Bank v Reno Auto-Sales Pty Ltd 160
Commonwealth Trading Bank of Australia v Sydney Raper Pty Ltd 151
Commonwealth v Amann Aviation Pty Ltd 81
Community Development Pty Ltd v Engwirda Construction Co 581, 582
Const v Harris 663
Construction Engineering (Aust) Pty Ltd v Hexyl Pty Ltd 649
Continental Trading Ltd v Dewe Patsy Trading as PSB Trade Store 112, 545
Cook v Deeks 302
Cooke v Eshelby 114
Co-ordinated Air Services Pty Ltd v Aircair Pty Ltd 89
Cornes v Kawerau Hotel (1994) Ltd 358, 360
Corpers (No 664) Pty Ltd v NZI Securities Australia Ltd 412
Corporate Affairs Commission (NSW) v Drysdale 277
Corporations Ltd v Brian Pty Ltd 638
Cotman v Brougham 396
Cotterall v Fidelity Life Assurance Co Ltd 359
Covington Railways Ltd v Uni-Accommodation Ltd 592, 599
Cox v Coulson 642
Cox v Hickman 636, 643
Crabtree-Vickers Pty Ltd v Australian Direct Mail Advertising and Addressing Co Pty Ltd 415, 416, 421, 423, 425, 435, 456
Creasey v Breachwood Motor Ltd 245
Cribb v Korn 639, 642
Cromwell Corporation Ltd v Sofrana Immobilier (NZ) Ltd 422, 425
Croton v R 141
Csolle (Trading as Lodi Timber Co) v ASP (NG) Ltd 50, 64, 66
Cuckmere Brick Co Ltd v Mutual Finance Ltd 545
Cue Energy Resources Ltd v Browse Petroleum Pty Ltd 364
Curragh Developments Ltd (in rec) v Rodewald 530
Curtain Bros (Qld) Pty Ltd and another v Independent State of Papua New Guinea 87, 98
Curtice v London City & Midland Bank 160
Custom Credit Corporation Ltd v Lynch 91, 94
Cuttwell v Lye 676

D Owen & Co v Cronk 557
Daewoo Australia Pty Ltd v Suncorp-Metway Pty Ltd 588
Daimler Co Ltd v Continental Tyre and Rubber Co (Great Britain) Ltd 272
Dairy Containers Ltd v Auditor-General 281
Dairy Containers Ltd v NZI Bank Ltd 281
Dalin More v The Independent State of Papua New Guinea 383
Dalton Time Lock Co v Dalton 483
Dan Kakaraya v The Ombudsman Commission 265
Danby v Coutts & Co 95
Daniels (formerly practising as Deloitte Haskins & Sells) v Anderson; Hooke v Daniels (formerly practising as Deloitte Haskins & Sells); Daniels (formerly practising as Deloitte Haskins & Sells) v AWA Ltd 319, 320
Danish Mercantile Co Ltd v Beaumont 103
Danziger v Thompson 112
Darvall v North Sydney Brick and Tile Co Ltd 300
Datasouth Holdings Ltd v Melco Sales (NZ) Ltd 597
David Gopalan v Uni Transport Pty Ltd 560, 607, 630, 607
David Wari Kofowei v Augustine Siviri 384
Davis v Contractors Ltd v Fareham U D C 117
Davis v Davis 641
Davis v Firman 680
Davis v Games 658
Davis v Pitzz 591
Day v Bank of NSW 169
Day v Bate 157
De Bussche v Alt Thesigen 106
Deadline Typesetting Ltd v Fuji Xerox New Zealand Ltd 597, 598
Dean v MacDowell 665
Decade Holdings Ltd v RKC Zeitler 294
Decro-Wall International v Practitioners in Marketing 62
Demby Hamilton & Co Ltd v Barden 42
Demondrille Nominees Pty Ltd v Shirlaw 627
Dennant v Skinner 36, 37
Deputy Commissioner of Taxation v Austin 280
DFC Financial Services Ltd v Coffey 530
Diamond v Graham 151
Dibbins v Dibbins 104
Dickinson v Lilwall 117
Dixon v Hammond 108
Donlan v Commonwealth of Australia 117
Dorchester Finance Co Ltd v Stebbing 332
Dosike Pty Ltd v Johnson 356

Downs Distributing Co Pty Ltd v Associated Blue Star Stores Pty Ltd (in liq) 619
Drakeford v Piercy 114
Drew v Nunn 117, 119
Drughorn (F) Ltd v Rederiaktiebolaget Trans-Atlantic 112
Drummond v Van Ingen 29
Dubai Aluminium Co Ltd v Salaam 384
Duffy v Super Centre Development Corporation Ltd 531, 532
Dynasty Pty Ltd v Coombs 357

E & S Ruben Ltd v Faire Bros. & Co Ltd 73
Eastern Distributors Ltd v Goldring 44
Eastern Petroleum Australia Ltd v Horseshoe Lights Gold Pty Ltd 465
Eastgate Real Estate Ltd v Walker 593
EBM Co Ltd v Dominion Bank 446
Ebrahimi v Westbourne Galleries Ltd 263, 568, 569, 673
Edge Computers Ltd v Colonial Enterprises Ltd 601
Edric Eupo v AGC (Pacific) Ltd 261
Eimco Corp v Tuth Bryant Ltd 157
Elder Smith Goldsbrough Mort Ltd v McBride Palmer 16
Elijah Harold v Regina Waim Harro (No 2) 528, 533
Emerson v American Express Co 139
Emhill Pty Ltd v Bonsoc Pty Ltd 590
Employers Federation of Papua New Guinea v Papua New Guinea Waterside Workers and Seamen's Union 364
English and Scottish Mercantile Investment Co Ltd v Brunton 442
Entwells Pty Ltd v National and General Insurance Co Ltd 412, 416
Equiticorp Industries Group Ltd (In Statutory Management) v Attorney-General (No 47) 455, 460
Equiticorp Industries Group Ltd (In Statutory Management) v The Crown (Judgment no 47) 455, 460
Equuscorp Pty Ltd v Perpetual Trustees Pty Ltd 597
Esso Petroleum Ltd v Commissioner of Customs and Excise 9
Evans v FCT 638
Evans v Rival Granite Quarries Ltd 503, 505, 539
Evans, Grey & Hood Ltd v Plantation Supply & Service Co Pty Ltd et al 75, 78, 79, 80

F E Hookway & Co Ltd v Alfred Isaacs & Sons 28
Fahey v Cooper 678
Falcke v Scottish Imperial Insurance Co 105
Far Eastern Bank v Bee Hong Finance Co Ltd 166
Farquharson Bros v King & Co 101

Farrar v Farrars Ltd 545
Farrow Finance Co Ltd (in liq) v Farrow Properties Pty Ltd (in liq) 465
Fatupaito v Bates 276
Ferguson v Tanglewood Forests Ltd 593, 600
Fernyhough v Rankin Nominees Ltd 326
Fexuto Pty Ltd v Bosnjak Holdings Pty Ltd 354, 355
Fine Art Society v Union Bank 165
Fire Nymph Products Ltd v The Heating Centre Pty Ltd 504
First City Corporation Ltd v Downsview Nominees Ltd (No 2) 513
First Energy (UK) Ltd v Hungarian International Bank Ltd 422
First State Computing Pty Ltd v Kyling 597
Firth v Staines 103, 470, 472
Flack v London and South Western Bank Ltd 165
Fleming v Bank of New Zealand 104
Fletcher Homes Limited v BE Ellis and S Baldick 594
Flight Centre (New Zealand) Ltd v Registrar of Companies 216, 217
Fliway–AFA International Pty Ltd v Australian Trade Commission 107
Floydd v Cheney 646
Fly River Provincial Government v Pioneer Health Services Ltd 394, 397
Foley v Hill 141
Forge Holding Ltd v Kearney Finance (NZ) Ltd 593
Forster v Maketu Contractors (1964) Ltd 368
Foss v Harbottle 232, 256, 260, 343, 344, 372, 373, 383
Foster Clark Ltd's Indenture Trusts, Loveland v Horscroft 540
Foster v Driscoll 647
Fowler v Commercial Timber Co 607
Franklin v Swethling's Arbitration 662
Fraser & Fraser (Trading as Wari Won Plantation) v ANG Co Pty Ltd 81, 82
Fraser Edmiston Pty Ltd v AGT 665
Fraser v BN Furnam (Productions) Ltd 106
Fray v Voules 106
Freeman and Lockyer (a firm) v Buckhurst Park Properties (Mangal) Ltd 99, 100, 101, 112, 411, 414, 416, 417, 418, 421, 423, 424, 425, 426, 428, 429, 433, 434, 455, 456
Freeman v Rosher 103
Fruehauf Finance Corporation Pty Ltd v Feez Ruthning (a firm) 107
Frykberg v Heaven and Ballymore Advertising Ltd 329, 376
Furs Ltd v Tomkies 305

Gabriel Velegamus v Paul Aisoli 532, 536, 573
Gadd v Houghton 116
Gamer's Motors Centre (Newcastle) Pty Ltd v Natwest Wholesale Australia Pty Ltd 52, 53, 56

Garina Pty Ltd v Action Holdings Ltd 368
Garnac Grain Co Inc v HMF Faure & Fairclough Ltd 93
Garner v Murray 681
Gartner v Beaton 95, 413
George A Bond & Co v Bond 301
George Barker Ltd v Eynon 541
George v Registrar of Companies 214
GFS Management Services Pty Ltd v Ground and Foundation Supports Pty Ltd 355
Giblin v McMullen 106, 157
Gibbons v Westminster Bank 163
Gibbons v Wright 132, 671
Gibson v Minet 134
Gilbert and Partners (a firm) v Knight 109
Gilford Motor Co Ltd v Horne 245, 259
Gippsland and Northern Co-operative Ltd v English, Scottish and Australian Bank Ltd 168
Glassington v Thwaites 665
Gloucester County Council v Richardson 11
Gobe Hongu Ltd v The National Executive Council 365
Godley v Perry 28
Golberg v Jenkins 650
Goldcorp Holdings Ltd v Greedus 588
Golobadana No 35 Ltd v Bank of South Pacific Ltd 364
Gomba Holdings (UK) Ltd v Minories Finance Ltd 538
Goode v Harrison 647
Goodwin v Robarts 135, 153
Governments, Stock and Other Securities Investment Co Ltd v Manila Railway Co Ltd 503
Graeme Rundle v MVIT 316
Grammar Corporation v Provetine and General Investments Ltd 433
Grant v Australian Knitting Mills Ltd 16, 19, 20, 23, 27, 79
Grant v NZMC Ltd 598
Grant v United Kingdom Switchback Railway Co 438
Grantham Holmes Pty Ltd v ANZ Banking Group Ltd 167, 169
Graves v Weld 9
Gray v Wilson 326
Great Western Railway Co v London and County Banking Co Ltd 128
Greenhalgh v Arderne Cinemas Ltd 222, 300, 326, 339
Greenwood v Martins Bank 147, 162
Grice v Kenrick 116
Grieve v Coromandel Kauri Company Ltd 376
Griffith v Peter Conway 19
Griffiths v Secretary of State for Social Services 541

Grover & Grover Ltd v Matthews 103
Guertin v Royal Bank of Canada 144

H Rowe & Co Pty Ltd v Pitts 157
Hadley v Baxendale 68, 75, 78, 81
Hallam v Ryan 240
Hamac Holdings Ltd v Sangara (Holdings) Ltd 439
Hamlyn v Houston 653
Hammer & Barrow v Coca Cola 61, 74
Handevel Pty Ltd v Comptroller of Stamps (Vic) 500
Handyside v Campbell 673
Hannes v MJH Pty Ltd 358, 359
Hardwick Game Farm v Suffolk Agricultural Products (alias Kendal (Henry) & Sons v Williams Lillico & Co Ltd) 19, 20, 23
Hardy & Co v Hillerns & Fowler 73
Harlington & Leinster Enterprises Ltd v Christopher Hull Fine Art Ltd 24
Harlowe's Nominees Pty Ltd v Woodside (Lakes Entrance) Oil Co NL 312, 314
Harrington v Browne 63
Harrisons & Crosfield (PNG) Ltd v Pous Trading Company Pty Ltd 76, 80
Hartner Trustee Ltd v Colin MacKenzie Plastering Ltd 592
Harvey v Harvey 658
Hawkesbury Development Co Ltd v Landmark Finance Pty Ltd 394, 395, 539
Hawkins v Bank of China 335, 336, 337
Hawksley v Outram 644
Hawtayne v Bourne 104
Hayman v Flewker 90
Heald v Kenworthy 114
Heap v Motorists' Advisory Agency Ltd 47, 48
Hedley Byrne & Co Ltd v Heller & Partners Ltd 106, 146
Heduru Transport Pty Ltd v Gairo Vegoli 386, 389
Helby v Matthews 12, 51
Heller Factors Pty Ltd v Toy Corporation Pty Ltd 156
Helmore v Smith 656
Hely-Hutchinson v Brayhead Ltd 100, 412, 413, 416, 417, 421, 429, 434, 437, 444
Herman Credit Ltd v Later 131
Hetherington v Carpenter 372
Hilbery v Hatton 103
Hilton International Ltd (in liq) v Hilton 326, 489

HL Bolton (Engineering) Co Ltd v TJ Graham & Sons Ltd 381, 382, 390, 429
Hodgson & Lee Pty Ltd v Mardonius Pty Ltd 152
Hogg v Cramphorn Ltd 310, 312
Hogg v Dymock 355
Holden v Architectural Finishes Ltd 305
Hollins v Fowler 164
Holroyd v Marshall 503
Hopley-Dodd v Highfield Motors (Derby) Ltd 540
Hospital Products Ltd v United States Surgical Corporation 303
Houghton (JC) & Co v Nothard, Lowe & Wills Ltd 418, 436, 442
Howard Smith Ltd v Ampol Petroleum Ltd 310, 311, 312, 313, 315
Howard v Patent Ivory Manufacturing Co 441, 444
Hudgell Yeates & Co v Watson 669
Hudley v Peacock 131
Huenerbein v Federal Bank of Australia 144
Hughes v NM Superannuation Board Pty Ltd 417, 437, 444, 472
Humble v Hunter 112
Humes Ltd v Unity APA Ltd (No 1) 368
Hutt Valley Energy Board v Hayman 219

IBF Investment Ltd v NCDC 265
Illingworth v Houldsworth 503
Imperial Loan Co Ltd v Stone 132
Importers Co Ltd v Westminster Bank Ltd 130, 166
In the Matter of the Organic Law on National and Local-Level Government Elections: Robert Lak v Paias Wingti 92
Income Tax Commissioner for City of London v Gibbs 667
Independent State of Papua New Guinea v Lohia Sisia 547
Industrial Development Consultants Ltd v Cooley 307
Industrial Equity Ltd v Blackburn 227
International Factors Ltd v Rodriguez 167
International Harvester Export Co v International Harvester Australia Ltd 540
International Harvester Co of Australia Pty Ltd v Carrigan's Hazeldene Pastoral Co 90, 91
International Paper Co v Spicer 97
International Sales and Agencies Ltd v Marcus 452
Investment Promotion Authority v Getrude Marika 271
Investment Promotion Authority v Niugini Scrap Corporation Pty Ltd 180, 207, 271
Inwards v Baker 651
IRC v Hamidian-Rad 259, 261, 270

Jacob Luke v John Ralda 82, 84, 252, 256
Jacobs v Morris 433
James Miller Holdings Ltd v Graham 540
Jay Mingo Pty Ltd v Steamships Trading Pty Ltd 108, 418, 430, 457
Jayson v Midland Bank 165
JB and BL Nominees Pty Ltd v McCormack 6, 7
Jebara v Ottoman Bank 104
Jelin Pty Ltd v Johnson 336
Jenkins v Bennett 665, 672
Jenkins v Enterprise Gold Mines NL 357, 360
Jennings v Baddeley 673
Jennings v Jennings 676
Jerome v Bentley & Co Ltd 45
Jivetuo v The Independent State of Papua New Guinea 548
JJ Leonard Properties Pty Ltd v Leonard (WA) Pty Ltd 514
Joachimson v Swiss Banking Corp 141, 142, 143, 159
John Bridge & Co v Magrath 643
John J Starr (Real Estate) Pty Ltd v Robert R Andrew (A'asia) Pty Ltd 356
John Kameku v Patilius Gamato 548
John Napi v Kundiawa General Hospital Board 267
John Shaw & Sons (Salford) Ltd v Shaw 297
Johns Period Furniture Pty Ltd v Commonwealth Savings Bank of Australia 151
Johns v Thomason 104, 470, 471, 629
Johnson v Gore Wood & Co (No 1) 333, 343
Jones v Lipman 245
Jones v Moy 671
Joseph & Co Pty Ltd v Harvest Grain Co 79
Judge Smith & Co v Renfrey 116, 117
Julius Harper Ltd v FW Hagedorn & Sons Ltd 620
Justin Seward Pty Ltd v Commissioner of Rural and Industries Bank 151

Kanssen v Rialto (West End) Ltd 444, 460
Kappo No 5 Pty Ltd v Wong 243, 250, 251
Kaye v Croydon Tramways Co 371
Keetley v Quinton 32
Keighley, Maxstead & Co v Durant 102, 111
Keith Spicer Ltd v Mansell 644
Kekedo v Burns Philp (PNG) Ltd 703
Kelly v Kelly 658
Kelner v Baxter 102, 115
Kendall v Hamilton 113, 653, 654

Kendall v London Bank of Australia 129
Kevin Masive v Iambakey Okuk 261
Kilgariff v Morris 661
Kilpatrick v Mackay 660
Kimbe International Primary School v Narpal 13, 14
Kinahan & Co Ltd v Parry 415
Kinsela v Russell Kinsela Pty Ltd (in liq) 300, 302, 326
Kirkham v Attenborough 39
KL Engineering and Constructions (PNG) Ltd v Damansara Forest Products (PNG) Ltd 449
Kleinwort v Comptoir 165
Knight v Bell 672, 673
Knightswood Nominees Pty Ltd v Sherwin Pastoral Co Ltd 368
Koenigsblatt v Sweet 469
Kokopo Building and Maintenance Ltd v Department of Police 274
Kokotovich Constructions Pty Ltd v Wallington 312, 315, 357
Kolta Development Pty Ltd v PNG Defence Force 383
Koorangang Investment Pty v Richardson and Wrench 115
Kreditbank Cassel GmbH v Schenkers 418
Kurt Reimann v George Skell 365
Kuwait Asia Bank EC v National Mutual Life Nominees Ltd 276, 332, 343
Kuya Kehi v Kelu Theodore 394

L J Hooker Pty Ltd v W J Adams Pty Ltd 110
Labouchere v Dawson 677
Ladbroke and Co v Todd 129
Lae Cordial Factory Pty Ltd v Dang Bros Pty Ltd 95, 393, 412, 413
Laing v Bank of NSW 141
Lamb (WT) & Sons v Goring Brick Co Ltd 89
Lang v James Morrison & Co Ltd 639
Latimer Holdings Ltd and Powell v SEA Holdings New Zealand Ltd 351, 353
Law v Law 664
Lease Management Services Ltd v Purnell Secretarial Services Ltd 95, 413
Lee v Griffin 10
Lee v Lee's Air Farming Ltd 229, 231
Leigh-Mardon Pty Ltd v Wawn 337
Lennard's Carrying Co Ltd v Asiatic Petroleum Co Ltd 381, 382, 383, 385
Levin v Clark 319
Levy v Napier 578

Lewis v Avery 48, 49
Lewis v Doran 586
LG Thorne & Co Pty Ltd v Thomas Borthwick & Sons (Australasia) Ltd 27
Lickbarrow v Mason 139
Linter Group Ltd v Goldberg 465
Liquidator of Contemporary Cottages (NZ) Ltd (in liq) v Margin Traders Ltd 514
Lister v Hesley Hall Ltd 384
Littlewoods Mail Order Stores Ltd v McGregor 239
Lloyd v Grace and Smith & Co 115, 381, 384, 655
Lloyds Bank Ltd v Savory 164
Lloyds Bank v Chartered Bank 164
Lloyds Bank v Savory (EB) 168
Loch v John Blackwood Ltd 569, 571
London and Cheshire Insurance Co Ltd v Laplagrene Property Co Ltd 517
London and River Plate Bank v Bank of Liverpool 161
London Bank of Australia v Kendall 129, 168
London Joint Stock Bank Ltd v Macmillan and Arthur 147, 161
Lothian v Richards 147
Lovegrove v Nelson 662
LS Harris v Power Packing Services Ltd 109
Lumsden v London Trustee Savings Bank 168, 169
Luxor (Eastbourne) Ltd v Cooper 110, 116
Lyford v Commonwealth Bank of Australia 454
Lyford v Media Portfolio Ltd 410, 451, 461
Lynch v Stiff 652
Lysaght v Edwards 4

M K Mutual Steamship Assurance Association v Nevill 112
Macaura v Northern Assurance Co Ltd 232, 475
MacDougall v Gardiner 344
MacFarlane v Barlow 377
Mackenzie v British Linen Co 162
Macleod v R 256
MacMillan Builders Ltd (in liq) v Morningside Industries Ltd 625, 626
Madden v Kirkegard Ellwood and Partners 648
Magill v Bank of North Queensland 163
Mahesan v Malaysia Govt Officers Co-op Housing Society 107, 108
Mahony v East Holyford Mining Co 438, 441
Mainzeal Property and Construction Ltd v Facility Finance Ltd 599
Manches v Trimborn 132
Manchester Trust v Furness 48

Manley v Sartori 678
Mann v D'Arcy 638
Mann v Hulme 655
Manukau City Council v Lawson 298
Marchesi v Barnes 325
Marfani & Co v Midland Bank Ltd 130, 168
Markscal Ltd v MRDC 364
Marlor Investments Pty Ltd v Symmons 75
Marquess of Bute v Barclays Bank Ltd 167
Marra Developments Ltd v BW Rofe Pty Ltd 491
Marsh v Joseph 107
Marshall v Colonial Bank of Australia 147
Marshall v Glanvill 117
Martin-Baker Aircraft Co v Canadian Flight Equipment Ltd 117
Martyn v Gray 652
Marzetti v Williams 163
Mash & Murrell Ltd v Joseph Emmanuel Ltd 41
Matthews v Brown and Co 128
Mattison v Gough 376
Max Umbu v Steamships Ltd 548
McEvoy v Incat Tasmania Pty Ltd 540
McHugh v Austral Group Investment Management Ltd 581, 582
McKay v PHC Holdings Ltd 376
McLaughlin v Daily Telegraph Newspaper Co Ltd 92
McLloyd v Dowling 668
McMahon v State Bank of New South Wales 530
Mellon v Alliance Textiles Ltd 476
Mercantile Credit Co Ltd v Garrod 650
Mercantile Credits Ltd v Foster Clark (Australia) Ltd 584
Meridian Global Funds Management Asia Ltd v Securities Commission 380, 385, 411
Metal Manufacturers Ltd v Lewis 238
Metropolitan Fire Systems Pty Ltd v Miller 338
Michael Kandiu v ANZ Banking Group (PNG) Ltd 607
Michael Yai Pupu v Tourism Development Corporation 104, 108, 393, 429, 431, 433, 451, 470, 471, 473
Microbeds AG v Vinhurst Road Markings Ltd 32
Midland Bank Ltd v Reckitt 168
Midland Counties Bank v Attwood 607
Millars' Karri & Jarrah Co v Weddel Turner & Co 61
Miller v Rice 135
Mills v Mills 300, 312, 313, 314
Minister for Lands v Frame 316
Miss Gray Ltd v Cathcart 105

Mistmorn Pty Ltd (in liq) v Yasseen 280
Mitchell v Jones 50
Mollwo March & Co v The Court of Wards 643
Mooney v Lipka 62, 63
Moran Development Corporation Ltd v Akida Investments Ltd 591, 592
Morgan Roche Ltd v Registrar of Companies 574, 582
Morgan v 45 Flers Avenue Pty Ltd 350, 352, 356, 569
Morgans v Launchbury 115
Morison v London County and Westminster Bank Ltd 165
Morley v Statewide Tobacco Services Ltd 337, 338
Morris v Kanssen 437, 438, 441, 444, 460
Moss v Elphick 668
Mousell Bros Ltd v London and North–Western Railway Co 386, 389, 390
Mt Hagen Urban Local Level Government v The National Housing Corporation 268
Mutual Life and Citizens' Assurance Co Ltd v Evatt 146
MYT Engineering Pty Ltd v Mulcon 399

National Australia Bank v Sparrow Green Pty Ltd 421, 460
National Bank of New Zealand v Walepole and Patterson 161
National Bank of New Zealand Ltd v Coltart 219
National Bank of New Zealand Ltd v Waitaki International Processing (NI) Ltd 625
National Bank v Silke 158
National Commercial Banking Corporation of Australia Ltd v Batty 655
National Employers' Mutual General Insurance Association Ltd v Jones 47
National Housing Corporation v Yama Security Services Pty Ltd 365
National Provident Fund Board of Trustees v Southern Highlands Provincial Government 265
National Provincial and Union Bank of England v Charnley 511
National Westminster Bank Ltd v Barclays Bank Ltd 160
National Westminster Bank plc v Spectrum Plus Ltd, Re Spectrum Plus Ltd, sub nom National Westminster Bank plc v Spectrum Plus Ltd 518
Nece Pty Ltd v Ritek Incorporation 416
Negiso Investments Ltd v PNGBC 545
Neilson v Mossend Iron Co 668
Nelson (EP) Ltd v Rolfe 117
Nelson v Rentown Enterprises Inc 488
Neville v Privatization Commission 246, 247, 253, 269

New Zealand Conference of Seventh-Day Adventists v Registrar of Companies 216, 217
New Zealand Couriers Ltd v Sutton 292
New Zealand Factors Ltd v The Farmers Trading Co Ltd 598
New Zealand Tenancy Bonds Ltd v Mooney 434
Newborne v Sensolid (Great Britain) Ltd 404
Newton of Wembley Ltd v Williams 52
Ngurli Ltd v McCann 302, 312, 314, 326
Niblett Ltd v Confectioners' Materials Co 24, 27, 29
Nicholls v Parkview Projects Ltd 360
Nicholson v Permakraft (NZ) Ltd 326
Nicoll v Cutts 540
Niord Pty Ltd v Adelaide Petroleum NL 348
Noami Vicky John v National Housing Corporation 267
Nolan v Watson 89
Norah Mairi v Alkan Tololo 364
North and South Trust Co v Berkeley 92
North Solomons Provincial Government v Bougainville Development Corporation Ltd 309, 315
Northside Developments Pty Ltd v Registrar-General 291, 399, 413, 417, 437, 442, 443, 446, 447, 449, 461, 466, 467
Nowra No 8 Pty Ltd v Kala Swokin, Minister for Lands and The Independent State of Papua New Guinea 547, 548

Obu v Strauss 109
Odata Ltd v Ambusa Copra Oil Mill Ltd and another 97, 180, 207, 241, 242, 244, 246, 249, 250, 251, 256, 257, 259, 449
Official Receiver v Tailby 521
Okam Sakarius v Chris Tep 266, 267, 268
Olympic Stationery Pty Ltd v Niugini Steel Corporation Pty Ltd 407, 413
Ome Ome Forests Ltd v Ray Cheong 227, 232, 239, 246, 256, 259, 260
O'Neill v Phillips 570
Ooregum Gold Mining Co of India Ltd v Roper 482
Oppenheimer v Attenborough & Son 47
Otter v Church 89
Otto Napi v NCDC 265
Overbrooke Estates Ltd v Glencombe Properties Ltd 422, 434

Pacific Motor Auctions Ltd v Motor Credits (Hire Finance) Ltd 47, 50
Paintin & Nottingham Ltd v Miller Gale and Winter 522
Pama Anio v Aho Baliki 365, 549
Panga Coffee Factory Pty Ltd v Coffee Industry Corporation Ltd 397

Pangia Constructions Pty Ltd v Papua New Guinea Banking Corporation 373
Panorama Developments (Guildford) Ltd v Fidelis Furnishing Fabrics Ltd 291, 419, 433
Papua New Guinea Forest Authority v Concord Pacific Ltd (No 2) 397
Paramac Wholesale Ltd v Family Boats Ltd 460
Parke v Daily News Ltd 339
Parkes v Batten and others 46
Parsons v Barclays & Co Ltd and Goddard 146
Partner v McKenna 664
Pathirana v Pathirana 678
Patten v Thomas Motor Pty Ltd 31
Patterson v NCDC 397
Paul Daintry Corporation Pty Ltd v National Tennis Centre Trust 94
Paul Torato v Sir Tei Abal 291, 419, 472
Pearce v Foster 672
Pearson v Rose & Young 47, 48
Pender v Lushington 371
Peoples Department Stores Inc (Trustees of) v Wise 326
Percival v Wright 330
Perkins v National Australia Bank 460
Permanent Building Society (in liq) v Wheeler 314, 320
Perrins v State Bank of Victoria 503
Peso Silver Mines Ltd v Cropper 308
Peter Aigilo v The Independent State of Papua New Guinea 383
Peters' American Delicacy Co Ltd v Heath 476
Phipps v Boardman 303, 304
Phoenix Organics Ltd v RD2 International Ltd 598
Pilcher v Rawlins 524
Pine Vale Investments Ltd v McDonnell and East Ltd 312
Pinpar Development Pty Ltd v TL Timber Development Pty Ltd 246, 254, 449
Playcorp Pty Ltd v Shaw 335
Plunkett v Barclays Bank 165
PNG Balsa Co Ltd v New Britain Balsa Co Ltd 593
PNGBC v Barra Amevo 549
PNGBC v Pala Aruai 545, 549
Pole v Leask 93, 433, 463
Polkinghorne v Holland 655
Pongakawa Sawmill Ltd v New Zealand Forest Products Ltd 523
Pooley v Driver 645
Portman Building Society v Gallwey 537
Portrait Express (Sales) Pty Ltd v Kodak (Australasia) Pty Ltd 597
Potel v Inland Revenue Commissioners 491

Powell v Fryer 335, 336
Powell v Powell 678
Prager v Blatspiel 104
Premdas v The Independent State of Papua New Guinea 246
Private Equity Management Co v Vianet Technologies Inc 326
Processed Sand Pty Ltd v Thiess Contractors Pty Ltd 595
Prosperity Ltd v Lloyds Bank Ltd 148
Prudential Assurance Co Ltd v Newman Industries Ltd (No 2) 333, 371
Public Trustee v Schultz 676, 680
Purcell v Public Curator of Queensland 539

Quan Resources Pty Ltd v ANZ (PNG) Ltd 605, 606, 607
Queen City Residential Ltd v Patterson Co-Partners Architects Ltd (No 2) 593, 594
Queensland Bacon Pty Ltd v Rees 163, 616
Queensland Mines Ltd v Hudson 301, 308
Quick v Stoland Pty Ltd 338

R v Australasian Films Ltd 386
R v Davenport 141
R v Gomez 256
R v Murray Wright Ltd 387
R v Registrar, ex p Central Bank of India 511
R v Roffel 255, 256
RA Price Securities Ltd v Henderson 551, 555, 558
Rabtrad Niugini Pty Ltd v ABCO Pty Ltd 10, 43
Rainbow Holdings Pty Ltd v Central Province Forest Industries Pty Ltd 99, 421, 423, 425, 426, 428, 432, 455, 456, 469
Raleigh v Atkinson 118
Rama Corporation Ltd v Proved Tin and General Investments Ltd 99, 422, 425
Raz v Matane 547
Re Accord Pty Ltd and the Companies Act 585
Re Adelaide Cooperative Society Ltd 127
Re Andrabell Ltd 523
Re Anntastic Marketing Ltd (in liq) 620
Re ANZ Savings Bank Ltd 142
Re Attorney-General's Reference (No 2 of 1999) 385
Re Austral Group Investment Management Ltd 581, 582
Re Automotive & General Industries Ltd 301
Re Bagot Well Pastoral Co Pty Ltd 359
Re Bank of New Zealand 216
Re Bolous 636
Re Bond Worth Ltd 514, 523

Re Bourne 680
Re Bright Pine Mills Pty Ltd 354
Re Broadcasting Station 2GB Pty Ltd 318
Re Buchanan & Co 643
Re Burnells Pty Ltd (In Liq) 574
Re Carl Hirth 239
Re City Equitable Fire Insurance Co Ltd 319, 332
Re Citybranch Group Ltd v Rackind 351
Re Civic Constructions Pty Ltd 470, 629
Re CL Nye Ltd 510
Re Coleman, ex parte Propsting 117
Re Commercial Pacific Lumber Exports Pty Ltd 568, 573, 578
Re Companies Act and Kawa Pty Ltd 612
Re Coslett 504
Re Dalkeith Investments Pty Ltd 358
Re Darby, ex parte Brougham 259
Re Diesels & Components Pty Ltd (receivers and managers appointed) 541
Re Efron's Tie and Knitting Mills Pty Ltd 446
Re Empire Building Ltd 350
Re Eric Holmes (Property) Ltd (In Liquidation) 510
Re Excel Freight Ltd (in liq) 620
Re Federal Land Company 585
Re Federated Fashions (NZ) Ltd 358
Re Fisher & Sons 636
Re Florence Land and Public Works Company, ex p Moore 505
Re Foster Clark Ltd's Indenture 540
Re Garwood's Trusts; Garwood v Paynter 662
Re General Rolling Stock Co 607
Re German Date Coffee Co 571
Re Glyn Wort 470
Re Harvey, ex parte Chapman 652
Re HR Harmer Ltd 359
Re Hydrodam (Corby) Ltd 276
Re Independent Quarries Pty Ltd 348
Re International Contract Co 111
Re Isle of Thanet Electricity Supply Co Ltd 480
Re James Allan Sannga 184, 190
Re John Willment (Ashford) Ltd 551
Re Leslie v Sneill 131
Re Lewis 101
Re Luabar Logging Pty Ltd 596
Re M Dalley & Co Pty Ltd 348
Re Mack Trucks (Britain) Ltd 540

Re Madi Pty Ltd 456
Re Maketu Contractors (1964) Ltd; Forster v Maketu Contractors 368
Re McMaster Construction Pty Ltd 680
Re Mechanisations (Eaglescliffe) Ltd 511
Re Megevand, ex parte Delhasse 644
Re Minimum Penalties Legislation 547
Re Modern Terrazzo Ltd (in liq); Bowden v Macdonald 620
Re Moore & Co v Landaur 60
Re Mowcon Ltd 102
Re Neath Harbour Smelting & Rolling Works 571
Re Neon Signs (Australasia) Ltd 559
Re New Cedas Engineering Co Ltd 438
Re Noble & Sons Ltd 353
Re Norvabron Pty Ltd (No 2) 350
Re Orbit Electronics Auckland Ltd (in liq) 625
Re Overton Holdings Pty Ltd 357, 359
Re Papua New Guinea Block Co Pty Ltd (in liq) 575, 576, 577
Re Paradise Real Estate 587, 595
Re Patridge 607
Re Peveril Gold Mines Ltd 580
Re Photo Holdings Pty Ltd 577
Re PMC Investments Pty Ltd 582
Re Polyresins Pty Ltd 349
Re Prime Link Removals Ltd 588
Re Rica Gold Washing Co Ltd 569
Re Row Dal Constructions Pty Ltd 511
Re Russley Hotel & Villas Ltd 376
Re Sairs Pty Ltd 584, 602
Re Samco Sargent Consolidated Ltd 531
Re Samoana Press Co Ltd 589
Re Severn and Wye and Severn Bridge Railway Co 491
Re Shearer Shaer 647
Re Shephard 131
Re Smith and Fawcett Ltd 299, 300, 350
Re Spargos Mining NL 357, 359
Re Standard Salt and Alkali Ltd 607
Re Stol Air Services Pty Ltd 584
Re Thames Freightlines Ltd (in rec) 584
Re Tiedmann and Ledermann Freres 102
Re Tisco Holdings (NZ) Ltd 531
Re Tivoli Freeholds Ltd 571, 572
Re TK (an Infant) 261
Re Tricorp Investments Ltd 551
Re Tru Grain Co 607

Re Tummon Investments Pty Ltd (in liq) 416
Re Tweeds Garages Ltd 585
Re W & M Roith Ltd 300
Re Wait 4
Re Waitikiri Links Ltd 356
Re Weddel New Zealand Ltd (in rec & liq) 556
Re Wenkam, ex parte Battams 648
Re White Star Line 483
Re William Hockley Ltd 581
Re Wragg Ltd 482
Re Yenidje Tobacco Co Ltd 673
Re Yenijde Tobacco Co Ltd 572
Re Yorkshire Woolcombers Association Ltd 504, 505
Rea v Chix Products (California) Ltd 529, 531
Read v Anderson 117
Reading v Attorney-General 107
Rebtrad Niugini Pty Ltd v ABCO Pty Ltd 71
Reckitt v Barnett Pewbroke and Slater Ltd 97
Regal (Hastings) Ltd v Gulliver 306, 307
Reid v Explosives Co Ltd 540
Reid v Metropolitan Police Commissioner 54
Rennie v Prospect Resources Ltd 598
Reuter v Electric Telegraph Co 469
Reynolds Bros (Motors) Pty Ltd v Esanda Ltd 504
RH Williston v British Car Option Ltd 165
Rhodes v Moules 655
Rice v Rice 524
Richardson v Landecker 399
Richardson v Richardson 143
Ricky Mitio v William G Gardner 285, 286, 410, 412
RJ Hayes Ltd v Innes-Jones 218
Robert James Reynolds v Kevin Walcott 261
Robert Lak v Paias Wingti 106
Roberts' Family Investments Ltd v Total Fitness Centre (Wellington) Ltd 598
Robin v Steward 163
Robinson v Ashton 658
Robinson v Graves 10, 11
Robinson v Rutter 116
Robson v Smith 539
Roka Coffee Estate Pty Ltd v Largo Gerebi 383
Rolled Steel Products (Holdings) Ltd v British Steel Corporation 442
Ross v Bank of New South Wales 145
Ross v Caunters 106

Ross v London County, Westminster and Parr's Bank 168
Ross McGartin Realty v Chard Holdings Pty Ltd (No. 2) 110
Rowland v Divall 30, 55, 71, 80
Royal Albert Hall v Winchelsea 116
Royal British Bank v Turquand 427, 428, 436–446, 449, 451–452
Ruben v Great Fingall Consolidated 425, 442, 467
Rundle v MVIT 316
Ryde Holdings Ltd v Sorenson 276

Sabatica Pty Ltd v Battle Mountain Canada Ltd 298, 299, 320, 333, 350, 351, 352
Sachs v Miklos 104
Safe Lavao v The Independent State of PNG (Re Kerema Town and Airstrip Land) 316
Said v Butt 113
Salomon v Salomon & Co Ltd 87, 228, 229, 237, 238, 239, 257, 615
Salvatore Algeri v Patrick Leslie 603, 620
Sandy Creek Gold Sluicing Ltd v McEachern 325
Sanford v Sanford Courier Service Pty Ltd 350, 356
Sangara (Holdings) Ltd v Hamac Holdings Ltd (In Liquidation) 98, 276, 325, 417, 428, 437, 439, 441, 443, 456, 465
Sarakuma Investment Ltd v Peter Merkendi 267
Saunders v Anglia Building Society 101
Savill v Chase Holdings (Wellington) Ltd 434, 435
Savings Bank of South Australia v Wallman 168
Savoy & Co v Lloyds Bank Ltd 130
Scarfe v Jardine 675
Schilling v Kidd Garrett Ltd 292
Schmalz v Avery 115
Schotsmans v Lancaster & York Ry 111
Scottish Co-operative Wholesale Society Ltd v Meyer 318, 354
Scottish Insurance Corporation Ltd v Wilsons and Clyde Coal Co Ltd 480
Sebulon Wat v Peter Kari (No 2) 391
Secretary for Law v New Guinea Development Corporation Ltd 295
Sednaoin Zarifta Nahas & Co v Anglo-Australian Bank 165
Segenhoe Ltd v Akins 489
Senanayake v Cheng 679
Sewell v Burdick 140
Shamsallah Holdings Pty Ltd v CBD Refrigeration and Airconditioning Services Pty Ltd 356
Sharp v Union Trustee Co of Australia Ltd 668
Ship Agencies Australia Pty Ltd v Fremantle Fishermen's Co-Operative Society Ltd 27

Shipton, Anderson v Well Bros 61
Sikkema v Kensington & Braham 514
Silkstone & Haigh Moor Coal Co v Edey 575
Silven Properties Ltd v Royal Bank of Scotland plc 544, 545
Sims v Midland Railways 104
Sipad Holding DDPO v Popovic 540
Sixty-Fourth Throne Pty Ltd v Macquarie Bank Ltd 461
Skaventos v Bevan McLean & Associates Pty Ltd (t/a Elders Real Estate Commercial 110
Smith v Anderson 638, 641, 647
Smith v Henniker-Heaton & Co 466
Smith v Prosser 153
Smith, Stone & Knight Ltd v Birmingham Corporation 250
Snow v Milford 672
Sobell v Boston 667, 675
South London Greyhound Racecourses Ltd v Wake 418
South Pacific Airlines of New Zealand Ltd v Registrar of Companies 214
Southern World Airlines Ltd v Auckland International Airport Ltd 584
Spackman v Evans 469
Spies v The Queen 340
Spirit Haus Ltd v Robert Marshall 180, 207, 298, 299, 300, 301, 317
Stadium Finance Ltd v Robbins 48
Standard Chartered Bank of Australia Ltd v Antico 335
Stanley-Hunt Earthmovers Ltd v Registrar of Companies 216
Stead Hazel & Co v Cropper 574
Steel v Matatoki International Ltd 531
Steiglitz v Egginton 94
Stein v Saywell 504
Stekel v Ellice 639, 646
Steven Naki v AGC (Pacific) Ltd 418, 431, 457
Stock Motor Ploughs v Forsyth 155
Story v Advance Bank Australia Ltd 447, 449, 452, 459, 462, 467
Straits Contracting (PNG) Pty Ltd v Branfill Investments Ltd 573
Summers v Solomon 433
Suncorp Finance Corp v Milano Assuisazioni SPA 102
Sunderland v Barclays Bank Ltd 145
Swansson v RA Pratt Properties Pty Ltd 378
Sylvanus Gorio v National Parks Board 394, 397
Symes v Laurie 9, 38, 41

Tai Hing Cotton Mill v Ching Hing Bank 148
Tapenda Ltd v Wahgi Mek Plantations Ltd 25, 26
Tarere v ANZ Bank 547, 548, 549, 550
Tasita Pty Ltd v Sovereign State of Papua New Guinea 449

Tatung (UK) Ltd v Galex Leisure Ltd 523
Taurus Transport v Taylor 298
Taxi Trucks Ltd v Nicholson 594, 596
Taylor Bros Ltd v Taylors Group Ltd 217, 218
Taylor v Smith 162
Taylors Textile Services Auckland Ltd v Taylor Bros Ltd 217, 218
TCB Ltd v Gray 466
Te Runanganui o Ngati Kahunguru Inc v Scott 531
Techflow (NZ) Ltd v Techflow Pty Ltd 375, 376
Teck Corporation Ltd v Millar 309
Teheran-Europe Co Ltd v S T Belton (Tractors) Ltd 20, 21
Tendering Tendring Hundred Waterworks Co v Jones 655
Tesco Supermarkets Ltd v Nattrass 385, 386, 390
Tetley v Administration of PNG 79
The Independent State of Papua New Guinea v Barclay Brothers (PNG) Ltd 397
The State v Danny Sunu 201, 316
The State v Graham Yotchi Wyborn 232, 244, 256
The State v Keboki Business Group Inc and Morobe Provinsel Gavman 394
The Waterboard v National Capital District Interim Commission 316
Theunissen v Filippini 669
Thexton v Thexton 330
Thomas v HW Thomas Ltd 351, 352, 353, 355
Thompson (W L) Ltd v Robinson (Gunmakers) Ltd 68, 69, 70
Thompson v Davenport 114
Thoneman v Holmes 157
Thorby v Goldberg 318
Thornett & Fehr v Beers & Son 25, 26
Thorrington v McCann 306, 376
Tian Chen Ltd v The Tower Ltd (No 1) 110, 433
Tikva Investments Pty Ltd v FCT 639
Timothy Lim Kok Chuan v Simon Goh Say Beng 180
Tinios v French Caledonia Travel Services Pty Ltd 368
TNT Australia Pty Ltd v Normandy Resources NL 479
Toba Motors Pty Ltd v Poole 41, 56, 57
Tonolei Development Corp Ltd v Lucas Waka, Minister for Forests 98, 402, 418, 468
Topfelt Pty Ltd v State Bank of New South Wales Ltd 589
Toplis & Harding Pty Ltd v Dadi Toka and Grandsen 112, 463
Tosich Construction Pty Ltd (in liq) v Tosich 627
Tournier v National Provincial and Union Bank of England 144
Tower Cabinet Co Ltd v Ingram 675
Townsend v Jarman 677

Trego v Hunt 677
Trevor Ivory Ltd v Anderson 245
Trevor v Whitworth 492, 495
Trimble v Golberg 665
Truck Wreckers (1979) Pty Ltd v Waters 26
Tsangaris v Graymark Investments Pty Ltd 425
Tse Kwong Lam v Wong Chit Sen 545
Tunier v National Provincial and Union Bank of England 145
Tunstall v Steigmann 245
Turley v Bates 38
Tussaud v Tussaud 217
Tynan v a'Beckett 116

Underwood (AL) Ltd v Bank of Liverpool 143, 165, 168, 442, 443
Underwood Ltd v Burgh Castle Brick Cement Syndicate 38, 41
United Australia Ltd v Barclays Bank Ltd 107
United Builders Pty Ltd v Mutual Acceptance Ltd 503, 505, 519
United Dominions Corporations Ltd v Brian Pty Ltd 638, 656, 665
United Dominions Trust (UDT) Ltd v Kirkwood 127
United Homes (1988) Ltd, United Homes (1994) Ltd v Workman 593, 600
United States v Milwaukee Refrigerator Transit Co 241
Universal Guarantee Pty Ltd v National Bank of Australasia 158
Universal Steam Navigation Co v McKelvie 116
Uxbridge Permanent Benefit Building Society v Pickard 442

Valentine v Michael Thomas Somare 547
Varker v The Commercial Banking Co (Sydney) 147
Varley v Whipp 16, 36, 72
Vrij v Boyle 375
Vujnovich v Vujnovich 350, 360, 569, 579

Waghi Security Service Pty Ltd v John Tembon and Western Highlands Provincial Government In Suspension 94, 402
Waikato Freight & Storage (1988) Ltd v Meltzer 620
Waitomo Wools (NZ) Ltd v Nelsons (NZ) Ltd 517
Walder v Cutts 117
Walker v European Electronics Pty Ltd (In Liq) 655
Walker v Hirsch 636
Walker v Mothram 677
Walker v Wimborne 227, 326, 340
Wallace v Safeway Caravan Mart 37, 41
Waller v Gipps 647
Walter Perdacher v PNGBC 545

Warner Holidays Ltd v Secretary of State (1983) Times 89
Warren Reid Wholesale Ltd v Custom Fleet (NZ) Ltd 593
Warren v Nuts Farms of Australia 9
Waterer v Waterer 658
Waters v Widdows 521
Watkins v Vince 92
Watson v Davies 104, 469
Watteau v Fenwick 97, 393, 415, 421
Waugh v Carver 652
Way v Latilla 109
Wayde v New South Wales Rugby League Ltd 350, 353
Weigall & Co v Runciman & Co 95
Weiner v Harris 645
Weld Weld-Blundell v Stephen 145
Westminster Bank v Hilton 160
Westminster Bank v Zang 169
Westpac Bank (PNG) Ltd v Henderson 545
Westpac Banking Corporation v Nangeela Properties Ltd (in liq) 626
Westpac Banking Corporation v Savin 460
WH Jones & Co (London) Ltd v Rea 625
White v Bank of New South Wales 165
White v Troups Transport 105
Whitehouse v Carlton Hotel Pty Ltd 310, 312, 314
Whitewell v Arthur 671
Wilkins v Jadis 157
Wilks v Howey 661
Willmott v Barber 652
Wilson v United Counties Bank Ltd 163
Wilton v Commonwealth Trading Bank of Australia 169
Winthrop Investments Ltd v Winns Ltd 302, 312
Wise v Perpetual Trustees Co 639
Withers v Reynolds 62
Wombat Nominees Pty Ltd v De Tullio 94
Wood v Odessa Waterworks Co Ltd 343
Woods v Martins Bank Ltd 133, 147
Woolfson v Strathclyde Regional Council 245
Worcester Works Finance Ltd v Cooden Engineering Co Ltd 48
WorkCover Authority of NSW v Placer (PNG) Exploration Ltd 227, 244, 246, 253, 255
Wright v Gibbons 671

Yango Pastoral Co Pty Ltd v First Chicago Australia Ltd 130
Yarlett v New Guinea Motors Pty Ltd 13
Yeoman Credit Ltd v Gregory 156

Yeomen Credit v Apps 30
YHA Hauka Coffee Pty Ltd v Kumul Kopi Export Pty Ltd and others 5, 8, 35, 36, 56
Yianni v Edwin Evans & Sons 106
Yonge v Toynbee 92, 117, 119
Young Marten Ltd v McManus Childs Ltd 11
Young v Grote 147

Table of Papua New Guinean Statutes

Accountants Act 1996 175, 236, 367, 576
Acts Interpretation (Interim Provisions) Act 1975 391
Agricultural Bank Act (Ch 139) 126
Aliens (Property) Act (Ch 14) 272
American Model Business Corporations Act 486
Assemblies of God in Australia (New Guinea) Mission Act (Ch 1002) 194
Associations Incorporation Act (Ch 142) 178, 193–195, 710
Audit Act 1989 270

Banking and Financial Institutions Act (Ch 137) 127
Banking Corporation Act (Ch 136) 126
Banks and Financial Institutions Act 125
Banks and Financial Institutions Act (Ch 137) 125, 582
Banks and Financial Institutions Act 2000 216, 535, 583
Bills of Exchange Act 128, 142, 149, 150, 152, 153, 154, 155, 157, 158, 159, 160, 161, 162, 165, 166, 167, 169
Bills of Exchange Act (Ch 240) 136
Bills of Exchange Act (Ch 250) 127, 128, 143, 149
Bills of Exchange Act 1909-1958 149
Bookmaking Act (Ch 265) 177
Building Act (Ch 301) 178
Business Groups Incorporation Act 234, 693, 708 716, 719
Business Groups Incorporation Act (Ch 144) 178, 185–187, 201, 202, 209, 705
Business Groups Incorporation Act 1974 202, 705
Business Names Act (Ch 145) 179–180, 647

Catholic Diocese of Aitape Act 2003 194
Catholic Diocese of Aitape Health Services Act 2003 194
Central Bank Act (Ch 138) 124
Central Banking (Foreign Exchange and Gold) Regulation (Ch 138) 124

Civil Aviation Act 2000 216
Claims By and Against the State Act 1996 264, 265–268, 270
Coffee Industry Corporation (Statutory Functions and Powers) Act 1991 190, 264, 287
Companies (Amendment) Act 1988 264, 441, 495
Companies (Co-operative Companies) Act 1975 692, 693
Companies Act (Ch 141) 509
Companies Act (Ch 145) 596
Companies Act (Ch 146) 181, 195, 198, 199, 200, 203, 204, 207, 209, 214, 215, 235, 264, 266, 278, 287, 296, 324, 325, 383, 394–396, 400, 402, 407, 425, 426, 445, 469, 470, 479, 481, 485, 486, 495, 502, 507, 509, 516, 517, 537, 562, 563, 564, 567, 568, 572, 574, 577, 578, 579, 582, 583, 587, 603, 606, 607, 609, 612, 613, 630, 708
Companies Act 1963 577, 578, 613, 692, 693, 703, 704
Companies Act 1997 87, 173, 175, 181, 182, 184, 186, 189, 191, 193, 194, 195, 198–225, 226–229, 234, 235, 239–241, 243, 246, 248, 249, 258, 259, 261–266, 269, 270, 273–299, 301, 309, 310, 311, 316–317, 319, 320, 321–335, 338, 339, 340, 342–345, 346, 347–351, 353, 358, 359–364, 365, 366–367, 368, 369, 370–372, 373–377, 380, 393, 394–397, 399–402, 405–412, 418, 421, 425, 436, 438, 441, 442, 447, 448–470, 472, 473, 474–503, 505, 506–527, 528–530, 534–537, 538, 541–546, 551, 552–561, 562–570, 572, 573–595, 597, 599–606, 607, 608–619, 621–623, 624, 626, 628–632, 640, 693, 704, 706, 711, 712, 718
Companies Regulation 1998 199, 211, 276, 481
Company Law Review Act 1998 444
Consumer Affairs Council Act 1993 5
Co-operative Societies Act 1965 692
Co-operative Societies Act 1982 689, 694
Co-operative Societies Regulation 2003 698
Copyright and Neighbouring Rights Act 2000 264
Customs Recognition Act (Ch 19) 200

Distillation Act (Ch 305) 177
District Courts Act (Ch 40) 531

Employment Act (Ch 373) 175
Environment Act 2000 178
Excise (Beer) Act (Ch 106) 177

Fairness of Transactions Act 1993 5, 83
Fisheries Management Act 1998 264
Fisheries Management Regulation 2000 233, 264
Food Sanitation Act 1991 178

Forestry Act 1991 190
Forestry Regulation 1998 264
Forsayth Prize Fund Trust Act (Ch 164) 196
Frauds and Limitations Act 1974 146
Frauds and Limitation Act 1988 94, 408

Gaming Act (Ch 270) 177
Gaming Machine Act 1993 177
Goods Act (Ch 251) 3, 111, 134, 241
Goods Act 1951 441
Goods Ordinance 1924 3

Hire Purchase Act (Ch 252) 5, 406

Income Tax Act 1959 175, 264, 270–271, 384, 385, 590
Income Tax (Salary or Wages Tax) (Rates) Act 1979 175
Income Tax Assessment Act 1959 639
Independent Consumer and Competition Commission Act 2002 217, 365, 387
Industrial Safety, Health and Welfare Act (Ch 175) 175, 178
Inflammable Liquid Act (Ch 311) 177
Informal Sector Development and Control Act 2004 175, 176–179, 182, 186, 187, 190
Insolvency Act (Ch 253) 180, 535
Instruments Act (Ch 254) 94, 118, 518, 519, 520
Insurance Act (Ch 256) 114
International Organizations (Privileges and Immunities) Act (Ch 87) 216
Interpretation (Interim Provisions) Act 1975 391
Interpretation Act (Ch 2) 177, 196, 264, 384–385, 391, 537, 588, 591, 592
Investment Promotion Act 1992 180, 206, 207, 208, 233, 264, 271

Judicial Proceedings (Interest on Debts and Damages) Act (Ch 52) 79

Koki Market-Place Trust Act (Ch 60) 54

Land (Ownership of Freeholds) Act (Ch 359) 233
Land (Tenure Conversion) Act 1963 233
Land (Tenure Conversion) (Amendment) Act 1987 190
Land Act (Ch 185) 547, 596
Land Act 1996 178, 264, 271, 272, 505
Land Disputes Settlement Act (Ch 45) 190
Land Groups Act 1974 202, 708

Land Groups Incorporation Act 233
Land Groups Incorporation Act (Ch 147) 187, 189, 190
Land Registration Act (Ch 191) 197, 519, 546
Lands Acquisition (Development Purposes) Act (Ch 192) 271
Laws Adoption and Adaptation Act (Ch 20) 241, 530
Lawyers Act 1986 175, 536
Licensing of Heavy Vehicles Act (Ch 367) 190, 264
Life Insurance Act 2000 535
Limited Partnership Act 1907 681
Liquor Licensing Act (Ch 312) 177
Loans and Assistance (International Agencies) Act (Ch 132) 196

Maintenance Orders Enforcement Act (Ch 279) 590
Marine Insurance (Adopted) Act (Ch 258) 241
Married Women's Property Act (Ch 281) 535
Merchant Shipping Act (Ch 242) 521
Mineral Resources Development Company Pty Limited (Privatisation) Act 1996 270
Mining Development Act (Ch 197) 535
Motor Dealers Act 1976 5

National Capital District Commission Act 2001 176
National Court Rules Act 648
National Court Rules Act (Ch 38) 45
National Housing Corporation Act 1990 196
National Institute of Standards and Industrial Technology Act 1993 216
Niugini Insurance Corporation Insurance Corporation Act (Ch 366) 196

Oil and Gas Act 1998 593

Packaging Act (Ch 285) 178
Partnership (Limited Liability) Act 1988 681
Partnership Act (PA) 87, 88, 635–637, 639, 641–642, 646, 647, 648, 650, 651, 653–655, 657, 658, 659, 661, 663, 664, 667, 668, 674, 676, 679
Partnership Act (Ch 148) 87, 182, 535
Partnership Act 1958 681
Personal Property Securities Act 199 507
Physical Planning Act 1989 178
Police Offences (Rubbish Dumping) Act 1969 389
Postal Services Act 1996 196
Pre-Independence Ordinances Interpretation Act 1949–1973 713
Prices Regulation Act 1949 388
Prices Regulations Act (Ch 320) 5

Privatization Act 1999 247, 269–270
Public Curator Act (Ch 81) 197
Public Finances (Management) Act 1995 264
Public Health Act (Ch 226) 178

Regulatory Statutory Authorities (Appointment to Certain Offices) Act 2004 286
Reserve Bank Act 1959 124
Roman Catholic Archdiocese of Rabaul Act (Ch 1012) 196

Sale of Goods Act 1979 4
Sale of Goods Ordinance 1921 3
Savings and Loan Societies Act (Ch 141) 191, 537
Savings and Loans Societies (Amendment) Act 1995 191
Scout Association of Papua New Guinea Incorporation Act (Ch 1032) 216
Second-hand Dealers Act (Ch 322) 178
Securities Act 1997 205, 365, 388, 535
Security (Protection) Industry Act 2004 175
Stamp Duties Act (Ch 117) 508, 509
Statute of Frauds (Amendment) Act 1828 146
Statutes of Frauds and of Limitations Act (Ch 330) 407
Summary Ejectment Act (Ch 202) 505
Summary Offences Act (Ch 264) 177
Superannuation (General Provisions) Act 2000 216, 535
Supreme Court Act 2001 268
Supreme Court Act 2003 200
Supreme Court Act (Ch 37) 531

Telecommunications Act 1996 196, 216, 365
The Workers' Compensation Act (Ch 179) 175
Tourism Development Corporation Act 1990 472
Trade Marks Act (Ch 385) 214
Trade Practices Act 1972 4
Trading Act (Ch 324) 178
Transactions Act 33

Unclaimed Goods Act (Ch 325) 45
Underlying Law Act 2000 240, 241
Underlying Law Act 2000 87, 200, 394
United Nations and Specialized Agencies (Privileges and Immunities) Act (Ch 88) 216

Wills, Probate and Administration Act (Ch 291) 197

Table of Statutes from Other Jurisdictions

Alberta Business Corporations Act, RSA 2000 464
Australian Corporations Act 2001 536

Banking Act 1959 (Cth) 126, 130
Banking Act 1979 (UK) 169
Banking Legislation (Amendment) Act 1989 (Cth) 126
Bills of Exchange Act 1971 (Cth) 150
Bills of Exchange Act 1882 (UK) 136, 154, 166

Cash Financial Transaction Reports Act 1988 (Cth) 130
Cheques Act 1957 (UK) 149
Cheques Act 1959 (UK) 166
Cheques and Payment Orders Act 1986 (Cth) 150, 152
Commonwealth Bank Act 1911 (Cth) 124
Commonwealth Bank Act 1959 (Cth) 124
Companies Act 1862 (UK) 230
Companies Act 1955 (New Zealand) 199, 322, 352, 507, 594, 625
Companies Act 1993 (New Zealand) 198, 199, 200, 201, 217, 240, 295, 298, 301, 308, 309, 317, 332, 334, 341, 345, 353, 358, 365, 372, 401, 418, 473, 480, 507, 536, 563, 576, 598, 601, 615, 616, 626
Companies Act 2001 (Australia) 626
Corporations Act 2001 (Australia) 335, 338, 350, 358, 444, 448, 507, 590
Corporations Act 2001 (Cth) 368
Corporations Regulations 2001 (Australia) 588
Crimes Act 1961 (New Zealand) 387
Crossed Cheque Act 1906 (UK) 166

Enforcement of Contract Act (UK) 1954 7
English Bankers' Books Evidence Act 1879 145
English Bills of Lading Act 1885 3
English Companies Act 1985 507, 518

English Factors Act 1889 46
English Partnership Act 635, 636, 675
English Sale of Goods Act 1893 3
English Solicitors Act 1957 669
European Communities Act 1972 (UK) 102
Exchange Act 1882 (UK) 136

Factors Act 1889 (UK) 3, 90
Fair Trading Act 1986 (NZ) 217

Insolvency Act 1986 (UK) 574

Limited Partnerships Act 1908 (Tas) 681
Limited Partnerships Act 1909 (WA) 681

Manitoba Corporations Act, RSM 1987 464
Merchant Shipping Act (UK) 381
Minors Property and Contracts Act 1970 (NSW) 131

Ontario Business Corporations Act (RSO 1990 462

Partnership Act 1892 (NSW) 681
Partnership Act 1908 (NZ) 681
Partnership Act 1958 (Vic) 681
Powers of Attorney Act 1971 (UK) 118
Property Law Act (Qld) 134
Property Law Act 1925 (UK) 134

Receiverships Act 1993 (NZ) 537

Saskatchewan Business Corporations Act, RSS 1978 464

Torts (Interference with Goods) Act 1977 (UK) 169
Trade Practices Act 1924 (Cth) 146

Workers' Compensation Act 1922 of New Zealand 231

Part I

Sale of Goods

By John Mugambwa

Chapter 1

Introduction to the Law of Sale of Goods in Papua New Guinea

Sources of the law

The law relating to the sale of goods in Papua New Guinea (PNG) is mostly contained in the Goods Act (Ch 251). Up to 1951, the Territory of Papua and the Territory of New Guinea had separate, although similar, sale of goods legislation: Sale of Goods Ordinance 1921 and Goods Ordinance 1924, respectively. The Goods Ordinance 1951[1] (which became the "Goods Act") repealed and replaced both pieces of legislation. This Act, just as the previous legislation, was a reproduction of the English Sale of Goods Act of 1893.[2] However, the Goods Act contains other provisions (ss 59–69), which were adopted from certain provisions of the English Bills of Lading Act 1885[3] and the Factors Act 1889.[4]

The English Sale of Goods Act 1893 was a code in the sense that it was a comprehensive and authoritative summary of this branch of English commercial law.[5] Hence, the Goods Act reflects English commercial law in the late nineteenth century. The Sale of Goods Act, ergo the Goods Act, was not intended to be exhaustive of the law relating to sale of goods. Section 58(2)[6] of the Goods Act expressly declares that the common law of England (including the law merchant), in particular the law of agency and the effects of fraud, misrepresentation, duress, coercion, mistake or other invalidating cause, continues to apply to contracts for the sale of goods. Obviously, the common law only applies to the extent that it is not inconsistent with express provisions of the Goods Act.

Whether the preservation of the common law includes the principles of equity is controversial. Traditionally, courts have been reluctant to invoke

1 Laws of the Territory of Papua and New Guinea 1949–1951 (at p 210), s 3.
2 56 and 57 Vict. c 71.
3 18 & 19 Vict., c III.
4 52 & 53 Vict., c 45.
5 *The Parchim* [1918] AC 157 at 160, per Lord Parker.
6 Compare with s 61(2) of the Sale of Goods Act 1893.

substantive rules of equity in commercial transactions. The case of *Re Wait*[7] is a classic illustration. In that case, a purchaser ordered and paid for goods in advance. Before property to the goods passed to the purchaser, the seller went into liquidation.[8] This meant that the purchaser stood to lose their money as unsecured creditor. The purchaser sought to argue that, though no legal title had passed, they acquired an equitable interest in the goods by virtue of a specifically enforceable contract. They submitted that the seller held the legal title to the goods as their (the buyer's) "trustee". To put the buyer's argument in perspective, if the subject matter of the sale was land, their argument would have been unassailable.[9] The question was whether the same equitable principle applied to goods. The House of Lords, by majority decision, rejected the purchaser's argument. Lord Atkins said that an equitable interest does not arise in favour of the purchaser by mere sale or agreement to sell goods. His Lordship observed that the Sale of Goods Act sets out elaborate rules for determining when property passes to the buyer and warned against the introduction of the principles of equity 'into territory where they are trespassers'. He added:[10]

> It would have been futile in a code intended for commercial men to have created an elaborative structure of rules dealing with rights at law, if at the same time it was intended to leave, subsisting with the legal rights, equitable rights inconsistent with, more extensive, and coming into existence earlier than the rights so carefully set out in the various sections of the Code.

Papua New Guinea was not the only jurisdiction to adopt the English Sale of Goods Act. All Australian states and most common law countries re-enacted it with little or no amendment. In England, the Sale of Goods Act was amended for the first time in 1973 and again in 1977. Two years later it was consolidated and re-enacted as the Sale of Goods Act 1979.[11] In PNG and in most other countries the Act remains practically as it was when first enacted in 1893.[12] Therefore, English cases (as well as cases of other

7 [1927] 1 Ch D 606.

8 See below for discussion of the rules regarding passing of property to the buyer.

9 In a contract of sale of land, which is enforceable by specific performance the purchaser acquires an equitable interest ahead of conveyance of a legal interest, see *Lysaght v Edwards* [1876] 2 Ch D 499.

10 *Re Wait* [1927] 1 Ch D 606 at 634–635. (Compare *Lysaght v Edwards*, ibid).

11 There were further amendments to the latter Act in 1994 and 1996. The amendments are mainly inserted for protection of consumers (end-users) as opposed to dealers. See Furmston, M, *Sale and Supply of Goods* (3rd edn, Cavendish, London, 2000), pp 1–6.

12 In Australia, for example, most states have made only minor amendments to the original Act. However, certain modern legislation overrides some of its provisions. For example, the Trade Practices Act 1972 implies certain non-excludable terms in a contract of sale of goods by a corporation to a consumer.

jurisdictions) interpreting similar provisions, though not binding on PNG courts, are highly persuasive.[13] Readers should of course exert caution when reading cases based on amended provisions.

Other sources

Apart from the Goods Act, several other statutes may directly or indirectly affect a sale of goods transaction. These include the Fairness of Transactions Act 1993; Consumer Affairs Council Act 1993; Hire Purchase Act (C 252); Prices Regulations Act (C 320); and the Motor Dealers Act 1976. In addition, s 58(2) of the Goods Act expressly preserves the application of the common law to contracts for the sale of goods. It is thought that customary law is not a source of law in this regard, though it might influence the judicial interpretation of the Goods Act. For example, the courts might take customary law into account when determining usage of trade or practice in relation to particular transactions.

Essence of a contract of sale of goods

The Goods Act applies only to a contract for the sale of goods. Section 3(1) of the Act defines such contract as one "where the seller transfers or agrees to transfer the property in goods to the buyer for a money consideration called the price". Thus, a contract of sale of goods has four essential elements: (i) a contract; (ii) the object of which is to transfer property; (iii) the subject matter is goods; and (iv) the consideration must be money. If any one of these elements is missing, then the transaction is not a sale of goods contract and the Goods Act does not apply to it. We shall briefly discuss these elements.

Contract

Subject to express provisions of the Goods Act, a contract of sale of goods must comply with the underlying law of contract. Hence, there must be offer and acceptance, intention to contract, capacity to contract, and consideration. Readers should refer to textbooks on the specialised law of contract for detailed discussion of these elements.[14]

Formalities

A contract for sale of goods may be oral, in writing, partly oral and partly in writing, or implied from the conduct of the parties.[15] However, s 6(1) of

13 *YHA Hauka Coffee v Kumul Kopi Export* [1991] PNGLR 331 at 334–335.

14 See generally Roebuck, Srivastava and Nongorr, *The Context of Law of Contract in Papua New Guinea* (UPNG Press, Port Moresby, 1984).

15 Goods Act, s 5.

the Goods Act provides that where the value of the goods is K20 or more, the contract is not enforceable unless a written note or memo of the contract is made and signed by the party being sued or their agent. For example, if the seller sues the buyer for breach of contract, the contract is not enforceable against the buyer unless the buyer signed a written note or memo of the contract. The same would be the case where the buyer sues the seller. However, it is not required for the person seeking to enforce the contract to have signed the memo.

For a note or memo to be effective, it must contain all essential terms of the contract. The case of *JB and BL Nominees Pty Ltd v McCormack*,[16] decided by the Supreme Court of Western Australia, illustrates this point. There, the defendant entered into a contract to sell a tractor to the plaintiff. They agreed that the defendant would deliver the goods within three days from the date of the contract. The defendant's agent signed a written note evidencing the contract. The note did not specify the delivery date or the date of payment. Subsequently, the parties verbally agreed to extend the date of delivery of the vehicle. In the event, the seller failed to deliver the goods and the buyer sued for breach of contract. The seller, in their defence, argued that the contract was unenforceable because the note they signed was not sufficient in that there was no mention of the delivery date and date of payment. The Supreme Court of Western Australia held that a memo sufficient to support a contract of sale of goods must contain all terms expressly agreed upon by the parties. In this case the note was not sufficient because it omitted the date for delivery of the goods and the payment date. The court rejected the buyer's submission that the defect was 'cured' by the subsequent verbal agreement to extend the delivery date. Burt CJ said that a memo must witness a complete contract. Therefore, if there was a subsequent verbal variation of the contract, it was further proof that the note the seller signed was insufficient.

Receipt and acceptance of the goods

The requirement for a written note or memo is dispensed with if the buyer accepts and actually receives the goods or part of the goods, or pays a deposit (Goods Act, s 6(1)(a)). It should be noted that the term "acceptance" has more than one meaning under the Goods Act. For the purposes of formation of a contract for the sale of goods, a buyer is deemed to accept the goods if their conduct in relation to the goods is indicative of an acknowledgement of a pre-existing contract. For example, in *Abbott and Co v Wolsey*,[17] the plaintiff entered into an oral contract to sell to the defendant

16 [1982] WAR 258.
17 [1895] 2 QB 97.

certain goods in accordance with a sample they supplied. When the plaintiff delivered the goods, the defendant, after examining the goods, said that they did not match the sample and rejected them. In an action for breach of contract the defendant contended, *inter alia*, that the contract was unenforceable because it was neither evidenced by a written note, nor had the goods been accepted. The issue was whether the defendant had accepted the goods within the meaning of the equivalent of s 6(3) of the Goods Act. It was held that a buyer accepts the goods if upon receipt of the goods he or she does anything in relation to the goods that shows the existence of a contract of sale. In this case, upon receipt of the goods, the defendant not only inspected the goods but also said that they did not match the sample, meaning a sample previously given under a contract of sale. Therefore, the defendant acknowledged the existence of a contract of sale of goods. The fact that the defendant rejected the goods was irrelevant to the matter at hand.

In practice, the statutory formalities are rarely an issue. The reason for this is that in most transactions the buyer accepts and receives the goods at the time of the contract or pays a deposit. In any case, legally, there is nothing to prevent the parties from proceeding with an oral contract for the sale of goods if they so wish, since failure to comply with the statutory formalities does not render the contract void *ab initio*. Rather, the contract is not legally enforceable by a court should one of the parties decide not to proceed with it.

The formal requirements for the formation of a contract of sale of goods, especially as to written memos, have been criticised by several writers. The original reason for the formalities was to curb fraudulent behaviour of people claiming or denying the existence of a contract of sale of goods. However, as the case of *JB and BL Nominees Pty Ltd v McCormack* demonstrates, the formalities, more often than not, perpetuate fraud by allowing the guilty parties to avoid an otherwise binding contract simply on the ground of the lack of a written memo. Interestingly, an oral contract to purchase shares in a company worth several hundred kina is binding, yet a contract to purchase a book worth K20 is not binding unless the contract is evidenced by a written note or otherwise complies with s 6(3) of the Goods Act. In England and in most states in Australia this requirement has been dispensed with.[18] It is suggested that PNG should do likewise.

Transfer and agreement to transfer property

Section 3(4) of the Goods Act, draws a distinction between "transfer" and an 'agreement to transfer' property in goods. The former refers to a contract of sale of goods whereby the property or ownership is conveyed at the

18 See for example, s 2 of the Law Reform (Enforcement of Contract Act) (UK) 1954.

time of the contract. The latter refers to a contract of sale of goods whereby the passage of property in the goods to the buyer is to take place in the future, or is subject to fulfilment of certain conditions. For example, if you sell your commercial law textbook to another student on the condition that property will not pass until she pays the purchase price, the contract is an agreement to sell because the passing of property is conditional on payment. It will become a sale when the condition is fulfilled (s 3(5)).[19] Meanwhile, the contract binds both parties. As we shall presently see, the passing of property to the buyer is a focal point on which several matters are resolved under the Goods Act.[20]

Property

The essence of a contract of sale of goods is for the seller to transfer possession and property in the goods to the buyer immediately or at some future time. Section 1 of the Goods Act defines the term "property" as the "general property in the goods and not merely a special property". Neither the expression "general property" nor "special property" is defined in the Act. At common law the term "general property" refers to the absolute legal interest in the goods, ownership. In contrast, "special property" refers to lesser or limited proprietary interests.[21] For example, if you hire a car from a car hire company, your right to possess and use the car during the hire period is "special property".[22] Your contract with the company is not a contract of sale of goods because its object is not to transfer general property in the goods; rather to give you a right of possession and use of the car for a limited period.

Goods

The subject matter of a contract of sale of goods must be "goods". Section 1, the interpretation section of the Goods Act, defines the term goods as including "all chattel personal other than things in action and money". Basically, this definition covers all forms of personal property except intangibles.[23] The definition of goods also includes "emblements". These are crops that are

19 See for example, *YHA Hauka Coffee v Kumul Kopi Export* [1991] PNGLR 331.

20 See below, p. 40.

21 'The very expression "special property" seems to exclude the notion of that general property which is the badge of property ownership': *The Odessa* [1916] 1 AC 145 at 158, per Lord Mersey.

22 In *The Odessa,* ibid, Lord Mersey thought that the term 'special interest' was a better expression than special property.

23 'Intangibles' or 'things in action' refer to property that the rightful owner can only recover from the wrongdoer by legal action and not by taking possession (self-help). Examples of things in action include company shares, bank cheques and trademarks.

planted and harvested within a period of twelve months, such as vegetables, potatoes and corn.[24] Fixtures or things attached to land may be sold as goods provided it is agreed to sever them before the sale or under the contract of sale. For example, a contract for the sale of a dismountable building, which was to be severed from the land, was held to be a contract of sale of goods.[25] Where there is no legal obligation to sever the fixture from the land, the transaction is not a contract of sale of goods but rather one of sale of land.[26]

Consideration

The consideration in a contract of sale of goods ("the price") must be money. A contract of sale where the parties exchange goods as consideration clearly is not a contract of sale of goods. The situation is more complicated where the consideration is partly money and partly goods. For example, suppose B buys a new car from Mosby Car Dealers trading in his old car as part of the purchase price, is the transaction a contract of sale of goods? We suggest that it is, on the basis that the trade-in of B's old car was intended as collateral or subsidiary arrangement to the contract of sale of the new car. Another way of looking at it is, if before the contract the parties agreed on the monetary value of the trade-in car, then the total of that value and the top-up money paid by B is the 'monetary' consideration for the new car.[27]

Contract of goods distinguished from other transactions

The Goods Act applies only to contracts of sale of goods. For this reason it may be important to determine whether a transaction involving goods is a contract of sale of goods or not. Let us consider some common examples.

Gift

The main distinguishing feature between a gift and a contract of sale of goods is, of course, the lack of consideration in a gift. The distinction is so obvious that it is rarely an issue whether a transaction is a gift or a contract of sale of goods. However, as the English case of *Esso Petroleum Ltd v Commissioner of Customs and Excise*[28] demonstrates, there may be cases where it is not clear whether a transaction is supported by monetary consideration or not.

24 *Graves v Weld* (1833) 110 ER 731. Crops that are not emblements include coffee and palm trees.
25 *Symes v Laurie* (1985) 2 Qd R 547.
26 *Warren v Nuts Farms of Australia* (1981) WAR 134.
27 Sutton, K C T, *Sales and Consumer Law* (4th edn, LBC Information Services, North Ryde, NSW, 1995), pp 55–57.
28 [1976] 1 All ER 117. Cf *Attorney General v L D Nathan and Co Ltd* (1990) 1 NZLR 129.

The case concerned a petrol sales promotion scheme, under which a world football cup souvenir coin was "given away" at petrol stations for every gallon of Esso petrol purchased. The issue was whether the coins were produced for "general sale" in terms of a certain legislative provision. A majority of the House of Lords held that the coins were not transferred for monetary consideration but in consideration of the customer entering into a collateral contract to purchase an appropriate amount of petrol. The coins were therefore not produced for "general sale" but rather for distribution by way of gift.

Bailment

Bailment is the delivery of goods by the owner (bailor) into the possession of another person (bailee) upon an express or implied condition that the goods must be restored to the bailor as soon as the purpose for which bailment was entered into is accomplished.[29] The main distinguishing feature between bailment and sale of goods is that bailment entails transfer of possession only and not property or ownership. For example, if one borrows a book from the library, the transaction is bailment. During the currency of the bailment the bailee has "special property" in the goods whilst the bailor retains the 'general property' in the goods. Bailment may be gratuitous (for example, where a friend lends another his or her book) or contractual.

Contract of service

Historically, it has been controversial whether a contract for the provision of service and labour is classified as a contract of service or sale of goods. For example, suppose I service my car at a garage and the garage charges me K50 for the parts and K200 for labour. Is that a contract of service or a contract of sale of goods? The problem is illustrated by the following famous English cases, *Lee v Griffin*[30] and *Robinson v Graves*.[31]

In *Lee v Griffin*, the plaintiff, a dentist, entered into an oral contract with his patient to make a set of false teeth for the patient. The plaintiff proceeded to make the teeth, but the patient died before the teeth were delivered. The executor of the deceased's estate (the defendant) refused to pay for the goods. In an action for breach of contract the defendant argued that the contract, being one of sale of goods, was not enforceable because it was not evidenced by a written note signed by the deceased. The plaintiff, in response, contended that the contract was not for sale of goods but rather for provision of service, hence, it was not necessary to evidence it in writing.

29 *Rabtrad Niugini Pty Ltd v ABCO Pty Ltd* (1990) PNGLR 155 at 160.
30 (1861) 1 B & S 272.
31 [1935] 1 KB 579.

The issue was whether the contract was for the sale of goods or for service. It was held that the test is as follows: where the end result of a contract was for the sale or transfer of property in a chattel, then it is a contract of sale of goods, no matter how great the skill involved. Conversely, if the end result of the contract is that a party has done work, which ends in nothing that can become the subject of a sale, then it is a contract of service. Applying the test to this case, it was held that the contract was one for the sale of goods because the outcome was the production of a chattel.

In contrast, in *Robinson v Graves*, the plaintiff, a painter, entered into an oral contract with the defendant to paint a portrait of a certain person. After the plaintiff had commenced painting the portrait, the defendant purported to repudiate the contract. In an action for breach of contract, the defendant argued that the contract was not enforceable, as it was not evidenced by a written memo. The issue was whether the contract was for the sale of goods or provision of service. It was held that if the substance of the contract is the production of a chattel, then it is one of sale of goods; but if it is the exercise of skill and labour, the production of the article being incidental, then it is a contract of service and material. In this case, the court found that the contract was essentially for the supply of skill and labour, hence it was enforceable.

Apart from the formal requirements for the formation of a contract of sale of goods, the distinction between a contract of sale of goods and provision of service is probably not that significant. Originally, the distinction was important because there are certain conditions that the Goods Act implies in a contract for the sale of goods, for example, as regards the quality of the goods.[32] However, dicta in some English authorities suggest that the common law implies similar conditions in a contract for work and the supply of materials.[33] If the PNG courts follow the latter authorities then the distinction between a contract for sale of goods and provision of work and material will cease to be legally significant, except in relation to formalities for creation of a contract for sale of goods.

Hire purchase and sale of goods

A contract of hire purchase is a form of bailment. In such a contract the owner of goods hires them out to another ("hirer") subject to periodic instalment payments over a specified period of time. At the end of the period the hirer has an option to purchase the goods by paying a final instalment. Even though hirers invariably exercise the option to purchase, a hire purchase contract is not a contract of sale of goods because during the currency of

32 See 'implied terms' below.

33 *Young Marten Ltd v McManus Childs Ltd* [1968] 2 All ER 1169 at 1179–80, per Lord Wilberforce. See also *Gloucester County Council v Richardson* [1968] 2 All ER 1181.

the agreement the hirer has no legal obligation to buy.[34] The contract becomes one of contract of sale of goods when the hirer exercises the option to purchase.[35] Until then, the Goods Act does not apply to the transaction.

34 *Helby v Matthews* [1895] AC 471 at 475–476; *Belsize Motor Supply Company v Cox* [1914] 1 KB 244 at 251.

35 *Helby v Matthews* [1895] AC 471 at 476.

Chapter 2

Terms of the Contract of Sale of Goods

Introduction

In the course of negotiating a contract of sale of goods, the parties make several statements to each other in relation to the contract. Some of the statements may be terms of their contract and others just mere representations.

Mere representations

These are statements, which might have induced the other party to enter into the contract, but which the parties did not intend to be terms of their contract. Whether the parties intended a particular statement to form a term of their contract is not always easy to determine. The courts employ several guidelines, none of which is conclusive, to resolve the issue. These include the importance of the statement to the parties, whether the statement was in writing, lapse of time between making of the statement and entering into the contract, and so on. For discussion of these guidelines and the remedies for misrepresentation, readers should refer to textbooks on the law of contract.

Terms

The terms of a contract may be express or implied. Express terms are terms that the parties agreed upon orally or in writing to form part of their contract. Where there are no express terms of the agreement, in certain circumstances the court may imply a term or terms if necessary to give business efficacy to the contract. In *BP Refinery Pty Ltd v Hastings Shire Council*,[1] the Privy Council stated certain guidelines used by the courts to determine

1 (1977) 52 ALJR 20 at 26. Cited with approval in *Yarlett v New Guinea Motors Pty Ltd* [1985] PNGLR 14 at 18. See also *Kimbe International Primary School v Narpal* [1987] PNGLR 442 at 444.

whether to imply a particular term to a contract:

> (1) it must be reasonable and equitable; (2) it must be necessary to give business efficacy to the contract, so that no term will be implied if the contract is effective without it; (3) it must be so obvious that "it goes without saying"; (4) it must be capable of clear expression; (5) it must not contradict any express term of the contract.

Usage of trade and statutory implied terms

A term may also be implied in a contract of sale of goods or any other commercial agreement in conformity with the usual custom of a particular trade or business.[2] In addition, and more importantly for our purposes, the Goods Act implies certain terms in a contract of sale of goods, which the parties are free to vary or exclude by express agreement or course of dealing.[3] We shall discuss these terms presently. Before we do, it is important for readers to understand the classification of contractual terms and the significance of this to the terms of a contract.

Classification of terms

Conditions and warranties

The Goods Act draws a distinction between a "condition" and "warranty". A condition is a term of a contract whose breach is so serious that it entitles the innocent party, if they so desire, to be relieved from any further performance of the contract.[4] In contrast, a warranty is a less serious term whose breach only entitles the innocent party to sue for damages, but not to terminate the contract.[5] Whether a term is a condition or warranty depends on the intention of the parties as gathered from the contract and all surrounding circumstances.[6] The mere fact that the parties called a particular term a condition or warranty is not conclusive.[7] As we shall see, under s 12(4) of the Goods Act, in certain circumstances a buyer is forced to treat the breach of a condition as a breach of a warranty, and is thereby denied the right of rejecting the goods and treating the contract as terminated.

2 *Kimbe International Primary School Narpal* [1987] PNGLR 442.
3 Goods Act, s 55.
4 Goods Act, s 12(2)(a).
5 Goods Act, ss 1(1) and 12(2)(b).
6 Goods Act, s 12(2).
7 Goods Act, s 12(3).

Conversely, a buyer may waive any condition to be fulfilled by the seller or elect to treat a breach of condition as a breach of warranty.[8]

Innominate terms

Although the Goods Act refers only to "conditions" and "warranties", it is established by several authorities that this classification is not exhaustive.[9] There are certain terms for which, at the outset, it cannot be said whether their breach would entitle the innocent party to repudiate the contract or only to sue for damages. Such terms are commonly known as "innominate" or "intermediary" terms. The consequence of breach of an innominate term depends on the seriousness of the breach. The English case of *Cehave NV v Bremer Handelsgesellschaft (The Hansa Nord)*[10] is a classic illustration of this point. In that case, the defendants entered into a contract to sell citrus pulp pellets to the plaintiffs for use in animal food. One of the terms of the contract was that the goods should be shipped in "good condition". The plaintiffs paid the purchase price in advance. The goods, when delivered, were in a damaged state and the plaintiffs rejected them, purportedly because the term "goods in good condition" was a condition of the contract whose breach entitled them to treat the contract as repudiated and to a refund of the purchase price. The defendant refused to refund the purchase price. The goods were left at the port and, subsequently, the port authority sold the goods to another person. Ironically, that other person later sold them to the plaintiffs at a fraction of the original price. Reportedly, the plaintiff used the goods for the same purpose as they originally intended to use them. The plaintiffs sued to recover the purchase price on the ground of total failure of consideration. The issue was whether the term "goods shipped in good condition" was a condition or a warranty. It was held that the term was neither strictly a condition nor a warranty: "It was one of those intermediate stipulations which give no right to reject unless the breach goes to the root of the contract."[11] The fact that the plaintiffs were able to use the goods in their "damaged" state showed that the breach was not sufficiently serious as to justify their rejection of the goods.

Terms implied by the Goods Act

The Goods Act implies the following terms in a contract of sale of goods:

- condition that the goods correspond with the description;
- condition that the goods are of merchantable quality;

8 Goods Act, s 12(1).
9 *Cehave NV v Bremer Handelsgesellschaft (The Hansa Nord)* [1975] 3 All ER 739 at 746.
10 [1975] 3 All ER 739.
11 Ibid, at 748, per Lord Denning MR.

- condition that the goods are fit for a particular purpose;
- condition that the goods correspond with sample;
- condition that the seller has title to the goods; and
- warranty of quiet enjoyment.

Each of the above terms will be examined in turn. It should be remembered that the implied terms are subject to any express agreement of the parties. The Goods Act is founded on the notion of freedom of contract, which means that the parties are generally free to insert any terms in their contract and to vary or exclude any term implied by the Act (s 55).

Correspondence with description

Section 14(1) provides that where goods are sold by description there is an implied condition that the goods shall correspond with the description given by the seller. This condition is only implied in a situation where the buyer relies on the seller's description of the goods. The obvious example is where the buyer has not seen the goods.[12] Thus, a contract to purchase unascertained or future goods (for example a computer to be imported by the seller) is necessarily one by description. At one time there was controversy as to whether a contract of sale of specific goods, or goods which the buyer examines before the contract, could be one by description. The view was that in such a situation the buyer could not claim to have relied on the seller's description of the goods. However, it has been established by several authorities that in certain circumstances sale of specific goods could be by description. In *Grant v Australian Knitting Mills Ltd,* the Privy Council held that a specific thing is sold by description "as long as it is sold not merely as the specific thing, but as a thing corresponding with a description".[13] For example, in *Beale v Taylor,*[14] the seller advertised their car for sale and described the car in the advertisement. The seller sought to argue that the contract was not one of sale by description because the goods were specific. It was held that the sale was by description because the buyer relied on the description of the car in the seller's advertisement.

The case of *Elder Smith Goldsbrough Mort Ltd v McBride Palmer*[15] also illustrates this point. The buyer purchased a bull at an auction sale. In the catalogue the bull was described as a "breeding bull". Also, at the auction, breeding bulls were separated from other bulls and the auctioneer reportedly told the buyer that the subject bull was a breeding bull. The bull turned out to be infertile. The buyer contended that the seller was in breach of the

12 *Varley v Whipp* [1900] 1 QB 513.
13 [1936] AC 85 at 100.
14 [1967] 3 All ER 253.
15 [1976] NSWLR 631.

implied condition that goods sold by description must correspond with the description. In response, the seller argued that it was not a contract of sale by description because the goods were specific and available for the buyer's inspection. It was held that normally where the buyer has an opportunity to inspect the goods, the contract is not by description. However, in this case, taking account of all circumstances (the catalogue, separation of the animals, auctioneer's statement) the contract was to supply a breeding bull. Therefore, "breeding bull" was part of the description identifying the goods.

Quality of the goods and description

A distinction must be drawn between statements relating to the quality of the goods and statements which are descriptive of the goods. Quality refers to the "state" or "condition" of the goods,[16] whereas description refers to the features by which the contract goods are identified. The distinction is illustrated in the House of Lords decision in *Ashington Piggeries Ltd v Christopher Hill Ltd*.[17] The defendants were mink farmers and the plaintiffs were manufacturers of animal foodstuff. Their contract was for the plaintiffs to compound foodstuff called "King Size" for feeding mink, in accordance with specifications supplied by the defendants. The defendants' minks, which were fed King Size, died of poisoning. It transpired that the poisoning was due to a chemical reaction with some of the ingredients. The defendants refused to pay the purchase price. When the plaintiffs sued for the purchase price, the defendants raised several defences and counter-claimed damages for breach of contract. One of the defences was that the goods did not fit their description because "King Size" was contaminated with poison. The issue was whether, because of the contamination, the goods (King Size) did not correspond with the description. It was held that statements that relate to the quality of the goods do not form part of the description except where they were necessary to identify the goods. In this case, although King Size was contaminated, it was still in accordance with the specifications described in the contract. The contamination was due to a chemical reaction, which affected the quality of the goods but not their description. As we shall presently see, the defendant won the case on other grounds.

In certain situations the quality and description of the goods may merge. For example, suppose a car dealer advertises for sale a "brand new" Toyota Hilux. The term "brand new" arguably refers both to the quality and the features by which the car is identified. Therefore, if the car is not brand new

16 Goods Act, s 1(1).
17 [1971] AC 441.

even if it is in a very good working condition, the seller would be in breach of s 14(1) of the Goods Act. In contrast, suppose the contract was to supply a 1999 Toyota Hilux. The seller supplies such a car but it is not in a good working condition. In the latter case the seller is not in breach of this provision because the goods fit the description, though the seller might be liable for breach of other implied terms that relate to the quality of the goods.

Right to reject

The buyer is entitled to reject the goods if there is any difference, other than trifling, between the goods tendered and the contractual description. For example, in *Arcos Ltd v Ronaasen and Sons Ltd*,[18] the buyer ordered timber in accordance with certain measurements. The goods delivered did not quite match those specifications and the buyer thereupon rejected the goods even though the difference in the measurements was not detrimental to their purpose. Their real reason for rejecting the goods was that the market price of timber had fallen substantially. It was held that:

> If the written contract specifies conditions of weight, measurement and the like, those conditions must be complied with. A ton does not mean about a ton, or a yard about a yard . . . If the seller wants a margin he must stipulate for it.[19]

In this case the court found that the goods did not correspond with their description, hence the buyer was entitled to reject them. Their motive was irrelevant. The only exception to the rule is with regard to microscopic deviations from the description that are commercially negligible.

Implied condition as to purpose and quality

Section 15(1) of the Goods Act opens with a general rule that in a contract of sale of goods there is no implied warranty or condition as to the quality or fitness of the goods for a particular purpose. This is a restatement of the classical common law proposition of *caveat emptor* or buyer be aware. The subsection then proceeds to state by way of exception that in certain specified circumstances the following conditions are implied in a contract of sale of goods: that the goods (a) are fit for a particular purpose and (b) are of merchantable quality. Though these two conditions have certain similarities, they are separate and distinct as explained below.

18 [1933] AC 470.
19 Ibid, per Lord Atkin at 479.

Fitness for a particular purpose – s 15(2)(a)

Where (i) a buyer makes known to a seller the particular purpose for which they require the goods, so as to show reliance on the seller's skill or judgment, and (ii) the seller is a dealer in goods of that description, there is an implied condition that the goods shall be reasonably fit for that purpose. The condition is not implied if the buyer purchased the goods under their trade name or patent. The meaning of this provision is discussed below.

Buyer must make known the particular purpose for which they require the goods

The buyer must expressly or impliedly make known to the seller the particular purpose for which the goods are required. It has been held that the expression "particular purpose" simply means that the buyer must state the purpose with sufficient clarity, so that a person in the seller's position can reasonably tell the extent to which their skill is required to provide the right goods or decline to contract if unable to do so.[20] Some goods have a single normal purpose, in which case it is not necessary for the buyer to inform the seller the purpose, except where the buyer wishes to use them for an unusual purpose.[21] For example, when you buy food from a take-away shop it is obvious that the purpose is for human consumption. In contrast, where the goods can be used for a range of purposes, the buyer must specify the particular purpose for which he or she requires the goods, otherwise the seller will not be liable if the goods do not fit the purpose for which the buyer requires the goods.

Similarly, where the buyer wishes to use the goods for an unusual purpose, he or she must inform the seller of that particular purpose, otherwise the seller will not be accountable if the goods do not fit the buyer's purpose. This point was emphasised by the House of Lords in *Ashington Piggeries Ltd v Christopher Hill Ltd*.[22] As may be recalled, in that case the buyer's minks were killed as the result of feeding on animal food compound (called "King Size") supplied by the defendant. Lord Wilberforce said that if the mink possessed an idiosyncrasy, which made the feed, as supplied, unsuitable for them though perfectly suitable for other animals, the seller was not liable unless the buyer informed them of the idiosyncrasy.[23] In *Griffith v Peter Conway*,[24]

20 *Hardwick Game Farm v Suffolic Agricultural Poultry Producers Association (alias Kendal (Henry) & Sons v Williams Lillico & Co Ltd)* [1968] 2 All ER 444 at pp 453–454, per Lord Reid.

21 *Grant v Australia Knitting Mills Ltd* [1936] AC 85 at 99; *Griffith v Peter Conway* [1939] 1 All ER 685.

22 Supra.

23 Supra, at 490. Although the court found that minks were more sensitive to the foodstuff than other animals, it held the sellers liable because on evidence there was a general unsuitability – not necessarily lethal – to all animals.

24 [1939] 1 All ER 685.

the plaintiff contracted dermatitis as a result of wearing a coat she purchased from the defendant. It transpired that she had particularly sensitive skin, as people with "normal" skin were not affected by the goods. It was held that the seller was not liable for breach of contract because the plaintiff did not tell them of her "abnormality". The fact that the plaintiff was not aware that her skin was particularly sensitive was immaterial.

RELIANCE

The buyer must not only disclose the particular purpose for which the goods are required, but must do so as to show to the seller that he or she is relying on the seller's skill to provide the appropriate goods. The question as to whether the buyer stated his or her purpose and or relied on the seller's skill or judgment is one of fact to be determined by examining all circumstances leading up to the transaction.[25] In *Grant v Australian Knitting Ltd*,[26] the Privy Council observed that although the reliance of the buyer must be brought home to the seller, this is seldom express. In most cases reliance arises by implication. For example, where a customer buys goods from a retailer or manufacturer, the reliance will generally be inferred from the fact that the buyer has gone to the shop or factory "in confidence that the seller has selected his stock with skill and judgement". Some authorities suggest that if, prior to the contract, the seller knows the purpose for which the goods are required or the buyer makes known to the seller the purpose for which he or she requires the goods, it raises a presumption that the buyer relies on the seller's skill.[27] Other authorities state that there is no such a presumption.[28] These assert that the test of reliance on the seller's skill is whether a reasonable person in the seller's position would have realised that the buyer was relying upon him or her to select the appropriate goods.[29] Where the contract of sale is between a buyer and a seller who are equally knowledgeable in relation to the subject matter of the sale, courts require strong evidence to infer that in the circumstances the seller ought to have realised that the buyer was relying on the seller's skill. The reason for this is that the courts take the view that, business being highly speculative, each person tends to rely on their own judgment.[30]

25 *Ashington Piggeries Ltd v Christopher Hill Ltd* [1972] AC 441 at 496, per Lord Wilberforce.

26 [1936] AC 85 at 99. See also *Teheran-Europe Co Ltd v S T Belton (Tractors) Ltd* [1968] All ER 886 at 894; *Hardwick Game Farm v Suffolk Agricultural Poultry Producers Association* [1969] 2 All ER 444 at 455.

27 *Hardwick v Kendall*, supra.

28 *Hardwick v Kendall*, supra, at 439, per Lord Reid.

29 *Ashington Piggeries*, supra, at 477, per Lord Guest. See also *Hardwick v Kendall*, supra, at 456, per Lord Reid.

30 *Ashington Piggeries*, supra, at 491, per Lord Wilberforce (cf *Hardwick v Kendall*, supra, at 466, per Lord Morris). In both cases, the respective court found that in the circumstances the seller ought to have realized that the buyer relied on their skill.

PARTIAL RELIANCE

Reliance on the seller need not be total or exclusive, it may be partial.[31] If the goods do not fit the buyer's purposes, the seller will only be liable if the defect is in that aspect of the work left to the seller's expertise. For example, in *Ashington Piggeries* the seller told the buyer that though they had experience in compounding animal food, they had no knowledge about mink food or its special requirements. They merely manufactured King Size in accordance with the formula supplied by the buyer, except that, with the buyer's consent, they substituted one ingredient, herring meal, for the more expensive fish meal. Accordingly, in the seller's submission they had not exercised any skill upon which the buyer could rely. It was held that although the buyer relied on their own judgment as to the suitability of the compound, they relied on the seller to select good quality ingredients of the kind stated in the formula and to combine them. One of the ingredients selected by the seller, herring meal, was harmful to mink. Therefore, the defect was in the area in which the buyer relied on the exercise of the seller's skill.

The fact that the seller has no skill or expertise in the area, or the fact that no one in the world has, is not a defence.[32] However, the seller's lack of knowledge, especially where the buyer is aware of it or is themselves more knowledgeable, might negative the inference of reliance.[33] Similarly, the fact that the buyer examined the goods prior to the contract is not a defence against implication of the condition of fitness for a particular purpose,[34] though it may be evidence that the buyer did not rely on the seller's skill.

Goods of a description, which it is in the course of the seller's business to supply

The House of Lords, in *Ashington Piggeries v Christopher Hill*, extensively discussed the meaning of this requirement. In that case, the seller sought to argue that this requirement was not satisfied because, though they were dealers in animal food stuff, it was their first time to compound mink food. The House of Lords dismissed this argument. Some of their Lordships found that the expression "goods of a description", in this context, was used in a wide sense to mean "goods of that kind". Hence, animal food

31 *Cammell Laird & Co v Manganese Bronze & Brass Co* [1934] AC 402 at 427, per Lord Wright.

32 The seller by holding themselves out as dealer in particular goods, led buyers to believe that they have the skill to select goods that fit the buyer's purposes, see *Ashington Piggeries*, supra, at 505, per Lord Diplock.

33 *Teheran-Europe Co Ltd v S T Belton (Tractors) Ltd* [1971] 1 QB 80.

34 Compare with implied term of merchantable quality, below.

stuff included mink food.[35] Lord Wilberforce went even further. He said that the requirements of the provision are satisfied if a seller agrees either generally or in a particular case to supply goods by way of business.[36] In other words, the test is whether the supply is by way of business; if it is then the goods are in the course of the seller's business to supply. The fact that it is the seller's first time to supply such goods is immaterial.[37] Conversely, if it is a non-business sale, for example, where a car is sold by private sale, the provision does not apply.

Goods reasonably fit for the particular purpose

Section 15(2)(a) does not impose on the seller the obligation to guarantee that the goods are absolutely fit for the buyer's purpose. The obligation is for the seller to supply goods that are *reasonably fit* for the particular purpose. What constitutes reasonable fitness obviously depends on the facts and circumstances of each case. The circumstances the courts may take into account include the gravity or consequence of the defect. For example, if a car supplied by the seller stalls or overheats, whether, for this reason, it is not reasonably fit for the buyer's particular purpose may depend on the number of times this happens, the chances of it happening again, the cost of repair if it did happen, whether the car is new or second hand and so on.[38] However, it should be emphasised that the seller does not escape liability by showing that they took all proper care to ensure that the goods were reasonably fit. Liability falls on the seller even if the defects that render the goods unfit were hidden or unknown to everyone at the time.[39]

Merchantable quality – s 15(2)(b)

Section 15(2)(b) of the Goods Act states that, where goods are bought by description from a seller who deals in goods of that description (whether a manufacturer or not), there is an implied condition that the goods are of merchantable quality. But if the buyer examined the goods prior to entering into the contract, the condition does not apply to defects that examination ought to have revealed.[40] We shall examine the key requirements of this provision.

35 At 495, per Lord Wilberforce; at 505, per Lord Diplock.
36 *Ashington Piggeries*, supra, at 495.
37 *Ashington Piggeries*, supra, at 494, per Lord Wilberforce.
38 See *Hardwick Game Farm*, supra, at 483, per Lord Pearce. See also *Bartlett v Sidney Marcus Ltd* [1965] 2 All ER 753.
39 *Hardwick Game Farm*, supra, at 457, per Lord Reid.
40 Section 15(4), Goods Act.

Merchantable quality

There is no definition of the expression "merchantable quality" in the Goods Act.[41] Nor is it defined in PNG case law. However, there are several English and Australian judicial statements that define a corresponding expression. One of the most often cited statements to this effect is that of Lord Reid in *Hardwick Game Farm*. In that case, his Lordship said that goods are deemed to be of "unmerchantable quality" if [42] –

> . . . in the form in which they were tendered were of no use for any purpose for which goods which complied with the description under which these goods were sold would normally be used, and hence were not saleable under that description.

Lord Reid added that the test whether the goods "were of no use for any purpose" is objective. It means that the goods "would not have been used by a reasonable man for any purpose . . .".

It is suggested that there are two key factors in Lord Reid's definition: the description of the goods in the contract; and, secondly, their commercial saleability. The description of the goods in the contract determines the range of purposes for which such goods would normally be used. The broader the description of the goods, the wider the range of purposes for which the goods can be used. If the goods are commercially saleable for any one of the range of purposes, then they are of merchantable quality even if that is not the purpose the buyer wished to use the goods for. Where the goods normally have only one purpose, if they are unfit for that purpose then they are not of merchantable quality.[43]

The case of *Hardwick Game Farm*, supra, illustrates the above points. In that case, K sold to G groundnut extract for compounding as food for cattle and poultry. G sold some of the extract to S who in turn sold to H. Many of H's pheasants that were fed on the extract died. Ultimately, it transpired that the extract contained a substance poisonous to poultry, which had no adverse effect on cattle where used in moderation. Indeed, cattle farmers continued to compound it in cattle food. The House of Lords held that the goods were of merchantable quality since they were commercially saleable under their contract description: animal food compound. It would have been different if the extract, though commercially saleable, for example, as a

41 The Act only defines "quality of goods" as includes "their state or condition": see s 1(1).

42 [1968] 2 All ER 444 at 451. In *B S Brown & Son v Craiks Ltd* [1970] 1 WLR 752 at 754, Lord Reid, whilst affirming his definition of merchantable quality in *Hardwick Game*, cautioned that it was not possible except in the vaguest terms to a frame that would apply to every case.

43 See for example, in *Grant v Australian Knitting*, supra, the goods (underpants), had only one normal purpose.

fertiliser, was poisonous to cattle as well. The reason for this is that use as a fertiliser does not fall within the description "animal food compound" under which the goods were originally sold.

PRICE REDUCTION

Whether the goods as tendered are commercially saleable is a question of fact depending on the circumstances of each case. In *Australian Knitting Mills v Grant*,[44] Dixon J proposed that goods are commercially saleable, hence are of merchantable quality, if they are saleable to a buyer fully acquainted with the defects without abatement of the price. However, subsequent cases attach less weight to the price reduction. For example, in *B S Brown & Son Ltd v Craiks Ltd*,[45] Lord Guest said that the price reduction had little or no significance in determining whether the goods as tendered were of merchantable quality, except where the reduction was so substantial that the goods could only be sold at a "give-away price". This is because several factors other than merchantability could influence the market price of the goods.

APPEARANCE

Goods that are otherwise fit for the purpose(s) such goods are normally used may nonetheless be unmerchantable because of their appearance. For example, suppose a retailer orders a dozen cartons of canned tuna fish from a wholesaler. At the date of delivery the tuna is perfect but the labels on the cans are damaged and dirty. If, because of the labels, the cans are not commercially saleable, then the goods are not of merchantable quality. This principle is illustrated by the case of *Niblett Ltd v Confectioners' Materials Co*.[46] In that case, a buyer imported goods from the USA to England. The goods were wrapped in such a way as to infringe the trademark of a third party. For this reason, the buyer could not lawfully remove the goods from custom without re-packaging. It was held that the labelling was as much a part of the state or condition of the goods as the content. Hence, the goods were not of merchantable quality.

Before we leave the definition of merchantable quality, it should be emphasised that care must be taken not to confuse this condition with that of fitness for a particular purpose. The fact that the goods do not fit the particular purpose for which the buyer requires them does not necessarily mean that the goods are not of merchantable quality. The converse is also true.

44 (1933) 50 CLR 387 at 418.
45 [1970] 1 WLR 752 at 757, 758.
46 [1921] 3 KB 387 (cf *Harlington & Leinster Enterprises Ltd v Christopher Hull Fine Art Ltd* [1991] 1 QB 564).

Goods bought by description from a seller who deals in goods of that description

To invoke the implied condition of merchantable quality the buyer must have purchased the goods by description and the seller must be a dealer in goods of that description. As we have seen, description refers to the nature or specification by which the goods are identified. Unascertained or future goods are necessarily bought by description. Specific goods may also be purchased by description.[47] A seller is deemed to be a dealer in goods of that description (whether a manufacturer or not) if they agree to supply them in the way of business, even if that occasion was their first time to sell such goods.[48] It follows, as with the implied condition of fitness for a particular purpose, that the condition of merchantable quality is not implied in a non-business sale. For example, if I sold you my car, unless it was otherwise agreed, the contract would be on the basis of *caveat emptor*.

Examination of the goods

The implication of the condition of merchantable quality is subject to the proviso that, if the buyer has examined the goods, there is no implied condition as regards defects that examination ought to have revealed (s 15(4)). The case of *Tapenda Ltd v Wahgi Mek Plantations Ltd*[49] illustrates the application of this proviso. The defendants purchased 24,400 kilograms of high-grade coffee from the plaintiff. The coffee turned out to be of low grade and, according to the court's findings, not of merchantable quality. The examination the defendant carried out, which at the time was the normal business practice, did not reveal the defect. The defect could only have been revealed by a relatively new and rather sophisticated examination process, which the buyer did not carry out. It was contended by the plaintiff that the implied condition of merchantable quality was excluded because the defendant had examined the goods. Woods J agreed. His Honour held that the defendants were given the opportunity to examine the goods, which they did not use to examine the goods thoroughly enough. If they had carried out a full and proper examination the defect would have been revealed.

Wood J's judgment seems to have followed the English case of *Thornett & Fehr v Beers & Son*.[50] In that case, glue was sold in casks and the seller allowed the buyer every opportunity to inspect the glue. The buyer had a casual look at the exterior of the cask but did not open them. It was held

47 See above at pp 16–17.
48 *Ashington Piggeries*, supra, at 495, per Lord Wilberforce.
49 N1787 of 1996.
50 [1919] 1 KB 486.

that if the buyer examines the goods he or she is deemed to have notice of defects which full examination of the goods would have revealed.

The foregoing decisions should be compared with that of the District Court of Western Australia in *Truck Wreckers (1979) Pty Ltd v Waters.*[51] The plaintiff purchased a second hand truck engine from the defendant. Prior to purchasing the engine, the buyer tested it by starting and revving the engine whilst cold. The engine emitted a significant amount of blue and white smoke from the exhaust. The plaintiff purchased the engine and later discovered that it consumed an excessive amount of oil. The plaintiff claimed that the engine was not of merchantable quality within the meaning of the relevant provisions of the Fair Trading Act 1987 (WA). The defendant argued that the plaintiff, having examined and started the engine, could not rely on the implied term as to merchantable quality, citing as authority the case of *Thornett & Fehr v Beers.* Yeats J, in delivering his judgment, observed that there was a difference in wording between the provisions of the Western Australian Fair Trading Act and the corresponding provisions of the English Sale of Goods Act. Whist the English Act refers to defects, which "*such*" examination ought to have revealed, the provision before him referred to defects "*that*" examination ought to reveal. His Honour continued:

> It seems to me that the language used in the Fair Trading Act requires the Court to focus on the actual examination and determine whether that examination ought to have revealed the defect. It is not concerned with whether that kind of examination or an examination of that nature ought to reveal a defect; the focus is on the actual examination that was conducted.

In other words, under the Western Australian provision, unlike the English provision, the focus is on the actual examination conducted by the buyer. If that examination ought to have revealed the defect in question, then the implied condition of merchantable quality was excluded as regards that defect. Applying the above test, his Honour held that, in the case of a used engine, starting the engine after it had been standing could not have revealed the excessive consumption of oil. The only examination which ought to have revealed the defect was dismantling the engine and examining the parts. For this reason the proviso did not apply to the contract.

The Courts in PNG might find the case of *Truck Wreckers* persuasive as the proviso in s 15(4) also refers to a defect "that" examination ought to reveal. If the same test was applied to the facts of *Tapenda Ltd v Wahgi Mek Plantations,* supra, it is most likely the results would have been different.

51 [1994] 10 SR (WA) 32.

On the other hand, the two cases can be distinguished. In *Truck Wreckers* the dispute was between a consumer and a trader and the court was interpreting a provision of a statute intended to protect consumers. In contrast, the dispute in *Tapenda* was between traders in circumstances where the buyer was at least as experienced in the particular business as the seller. Moreover, the Goods Act is not aimed at consumer protection.

Interestingly, it would seem that the proviso does not apply where the buyer did not attempt to examine the goods at all, nor where no examination the buyer could or would normally have made would have revealed the defect.[52]

PERFECT TENDER

Merchantability is determined as at the time of delivery. Therefore, where the seller delivers goods that are of unmerchantable quality the buyer is entitled to reject them even if the defect could easily be cured.[53] Of course, in practice it is most likely the buyer would give the seller a leeway to cure defects that could easily be cured in order to make the goods merchantable.

Implied condition in a contract of sale by sample – s 16

A sample is a physical illustration or guide as to the type and grade of the goods the seller seeks to sell to a buyer. Whether a contract of sale is by sample depends on the intention of the parties expressed or implied in their contract.[54] The fact that in the course of the negotiations leading up to the sale the seller produces a sample of the goods is strong, but by no means conclusive, evidence that the sale is by sample. For example, in *LG Thorne & Co Pty Ltd v Thomas Borthwick & Sons (Australasia) Ltd*,[55] during negotiations to purchase drums of oil, the buyer demanded to see a sample of the oil. The seller produced a sample, which the buyer inspected. After inspection of the sample the parties entered into a written contract, which made no reference to the sample. The issue was whether the contract was by sample. It was held that the fact that the buyer was shown a sample did not necessarily mean that the parties intended their contract to be by sample. If the parties intended their contract to be by sample they would have included it in their written contract.[56]

52 *Grant v Australian Knitting*, supra, at 100 (cited with approval in *Tapenda Ltd v Wahgi Mek Plantation Ltd*, supra).

53 *Grant v Australian Knitting*, supra, at 100. See also *Niblett Ltd v Confectioners' Material* [1921] 3 KB 387.

54 Goods Act, s 16(1).

55 [1956] SR (NSW) 81.

56 Compare with *Ship Agencies Australia Pty Ltd v Fremantle Fishermen's Co-Operative Society Ltd* [1991] 8 SR (WA) 109.

If a contract is by sample, s 16(2) implies in such contract a condition that:

(a) the bulk of the goods will correspond with the sample;
(b) the buyer will have a reasonable opportunity to compare the bulk with the sample; and
(c) the goods are free from any defect making them unmerchantable that could not be apparent on reasonable examination.

Correspondence with the sample means visual correspondence as is usual in the particular industry or trade. Differences that can only be detected by rigorous or microscopic examination go to obligations as to merchantable quality or description but not correspondence with sample.[57] The requirement to provide the buyer a reasonable opportunity to compare the sample with the bulk is obviously intended for the buyer to ascertain that they correspond. The legal significance of the provision is that a buyer who has accepted delivery of the goods does not lose his or her right to reject the goods, until he or she has had a reasonable opportunity to compare the bulk with the sample.[58]

Hidden defects

The fact that the goods correspond with the sample is not enough to discharge the seller's obligation. Section 16(2)(c) implies a further obligation against the seller that the goods have no hidden defects rendering them unmerchantable, which reasonable examination of the sample would not reveal. Put differently, the seller is not liable for defects which a reasonable examination of the sample would have revealed. The case of *Godley v Perry*[59] provides a good illustration of the judicial interpretation of "reasonable examination" in a corresponding provision. A boy was injured whilst playing with a catapult he purchased from the defendant (a retailer). He successfully sued for damages for breach of contract on the ground, *inter alia*, that the goods were not of merchantable quality. The retailer in turn sued the wholesaler from whom he purchased the catapult, alleging that the sale was by sample and that the wholesaler was in breach of a provision corresponding with s 16(2)(c), that the catapults would be free of any defect rendering them unmerchantable which was not apparent on reasonable examination of the goods. The retailer claimed that when the catapults were delivered she tested them by pulling the elastic back and they appeared to be sound. The wholesaler in their defence denied that the test

57 *F E Hookway & Co Ltd v Alfred Isaacs & Sons* [1954] 1 Lloyd's Rep 491.
58 See also Goods Act, s 34. See below (pp 72–73) for discussion of the relationship between acceptance of the goods and the right to reject defective goods.
59 [1960] 1 All ER 36.

conducted by the retailer was sufficient. They argued that if the retailer had conducted a proper examination of the goods, for example, by holding the sling down on one foot and pulling the elastic more strongly, squeezing together the two prongs, the defect would have been revealed. It was held that the provision only requires a process of "reasonable examination" as that phrase would be understood by "the common sense standards of everyday life". The tests suggested by the wholesaler, though "practical", went beyond "reasonable examination" required by the Act. Accordingly, the court found that in the circumstances the examination conducted by the retailer was reasonable and the defect could not have been revealed by such examination.

The fact that a contract is by sample does not necessarily exclude the other conditions implied by the Goods Act. For example, in an appropriate case, supplying goods that correspond with the sample does not relieve the seller of the obligation that the goods fit the particular purpose.[60] Similarly, where goods are sold both by description and by sample they must comply with both conditions.[61]

Implied undertaking as to title

We have seen that a contract of sale of goods is one whereby a seller transfers or agrees to transfer property in goods to a buyer for a monetary consideration. As a corollary, s 13 of the Goods Act provides that unless the circumstances show a different intention, there is an implied condition on the part of the seller that he or she has a right to sell the goods at the time of sale, or in the case of future goods, will have a right to sell. In most cases the seller is the owner of the goods in question, but this need not be the case provided he or she has a right to sell the goods or will have a right to sell at the appropriate time. For example, suppose a person enters into a contract with the University of PNG to sell it ten personal computers, which they intend to import from Malaysia. Obviously, at the time of the contract they do not have ownership of the computers or even a right to sell them. However, there is an implied undertaking on the seller's part that they will have a right to sell the computers at the time of delivery.

On the other hand, the fact that the seller owns the goods does not necessarily discharge his or her implied obligation as to title. For example, in *Niblett Ltd v Confectioners' Materials Co Ltd*,[62] the seller, an American company, exported certain goods to the buyer in England. Upon arrival in England the goods were confiscated by customs because the labels on the goods infringed another company's trademark. The issue was whether the

60 *Drummond v Van Ingen* (1887) 12 App Cas 284.
61 Goods Act, s 14(2).
62 [1921] 3 KB 387.

seller was in breach of the implied condition as to title corresponding with s 13(a) of the Goods Act. It was held that there is a breach of this provision if the seller can be stopped by legal means from selling the goods. In this case, though the sellers were the owners of the goods at the time of delivery, they were in breach of the condition as to title because they had no right to sell the goods in the UK.

Total failure of consideration

Breach of the implied condition as to title constitutes a total failure of consideration, which entitles the buyer, in addition to any other remedies, to recover the purchase price if paid in advance without obligation to account to the seller for the intermediary use of the goods. The authority for this proposition is the judgment of the English Court of Appeal in *Rowland v Divall.*[63] In that case the plaintiff purchased a second-hand car from the defendants and used it for about four months. It then transpired that the defendants had no title to the car and the plaintiff was forced to return the car to X, the true owner (unknown to the defendants, the person who originally sold the car to them had stolen it from X). The plaintiff sued the defendants to recover the purchase price he had paid, on grounds of total failure of consideration. The defendants argued that there was no total failure of consideration since the plaintiff had used the car for four months. Moreover, they argued that the plaintiff could not claim a refund since he was not in a position to return the car to the seller. It was held that, notwithstanding that the plaintiff had used the car for four months, there was total failure of consideration because the plaintiff did not get what he bargained for. He bargained for the property in, and the lawful possession of, the car. Instead, he received an unlawful possession, which exposed him to a possible action for conversion by the true owner. The court also held that though normally an order for refund is only made where the plaintiff had returned the defective goods, this case was different because the defendant's lack of title was the very reason the plaintiff was unable to return the goods.

Curing the defect

Some authorities suggests that in appropriate circumstances a seller in breach of the implied condition as to title can cure the defect if he or she acquires title to the goods or a right to sell. For example, in *Butterworth v Kingsway Motors Ltd*,[64] H purchased a car from HP Ltd under hire purchase terms.

63 [1923] 2 KB 500 (Compare this case with that of *Yeomen Credit v Apps* [1966] 1 QB 520).
64 [1954] 2 All ER 694.

She sold the car to a third party, mistakenly thinking that she had a right to do so as long as she kept paying the instalments. The third party sold the car to the defendants who in turn sold it to the plaintiff. None of the parties was aware that their respective seller had no right to sell. Meanwhile, H continued paying the instalments to HP Ltd, except for the final instalment. Whereupon HP Ltd demanded that the plaintiff either hand over the car, or pay them the outstanding final instalment. The plaintiff chose to return the car to HP Ltd and demanded from the defendant a full refund of the purchase price on account of a total failure of consideration. A week later X paid the outstanding instalment to HP Ltd and, as far as HP Ltd were concerned, they had no more interest in the car. Thus, notwithstanding, the plaintiff rejected the car and sued the defendant to recover the purchase money he had paid. The defendant sought to argue that when H got the title it retrospectively "cured" (or "fed") the defective title of subsequent buyers, including the plaintiff. Hence, the defendants submitted that they were not in breach of condition as to title. It was held, *obiter dictum*, that there might be cases where the seller could cure a defective title, by acquiring title from the rightful owner. However, in this case it was too late as the purported cure occurred *after* the plaintiff had terminated the contract.[65]

Implied warranties

In addition to the implied condition as to title, s 13 implies two warranties on the part of the seller: (i) that the buyer will have and enjoy quiet possession of the goods; and (ii) that the goods are free from any third party incumbrance not declared before or at the time of the contract.[66] Breach of any of these warranties only entitles the buyer to damages for breach of contract.

Quiet enjoyment

The implied warranty of quiet enjoyment is analogous to the covenant of quiet enjoyment implied by the common law against a landlord. The object of the provision is to protect the buyer from interference with the goods by

65 See also *Patten v Thomas Motor Pty Ltd* [1965] NSWLR 1457. In this case, the New South Wales Supreme Court held that where the seller obtained title, for example, by paying off the true owner before the buyer rescinded the contract, the buyer could not rescind the contract because the defect would have been cured. Under the Goods Act of the Australian State of Victoria, s 98, a buyer is prohibited from rescinding the contract for breach of a condition corresponding with s 13(2) of the Goods Act (PNG), without first giving the seller an opportunity to cure the defect. Moreover, the courts have a discretion to order the buyer to pay for intermediary use and enjoyment of the goods.

66 Section 13(b) and (c).

the seller or seller's agents after the sale. For example, in *Keetley v Quinton*,[67] the buyer defaulted in payment of the purchase price, which was payable in instalments. The seller thereupon seized the goods. It was held that once the seller parted with possession of the goods he or she was not entitled to physically repossess them. The court found that the seller's interference with the goods constituted breach of a warranty of quiet enjoyment implied by a provision corresponding with s 13(b) of the Goods Act. In *Microbeds AG v Vinhurst Road Markings Ltd*,[68] it was held that the seller's liability under this provision is not only with respect to defects as to title at the time of sale, but also to defects which emerge in the future. In that case the seller sold certain machinery to the buyer. Unknown to both parties, at the time of sale a third party (TP) had applied for a patent in relation to similar machines, but the specification had not been granted. Two years later the patent was granted to TP, who then brought a patent action against the buyer. Meanwhile, the buyer claimed against the seller for breach of the implied condition as to title and breach of the implied warranty as to quiet possession under provisions corresponding to s 13(a) and (b), respectively. It was held that the seller was not in breach of the former provision because at the time of sale they had a right to sell the goods. However, the court found the seller liable for breach of warranty of quiet enjoyment because the subsequent grant of a patent to TP exposed the buyer to possible interference with their possession and use of the goods. It seems the seller's liability continues until expiration of the limitation period.

Seller's warranty that the goods are free from undisclosed incumbrances or charges

Section 13(c) of the Goods Act, implies a warranty on the part of the seller that there are no incumbrances or charges not disclosed or known to the buyer at the time of sale. "Incumbrances" refers to third party title claims against the goods. The provision covers an unusual situation where the seller has or may have limited interest in the goods. For example, suppose the seller acquired the goods as a finder. If at the time of sale he or she disclosed this to the buyer or the buyer was aware of it, the effect of the provision is that, if the true owner subsequently claimed the goods, the buyer would have no recourse against the seller. Similarly, if the goods were subject to payment of statutory charges (e.g. custom duty) and the buyer was aware of it, he or she could not complain if later the charges were levied against the goods. The seller would be in breach if the buyer was unaware of the defects.

67 [1991] 4 WAR 133.
68 [1975] 1 All ER 529.

Exclusion clauses

The Goods Act was largely based on the philosophy of freedom of contract. Accordingly, the Act gives the parties a right to exclude or vary any term implied by the Goods Act. The parties can do this by express agreement, course of dealing between the parties, or usage of trade where such usage binds both parties.[69] In practice, sellers are usually more economically powerful than the buyers, and invariably take advantage of the provision to exclude or limit the scope of the terms implied by the Goods Act. The courts, being aware of the buyers' weak bargaining position, tend to construe exclusion clauses strictly and against the sellers. Moreover, the Fairness of Transactions Act[70] gives the courts extensive powers to review contracts, "to ensure overall fairness" in situations such as where due to unequal bargaining strength of the parties, the weaker party had no real freedom of contract or where the terms of a contract are manifestly unfair. It is submitted that, in appropriate cases, the courts could use these powers to nullify an unfair attempt by a seller to exclude his or her obligations under the Goods Act. A detailed discussion of exclusion clauses is outside the scope of this work. Readers interested in this topic should refer to specialised law of contract textbooks.

69 Section 55, Goods Act.
70 Act No 28 of 1993.

Chapter 3

Effects of the Contract of Sale of Goods

Introduction

In this chapter we shall cover two main topics: transfer of property from seller to buyer; and transfer of title by a non-owner of the goods.

Transfer of property between seller and buyer

The objective of a contract of sale of goods is not only to transfer possession of the goods, but also to transfer property or ownership in the goods to the buyer. The Goods Act sets out rules for determining when property passes to the buyer. As we shall presently see, the passing of property to the buyer has several legal consequences as between the parties and in some instances in relation to other people. For example, it may determine who bears the risk of loss or accidental damage to the goods and whether the seller is entitled to sue for the purchase price. Hence, it is important to ascertain the exact time when property passes.

Classification of goods

For the purpose of determining the moment when property passes to the buyer, the Goods Act classifies goods into: "specific goods", "future goods", "unascertained goods" and "ascertained goods". The term "specific goods" refers to goods that are identified and agreed upon at the time of the contract (s 1). For example, if X enters into a contract to sell Y her car, that is a contract of sale of specific goods. "Future goods", on the other hand, refers to goods to be manufactured or acquired by the seller after entering into the contract. For instance, if S enters into a contract to sell B ten computers, which S does not have in stock but which he intends to import from Australia, the contract is one for the sale of future goods. S's obligation would be to supply any ten computers that correspond with the contractual description.

The term "unascertained goods", although used in s 17 of the Goods Act, is not defined in the Act. Arguably, the term could embrace future goods, such as goods yet to be manufactured at the time of the contract. The term also could denote goods in bulk, where the buyer's share is yet to be set aside. For example, if Y has ten cartons of tuna fish and she agrees to sell three of them to X, the contract is one of sale of unascertained goods. The goods become "ascertained goods" once the actual contractual goods are identified and set aside from the bulk.

When does property pass in specific *and* ascertained goods?

Section 18(1) of the Goods Act provides that property in specific and ascertained goods passes from the seller to the buyer when the parties intend it to pass. Section 18(2) states that for the purpose of determining the parties' intention the courts must take into account the terms of the contract and all relevant circumstances.[1]

The case of *YHA Hauka Coffee Pty Ltd v Kumul Kopi Export Pty Ltd and others* illustrates the application of the above provision. In that case, the plaintiff sold coffee to the first defendant which, to the knowledge of the plaintiff, the defendant intended to export. The contract was subject to a term that the coffee remained the property of the seller until paid for in full. As per previous transactions between the parties, upon delivery of the coffee it was loaded and shipped to the third defendant, in Australia. The latter remitted their payment for the coffee to the first defendant's Westpac Bank account, in Mt Hagen. The normal practice was for the bank to transfer the funds into the plaintiff's Westpac Bank account in Lae. It would appear that the bank in Mt Hagen put the payment received into an account, but for unknown reasons did not transfer the proceeds into the plaintiff's account. As the plaintiff had not received payment, they brought these proceedings for a declaration that title never passed to the other parties. The issue was whether property had passed to the buyer (first defendant) to enable them to pass it to any of the other defendants. Doherty J observed that s 18 of the Goods Act provides that property in the goods does not pass to the buyer until the terms of the contract are fulfilled. Her Honour found that the terms of the present contract clearly stipulated that property in the goods would not pass to the buyer until payment. On the basis of the evidence tendered she held that "despite the transfer of moneys to the first defendant the seller had never received payment for the goods" as agreed by the parties, accordingly the coffee remained the seller's property.[2]

1 See for example, *YHA Hauka Coffee Pty Ltd v Kumul Kopi Export Pty Ltd and others* [1991] PNGLR 331.

2 Ibid, at 334–335, Doherty J observed that under s 18 of the Goods Act, the fact that a buyer hands over the goods to the seller's shipping agent was not conclusive of transfer of property in the goods. Her Honour also noted that s 19 of the Act permits a seller to reserve the right of disposal of the goods until certain conditions were fulfilled notwithstanding delivery of the goods to the buyer or their agent for purposes of consignment to the buyer.

Presumptive intention of the parties

Most contracts do not spell out the time as to when property would pass to the buyer. In the event, s 18(3) of the Goods Act lays down five presumptive rules to ascertain the moment the parties intended property to pass. The first four rules relate to specific goods, and the fifth applies to future and unascertained goods. The presumption under the rules is rebuttable by evidence of a contrary intention.[3]

Rule 1

Section 18(3)(a) provides that:

> [W]here there is an unconditional contract for the sale of specific goods in a deliverable state –
>
> (i) the property in the goods passes to the buyer when the contract is made; and
>
> (ii) it is immaterial whether the time of payment or the time of delivery or both are postponed . . .

The meaning of the expression "unconditional contract" is controversial. Some authorities suggest that it means a contract where there are no fundamental terms.[4] If this is the correct interpretation of the expression, Rule 1 would hardly apply to any contract as it is almost inconceivable for parties to enter into such a contract. Others interpret the expression to mean a contract where there is no condition precedent to the passing of property to the buyer.[5] For example, the contract in *YHA Hauka Coffee v Kumul Kopi Export*, supra, was not conditional in this sense because the transfer of property to the buyer was subject to payment of the purchase price.

The English case of *Dennant v Skinner*[6] is often cited to illustrate the application of the equivalent of Rule 1. In that case, at an auction sale, a rascal going by the name of "Mr King" successfully bid for a car. He tendered a cheque for the purchase price, but the seller declined to let him take the car until the cheque was cashed. Eventually, he let King take the car, after King signed a document acknowledging that property in the car remained with the seller until the cheque was cashed. The cheque bounced, but by then King had already sold the car to the defendant, who was a bona fide purchaser. The seller instituted these proceedings for conversion

3 See for example, *YHA Hauka Coffee Pty Ltd v Kumul Kopi Export Pty Ltd and others*, supra.
4 *Varley v Whipp* [1900] 1 QB 513.
5 See generally, Sutton, K C T, *Sales and Consumer Law* (4th edn, LBC Information Services, North Ryde NSW 1995), pp 202–205, and 388–389.
6 [1948] 2 KB 164.

against the defendant. The issue was whether property had passed to King when he purportedly sold the car to the defendant, if it had not passed the defendant was liable for conversion.[7] It was held that, at an auction sale, the contract is concluded at the fall of the hammer. Since the contract was unconditional, property in the car passed to King at that time. The document King signed, which purported to make the contract conditional, had no effect as by then property had already passed to him.[8]

DELIVERABLE

For Rule 1 to apply, the goods must be in a deliverable state. Goods are in a "deliverable" state when they are in such a state that the buyer would be legally obliged to accept them.[9] In other words, the seller has done everything he or she is required to do under the contract in relation to the goods.

It has been suggested that, in practice, the case of *Dennant v Skinner* is more likely to be the exception than the rule. In most cases where a buyer pays by cheque, the courts will more than likely find that the intention of the parties was that property should not pass to the buyer until the cheque is cashed.[10] For this reason, plus the uncertainty surrounding the meaning of the expression "unconditional contract", the scope for the application of Rule 1, appears to be very limited.

Rule 2

Section 18(3)(b) provides that:

> [W]here –
> (i) there is a contract for the sale of specific goods; and
> (ii) the seller is bound to do something to the goods for the purpose of putting them into a deliverable state, the property does not pass until –
> (iii) the thing is done; and
> (iv) has notice that it is done . . .

The Supreme Court of Queensland case of *Wallace v Safeway Caravan Mart*[11] provides a good illustration of this rule. In that case, S sold a caravan to B subject to S doing certain relatively minor repairs to the van before its delivery. B paid the purchase price in advance. Overnight, the van was stolen

7 See below, "Transfer of title by a non-owner".
8 The seller should have exercised their right of lien: see s 40 of the Goods Act.
9 See s 1(4), the interpretation section of the Goods Act. For illustration of the term, see the cases cited under Rules 2 and 3, below.
10 See Bridge, M G, *Sale of Goods* (1988, Butterworths, Toronto) generally and at pp 118–121.
11 [1975] 3 Qd R 224.

before S had done the repairs. The issue was whether property had passed to B at the time of the theft. It was held that property had not passed because the van was not in a deliverable state. Hence, the risk of loss was on the seller.[12]

Rule 3

Section 18(3)(c) provides that:

> [W]here –
>
> (i) there is a contract for the sale of specific goods in a deliverable state; and
>
> (ii) the seller is bound to weigh, measure, test or do some other act or thing with reference to the goods for the purpose of ascertaining the price,
>
> the property does not pass until –
>
> (iii) the act or thing is done; and
>
> (iv) the buyer has notice that it is done . . .

The point to note in this rule is that the act or thing is to be done by the seller with a view to ascertain the price of the goods. For example, suppose S agrees to sell to B all the scrap metal in S's garage at K1 per kilogram, and S is bound to weigh the goods in order to determine their weight and, consequently, the price. The presumption under Rule 3 is that property will not pass until S has weighed the goods and B has notice that it has been done.[13] But if the weighing is to be done by the buyer, then Rule 3 would not apply to determine the passing of property.[14] In the latter case, if the only act remaining was for the buyer to weigh the goods in order to ascertain the price, the goods are deemed to be in a deliverable state and the property would pass under presumptive Rule 1, unless the parties expressed a contrary intention.

Rule 4

Section 18(3)(d) provides that:

> [W]here goods are delivered to the buyer on approval or "on sale or return" or other similar terms, the property in the goods passes to the buyer –
>
> (i) when he signifies his approval or acceptance to the seller, or does any other act adopting the transaction; or

12 See also *Underwood Ltd v Burgh Castle Brick Cement Syndicate* [1922] KB 343. Compare with *Symes v Laurie* [1985] 2 Qd 547.

13 See for example, *Turley v Bates* (1863) 159 ER 83 (Exch).

14 See Bridge, M G, *Sale of Goods*, supra, at p 123.

> (ii) if he does not signify his approval or acceptance to the seller but retains the goods without giving notice of rejection, then –
>
> (A) if a time has been fixed for the return of the goods – on the expiration of that time; or
>
> (B) if no such time has been fixed – on the expiration of a reasonable time . . .

A contract of sale or return is one where, for example, a book publisher supplies 100 textbooks to the University Bookshop upon terms that the bookshop will only pay for books it sells, or wishes to keep, and return the rest. Under Rule 4, property passes when the bookshop informs the publisher of the number of the books it has sold or retained; or when the bookshop adopts the contract. A buyer is deemed to adopt the contract if he or she does any act in relation to the goods, which is inconsistent with the seller's right to regain possession of the goods. For example, if the buyer pledges or uses the goods he or she is deemed to have adopted the contract.[15] Property in goods under a contract of sale or return also passes after lapse of time fixed in the contract or if no such time is expressed, after lapse of a reasonable time.

When does property pass in **future** *and* **unascertained** *goods?*

Section 17 of the Goods Act states the first rule in relation to passing of property in future and unascertained goods. It states that in a contract of sale of unascertained goods "no property in the goods is transferred to the buyer unless and until the goods are ascertained".[16] This is a mandatory rule, which applies irrespective of the parties' intention or agreement. Subject to this rule, property in unascertained and future goods passes in accordance with the intention of the parties. Presumptive Rule 5 assists the courts in determining the parties' intention.

Rule 5

Section 18(3)(e) provides that:

> [W]here –
>
> (i) there is a contract for the sale of unascertained or future goods by description; and
>
> (ii) goods of that description and in a deliverable state are unconditionally appropriated to the contract –

15 *Kirkham v Attenborough* [1897] 1 QB 201.

16 Although the section does not mention "future" goods, clearly the term "unascertained" goods was intended to include future goods (e.g. see s 18(3)(e), where both are mentioned).

(A) by the seller with the assent of the buyer; or
(B) by the buyer with the assent of the seller,

the property in the goods passes to the buyer on the appropriation.

For example, suppose S enters into a contract to sell B a bottle of milk from a carton in S's store, property in the goods will not pass, irrespective of the parties' express agreement to the contrary, until goods fitting that description are unconditionally appropriated to the contract by S (seller) with B's consent, or by B (buyer) with S's consent.

UNCONDITIONAL APPROPRIATION

The meaning of the expression "unconditionally appropriated" was discussed in the famous English case of *Carlos Federspiel & Co v Charles Twigg & Co Ltd.*[17] The facts of the case were as follows. A buyer paid in advance for bicycles to be manufactured by the seller. Bicycles fitting the contract description were made and packed in containers bearing the buyer's name and kept in store awaiting shipment to the buyer. Before the goods were despatched, the seller went bankrupt. In the circumstances the buyer stood to lose the money they paid in advance. Their only option was to claim that property in the bicycles had passed to them before the seller went bankrupt. The issue was whether the goods were unconditionally appropriated to the contract so that property passed under the equivalent of Rule 5. It was held that to constitute appropriation of goods to the contract there must be an intention to attach the contract irrevocably to the particular goods and no other. In this case the seller merely set aside the goods they intended to use in the performance of the contract but legally there was nothing to stop them from substituting them with other bicycles. Hence, property did not pass to the buyer.

Consequences of the passing of property

Two main consequences flow from the passing of property to the buyer: (i) risk of loss or damage; and (ii) right of the seller to the purchase price. We shall only consider the former in this chapter, the latter is discussed in the following chapter under Remedies.

Risk

The Goods Act does not define the term "risk", but clearly it refers to loss through damage or theft of the goods as opposed to financial loss as a result of market price fluctuation. Where the goods are accidentally damaged or

17 [1957] 1 Lloyd's Rep 240.

are stolen before or after delivery, the issue becomes who bears the loss, the seller or the buyer?

Risk passes with property

Section 20(1) of the Goods Act states that in the absence of a contrary agreement the risk passes with property. In other words, whoever is the owner of the goods at the time bears the risk of loss and it matters not whether delivery has taken place or not.[18] This means that if the risk had passed to the buyer at the time the goods were lost, he or she must pay the purchase price. This is the case even though, because of the loss, the seller is unable to deliver the goods.[19] The parties may, however, express a different intention. For example, in a sale or return contract, where under presumptive Rule 5, property does not pass to the buyer until the goods are appropriated to the contract, the parties may nonetheless agree that the buyer bears the risk of loss of the goods in their possession. A contrary intention might also be expressed by course of dealing between the parties or usage of trade. For example, in international sales under "FOB" (Free on Board) terms, according to custom the risk passes to the buyer when the goods are loaded on board the carrier, yet property does not pass till the bill of lading is delivered to the buyer or the buyer's agent.[20]

Goods delivered to the buyer

Section 29(1) of the Goods Act, also illustrates a situation where property passes but the risk remains with the seller until delivery of the goods. The subsection envisages a contract where the seller is required to send the goods to the buyer. It provides that in such a contract, unless the contrary is shown, delivery to the carrier is deemed to be delivery to the buyer. Though the subsection does not expressly say so, it is implicit in the provision that the risk passes to the buyer upon delivery to the carrier in the absence of any agreement to the contrary. This seems to be the interpretation of the provision in the Supreme Court judgment in *Toba Pty Ltd v Poole*.[21] In that case, the seller sought to argue on the basis of s 29(1) that their liability ceased once they delivered the goods to the shipper. The Supreme Court

18 See for example, *Underwood Ltd v Burgh Castle Brick Cement Syndicate* [1922] KB 343; *Symes v Laurie* [1985] 2 Qd 547; and *Wallace v Safeway Caravan Mart* [1975] 3 Qd 224.

19 This effectively constitutes an exception to s 28 of the Goods Act, which says that payment and delivery are concurrent conditions.

20 *Carlos Federspiel & Co v Charles Twigg & Co Ltd and another* [1957] 1 Lloyd's Rep 240. See also under s 33 of the Goods Act (risk where goods are delivered at a distant place). Also in *Mash & Murrell Ltd v Joseph Emmanuel Ltd* [1962] 1 All ER 77, it was held that in the case of perishable goods it is implied that the seller carries the risk of deterioration of the goods whilst in transit in a normal journey, even though property has passed.

21 [1984] PNGLR 94.

held that the provision did not apply to the parties' contract because they expressed a different intention. Hence, the risk of damage to the goods remained with the seller.

Exceptions

Apart from where the parties express a contrary intention, the operation of s 20 is subject to two provisos: wrongful delay and bailee's duties.

DELAY

Section 20(2), provides that:

> Where delivery has been delayed through the fault of the buyer or seller, the goods are at the risk of the party in fault as regards loss that might not have occurred but for the fault.

The effect of the proviso is to reverse the passing of the risk by reason of the fault of the other party to deliver or accept delivery on time, as the case might be. For example, in *Demby Hamilton & Co Ltd v Barden*,[22] a seller agreed to supply a buyer 30 tons of apple juice. The seller crushed enough apples and waited for the buyer's instructions as to the place of delivery. The buyer in breach of contract delayed to issue the instructions. Meanwhile, the juice had gone bad. It was held that the deterioration of the juice was due to the buyer's delay in taking delivery; hence the loss fell on the buyer.

The New South Wales case of *Allied Mills Ltd v Gwydir Valley Oilseed Pty Ltd*[23] illustrates a similar point where delivery is delayed due to the seller's fault. The parties entered into a contract for the unconditional sale of specific goods, which were in the seller's store. The goods were in a deliverable state so that property passed at the time of the contract. The seller, in breach of contract, delayed to deliver part of the goods. Later, a fire accidentally destroyed the goods retained by the seller. The trial judge found that the goods were at the risk of the seller because of its breach of contract and, further, that the loss which was suffered might not have occurred but for such fault on the part of the seller. The seller appealed against the award of damages. They argued that the proviso corresponding with s 20(2) of the Goods Act, only exonerated the buyer from the necessity of paying for the goods that were burnt, but did not give the buyer a cause of action in damages. The Court of Appeal of New South Wales held that the first proviso does not only relieve the buyer from liability to pay for the goods; it also gives such buyer a cause of action in damages for

22 [1949] 1 All ER 485.
23 [1978] 2 NSWLR 26.

breach of contract. The court also dismissed the seller's argument that the contract was frustrated.

BAILEE'S DUTIES

Section 20(3) states that the passing of the risk does not relieve the party in possession of the duties or liabilities of a bailee. A bailee is a person entrusted with possession of another person's goods. At common law a bailee has an obligation to take reasonable care of the goods in their possession. The effect of the second proviso is to preserve that obligation. For example, where the property and the risk pass to the buyer, but the goods remain in the seller's possession, the latter as a bailee "for reward", must take reasonable care of the goods.[24]

Transfer of title by a non-owner

The fundamental principle of the common law is *nemo dat quod non habet* (or simply *nemo dat*), which means that a person cannot transfer or give a better title than he or she has. This common law rule was enacted in s 21(1) of the Goods Act. Thus, if one purchases stolen goods, one does not acquire a better title than the person who sold the goods to them, even if he or she is a bona fide purchaser for value without notice. Moreover, the purchaser will be liable in damages to the true owner for conversion. The underlying policy of the rule is to protect private property.

Exceptions to nemo dat

The *nemo dat* rule is not absolute; it is subject to several exceptions set out in the Goods Act. The underlying policy for the exceptions are eloquently explained in Lord Denning's judgment in *Bishopsgate Motor Finance Corporation Ltd v Transport Brakes Ltd* as follows:[25]

> In the development of [English] law, two principles have striven for mastery. The first is for the protection of property: no one can give a better title than he himself possesses. The second is for the protection of commercial transactions; the person who takes in good faith and for value without notice should get a good title. The first principle has held sway for a long time, but it has been modified by the common law itself and by statute so as to meet the needs of our own times.

24 See for example, *Rabtrad Niugini Pty Ltd v ABCO Pty Ltd* (1990) PNGLR 155. The seller may charge the buyer storage charges and hold them accountable for any consequential damages: see s 37 of the Goods Act.

25 [1949] 1 KB 322 at 336–337.

The exceptions are:

(i) estoppel – s 21(1);
(ii) sale under court order, common law or statutory power – s 21(2);
(iii) sale by an agent – s 58(2)(b);
(iv) disposition by a mercantile agent – s 61;
(v) sale under a voidable title – s 22;
(vi) disposition by seller in possession – s 25(1);
(vii) disposition by buyer in possession – s 25(2);
(viii) sale in a market overt – s 23.

Each one of these exceptions will be considered in turn. When reading the exceptions, readers should critically consider whether or not, in the socio-economic circumstances of PNG, the exceptions strike a fair balance between the protection of individual property and facilitation of trade, or business convenience.

Estoppel

Section 21(1) of the Goods Act, after stating the *nemo dat* rule, adds the following rider, "unless the owner of the goods is precluded by his conduct from denying the seller's authority to sell". The qualifying words embody the principle of estoppel. In those circumstances the buyer acquires a better title than the person who sold the goods to them.

The common illustration of this exception is the English case of *Eastern Distributors Ltd v Goldring*.[26] In that case, O owned a van, which he used in his business. He wished to purchase a second-hand car from CD (a car dealer) but did not have enough funds. CD and O conspired to obtain finance from the plaintiff (P), a finance company. In their plan, CD lied to P that he was the owner of a van and a car, both of which O wished to purchase on hire purchase terms. CD submitted to P the appropriate application forms for finance and hire purchase duly signed by O. Under the plan P would buy the two cars and immediately sell them to O on hire-purchase terms. Unfortunately for the conspirators, the plan fell through because P was not interested in buying the car. However, P expressed interest in purchasing the van. Without O's knowledge or consent, CD purportedly sold the van to P and kept the proceeds of the sale. P purported to sell the van to O on hire-purchase terms using the form signed by O. At all material times O retained possession of the van.

Later, O sold the van to D (the defendant) a bona fide purchaser without notice. When P learned what had happened, they brought these proceedings against D for conversion. D contended that P had no title to the van since the person who sold it to them, CD, was neither the owner nor had O's authority

26 [1957] 2 QB 600.

to sell it. P, in response, invoked the principle of estoppel against O. It was held that O, having armed CD with signed documents that represented to P that CD was the owner of the van, was estopped from denying that CD was the owner or had the authority to sell the van. Therefore, P acquired a title that was good not only against O, but also against the whole world. It further followed when O purported to sell the van to D, he no longer had property in the goods.[27] D was found liable for conversion of the van.

Note that, for the principle of estoppel to apply, the representation must be made to the buyer by the owner of the goods, and not merely by the seller. For example, in *Eastern Distributor Ltd,* it would not have sufficed if CD simply went to P pretending to be the owner or to have the owner's authority to sell the van. O made the representation in the application forms submitted to P. Secondly, not any conduct of the owner would invoke the principle, even if it misleads another person. The conduct must be such that the law recognises it as misleading. For example, the mere fact that I let X drive my car does not estop me from denying that she had my authority to sell it.[28] Nor is carelessness by itself sufficient to invoke estoppel. For example, suppose my car is stolen and subsequently the thief sells it to a bona fide purchaser for value without notice. The fact that I parked the car, unlocked, in an area notorious for theft would not be enough to invoke the principle of estoppel, unless the purchaser proved that I owed them a duty of care not to park the car in the particular park or not to leave my car unlocked.[29] It would be almost impossible for the courts to hold that such a duty existed.

Sale under court order, common law or statutory power – s 21(2)

This provision safeguards the validity of sales ordered by the courts under any law and sales conducted under the common law or other statutory provisions.[30]

Sale by an agent

Under the general law of agency, where an agent sells goods within their actual, usual, implied or ostensible authority, the buyer acquires a good title. Section 58(2)(b) of the Goods Act saves the application of the common law of England relating to the law of agency. For example, if an agent sells goods to T without the actual authority of her principal, or contrary to the principal's

27 Of course, D could have sued O for breach of contract, and the latter could have sued CD for conversion. Perhaps neither O nor CD was worth suing.

28 *Jerome v Bentley & Co Ltd* [1952] 2 All ER 11.

29 See above. See also *Central Newbury Car Auctions Ltd v Unity Finance Ltd* [1957] 1 QB 371.

30 For example, sale by a sheriff of a judgment debtors' goods to recover damages awarded by a court, see Order 13, National Court Rules Act (Ch 38). See also s 4 of the Unclaimed Goods Act (Ch 325).

express instructions, T will acquire a good title so long as the agent was acting within her ostensible or usual authority. For detailed discussion readers should refer to specialised textbooks on the law of agency.

Disposition by a mercantile agent

Section 61(1) provides that:

> Where a mercantile agent is, with the consent of the owner, in possession of goods or of the documents of title to goods, a sale, pledge or other disposition of the goods made by him when acting in the ordinary course of business of a mercantile agent is, subject to this part, as valid as if he were expressly authorized by the owner of the goods to make it if the person taking under the disposition –
>
> (a) acts in good faith; and
> (b) has not, at any time of the disposition, notice that the person making the disposition has no authority to make the disposition.

The section is concerned with providing for the validity of sales, pledges and other dispositions by mercantile agents who are "with the consent of the owner" in possession of the goods or documents of title to the goods. The section provides that such transactions shall be valid as if they were authorised by the owner. This provision is almost a verbatim reproduction of s 2(1) of the English Factors Act 1889. The Factors Acts, which go back to 1823, were enacted by the English Parliament to consolidate and expand the scope of the common law of agency in relation to the agent's apparent authority. The aim was to protect persons dealing with, mainly, professional agents with a view to encourage commercial transactions.

MERCANTILE AGENT

A "mercantile agent" is defined in s 1(1) of the Goods Act, as "a mercantile agent having in the customary course of business as such agent, authority" to sell, buy, consign or raise money on security of goods or documents of title. The use of the words "course of business" suggest that the legislature might have had in mind professional agents such as (modern examples), stockbrokers, auctioneers, car salespersons, real estate agents and the like. However, several English and Australian authorities state that a mercantile agent includes any person who agrees to act as an agent in a business capacity, even if it is a one-off job.[31]

31 *Budberg v Jerwood & Ward* (1934) 51 TLR 99; *Belvoir Finance Co Ltd v Harold (G) Cole & Co Ltd* [1969] 2 All ER 904; *Parkes v Batten and others* [1985] 3 SR (WA) 110.

CONSENT TO POSSESSION

The provision only applies if the agent obtains possession of the goods or documents of title[32] with the consent of the owner.[33] Does any consent to possession suffice? English authorities interpreting a similar provision hold that the consent, which enables the provision to operate, must be consent to the possession of the goods by a mercantile agent *as a mercantile agent.*[34] For example, suppose X took her car for service at Highlands Garage, which also happens to sell second-hand cars. Without X's authority Highlands sells the car to TP, a bona fide purchaser for value without notice. If X sues TP for conversion, s 61(1) would not avail TP as a defence because X only consented to Highlands' possession of her car in their capacity as *repairers* and not as *dealers*.[35] If the rule were otherwise, owners would be exposed to too much risk of losing their property left in possession of dealers who wear more than one hat.

However, the provision would apply to a situation where the owner consented to the mercantile agent having possession of the goods for a purpose which is related to their business as dealers. For example, suppose you left your car with a car-dealer to solicit for offers or for display only. If, without your authority, the dealer sold the car, the dealer would be deemed to be a mercantile agent in possession of the goods with your consent.[36] Consent to possession includes fraudulently obtained consent.[37] Moreover, the termination of consent does not affect the purchaser unless he or she is aware of the termination.[38]

It should be noted that the word "owner" refers to the person with whose consent the agent is in possession. If that person is not the owner of the goods, for example he or she stole the goods or derived title from a thief, the provision will not apply to deprive the lawful owner of their title to the goods.[39]

ORDINARY COURSE OF BUSINESS

The mercantile agent's conduct must be in the ordinary course of business. In *Oppenheimer v Attenborough & Son*[40] Lord Buckley said, with reference

32 "Document of title" is an instrument that represents the goods identified in the document. A typical example of such a document is a bill of lading (see ss 66 and 67 of the Goods Act).
33 *Heap v Motorists' Advisory Agency Ltd* [1923] 1 KB 577.
34 *Pearson v Rose & Young* [1951] 1 KB 275 at 288, per Lord Denning.
35 Per Lord Denning, ibid. See also *Astley Industrial Trust Ltd v Miller (Oakes)* [1968] 2 All ER 36.
36 Per Lord Denning, ibid.
37 *Pearson v Rose & Young* [1951] 1 KB 275.
38 Section 61(2), Goods Act.
39 *National Employers' Mutual General Insurance Association Ltd v Jones* [1990] 1 AC 24.
40 [1908] 1 KB 222 at 230. See also *Pacific Motor Auctions Pty Ltd v Motor Credits Ltd* [1965] AC 867 (a car sold by a mercantile agent outside office hours).

to the equivalent English provision, that the phrase "ordinary course of business" meant acting within business hours at a proper place of business and in all respects acting in the ordinary way a mercantile agent would act. For example, several English cases hold that the sale of a second-hand car without the registration book cannot be in the ordinary course of business of a mercantile agent, though there might be special circumstances in which it might.[41] Whether this is also the case in PNG might depend on the common practice and expectation of the people in that type of trade.

GOOD FAITH

The buyer from a mercantile agent must act in good faith. The term "good faith" connotes "honesty". Clearly, a buyer cannot act honestly if he or she had notice of the mercantile agent's lack of authority to dispose of the goods. Notice means actual notice, "that is knowledge of [the mercantile agent's lack of authority] or deliberately turning a blind eye to it".[42] English courts have steadfastly rejected the notion of constructive notice (negligent failure to make proper inquiry) in commercial transactions.[43] However, there may well be circumstances where failure to inquire might lead to an inference that the buyer did not act in good faith.[44] There is no direct PNG judicial authority as to the meaning of "good faith" in this context. The courts, unlike their English counterparts, might consider constructive notice as sufficient to establish lack of good faith.

Sale under a voidable title – s 22

VOID AND VOIDABLE

A contract of sale of goods induced by fraud, misrepresentation or duress could be void or voidable.[45] Whether a contract is void or voidable depends on the circumstances of each case. If it is void, from the very beginning, no title passes to the buyer. If the contract is voidable, the buyer acquires a good title but the contract is liable to be set aside at the instance of the innocent party, so long as they do so before a bone fide purchaser for value acquires an interest in the goods.

41 See for example, *Pearson v Rose & Young*, supra; and *Stadium Finance Ltd v Robbins* [1962] 3 All ER 633.

42 *Worcester Works Finance Ltd v Cooden Engineering Co Ltd* [1972] 1 QB 210 at 218, per Lord Denning.

43 *Manchester Trust v Furness* [1895] 2 QB 539 at 545, per Lindley LJ.

44 See for example, *Heap v Motorists' Advisory Agency Ltd* [1922] All ER 251 (held that the buyer did not act in good faith because the price of the goods was so low that it ought to have raised the buyer's suspicion).

45 It is not always easy to determine whether a contract is void or voidable, see for example, *Lewis v Avery* [1971] 3 All ER 906 and the authorities cited therein.

Section 22 of the Goods Act provides that where, before the title is avoided, the buyer, under a voidable contract, sells the goods to another person, the latter acquires a good title to the goods if he or she buys them in good faith and without notice of the seller's defect of title. This exception to the *nemo dat* rule is illustrated by the English case of *Lewis v Avery*.[46] In that case a rascal represented himself to O as a famous actor to convince him to accept a cheque for the purchase of a car. After confirming the rascal's identity, O let him take the car. When the cheque was dishonoured, O attempted to avoid the contract, but by then the rascal had sold the car to BP, a bona fide purchaser without notice. O sued BP for conversion. It was held that the contract between O and the rascal was voidable; hence the rascal had a voidable title that had not been avoided by the time he sold the car to BP. Consequently, BP had a good title to the goods.

If the original seller avoids the contract, they must take reasonable steps to inform the public of their decision. What constitutes reasonable steps will of course depend on the circumstances of each case. Such steps would include reporting the matter to the police, and possibly publishing an advertisement to that effect in a local daily or some prominent public place in the local area.[47]

Disposition by seller in possession – s 25(1)

Section 25(1) of the Goods Act provides that:

> Where a person who has sold any goods is in possession of the goods or of the documents of title to the goods, the delivery or transfer by him, or by a mercantile agent acting for him, of the goods or documents of title under a sale, pledge or other disposition of the goods to a person receiving them in good faith and without notice of the previous sale has the same effect as if the person making the delivery or transfer were expressly authorized by the owner of the goods to make it.

For example, suppose S sells her car to Y with the intention of both parties that the property in the car passes to Y immediately. However, for some reason S retains possession of the car. Later, S sells and delivers the same car to BP, who is a bona fide purchaser for value without notice. The effect of the provision is that BP acquires a good title, even though at the time of purchase S no longer had title to the car. The justification for this exception to *nemo dat* is to protect innocent members of the public, who are unaware

46 Ibid. Compare with *Car and Universal Finance v Caldwell* [1965] 1 All ER 290.
47 See *Car and Universal Finance v Caldwell*, ibid.

of the legal transfer, from being deceived by the appearance of ownership, which goes with uninterrupted possession of the goods or document of title.[48]

SELLER CONTINUES IN POSSESSION

It is imperative that the seller continues in possession after selling the goods; if continuity is broken the provision does not apply. What constitutes continuous possession was discussed by the Privy Council in *Pacific Motor Auctions Pty Ltd v Motor Credits*.[49] M Ltd, car dealers, sold several cars to the plaintiff but the cars remained in M Ltd's possession for display in its showroom. Under a separate contract, the plaintiff authorised M Ltd to sell the cars on behalf of the plaintiff. Later, when the plaintiff heard that M Ltd was in serious financial difficulties, they revoked M Ltd's authority to sell the cars. Notwithstanding, M Ltd sold one of the cars to the defendant, moreover, outside working hours. The defendant purchased the car in good faith and without notice of M Ltd's lack of authority to sell. The plaintiff sued the defendant for conversion. The defendant relied on the exception to *nemo dat* under the equivalent of s 25(1) of the Goods Act.[50] The plaintiff in reply contended that the provision did not apply because, after they withdrew M Ltd's authority to sell the cars, M Ltd remained in possession not as a "seller" but as a "bailee". The issue was whether M Ltd continued in possession after selling to the plaintiffs. It was held that being "in possession" meant retention of physical control of the goods, regardless of any private instructions between the buyer and the seller, which might alter the legal capacity in which M Ltd held the cars. Therefore, M Ltd was a seller who had "continued in possession" of the car after selling it.

The s 25(1) exception to *nemo dat* does not apply where there is a break in the seller's physical possession of the goods after the sale. For example, suppose in the above case, after the sale the plaintiff had taken physical delivery of the car in question and later returned it to M Ltd's premises. Section 25(1) would not have applied to the transaction. The reason for this is that when the buyer takes possession of the goods, the relationship of the parties as "buyer and seller" comes to an end. Therefore, when the "buyer" returns the goods, the "seller" receives them not in the capacity of a seller, but as a bailee.[51]

48 *Pacific Motor Auctions Ltd v Motor Credits (Hire Finance) Ltd* [1965] AC 867 at 886, per Lord Pearce.

49 Ibid.

50 The defendants also relied on sale by a mercantile agent under the equivalent of s 61(1), but this argument was dismissed because the sale took place outside working hours.

51 *Mitchell v Jones* [1905] 24 NZLR 932, cited with approval in *Pacific Motor Auctions*, supra. See also the Supreme Court judgment in *Csolle (Trading as Lodi Timber Co) v ASP (NG) Ltd* [1967-68] P & NGLR 301 at 305.

GOOD FAITH

As with the other exceptions to *nemo dat*, the purchaser must act in good faith without notice of the previous sale.[52]

Disposition by buyer in possession – s 25(2)

Section 25(2) of the Goods Act provides that:

> Where a person who has bought or agreed to buy any goods obtains, with the consent of the seller, possession of the goods or of the documents of title to the goods, the delivery or transfer by him, or by any mercantile agent acting for him, of the goods or documents of title under a sale, pledge or other disposition of the goods to a person receiving them in good faith and without notice of a lien or other right of the original seller in respect of the goods has the same effect as if the person making the delivery or transfer were a mercantile agent in possession of the goods or documents of title with the consent of the owner.

If the conditions stated in the provision are satisfied, the purchaser acquires a good title even though the person from who they acquired the goods had no title or authority to deal with the goods.

BUYER IN POSSESSION

The first focus is on the transaction, if any, between the owner of the goods and the person who purportedly disposed of the goods without their authority. The provision requires that the latter must be a person who "bought or agreed to buy" the goods from the owner. This means that, at the outset, there must have been a binding contract of sale or an agreement to sell between the two persons.[53] The provision does not apply if the person was in possession of the goods under, for example, a contract of hire purchase or lease of the goods.[54]

CONSENT TO POSSESSION

Secondly, at the time of the transaction, that person must be in possession of the goods or documents of title with the consent of the owner of the goods.

52 See above (p 48) for meaning of "good faith".

53 Obviously, the assumption is that property had not passed; if it had the buyer's title would at least be "voidable", see discussion above of s 22 of the Goods Act.

54 See for example, *Helby v Matthews*, supra, it was held that a purported sale of goods by a hirer, under a hire purchase agreement to a bona fide purchaser, did not come under the equivalent provision.

This obviously excludes a thief or a person who acquired the goods from a thief. However, consent to possession suffices even if it was fraudulently obtained or had been withdrawn at the time of the purported sale to the third party. For example, in *Newton of Wembley Ltd v Williams*,[55] the plaintiffs sold a car to Andrew (A) in exchange for a cheque and allowed him to take it away. When the cheque was dishonoured, the plaintiff decided to terminate the contract. They failed to trace A or the car but took all reasonable steps to notify him and the public of their action. Later, A sold the car to B at a street market in the city of London. Subsequently, B sold it to the defendant, a bona fide purchaser. The plaintiffs sued the defendant for conversion. In his defence, the defendant sought to rely on the equivalent of the s 25(2) exception to *nemo dat*. In response, the plaintiffs submitted that the provision did not apply because, though at the outset A was a person who had obtained, with the consent of the plaintiffs, possession of the goods, at the time he purported to sell the car to B (under whom the defendant claimed title) that consent had been withdrawn. The issue was whether at the time A sold the car to B he was still "a buyer in possession". It was held that, notwithstanding the plaintiffs' termination of the contract and withdrawal of their consent, "they had in fact – true, through inability to do otherwise – left the possession of their car with Andrew".[56] Therefore, the requirements of this part of the provision were satisfied.

DELIVERY OF THE GOODS

Thirdly, there must be delivery of the goods or documents of title to the purchaser. For example, suppose O enters into a contract to sell her car to X, and she allows him to take the car on the condition that title will not pass until X pays the purchase price in full. X, without O's authority, purportedly sells the car to BP, but X retains possession of the car. BP cannot invoke s 25(2) because he did not take delivery of the car. In *Gamer's Motors Centre (Newcastle) Pty Ltd v Natwest Wholesale Australia Pty Ltd*,[57] the High Court of Australia, interpreting a similar provision, held that in this context, delivery need not be actual, it could be constructive.

TRANSACTION IS AS IF THE SELLER WERE MERCANTILE AGENT

The provision concludes that if all the requirements of the provision are satisfied, the transfer shall have the same effect "*as if the person making the delivery or transfer were a mercantile agent*" (emphasis added) entrusted by the owner with the goods. The judicial interpretation of the clause in italics is controversial. On one hand, in *Newton of Wembley v Williams*, the

55 [1965] 1 QB 560.
56 Ibid, at 573–574, per Sellers LJ.
57 [1987] 163 CLR 236.

English Court of Appeal held that the equivalent clause meant that the person (i.e. the buyer in possession who wrongfully disposes of the goods to the third party) when selling or delivering the goods must act as a mercantile agent in ordinary course of business. For example, the sale must take place during working hours, in business premises and otherwise behave as a mercantile agent. On the other hand, Australian and New Zealand authorities interpret the equivalent provision to mean that once the conditions stated in the subsection are satisfied, "the delivery of the goods is to have the same effect as if the sale of the goods had been legally effected by a mercantile agent, that is as if it had been in the ordinary course of business of a mercantile agent".[58] In other words, according to the latter interpretation, the buyer in possession need not have disposed of the goods in the ordinary course of his or her business as a mercantile agent.

To date, no PNG court has yet considered the clause in question. When the issue arises, the courts will have a choice between the English interpretation, which severely limits the scope of s 25(2) exception to the *nemo dat* rule, and the Australian/New Zealand interpretation, which gives it a much wider scope. The judicial dilemma will be whether, in the socio-economic circumstances of PNG, the law should give more protection to the owners of property or to commercial convenience. It is submitted that, as a matter of policy, the Australian/New Zealand interpretation is, perhaps, better because it avoids unnecessary technicalities, such as what constitutes the ordinary course of business of a mercantile agent in PNG. The owners are still protected by the fact that the buyer must be a bona fide purchaser for value. Thus, a purchaser of a car at night in the back street of Port Moresby would be hard pressed to prove that he or she is a bona fide purchaser.

GOOD FAITH

The third party (purchaser) must accept delivery in good faith and without notice of the seller's lack of authority to dispose of the goods.[59]

Sale in a market overt – s 23

Section 23 of the Goods Act, provides that where goods are sold in a market overt, according to usage of the market, the buyer acquires a good title from the seller provided he or she purchased the goods in good faith and without notice of the seller's lack of title. "Market overt" is an anachronistic common law doctrine. It relates to sales conducted in an open, public and legally

58 *Gamer's Motors Centre (Newcastle) Pty Ltd v Natwest Wholesale Australia Pty Ltd*, ibid, at 242, per Mason CJ.

59 See above (p 48) for the meaning of "good faith".

constituted market.[60] To invoke this exception to the *nemo dat* rule, the sale must take place in accordance with the customary practices and usages of the particular market. For example, the goods must be of a type that is usually sold in that market. Moreover, the sale must be concluded between sunset and sunrise. This is to ensure that the goods were openly on sale at a time when customers could see them. According to the English case of *Reid v Metropolitan Police Commissioner*,[61] the fact that the rules of a particular market allow the market to operate beyond sunrise does not affect this requirement.

Unlike the other exceptions to *nemo dat*, the market overt rule affords protection to a buyer even with respect to stolen goods. However, s 24(1) of the Good Act provides that where any person is convicted for the theft of such goods, the property in the goods reverts to the true owner irrespective of any intermediary dealings with them. Subsection 24(2) makes it clear that if the goods were obtained by fraud, which does not amount to "larceny" property does not revert to the owner.

60 This includes a market created under statutory power: *Bishopsgate Motor Finance Ltd v Transport Brakes Ltd* [1949] 1 KB 322 at 337, per Lord Denning. The Koki market place, in Port Moresby, originally established under the Koki Market-Place Trust Act (Ch 60), repealed by Act 47 of 1986, would qualify as a market overt.

61 [1973] 3 All ER 97.

Chapter 4

Performance of the Contract of Sale of Goods and the Remedies

Introduction

The buyer and seller perform the contract by carrying out their respective duties in accordance with the terms of their contract. Section 27 of the Goods Act stipulates that it is the seller's duty to deliver the goods and the buyer's duty to accept and pay for the goods as provided in the contract. In this chapter we analyse what constitutes performance and the remedies available to the parties in the event of a breach by the other party.

Performance

Duties of the Seller

Transfer of title

Although s 27 mentions only the duty to deliver, clearly the seller's duty includes transfer of property in the goods to the buyer. As we have seen, a contract of sale of goods is one where the seller transfers or agrees to transfer property in goods to a buyer for monetary consideration. Indeed, if the seller delivers goods which the seller has no right to sell, that constitutes a total failure of consideration.[1]

Delivery of possession

The Goods Act defines the term "delivery" as the voluntary transfer of possession of the goods from the seller to the buyer.[2] There is no definition in the Act of the word "possession". In popular parlance it means having physical or actual custody of the goods. However, in law, the expression "possession" additionally means having constructive control of the goods.

1 See for example, *Rowland v Divall* [1923] 2 KB 500. See above, "implied condition as to title".

2 Goods Act, s 1(1),

Thus, delivery of possession may be effected by physical transfer of the goods to the buyer or constructively. An example of constructive delivery is where the seller hands over to the buyer the document of title to the goods or the key to the warehouse where the goods are kept.[3] Delivery of possession could also be effected by "attornment" as provided by s 29(3) of the Goods Act. Basically, this is where, at the time of the sale, the goods are in the possession of a third party and the latter acknowledges to the buyer that they hold the goods on their behalf.

DELIVERY AND PROPERTY

In practice, property usually passes upon delivery of the goods, but this need not be the case. A contract may provide for delivery without transfer of property until, for example, the buyer pays the purchase price.[4] Conversely, a contract may provide for the transfer of property in the goods before delivery of the goods.

SIGNIFICANCE OF DELIVERY

Delivery of the goods is legally significant in several respects. For example, the seller's right to demand payment might depend on whether the seller delivered the goods. Section 28 of the Goods Act provides that, unless otherwise agreed, delivery and payment are concurrent conditions. This means that at the agreed moment of delivery the seller must be ready and willing to hand over possession of the goods in exchange for the price. Likewise, the buyer must be ready and willing to accept delivery and to pay the agreed purchase price. Most everyday contracts, such as where a customer purchases goods in a shop or market, are of this nature. Some other contracts allow the buyer to take possession of the goods immediately and pay later.

The risk of accidental loss or damage to the goods might also depend on whether, at the material time, the seller had delivered the goods.[5] Moreover, where the buyer wrongfully fails to pay for the goods, the rights of the seller to deal with the goods might depend on whether delivery was complete or not. This is particularly important where the buyer is insolvent.[6] These examples underpin the importance of determining what constitutes delivery.

3 *Gamer's Motors Centre (Newcastle) Pty Ltd v Natwest Wholesale Australia Pty Ltd* [1987] 163 CLR 236.
4 *YHA Hauka Coffee Pty Ltd v Kumul Kopi Export Pty Ltd and others*, supra.
5 See for example, *Toba Motors Pty Ltd v Poole* [1984] PNGLR 94.
6 See seller's remedies discussed below (pp 67–70).

RULES FOR DETERMINING DELIVERY

Generally it is for the parties to stipulate when and where to deliver the goods. In the absence of such an agreement or usage of trade or custom, the Goods Act lays down certain rules to determine when and where delivery takes place and the consequences of late or non-delivery of the goods.

PLACE OF DELIVERY

Prima facie the place of delivery is the seller's place of business (shop or factory), if any, or residence.[7] This is just a presumption. The agreement of the parties might show that the parties intended delivery to take place at the buyer's place or some other place. Such intention may be inferred from the circumstances of the case, trade usage or course of dealing between the parties. For example, where the buyer orders goods to be sent to them, most likely the buyer's premises is the intended place of delivery.[8] In the case of a contract for the sale of specific goods which, to the knowledge of both parties, are in some other place at the time of the contract, delivery takes place where the goods are situated.[9] For example, if I enter into a contract with you to sell you my car, which both of us know is parked in a certain garage in Lae, prima facie the garage in Lae is the place of delivery. In this example, if the car is in the possession of a third party, there is no delivery until that person acknowledges to you, the buyer, that he or she holds it on your behalf.[10]

DELIVERY TO A CARRIER

Section 32(1) of the Goods Act provides that, if in a contract the seller is authorised or required to send the goods to the buyer, delivery of the goods to a carrier (for example, airline or shipper), for the purpose of transmission to the buyer prima facie is deemed to be delivery to the buyer. This is so whether or not the buyer nominated the carrier. The presumption can be rebutted by evidence of a contrary intention as illustrated by the Supreme Court judgment in *Toba Pty Ltd v Poole*.[11] In that case the respondent (plaintiff), a resident of Kieta, entered into a contract to buy a vehicle from the appellant (seller) in Port Moresby. Under the contract the appellant was required to organise for the vehicle to be put in a suitable container before shipping it to Kieta. The appellant delivered the vehicle to the carrier for shipment to Kieta, without a container. The vehicle was damaged en route.

7 Goods Act, s 29(1), (2).
8 However, see the presumption in Goods Act, s 31(1), discussed below.
9 Goods Act, s 29(3).
10 Goods Act, s 29(5).
11 [1984] PNGLR 94.

The trial judge found that the appellant bore the risk of damage and awarded damages to the respondent. On appeal, the appellant contended that by operation of s 32(1) and (2) of the Goods Act, delivery to the shipper is delivery to the buyer; hence, their liability ceased when they delivered the vehicle to the shipper.

In a unanimous decision, the Supreme Court held that the deeming of delivery to the carrier as delivery to the buyer in s 31(1) is a rebuttable presumption. The provision "does not say that delivery to the carrier is delivery to the buyer. It merely means that unless the contrary is shown, delivery of the goods to the carrier is delivery to the buyer".[12] In this case the court found that a contrary intention was shown by the express requirement for the appellant to deliver the vehicle to the shipper in a container, which they did not do. Therefore, the appellant's liability did not cease on delivery of the vehicle to the wharf in Port Moresby.

We shall digress from our narrative of place of delivery to comment on some other aspects of the above case. It is submitted that the case illustrates two further points, neither of which was argued, regarding the passing to the buyer of the risk of damage or loss of the goods. The first is, that in a contract where the goods are to be delivered to the buyer, unless otherwise agreed, the risk of loss or damage remains with the seller until, *at the earliest*, the goods are delivered to the carrier. Where, as in the present case, delivery to the carrier is not intended to be delivery to the buyer, it would seem that the risk remains with the seller until the goods are actually delivered to the buyer. The buyers could also have argued that their contract was for the sale of specific goods, but that the goods were not in a deliverable state because the seller did not put them in a container. Therefore, under Rule 2, s 18(3)(b) of the Goods Act, property in the goods and the risk did not pass to the buyer.[13]

TIME OF DELIVERY

The parties are free to express in their contract the time when the seller should deliver the goods. Section 29(4) of the Goods Act provides that in the absence of stipulation as to time, if under the contract the seller is bound to send the goods to the buyer, the goods must be sent within a reasonable time. Also, s 29(6) provides that demand or tender of delivery may be treated as ineffectual by the other party unless made at a reasonable hour. What constitutes reasonable hour obviously depends on the facts of each case.

12 Ibid, at 96, per Kidu CJ.
13 See above (pp 36–37) for detailed discussion of the rules for passing of property.

CONSEQUENCES OF DELAY

The Goods Act is silent as to whether failure to deliver the goods on time constitutes breach of an essential term of the contract, which entitles the buyer to reject the goods; or is merely a breach of a warranty, which entitles the buyer only to damages. At common law, whether time of delivery is an essential term of the contract depends on the parties' intention. The English House of Lords, in *Bunge Corporation v Tradax Corporation*,[14] summarised the guidelines the courts use to determine that intention. As a general rule, in a commercial contract, unless the contrary is expressed, the courts consider time to be an essential term of the contract. The reason for this is that in commercial contracts, certainty is of great importance because such contracts usually involve a string of other contracts.[15] For example, suppose X enters into a contract to supply B with 2,000 kilograms of beef. On the basis of this contract, B enters into a contract to supply beef to a number of restaurants and supermarkets. Failure by X to deliver the goods on time to B could lead to a string of legal actions.

In non-commercial contracts time is not regarded as an essential term unless the contract expressly stipulates that time must strictly be observed; or the nature of the contract, the subject matter or the circumstances of a particular case, require precise compliance with time. For example, suppose you order a wedding cake to be delivered before 9 am on the day of the wedding. Let us suppose further that there is no express provision in the contract that requires strict observation of the time of delivery. The seller in breach of contract delivers the cake a day after the wedding. Is time of delivery an essential term? Since this is a non-commercial contract, prima facie it is not. However, the circumstances might show that the parties intended that the time of delivery must strictly be complied with.

Where time of delivery is not an essential term of the contract, but the seller unreasonably delays delivery of the goods, the buyer may give the seller notice making time the essence of the contract. However, the length of the notice must be reasonable.[16]

WAIVER

Even where time is of the essence of the contract, delay does not automatically lead to the termination of the contract. The buyer may expressly or impliedly waive his or her right to repudiate the contract, by accepting late delivery or by giving the seller more time within which to deliver the goods. If the buyer extends the time of delivery, time ceases to be an essential term.

14 [1981] 1 WLR 711 at 728–729, per Lord Roskill.
15 Ibid, per Lord Roskill.
16 *Bunge Corporation v Tradax*, supra; *Charles Rickards Ltd v Oppenheim* [1950] 1 All ER 420.

However, the buyer could reinstate time of delivery as an essential term by giving the seller reasonable notice to that effect.[17]

DELIVERY OF WRONG QUANTITY – S 30[18]

The seller must deliver the agreed quantity of the goods. Section 30(1) of the Goods Act provides that if the seller delivers less than what they contracted to deliver, the buyer may reject the goods or accept them as they are. Either way, the buyer would be entitled to sue the seller for damages for breach of contract. Where the buyer decides to accept delivery, they must pay a proportionate part of the purchase price. For example, in *Behrend v Produce Brokers Co*,[19] the seller agreed to deliver a specified quantity of cottonseed arriving in London on a named ship. The ship arrived on time with the right quantity of the goods, but due to technical difficulties, only half of the goods were off-loaded before the ship proceeded to another port. The ship came back two weeks later with the rest of the goods. The buyer accepted the lot delivered on time and rejected the rest. It was held that the contract was to deliver an indivisible whole and not by instalments. Therefore, on the basis of the equivalent of s 30(1), the buyer was within their right to reject the second lot. Similarly, where the seller delivers more than the agreed quantity, the buyer has three choices. They could reject the whole lot, accept only the agreed quantity or accept the whole lot. Where they choose to accept the whole lot, they must pay for the excess goods at the contract rate.[20] The buyer would be entitled to sue for any damages resulting from the breach.

MIXED DELIVERY

Delivery is also wrongful if the contract goods are mixed with non-contract goods. For example, suppose the seller promises to deliver at the buyer's shop 30 bags of rice, and they deliver 30 bags of rice and five bags of salt. Under s 30(3) of the Goods Act, the buyer is entitled to reject the whole lot or accept the goods that are in accordance with the contract and reject the non-contract goods. Unlike under subsections (1) and (2), in this instance the buyer has no right to accept the non-contractual goods. It would seem that the reason for this is that in the event of a dispute between the parties regarding the purchase price for the non-contract goods, there is nothing in

17 *Charles Rickards Ltd v Oppenheim* [1950] 1 All ER 420

18 Delivery of the wrong quantity in some instances may also constitute breach of the implied condition in Goods Act, s 13 (correspondence with the description). See for example, *Re Moore & Co v Landaur* [1921] 2 KB 519.

19 [1920] 3 KB 530.

20 Goods Act, s 30(2).

the contract that could assist the courts to determine the appropriate price for the non-contractual goods.

It should be remembered that the operation of the foregoing rules is subject to any trade usage, special agreement or course of dealing between the parties. Readers should also be mindful of the common law maxim: *de minimis non curat lex* (or the law does not bother with trifling). In this context it means that the buyer is not entitled to reject the goods for trifling or microscopic deviations. What constitutes "trifling" obviously is a question of fact depending, inter alia, upon the nature of the contract and trade usage.[21]

INSTALMENT DELIVERY

A buyer is not bound to accept delivery by instalments, except where the contract provides so. For example, a contract may provide for the seller to supply 2,400 tonnes of cement to be delivered in 12 different instalments over a period of six months. The contract is one and entire, even though performance is not rendered all at once. Suppose in such a contract the second instalment is defective or short, is the buyer entitled to reject the defective instalment and to rescind the contract in relation to future instalments? Section 31 of the Goods Act provides that, in such a case, if the contract provides for separate payments for each instalment, whether the breach entitles the buyer to terminate the contract or only to a claim for damages with regard to that instalment, is a question of fact depending on the terms of the contract and all circumstances of the case. Generally, if the breach is of such a kind or takes place in such circumstances as reasonably to lead to the inference that similar breach will be committed in the future, then the buyer may be entitled to treat the whole contract as at an end.[22]

The New Zealand case of *Hammer & Barrow v Coca Cola*,[23] illustrates the judicial interpretation of a similar provision. In that case, the plaintiff contracted to deliver 200,000 yoyos by instalments to the defendants. The defendants terminated the contract when just less than half of the goods had been delivered. The plaintiff sued the defendant for breach of contract. The court held that in determining whether the buyer was justified to terminate future delivery, two key factors had to be taken into account: (i) the quantitative ratio of the breach to the whole contact; and (ii) the degree of probability that the breach would be repeated. In this case, the court found that of the lot delivered, 80 per cent were defective, which in their Lordships' opinion was considerable and there was no evidence that the breach would not be repeated. Moreover, the court found that the consequences of the breach were detrimental to the defendant's promotional exercise.

21 *Shipton, Anderson v Well Bros* [1912] 1 KB 574.
22 *Millars' Karri & Jarrah Co v Weddel Turner & Co* [1908] 100 LT 128.
23 [1962] NZLR 723.

Duties of the buyer

The buyer performs the contract by payment of the purchase price and acceptance of delivery of the goods in accordance with the terms of the contract.[24]

Payment

It has been seen that under s 28 of the Goods Act, unless otherwise agreed, the buyer must pay when the seller delivers the goods. Quite often the parties agree for payment to be made after delivery (credit sale) or in advance of delivery. The legal effect of the former is that the seller cannot withhold delivery on account of non-payment, whilst under the latter agreement the seller can sue the buyer for the price before delivery or passage of property.

TIME OF PAYMENT

Many contracts state the time or period within which payment should be made. The question is, where the buyer is late in payment, is the seller entitled to treat the breach as a repudiation, which gives the seller a right to terminate the contract? According to s 11 of the Goods Act, as a general rule, it is presumed that the parties do not intend a stipulation relating to time of payment to be essential term.[25] The presumption can be displaced by evidence of a contrary intention expressed or implied in the contract and all surrounding circumstances. For example, in the Canadian case of *Mooney v Lipka*,[26] the defendant agreed to sell to the plaintiff a cartload of potatoes, payment to be made upon the seller loading the cart. The seller loaded the cart as agreed. The plaintiff tendered payment two days later, by which time the defendant had already sold the potatoes to another person. In an action for breach of contract, the defendant claimed that he treated the delay in tendering the purchase price as breach of condition, which entitled him to terminate the contract. It was held that in commercial contracts a stipulation of time of delivery is presumed to be an essential term, and since in this case payment was supposed to be made upon delivery the parties must have intended punctuality of payment to be an essential term. However, it should be stressed that each case depends on its own facts.[27] Also, even where, at the outset, time of payment is not an essential term, it could become one in case of excessive delay.[28]

24 Goods Act, s 27.
25 For illustration see *Decro-Wall International v Practitioners in Marketing* [1971] 2 All ER 216.
26 (1926) 4 DLR 647. See also *Withers v Reynolds* (1831) 2B & AD 882.
27 See for example, *Decro-Wall International v Practitioners in Marketing*, supra.
28 Bridge, *Sale of Goods*, supra, at p 409.

Acceptance of delivery

It is the buyer's obligation to take delivery of the goods. Section 37(1) of the Goods Act states that where the seller is ready and willing to deliver and requests the buyer to take delivery, if the buyer fails to do so within a reasonable time he or she will be liable to the seller for any loss occasioned by the delay plus reasonable charges for storage of the goods. Whether the buyer's obligation to take delivery at the stipulated time is an essential term of a contract, the breach of which would entitle the seller to treat the contract as repudiated, or whether it is an intermediary term or a warranty depends on the intention of the parties. As we have seen, in commercial contracts prima facie, time is regarded as an essential term. Nevertheless, it would seem that generally a seller is not entitled to rescind a contract on account of the buyer's delay to accept delivery on time, except where the subject matter or circumstances require precise compliance.[29] For example, in the case of perishable goods, spot contracts that require immediate payment[30] and in livestock trade,[31] timely acceptance of delivery is likely to be an essential term. In other situations, the courts will most likely treat time for acceptance of delivery as an intermediary term.

Remedies of the parties

In this part we shall discuss the range of remedies available to the buyer or seller, as the case may be, in the event of breach of contract. Needless to say, the available remedies and choice depend on the term breached and other circumstances as explained below.

Seller's remedies

For convenience, the seller's remedies are broadly divided into two, action against the goods and action for money. The former is a self-help remedy whilst the latter action must be pursued through the courts, unless of course the matter is settled out of court.

Action against the goods

In certain circumstances an unpaid seller's best remedy might be to retain or resume possession of the goods. For example, where the buyer is bankrupt or is in serious financial difficulties, suing him or her for damages or for the purchase price in most cases would be a pointless and expensive exercise.

29 See *Bunge Corporation v Tradax*, supra.
30 See for example, *Mooney v Lipka*, supra.
31 *Harrington v Browne* [1917] 23 CLR 297. See Bridge, *Sale of Goods*, supra, at pp 364–366.

The Goods Act, in certain specified situations, empowers an unpaid seller (i) to withhold delivery (lien) and (ii) to stop delivery of the goods in transit. Both remedies are only available where the seller is "unpaid". Section 38(b) defines an "unpaid seller" as including a seller in a case where the whole of the purchase price has not been paid, or if paid by a negotiable instrument (such as a cheque) it is dishonoured.

Lien

Lien is the right of an unpaid seller to retain possession of the goods till he or she is paid. For the purpose of exercising a seller's lien, a seller of goods on credit is not "unpaid" as long as the time for payment is not yet due, except if the buyer is insolvent.[32] This remedy is exercisable as long as the seller is in possession of the goods, irrespective of whether property in the goods has passed to the buyer.[33] Conversely, the seller loses his or her right of lien if the goods are delivered to a carrier without the seller reserving a right of disposal; or where the buyer lawfully obtains possession of the goods; or where the seller waives his or her right of lien.[34]

LOSS OF LIEN

Once the seller allows the buyer to take possession, the right of lien is lost and cannot be revived even if the seller regained possession.[35] The case of *Csolle (Trading as Lodi Timber Co) v ASP (NG) Ltd*[36] illustrates this point. In that case, the respondents sold to the appellants on credit a motor-driven saw and the appellants took possession of the goods. Two weeks later the appellants returned the saw for repair and left it with the respondents. After the saw was repaired, the parties could not agree as to which one of them was to pay the repair bill. The respondents retained the saw and the appellants purchased a replacement saw from other sources. Nine months after the original sale, the respondents, without notifying the appellants, sold the saw to a third party at a price less than the original purchase price. The respondents initially sued the appellants for the purchase price[37] but amended their plea and claimed damages for breach of contract assessed as the difference between the original purchase price and the re-sale price of the saw, plus the cost of repair. The trial magistrate

32 Goods Act, s 40(1).
33 Goods Act, s 39(1). If property has not passed to the buyer, the seller's lien is in addition to any other rights the seller has under the contract, s 39(2).
34 Goods Act, s 42.
35 However, in case of insolvency of the buyer, the seller may stop delivery to the buyer of goods that have left the seller's possession, see below "stoppage in transit".
36 [1967–68] P & NGLR 301.
37 This point is discussed below under "Action for the price".

found that the respondents were not responsible for the repair bill and awarded the respondents damages on the basis that, in reselling the saw, the respondents were exercising their right as an unpaid seller under s 48(3) of the Goods Act.

On appeal to the Supreme Court, the appellants argued that s 48(3) did not apply because the respondents at the time of sale were not in possession of the goods as a seller but as bailee. Moreover, they did not give the statutory notice to the appellants prior to reselling the saw. The respondents sought to argue that the return of the saw to them restored them to the position of an unpaid vendor still in possession of the goods sold. In response to the contention that they did not give the appellants the statutory notice, the respondents argued that they did not need to give the notice because the saw was of a "perishable" nature. It was held that when the respondents gave possession of the saw to the appellants the respondents ceased to be "an unpaid seller in possession" of goods sold. When they resumed possession they did so not as seller but as bailee with obligations to take care of the goods, but with no right of resale. The court also dismissed the respondents' claim that the saw was of a perishable nature. It was held that the term "perishable" applies only to goods that are "likely to deteriorate so rapidly that the delay involved in giving notice would result in unnecessary loss and that was not the position here."[38]

Stoppage in transit

Section 43 of the Goods Act provides that where the buyer becomes insolvent, the unpaid seller has a right of "stoppage in transit". This remedy envisages a situation where the goods have left the seller's possession en route to the buyer and the latter becomes insolvent whilst the goods are still in transit (by sea, road or air). In that case, an unpaid seller has a right to stop delivery of the goods to the buyer and to keep the goods until he or she is paid.[39] Goods are deemed to be in transit until the buyer or their agent takes delivery of the goods from the carrier.[40] The seller may effect his or her remedy either by physically taking possession of the goods, or by serving notice of his or her claim to the carrier or bailee.[41]

CONSEQUENCES OF EXERCISING SELLER'S RIGHT OF LIEN OR STOPPAGE IN TRANSIT

The fact that the seller exercises his or her right of lien or stoppage in transit does not automatically terminate the contract. The contract only terminates

38 [1967–68] P & NGLR at 306–307. At 308, Clarkson J observed, *obiter dictum*, that the respondent was liable to the appellant for damages for conversion.

39 Goods Act, s 44.

40 Goods Act, s 45.

41 Goods Act, s 46.

when the seller re-sells the goods. Section 48(3) gives an unpaid seller, who has exercised a right of lien or stoppage in transitu, the power to re-sell goods immediately in the case of perishable goods. In other cases this power is exercisable after the seller serves notice on the buyer and the buyer fails to tender the money due within a reasonable time. The seller may also re-sell the goods where the power to do so is reserved in the contract. In all situations the buyer remains liable to the seller for loss suffered as result of the buyer's breach of contract.[42]

Action for money

The seller may sue the buyer for the price of the goods and/or for damages for breach of contract. In an action for the price, the seller sues for the amount agreed upon plus damages for any consequential loss (such as the cost of storage of the goods). In an action for damages, on the other hand, the seller is suing for loss suffered as a result of the buyer's wrongful delay or failure to take delivery. The seller must prove that his or her loss resulted from the breach. As we shall presently see, a seller suing for damages must attempt to mitigate his or her loss by re-selling the goods to other persons. But a seller who is entitled to sue for the price is under no such obligation. The reason for this is that the property and the risk in the goods would have passed to the buyer and it is up to the buyer to take whatever action he or she wants with respect to the goods.[43] Therefore, from the seller's point of view, if he or she can sue for the price, usually it is the best remedy, except of course where the buyer is not worth suing. We shall discuss in detail the two remedies.

PURCHASE PRICE

Section 49 of the Goods Act specifies two situations in which a seller may sue for the price. First, the seller may sue for the price where property has passed to the buyer and the buyer *wrongfully* rejects or neglects to pay the purchase price.[44] Refusal to pay is not wrongful where the buyer rightfully rejects the goods on the ground that the seller is in breach of an essential term of the contract, such as the case where goods do not correspond with the description or do not fit the particular purpose. Nor is the refusal to pay the purchase price wrongful where the buyer purchased the goods on credit and the time allowed has not expired. Secondly, the seller may sue for the

42 Goods Act, s 48(3)(d) and (4).
43 See for example, *Colley v Overseas Exporters* [1921] All ER 596.
44 See for example, *Csolle (Trading as Lodi Timber Co) v ASP (NG) Ltd,* supra. In that case, it was held that where property has passed this is the only remedy available to the seller after the goods have left their possession.

price if the contract stipulates for payment in advance irrespective of delivery, and the buyer wrongfully refuses or neglects to pay. In such a case it is irrelevant whether or not the property has passed or the goods have not been appropriated to the contract.[45]

The English case of *Colley v Overseas Exporters Ltd*[46] illustrates the application of a provision corresponding with s 49 of the Goods Act. The plaintiffs agreed to sell to the defendants a specified quantity of goods on terms, which included FOB terms.[47] The plaintiffs were under obligation to deliver the goods on board a ship to be nominated by the defendants and the price was payable upon delivery. The plaintiffs sent the goods to the docks to be loaded on the nominated ship, but the ship had been withdrawn and the defendants, in breach of contract, failed to nominate another ship. The plaintiffs left the goods at the docks, and subsequently the goods perished. The issue was whether the plaintiffs were entitled to sue for the price. It was held that, in the absence of a special contract, a seller is not entitled to sue for the price unless the property has passed to the buyer. In a contract subject to FOB terms, property does not pass till the shipping documents are delivered to the buyer. Since, in this case, there were no shipping documents and the goods were not put on board a ship, property did not pass to the buyer. Accordingly, the plaintiffs were not entitled to sue for the price. Their only remedy was action for damages.[48] The fact that it was the defendants' fault that prevented the property passing was irrelevant.

DAMAGES

The award of damages is the most common remedy for aggrieved sellers and buyers. A seller may sue for damages under s 37 (delay or refusal to take delivery) and or s 50 (non-acceptance of delivery) of the Goods Act.

Wrongful delay or refusal to take delivery Section 37 contemplates a situation where the seller is ready and willing to deliver the goods and requests the buyer to take delivery. If the buyer wrongfully delays or refuses to take delivery within a reasonable time thereafter, he or she will be liable to the seller for loss suffered as a result and a reasonable charge for the care of the goods. The charges may include, for example, rent for storage of the goods, provision of security guards and insurance. It should be remembered that the buyer's delay or refusal to take delivery within a reasonable time does

45 Goods Act, s 49(2).
46 [1921] 3 KB 302.
47 Under FOB (free on board) terms, the risk passes when the goods are on board on a carrier and property passes when the title documents (e.g. bill of lading) are handed over to the buyer.
48 If they sued for damages, the damages would have been substantially reduced because they did not attempt to mitigate their loss by reselling the goods, see below "mitigation of damages".

not automatically relieve the buyer of the obligation to deliver the goods, except where time is the essence of the contract or the buyer's action amounts to a repudiation of the contract. Also, s 37(2) stresses that if the breach amounts to a repudiation of the contract, these remedies are in addition to any other remedies the seller is entitled to seek.

Wrongful non-acceptance of delivery Section 50(1) of the Goods Act provides that if the buyer wrongfully refuses to accept and pay for the goods, the seller may sue him or her for damages for non-performance of the contract. In the absence of a special agreement between the parties, action for damages is the appropriate remedy for the seller where property in the goods has not passed to the buyer.

QUANTUM OF DAMAGES

It is common knowledge that the object of awarding damages is to put the losing party in as good a position as they would have been in had the contract been performed. As we shall presently see, the principle for assessment of the buyer's and seller's damages is the same. For the seller, s 50(1) of the Goods Act states that the measure of damages is the "estimated loss directly and naturally resulting in the ordinary course of events from the buyer's breach of contract". Readers will no doubt recognise that the subsection re-states the well-known principle in *Hadley v Baxendale*.[49] Section 50(2) qualifies this provision to the effect that, where there is an available market for the goods in question, then the measure of damages prima facie is to be assessed as the difference between the contract price and the market or current price prevailing at the time the buyer was supposed to take delivery or, in the absence of stipulated time, at the time he or she rejected the goods.

Available market The "contract price" is the purchase price for the goods stipulated in the contract. The term "available market" does not mean a physical place. Rather, it presupposes a situation where the goods could be purchased in accordance with the economic rule of demand and supply. In *Central Province Forest Industries Pty Ltd (Provincial Liquidator Appointed) v Rainbow Holding Pty Ltd*,[50] Kapi J cited with approval the following definition of "available market" by Upjohn J in *Thompson (W L) Ltd v Robinson (Gunmakers) Ltd*:[51]

> [A]n available market merely means that the situation in the particular trade in the particular area was such that the particular goods could

49 (1854) 9 Ex Ch 341.
50 N321 of 1980.
51 (1955) Ch 177 at 187.

> freely be sold; and that there was a demand sufficient to absorb readily all the goods that were thrust on it, so that if a particular purchaser defaulted, the goods in question could readily be disposed of.

For example, suppose that S contracts to sell a car to B for K20,000, and B wrongfully rejects the goods. As we shall see, S is supposed to take reasonable steps to mitigate their loss by attempting to sell the car to other people. Let us assume that S manages to sell the car to TP for K15,000. S's damages are measured as the difference between the price for which he or she originally agreed to sell the car to B and the price for which he or she sold the car to TP, which is K5,000. In addition, S could claim damages under s 37, if applicable. It follows that if S sells the car to TP for the same or more than the original contract price he or she suffers no loss; hence no damages will be awarded except for nominal damages.

No available market The market price rule is a general or prima facie rule. There may be circumstances when it is not an appropriate measure of the seller's loss. For example, suppose S and B enter into a contract whereby S agrees to sell her lecture notes to B for K500. Later, B wrongfully rejects the goods because he realises that the law has changed substantially and, accordingly, the notes are outdated. S tries to sell the notes elsewhere but to no avail. In such a case the market rule cannot be used as a yardstick for S's damages as there is no market for the goods. The courts would therefore resort to the more general formula under s 50(1)(b), estimated loss directly and naturally resulting in the ordinary course of events from the buyer's breach, and try to work out a fair estimate of S's loss.

The foregoing provisions were discussed in the judgment of the National Court of Justice in *Central Province Forest Industries Pty Ltd (Provisional Liquidator Appointed) v Rainbow Holdings Pty Ltd.*[52] In that case, the plaintiff contracted to sell to the defendant a certain amount of logs at a total price of K270,000. The defendant, in breach of contract, refused to accept the goods, whereupon the plaintiff, rightly, terminated the contract. Thereafter, the plaintiffs attempted to resell the goods, but were unable to obtain corresponding offers because the logs had deteriorated. Subsequently, the plaintiffs managed to sell the logs for K50,000, and sued the defendants for damages for breach of contract. The issue was whether the damages ought to be assessed by reference to s 50(1)(b) formula or by the market price rule under s 50(2). It was contended for the plaintiff that the market price rule was inapplicable because there was no market for the goods.

Kapi J, after citing with approval Lord Upjohn's definition of "available market" in *Thompson (W L) Ltd v Robinson (Gunmakers) Ltd,* quoted

52 WS 713 of 1980 (N321) (unreported judgment).

above, agreed with the plaintiff's submission that there was no available market for the subject goods. In the circumstances, his Honour held that the difference between the contract price and the price for which the plaintiff sold the logs was the appropriate measure of the plaintiff's loss which "directly and naturally resulted from the breach".

Lost volume The market rule is also not an appropriate measure of damages where the seller has more supply of the particular goods than there is demand. For example, suppose S, dealers in new cars, have in stock ten Toyota vans for sale. They buy the vans for K20,000 and resell them, on average, for K30,000. S enters into a contract to sell one of the vans to B for K30,000. Later, B wrongfully rejects the van. S manages to sell the same van to TP on the same day for the same price. If we apply the market rule, S suffered no loss since they managed to resell the van for the same price as the original contract price. However, in reality that is not true. If B had not breached the contract, S could have sold two cars, one to B and another to TP, making a gross profit of K10,000 on each car. Clearly, applying the market rule would result in S not being compensated for lost volume of trade. To avoid this, in such a situation the courts would use the general formula under s 50(1)(b) to arrive at a fair assessment of the seller's loss. In our example, the loss of profit of K10,000 would be the appropriate award, being "loss directly and naturally" resulting from B's breach.[53]

It should be noted that the above argument only applies where the seller has other goods in stock for sale. For instance, suppose in the above example S had only one car to sell, and when B breached, S sold the car to TP at K29,000. S could not claim lost volume of sale, as they had no other cars in stock to sell. In that case the market rule would be the appropriate measure of S's damages.[54]

Mitigation of damages The seller has a duty to mitigate their loss, for example, by trying to resell the goods to other people. If the seller fails to take reasonable steps to mitigate their loss, the damages awarded would be reduced by the amount they would have saved had they attempted to mitigate the loss.[55]

Buyer's remedies

The buyer has two basic remedies: (i) rejection of the goods; and/or (ii) action for damages. In addition, in appropriate cases the buyer could (iii) seek an order of specific performance.

53 *Thompson (W L) Ltd v Robinson (Gunmakers) Ltd* [1955] Ch 177.
54 *Charter v Sullivan* (1957) 2 QB 117.
55 See below (p 80) for further discussion.

Right to reject the goods

A buyer is entitled to reject the goods if the seller delivers less or delivers more than the agreed quantity of the goods.[56] Secondly, a buyer may reject the goods if the seller breaches any condition implied in the contract by sections 13 to 16 of the Goods Act, or breaches any express essential terms of the contract.[57]

CONSEQUENCES OF REJECTION

If the buyer rightfully rejects the goods, he or she is entitled to a refund of the purchase price, if already paid, as a breach constitutes a total failure of consideration.[58] In addition, the buyer may sue the seller for damages for non-delivery of the goods.[59] If the seller had delivered the goods, unless otherwise agreed, the buyer has no obligation to return the rejected goods to the seller. It suffices for the buyer to inform the seller of their decision to reject the goods.[60] The property and or risk, if passed to the buyer, revert to the seller. However, pending collection of the goods, the buyer bears the usual common law obligations of a bailee in possession.[61]

LOSS OF RIGHT TO REJECT

Under s 12 of the Goods Act, a buyer may elect or, in certain stipulated circumstances, may be compelled, to treat breach of a condition as a breach of warranty and not as a ground for rejecting the goods. Section 12(4) provides that unless otherwise agreed, a buyer loses his or her right to reject the goods, in a contract which does not provide for instalment delivery if: (i) the contract is for the sale of specific goods the property in which has passed to the buyer; or (ii) the buyer accepts the goods or part thereof. We shall elaborate the provision below.

SALE OF SPECIFIC GOODS

The interpretation of the equivalent of s 12(4)(b) of the Goods Act (namely, "in a contract of sale of specific goods the buyer loses the right to reject the goods upon the passing of property") when read with presumptive Rule 1, s 18(3)(a), has been problematic in England and other jurisdictions. As it may be recalled, presumptive Rule 1 stipulates that in an unconditional

56 See discussion above (p 60): seller's duty to deliver.
57 See above discussion of terms of contract of sale of goods.
58 Goods Act, s 54(b), see for example, *Rowland v Divall* [1923] 2 KB 500.
59 See measurement of damages, below (p 75).
60 Goods Act, s 36.
61 See for example, *Rebtrad Niugini Pty Ltd v ABCO Pty Ltd* [1990] PNGLR 155.

contract for the sale of specific goods in a deliverable state, property passes the moment the parties enter into the contract. The problem can be illustrated by the following example. Suppose B purchases a can of fish from a store. Upon opening the can B discovers that the fish is rotten. A literal interpretation of the two provisions means that B cannot reject the goods because property passed to him or her the moment he or she entered into the contract. Clearly, such interpretation, if right, renders the buyer's right to reject non-complying goods virtually meaningless and unfair to the buyer. To avoid this undesirable outcome, the oft-cited English case of *Varley v Whipp*[62] narrowed down the scope of the equivalent of Rule 1, s 18(3)(a).

The facts of *Varley v Whipp* were as follows. The plaintiff sold to the defendant a machine, which in the contract was described as near new. The buyer had not previously seen the machine. When it was delivered it turned out to be a much older machine and the buyer purported to reject it on the ground that it did not fit the description. The plaintiff sued for the purchase price arguing that the defendant had lost their right to reject the goods because the property had passed under the equivalent of Rule 1 read with s 12(4)(b). It was held that Rule 1 applies only where the contract is "unconditional". The court said that the term "unconditional" not only refers to condition precedent, but also to essential terms. In the present case, the contract was not unconditional because it was subject to a condition that goods must fit the description. Therefore, property did not pass at the time the parties entered into the contract and, hence, the buyer was entitled to reject the goods.

The effect of the judgment is that a buyer of specific goods under a contract subject to any implied or express essential terms does not lose the right to reject the goods for breach of any of these terms, unless the buyer accepts the goods. Since invariably all contracts are subject to some essential terms, this interpretation renders Rule 1 devoid of any practical effect. *Varley v Whipp* has been widely criticised in some circles for its interpretation of presumptive Rule 1.[63] However, the primary cause of the problem is s 12(4)(b), which links the passing of property with the buyer's right to reject the goods. In some Australian jurisdictions, the equivalent provision has been omitted from the legislation. In those jurisdictions the buyer only loses the right to reject if they accept the goods. It is suggested that the Goods Act should likewise be amended.

ACCEPTANCE

The buyer loses the right to reject the goods once he or she accepts the goods. Under s 35 of the Goods Act, the buyer is deemed to have accepted

62 [1900] 1 QB 513.

63 For detailed discussion of this case and related cases, see Sutton, *Sales and Consumer Law,* supra, pp 202–205.

the goods when he or she informs the seller that he or she has accepted the goods; or if the goods are delivered and the buyer does an act in relation to the goods that is inconsistent with the seller's ownership; or after lapse of a reasonable time the buyer retains the goods without advising the seller he or she has rejected them. A common example of an inconsistent act is where the buyer uses or consumes the goods, so that the buyer is unable to return the goods in substantially the same condition. Selling or pledging the goods as security for a loan is also regarded as doing an act that is inconsistent with the seller's ownership, and therefore it is deemed to be acceptance of the goods.[64]

RIGHT TO EXAMINE THE GOODS

Section 34 of the Goods Act states that where goods are delivered to the buyer, which the buyer has not previously examined, the buyer "shall" not be deemed to have examined them until the buyer has had a reasonable opportunity of examining them for the purpose of determining whether the goods comply with the contract. In certain situations this provision and s 35, above, appear to conflict. Suppose that B orders ten computers from XP in Port Moresby, which B intends to resell to TP in Lae. B instructs XP to deliver the computers directly to TP in Lae. When the computers arrive in Lae, TP upon examination finds that they do not correspond with the description and he rejects them. As between B and XP, the latter is entitled to reject because he had not previously examined the goods and had not accepted them. As between B and TP, the question is whether (assuming that the computers do not correspond with the description in their contract) B is also entitled to reject them. On the one hand, under s 34, B is not deemed to have accepted the goods because B never had the opportunity to examine them. On the other hand, selling the computers to TP is doing an act that is inconsistent with XP's ownership, which under s 35 is deemed to constitute acceptance of the goods, which in turn disentitles B to reject the goods.

There are no PNG cases dealing with the apparent conflict between the two provisions. Several English and other jurisdiction cases have considered the equivalent provisions. In the English Court of Appeal judgment in *Hardy & Co v Hillerns & Fowler*,[65] it was held that the equivalent of s 35, is independent of s 34, and that it was immaterial for the purposes of the former provision that the buyer had not had a reasonable opportunity to examine the goods when the buyer performed the inconsistent act. In other words, if the buyer does any act to the goods, which is inconsistent with the

64 See for example, *E & S Ruben Ltd v Faire Bros. & Co Ltd* [1949] 1 KB 254.
65 [1923] 2 KB 490.

seller's right, the buyer loses his or her right to reject the goods irrespective of the fact that the buyer had not previously examined the goods. The New Zealand case of *Hammer & Barrow v Coca-Cola*[66] summarised the legal position as follows. If the goods are delivered and the buyer, upon receipt of the goods, delivers them to the sub-buyer or the buyer instructs the seller to deliver the goods directly to the sub-buyer, the buyer's act is deemed to be inconsistent with the seller's ownership. If we applied this rule to our example above, B would not be entitled to reject the goods as against the original seller. B's only remedy would be to sue TP for damages for breach of contract. Where the buyer merely enters into a contract to resell the goods to a third party before the seller delivers the goods, that by itself is not regarded as being inconsistent with the seller's ownership.

LAPSE OF REASONABLE TIME

If the buyer retains the goods for more than a reasonable time without objection, he or she loses the right to reject the goods if, upon examination, the goods are defective. What constitutes reasonable time depends on the circumstances of each case. Generally reasonable time refers to sufficient time necessary to discover the defect.

Damages

As already seen, the object for awarding damages is to compensate the innocent party for their loss resulting from the breach of contract by the other party. The rules for the assessment of the buyer's damages are basically the same as those for assessing the seller's loss discussed above. We discuss them under separate headings mainly for convenience.

DAMAGES FOR BREACH OF WARRANTY

The buyer may sue the seller for damages for breach of a warranty expressed or implied in the contract. For example, if the seller wrongfully interferes with the buyer's use or enjoyment of the goods the buyer may sue him or her for damages for breach of the implied warranty of quiet enjoyment under s 13(b) of the Goods Act. The buyer may also sue the seller for damages for breach of a condition of the contract where the buyer elects to treat the breach as grounds for termination of the contract or where the buyer is compelled to treat the breach as if it were a breach of warranty.[67] Section 53(2) states that the measure of damages for breach of warranty is the

66 [1962] NZLR 723.
67 See Goods Act, ss 12(1), (4), 35 and 53.

estimated loss directly and naturally arising from the breach.[68] The rule, as may be recalled, is designed to exclude loss that is too remote from the breach.[69]

Wrong quality Where the breach relates to the quality of the goods, prima facie the measure of the buyer's damages is the difference between the value of the goods at the time of delivery, and the value which they would have had if they had answered the warranty.[70] For example, in *Marlor Investments Pty Ltd v Symmons,*[71] the defendant sold a tractor to the plaintiff, which the defendant warranted to be in good working order. It transpired that the tractor was not in working order. Frost J upheld the trial magistrate's award of damages of $2,000 as being the estimated value of the tractor had it answered the warranty.

NON-DELIVERY

A buyer may sue the seller for damages for wrongful non-delivery of the goods. Non-delivery is where the seller, in breach of contract, refuses or neglects to deliver the goods or delivers goods in such circumstances that the buyer is entitled to treat, and does treat, the breach as a repudiation of the contract. Section 51(1)(b) of the Goods Act, states that the measure of the buyer's damages shall be the estimated loss directly and naturally resulting from the ordinary course of events from the seller's breach. This general rule is subject to s 51(2), which provides that where there is an available market for the goods, then prima facie the measure of damages is the difference between the contract price and the market price. These provisions are worded in exactly the same way as s 50(1)(b) and (2), respectively, of the Goods Act, which deal with the measurement of the seller's damages. Our earlier discussion of the latter provisions would equally apply to the former provisions.

No available market Where there is no market for similar goods, the court must make its own assessment of the buyer's loss. The judgment of the National Court of Justice in *Evans, Grey & Hood Ltd v Plantation Supply & Service Co Pty Ltd et al.*[72] illustrates the application of this rule. The defendants agreed to sell to the plaintiffs 3 tons of PNG chillies for the price

68 Alternatively, the buyer may use a breach of warranty as a counterclaim against the seller to diminish or extinguish the price, s 53(1)(c).
69 See *Hadley v Baxendale*, supra.
70 Goods Act, s 53(3).
71 [1967–68] P & NGLR 292.
72 [1979] PNGLR 34.

of £738 sterling per tonne. The defendants, in breach of contract, failed to deliver. The plaintiffs failed in their endeavour to find sufficient quantities of alternative supplies of chillies in PNG or elsewhere, as there was a world-wide scarcity of chillies. The issue was how to assess the buyers' loss. Wilson J, after reviewing the evidence, concluded that the market price was not an appropriate measure of the plaintiffs' damages because chillies were in such short supply that it could properly be said that at the time of the breach (the relevant time for measuring the damages) there was no available market for the goods in question. In the circumstances, his Honour held that the measure of damages was the difference between the contract price and the re-sale price, or the loss of anticipated profit. His Honour stressed that the circumstances he had in mind were the fact that the chillies were sold on a commodity and produce market and that the defendants should have reasonably contemplated that the goods were for resell.

Wilson J, also noted that even if the market rule was employed to assess the damages, in the circumstances of the case, the result would have been the same, as the price at which the plaintiffs had agreed to sell the goods appeared to be the prevailing market price in London at the material time. His Honour determined that in the circumstances of this case, the market of chillies in London was the market price (if one was available). He stressed that the plaintiffs were not under any legal obligation to explore the world for better prices.

The National Court judgment in *Harrisons & Crosfield (PNG) Ltd v Pous Trading Company Pty Ltd*[73] illustrates the difficulty of applying the rules for the measurement of damages to concrete facts. In that case, the plaintiffs, coffee exporters, entered into a contract to purchase from the defendants 195 tons of Y grade coffee at 72.75t per kilogram, delivered at Mt Hagen. The defendants, in breach of contract, failed to deliver the goods. The plaintiffs had contractual obligations to supply coffee to their overseas clients and faced stiff penalties if they failed or delayed to deliver. Coincidentally, at the material time there was a dramatic increase in the demand for coffee in the international market, which triggered a price upsurge internationally and, inevitably, domestically. Within a space of two weeks the price of coffee jumped up to 140t per kilogram on the domestic market, and because of the high demand there was a general scarcity of coffee in the country. The plaintiff, faced with a stiff penalty, purchased coffee from various sources in the country to get enough quantity to supply their overseas clients. In some cases the plaintiffs were forced to pay higher than the prevailing market price and to purchase superior quality coffee than Y grade. In their action against the defendants for damages for breach of contract, the plaintiffs claimed loss of profit of K3792.36 and damages for loss they made on the buying of coffee from alternative sources. They calculated the latter

73 [1976] PNGLR 106.

loss as the difference between the contract price and the average price they paid to purchase coffee elsewhere:[74]

Contract price for 195 tonnes × 72.75t @ kilogram	= K141,862.50
Freight	= K4,442.10
Total	= K146,304.60
Buy-in price for 195 tonnes × K121.19 (average) @ kilo inclusive of freight	= K236,320.50
Loss: 236,320.50 − 146,304.60 = K90,015.90.	

It seems from the facts that the defendants conceded to the plaintiffs' claim of loss of profit of K3,792.36, but objected to the assessment of the plaintiffs' alleged loss on buy-in from other sources. Apparently, the defendants objected on the grounds that the plaintiffs in some instances paid more than the market price and also that the quality of some of the coffee they purchased was superior to the contract coffee. The issue was whether the plaintiffs were justified in the steps they took and whether the price they paid for the coffee was the market price.

Frost CJ, in delivering his judgment, observed that the application of s 51 of the Goods Act depends upon whether, in the circumstances, there was an available market. His Honour said that if there was no available market "then the measure of damages is the amount a reasonable man, acting sensibly and on his own behalf and at his own risk would be willing to pay in order to get the goods at the place and time stipulated".[75] On the facts of the case, he found that there was no available market for the goods "in a sense that the entire contract quantity could have been purchased on 25 July at a single price lower than the prices paid by the plaintiff". Accordingly, Frost CJ held that the plaintiffs were justified to purchase coffee from alternative sources and at the price they paid for it. His Honour awarded the plaintiffs damages of K3,792.36 for lost profit and K92,905.06 for loss on buying in 195 tonnes from alternative sources (total K96,697.42).

With respect, Frost CJ's conception of "available market" is a bit confusing. In our view, there was an available market for coffee in the sense that there were willing sellers, but the price was well above the contract price. The issue should have been whether the price paid by the plaintiffs was the prevailing market price at the time of breach. In the circumstances of the case it would

74 Readers who have read the case may note that our figures are different from those in the judgment. The reason is that the sums in the judgment do not seem to add up. This might be because in the judgment they calculated the total weight of the coffee as 195 imperial tons (which they converted into metric tonnes), whilst we assumed the total weight to be 195 tonnes. For present purposes, the difference is not material as we follow the same formula as used in the judgment.

75 Ibid, at p 110.

seem that that was indeed the case. Interestingly, although his Honour found that there was no available market for the goods, he used the market rule to assess the plaintiffs' damages from buying-in coffee from alternative sources. His Honour's award to the plaintiff of damages of K92,905.06 appears to be correct. However, with respect, in our view the additional award to the plaintiff of K3,792.36 in lost profit, amounted to over-compensation. It is submitted that the plaintiffs' lost profit was covered in the damages awarded for loss on buying in. That sum represents the extra money they were forced to spend to purchase enough coffee from alternative sources in order to fulfil their overseas contractual obligations.

The point we are trying to make is best explained with an illustration. Suppose for our present purposes that the plaintiffs contracted to resell to their overseas clients 195 tonnes (195,000 kilograms) of coffee at 82.75t per kilogram: 195,000 kilos × 82.75t = K161,362.50. Their gross profit would have been K15,057.90 (which is the difference between the resale price and the purchase price: K161,362.50 – K146,304.60). Because of the breach they were forced to spend an extra K90,015.90 (K236,320.50 – K146,304.60) to purchase coffee from elsewhere. If they sold the coffee to their overseas clients at 82.75t @ kilogram, instead of making a gross profit of K15,057.90 they would make a gross loss of K74,958 (K236,320.50 – K161,362.50). However, the compensation they would receive for the extra money they spent to acquire the coffee from elsewhere, would wipe out this loss (K90,015.90 – K74,958) leaving them a gross profit of K15,057.90.

Resell Where there is an available market for the particular goods the fact that the buyer intends to resell the goods at a profit does not affect the operation of the market rule. The buyer has simply to purchase similar goods from elsewhere and claim compensation from the seller for the extra cost, if any, to purchase the goods. If there is no available market, the right of the buyer to claim compensation would depend on whether the loss was within the reasonable contemplation of both parties,[76] as is discussed below.

Interest, special damages and refund

Section 54 of the Goods Act, expressly saves the right of a seller or buyer to recover special damages or interest whereby under any law such damages or interest are recoverable, and the buyer's right to recover money paid in the event of total failure of consideration.

SPECIAL DAMAGES

At common law, a buyer or seller may claim compensation for special damages under the second limb of the principle of *Hadley v Baxendale.*

76 *Evans, Grey & Hood Ltd v Plantation Supply & Service Co Pty Ltd et al.*, supra, at 40.

Essentially, it provides that the innocent party is entitled to recover damages for loss which, at the time of the contract, was reasonably foreseeable by both parties as being sufficiently likely to occur.[77] For example, under this rule, the buyer (or seller, as the case may be) may recover damages for expenses incurred in preparation for delivery of the goods, such as non-refundable freight and insurance charges paid in advance. The extent and nature of damages recoverable under this rule depends on the circumstances of each case. For example, S agrees to sell to B a certain gadget. In anticipation, B enters into a contract to sell the gadget to TP at a profit. S wrongfully fails to deliver the gadget. Let us assume that the gadget in question is the only one of its kind. S is liable to B for breach of contract. At the same time B is liable to TP for breach of contract. The issue is whether B is entitled to recover from S not only damages for loss of profit on the resell to TP but also damages for which B would be liable to TP for breach of contract. It is suggested that neither loss "directly and naturally" results from the breach in the ordinary course of events; hence it is "special" loss. Whether B would recover such loss from S would depend on whether the loss was reasonably within the contemplation of both parties at the time they concluded the contract. For example, if S knew that B was in the business of buying and selling such gadgets then chances are that the loss was within the reasonable contemplation of both parties.[78]

Another example: B purchases from S an electric saw, which unknown to both parties has defects. As a result of using the saw, B suffers serious injuries. The damages for the injuries suffered by B would be "special damages". B could, in the alternative, sue S in tort for damages, but action for breach of contract would be easier to prove as liability for breach of contract, unlike negligence, is strict.[79]

INTEREST

The court may, in an appropriate case, award interest on damages. The power to award such interest arises from s 1 of the Judicial Proceedings (Interest on Debts and Damages) Act.[80] The power is discretionary and must be exercised according to law.[81]

77 Cited in *Tetley v Administration of PNG* [1971] PNGLR 65.
78 *Evans, Grey & Hood Ltd v Plantation Supply & Service Co Pty Ltd et al.*, supra, at 4. For a detailed discussion of a similar scenario see *Joseph & Co Pty Ltd v Harvest Grain Co* [1996] 39 NSWLR 722, and the authorities cited in that case.
79 See for example, *Grant v Australian Knitting*, supra.
80 Ch 52.
81 *Central Province Forest Industries Pty Ltd (Provisional Liquidator Appointed) v Rainbow Holdings Pty Ltd* N321 of 1980.

REFUND

Where the buyer pays the purchase price in advance, and there is a total failure of consideration, the buyer is entitled to a refund of the purchase price in addition to any other damages he or she might be entitled to claim against the seller for breach of contract.[82]

Mitigation of damages

In the event of breach of contract the aggrieved party should not just sit back and let damages accumulate. He or she must take reasonable steps to mitigate his or her loss. Thus, if the seller wrongfully fails to deliver the goods, the buyer should mitigate his or her loss by purchasing alternative goods elsewhere. The measure of the buyer's loss would be the extra cost incurred, if any, to purchase those goods.[83] Likewise, if the buyer wrongfully refuses to take delivery of the goods, the seller should take reasonable steps to find an alternative buyer for the goods.[84] The obligation of the aggrieved party is to act reasonably. For example, in the case of an aggrieved buyer, usually his or her obligation is to purchase similar goods in a market place contemplated by both parties. The buyer is not bound to go "hunting the globe" for a better market.[85] The same principle applies to an aggrieved seller. However, it should be stressed that what constitutes "reasonable" steps depends on the circumstances of each case. There may well be cases where the aggrieved party is expected to go "globe hunting" for an alternative market for the goods, if that was the contemplation of both parties. Similarly, though the alternative goods should be of the same quality as the contract goods, there may be circumstances where an aggrieved buyer is justified to purchase superior or more expensive alternative goods, if that was within the reasonable contemplation of both parties.[86]

Concluding remarks on the assessment of damages

As readers would have by now appreciated, it is not always easy to assess the innocent party's loss or determine the appropriate rules to apply. It is proper that we conclude this section with the following words of wisdom

82 See for example, *Rowland v Divall*, supra.

83 See for example, *Evans, Grey & Hood Ltd v Plantation Supply & Service Co Ltd and another* [1979] PNGLR 34.

84 See for example, *Central Province Forest Industries Pty Ltd (Provisional Liquidator Appointed) v Rainbow Holdings Pty Ltd* N321 of 1980.

85 *Evans, Grey & Hood Ltd v Plantation Supply & Service Co Ltd and another* [1979] PNGLR 34 at 40.

86 See for example, *Harrisons & Crosfield (PNG) Ltd v Pous Trading Company Pty Ltd* [1976] PNGLR 106.

stated in the judgment of Deane J in the High Court of Australia case of *Commonwealth v Amann Aviation Pty Ltd*:[87]

> It has been truly said that the assessment of damages in contract and tort is a "pragmatic subject [which] does not lend itself to hard and fast rules"... The explanation of that is to be found in the fact that the assessment of common law damages for breach of contract or tort was traditionally seen as a matter for the good sense of the jury... Within the context of the principle laid down in *Hadley v Baxendale*... the more particular rules for assessing damages for repudiation or breach of contract should be treated not as "rigid rules of universal application" but "as prima facie rules which my be displaced or modified" whenever it is necessary to do so in order to achieve a result which provide reasonable compensation... without imposing a liability upon the other party exceeding that he could fairly be regarded as having contemplated and willing to accept.

Although his Honour was not dealing with a case of sale of goods, it is submitted that those words could aptly apply to the assessment of damages in such contracts as well.

Specific performance – s 52

Specific performance is an equitable remedy by which the court orders the wrongdoer to perform his or her contractual obligation. Section 52 of the Goods Act expressly preserves the buyer's (*not* the seller's) remedy of specific performance. It provides:

> (1) In an action for breach of contract to deliver specific ascertained goods, if it thinks fit the court, on the application of the plaintiff, at any time before judgment, may, by its judgment direct the contract be specifically performed without giving the defendant the option of retaining the goods on payment of damages.
> (2) The judgment may be –
> (a) unconditional; or
> (b) on such terms and conditions as to damages, payment of the price and otherwise as to the court seems just.

It should be noted that a buyer can only claim specific performance if the goods are "specific ascertained" goods. The meaning of this expression is not clear.[88] The English Sale of Goods Act equivalent provision states "specific *or* ascertained" goods. In the case of *Fraser & Fraser (Trading as Wari Won*

87 [1991] 174 CLR 64 at 119–120.
88 See classification of goods, above (Chapter 2).

Plantation) v ANG Co Pty Ltd, Frost CJ, observed in passing that the difference in wording between the two provisions had to be taken as significant. His Honour declined to interpret the provision as it was irrelevant to the facts of the case before him. Other writers blame the draftsman of the Goods Act for "inaccurately copying from the colonial Act".[89] We are inclined to agree with the latter. In any case, clearly whatever "specific ascertained" means, it does not include unascertained goods.[90]

It should be remembered that specific performance is only awarded if the court "thinks" it fit. In practice the courts are unlikely to award this remedy except where in the circumstances of a particular case damages are not a sufficient relief.

Fairness of transactions

The courts have, by both underlying law[91] and statutory law, general powers to intervene in transactions which are blatantly unfair to the weaker party, invariably the buyer.

Underlying law principle of fair dealing

The scope of this principle is not very clear, except that it was the basis of the National Court's judgment in *Jacob Luke v John Ralda*.[92] In that case, a number of village people contributed funds towards the purchase of a second-hand bus. Their representative, the plaintiff, paid the defendant K4,800 upon delivery of the bus. The plaintiff found the bus to not be in good working order and returned it to the defendants. According to the plaintiff, he returned the bus for repair, whilst the defendant claimed that the reason was that the plaintiff wanted to exchange the bus for another vehicle. The parties also gave conflicting versions as regards the purchase price. According to the plaintiff, the K4,800 he paid was the full purchase price, whilst the defendant claimed it was partial payment. The defendant did, however, concede that he refunded approximately half of the money to some of the original contributors because "he felt sorry for them". Neither party had any document to support their version of the events. The trial magistrate found that the amount paid by the plaintiff was the full purchase price.[93] The defendant appealed to the National Court.

89 Roebuck, Srivastava and Nonggorr, *The Context of Contract in Papua New Guinea*, supra, at p 127.

90 See *Fraser & Fraser (Trading as Wari Won Plantation) v ANG Pty Ltd*, supra.

91 Section 20, Schedule 2.3–2.4, of the Constitution gives the National and Supreme Court power to develop the underlying law.

92 [1992] PNGLR 549.

93 Unfortunately, the judgment is badly reported. It is not very clear whether the action was for refund of the purchase price or for damages. Possibly, it was the former.

Woods J, in the course of his judgment, observed that the facts of the case were muddled because the events were more than five years old and that "neither party seemed to be concerned about or have any understanding of prudent business practice".[94] Since the defendant was in the business of buying and selling cars, he had the onus to prove his version of the events. His Honour found that the fact that the defendant refunded some of the money was, in his Honour's view, indicative of an admission of "some warranty or obligation" on his part. Accordingly, Wood J upheld the trial magistrate's judgment, "which, in effect, is applying principles of an underlying law, requiring fair dealings".[95]

With respect, the facts of the foregoing case as well as Justice Woods' judgment are confusing. His Honour neither discussed nor cited any authority for the underlying law principle requiring fair dealing, which he invoked. Hence, the scope of this principle is not clear.[96] Fortunately, the statutory powers discussed below will probably render it unnecessary to rely on this principle.

Statutory power

The Fairness of Transactions Act[97] gives the courts extensive general powers of intervention in contractual and other transactions. The preamble to this Act reads in part:

> Being an Act relating to the effect of certain transactions to ensure that they operate fairly without causing undue harm to . . . any person, and in such a way that no person suffers unduly because he is economically weaker than . . . another person.

Section 1 declares that the purposes of the Act are to "ensure the overall fairness of any transaction" (i) entered into between persons in circumstances whereby one party was predominant (due to economic or other advantages) and as a result the other party did not exercise a free choice, or (ii) which for various reasons appear to be manifestly unfair. Section 4 defines the concept of "fairness" as "the just and equitable distribution to and among parties to a transaction of the rights, privileges... benefits and duties... of the transaction in proportion and relative to a party's... contribution to the transaction, and according to business principles and practices appertaining

94 [1992] PNGLR at 550.
95 Ibid at 551.
96 Schedule 2.4 of the Constitution enjoins the judiciary to ensure that the underlying law develops as a "coherent system in a manner that is appropriate to the circumstances of the country from time to time".
97 No. 28 of 1993.

to the particular transaction...". In determining whether a particular transaction is fair, courts are required to take into account all circumstances of the parties existing before, at and after entering into the transaction.[98]

Where a court finds a transaction to be unfair within the meaning of the Act, it must, in the first instance, order the parties to attempt to resolve the matter through mediation. If mediation fails, the court has the power to make any such order, as it deems proper consistent with the underlying policy objective of the Act.[99]

Although the Fairness of Transactions Act has been in operation for more than ten years, to our knowledge there is no judgment (at any rate concerning sale of goods contract) where it has been invoked or argued. This is rather surprising, considering its wide scope and potential for a remedy outside the Goods Act. The facts of the case of *Jacob Luke v John Ralda*, supra, most likely would have justified judicial intervention under the Act.

98 Section 4(2).
99 Section 8.

Part II

Law of Agency

By Alex Amankwah

Chapter 5

Agency Law in Papua New Guinea

Introduction

Agency is an indispensable apparatus in the mechanism of business and commerce. Without it, most business activities are well-nigh impossible of execution or implementation. The phenomenon simply accentuates the limitations on the human capacity to go it alone and underscores the importance of actors beyond the individual human entity. For example, since a person cannot be in two places at the same time, a person may sometimes require other people to represent him/her, on occasions in other places. Again, a person who lacks the legal capacity to carry out a certain function may require others endowed with the requisite legal capacity to undertake such function on his/her behalf. Even where a person has the legal capacity to perform a certain function, he/she may still need the assistance and support of others in order to carry out a commercial or business enterprise. Such people are consequently endowed in law with the power to act for and on behalf of other people.[1] A registered company acquires upon incorporation a legal personality and can also employ human actors to act on its behalf.[2]

Papua New Guinea's law of agency derives essentially from the common law, which, by virtue of the Constitution of the Independent State of Papua New Guinea,[3] the courts are mandated to apply as part of the underlying law. Some of the common law principles of agency have been incorporated into the Papua New Guinea Partnership Act.[4]

1 See Partnership Act (PA) Ch 148, s 6.

2 Companies Act No. 10 1997, ss 16, 17, 19 and 155; *Salomon v Salomon & Co* [1897] AC 22. Agency law relating to corporations and other entities with legal personality is more fully covered in Chapter 8.

3 In *Curtain Bros (Qld) Pty Ltd and another v Independent State of Papua New Guinea* [1993] PNGLR 285 the Supreme Court affirmed that the law of agency in PNG is the law deriving from the common law, and "which is applicable" by virtue of Schedule 2.2 of the Constitution of Papua New Guinea, per Kapi DCJ and Hinchliffe J at 296. See now the Underlying Law Act 2000, s 3.

4 Agency law relating to business partners is covered in greater detail in Chapter 15.

Definition

It is possible to conclude from the preceding discussion that agency is a tripartite relationship which comes into existence where a person (agent) effects a business transaction with another person (third party) on behalf of some other person (principal).[5] Though agency is essentially a common law doctrine in its origin, equity has exerted its usual ameliorating influence to ensure fair and just outcomes, which meet the parties' expectations.

Equitable principles which govern the agent–principal relationship include the fiduciary duty of an agent to the principal, the agent's duty to account for his/her stewardship and the need for the agent to avoid conflict of interest situations from arising in the execution of his/her authority. Finally, legislation can affect agency as well.[6]

Dorwick concludes, after a thorough review of the anomalies, contradictions and inconsistencies that characterise principal–agent relations:

> The essential characteristic of an agent is that he is invested with a legal power to alter his principal's legal relations with third persons: the principal is under a correlative liability to have his legal relations altered. *It is . . . this power-liability relations [that] is the essence of the relationship of principal and agent.* The rules which normally attach to the parties, the normal incidents of the relation, are ancillary to this power-liability relation. To satisfy principals' claims in a myriad of cases the judges have imposed on agents certain rules constituting safeguards against the abuse of their powers. To satisfy agents' claims for reimbursement the judges have granted certain rights to agents. But the parties, the best judges of their own interests, may exclude these normal incidents of the relation by their agreement.[7] (Emphasis added.)

The difficulties inherent in this area of the law may be exemplified by two situations:

(i) *Where an agent is not an agent.* In distributorship agreements, a person described in such agreements as "sole agent" is merely granted monopoly selling rights over goods produced or manufactured by a particular manufacturer. Consequently, contracts entered into by such an "agent"

5 A legal relationship is effected between two of these (principal and third party) through a medium as a conduit (agent). There is no direct contact between the principal and third party.

6 Partnership Act, s 3 (agency of partners); Insurance Act No 23 1995, s 39 (insurance agency).

7 Dowrick, F E, "The Relationship of Principal and Agent" (1954) 17 *MLR* 24 at 36.

with third parties are contracts by him/her as principal in his/her own right and not on any one else's behalf.[8]

(ii) *Where absence of authority may nevertheless create agency relation.* Similarly, an insurance agent who lacks the power to effect insurance contracts of the appellant insurance company could create vicarious liability for the company in respect of defamatory remarks made by him/her against a claimant.[9]

Agency distinguished from other relationships

Agency has an appearance similar to that of other types of legal relationships, notably independent contracting, employment of servants, bailment and trusteeship. The distinction between agency and these others is useful in delineating more accurately agency relationship. What is attempted here is merely an overview and not a detailed analysis of the positions.

Independent contracting

An independent contractor undertakes (under a contract) to perform designated or specified assignments or tasks and is free to determine his/her own (*modus operandi*) method and is not under anyone's direction as to the manner in which the tasks are to be executed or performed. He/she is "in business on his own account".[10] An example of this person is an electrician who contracts to supply and install power in a building.

Employment of servants

A servant is under the control of his/her employer who determines *what* task is to be carried out and *how* it should be undertaken.

Bailment

A contract of bailment is one in which the bailee takes possession of goods from or for the owner for a specific purpose. For example, the retention of the goods until such time as the owner requires them.[11]

8 *Lamb (WT) & Sons v Goring Brick Co Ltd* [1932] 1 KB 710; see also *Nolan v Watson* (1965) 109 SJ 288.

9 *C M L Life Assurance Society Ltd v Producers and Citizens Co-operative Assurance Co of Australia Ltd* (1931) 46 CLR 41; see also *Otter v Church* [1953] 1 Ch 280 in respect of liability in negligence.

10 *Warner Holidays Ltd v Secretary of State* (1983) *Times*, 3 January, cited in Lowe, R, *Commercial Law* (6th edn, Sweet & Maxwell, London, 1983), p 9. See also, Fisher, S, *Agency Law* (Sydney, Butterworths, 2000) p 9.

11 *Co-ordinated Air Services Pty Ltd v Aircair Pty Ltd* [1988–89] PNGLR 549.

Trusteeship

The analogy often drawn between agency and trust obfuscate rather than elucidate the distinction between the two, for while it is perhaps correct to say an agent genuinely represents the principal, a trustee does not represent the beneficiaries. In so far as an agent can be said to be a fiduciary, this is so only in relation to the duty owed the principal by the agent in the performance of the agency obligation. Agency does not establish a general fiduciary relationship as such between principal and agent. The fiduciary duty operates only to restrain the agent from acting in his/her own self-interest rather than in the interest of the principal.[12] The dichotomy of legal-equitable interests which reside in two different persons in a trust situation has no application to agency. Agency approximates more creditor–debtor relationship than anything else.

The congruency of agency and the four non-agency relationships

Agency cannot be placed in a water-tight compartment apart from the five relationships it has been differentiated from. There is a necessary overlap between all five.[13] For example, in England some statutory provisions make reference to both agents and servants while others refer solely to agents.[14] Again, at common law the view is prevalent that an agent has a greater latitude of independence of action and absence of external control and direction than has a servant.[15] Such a distinction is hard to sustain in the case of a sales representative, for example, and there is ongoing disputation concerning the issue whether there may be situations where an agent is neither servant nor independent contractor.[16] With respect to bailment, while agents such as brokers and real estate agents are not bailees for absence of possession of a *res*, many bailees are not agents in the sense of being the representatives of their bailors.[17] An agent, however, just as a trustee must not make a secret profit and avoid a conflict of interest situation from arising in the performance of the agency duties.

12 See p 107 infra, on Fiduciary duty.
13 *Buttomley v Harrison* [1952] 1 All ER 368. See also Dowrick, note 7, supra.
14 *Factors Act* 1889 (UK).
15 *Hayman v Flewker* (1863) 13 CB (NS); *Bailee v Goodwin* (1886) 33 CLD 604.
16 Powell, S, *Law of Agency* (2nd edn, Sweet & Maxwell, London, 1980) pp 7–24; Fridman, G, *Law of Agency* (7th edn, Butterworths, London, 1996) pp 26–32; Chitty, J D, *Chitty on Contracts* (Guest, A G (ed)) (27th edn, Sweet & Maxwell, London, 1994) Vol. 2 Chapter 9; Reynolds, F M, *Bowstead and Reynolds on Agency* (16th edn, Sweet & Maxwell, London, 1996) Arts 1–2.
17 See Lowe, note 10 supra at p 10; *International Harvester Co of Australia Pty Ltd v Carrigan's Hazeldene Pastoral Co* (1958) 100 CLR 644.

The guiding test

The test of agency is therefore substance and not the form it takes or the description or designation given it. Thus, where a person who introduced a client to a financier who paid him a fee for the introduction, it was held that such payment was not sufficient in itself to make such a person an agent of the financier in respect of a contract concluded between the financier and the person so introduced.[18] In the same vein, the purchase of machinery from vendors described merely as "machinery and general agents" did not constitute such vendors into agents of the manufacturers of such machinery.[19]

The perimeters of the power to act through an agent

The common law position is exemplified by the Latin maxim *qui facit per alium per se*, which literally means: what one can do by himself/herself, one can do through others.[20] There is thus virtually no limit on the power of a person to act through other people as agents. There is, however, one recognised exemption to the rule: it is the case where a person occupies a position which requires him/her to perform certain functions personally. This is analogous to an express or implied provision of a contract which prohibits delegation of functions to an agent.[21]

Capacity to act as principal or agent

Principal

The general principle is that the capacity of a principal to act through an agent is coterminous with capacity to enter into a contract. The problem areas concern infants and people of unsound mind.

INFANTS

Infants lack full contractual capacity. However, they will be bound to the same extent they would have been for liabilities contracted on their behalf by agents if they had acted themselves.[22]

18 *Custom Credit Corp Ltd v Lynch* [1993] ASC Rep 58.
19 *International Harvester Co of Australia Pty Ltd v Carrigan's Hazeldene Pastoral Co* (1958) 100 CLR 644.
20 *Bevan v Webb* [1901] 2 Ch 59 at 77, per Stirling J.
21 Ibid.
22 *G v G* [1970] 2 QB 643 at 652, per Denning LJ; *Christie v Permewan, Wright and Co Ltd* (1904) 1 CLR 693.

PERSONS OF UNSOUND MIND

The principle was enunciated in *Yonge v Toynbee*[23] that the insanity of a principal terminates forthwith the agent's authority, even though the agent had no knowledge of the principal's insanity.

Agent

The rule at common law is to the effect that any person of sound mind may act as an agent notwithstanding the fact that such a person lacks contractual capacity.[24] The rationale of the rule is that an agent is a mere conduit or link between the real contracting parties. And it is possible for one agent to represent both parties as long as this does not give rise to a conflict of interest situation.[25] These principles are of equal validity to PNG's legal system by virtue of the underlying law mandate under the Constitution of Papua New Guinea, 1975.[26]

The nature of the authority in agency

The critical feature of agency is the agent's authority to effect a change in the legal position of the principal. It has been pointed out that agency creates a power–liability relationship. The agent's power to alter the principal's legal position relates to contract formation and disposition of property for and on behalf of the principal.[27]

The power may arise by:

1. consent; and
2. operation of law.

The authority must be executed in a lawful manner. Thus, where the agent's act contravenes mandatory statutory prescriptions, the fact that the state

23 [1910] 1 KB 215. See contra, however, *McLaughlin v Daily Telegraph Newspaper Co Ltd* (1904) 1 CLR 243.

24 *Watkins v Vince* (1818) 171 ER 675. This has been modified by statutory restrictions on unqualified people operating as professionals.

25 *North and South Trust Co v Berkeley* [1971] 1 WLR 470, [1971] 1 All ER 980.

26 See note 3 supra.

27 Thus in *In the Matter of the Organic Law on National and Local-Level Government Elections: Robert Lak v Paias Wingti* case No. N2358, 2002 where the complaint was that the respondent instructed someone to bribe persons in certain electoral districts during the 2002 national election to vote for him with the promise of monetary reward if the respondent won the election. The issue arose whether or not the person so instructed had the authority of the respondent so as to become the respondent's agent. The National Court held, per Kapi DCJ, that in the absence of proof of authorisation (which was found to be lacking) agent–principal relationship cannot be established in law.

incorporates a business entity to carry out development projects on behalf of the state does not relieve that entity as an agent of the state, of the duty to comply with mandatory provisions on contract formation involving disbursement of public funds. Accordingly, any such contract entered into by the agent is void and does not bind the state as principal.[28]

Consent or agreement

The consent of the principal to be bound by the agent's acts may be express or implied from the nature of the act done.[29] Where consent is implied, it operates as an apparent authority to bind the principal. The consent may be precedent or subsequent to the act. In the latter case, the agent's act is subsequently adopted by the principal who had previously not granted express consent for the doing of the particular act performed by the agent. This position is known as ratification.

Operation of law

Absence of the principal's consent notwithstanding, in appropriate circumstances, the principal will still be bound by the agent's acts. This is the consequence of the operation of the law.

Estoppel

In other circumstances, a principal who has not granted an agent his or her express authority to act may still be held to be bound due to the conduct of the principal which sometimes manifests in the principal representing some person to the world as having his authority to act on his/her behalf. This is called estoppel by representation or holding out.[30]

Formation (creation) of agency relationship

The various forms of agency have been outlined above. This section deals with the method of *creating* them or bringing them into existence.

Agency may be an express or implied agreement. No legal formalities are required for bringing this into fruition. Lord Cranworth said in *Pole v Leask*:[31]

> No one can become the agent of another person except by the will of that other person. His will may be manifested in writing or orally or

28 *Bayclay Brothers (PNG) Ltd v Independent State of Papua New Guinea*, Unreported Case, N2090 (2002).
29 *Garnac Grain Co Inc v HMF Faure & Fairclough Ltd* [1968] AC 1130, at 1137; [1967] 2 All ER 353 at 358, per Lord Pearson LJ.
30 See below (pp 97–100) for further discussion.
31 (1863) 33 LJ Ch 115.

> simply by placing another in a situation in which . . . according to the ordinary usages of mankind that other is understood to represent and act for the person who has so placed him.[32]

It has been pointed out above that to determine whether an agency exists or not is a matter of substance rather than form or designation. Thus, an attempt to disguise an agency relationship by employing ambiguous language in the written agreement will not obliterate the substance of the agreement as one intended to create an agency agreement.[33] By the same token, the fact that the parties designate a commercial relationship agency does not in law impress the relationship with the imprimatur of agency.[34]

One notable exception to the absence of any requirement on observance of formalities in the creation of an agency agreement is the rule in relation to land transactions and conveyance, i.e. acquisition, disposition and transfer of interests in land.[35] Thus, an agent authorised to execute a deed in relation to such matters must have a deed of authority, for example, power of attorney to do so.[36] Additionally, there is no requirement for the giving of consideration, although in an express or implied agreement, provision is often made for payment of remuneration. Indeed, agency may be gratuitous – for example, in circumstances in which a wife pays for goods and services on behalf of her husband.

The content and scope of the agent's authority

This section details the scope of the agent's authority to contract with third parties and to act in other ways with a third party, which attracts liability for the principal. The law recognises several categories most of which have been touched on in the preceding sections. For convenience they are set out again below:

(i) express (actual) authority;
(ii) implied authority;

32 Ibid, at 161–162.

33 See *Custom Credit Corporation Ltd v Lynch*, note 16, supra; also *Wombat Nominees Pty Ltd v De Tullio* (1990) 98 ALR 307; and *Paul Daintry Corporation Pty Ltd v National Tennis Centre Trust* (1990) ATPR.

34 Ibid.

35 Frauds and Limitation Act No. 3 1988, s 2.

36 *Steiglitz v Egginton* (1815) Holt NP 141. In *Waghi Security Services Pty Ltd v John Tembon and Western Highlands Provincial Government In Suspension* [1994] PNGLR 138, an unstamped document was held to be insufficient evidence of a contract purportedly executed on behalf of the company and the Provincial Government, per Woods J. See the Instruments Act (Ch 254).

(iii) usual authority;
(iv) apparent (ostensible) authority;
(v) ratification; and
(vi) agency by operation of law.

Express authority

The principal's express authority given to his/her agent may be oral or written; and if written, it may or may not be under seal. If the authority is under seal or by deed, it is known as power of attorney and is construed in the usual way documents under seal are construed.[37]

A principal who grants an ambiguous express authority will have only his/herself to blame if the agent acts in accordance with a reasonable interpretation of the instructions, though not what was in fact intended by the principal.[38]

Implied (actual) authority

An agent's authority may sometimes extend beyond the performance of specific functions detailed in the express authority to cover acts which are "necessary for, or incidental to, the execution of his express authority".[39] This is the essence of the implied authority of an agent. "This implied authority is a real authority and it arises from the construction of the express authority."[40] For example, an agent authorised to sell a house must necessarily have the additional (implied) power to sign the contract, although this may not be spelt out in the express authority granted. The case of *Lae Cordial Factory Pty Ltd v Dang Bros Pty Ltd*[41] illustrates the situation of a person being given implied actual authority to bind the company from the conduct of the company (through its managing director, Mr Davis, who had authority to give such permission).[42] In that case, the respondent (Dang) sued the appellant

37 *Danby v Coutts & Co* (1885) 29 Ch D 500.
38 *Weigall & Co v Runciman & Co* (1916) 85 LJ KB 1187.
39 Lowe, note 10, supra at 35.
40 Ibid.
41 (1978) N176. Roebuck, D, Srivastava, D K, Nonggorr, J, *The Context of Contract in Papua New Guinea* (University of Papua New Guinea Press, Waigani, 1984), p 149 treats this case as one of "ostensible authority", claiming that "The facts showed that the defendant [Lae Cordial Factory Pty Ltd or Mr Davis] held out the tenant [Mr Blackwell] as its agent." See *Gartner v Beaton* [1993] 2 Lloyd's Rep 369 and *Lease Management Services Ltd v Purnell Secretarial Services Ltd* [1994] CCLR 127. See also Tettenborn, A, "Agents, Business Owners and Estoppel" (1998) *Cambridge Law Journal* 274.
42 The circumstances which give rise to inferring an implied actual grant of authority may also provide the basis for holding that the agent was given apparent or ostensible authority. See Diplock LJ in *Freeman and Lockyer (a Firm) v Buckhurst Park Properties (Mangal) Ltd* [1964] 2 QB 480. It is suggested that this case straddles these two areas of authority.

(Lae Cordial) for breach of contract, for non-payment for goods (sugar) sold and delivered. Lae Cordial denied having ordered or received the goods. The main argument advanced by the appellant was that the magistrate in the court below was wrong in law in finding that the appellant company (Lae Cordial) held a Mr Blackwell out to be its agent and that even if it were estopped from denying this the respondent was put on inquiry by Blackwell's actions that something was amiss and did nothing about it; i.e., they were put on due inquiry and failed to investigate the matter.[43]

Lae Cordial, under the direction of its part owner and managing director, Mr Davis, used to manufacture soft drinks from premises in Lae. Mr Davis then leased the business (the premises as well as the soft drink manufacturing equipment) to Mr Blackwell, and went to Port Moresby, leaving the company "in existence, at the place where it had always been and in the possession and under the *de facto* control in its day to day operation of Blackwell". Blackwell continued to operate the business in a similar fashion to the way in which the company operated under Mr Davis. The court below held that Lae Cordial, "being a legal person in its own right continued to have its legal existence at the factory premises right throughout the period over which [the] events took place". It further held that "in fact *actual authority was to be implied* from the conduct of Davis in letting Blackwell take possession of the company premises and equipment in the way he did". (Emphasis added.) On appeal to the National Court, Pritchard J said:

> Whichever way one looks at it [Mr Davis] left this company in existence, at the place where it had always been and in the possession and under the *de facto* control in its day to day operation of Blackwell. Whatever Mr Davis may have intended the legal consequences of his action to have been, and whatever else was contained in the mysterious agreement which was never produced, except for the customers Davis did tell that Blackwell had taken over (assuming he did), to the world at large the company continued to exist and carry on business at the place it always had, and in fact it was under the control of Blackwell, who Mr Davis himself had let into possession knowing full well he was going to continue on in precisely the same business the company had always been engaged in. *I can imagine no clearer case of holding out by Davis that Blackwell had the control of the company*, despite his subsequent protestations that this was not so. (Emphasis added.)

43 The case also raised the issue of whether Dang was estopped from relying on the company holding out Blackwell to be its agent, as it had been put on inquiry by circumstances surrounding the payment that "something was wrong" and ought to have made further inquires. The judge rejected this argument.

His Honour concluded:

> By utter neglect of his responsibilities as Managing Director of the appellant company Mr Davis was the author of its misfortune. He had those responsibilities and responsibilities on behalf of the company to the public who dealt with it. The public is entitled to be protected against people who meddle with corporations in this fashion.

Usual authority

This authority is in fact an extension of the implied authority unless specifically restricted or negated. It applies especially to trade, professional or business agents such as factors, auctioneers, estate agents and stockbrokers who are expected to perform such acts as are "usual" in their trade, profession or business. What is usual in a trade or profession will often be a matter for expert evidence.[44]

Apparent (ostensible) authority

Apparent authority is very important from the point of view of a third party dealing with an agent and who has no way of ascertaining the perimeters of the agent's authority. Thus it has become axiomatic that, so far as the third party is concerned, the apparent authority is the real authority. The third party's only guide is whether there seems to be authority on the agent's part to act – i.e. an appearance of authority.[45]

In *Odata Ltd v Ambusa Copra Oil Mill Ltd and another*[46] the second defendant, National Provident Fund (NPF), incorporated the first defendant in order to engage in production and sale of copra oil. The first defendant then entered into a contract with the plaintiff for the installation of a copra mill for the production of copra oil. The contract was terminated upon legal advice that the venture was a bad investment. The plaintiff sued for damages for breach of contract. One of the issues in the case was the nature of the relationship between the first and second defendant and involved lifting of the corporate veil. The capital shares issued were held by the defendants equally 50:50. However, most decisions were taken by NPF (second defendant)

44 In *Watteau v Fenwick* [1893] 1 QB 346, [1891–94] All ER Rep 897, where cigars were sold to a hotel manager who was forbidden by the hotel proprietors to buy cigars, the vendor's action against the hotel proprietors for the price was allowed, because cigars were "such as would usually be supplied to and dealt with in such an establishment". The authority of this case has been doubted by the High Court of Australia: *International Paper Co v Spicer* (1906) 4 CLR 739 at 763, per Isaacs J; and by academic writers: see Stoljar, S J, *The Law of Agency* (Sweet & Maxwell, London, 1961) pp 75–78 and Powell, S, *Law of Agency* (2nd edn, Sweet & Maxwell, London, 1980) pp 55–59, who argued that this decision should have been based on estoppel by conduct rather than on usual authority.

45 *Reckitt v Barnett Pewbroke and Slater Ltd* [1928] 2 KB 244 at 257, per Scrutton LJ.

46 Unreported case No. N2106 (2001).

officials. The corporate secretary was an employee of NPF and board meetings were held on NPF premises (NPF Board Room). Kandakasi J rested his ruling on the finding that in fact the first defendant was either an extension or a subsidiary company of the second defendant and the consequence of this in law was that agency relationship was established between the second defendant as the parent company and the first defendant as subsidiary company. Further, his Honour was inclined to the view that the first defendant was a "façade" behind which the second defendant operated.

His Honour took into account the relative ignorance of members of the first defendant company who were mostly illiterate land owners ("local ill-equipped landowners") without any knowledge of corporate structure and management and who simply went along with decisions taken by management of second defendant company. In lifting the corporate veil, his Honour was actually revealing the actors behind the scene, that is, NPF and its officers.

It is submitted that it would have been instructive if his Honour considered the matter from the perspective of the plaintiff to determine whether the plaintiff considered the first defendant to be the *alter ego* of the second defendant.

Again, in *Curtain Bros (Qld) Pty Ltd v Independent State of Papua New Guinea*,[47] where a minister concluded an agreement settling a large claim for damages against the government, the Supreme Court held the government bound by the settlement agreement, their Honours made no attempt to delineate or categorise the type of agency which is constituted between the state and its servants such as ministers when such ministers act in their official capacity. To most ordinary people, ministers appear to be clothed with the garment of the government and consequently of the state when they act. This is the gist and crux of the doctrine of apparent power or authority (i.e. appearance) which third parties dealing with other people's representatives presume. It is not instructive enough to simply postulate: "The general rule is that, in a contract, the State is bound by a servant or agent acting within his or her authority... and the Acting Solicitor General [is an] agent of the State . . ."[48]

In *Sangara (Holdings) Ltd v Hamac Holdings Ltd (In Liquidation)*,[49] a case involving a commercial enterprise, however, the sale of a substantial portion of a company's assets by a single director of the company was held to be

47 (Per Kapi Dep CJ, Hinchliffe and Jalina JJ) note 3, supra.

48 Ibid at 296. See also *Tonolei Development Corp Ltd v Lucas Waka, Minister for Forests* (1983) N 404 (L) on the ability or otherwise of a government minister to enter into a contract on behalf of the National Government and to revoke the offer relating to such contract.

49 [1973] PNGLR 504, per Frost J.

so "unusual" as to be beyond such a director's ostensible or apparent authority.

In all such cases, the law takes the position that where a person (principal) represents to a third party that another person (agent) has the power or authority to act on his/her behalf in a particular manner, and the third party in reliance upon that representation alters his/her legal position to his/her detriment, the acts become binding on the principal notwithstanding the fact that the agent was in fact not endowed with the principal's authority to act for the principal. The consequence of this is that the principal will be estopped from denying the state of facts represented. It is therefore an aspect of estoppel by conduct and is also sometimes referred to as ostensible authority. The principle was succinctly stated in *Rama Corporation v Proved Tin and General Investments Ltd.*[50] In that case Slade J said:

> Ostensible or apparent authority which negatives the existence of actual authority is merely a form of estoppel and a party cannot call in aid an estoppel unless three ingredients are present: (1) representation, (2) a reliance on that representation, and (3) an alteration of his position resulting from that reliance.[51]

Apparent authority, it has been noted above, is the result of representations made by a principal to a third party that the agent has the principal's authority to engage in the function in question on the principal's behalf. In the leading case of *Freeman and Lockyer v Buckhurst Park Properties*,[52] Diplock LJ, in an effort to bring out clearly the scope of this authority, contrasted it with actual authority. His Lordship said in that regard:

> It is necessary at the outset to distinguish between an "actual" authority of an agent on the one hand, and an "apparent" or "ostensible" authority on the other. Actual authority and apparent authority are quite independent of one another. Generally they co-exist and coincide, but either may exist without the other and their respective scopes may be different . . .
>
> An "actual" authority is a legal relationship between principal and agent created by a consensual agreement to which they alone are parties. Its scope is to be ascertained by applying ordinary principles of construction of contracts, including any proper implications from the express

50 [1952] 2 QB 147, [195*] 2 All ER 554. This case was followed in *Rainbow Holdings Pty Ltd v Central Province Forest Industries Pty Ltd* [1983] PNGLR 34, where a solicitor sold timber logs "as solicitor for Rainbow Holdings Pty Ltd", the Supreme Court (Pratt, Bredmeyer and McDermott JJ) held that there was a "strong holding out" by the solicitor. See also *AGCPacific Ltd v Woo International Pty Ltd* [1992] PNGLR 100 at 106, per Sakora J.

51 Ibid at 556.

52 [1964] 2 QB 480 at 501–501; [1964] 1 All ER 630 at 644.

> words used, the usages of the trade, or the course of business between the parties. To this agreement the contractor [third party] is a stranger; he may be totally ignorant of the existence of any authority on the part of the agent. Nevertheless, if the agent does not enter into a contract pursuant to the "actual" authority, it does not create legal rights and liabilities between the principal and the contractor . . .
>
> An "apparent" or "ostensible" authority, on the other hand, is a legal relationship between the principal and the contractor created by a representation, made by the principal to the contractor, intended to be and in fact acted on by the contractor, that the agent has authority to enter on behalf of the principal into a contract of a kind within the scope of the "apparent" authority, so as to render the principal liable to perform any obligations imposed on him by the contract. To the relationship so created the agent is a stranger. He need not be (although he generally is) aware of the existence of the representation. The representation, when acted on by the contractor by entering into a contract with the agent, operates as an estoppel, preventing the principal from asserting that he is not bound by the contract. It is irrelevant whether the agent had actual authority to enter into the contract.

There are four requirements for the establishment of apparent authority. These are:

(a) There must be a representation by the principal that the person is his or her agent. The representation may be expressed by word of mouth or in writing. More often the representation is implied from the principal's conduct, for example, the owners of a supermarket by putting a person behind the counter gives the appearance that that person has the authority to sell the goods in the store and receive payment on their behalf. As a general rule, the representation must be made by the principal. A representation by the agent that he or she has the authority to act on the principal's behalf, usually, is not enough to bind the alleged principal.[53] Where the principal is a human being, it is relatively easy to establish whether he or she held out the person in question as his or her agent. The identity of the person making the representation is more difficult to establish where the alleged principal is a corporation. In *Hely-Hutchinson v Brayhead Ltd*,[54] Lord Pearson alluded to the issue when he said:

> There is, however, an awkward question arising in such cases [as to how] how the representation which creates the ostensible authority is made by the principal to the outside contractor. There is this difficulty. I agree

53 *Freeman and Lockyer v Buckhurst Park Properties*, supra.
54 [1968] QB 549.

> entirely with what Diplock LJ, said [in *Freeman and Lockyer v Buckhurst Properties (Mangal) Ltd*] that such representation has to be made by a person or persons having actual authority to manage the business. Be it supposed for convenience that such persons are the board of directors. Now there is not usually any direct communication in such cases between the board of directors and the outside contractor. *The actual communication is made immediately and directly, whether it be express or implied, by the agent to the outside contractor*. It is, therefore, necessary in order to make a case of ostensible authority to show in some way that *such communication which is made directly by the agent* is made ultimately by the responsible parties, the board of directors. That may be shown by inference from the conduct of the board of directors in the particular case by, for instance, placing the agent in a position where he can hold himself out as their agent and acquiescing in his activities, so that it can be said that they have in effect caused the representation to be made. They are responsible for it and, in the contemplation of law, they are to be taken to have made the representation to the outside contractor.

The third party must therefore, establish categorically that the principal himself/herself/itself made a representation on which he/she/it relied and that the agent had the authority to do so.

(b) The representation must be one of fact.[55] Thus, where the reserved price of property being auctioned was not varied the mere fact that the auctioneer and the vendor were at cross purposes during the auction would not operate to vary the price.[56]
(c) The representation must be made known to the party seeking to hold the principal liable (i.e. third party). Thus, in *Farquharson Bros v King & Co*[57] where as a result of an agent's fraud, the buyer of goods (timber) did not know who the vendor (principal) or the clerk of the vendor (agent) was, the buyer's plea of apparent authority was struck down by the court.
(d) The representation caused the third party to alter his/her position to his/her detriment. Thus, it is not enough to establish merely that the principal made a representation which the third party believed.[58]

Ratification

Ratification, it has been pointed out, is the subsequent adoption by a principal of an agent's otherwise unauthorised act. This is really tantamount to

55 See *Saunders v Anglia Building Society* [1971] AC 1004, [1970] 3 All ER 961, HL.
56 *Boulas v Angelopoulos* (1991) Aust Cont Rep 90-004.
57 [1902] AC 325.
58 *Re Lewis* [1904] 2 Ch 656.

post facto grant of actual authority.[59] Ratification is effective only if certain conditions are fulfilled.[60] These will be considered *seriatim*.

The principal must be in existence

A non-existent entity or personal is incapable of having an agent when the act of the "agent" purportedly took place. Thus, it has been held that where a company had not yet been incorporated it was incapable of ratifying pre-incorporation contracts purportedly entered into on its behalf.[61] It is perhaps possible to regard the so-called agent as personally liable for contracts entered into in such circumstances by treating him/her as acting on his/her own behalf.[62] Conversely, presumably, the so-called agent may personally sue on those contracts.

The principal must be ascertainable

The principal on whose behalf the agent purported to have acted must have been named or described to the third party at the time the act was carried out. It is impossible, it has been held, for an undisclosed principal to ratify.[63] In *Keighley Maxstead & Co* an agent who was unable to buy wheat at a certain price authorised by his principal bought the commodity in his own name but at a higher price. The principal however purported to ratify the purchase but later refused to take delivery of the wheat. The seller sued the principal for the price. The House of Lords held that the agent's act was in the first place not authorised and since the principal was not disclosed to the seller, at the time of sale, the principal could not ratify the purchase in those circumstances and was, therefore, not liable to pay the price. In the opinion of Lord Macnaghten LJ, "civil obligations are not to be created by or founded upon undisclosed intentions".[64] It is not clear from this dictum whether the important matter here is the fact that the principal is undisclosed or that the agent's intentions are undisclosed and remained locked in the agent's bosom. It is clear from the decision in *Re Tiedmann and Ledermann Freres*,[65] however, that the most important consideration is, the circumstances of the case viewed from the perspective of the third party. The problem relates to the identity of the person or entity making the representation.

59 See *Re Mowcon Ltd* [1969] 1 WLR 78, [1969] 1 All ER 188.
60 *Suncorp Finance Corp v Milano Assuisazioni SPA* [1993] 2 Lloyd's Rep 225 at 234, per Waller J.
61 *Kelner v Baxter* (1866) LR CP 174.
62 See European Communities Act 1972, s 9(2) (UK).
63 *Keighley, Maxstead & Co v Durant* [1901] AC 240.
64 Ibid at 246.
65 [1899] 2 QB 66, [1968] 1 QB 549.

The principal must have legal capacity to act (ratify)

At the time the agent performed the function in question, the principal must have had the legal capacity to do what the agent did. This is directed perhaps at *ultra vires* corporate acts and situations in which ratification is simply impossible as where the purported agent was dead or insane at the time of the act. And, the principal must also have the legal capacity at the time of the purported ratification.[66]

The act must be ratifiable

The agent's act in question must be one which can be lawfully ratified. Thus, an *ultra vires act* undertaken on a company's behalf is incapable of subsequent ratification by the company.[67] For similar reasons, a forgery being a legal nullity cannot be ratified.[68] Such transactions are in the eye of the law void *ab initio* and it were as if the transaction never took place. However, when the act in question is merely voidable, the cases seem to suggest that such an act can be ratified.[69]

The principal must have knowledge of the facts

The principal can ratify only if the factual situation is within his/her knowledge.[70]

Effect of ratification

The legal effect of ratification (subject to the exemptions outlined below) is that it operates retrospectively, that is to the date of the original act. In *Bolton Partners v Lambert*,[71] an agent acting on behalf of a principal, without the authority of the principal, agreed to sell a plot of land to a third party; the third party subsequently purported to repudiate the agreement. In the meantime, the principal had ratified the agreement. The Court of Appeal held that the principal's ratification related back to the time of the original contract, with the result that the third party's withdrawal was of no legal consequence.

66 See *Grover & Grover Ltd v Matthews* [1910] 2 KB 401, where a fire insurance policy was purportedly ratified after the risk insured, i.e. loss or damage through fire.

67 See *Ashbury Ry Carriage and Iron Co v Riche* (1875) LR 7 HL 653; see also *Bolton Partners v Lambert* (1889) 41 Ch D 295. See Chapter 7 on the *ultra vires* doctrine.

68 See *Brook v Hook* (1871) LR 8 Exch 89. However, the issue whether a forgery can be *adopted* is debatable: See Hanbury, *The Principles of Agency*, note 39 supra, p 264 for an interesting discussion of the issue.

69 See for example, *Danish Mercantile Co Ltd v Beaumont* [1951] Ch 680, [1951] 1 All ER 925, where steps taken in proceedings on behalf of a company were purportedly ratified by the liquidator of the company. The Court of Chancery upheld the validity of the liquidator's ratification of those steps.

70 See *Freeman v Rosher* (1849) 18 LJ QB 340. Contra, *Hilbery v Hatton* (1864) 2 H & C 822.

71 (1889) 41 Ch D 295, at 302. See also *Firth v Staines* [1897] 2 QB 70 at 75, per Wright.

The difficulties inherent in this decision (Lindley LJ, as he then was, was also a member of the panel of the Court of Appeal) has been highlighted ten years later by the learned Lord Justice in *Fleming v Bank of New Zealand*.[72] On this occasion Lord Lindley LJ said: "The decision... presents difficulties and their Lordships reserve the liberty to reconsider it if on some further occasion it should become necessary to do so."[73]

Ratification has been accepted to be an applicable common law doctrine within the PNG jurisdiction.[74]

Exceptions to the rule on the effect of ratification

There are generally two exceptions to the rule:

(a) Vested rights remain where they have accrued and cannot be divested.[75]
(b) The rule in *Watson v Davies*[76] to the effect that an offer "accepted subject to ratification" affords the offeror the right to withdraw before ratification and when the offeror withdraws nothing remains thereafter to ratify.

Agency by operation of law

The law presumes agency to exist in a few circumstances; for example:

(a) agency of necessity; and
(b) agency by cohabitation.

Agency of necessity

In an emergency situation involving the property or interests of a principal, the law appears to mandate prompt and reasonable action by an agent in proximate relationship with the goods and property to protect them.[77] Stringent conditions are placed on the applicability of the doctrine to prevent its abuse and misuse, for example: the existence of a genuine emergency, commercial impracticability to

72 [1900] AC 577 (PC).
73 Ibid at 587.
74 *Michael Yai Pupu v Tourism Development Corporation* N 2258 (2002). See also *Johns v Thomason* [1976] PNGLR 15 at 19–20, per Frost.
75 *Bird v Brown* (1850) 4 Exch 486; *Dibbins v Dibbins* [1896] 2 Ch 348. This principle was affirmed in *Bolton Partners v Lambert* at 306, per Lord Cotton.
76 [1931] 1 Ch 455.
77 In *Hawtayne v Bourne* (1841) 7 M & W 595 at 599 Parke B cited the examples of a ship-master's powers of sale of the cargo and ship to buy necessaries and an acceptor of a bill of exchange for the honour of the drawer. Today, carriers of goods on land have been invested with similar powers: *Sims v Midland Railways* [1913] 1 KB 103. See also *Prager v Blatspiel* [1924] 1 KB 566 at 570, per McCardie J; *Jebara v Ottoman Bank* [1927] 2 KB 254 and *Sachs v Miklos* [1948] 2 KB 23 at 26, [194*] 1 All ER 67 at 67 per Lord Goddard CJ.

get owner's instruction, acting in good faith and owner's benefit not merely agent's convenience, for, as Bowen LJ said, "Liabilities are not to be forced upon people behind their backs".[78]

Agency by cohabitation

No distinction exists today between married couples and people living together in a *de facto* relationship. There is a presumption, where a man and woman cohabitate and maintain a household, that the woman has the actual or apparent authority of the man to pledge the man's credit for necessities supplied her to support their lifestyle. Again, the rule being that of presumption of fact is rebuttable by other evidence to the contrary.[79] Such evidence include the fact that:

(i) the goods supplied were excessive in the circumstances;
(ii) the man had forbidden the woman to pledge the man's credit; and
(iii) the woman was currently in receipt of adequate allowance.

How much of all this can stand legal scrutiny in today's changing world, permeated by women's liberation culture and financial independence, remains to be seen.

The relationship between the parties – principal, agent and third party

This section explores the *rights* and *obligations* of the parties in the tripartite relation which agency establishes. The section consists of three subsections, namely:

1. the rights and obligations of agent and principal, *inter se*;
2. the rights and obligations of principal and third party, *inter se*; and
3. the rights and obligations of agent and third party, *inter se*.

Agent and principal inter se

Agent's duties

The agent's duties are primarily those that arise under the common law. However, superimposed upon these are duties deriving from equity. Under the common law, the agent owes the principal the following duties: *obedience*, *care and skill*, and *personal performance*.

78 *Falcke v Scottish Imperial Insurance Co* (1886) 34 Ch 234 at 238. See also *Bistead v Buck* (1776) 2 Wm Bl 1117, where a good Samaritan's action for the cost of feeding a lost dog against the owner failed. However, freeing a car jammed under a bridge in a city thoroughfare qualified: *White v Troups Transport* [1976] CLY 33.
79 *Miss Gray Ltd v Cathcart* (1922) 38 TLR 562.

The duty of obedience connotes the strict discharge of the agency contract's obligation by the agent even if in doing so, the principal's interest would be prejudiced. This principle was applied in *Fray v Voules*,[80] where a solicitor in order to protect his client's interest failed to carry out his given instructions. Similarly, it was held that where an agent was instructed to sell stock at a certain price, he had no discretion to wait for an appreciation in the value of the stock in order to sell at a higher price.[81] An agent, however, is not under any obligation to perform an illegal act or one which at law is void as contrary to public policy.[82]

The duty to exercise due care and diligence flows from the requirement of the tort of negligence. The initial dichotomy between paid and unpaid or gratuitous agents no longer exists.[83] Today the position depends on the kind of skill the agent professes to possess.[84]

Duty not to delegate

The duty of personal performance forms the basis of the *delegatus non potest delegare* maxim and rests on the intimate relationship between a principal and an agent which requires that the agent perform himself/herself the assignment he/she has undertaken to execute. There are, however, a few exceptions to the rule, namely: (i) where the principal expressly authorises the agent to delegate his/her powers; (ii) where it is possible to imply, from the circumstances of the case, the power to delegate. In *De Bussche v Alt Thesigen*[85] LJ explained the position thus:

> An authority [to delegate] may and should be implied where from the conduct of the parties to the original contract of agency, the usage of trade or the nature of the particular business which is the subject of the agency it may reasonably be presumed that the parties to the contract of agency originally intended that such authority should exist or where, in the course of the employment, unforeseen emergencies arise which impose upon the agent the necessity of employing a substitute.[86]

80 (1859) E & E 839.

81 *Bertram Armstrong & Co v Godrey* (1830) 1 Knapp 381 (PC); See also *Fraser v BN Furnam (Productions) Ltd* [1967] 1 WLR 898, [1967] 3 All ER 57, CA.

82 *Cohen v Kittell* (1889) 22 QBD 680. See also *Robert Lak v Paias Wingti*, N2358 (2002).

83 See *Giblin v McMullen* (1868) LR 2 PC 317.

84 *Hedley Byrne v Heller and Partners* [1964] AC 465. See also *Ross v Caunters* [1979] 3 WLR 605; *Yianni v Edwin Evans & Sons* [1981] 3 WLR 843.

85 (1878) 8 Ch D 286.

86 Ibid at 311.

Additionally, purely administrative acts requiring no specified skill may be delegated.[87] Where, however, a contrary intention negates the power to delegate, an agent is barred from delegating his/her powers.[88]

Equitable duties

The agent's equitable obligations arise from the confidential/personal nature of the relationship which requires the imposition of fiduciary duties in equity on the agent to ensure probity and transparency in the agent's execution of his/her authority. There are three such duties, namely, good faith, account and estoppel.

GOOD FAITH

It must be pointed out that, although agency does not create a fiduciary relationship between the agent and the principal, equity subjects an agent to fiduciary duties for the purposes of the specific acts to be performed by the agent. This ensures that the agent is prohibited from engaging in certain acts. Notable among such acts are conflict of interest situations and making of secret profits. An agent must act solely in the furtherance of the principal's interest and subjugate his/her own personal interests while acting for the principal. The *locus classicus* is *Mahesan v Malaysia Govt Officers Co-op Housing Society*.[89] In that case, a director in charge of land acquisition for the appellant's housing development purposes colluded with a land owner and had the land sold to him by the owner in return for a quarter share of the profit to be made when the director resold the land to the appellant at about twice the amount paid for it. The appellant succeeded in their action to recover the profit made by the director.[90] While it is not possible to delineate all conflict of interest situations, some such situations would involve serving two principals where the interests are the same – conflict of duty and duty situations – and extends to circumstances in which the agent after acting for the principal in one transaction acts against the same principal's interest in a subsequent transaction.[91]

87 *Marsh v Joseph* [1897] 1 Ch 213; *Allam v Europa Poster Services* [1968] 1 All ER 826.

88 *Bell v Balls* [1897] 1 Ch 663.

89 [1978] 2 All ER 405.

90 See also *United Australia Ltd v Barclays Bank Ltd* [1941] AC 1; *Fliway – AFA International Pty Ltd v Australian Trade Commission* (1992) 39 FCR 446; *Reading v Attorney-General* [1951] AC 507, [1951] 1 All ER 617.

91 See *Fruehauf Finance Corporation Pty Ltd v Feez Ruthning (A Firm)* [1991] 1 Qd R 558, involving legal practitioners professional responsibilities in their representation of clients.

DUTY TO ACCOUNT

The duty to account is an aspect of the duty of the agent to act in good faith in his representation of the principal. A proper account of all transactions entered into on the principal's behalf must be rendered by the agent to the principal or some other person appointed by the principal. The agent must also give the principal all moneys received by him or her for the principal's benefit.[92] A great deal of the law on legal professional responsibility falls into this area as well.

ESTOPPEL

The doctrine of estoppel operates to bar an agent from denying the title of his/her principal to property or money in respect of which the agency relationship arose. The rationale of the principle is that, but for the agency relationship, such property or money would not have come into the agent's sphere of control.[93] An exception to the rule is to the effect that where the agent is in possession of goods as a bailee he/she may set up a third party's title in an action against him/her by the principal, subject of course to the third party's consent.[94]

Principal's remedies for agent's breach of duty

Where an agent is in breach of an obligation, as discussed above, the principal may take any of the following courses:

(i) If the obligation is contractual, sue for damages for breach of contract. In appropriate circumstances, injunctive remedies are also available to him.
(ii) If the breach relates to a duty of care, an action can be maintained in tort (for example, the tort of conversion in retaining the principal's property and refusing to return it) for damages.
(iii) If the breach relates to a fiduciary duty (for example, secret profit), the principal may sue for money had and received or for an account.[95]

92 *Blaustein v Maltz, Mitchell & Co* [1937] 2 KB 142, [193*] 1 All ER 497.

93 *Dixon v Hammond* (1819) 2 B & Ald 310 at 313, per Abbott CJ. See also Tottenborn, A, "Agents, Business Owners and Estoppel" (1998) *Cambridge LJ* 274. In *Jay Mingo Pty Ltd v Steamships Trading Pty Ltd* [1995] PNGLR 129, Sevua J amplified the doctrine of estoppel to hold a national statutory corporation liable for leasing land to the defendant/respondent Steamship Trading Pty Ltd; see also *Michael Yai Pupu v Tourism Development Corporation* N 2258 (2000).

94 See *Biddle v Bond* (1865) 6 B & S 225.

95 In *Mahesan v Malaysia Govt Officers Co-op Housing Society* [1979] AC 374, [1978] 2 All ER 405, the House of Lords made it clear that a principal who has two courses of action – one for money had and received for the principal's benefit and one for damages – must elect one of the two as such a plaintiff is not entitled to two remedies.

(iv) A principal may opt for the dismissal of the agent for a serious breach of duty (for example, the agent's disclosure of the principal's confidential information) and in that event the principal may forfeit any remuneration due payable to the agent.[96]
(v) Depending on the circumstances (i.e. the terms of the contract and the nature of the agent's breach of duty), the principal may refuse to indemnify the agent for expenses incurred in the course of the agency relationship.[97]

The rights of the agent

Generally, the principal owes the agent two primary obligations:

(i) Pay remuneration or commission;
(ii) Provide indemnity for expenses incurred.

REMUNERATION

This is the *quid pro quo* for the agent's performance of his/her obligation under the agency agreement. This is usually a contractual term which may be express or implied. In the absence of a contract, provided the principal consented to the task undertaken by the agent, a reasonable sum is payable on the basis of principles of restitution often referred to as *quantum meruit*.[98] Difficult issues often arise in this area of the law and involves especially commission agents':

(a) whether the agent is *entitled* to remuneration;
(b) what is the *quantum* of remuneration; and
(c) whether remuneration has *accrued* or *been earned.*

Remuneration is buttressed in the expectation to be paid for the services rendered. Ordinarily, in commercial transactions this expectation is obvious and may be presumed even in the absence of a contract.[99] It is for the parties to determine the quantum of remuneration on the basis of the particular contractual obligation to be undertaken by the agent. In the absence of a contract, as stated earlier, the principles of restitution are resorted to by the courts. However, the courts will not fix the rate of commission payable where the contract leaves the decision in that regard "to the discretion" of the principal.[100]

96 *LS Harris v Power Packing Services Ltd* [1970] 2 Lloyd's Rep 65.
97 This is elaborated upon below.
98 *Way v Latilla* [1937] 3 All ER 759.
99 See *Way v Latilla* [1973] 3 All ER 759.
100 *Obu v Strauss* [1951] AC 243 (PC); *Gilbert and Partners (A firm) v Knight* [1968] 2 All ER 248, CA.

The issue here revolves around a determination of the question whether the specific event on the happening of which payment of remuneration depends has actually taken place. As Lord Russell of Killowen put the matter:[101] "[i]f according to the true construction of the contract the event has happened of which the agent has acquired a vested right to the commission... then no act or omission by the principal or anyone else can deprive the agent of that right."[102]

In relation to real estate agents, for example, who are under contract to sell property, the High Court of Australia said:[103]

> When an agent is employed to sell property, or find a purchaser, he does not earn his commission simply by finding some one who is ready, willing and able to purchase it, or who offers to buy... [It] is at least necessary that a binding contract of sale should... [be] executed...

The principle was applied in *Tian Chen Ltd v The Tower Ltd*[104]

INDEMNITY AND REIMBURSEMENT

The agent may commence action to recover the cost of expenses and other liabilities lawfully incurred in connection with his or her performance of his agency.

MISCELLANEOUS REMEDIES: LIEN AND STOPPAGE IN TRANSIT

If the principal does not pay the agent his/her remuneration or indemnity, in addition to instituting action to claim any of the above, the agent may exercise a lien over the principal's goods in his or her possession or if the goods are with a carrier, the right of *stoppage* in transit. A lien is a right of retention of possession of the goods of another person as security for repayment of a debt owing. It is rooted in possession and the right is therefore exercisable only if possession of the goods is lawful. There are two kinds of lien, namely, special and general. The law frowns on general liens and allows it only by the way of trade usage in such professions or trades as factors, bankers, solicitors and stockbrokers.

Where the goods are no longer in the agent's possession but with a carrier who is charged with transportation of the goods to a different destination, the agent may cause the detention of the goods. As Cairns LJ observed: "The essential feature [of stoppage is that goods should be... in transit] in

101 *Luxor (Eastbourne) Ltd v Cooper* [1941] AC 108, [19**] 1 All ER 33.

102 Ibid at 129; 46–67.

103 *L J Hooker Pty Ltd v W J Adams Pty Ltd* (1977) 138 CLR 52 at 66–67, 13 ALR 161 at 172, per Gibbs J. See also *Ross McGartin Realty v Chard Holdings Pty Ltd (No. 2)* [1991] 1 Qd R 182; *Skaventos v Bevan McLean & Associates Pty Ltd (t/a Elders Real Estate Commercial* (1994) 62 SASR 334.

104 N2313 (2000), per Kandakasi J.

the possession of a middleman."[105] As in the case of the right of lien, stoppage in transit operates as security for a debt. Stoppage in transit is now governed in PNG by The Goods Act (Ch 251).

The rights and obligations of principal and third party

Problems with designation

This area may be confusing to readers due to nomenclature and designation of the status of the principal on whose behalf the agent purports to act. The principal may be *named*, *disclosed* or *undisclosed*. This necessarily has implications for the nature of the principal's liability to the third party and vice versa.

Named and disclosed principal

A principal is said to be *named* where the agent *identifies* the principal *by name* to the third party. An agent may, however, merely tell the third party that he/she is acting on behalf of a principal whose *identity* he/she refuses to *disclose*. The principal is then said to be *disclosed* but *unnamed*. In both cases the legal rights and liabilities of the principal and the third party are the same. The agent's task is accomplished and he/she drops out of the picture as merely the conduit of bringing the parties into contractual relationship. The principal will be bound if the agent has his authority – express, implied or usual – or if he opts to ratify the agent's act *ex post facto*. And the third party can sue the principal if he/she defaults on the contract. There is only one exception to the principle, namely, a principal cannot sue on a deed executed by his/her agent unless the (principal) is described in the deed as a party and the person on whose behalf the deed is executed.[106] This exception is also subject to equitable doctrines on trusteeship and the right of an agent who executes a deed on the basis of a power of attorney.

Undisclosed principal

A principal is said to be undisclosed where an agent with the necessary authority concludes a contract on behalf of his/her principal whose existence he/she does not disclose to the third party. In respect of such a principal, the general rule is that he/she can sue and be sued on the contract entered into by the agent on his/her behalf. As Lord Lindley observed:[107]

> [M]iddle-men through whom contracts are made, are common and useful in business transactions and in the great mass of contracts it is a

105 *Schotsmans v Lancaster & York Ry* (1867) 2 Ch App 332 at 338.
106 *Re International Contract Co* (1871) LR 6 Ch 525.
107 *Keighley, Maxstead v Durant* [1901] AC 240 at 261–262.

> matter of indifference to either party whether there is an undisclosed principal or not. If he exists, it is, to say the least, extremely convenient that he should be able to sue and be sued as a principal and he is only allowed to do so upon terms which excludes injustice.

The rationale for the principle, it has been suggested is, the avoidance of circuity of action, "for the principal could in equity compel the agent to lend his hand to enforce the contract against the contractor, and would at common law be liable to indemnify the agent in respect of the performance of the obligations assumed by the agent under the contract".[108] Thus, in *Continental Trading Ltd v Dewe Patsy Trading as PSB Trade Store*,[109] the respondent bought a new generator from Pacific Merchants Ltd (PML). Within a matter of days the generator had developed mechanical problems necessitating its return by the respondent to PML, the seller. Since PML's merchandise was supplied by Docke & Co, a German corporation, when PML went into liquidation, Docke & Co instructed the appellant to seize and sell all the goods in PML's custody and possession. The goods included the defective generator which had been paid for by the respondent. At the time of the sale the respondent had no knowledge of PML's principals in Germany. The court, per Manuhu J, found the appellant auctioneer liable for the cost of the generator for performing a function on behalf of the undisclosed German principal, Docke & Co, and did so negligently for not selling at a fair price but rather at a ridiculously low price.[110]

Be that as it may, there are a few exceptions to the principle, that is, circumstances in which the principal is prevented from suing. These are:

(i) Where the contract between the agent and the third party expressly stipulates that the agent is the sole principal.[111]
(ii) Where the terms of the contract are inconsistent with agency. In *Humble v Hunter*[112] an agent signed a charter-party in his own name and described himself as "owner" of the ship. The court held that in those circumstances his undisclosed principal had no right to sue on the charter-party.[113]
(iii) Where the identity of the principal is *material* to the third party. An example is where the contract between the agent and the third party is

108 *Freeman and Lockyer v Buckhurst Park Properties* [1964] 2 QB 480 at 644, per Diplock LJ.
109 Unreported Case No. N2503 (2000).
110 See also *Toplis & Harding Pty Ltd v Dadi Toka and Grandsen* [1982] PNGLR 321.
111 *M K Mutual Steamship Assurance Association v Nevill* (1889) 19 QBD 110.
112 (1848) 12 QB 310.
113 See, however, contra *Drughorn (F) Ltd v Rederiaktiebolaget Trans-Atlantic* [1919] AC 203 and *Danziger v Thompson* [1944] KB 654, [1944] 2 All ER 151, where the undisclosed principals were allowed to sue.

of a *personal* nature as where a friend bought a ticket for another to a show because the theatre operator would definitely not sell a ticket to this other due to personal differences between them. This other was denied a seat at the show when his identity was recognised by the theatre operator. He sued the theatre operator for the cost of the ticket and lost the action.[114]

Remedy of the principal

The principal may intervene to either enforce the contract or sue for damages for any loss or liability incurred by him/her as a result of the contract. The contract is, however, subject to the third party's right of election is discussed below. Until the principal intervenes, the agent may enforce the contract against the third party and vice versa.

Remedy of the third party

On the third party realising that the agent was acting for the principal, he/she may elect to sue either the principal or the agent. This potential for the agent to be liable on a contract made on behalf of an undisclosed principal is the reason why such contracts are not favoured in the commercial and business world. This right to elect to sue either the principal or the agent is called Third Party Election and operates to bar a second action against the other person potentially liable should the action against the person sued fail. It is based on the law's policy of discouraging protracted litigations. There was only one cause of action and therefore only one available remedy.

Should the third party make an unequivocal election to proceed against the agent, for example, the principal will be discharged from liability to the third party. The law then treats the principal's liability as utterly extinguished, even if the judgment remains unsatisfied. The reason for this is that the cause of action is subsumed by the judgment.[115] It has been held that whether such an election has been made is a matter of fact.[116]

Miscellaneous contractual issues

SETTLEMENT WITH AGENT

Settlement with agent sounds in situations where the principal pays a sum of money to the agent who was in turn to pay the money over to the third

114 *Said v Butt* [1920] 3 KB 497.
115 *Kendall v Hamilton* (1879) 4 App Cas 504.
116 *Calder v Dobell* (1871) LR 6 CP 486; *Clarkson Booker v Andjel* [1964] 2 QB 775, [1964] 3 All ER 260.

party and the agent some how failed to account to the third party. The question is then whether the principal can be made to pay the third party a similar sum of money all over again. The answer to that question would seem to be in the affirmative on the principle that in a contractual setting a debtor must seek out his/her creditor and pay the creditor.[117] Clearly, there ought to be exceptions to the enforcement of the strict letter of the law where it manifests in injustice. However, the cases have not provided consistency in the resolution of the issue.[118] Conversely, a third party does not generally escape liability for a debt he/she owes the principal merely because he/she has paid the agent, unless the agent had authority to act in his/her own name, such payment is not good as against the principal.[119]

INSURANCE AGENTS AND BROKERS

Insurance agents and brokers receive payments from persons seeking insurance coverage (life, property, accident, annuity, etc). Such agency is governed by the Insurance Act.[120]

RIGHT OF SET-OFF

Where a debt is due from the agent to the third party, the question is whether the third party dealing with the agent can set off the debt due from the third party to the principal. If the principal is disclosed, then it is patently clear that the third party is bound to pay the principal. However, in a situation where the principal is undisclosed the rule is that the principal must take the contract between the agent and the third party as he finds it, and is consequently caught by the third party's right of set-off. This rule can obviously work hardship if applied rigorously to every situation. As a result some cases seem to suggest that an undisclosed principal is not bound by the third party's right of set-off unless the agent was armed with actual or apparent power to contract as principal. It was in respect of this position that Lord Watson LC observed:

> It is not enough to show that the agent sold in his own name. It must be shown that he sold the goods as his own and it must also be shown that the agent was enabled to appear as the real contracting party by the conduct, or by the authority, express or implied, of the principal.[121]

117 *Heald v Kenworthy* (1885) 10 Exch 739.
118 See *Thompson v Davenport* (1829) 2 B & C 78; *Heald v Kenworthy*, supra; and *Armstrong v Stokes* (1872) LR 7 QB 598.
119 *Drakeford v Piercy* (1866) 7 B & S 515.
120 Ch 256.
121 *Cooke v Eshelby* (1887) 12 App Cas 271 at 278, HL.

Liability for torts

DECEIT

The inflexible contract – tort dichotomy in the law appears to have been jettisoned by the courts, thus making it possible in agency relationships to establish liability for tort as well, especially the tort of deceit. The principle was enunciated in *Lloyd v Grace Smith*,[122] where a managing clerk defrauded his company's clients. In that case, the rule was laid down that where an agent, acting within his/her actual, usual, or apparent authority commits the tort of deceit, both the principal and the agent will be liable and it is immaterial whether the agent acted to promote his/her principal's interest or his/her own.[123]

MOTOR-CAR CASES

The owner of a vehicle who gives his/her consent to another to drive his/her motor vehicle for that owner's purposes under delegation of task or duty situations creates an agency relationship between himself/herself and the driver of the motor vehicle such as renders him/her liable for the driver's negligence.[124]

The rights and obligations of agent and third party

The agent, being a mere conduit, can, as a general rule, neither sue nor be sued on a contract concluded by his/her principal and the third party. There are a few exceptions to this general rule, some of which have been touched upon already in preceding sections of this chapter.

Contract

In relation to contract, the first exception is that an agent is liable to the third party if the agent is in fact the principal. The agent is so to speak, no different from the principal. Thus, in a charter party the person who was described as "agent for the freighters" was held personally liable when evidence showed that he was in fact the freighter.[125] On the basis of similar reasoning, an agent who signs a contract on behalf of a non-existent principal will be personally liable.[126] The matter comes down ultimately to the construction of the contract

122 [1912] AC 716; see also *Armstrong v Strain* [1951] 1 TLR 856.
123 See, however, *Koorangang Investment Pty v Richardson and Wrench* [1981] 3 WLR 493, PC for the position in negligence.
124 See *Morgans v Launchbury* [1973] AC 127, [1972] 2 All ER 606, HL.
125 *Schmalz v Avery* (1815) 16 QB 655.
126 *Kelner v Baxter* (1866) LRZ CP 174.

and the signature which appears on the contract.[127] The second exception is where the agent signs a contract in a dual capacity, for example, where a dealer makes a representation in respect of goods which are sold to a finance company which ultimately let out the goods on hire purchase to a hirer-purchaser.[128]

Remedies of the parties

THIRD PARTY

The third party can sue the agent in contract in those circumstances outlined above where the agent is in fact the principal. Also, he/she may sue in tort for loss incurred through the agent's tort.

AGENT

Conversely, the agent may sue the third party in contract where there is a settlement between the principal and the agent. This will have no effect on the agent's right to sue if the agent has a lien on any property involved.[129] Again, the agent may sue for any loss suffered by him/her as a consequence of a tort committed by the third party.

TORTS

There could be liability here as well on the basis of loss through deceit or negligence as discussed above.

Termination of agency

Modes of termination

The principal/agent relationship may be determined in any of the following ways:

(a) By act of the parties, namely:
  (i) mutual agreement;
  (ii) withdrawal of the original agreement, for example the principal's revocation of the agent's authority which may be done expressly[130] or impliedly.[131]

127 *Royal Albert Hall v Winchelsea* (1891) 7 TLR 362; See also *Gadd v Houghton* (1876) 1 Exch D 357; *Universal Steam Navigation Co v McKelvie* [1923] AC 492; *The Swan* [1968] 1 Lloyd's Rep 5.

128 See Sale of Goods, pp 44–45.

129 *Robinson v Rutter* (1855) 4 E & E 954. See, contra, *Grice v Kenrick* (1870) LR 5 QB 340.

130 *Judge Smith & Co v Renfrey* (1920) 22 WALR 41; *Tynan v a'Beckett* (1923) VLR 412.

131 *Luxor (Eastbourne) Ltd v Cooper* [1941] AC 108, [1941] 1 All ER 33.

(b) By operation of law, namely:
   (i) performance resulting from the execution of the authority on expiration of the period for which the authority was granted;[132]
   (ii) death,[133] bankruptcy[134] or insanity[135] of either party such as renders them legally unfit to perform their respective duties.
   (iii) frustration of contract.[136]

Limitation on termination

Any termination of agency, whether by act of a party or by operation of law, is inoperative and ineffectual in the following circumstances.

VESTED RIGHTS

Rights acquired, or accrued and became vested before the termination event remain valid and unaffected. Consequently, agency commission due to the agent or indemnity from the principal cannot be divested or withheld.[137] The principal also may on his/her part sue the agent for damages for the agent's breach of duty which provoked the principal's revocation of the agent's authority.[138]

NOTICE REQUIREMENT

Where the agency agreement provides for the giving of reasonable notice by either party before termination, the right to terminate is conditional upon the giving of such notice. A great deal, however, depends on the nature of the agency. For example, in the case of a real estate agent, the property owner may revoke the agency summarily.[139] However, where the agency is analogous to a contract of employment the giving of reasonable notice is a condition precedent to the exercise of the right of termination.[140]

132 *Dickinson v Lilwall* (1815) 4 Camp 279; *Walder v Cutts* (1909) VLR 261.
133 *Blades v Free* (1829) 9 B & C 167.
134 See Lowe, supra, at 60.
135 *Yonge v Toynbee* [1910] 1 KB 215. In *Drew v Nunn* (1879) 4 QBD 661, it was held that the party's insanity must be known to the third party. See also *Re Coleman, ex parte Propsting* (1929) 24 Tas LR 22; *Donlan v Commonwealth of Australia* (1953) 54 SR (NSW) 67.
136 *Marshall v Glanvill* [1917] 2 KB 87; *British Movietonews v London & District Cinemas Ltd* [1952] AC 166, [1951] 2 All ER 617; *Davis v Contractors Ltd v Fareham UDC* [1956] AC 696, [1956] 2 All ER 145; *Codelfa Construction Pty Ltd v State Rly Authority of New South Wales* (1982) 149 CLR 337, 41 ALR 367.
137 *Read v Anderson* (1884) 13 QBD 779.
138 *Nelson (EP) Ltd v Rolfe* [1950] 1 KB 139, [1949] 2 All ER 584.
139 *See Judge Smith & Co v Renfrey* supra at 122.
140 *Martin-Baker Aircraft Co v Canadian Flight Equipment Ltd* [1955] 2 QB 556, [1955] 2 All ER 722.

AUTHORITY COUPLED WITH AN INTEREST

Where the authority is coupled with an interest, the authority cannot be revoked. An interest in this context is quite often a debt due to the agent from the principal. The authority therefore provides the necessary security for the repayment of the debt. The case *Raleigh v Atkinson*[141] illustrates this position of the law. In that case, the principal entrusted goods to the agent to be sold by the agent. Occasionally, the agent would advance money to the principal and then recoup the amount so advanced from the proceeds of a sale when authorised by the principal to sell. It was held that the authority was irrevocable as it was coupled (tied up inextricably) with an (agent's) interest.

Irrevocable powers of attorney

As a consequence of recommendations made by the British Law Reform Commission,[142] a change was effected to the common law on powers of attorney to make room for the granting of irrevocable powers of attorney. This change became necessary due to the hardship experienced by third parties who dealt with the donees of powers of attorney where revocation, especially by operation of law occurred.[143] The necessary changes were brought about through the passage of the Powers of Attorney Act 1971 (UK) and in PNG by the Instruments Acts and may be summarised as follows:

(i) A third party dealing with the donee of the power of attorney is protected if, at the time of the disposition, he had no knowledge of any revocation or of any event giving rise to revocation, e.g. the donor's death.
(ii) A purchaser from the third party can safely assume that the third party had no knowledge of revocation if: (a) the disposition to the third party took place within 12 months of the power coming into operation; or (b) the third party makes a statutory declaration before or within three months after completion that he had no such knowledge.
(iii) If the power is given to secure some proprietary interest of the donee and if it is expressed to be irrevocable, it cannot be revoked (even by operation of law) without the donee's consent.[144]

Effect of termination

Principal and agent

The consequence of the termination of agency is, as between the principal and the agent, that it operates to extricate the legal bond between them

141 (1843) 6 M & W 870.
142 See Liddle, C K, "Powers of Attorney Act 1971" (1971) 68 *Law Soc Gazette* 434.
143 See Lowe, supra at 62.
144 Instruments Act Ch 254, s 7.

prospectively except with regard to vested rights which, as noted previously, are not extinguished.

Principal and third party

With respect to the principal and third party, however, the position is problematic. Take, for instance, the situation of the third parties who dealt with the principals in *Drew v Nunn*,[145] where a wife continued to pledge the husband's credit even after the husband became a person *non mentis compos* and *Yonge v Toynbee*,[146] where solicitors entered an appearance and took the other legal steps in an action on behalf of a client, the defendant, in the action while the client was suffering from lunacy. In both cases the third parties were the supplier of goods (and the plaintiff in the second) who had no knowledge of the principal's incapacitation. In *Drew*, the third party's action against the principal succeeded. However, in *Yonge*, the action succeeded only against the agent and not the principal, because there was not a holding out by the principal of an agent. The principle was not formulated in *Yonge* but in *Drew* where Brett LJ observed:

> In my opinion, if a person *who has not been held out as agent* assumes to act on behalf of a lunatic *the contract is void as against the supposed principal* and the pretended agent is liable to an action for misleading an innocent person.[147] (Emphasis added.)

145 (1879) 4 QBD 661.
146 [1910] 1 KB 215.
147 *Drew v Nunn* at 686, per Brett LJ.

Part III

Law of Banking

By Alex Amankwah

Chapter 6

Law of Banking in Papua New Guinea

Introduction

Banks are an important component of the aggregation of financial institutions (credit unions, building societies, finance companies and insurance companies) which together propel a modern economic system.[1] Without banks, exchange activities will be well-nigh impossible, capital intensive projects cannot be carried out, commercial lending and borrowing will simply not exist.

Beginning from the initial practice of the merchant class of facilitating the transfer of cash across national frontiers for goods sold or purchased, through the medium of commercial or designated agents culminating in the genesis of the concept of negotiability,[2] banks have flourished worldwide to become today the lifeline of the international economic system.

With regard to PNG, banking is inextricably linked to the British Annexation of the Territory of Papua New Guinea in 1884 and the resulting inauguration of a market economy. It is trite learning that banking is a handmaiden of commerce and trade. With the establishment of Australia's first bank, Bank of New South Wales (now Westpac), in 1817, it is little wonder that the operation of that bank was extended to the Territory of Papua under Australian Administration. Westpac (West Pacific Bank) is thus PNG's oldest bank.

The nature and functions of banks and financial institutions in PNG

Banks are known by different designations and they perform distinct and varying functions. While some banks undertake the prudential regulation of

1 Blay, S N and Clark, U, *Australian Law of Financial Institutions* (Harcourt Grace & Co, Sydney, 1993); Conrick, B, *The Law of Negotiable Instruments in Australia* (Butterworths, Sydney, 1989) pp 2–4.

2 Lord Chorley, R S, *The Law of Banking* (6th edn, Sweet & Maxwell, London, 1974) pp 3–5; Paget, J, *Law of Banking* (10th edn, Butterworths, London, 1982).

banks, others engage in trading and still others, through trading, operate in specialised portfolios.

The Central Bank

The Central Bank or Reserve Bank is a regulator of the banking business in many countries. In PNG, the Central Bank Act[3] inaugurated the Bank of PNG and charged it with the responsibility of acting as the nation's Central Bank and custodian of its monetary system.[4] The progenitor of the PNG Central Bank was the Commonwealth Bank of Australia which was similarly established by the Commonwealth Bank Act 1911 (Cth). It later metamorphosed into the Reserve Bank by the passage of the Reserve Bank Act 1959 (Cth). The trading operation of that bank was carried forward by the Commonwealth Bank Act 1959 (Cth).

The bank also manages and issues PNG currency and acts as the official bank of the PNG government while acting in the same capacity to the commercial and trading banks.[5] An aspect of the Central Bank's regulatory function is its administration of the country's exchange control system.[6] The bank is administered by a Board,[7] which is responsible for its policy direction.[8] The Board is constituted by a chairman who is also Governor of the Bank, his deputy, the Head of the Finance Department of the bank and six to eight nominees of the Head of State (Governor General).[9]

In order to keep the government apprised of the condition of the nation's financial affairs, it is important for the Governor of the Bank and the Secretary to the Treasury to maintain robust rapport between themselves.[10] The bank is enjoined to direct its fiscal and banking policy towards:

(i) securing the maximum advantages for Papua New Guineans; and
(ii) "promoting monetary stability and a sound and efficient financial structure".[11]

The functions and powers of the bank set out in ss 5 and 6 embrace the bank's regulation of trading bank liquidity; supervision of savings bank

3 Ch 138.
4 Section 4(1).
5 Section 5.
6 Section 6. See also Central Banking (Foreign Exchange and Gold) Regulation Ch 138.
7 The PNG Bank Board; s 7.
8 Ch 138, s 8.
9 Ibid, s 11.
10 Section 10.
11 Section 4(2).

investment policy; control of bank lending; determination of bank interest rates; and open market operation system.

As custodian of the nation's gold and foreign exchange reserves, the bank ensures that PNG's exchange rate policy and similar aspects of external economic relations between PNG and the outside world are properly adjusted. The bank therefore oversees the processes involving exchange of domestic and foreign currencies, PNG's relations with international institutions and negotiations with such institutions which affect the international monetary system and structure.[12]

The bank's monopoly in regulating all banking activities in PNG is buttressed by the Banks and Financial Institutions Act.[13] The bank also wields monopoly in fixing exchange rates and the issue of PNG currency.[14] Currency issued by the bank is legal tender throughout PNG.[15] As the government's banker, the bank operates as the government's financial agent[16] and the conduit for loan granted the government from both domestic and international sources.

Trading banks

Trading banks generally deal in commercial banking and traditionally engage in using the deposits of customers to finance investors.[17] They also accept money or deposits on current accounts, or on other fixed-term basis and make loans to their customers by way of overdraft facilities and bankcard. Today, trading banks perform a great deal more functions than those enumerated above, functions which are advertised in booklets and other publications issued by particular banks themselves.

There are six trading banks in PNG:

(i) Australia and New Zealand Banking Group Limited (ANZ).[18]
(ii) The Westpac Bank (formerly Bank of New South Wales).[19]

12 Section 23.
13 Ch 137, s 3.
14 Sections 46 and 47.
15 Section 50.
16 Section 19.
17 See Blay and Clark, supra, at p 1.
18 The Australia and New Zealand Bank was formed by the amalgamation of the Bank of Australia and the Union Bank of Australia Limited in 1837. In January 1969 the ANZ Banking Group Ltd was incorporated for the purpose of the merger in October 1970 of the ANZ with the English, Scottish and Australian Bank Ltd. This bank, just as its predecessors did, has its registered head office in London. The majority of its shareholders are British residents, but its banking business is almost exclusively confined to Australia, New Zealand and the Pacific area including PNG. It is the second largest private trading bank in Australia.
19 This is Australia's oldest and the largest private bank with over 1,280 branches and agencies in Australia.

(iii) The Bank of South Pacific (BSP).[20]
(iv) The Bank of Hawaii.[21]
(v) The May Bank (PNG) Limited.[22]
(vi) The Papua New Guinea Banking Corporation (PNG BC).[23]

Savings banks

Savings banks historically engaged in receipt of deposits which were paid back upon demand. Such banks did not initially provide current account facilities. In Australia, current account facilities became available in 1984. In Australia, savings banks were regulated under the subsidiary legislation, Banking (Savings Banks) Regulation promulgated under the Banking Act 1959 (Cth). Since 1989 and with the passage of the Banking Legislation (Amendment) Act 1989 (Cth) the distinction between trading and savings banks had become otiose in an age of deregulation of banks.[24]

Specialist banks

These banks are designed and inaugurated to provide financial assistance to specialised sectors of the economy. In PNG the most apposite example of these banks is the Agricultural Bank previously known as the Development Bank. The Agricultural Bank was established by legislation, i.e. the Agricultural Bank Act.[25] The purpose of the Agricultural Bank was to provide the rural community easily accessible means for business opportunities ordinarily beyond their reach. This bank is now merged with the PNG Banking Corporation. It is not clear whether the merger of these banks, which were established with differing objectives, will prove beneficial to the nation in the long run.

The legal nature of a bank

It is customary to begin the study of the law of banking with an exploration of ideas as to what constitutes a bank or what functions a bank performs.

20 This bank was established on 1 October 1994. The BSP, as it is commonly known, is the only bank in which Papua New Guineans are the majority shareholders. It owes its origin to the National Bank of Australia (Ltd).

21 This bank merged with the Indosuez Bank and it is quite new in PNG. It has branches in Lae and Port Moresby only. It was established on 22 April 1982.

22 This is an Asian controlled bank having only one branch in Port Moresby. It is a small bank compared with the other trading banks. It began operations on 24 April 1994.

23 This bank was established on 22 April 1974 and it is the largest trading bank in PNG. It is owned by the state and it is the biggest trading bank in PNG. It is commonly known as people's bank. It acquired assets of the Commonwealth Bank of Australia, its parent bank. It was established under the Banking Corporation Act (Ch 136).

24 See Blay and Clark, supra, at p 12.

25 Ch 139.

The PNG Bills of Exchange Act[26] provides no definition for the word bank. Instead, s 1 provides a clue by its definition of the word banker. It states:

> Banker includes a body of persons, whether incorporated or not who carry on the business of banking.

This sounds like arguing circumlocutorily, i.e. a banker does the business of banking.[27] The question, therefore, is: what are the implications of the phrase "carrying on the business of banking"?[28] It is at this point that Lord Herschell's dicta becomes a useful guide. Where a statute codifies the common law and leaves gaps in the process, resort may be had to "the previous state of the law... with inquiring how the law previously stood".[29]

In the UK, it is taken for granted that a banker must perform the following functions: conduct current account, pay cheques drawn on itself; and collect cheques for its customers.[30]

In Australia, the High Court enunciated a set of principles as those that determine the perimeters of banking business. In *Commissioners of the State Savings Bank of Victoria v Permewart Writh & Co Ltd*,[31] Isaacs J, with whom the majority agreed, said the principal characteristics of the business of banking comprise the collection of money by receiving deposits upon loan; repayment of money when and as expressly or impliedly agreed upon; and the utilisation of money collected by lending it again in such sums as are required.[32]

This appears to be the current position of the law.[33] For PNG it is argued that the expanded Australian judicial meaning of business of banking should be preferable to the limited scope given the phrase by the British courts, because an important aspect of the business of banking today is the

26 Ch 250.

27 The difficulty of doing this stems from the variegated functions a bank undertakes in the modern world and which was recognised in *Bank of NSW v The Commonwealth* (1948) 76 CLR 1. Dixon J said in that case: "To give an inclusive definition of such a concept as banking is almost impossible ... the theory and practice of banking have varied from age to age and still vary from country to country" (at 334).

28 Section 1 of the Banking and Financial Institutions Act (Ch 137), however, defines a bank as "a corporation licensed as a bank" and doing "banking business".

29 *Bank of England v Vagliano Bros*, note 32, supra.

30 *United Dominions Trust (UDT) Ltd v Kirkwood* [1966] 2 QB 431 at 446, per Denning LJ. See also *Bank of Chettinad v CIT Colombo* [1948] AC 378.

31 (1914) 19 CLR 457.

32 Ibid at 471.

33 In *Australia Independent Distributors Ltd v Winter* (1964) 112 CLR 443, the correctness of the *State Savings Bank of Victoria* was affirmed, per Kitto, Taylor and Owen JJ at 455. See also *Re Adelaide Cooperative Society Ltd* (1964) 5 SASR 266.

lending of money to clients, a function which is not mentioned in the British position.

The Legal Status of a customer

Although the term "customer" appears in many places in the Bills of Exchange Act, no definition or explanation of the term has been offered anywhere. The courts assume that a bank provides services to its customers. This is central to all of a bank's functions. It is germane to an appreciation of the complex relationship that exists between a bank and its customer that the position of a customer be clearly defined, for it cannot be said legally that any person who transacts some business with a bank is a customer of that bank. For many practical reasons, therefore, it is critically important to define the word customer. It is appropriate perhaps, as Lord Chorley observed, to clarify the position of a customer before engaging in the task of examination of that person's relationship with a bank. In the first place, the definition of the term customer, as Lord Chorley observed, is "of greater practical importance than the definition of banking; for banks are few, the people whom banks have to do business are innumerable".[34]

Secondly, since the bank renders services to the customer, the relationship becomes one of banker–customer relationship. Thirdly, the governing legislation, the Bills of Exchange Act[35] affords a bank statutory protection when it deals with cheques for a customer. For example, under s 65, where the bank honours a customer's forged cheque in good faith and in the ordinary course of business, or under s 91, where a bank collects a cheque for a person who has no title to it, in both situations the banks are clothed with immunity from actions in conversion and negligence. Finally, the law imposes certain duties on a bank in its dealings with a customer.

Initially, the common law required the establishment of regularity or "use and habit" so that "one transaction" was considered insufficient to constitute a person being a customer of a bank.[36] Additionally, a person's dealings with the bank must be in the general and regular course of banking business. Thus cashing cheques for over 20 years and therefore being well known at the branch of the bank in the absence of having an account there would not meet the requirement of regularity.[37]

An account with the bank

Subsequently, the courts appear to make the fact of possession of an account at a bank the *sine qua non* of customer status. Thus, opening a

34 *Law of Banking*, supra, at p 35.
35 Ch 250.
36 *Matthews v Brown and Co* (1894) 10 TLR 386.
37 *Great Western Railway Co v London and County Banking Co Ltd* [1901] AC 414.

bank account with a stolen cheque was sufficient to make even a thief a customer of the bank. There was no need even to withdraw any money from the account so opened.[38]

Duration of the relationship

It has been consistently held that to be a customer of a bank, duration is not of the essence of the relationship. The Australian case directly in point is *Commissioners of Tax v English Scottish and Australian Bank*.[39] In this case a thief stole a cheque, the property of the Department of Taxation, then opened an account with the defendant bank into which he deposited £20. The following day he deposited into the account the stolen cheque. Apart from a chequebook which the bank issued, the thief had no other business with the bank. In spite of the tenuousness of the relationship, the Privy Council held that the thief was a customer of the defendant bank. Delivering the judgment of Judicial Committee of the Privy Council (House of Lords), Lord Dunedin observed:

> [T]heir Lordships are of the opinion that the word "customer" signifies a relationship in which duration is not of the essence. A person whose money has been accepted by a bank on the footing that they undertake to honour cheques up to the amount standing in his credit is, in the view of their Lordships, a customer of the bank in the sense of the Statute, irrespective of whether his connection is of short or long standing. The contrast is not between a habitué and a newcomer, but between a person for whom the bank performs a casual service, such as, for instance, cashing a cheque for a person introduced by one of their customers, and a person who has an account of his own at the bank. Thallon was, therefore, a customer, though of short standing.[40]

A similar judicial view was expressed by New South Wales Supreme Court in *Kendall v London Bank of Australia*[41] and affirmed by the High Court[42] of Australia where the bank allowed a person to open an account with £5 and four crossed cheques of the defendant bank. This person then drew out nearly all the amount in the account the following day. The court did not consider this person a "casual stranger" merely cashing a cheque but one with whom the bank conducted banking business "upon a current account".

38 *Ladbroke and Co v Todd* (1914) 30 TLR 43.
39 [1920] AC 683.
40 Idid at 687.
41 (1918) 18 SR (NSW) 394.
42 *London Bank of Australia v Kendall* (1920) 28 CLR 401.

Customer judicially defined

A composite definition of customer that emerges from the decided cases appears to be that a customer is a person who keeps an account at the bank; the type of account is not a matter of consequence nor is the duration of the relationship; and a person is a customer regardless of whether he/she operates under a false or assumed name[43] and whether the account is overdrawn.[44]

In Australia, legislative change has altered the common law position. The Cash Financial Transaction Reports Act 1988 (Cth), s 24(1) prohibits the opening of an account by any person in a false name. Section 24(2) apprehends those who succeed in opening an account by prohibiting operation of the account. Whether the illegality, which the opening of an account in a false name constitutes, does have any effect on bank customer relationship is debatable. However, the High Court has decided in *Yango Pastoral Co Pty Ltd v First Chicago Australia Ltd*[45] that breach of the Banking Act 1959 (Cth) did not relieve a customer debtor of the obligation to pay back a loan obtained from the banker creditor.

Who qualifies to be a customer?

The capacity to become a customer of a bank is coterminous with that to enter into a contractual relationship.[46] This is subject to the bank obtaining suitable references before accepting an application to open a current account.[47]

Bank as customer

A bank may operate as the bank of another bank. In *Importers Co Ltd v Westminster Ltd*,[48] Bankes LJ said:

> What does the expression "customer of bank" cover? The most ordinary meaning I suppose, is "a person who keeps an account at a bank". Such a person is obviously a customer but banks do various kinds of business, and in all those individuals or the companies with whom they do the business may be properly called customers; and they can properly be so called whether they are individuals or whether they are banks. In this

43 *Clarke v London County Bank Ltd* [1897] QB 552.
44 *Barclays Bank Ltd v Okenarhe* [1966] 2 Lloyd's Rep 87.
45 (1978) 139 CLR 410.
46 See for example, the Australian Cheques and Payment Orders Act 1986 (Cth), s 30.
47 *Savoy & Co v Lloyds Bank Ltd* [1932] All ER 10; affirmed on appeal [1933] AC 201. See, however, *Marfani & Co v Midland Bank Ltd* [1967] 3 All ER 967.
48 [1927] 2 KB 297, [1927] All ER 683.

> case the class of business of collecting cheques was done between bank and bank, and it seems to me impossible to contend, as a matter of law, that the bank for which the respondents were doing business were not, in reference to that business, their customer.[49]

Minors

In PNG a person of 18 years attains the age of majority and therefore possesses full legal capacity to enter into binding contractual relationships. Persons under the age of 18 are at common law incapacitated due to their lack of the power to make informed judgment. The cases *R Leslie v Shiell*[50] and *Herman Credit Ltd v Later*[51] illustrate the incapacity under which minors labour in their bid to enter into contractual relations with other people not under any legal disability. However, minors are liable for necessaries supplied them by others.[52] With respect particularly to the ability of minors to engage in banking activities, for example to draw a cheque, this is a conundrum. It has been held, for example, that although a minor cannot draw a valid cheque, he or she may be a party to a valid cheque.[53]

The issue then is whether such minor can be held liable on the valid cheque. Here, both the English and Australian authorities provide a negative answer.[54] On the issue whether a minor who has an account with a bank may authorise an adult to operate the account on his behalf, it has been held that such authorisation would be prejudicial to the minor's interest as he is "all too likely to choose the wrong man".[55] In *Re Shephard*[56] Denning LJ characteristically observed further:

> [T]he authority signed by the children [him] was absolutely void. It was on the face of it, an authority to the bank authorizing them to honour the father's signature to withdrawals from the [children's] deposit account. In other words [the children] authorized the testator to draw out [their] money. That is a transaction so manifestly prejudicial to [the children] that the law regards it not merely as voidable, but as void.

49 [1927] 2 KB 297 at 305. Atkin LJ echoed an identical view when he said (at 310): "it seems to me that if a non-clearing bank regularly employs a clearing bank to clear its cheques, the non-clearing bank is the 'customer' of the clearing bank."
50 [1914] 3 KB 607.
51 [1961] 2 All ER 294.
52 Section 19 Minors Property and Contracts Act 1970 (NSW).
53 *Colland v Lloyd* (1840) 151 ER 118.
54 See *Hudley v Peacock* [1913] 13 TLR 42 and *Avoney v Ausitianus* (1915) SR (NSW) 118; *Campbell v Ridgeway* (1887) 13 VLR 701.
55 [1953] Ch 728 at 755, [1953] 2 All ER 608 at 618–619.
56 Ibid.

> It is very like the appointment by [an infant] of an agent, which has always been held void . . . if [an infant] purports to appoint an agent, not only is the appointment itself void, but everything done by the agent on behalf of the infant is also void and incapable of ratification.[57]

Lord Denning's dictum needs some qualification. The correct position appears to be that a minor could not appoint an agent to dispose of his property so as to bind him irrevocably.[58]

The mentally unwell

At common law a contract entered into by a person labouring under mental disorder is voidable at the instance of such a person. The issue to be determined in such a case is whether or not, at the time of the contract, the subject understood the nature of the agreement.[59] A clue to the right to avoid obligations arising from such a transaction is whether the other contracting party was aware or ought to be aware of such mental incapacity.[60]

In the leading English case[61] where the defendant signed a promissory note as surety and later alleged that when he signed the document he was so insane as not to know what it was about, Lopes LJ explained the position thus:

> A contract made by a person of unsound mind is not voidable at that person's option, if the other party to the contract believed at that time he made the contract that the person with whom he was dealing was of sound mind. In order to avoid a fair contract on the ground of insanity, the mental incapacity of the one must be known to the other contracting party. *A defendant who seeks to avoid a contract on the ground of insanity must plead and prove, not merely his incapacity, but also the plaintiff's knowledge of that fact, and unless he proves these two things he cannot succeed.*[62] (Emphasis added.)

Inception of banker–customer relationship

Difficult questions often arise in relation to the issue: at what point in time does a person become a customer of a bank? Some answers may be gleaned

57 Ibid.
58 *G v G* [1970] 2 QB 643 at 652.
59 *Gibbons v Wright* (1954) 91 CLR 423.
60 *Manches v Trimborn* (1946) WN 62.
61 *Imperial Loan Co Ltd v Stone* [1892] 1 QB 599.
62 Ibid at 602–603.

from the decision in *Woods v Martins Bank Ltd*.[63] In this case the plaintiff sought investment advice from the branch manager of the defendant bank in May and proceeded to invest £5,000 in a company, which was also a customer of the bank. The plaintiff signed an authority note instructing the bank to make payments on his behalf, out of the plaintiff's other investments, and to retain any balance of such proceeds to the order of the plaintiff. However, no current account was opened for the plaintiff by the bank until June. In the meantime, the plaintiff had lost all his investments. He therefore sued the bank for negligence. A duty of care on the part of the bank to the plaintiff would arise from the time the plaintiff became a customer of the bank and the question therefore was: when did the plaintiff become a customer of the bank? The bank argued that the plaintiff could not be its customer before June. Salmond J, rejecting the bank's argument, observed that upon accepting the plaintiff's note of authority and instructions to pay on his behalf, the bank was acting as the plaintiff's bank and a duty of care to him arose from that date.

It may be said, therefore, that although the opening of a bank account is an essential aspect of banker–customer relationship, the account may be subsequent to the establishment of a relationship in which it is apparent that a person had accepted to leave some aspects of his/her financial matters to be managed by a bank.

Negotiable instruments

Banking involves the transfer of securities and money between individuals and their bankers and between the bankers themselves. This process gave rise to the concept of negotiability, principally by means of negotiable instruments.

A great deal of the law of negotiable instruments originates from the common law which, under the Constitution of the Independent State of Papua New Guinea, the courts are enjoined to apply as part of the "Underlying Law".[64]

The concept of negotiability

Negotiability is a salient aspect of the transfer of property from one person to another by way of a document evidencing a contractual undertaking to pay a sum of money or to deliver some other security for a sum of money. This kind of transfer effects a change of ownership by mere delivery or in some cases by the owner endorsing the document at the back (with his/her signature) and

63 [1959] QB 55, [1958] 3 All ER 166.
64 Ch 1 (1975), Sch 2.2; Underlying Law Act 2000.

delivering same. In this way, a transferee who takes such a document in good faith and for value acquires a title superior to that of the transferor and enables such a person to sue in his/her own name as the absolute owner. The transferee's title is thus free from any and all defects antecedent to his/her ownership.

It is apparent that, unlike the position relating to other forms of property, realty or personalty, where a person cannot transfer a title unless he or she is the owner; the principle being *nemo dat quod non habet*[65] (with exceptions which need not delay us here), a transferee of a negotiable instrument can acquire good title from a non-owner transferor. This was the result of the ingenuity of merchants who in the distant past developed the means by which commerce and trade was unimpeded and free from the restraints of cumbersome rules and procedures characteristic of property law.[66] This was achieved through the development of the concept of negotiability.

Of this legal contrivance, Eyre CJ said:[67]

> The wit of man cannot devise anything better calculated for circulation. The value of the writing, the assignable quality of it, and the particular mode of assigning it are created and determined in the original frame and constitution of the instrument itself; and the party to whom such a Bill of Exchange is intended has only to read it, need look no further, and has nothing to do with any private history that may belong to it.

A brief history of negotiability

Around the turn of the twelfth century, medieval merchants who traded goods for gold and silver began to reckon with the hazards of transferring large quantities of precious metals across the seas (pirates and shipwrecks) and experimented with a method of transmitting written orders between themselves with direction that the debtor made payment in a particular manner to an agent, usually a creditor. A further source of irritation was the aspects of diverse laws of the maritime nations which militated against the development of universal business trade. For example, the English common law's insistence on privity of contract flew in the face of contract with non-resident parties. Again, when the common law eventually permitted assignments (whether statutory or equitable) of choses in action, these were subject to equities.

The merchants circumvented the inconveniences of the law and other impediments to the growth of international trade by devising their own

65 Goods Act, s21 (1) Ch 251. See p 43 above.

66 For example, at common law choses in action were not assignable. The Property Law Act 1925 (UK), s 136 now allows it as well as in equity; also the Property Law Act (Qld), s 199.

67 *Gibson v Minet* (1791) 1 H Bl 569 at 606, 126 ER 326 at 347.

solution, viz the inauguration of a substitute for currency. The merchants by agreement among themselves adopted the usage and practice that:

> [A] document evidencing a single debt must be capable of being transferred freely by delivery alone or, in appropriate cases, by delivery plus endorsement of the payee thereby constituting the transferee, the holder of it in his own right and payment to him or to his order constituted an effective discharge. Merchants devised the negotiable instrument as a substitute for currency. From their point of view it was essential that it should serve the same purpose. Hence, a transferee must be able to enforce payment on it free from any defences that may have been available against prior parties. There is no room here for the application of the *nemo dat* rule. This is the result they achieved.[68]

The composite of the practices and usages of the merchant class came to be regarded as their customary rules *lex mercatoria*. In his work *Ancient Law Merchant*, published in 1622, Gerard de Malynes described *lex mercatoria* as "a customary law approved by the authority of all Kingdoms and Commonwealths, and not a law established by the authority of any place".[69] A veritable international law.

England resisted the assimilation of *lex mercatoria* into English law for a while until, under the steady guidance of the common law judges such as Holt CJ and Lord Mansfield CJ, it began to be imperceptibly incorporated into the common law.[70]

Another judge of the common law courts, Cockburn CJ, was finally and authoritatively to state the status of the *law merchant* in England. He said in *Goodwin v Robarts*[71] that a law merchant is:

> Neither more nor less than the usages of merchants and traders in the different departments of trade, ratified by the decisions of courts of law which, upon such usages being proved before them, have adopted them as settled law with view to the interests of trade and the public convenience, the court proceeding herein on the well-known principle of law that, with reference to transactions in the different departments of trade, courts of law, in giving effect to the contracts, and dealings of the parties, will assume that the latter have dealt with one another on the

68 Conrick, B, *The Law of Negotiable Instruments in Australia* (2nd edn, Butterworths, Sydney, 1989), p 3.

69 Ibid.

70 See for example, *Miller v Rice* (1758) 1 BURR 452, 97 ER 398, where Lord Mansfield CJ said the bank note: ". . . is constantly and universally, both at home and abroad, treated as money . . . it is necessary for the purpose of commerce that their currency should be established and secured" (at 459, 401).

71 (1875) L R 10 Exch 337; affirmed (1876) 1 App Cas 476.

> footing of any custom or usage prevailing generally in the particular department. By this process, what before was usage only, unsanctioned by legal decision, has become engrafted upon, or incorporated into, the common law, and may thus be said to form part of it.[72]

On the possibility of the development of new customary rules and therefore their position in the common law scheme of things, Cockburn CJ saw no reason why they should not have the same force of law as the older ones:

> Usage adopted by the courts, having been thus the origin of the whole of the so-called law merchant as to negotiable securities, what is there to prevent our acting upon the principle acted upon by our predecessors, and followed in the precedents they have left to us? Why is it to be said that a new usage which has sprung up under altered circumstances, is to be less admissible than the usages of past times? Why is the door to be now shut to the admission and adoption of usage in a matter altogether of cognate character, as though the law had finally been stereotyped and settled by some positive and peremptory enactment?[73]

The Bills of Exchange Act 1882 (UK) has assured *lex mercatoria* a permanent place in English law:

> The rules of common law including the law merchant, save in so far as they are inconsistent with the express provisions of this Act, shall continue to apply to bills of exchange, promissory notes and cheques.[74]

It is instructive, however, to bear in mind Lord Herschell's well-known dicta in *Bank of England v Vagliano Bros*[75] in relation to the limitation on *lex mercatoria* as part of English law where a statute exists on a particular subject:

> I think the proper course is in the first instance to examine the language of the statute and to ask what its natural meaning, uninfluenced by any considerations derived from the previous state of the law, and not to start with inquiring how the law previously stood, and then, assuming that it was probably intended to leave it unaltered, to see if the words of the enactment will bear an interpretation in conformity with this view.

72 Ibid at 346.
73 Ibid at 352.
74 Ibid, s 92(2); see also the Bills of Exchange Act (Ch 240), s 5; *Stock Motor Ploughs v Forsyth* (1937) 58 CLR 618, per Starke J at 630. Also *Bank of Baroda v Punjab National Bank* [1944] AC 176 at 183, PC.
75 [1891] AC 107.

> If a statute, intended to embody in a code a particular branch of the law, is to be treated in this fashion, it appears to me that its utility will be almost entirely destroyed, and the very object with which it was enacted will be frustrated. The purpose of such a statute was that on any point specifically dealt with by it, the law should be ascertained by interpreting the language used instead of, as before, roaming over a vast number of authorities in order to discover what the law was, extracting it by a minute critical examination of the prior decisions.[76]

Nature of negotiable instruments

Bill of exchange

The traditional form of a negotiable instrument is a bill of exchange, which currently is seldom employed in the area of inland trade. It is, however, the essence of export trade. Additionally, there is a particular form of bill of exchange in constant use today; this is the cheque. It is therefore critically important to preface the study of banking law with an exploratory overview of a bill of exchange.

The functions of a bill of exchange are as follows. First, to enable a seller to procure payment and the buyer to secure credit at the same time. The seller does not have to wait to be paid only after the buyer has sold the goods and the buyer who cannot afford to pay immediately may obtain time to pay under the bill. Secondly, it facilitates an action for the recovery of debt upon the buyer's default in making payment, since all that the seller does is sue on the bill for default in payment. Finally, in bankruptcy proceedings, holders of negotiable instruments are given priority over ordinary creditors.

A bill of exchange may be described as an unconditional order for the payment of money wholly independent of any underlying transactions and

K50,000		Place: Port Moresby Date: 19 December 2003
stamp	30 days after date pay Supplier (Pty) Ltd the sum of PNG Kina Fifty thousand only for value received.	
	Signed	David Kinu Managing Director Supplier (Pty) Ltd
	To:	Manufacturer Waigani NCD

76 Ibid at 144–145.

was used by exporters to obtain payment from buyers of goods who were not in a position to pay immediately for the goods. A bill of exchange may be depicted diagrammatically as above.

A bill of exchange may also serve as a medium for raising short- and medium-term finance. In this regard it takes the form of a commercial bill which can be negotiated or discounted for cash by a customer with his/her bank. The commercial bill is attractive for a number of reasons, the salient ones being:

(a) it affords flexibility in business dealing;
(b) it is easily marketable; and
(c) its discounting has been held to be distinct from money-lending.[77]

Cheques

The bill of exchange which the ingenuity of the medieval merchant minds contrived for purposes of international financial transactions took on a new role in eighteenth-century England. It was adapted for use as an order on a bank and served to settle debts. The name "cheque" or "check" derives from the practice of having the forms printed as composite booklets which contained a counterfoil or check. The cheque is still widely used in the settlement of accounts in spite of the more modern forms of settlement of debts and bills such as the credit card, bankcard and other electronic paying systems.

Promissory notes

These serve as security in money lending transactions. As a form of bill of exchange, a promissory note is perfectly negotiable, however, it remains only a promise by one person to pay another a debt. It is not an order by one person addressed to another.

Analogous instruments

A few instruments in current vogue give the misleading appearance that they possess the qualities of the bill of exchange which are, however, not of the genre of a bill of exchange. Typical examples are travellers' cheques and bills of lading.

Travellers' cheques

The popular types of travellers' cheques, Citibank, Thomas Cook and American Express, are cheques drawn by a bank on itself to enable a traveller

77 *Chow Yoong Hong v Choong Fah Rubber Manufactory* [1962] AC 209.

to obtain currency in a foreign country at the prevailing rate there. It has to be signed once by the purchaser in the presence of an officer of the issuer and again countersigned before an authorised dealer prior to its conversion into cash. The requirement to countersign a cheque appears to be a condition precedent to the right to obtain cash which negates its quality as a bill or note. There is lack of unanimity on the issue whether a travellers' cheque should be treated as a bill of exchange or not. In *Emerson v American Express Co*,[78] the Court of Appeal for the District of Columbia said:

> Whatever may be its effect in the case of ordinary bank cheques, the lack of a named payee in the body of a travellers' cheque does not render the instrument incomplete as to subsequent holder for value. On the contrary, we think that the very nature of a travellers' cheque is such that, having been signed and countersigned by the purchaser, it may be regarded as having been endorsed in blank and rendered subject to negotiation by delivery; and that a party cashing such a cheque containing identical signature and countersigning is entitled to collect from the issuer.[79]

With the greatest respect, the judgment goes against the weight of authority on the nature of a bill of exchange. A travellers' cheque is not an unconditional order to pay. On the other hand, it is a perfectly valid argument that it ought to be treated as a new species of negotiable instruments and has been considered as such by a universal mercantile usage.[80]

Lord Chorley, a notable authority, argues to the contrary, however, that:

> Proof of such universal acceptance might be difficult to obtain. The well-recognised practice of many money-changers to require identification of the payee, suggests the contrary.[81]

Bills of lading

A bill of lading also has the appearance of a bill of exchange. It is a document which a ship owner issues, covering goods shipped by him to a buyer, in which the ship-owner undertakes that the goods had been shipped in apparent good order and condition. A bill of lading is one of the forms in regular use in the mercantile world in much the same way as the bill of exchange. The cases, commencing with *Lickbarrow v Mason*[82] through

78 (1952) 90 Atlantic Rep 2d 236.
79 Ibid 241.
80 See *Ashford v Thomas Cook & Sons (Bankers) Ltd* (1970) 471 P 2d 531 at 532.
81 Lord Chorley, supra, at 260.
82 (1794) 5 TR 683.

Sewell v Burdick,[83] judicially recognise the functions of a typical bill of lading as:

(a) a receipt acknowledging shipment of goods;
(b) evidence of the contract of carriage of goods by sea; and
(c) a document of title to the goods represented thereby.

Such a document is negotiable and may be negotiated in the way a negotiable instrument is usually treated. It is transferable by delivery or endorsement plus delivery and may be sold and may be mortgaged. A bill of lading symbolises the goods and where a bill is endorsed to a bank it creates only a charge against the goods, it does not effect a complete transfer of property in the goods to the banker. Bowen J noted in this regard:

> The freedom of disposition which owners of property possess when their property is on shore, belongs to them equally when it is afloat. They can if they please, sell the bill of lading, or transfer it upon terms which amount either to a mortgage or a pledge. For a bill of lading is a symbol of the goods themselves. The cargo being at sea, no actual delivery of it is possible before the ship arrives. During this period of floatation and transit the bill of lading becomes and remains a token or symbol of the goods, and the delivery and endorsement of the bill of lading is equivalent, so far as the passing of property is concerned, to a symbolical delivery of the goods.[84]

It must be emphasised that a bill of lading is not a fully fledged negotiable instrument because, as his Lordship has pointed out, a transferee may on occasions take a bill negotiated to him/her subject to equities. It is thus perhaps more accurate to describe a bill of lading as a 'quasi-negotiable' instrument.

The legal nature of banker–customer relationship

The relationship between the banker and customer is generally that of contract and comprises a set of complex reciprocal rights and duties, some of which are based on the practices and usages prevailing in the banking community. Some of the terms of the contract may be express. A great many, however, are implied and derive from banking usages and practices. The relationship may create a bailment situation, as where the banker has the goods of the customer in its custody; or an agency situation, as where the bank acts on behalf of the customer for instance, buying shares for the customer; or create a mortgage situation, as where the banker loans money to the customer on the security of the customer's property.

83 (1884) 10 App Cas 74.
84 *Burdick v Sewell* (1883) 10 QBD 363.

The necessity of the customer maintaining an account

It has been observed previously that the banker–customer relationship is buttressed in the fact that the customer has opened an account with the bank. It is not easy to determine the exact resultant legal position between a depositor and the bank where the money is deposited.

In *Foley v Hill*,[85] the House of Lords held that banker–customer relationship is grounded in contract, which is really one of creditor and debtor in which the bank borrows from the customer each time the customer pays money into the account and promises at the same time to pay it back to the customer when the customer makes a demand in writing. A detailed discussion on the position was undertaken in the well-known case *Joachimson v Swiss Banking Corp*.[86] Atkin LJ amplified the relationship thus:

> I think that there is only one contract made between the bank and its customer. The terms of the contract involve obligations on both sides, and require careful statement. They appear upon consideration to include the following provisions. The bank undertakes to receive money and to collect bills for its customer's account. The proceeds so received are not to be held in trust for the customer, but the bank borrows the proceeds and undertakes to repay them. The promise to repay is to repay at the branch of the bank where the account is kept, and during banking hours. It includes a promise to repay any part of the amount due against the written order of the customer, addressed to the bank at the branch, and, as such written orders may be outstanding in the ordinary course of business for two or three days, it is a term of the contract that the bank will not cease to do business with the customer, except upon reasonable notice. The customer on his part undertakes to exercise reasonable care in executing his written orders so as not to mislead the bank or facilitate forgery. I think it is necessarily a term of such contract that the bank is not liable to pay the customer the full amount of his balance until he demands payment from the bank at the branch at which the current account is kept.[87]

One implication of the idea that a customer loans money to his/her banker when he/she deposits money with the bank is that the bank's right to the money is a chose in action and not a chose in possession and therefore not "susceptible of larceny".[88]

85 (1848) 2 HL Cas 28, 9 ER 1002.
86 [1921] 3 KB 110.
87 Ibid at 127.
88 *Croton v R* (1967) 41 ALRJ at 289–291; see also *R v Davenport* [1954] 1 WLR 569, [1954] 1 All ER 602; *Laing v Bank of NSW* (1952) 69 WN (NSW) 318; affirmed on appeal [1954] AC 135.

In sum, the banker–customer relationship encompasses the notion that the bank undertakes to receive money and collect bills for the account of its customer, borrows the proceeds realised and promises to pay back to the customer, during regular working hours at the customer's written order which should be addressed to the particular branch where the account is held. The bank also undertakes that it will not discontinue business with the customer except upon giving the customer reasonable notice. On his/her part, the customer undertakes to exercise reasonable care in the execution of his/her orders in order not to mislead the bank or facilitate fraud or forgery.

Some special aspects of the debtor–creditor relationship

Though the banker–customer relationship is based on contract, the debtor–creditor aspect is quite peculiar because, here, it is the creditor, i.e. the customer, who must go after the debtor for payment and not the other way around as in ordinary debtor–creditor relationship. The bank (debtor) undertakes to "repay at the branch of the bank where the customer's account is kept during working hours".[89] This is the legal position in Australia also.[90]

The obligation to pay is conditional on the customer making a written demand (written order). The question arises, therefore, concerning what precise act of the customer constitutes a demand. According to banking practices, a cheque drawn by the customer on the banker and presented at the branch where the customer's account is held constitutes such demand. However, there is no law which explicitly requires that a customer's demand must be in the nature of a cheque, for as Mocatta J observed:

> Unless otherwise agreed, the customer's written order need not be in any particular form, though no doubt in the vast majority of cases the customer today, uses cheque forms supplied by his banker...[91]

It does appear, therefore, that a customer's demand may be made on an ordinary paper subject of course to existing banking practice.[92]

Requirements of a valid cheque

A cheque, to constitute demand for payment, must be drawn in the manner required by law. The requirements according to the English authorities

89 *Joachimson v Swiss Banking Corp* [1921] 3 KB 110 at 127.
90 See *Bank of NSW v Laing* [1954] AC 135; and *Re ANZ Savings Bank Ltd* [1972] VR 690.
91 *Burnett v Westminster Bank Ltd* [1966] 1 QB 742 at 760, [1965] 3 All ER 81 at 85.
92 An inchoate bill of exchange is created simply by affixing an impress duty stamp on a blank paper which bears the signature of the person delivering it: s 25(1), Bills of Exchange Act.

which are persuasive in many common law jurisdictions and presumably in PNG jurisdiction are as follows:

(a) The cheque must be signed by the drawer or by some other person authorised by the drawer to do so;
(b) The payee's name, the amount of the cheque and the date of payment must be clearly written on the cheque;
(c) Alterations, if any, must be properly countersigned by the drawer or his/her authorised agent;
(d) The amount payable should be written in both words and figures which must agree correspondingly; and
(e) The cheque must be due for payment.

A cheque which does not meet these requirements will be considered invalidly drawn and justification for a banker's refusal to pay.[93]

Additionally, a banker must only pay under the following conditions:

(a) the cheque is presented during regular business hours[94] at the branch where the customer maintains an account;[95]
(b) the customer has sufficient funds to his credit to meet the amount covered by the cheque or if in excess, the customer has made prior arrangement with the bank for payment of the cheque;[96] and
(c) there is no legal impediment to the payment of the cheque.[97]

In all circumstances the banker must carry out, to the letter, the customer's mandate or order. Thus, where a customer overdraws his current account, the bank cannot, in the absence of the customer's specific instructions, use the customer's deposit to reduce any current deficit the consequence of which would be the bank's inability to pay cheques in respect of which the

93 *Joachimson v Swiss Banking Corp* [1921] 3 KB 110 at 127; *Commercial Bank of Australia Ltd v Hulls* (1884) 10 VR 110; see also *Bills of Exchange Act* (Ch 250), s 8.

94 In *Baines v National Provincial Bank* (1927) 137 LTR 631, payment of cheque five minutes after closing time was held to be payment in the ordinary course of business.

95 *Richardson v Richardson* (1927) 43 TR 631. The availability of automatic teller machines (ATMs) does not change the situation. ATMs merely enable customers to access their accounts from the ATMs.

96 *Bank of NSW v Laing* [1954] AC 135 where the parties have an agreement to pay against uncleared cheques the customer is entitled to that privilege. See also *Underwood (AL) Ltd v Bank of Liverpool* [1924] 1 KB 775.

97 A legal bar to payment includes notice of the customer's countermand winding up and bankruptcy proceedings involving the customer garnishee or sequestration and injunction orders made against the customer. See infra for detailed discussion.

customer made the deposit.[98] Any such instruction given by the customer must be unambiguously clear.[99]

Banker's duty to customer

A banker owes the customer the following duties:

(i) pay the customer;
(ii) observe secrecy;
(iii) offer advice.

Duty to pay

The primary duty of the banker, as discussed above, is to pay the customer's cheque.

Secrecy

This duty relates to the customer's account, which the banker must maintain with the utmost confidentiality. It arises out of the confidential nature of the banker–customer relationship, as enunciated in *Tournier v National Provincial and Union Bank of England*,[100] where because the customer's banker discussed the customer's financial problems (he had overdrawn his account and was making weekly payments to pay back) with the customer's employer, the employer refused to renew the customer's employment contract. Atkin LJ observed:

> To what information does the obligation of secrecy extend? It clearly goes beyond the state of the account, that is, whether there is a credit or a debit balance. It must extend at least to all the transactions that go through the account, and to the securities, if any, given in respect of the account; and in respect of such matters it must, I think, extend beyond the period when the account is closed, or ceases to be an active account.[101]

The duty of secrecy extends also to information obtained by the banker for the purposes of its business with the customer. The banker must not use such information to benefit itself to the prejudice of the customer.[102]

98 *Huenerbein v Federal Bank of Australia* (1892) 13 LR (NSW) 244.
99 *Commercial Banking Co of Sydney Ltd v Jalsard Pty Ltd* [1973] AC 279.
100 [1924] 1KB 461.
101 Ibid at 485.
102 *Guertin v Royal Bank of Canada* [1983] 1 DLR 68

The duty of secrecy, however, is hedged around with limitations which Bankes LJ delineates carefully in *Tournier*'s case. He says:

> On principle . . . the qualifications can be classified under four heads:
> (a) where there is a compulsion by law to disclose the information;
> (b) where there is a duty to the public to disclose;
> (c) where the interests of the bank require disclosure; and
> (d) where the disclosure is made by the express or implied consent of the customer.[103]

Bankes LJ proceeds to provide examples of the legal qualifications. An example of the first limitation is the English Bankers' Books Evidence Act 1879, under which a banker or its officers cannot be compelled to give evidence or produce the banker's books in any proceedings in which the banker itself is not a party if the contents can be proved in court under the statute. In other words, by these provisions, the banker's books are considered prima facie evidence of whatever records may be required in the case if the banker is not a party.

It goes without saying that, where the banker is a party to the proceedings in court, it is compellable to produce the real books and not just copies.

An example of the second qualification is the call to higher duty over and above duty to self as where "danger to the state or public duty may supersede the duty of the agent to the principal".[104] In this era of global insecurity and terrorism, perhaps it could be said that payment in favour of proscribed terrorist organisations or money laundering are glaring examples. An example of the third qualification is where the banker's own interest is in issue as where it is suing or being sued. In one case, a bank's disclosure of a customer's insufficient funds in her account, which the bank attributed to the customer's cheque payments made to bookmakers, was held to be within the bank's right to make such disclosure.[105] An example of the last exception is in Bankes LJ's own words "where the customer authorises a reference to his bank".[106] Here the customer himself/herself provides particulars such as his/her name, address and account, in a loan or credit application to other banks.[107]

It has been held that where the practice of providing banker's reference is well known, the consent of those concerned may be dispensed with.

103 Ibid at 473.
104 *Weld Weld-Blundell v Stephen* [1920] AC 956 at 965, per Finlay LJ.
105 See *Sunderland v Barclays Bank Ltd* (1938) 5 Legal Decisions Affecting Bankers 163, *Times*, 25 November.
106 *Tunier v National Provincial and Union Bank of England* [1924] 1 KB 461 at 473.
107 See *Ross v Bank of New South Wales* (1928) SR (NSW) 539.

In other words, where the practice is one of common knowledge there is no need for a banker to obtain the consent of a customer when a reference has been requested. Judicial opinion in Australia is divided on the matter.[108]

It is possible for a banker, who provides information of the kind normally requested by banks in connection with loan or credit applications by a customer from another bank, to add a disclaimer of any liability. This practice, which negated negligent misstatements, was upheld in *Hedley Byrne & Co Ltd v Heller & Partners Ltd*[109] in respect of a banker's disclaimer added to a reference. In *Mutual Life and Citizens' Assurance v Evatt*, Barwick CJ said, however:

> The duty of care, in my opinion, is imposed by law in the circumstances. Because it is so imposed, I doubt whether the speaker may always except himself from the performance of the duty by some express reservation at the time of his utterance. But the fact of such a reservation, particularly if acknowledged by the recipient, will in many instances be one of the circumstances to be taken into consideration in deciding whether or not a duty of care has arisen and it may be sufficiently potent in some cases to prevent the creation of the necessary relationship. Whether it is so or not must, in my opinion, depend upon all the circumstances of and surrounding the giving of the information or advice.[110]

In providing a reference, a banker must provide fair and accurate information and must avoid, in particular, fraudulent misrepresentation.[111]

In England, s 6 of the Statute of Frauds (Amendment) Act 1828 requires a document to be written and signed by the author in order for an action to be maintained against the author.[112] The legal position appears to be the same in PNG under the country's Frauds and Limitations Act 1988. In Australia, however, the defence of absence of written document will not absolve a defendant from misconduct under the Trade Practices Act 1974 (Cth).

108 *Mutual Life and Citizen's Assurance Co v Evatt* (1969) 122 CLR 556.

109 [1964] AC 465. Note, however, Barwick CJ's reservation in *Mutual Life and Citizens' Assurance Co Ltd v Evatt*, supra.

110 Ibid at 570.

111 *Commercial Banking Co (Sydney) v RH Brown & Co* (1972) 126 CLR 337.

112 *Parsons v Barclays & Co Ltd and Goddard* (1910) 2 TLR 628. In *Commercial Banking Co (Sydney) v RH Brown & Co*, supra, the defence of lack of signature was not raised even though the reference was not signed.

Banker's duty in the provision of investment advice

It has been noted that courts recognise that bankers render a multitudinous range of services to their customers, some of which include providing customers with investment advice.[113]

This area of banking law is fraught with difficulties due to inconsistent judicial pronouncements in the cases. In the Canadian case of *Bank of Montreal v Young*[114] it was held that the branch manager of the defendant chartered bank had no authority of the defendant bank to offer investment advice. It is not clear whether the matter of authority to bind the banker in this situation depends on the rank of the officer giving the advice or on the fact that indeed the advice was intended to be acted upon and was indeed acted upon by the customer to the customer's detriment.

Perhaps a banker's liability for the negligence of a branch manager's financial advice given to the banker's customer could rest on the principle of vicarious liability: "*respondeat superior*".[115]

Customer's duty to banker

We have noted already the customer duty to:

(a) take reasonable care in the drawing up of cheques so as not to facilitate forgery;[116] and
(b) notify the banker as soon as he/she discovers that cheques ostensibly drawn by him/her are in fact forgeries.[117]

In Australia, this principle took a long time in taking root. Initially, the courts rejected the rationale of the principle by refusing to follow one of the earliest authorities on the issue.[118] The Australian courts consistently rejected *Young v Grote* until 1972.[119]

The High Court stamped its imprimatur on the *Macmillan* and *Greenwood* principle when, in rejecting the rule in *Marshall*, it embraced rather the New South Wales Supreme Court decision in *Varker v The Commercial Banking Co (Sydney)*,[120] where, in spite of the plaintiff's own

113 *Woods v Martins Bank* [1959] 1 QB 55.
114 (1966) 60 DLR (2d) 220.
115 See *Bank of Montreal v Young* (1966) 60 DLR (2d) at 232.
116 *London Joint Stock Bank Ltd v Macmillan and Arthur* [1918] AC 777.
117 *Greenwood v Martins Bank* [1933] AC 51.
118 *Young v Grote* (1827) 4 Bing 253 NC.
119 See *Marshall v Colonial Bank of Australia* (1904) 1 CLR 632; followed in *Austin v Austin* (1906) 3 CLR 516; *Lothian v Richards* (1911) 12 CLR 165.
120 [1972] 2 NSWLR 967.

contributory negligence in the drawing of his cheque, the defendant bank was held liable for the debit to his account.

In *Commercial Trading Bank of Australia v Sydney Wide Stores Pty Ltd*,[121] Murphy J in a separate judgment[122] opined that as a matter of social policy, the loss must fall on the banker rather than on the customer, the "deep pocket" policy on apportionment of loss.[123]

Termination of relationship

Banker–customer relations, being contractual, may be terminated at the option of either party. However, while the customer may terminate the relationship at anytime, by, for instance, closing the account, it has been held that the banker does not enjoy the privilege of unilateral termination of the relationship. The banker must give the customer reasonable notice to terminate the relationship.[124] What constitutes reasonable notice is a matter of fact and depends on the circumstances of each particular case.[125]

Alteration of contract or change in relationship

As with all contracts, change or alteration of the terms is not subject to unilateral action by a party. In the computer age, in particular, where most business processes are computerised, it is important that bankers notify their customers of any changes they effect in their business procedures involving the use of computers.[126] Changes by the banker in the contractual terms, especially an express term which effectively alters an implied term, will be construed against the bank.[127] Lord Scarman's observation in this regard is pertinent. He said:

> If banks wish to impose upon their customers an express obligation to examine their monthly statements and to make those statements, in the absence of query, unchallengeable by the customer after expiry of a time limit, the burden of the objection and of the sanction imposed must be brought home to the customer the provisions which they have

121 (1981) 55 ALJR 574.

122 Ibid at 578–579.

123 See further: Burton, G, and Jamieson, P, 'Modern Banking Services on Rights and Liabilities' (1989) *Austr LJ* 595; Carter, J W, 'A Customer's Duty Towards his Banker' (1982) 98 *Law Quarterly Review* 19; and White, T J, 'The Scope of the Depositor's Duty to Prevent and Discover Alterations and Forgeries of his Checks' (1963) 16 *Vanderbilt Law Review* 1201.

124 *Prosperity Ltd v Lloyds Bank Ltd* (1923) 39 TLR 372.

125 Ibid.

126 *Burnett v Westminster Bank* [1965] 3 All ER 81.

127 *Tai Hing Cotton Mill v Ching Hing Bank* [1985] 2 All ER 947, [1986] AC 80.

> set out do not meet this undoubtedly rigorous test. The test is rigorous because the bankers would have their terms of business so construed as to exclude the rights which the customer would enjoy if they were not excluded by express agreements.[128]

Cheques and banker–customer relationship

Papua New Guinea does not currently have a Cheques Act. It seems PNG's continued dependence on the Bills of Exchange Act[129] as the source of its banking law inhibits efforts to modernise the nation's law of banking. The inclusion of cheques in the Bills of Exchange Act[130] appears to be incongruous, because while the dominant purpose of a bill of exchange is the facilitation of extension of credit, that of a cheque today is the payment or settlement of debt. Today the bulk of the functions of bankers revolve around the handling of cheques.

It is this realisation that led, in England, to the passage of the Cheques Act 1957 (UK) following the deliberations of the Mocatta Committee. As Brian Conrick notes:

> The Cheque... had virtually ceased to be negotiable instrument and has become effectively a non-transferable document, no useful purpose was served by insisting on the payee's endorsement on it. It was estimated that 97% of the cheques were paid directly into the payee's own bank accounts and that seven thousand man hours were being needlessly wasted on this superfluous formality.[131]

In Australia, similar consideration led to the setting up of the Manning Committee in April 1962. The Manning Committee's terms of reference were:

(a) To consider the provisions of the Bills of Exchange Act 1909-1958 and to recommend any alterations to that Act that may be thought desirable.
(b) In particular to consider whether any of the changes effected in the British law by the Cheques Act 1957, should be adopted in Australia.
(c) For the purposes of the foregoing, to seek and consider expressions of opinion from relevant bodies and members of the public.
(d) To report to the government the conclusions of the committee with regard to 1 and 2 above.[132]

128 Ibid at 947, 110.
129 Ch 250.
130 Part III, ss 79–92.
131 *The Law of Negotiable Instruments in Australia*, supra at 7.
132 Ibid at 8.

The Manning Committee Report was submitted to the Commonwealth Government in May 1964 after protracted consultation with business and professional bodies and the general public and concludes:

> While bills of exchange are used in the conduct of most overseas trading transactions, cheques are used overwhelmingly if not entirely for local transactions. Thus, they are the strongest reasons for maintaining uniformity with Great Britain and other Commonwealth countries in legislation dealing with bills of exchange, but the need to do so with regard to cheques is virtually non-existent.

Accordingly, the Committee felt reluctant to "propose any major amendments to the law as to bills, while, on the other hand, it has felt at liberty to consider proposals to amend the law as to cheques entirely on what are regarded as their merits".[133] Consequently, the Committee recommended two separate Acts for cheques and bills of exchange and promissory notes. The first, the Bills of Exchange Act 1971 (Cth), was passed. It was not until 15 years later that the second, the Cheques and Payment Orders Act 1986 (Cth), was promulgated.

In the case of PNG, s 1 of the Bills of Exchange Act defines a cheque as "a bill drawn on a banker payable on demand". Thus, under PNG law, although cheques are specifically covered in Part III (ss 79–92) relevant sections of the entire legislation must be carefully scrutinised in order to ascertain the purview of the law relating to cheques and banking in PNG.

Cheques and bills compared

Although the rules governing cheques are generally the same (subject to a few exceptions) as those which govern bills, there are enormous differences in the rules. These include the following:

(a) Cheques do not require acceptance, consequently the rules relating to acceptance of a bill do not necessarily apply.
(b) Since most cheques are used simply in the payment of debts, cheques are therefore usually not "negotiated". Consequently, the rules relating to negotiation have little practical relevance to cheques.
(c) Cheques are normally used for internal transactions while bills of exchange feature mostly in external trading.
(d) Delay in the presentation of a cheque for payment does not discharge the drawer, unless the drawer suffers actual loss through the delay.

133 Ibid at 8.

(e) The rules on crossings operate only in respect of cheques and do not therefore apply to other bills.
(f) Payment of an order cheque which bears a forged or unauthorised endorsement discharges the paying bank whereas if this were the case involving a bill, the acceptor of such a bill would not be discharged.
(g) A cheque is only drawn on a financial institution.

Types of cheques

There are a variety of cheques in vogue in the banking industry. The common forms are listed below:

Bank cheque and band draft

A bank cheque is a cheque drawn by a bank on itself. Technically, a bank cheque does not conform to the definition of a bill as an instrument drawn by one person on another person. Usually, a customer who wishes to send money to another person pays to the banker an amount equal in value to the cheque amount plus a fee or other such charges. A bank cheque is a bearer cheque with the words "not negotiable" written on the face of it. The popularity of bank cheques rests in the perception that they are not likely to be dishonoured.[134] The circumstances include forgery, material alteration of a cheque, stolen or lost cheques, court order restraining payment of a cheque by the bank and absence of valuable consideration for the cheque.[135] A bank draft is quite similar to a bank cheque. A bank draft may be defined as "an instrument by which a branch of a bank orders another branch of the head office to make a payment".[136]

Agency cheque

This is a mechanism by which financial institutions such as credit unions and building societies (non-banking financial institutions (NBFI)) offer their members a trading or cheque account facility. Again, it must be pointed out

134 There are, however, circumstances justifying non-payment of a bank cheque by a bank: *Commonwealth Trading Bank of Australia v Sydney Raper Pty Ltd* (1975) 25 FLR 217; *Justin Seward Pty Ltd v Commissioner of Rural and Industries Bank* (1982) 60 FLR 51.

135 *Johns Period Furniture Pty Ltd v Commonwealth Savings Bank of Australia* (1980) 24 SASR 223; *Diamond v Graham* [1968] 1 WLR 1061. See further Lane, P, "When is a Bank Cheque Not a Bank Cheque?" (1984) *NSW Law Soc J* 88.

136 Weerasooria, W S, *Banking Law and the Financial System in Australia* (Butterworths, Sydney 1988) pp 204–205. Section 5(1) and (2) of the Australian Cheques and Payment Orders Act 1986 provides that in that legislation reference to bank orders includes reference to bank drafts as well.

that an agency cheque would not answer the definition of a cheque in the conventional sense as an order addressed by one person to another.[137]

Payment order

This is an innovation of the Australian Cheques and Payment Orders Act 1986. It is the creation of a new type of negotiable instrument, a bill drawn not on a banker; rather it is drawn on a NBFI. Section 101(1) defines a payment order as an unconditional order in writing that:

(a) is addressed by a person to another person (being a non-bank financial institution);
(b) is signed by the person giving it;
(c) requires the non-bank financial institution to pay on demand a sum certain in money; and
(d) clearly bears the words "payment order" on the front of the instrument.

This type of cheque may not be in use in PNG currently. It is, however, worthy of noting due to the extent of linkage of the economy of PNG with that of Australia.

Order cheques

The most common type of the cheque is the cheque in ordinary daily use by customers, drawn on those banks and "payable on demand"[138] and discussed hereafter.

Formalities

The requirements for a valid bill apply with equal force to a cheque also.[139] However, an order cheque requires a bank to pay to or to the order of, and only to the order of the person specified on the cheque as payee or endorsee. An order cheque is "negotiated" by endorsement. A cheque is not invalid because it is antedated or post-dated.[140] However, the drawer of a cheque

137 Agency cheques are regularised and protected under the Australian Cheques and Payment Orders Act 1986, ss 96–100.

138 Section 1, Bills of Exchange Act.

139 Section 8, Bills of Exchange Act: a cheque must bear the signature of the drawer, date or time of payment and amount to be paid.

140 Section 18(2), Bills of Exchange Act. See *Hodgson & Lee Pty Ltd v Mardonius Pty Ltd* [1986] 5 NSWLR 496; *Brien v Dwyer* (1978) 141 CLR 378 at 394.

may intend the details (including the date of payment) of a cheque to be filled in later and so draws a blank cheque. Such a cheque qualifies as an inchoate instrument.[141]

Brett LJ's dictum in *Bexandale v Bennet*[142] applies with equal force to such a cheque. In that case Brett LJ said:

> The law as to the liability of a person who accepts a bill in blank is that he gives an apparent authority to the person to whom he issues it to fill it up to the amount that the stamp will cover; he does not strictly authorise him, but enables him to fill it up to a greater amount than was intended. Where a man has signed a blank acceptance, and has issued it, and has authorised the holder to fill it up, he is liable on the bill, whatever the amount may be, though he has given secret instructions to the holder as to the amount for which he shall fill it up; he has enabled his agent to deceive an innocent party, and he is liable.[143]

Because a cheque is a bill of exchange designed to be freely transferable, the transferee should be able to treat it as cash.[144] The liabilities which arise and defences which can be raised are quite limited and different from those relating to the initial transaction. Assume, for example, that X buys goods from Y and pays by drawing a cheque. X finds that the goods are defective and attempts to retrieve the cheque. Unless there is a total failure of consideration, X cannot raise the defects either as a defence or by way of set-off or counterclaim. It follows that Y can obtain judgment on the bill and can enforce that judgment unless the court grants a stay of execution.

Thus, for example, a drawee who also does not accept the cheque for payment is not liable on it, although he/she may be liable on the original debt for which the cheque was drawn.[145]

A drawer by drawing a cheque:

(a) engages that on due presentation it will be accepted and paid according to its tenor, and that if it is dishonoured he/she will, if the requisite proceedings in dishonour are taken, compensate the holder or any endorser who is compelled to pay it; and
(b) is precluded from denying to a holder in due course the existence of the payee and his capacity at that time to endorse.[146]

141 Section 25, Bills of Exchange Act.
142 (1873) 3 QBD 525.
143 Ibid at 531. See also *Smith v Prosser* [1907] 2 KB 735 at 753–754, per Fletcher Moulton LJ.
144 *Goodwin v Robarts* (1875) LR 10 Exch 337; affirmed (1876) 1 App Cas 476.
145 Section 58, Bills of Exchange Act.
146 Section 60(1) Bills of Exchange Act.

An endorser, by endorsing a cheque:

(a) engages that on due presentation it will be accepted and paid according to its tenor, and that if it is dishonoured he will compensate, if the requisite proceedings on honour are taken, the holder or a subsequent endorser who is compelled to pay it; and
(b) is precluded from denying to a holder in due course the genuineness and regularity in all respects of the drawer's signature and all previous endorsements; and
(c) is precluded from denying to his immediate or a subsequent endorsee that the bill was at the time of his/her endorsement a valid and subsisting bill, and that at that time he/she had a good title to the bill.[147]

Holder in due course

A holder is a payee or indorsee in possession of a cheque. Possession may be actual or constructive. It should be observed that possession *simpliciter* does not transform a person into a holder, for example a person in possession of a cheque payable to another is not a holder while the cheque remains unendorsed. A thief in possession of a bearer bill, on the other hand, is a "holder", therefore would be capable of passing good title to a bona fide transferee for value. A person may improve his/her standing by giving value in exchange for the cheque. The holder in the most fortified position is the so-called holder in due course. This person can enforce the cheque against all persons in the world. Section 43(1)(b) provides that a holder in due course:

(i) holds the bill free from any defect of title of prior parties as well as from mere personal defences available to prior parties among themselves; and
(ii) may enforce payment against all parties liable on the bill.[148]

147 Section 60(2) Bills of Exchange Act.

148 This is an abbreviated version of s 29 of the English Bills of Exchange Act 1882 which reads:

(1) A holder in due course is a holder who has taken a bill, complete and regular on the face of it, under the following conditions; namely,
  (a) That he became the holder of it before it was overdue, and without notice that it had been previously dishonoured, if such was the fact;
  (b) That he took the bill in good faith and for value and that at the time the bill was negotiated to him he had no notice of any defect in the title of the person who negotiated it.
(2) In particular the title of a person who negotiates a bill is defective within the meaning of this Act when he obtained the bill, or the acceptance thereof, by fraud, duress, or force and fear, or other unlawful means, or for an illegal consideration, or when he negotiates it in breach of faith, or under such circumstances as amount to a fraud.

Defect of title vitiates and voids title and it includes illegal consideration and other forms of illegality. Personal defences encompass all available defences at law and include legal as well as equitable set-offs.[149]

Endrosements

Generally, the parties to a cheque are the drawer (customer), the drawee (banker) and the payee (person designated to receive payment). Although payment cheques generally require no endorsement, a person may become a party by merely appending his or her signature to a cheque. Thus, a total stranger may become party by signing the cheque.[150]

Endorsement and signature go hand in hand. Thus, an endorsement in blank is nothing more than the simple signature of the endorser on the cheque.[151]

There are the following types of endorsements:

(a) in blank,[152] which operates as payable to bearer;
(b) special;[153]
(c) restrictive,[154] which gives the endorsee the right to receive payment of the cheque; and
(d) conditional,[155] in which case the condition may be disregarded by the payer.

An endorsement is effected by writing or placing any relevant words and signature on the cheque, which then becomes part of the cheque. However, because an endorser of a cheque may become a party to it, the cheque adopts a different hue after an endorsement, thus bringing along with it issues of regularity which go to the nature of liability under the cheque.

A cheque may be regular on the face of it and still be invalid. It is therefore necessary to distinguish regularity from validity. In *Arab Bank v Ross*,[156] Denning LJ observed:

> Regularity is a different thing from validity. The Act itself makes a careful distinction between them. On the one hand an indorsement which is quite invalid may be regular on the face of it. Thus the indorsement may be forged or unauthorized and, therefore, invalid but nevertheless

149 *Stock Motor Ploughs v Forsyth* (1932) 48 CLR 138; s 61, Bills of Exchange Act.
150 Section 61 Bills of Exchange Act.
151 Section 73(1)(a).
152 Section 37(5)(a); s 39, Bills of Exchange Act.
153 Section 37(5)(a); s 39, Bills of Exchange Act.
154 Section 37(5)(b).
155 Section 38, Bills of Exchange Act.
156 [1952] 1 All ER 705.

> there may be nothing about it to give rise to any suspicion. The bill is then quite regular on the face of it. Conversely, an indorsement which is quite irregular may nevertheless be valid. Thus, by a misnomer, a payee may be described on the face of the bill by the wrong name, nevertheless, if it is quite plain that the drawer intended him as payee, then an indorsement on the back by the payee in his own true name is valid and sufficient to pass the property in the bill, but the difference between front and back makes the indorsement irregular unless the payee adds also the misnomer by which he was described on the front of the bill.[157]

Additionally, the fact that a cheque is regular on the face of it does not affect the issue of liability on it. Thus, again in *Arab Bank v Ross*,[158] Lord Denning draws a distinction between regularity and liability. His Lordship said:

> Regularity is also different from liability. The Act makes a distinction between these two also. On the other hand, a person who makes an irregular indorsement is liable thereon despite the irregularity. Thus, if a payee, who is wrongly described on the front of the bill, indorses it in his own true name, the indorsement is irregular, but he is liable to any subsequent holder and cannot set up the irregularity as a defence; or if he is rightly described on the front of the bill, but indorses it in an assumed name, the indorsement is irregular, but he is liable thereon as if he had indorsed it in his own name.

Conversely, a regular endorsement will not impose liability if it is forged or unauthorised. Thus, where a firm is the payee, but is described in an unauthorised name which is substantially different from its real name, an endorsement by one partner in that name does not impose liability on the other partner. It would be otherwise if the name was substantially the same.[159]

Presentation for payment

Because a cheque is "drawn on a bank payable on demand", it follows that a holder must duly present the cheque for payment, otherwise the drawer and endorsers, if any, are discharged.[160]

157 Ibid at 715.
158 Ibid.
159 Ibid; see also *Heller Factors Pty Ltd v Toy Corporation Pty Ltd* [1984] 1 NSWLR 121.
160 Section 50(2) See also *Yeoman Credit Ltd v Gregory* [1963] 1 All ER 245.

Presentation must be made "at a reasonable hour on a business day, at the place of payment specified on the cheque".[161] Note, however, that a few minutes of lateness may be excused: "*de minimis non curat lex*",[162] so goes the Latin maxim. Delay in the presentation of a cheque may be excused in appropriate circumstances.[163] Additionally, presentation may be dispensed with according to the circumstances of the cheque.[164]

Crossings on cheques

Crossings, just as anything written or inscribed on the face of a cheque, carry a significant message of the drawer of a cheque.[165] Emanating historically from the mechanism of Clearing House of Bankers nominating particular banks as payees, "so that payment would be made only to the banker named in the crossing",[166] drawers of cheques today have become the main beneficiaries of the practice and employ it as useful apparatus and safeguard against the loss or theft of a cheque.

Types of crossings

There are two types of crossings in common use:

(a) general crossings; and
(b) special crossings.

General crossing

This consists of two parallel traverse lines across the face of the cheque, with or without the words "and company", or an abbreviation of that expression.

Special crossing

This is the situation where a cheque bears across its face the name of the banker. The Bills of Exchange Act has introduced the use of the words

161 Section 50(6) and (7).
162 *Eimco Corp v Tuth Bryant Ltd* (1970) 18 FLR 50; *Day v Bate* (1979) 41 FLR 22; *City Bank v Australian Joint Stock Bank* (1870) 95 SCR NSW 259; *Thoneman v Holmes* [1945] SASR 227; *Baines v National Provincial Bank* (1927) 32 Com Cas 216; *Wilkins v Jadis* (1831) 109 ER 1213; and *H Rowe & Co Pty Ltd v Pitts* [1973] 2 NSWLR 159.
163 Section 51(1) and (2).
164 Section 51(3).
165 *Giblin v McMullen* (1868) LR 2 PC 317.
166 See Holder, J M, *History of Negotiable Instruments in English Law* (Pitmans, London, 1955); Holder, J M, *The Law and Practice of Banking* (Pitmans, London, 1974) pp 132–133.

"not negotiable" in addition to crossings.[167] The effect of that innovation is expressed in s 88 of the Act. It provides:

> A person who takes a crossed cheque bearing the words "not negotiable" does not have and is not capable of giving a better title to the cheque than the person had from whom he took it.

A "not negotiable" crossing thus affords considerable protection where a cheque is a bearer cheque. For example, suppose X to be owner of a bearer cheque (an order cheque endorsed in blank[168]) and Y steals it from X and delivers it to Z. If Z is a holder in due course, he gets good title. On the other hand, if X's cheque were a crossed cheque with the words "not negotiable" also on it, Z would only have acquired the same title as Y the thief, that is, no title at all.

It must be emphasised that the words "not negotiable" on an uncrossed cheque may probably not have any effect, though perhaps transferable in the usual way.[169]

Account payee crossings

Though the words "account payee" on the face of a crossed cheque are not mentioned in the Act, they are regarded as an instruction to the collecting banker to credit the account of the payee with the proceeds of the cheque. In *National Bank v Silke*[170] it was held that a cheque bearing those words on the face of it remained freely negotiable. The words "account payee only" would seem to have the same effect as "account payee".[171]

Negotiation of a cheque

Although order or payment cheques are not intended to be negotiated,[172] because they are bills of exchange, they may be negotiated in the same manner as all bills are negotiated, should the need arise to negotiate them. A cheque is thus negotiated by transfer from a holder to a recipient who is thus constituted a holder also.[173] While order cheques are negotiated by

167 Section 83(2)(a) and (b).

168 Section 13(3)(b), Bills of Exchange Act.

169 Section 13(1)(b), Bills of Exchange Act.

170 [1891] 1 QB 435.

171 *Universal Guarantee Pty Ltd v National Bank of Australasia* [1965] 1 WLR 691 at 996, [1965] 2 All ER 98 at 102, PC.

172 See Ellinger, E P, "Is there a need for Non-Transferable Cheques" (1992) 108 *Law Quarterly Review* 15.

173 Section 36(1), Bills of Exchange Act.

endorsement and delivery,[174] bearer cheques are negotiated by mere delivery.[175] A cheque is negotiable until restrictively endorsed or discharged by payment.[176]

Stale cheques

A cheque which has been in circulation for an unreasonable period is deemed to be overdue or "stale". What amounts to an unreasonable time is a matter of fact.[177]

Liabilities of the banker

A banker runs the risk of incurring legal liabilities in its dealing with and treatment of the cheques of a customer. Some liabilities arise from the fact of the contractual relationship between the banker and the customer. Others flow from the legal effect of a banker's conduct in relation to the customer's cheques such as conversion and defamation.

Observance of the customer's mandate

Central to banker–customer relationship is the duty on the banker to honour the customer's order to pay when the customer has sufficient funds to his credit in his/her account.[178] Wrongful failure to honour the customer's mandate is tantamount to dishonour of the customer's cheque. Such dishonour has serious legal consequences and could attract liability for:

(a) breach of contract;
(b) conversion; and
(c) the tort of defamation or libel.

The customer may, however, stop payment of a cheque by countermand.[179] And if the banker pays such a countermanded cheque, the banker would be acting contrary to the customer's mandate not to pay. In *Bank of Hawaii v PNG Banking Corporation and Others*,[180] an uncrossed cheque of the

174 Section 36(2), Bills of Exchange Act.
175 Section 36(3), Bills of Exchange Act.
176 Section 41(3)(a) and (b).
177 Section 41(2), Bills of Exchange Act. Under the Australian Cheques and Payment Orders Act 1957, the period for this is 15 months from the date of the drawing as appears on the face of the cheque: s 3(5).
178 *Foley Hill*, supra, note 79 (1848) 2 HL Cas 28, 9 ER 1002; *Joachimson v Swiss Banking Co*, [1921] 3 KB 110.
179 A countermand amounts to the withdrawal or revocation of the mandate – s 82(a), Bills of Exchange Act and operates to determine the banker's duty and authority to pay a cheque.
180 Unreported judgment, Supreme Court N2095, 2000.

plaintiff's customer was made payable to one "Avoa Maria". The cheque was apparently stolen and endorsed to the second defendant with the forged signature "Avoa Maria John". The second defendant as endorsee deposited the cheque in its current account with the first defendant and requested that it be cleared through the first defendant's "special clearance" system. The first defendant obliged. The first defendant credited the second defendant's account with the proceeds.

When the forgery was subsequently detected, the plaintiff brought this action to recover from the defendants the amount involved. The first defendant denied the plaintiff's right to recover the sum claimed as the cheque was specially cleared. The plaintiff countered that argument with the submission that the cheque was, in all material respects, regular on the face of it and that the forgery, not being obvious, brought the plaintiff's conduct within the protection of the s 29 exception of the Bills of Exchange Act.

Kandakasi J upheld the plaintiff's submission and, relying on *National Westminster Bank Ltd v Barclays Bank Ltd*[181] said:

> . . . [A] party seeking to prevent a paying bank as in this case, from recovering a payment under a forged cheque, must prove that, the paying bank was in fact negligent in making the payment. It is not simply good enough to claim that, because the paying bank honoured a forged cheque, it was negligent. There must be some evidence of a demonstrable failure on the part of the paying bank to form the foundation for an argument that it was negligent in allowing the payment as opposed to believing the signatures on the cheque were genuine.[182]

On the proper legal relationship that must exist between the parties for the plaintiff to succeed, his Honour said: "there was no relationship between the plaintiff's customer and the rogue or the plaintiff and the rogue."[183]

To be a valid countermand, it must be clear and unambiguous[184] and communicated to the bank before presentation of the cheque for payment.[185] Where a bank pays a cheque after a valid customer countermand, the bank cannot debit the account of the customer.[186] Where the bank pays after a countermand in error and the legal position of the payee has not changed, the banker may recover from the payee.

181 *National Westminster Bank Ltd v Barclays Bank Ltd* [1974] 3 All ER 834 at 849–850, per Kerr J.
182 Ibid, 13–14.
183 Ibid at 18.
184 *Westminster Bank v Hilton* [1926] 43 TLR 124 at 129–130.
185 *Curtice v London City & Midland Bank* [1908] 1 KB 293; *Commonwealth Trading Bank v Reno Auto-Sales Pty Ltd* [1967] VR 790.
186 *Barclays Bank Ltd v WJ Simms Sons & Cooke (Southern) Ltd* [1980] 1 QB 677; *Commercial Bank of Australia Ltd v Younis* [1979] NSWLR 344.

In *London and River Plate Bank v Bank of Liverpool*,[187] Matthew J explained the banker's right to recover from the payee as follows:

> In *Cocks v Masterman* 9 B & C 902 the simple rule was laid down in clear language for the first time that when a bill becomes due and is presented for payment, *the holder ought to know at once whether the bill is going to be paid or not*. If the mistake is discovered at once, it may be the money can be recovered back; but if it be not, and the money is paid in good faith, and is received in good faith, and there is an interval of time in which the position of the holder may be altered, the principle seems to apply that money once paid cannot be recovered back. The rule is obviously, as it seems to me, indispensable for the conduct of business.[188] (Emphasis added.)

Where the bank pays a cheque on which the customer's signature is forged, the banker cannot debit the account of the customer with the amount so paid "because a cheque on which the signature of a customer is forged, is not the customer's mandate or order to pay".[189] Richmond J states succinctly the legal principle in *National Bank of New Zealand v Walpole and Patterson*:[190]

> When a banker pays out a cheque he is not thereby paying away funds of the customer. The money or credits used by the banker to meet a cheque are his own. If the banker has no valid mandate from his customer then he has no authority to debit payment in current account as between himself and his customer. If the banker makes an unauthorised debit entry the customer does not thereby suffer a loss equivalent to the amount of the cheque. The wrongful debit entry may cause the banker to dishonour a subsequent valid cheque and in that case the customer will have his remedy for the wrongful dishonour. Again, if the customer demands payment from the banker of the true amount standing to his credit then the unauthorised debit entry cannot avail the banker as a defence.[191]

Forgery also encompasses situations of multiple signatures, as where the mandate to the bank is to the effect that two or more persons be joint signatories to a cheque and one or more signatories having signed, they then

187 [1896] 1 QB 7; see also *ANZ Banking Group Ltd v Westpac Banking Group* (1988) 62 ALJR 292.
188 Ibid at 11.
189 *London Joint Stock v Macmillan and Arthur* [1918] AC 777 at 790, per Lord Finlay LC; see also s 29(1), Bill of Exchange Act, which provides that the signature is wholly inoperative.
190 [1975] 2 NZLR 7.
191 Ibid at 12.

forge the signatures of the others.[192] However, the banker's payment of a forged cheque may be excused on grounds of estoppel or ratification.[193]

Estoppel operates to foreclose the customer's ability to repudiate his/her signature. In *Greenwood v Martins Bank*,[194] Tomlin J set out the salient elements of such conduct of the customer as foreclose the customer's right to repudiate the signature on his/her cheque:

> The essential factors giving rise to estoppel are I think:
>
> (1) A representation or conduct amounting to a representation intended to induce a course of conduct on the part of the person to whom the representation is made.
> (2) An act or omission resulting from the representation' whether actual or by conduct, by the person to whom the representation is made.
> (3) Detriment to such person as a consequence of the act or omission. Mere silence cannot amount to a representation, but when there is a duty to disclose deliberate silence may become significant and amount to a representation.

Ratification, on the other hand, is such conduct of adoption of an otherwise unauthorised action not amounting to forgery as can support a defence of estoppel.[195]

Paying against tenor of crossing

Since the banker's primary duty to the customer is to pay the customer's written order, except in the case of a cheque crossed for collection, a banker is in breach of the duty to pay if it pays a crossed cheque; for this is against the instructions of the customer written on the face of the cheque.[196] A crossing, it has been noted, is a material part of a cheque.[197]

192 *Arden v Bank of New South Wales* [1956] VLR 569.
193 Section 29(1) and (2), Bills of Exchange Act.
194 [1933] AC 51 at 57.
195 Section 29(2) See *Taylor v Smith* (1926) 38 CLR 48 at 60, per Rich J and *Brook v Hook* (1871) LR 6 Ex 89. Contra, *Mackenzie v British Linen Co* (1881) 6 App Cas 82, where Lord Blackburn LJ said: "I wish to guard against being supposed to say that if a document with an unauthorized signature was altered under such circumstances of intent to defraud that it amounted to the crime of forgery, it is in the power of the person whose name was forged to ratify it so as to make a defence for the forger against a criminal charge. I do not think he could. But if the person whose name was without authority used chooses to ratify the act, even though known to be a crime, he makes himself civilly responsible just as if he had originally authorised it. It is quite immaterial whether this ratification was made to the person who seeks to avail himself of it or to another", at 99.
196 Under s 86(2) the banker is liable to the true owner "for any loss that he sustains owing to the cheque having been so paid".
197 Section 85, Bills of Exchange Act.

Action for breach of contract

Ordinarily, the legal remedy for the breach of the banker's obligation to honour the customer's order to pay money out of his/her account in which he/she has sufficient funds is damages.[198] Since damages are awarded on the basis of a plaintiff's loss flowing from the breach, it follows that the quantum will vary according to the circumstances of particular cases. It has been held that a factor which features in the determination of the quantum of damages is whether the plaintiff is a trader or non-trader.[199] Loss to a trader obviously entails harm to business reputation and credit.[200] Whether a plaintiff falls within the category of trader is a matter of both fact and law.[201] Whereas a trader may recover substantial damages, a non-trader is not so entitled in the absence of proof of special damage.[202]

In awarding substantial damages in the absence of proof of special damages, Williams J observed in *Robin v Steward*:[203]

> When it is alleged and proved that the plaintiff is a trader, I think it is equally clear that the jury, in estimating the damages, may take into their consideration the natural and necessary consequences which must result to the plaintiff from the defendant's breach of contract; just as in the case of an imputation of insolvency on a trader, the action lies without proof of special damages.[204]

In the case of a non-trader plaintiff, the courts are not so generous. In *Gibbons v Westminster Bank*,[205] where as a consequence of the bank's dishonour (through error) of the plaintiff's cheque in payment of rent to the landlord, the landlord insisted on cash payment for future rents; the tenant was rewarded 40 shillings nominal damages for the action for damages. Lawrence J said:

> The authorities which have been in argument all day lay down that a trader is entitled to recover substantial damages for the wrongful dishonour of his cheque without pleading and proving actual damage,

198 *Bank of NSW v Laing* [1954] AC 135; *Bell v Capital and Counties Bank* (1887) 3 TLR 540.

199 *Magill v Bank of North Queensland* (1895) 6 QLJ 262; *Bank of New South Wales v Milvain* (1884) 10 VLR 3; *Baker v ANZ Bank Ltd* [1955] NZLR 907.

200 *Marzetti v Williams* [1830] B & Ad 415; *Robin v Steward* (1854) 14 CB 595.

201 *Magill v Bank of North Queensland* (1895) 6 QLJ 262.

202 *Robin v Steward* (1854) 14 CB 595.

203 (1854) 14 CB 595.

204 Ibid at 607; see also *Wilson v United Counties Bank Ltd* [1920] AC 102; *Bailey v Bank of Australia* (1906) 6 SR (NSW) 686; *Queensland Bacon Pty Ltd v Rees* (1967) 115 CLR 266.

205 [1939] 2 KB 882.

> but it has never been held that the exception to the general rule as to the measure of damages for breach of contract extends to anyone who is not a trader . . . In my opinion this matter should be treated as covered by the authorities and I hold accordingly that the corollary of the proposition laid down by them is the law – namely that a person who is not a trader is not entitled to recover substantial damages for the wrongful dishonour of his cheque, unless the damage which is suffered is alleged and proved as special damage.

Action of conversion

In paying a customer's cheque or collecting a cheque for a customer, the banker runs the risk of paying the money over to a person not entitled to receive it, or crediting the customer's account with money to which he/she is not entitled. Both situations could render the banker liable to the "true owner" for conversion. In *Lloyds Bank v Chartered Bank*,[206] Atkin LJ expatiates on the legal position thus:

> Conversion, primarily, is conversion of chattels . . . but a series of decisions binding on this court, culminating in *Morrison's Case* and *Underwood's Case* have surmounted the difficulty by treating the conversion as of the chattel, the piece of paper [i.e. the paper on which the cheque is written] and the value of the chattel as the money received under it.[207]

Since conversion is a tort of strict liability, neither honesty nor the observance of due care and attention are material or are good defences, for, as Lord Wright LJ observed in *Lloyds Bank Ltd v Savory*:[208]

> In an ordinary action of conversion, once the true owner proves his title and the act of taking by the defendant, absence of negligence or of intention or knowledge are alike immaterial as defences.

The essence of the tort of conversion is the dealing with the property of another in such a manner as to deprive that person of ownership in the property. Thus, in the case of a collecting bank, it is the fact of possession of the cheque which attracts liability. In *Hollins v Fowler*,[209] the principle was enunciated thus:

> [A]ny person "who however innocently, obtains possession of the goods of a person who has been fraudulently deprived of them and

206 [1929] 1 KB 40.
207 Ibid at 44.
208 [1933] AC 201 at 229.
209 (1875) LR 7 HL 757.

> disposes of them, whether for his own benefit or that of any other person, is guilty of conversion".[210]

That statement of the law was approved in *RH Williston v British Car Option Ltd*[211] by the Court of Appeal. Scrutton LJ put the matter even more succinctly in relation to collecting banks in *Underwood (AL) Ltd v Bank of Liverpool*,[212] where he said:

> Now banks who collect, borrow from their customers the proceeds when collected, and in collecting exhaust the operation of the cheque. These operations have been held to be conversion in such cases as *Kleinwort v Comptoir*, and *Arnold v Cheque Bank*, *Fine Art Society v Union Bank*, and by Lord Reading in this court in *Morrison v London County and Westminster Bank Ltd*. Unless, therefore, the defendant bank can show some excuse in law, they are guilty of conversion.[213]

Action in defamation

Where a banker dishonours a customer's cheque even though the customer has sufficient funds in his/her account, the banker risks being sued by the customer in defamation. Since the banker's indication of dishonour normally appears on the face of the cheque, such written instruction constitutes libel.[214]

In *Sednaoin Zarifta Nahas & Co v Anglo-Australian Bank*,[215] it was held that the customer had the option either to present the cheque again for payment or regard it immediately as dishonoured. These written words are false because the true position is that the customer actually has sufficient funds in the account, and they are capable of defamatory meaning, in that they tend to lower the customer in the estimation of right-thinking members of society generally. They imply "insufficient funds" and may harm the reputation, standing or credit of the customer. The quantum of damages recoverable depends on similar considerations as in an action for breach of contract.[216]

210 Ibid at 795, per Lord Chelmsford LJ.
211 [1978] 1 WLR 438, CA.
212 [1924] 1 KB 775.
213 Ibid at 791.
214 For example, the banker writes on the cheque "refer to drawer": *Flack v London and South Western Bank Ltd* (1915) 31 TLR 334; *Plunkett v Barclays Bank* [1936] 1 All ER 653; *Jayson v Midland Bank* [1967] 2 Lloyd's Rep 563; or "present again": *Baker v ANZ Banking Group Ltd* [1958] NZLR 907.
215 (1909) 30 *Journal of the Institute of Bankers* 413. See also, Gabi, S R, 'Wrongful Honour and Dishonour of Customer's Cheque: Customer's Remedies against the Paying Bank (1979) 7 *Melanesian LJ* 82.
216 See supra; See also s 62(2), Bills of Exchange Act. The customer's foreknowledge of circumstances which could lead to the dishonour of his/her cheque may have effect on the quantum of damages recoverable: *White v Bank of New South Wales* (1883) 2 SCR (NSW) 17.

Negligence and banker protection

Section 91 of the Bills of Exchange Act safeguards the conduct of a banker where the banker is engaged in the collection of customers' payment cheques. The section requires *in extenso* quote. It reads:

> (1) Where –
> (a) a banker, in good faith and without negligence –
> (i) receives payment for a customer of a cheque; or
> (ii) having credited a customer's account with the amount of a cheque for himself; and
> (b) the customer has no title, or has a defective title, to the cheque, the banker does not incur any liability to the true owner of the cheque by reason only of having received payment of the cheque.
> (2) Subject to subsection (3), a banker shall not, for the purposes of this section be deemed to have been negligent by reason only of his failure to concern himself with the absence of endorsement, or an irregularity in the endorsement of a cheque.
> (3) Subsection (2) does not apply in relation to a cheque unless the name appearing on the cheque as the name of the payee –
> (a) is the same as the name of the customer; or
> (b) is so similar to the name of the customer that it was reasonable, in all the circumstances, for the banker to assume that the customer was the person intended by the drawer to be the payee.
> (4) This section applies in relation to a draft drawn by a banker on himself and payable on demand as it applies in relation to a cheque, whether the draft is payable at the head office or at some other office of the banker.

This provision has its roots in s 82 of the English Bills of Exchange Act 1882 (UK), as amended by the Crossed Cheque Act 1906 (UK) and further expanded by the Cheques Act 1959 (UK). The protection extends to crossed cheques only.[217] The collecting bank may be acting as agent of another bank.[218]

The sections indemnifies the banker if it can establish that:

(a) it acted in good faith;
(b) without negligence;[219] and

217 *Capital and Counties Bank v Gordon* [1903] AC 240.
218 Section 87. See also *Importers Co Ltd v Westminster Bank Ltd* [1927] 2 KB 297; *Far Eastern Bank v Bee Hong Finance Co Ltd* (1971) 2 Malayan LJ 28.
219 Section 91(1)(a)(i), Bills of Exchange Act.

(c) its act consists in receipt of payment for a customer of a cheque, or crediting of a customer's account with the proceeds of a cheque received by it;[220] or
(e) pays to another bank or its agent a crossed cheque for collection.[221]

The legal concern here is directed at the "true owner" of the cheque and not the banker's customer. Denman CJ observed in *Bissell & Co v Fox Bros & Co*[222] that negligence in this regard is:

> The neglect of such reasonable precautions as ought to be taken with reference to the interests, not of the customer who purports to have the authority, but of the principal whose authority he purports to have, the section being framed wholly with reference to the liability of the banker to the "true owner" of the cheque, and not with reference to his liability to his customer.

It is, however, not always easy to identify the "true owner" and the most salient factor the courts, on occasions, take into account in making the identification of entitlement to the property is the cheque ownership[223] or the right to immediate possession of same.[224]

Good faith (in the collection of a cheque) connotes honesty and diligence in the operations of the banker.[225]

Negligence implies want of reasonable care. The standard of care is to be measured with reference to that prevalent among reasonably minded bankers who transact banking business in a manner that safeguards their interests and those of others against fraud.[226] In *Commissioners of State Savings Bank of Victoria v Permewan Wright & Co Ltd*,[227] the standard formulated was as follows:

> The test of negligence is whether the transaction of paying in any given cheque was so out of the ordinary course it ought to have aroused doubt in the bankers' mind, and caused them to make enquiry.

220 Section 91(1)(a)(ii), Bills of Exchange Act.
221 Section 87, Bills of Exchange Act.
222 (1884) 51 TLR 663.
223 *Marquess of Bute v Barclays Bank Ltd* [1955] 1 QB 202 at 211, per McNair J; *Commercial Banking Co (Sydney) Ltd v Mann* [1961] AC 1. See, however, *Grantham Holmes Pty Ltd v ANZ Banking Group Ltd* (1980) ACTR 1.
224 *Grantham Holmes Pty Ltd v ANZ Banking Group Ltd* (1980) ACTR 1; *International Factors Ltd v Rodriguez* [1978] 3 WLR 877.
225 *Bank of Borada v Punjab National Bank* [1944] 2 All ER 83 at 92, [1944] AC 176 at 194, PC, per Lord Wright.
226 Ibid.
227 (1914) 19 CLR 457 at 468, per Isaacs J.

The test was adopted by the Privy Council in *Commissioner of Taxation v English Scottish and Australian Bank Ltd.*[228] In that case the Judicial Committee of the Privy Council said:

> The test of negligence is whether the transaction of paying in any given cheque (coupled with the circumstances antecedent and present) was so out of the ordinary course it ought to have aroused doubt in the bankers' mind, and caused them to make enquiry.[229]

The test as amended by the Judicial Committee of the Privy Council has since been accepted by the High Court of Australia as the best formulation of the principle and has finally settled, for Australia, the test of negligence.[230]

It is not advisable, therefore, for a banker in the absence of inquiry to collect a cheque in the following circumstances, as they might have been misappropriated from the true owner:

(i) collect payment for a private account of a cheque payable to a public official;[231]
(ii) collect for an employee's private account a cheque drawn by, or in favour of, his/ her employer;[232]
(iii) collect for an agent's private account a cheque drawn in favour of the principal[233] or a cheque drawn by the agent (on behalf of the principal) in favour of the agent personally;[234]
(iv) collect for a director's private account a cheque payable to a "one man" company;[235] and
(v) collect a cheque marked "account payee" or "account payee only".

Contributory negligence of true owner

It is not clear whether the defence of contributory negligence is open to the banker. In the UK, if raised and successfully pleaded and upheld by the

228 [1920] AC 683.
229 Ibid at 688.
230 *London Bank of Australia v Kendall* (1920) 28 CLR 401. The more recent cases include *Marfani v Midland Bank Ltd* [1968] 2 All ER 573, 1 WLR 956, CA; *Savings Bank of South Australia v Wallman* (1935) 52 CLR 688; *Cary v Rural Bank of NSW* [1967] 2 DCR (NSW) 49; *Gippsland and Northern Co-operative Ltd v English, Scottish and Australian Bank Ltd* [1922] VLR 670. In *Lumsden v London Trustee Savings Bank* [1971] 1 Lloyd's Rep 114, Donaldson J gave extensive practical observations on the appropriate enquiries which a bank might make when opening an account.
231 *Ross v London County, Westminster and Parr's Bank* [1919] 1 KB 678.
232 *Lloyds Bank v Savory (EB)* [1933] AC 201. *Carpenters' Co v British Mutual Banking Co* [1938] 1 KB 511.
233 *Bute v Barclays Bank* [1955] 1 QB 202, [1954] 3 All ER 365.
234 *Midland Bank Ltd v Reckitt* [1933] AC 1, [1932] All ER Rep 90.
235 *Underwood (AL) Ltd v Bank of Liverpool* [1924] 1 KB 775, [1924] All ER Rep 230.

court, it operates in mitigation or diminution of the bank's liability to the true owner. In *Lumsden v London Trustee Savings Bank*,[236] plaintiff's damages were reduced by 10 per cent, this being the measure of loss by way of his own negligence. In the UK the defence was abolished[237] and then revived again.[238]

In Australia, however, the courts have consistently rejected the availability of the defence of contributory negligence to a collecting bank.[239]

Paid cheque as receipt

Section 90(1) of the Bills of Exchange Act provides:

> An unendorsed cheque payable to order that appears to have been paid by the banker on whom it is drawn is evidence of the receipt by the payee of the sum payable by the cheque.

This appears to be the language of s 3 of the English Cheques Act 1957 (UK). It extends to unendorsed cheques the same result in law as payment of endorsed cheques by a banker. The evidence of payment is however not conclusive, though perhaps strong.[240] This weakens perhaps the legal protection of payers at law.

236 Supra [1971] 1 Lloyd's Rep 114.
237 Torts (Interference with Goods) Act 1977 (UK).
238 Banking Act 1979 (UK), s 47.
239 *Wilton v Commonwealth Trading Bank of Australia* [1973] 2 NSWR 644; *Day v Bank of NSW* (1978) 19 ALR 32; and *Grantham Holmes Pty Ltd v ANZ Banking Group Ltd* (1980) 26 ACT R 1.
240 *Westminster Bank v Zang* [1966] AC 182, [1966] 2 WLR 110.

Part IV

Company Law

By Val Haynes

Chapter 7

Introduction to Company Law in Papua New Guinea

Introduction

When an individual or a group of people decide that they want to engage in business, one of the first questions that must be decided is what form of business organisation to use. There are various types of legal entities that may be used, each with its own advantages and disadvantages; and not every entity will suit the person's business, financial and family needs. The single individual or group may decide to trade on their own account, i.e. in their own name (Vada Henao) as a sole trader (or sole proprietor), or under a registered business name (Vada Henao Builder or even Gut Haus Bilders). The group may decide to establish a formal partnership[1] or even a co-operative if they meet the necessary requirements.[2] In all of these cases except co-operatives, no separate legal body is formed: the individuals continue to contract and incur debts and liabilities as individuals and therefore remain personally liable for the obligations they incur. Provided that the requirements set out for an incorporated land group or business group are established, the individuals may decide to form such entities.[3] If the individual or group of persons decides to form a company under the Companies Act 1997, a separate legal person comes into existence, and that entity will become liable for any debts or obligations it incurs. Furthermore, the persons who set up (incorporate) the company will not normally be liable for any of the debts or liabilities incurred by the company. The company will be able to buy and sell property on its own account. The persons who own the company will not directly own these assets but will own "shares" in the company which will entitle them to control what the company does.

1 See Chapter 15 for discussion of the law relating to partnerships.
2 See Chapter 16 for discussion of the law relating to co-operatives.
3 Chapter 17 for discussion of the law relating to business groups. For discussion of the law and practice of land group incorporation see Power, A (ed), *Land Group Incorporation: Part I – Village and Legal Guides* (AusAID, Port Moresby, 1999).

One of the first things that must be done, therefore, is to decide whether to trade as individuals, and if not, what corporate vehicle to use. The possible business structures include:

- sole proprietorship;
- trust;
- partnership;
- joint venture;
- unincorporated group;
- incorporated association;
- incorporated business group;
- incorporated land group;
- co-operative;
- savings and loans society;
- statutory authority;
- company.

In deciding which commercial business organisation best caters for the individual's or group's needs, several matters will be taken into consideration, including the following:

- costs involved in establishing and operating the business organisation;
- flexibility of the structure;
- purpose of the structure;
- whether control of the structure is to be shared and to what extent;
- whether outside finance is required and what structure can best secure it;
- whether the advantages of establishing a separate entity structure outweighs operating as a sole proprietorship, in particular the risk and potential liability involved;
- intended size and potential growth of the business;
- taxation implications;
- the extent to which the organisation will be regulated, e.g., by reporting and supervisory government requirements.

Unincorporated businesses

Sole proprietorship (sole trader)[4]

Sole proprietorship or ownership is the oldest and simplest method to conduct business, and it is still the most widely used way in which Papua New

4 Tashjian, P C, *Business Organisations in Papua New Guinea* (Law Book Co, Sydney, 1989), Chs 1 and 2.

Guineans engage in business. The formalities and costs of creating and using this structure are minimal: it is easy for a person to carry on business as a sole trader.[5] The law does not lay down any formalities to make a person a sole trader. Unlike companies formed under the Companies Act 1997, there is no need to audit the business finances, or to file annual financial reports and other business details with regulatory agencies. However, there may be incidental legal requirements. For example, the person may be required to apply for a licence for the particular business that he or she intends to engage in. Thus, if the person wanted to open a hotel, or run a supermarket or gambling or betting shop, they may need to obtain a licence from the relevant authority.[6] Not only may small businesses like tradestores, carpenters and builders operate as sole traders, but so also may professionals. Lawyers and accountants, for example, may also operate as sole proprietors: however, they would need to comply with the requirements of the Lawyers Act 1986 and the Accountants Act 1996.

The Employment Act (Ch 373) continues to apply to small businesses. So, for example, children under the age of 11 may not be employed by anyone, and children between the ages of 11 and 16 may be employed only in family businesses or with the written permission of their parents. The number of hours that a person may work every day is generally restricted and in some cases the employees of the small business must allow their employees sick leave. In the past the Industrial Safety, Health and Welfare Act (Ch 175) used to apply to small businesses to ensure that the workplace was clean and safe. The Workers' Compensation Act (Ch 179) still applies to employees of small businesses allowing for claims to be made when workers are injured whilst carrying out their duties, and the sole trader is liable to pay income tax and to deduct salary tax from payments made to his or her employees.[7]

After many years of criticism and calls for the removal of restrictions on informal businesses, the National Parliament has recently enacted legislation

5 Although "sole" means "one", it does not mean that only one person is engaged in the business. The business may be "owned" by one person who then employs several other people (employees or consultants) to help him or her with the business.

6 For example, licences for selling alcoholic beverages. Although, as we discuss below, the legal requirements to operate businesses in the informal sector have recently been relaxed (Informal Sector Development and Control Act 2004), in at least one other area, the law has sought to more tightly regulate another industry. Up until quite recently it was relatively easy for an individual to perform security guard services without the need for licences or fulfilment of other conditions. However, in 2004, the National Parliament enacted the Security (Protection) Industry Act 2004 which prescribes stringent requirements regulating this industry, including the establishment of a Security Industries Authority and Security Industries Council to administer the Act's requirements.

7 Under the Income Tax Act 1959 and Income Tax (Salary or Wages Tax) (Rates) Act 1979 respectively.

to encourage Papua New Guineans to set up small businesses.[8] The Informal Sector Development and Control Act 2004, in setting out its purposes, provides that it is an Act:

(a) to provide the facilities and encourage the development of informal businesses in urban and rural areas; and
(b) to regulate and control the development of informal businesses for the protection of public health and safety.

This Act has made it easier for Papua New Guinean *grassroots* to engage in small business without having to comply with bureaucratic "red tape", i.e. the need to obtain licences and comply with other regulatory requirements. The Act provides that an informal business conducted by no more than five Papua New Guinean citizens[9] may engage in an "informal business" without having to comply with various Acts which would otherwise have applied, and required them to obtain licences and fulfil other administrative requirements. The Act applies to all parts of PNG whether declared to be informal business areas or not:[10] where an Administering Authority has declared an area to be an informal business area for the purposes of the Act, the requirements set out in the Act apply, but, in addition, the Administering Authority may restrict the kinds of informal business that may be operated in the area and impose additional conditions on the operation of these informal businesses.[11] In areas in respect of which no such declaration has been made, only the provisions of the Informal Sector Development and Control Act 2004 apply.

8 For criticism of the impact of pre-existing laws on businesses in the small or informal sector, see in particular Nash, G P, "Legal Structure and Indigenous Business Enterprise: The Need for Change", in *The Indigenous Role in Business Enterprise* (New Guinea Research Bulletin No 35, New Guinea Research Unit, ANU, Canberra, 1970) pp 27–46; Graziano, E F, *Forms and Functions of Business in Papua New Guinea* (Occasional Paper No 13, Law Reform Commission of Papua New Guinea, Port Moresby, 1980); Fitzpatrick, P and Blaxter, L, "Imposed Law in the Containment of Papua New Guinea Economic Ventures" in Barman, S B, and Harrell-Bond, B E (eds), *The Imposition of Law* (Academic Press, New York, 1979), pp 115–126; Goldring, J L, "Business and the Law in Papua New Guinea" (1974) 2 *Melanesian Law Journal* pp 224–247; Ghai, Y P, The Development of Indigenous Business Organizations in Papua New Guinea", in *Third World Legal Studies 1982: Law in Alternative Strategies of Rural Development*, p 193.

9 See definition of "informal business" in s 2 of the Informal Sector Development and Control Act 2004. See also s 8(1).

10 Informal Sector Development and Control Act 2004, s 8(1).

11 Informal Sector Development and Control Act 2004, s 3(2)(a), (3). Laws made under the National Capital District Commission Act 2001 and the Organic Law on Provincial Governments and Local-level Governments having an impact on small businesses need to be "consistent with the provisions of [the Informal Sector Development and Control Act 2004]", otherwise they will be invalid: see s 8(2)(e). *Sed quaere* whether an ordinary Act like the Informal Sector Development and Control Act 2004, can control the operation of provincial legislation enacted pursuant to the Organic Law on Provincial Governments and Local-level Governments.

Section 2 of the Informal Sector Development and Control Act 2004 defines "informal business" to mean, subject to s 3(3),[12] a business carried on by citizens comprising not more than five persons, and which is characterised by the following:[13]

(a) it is a very small-scale unit—
  (i) producing goods; or
  (ii) distributing goods; or
  (iii) producing and distributing goods; or
  (iv) selling goods; or
  (v) providing services; or
(b) it operates with no or very little capital; or
(c) it utilizes low levels of skills or technology; or[14]
(d) it does not engage in activities which constitute an offence under—
  (i) the *Criminal Code* (Chapter 262); or
  (ii) the *Summary Offences Act* (Chapter 264); or
  (iii) the *Gaming Act* (Chapter 270); or
  (iv) the *Gaming Machine Act* 1993; or
  (v) the *Liquor Licensing Act* (Chapter 312); or
  (vi) the *Distillation Act* (Chapter 305); or
  (vii) the *Bookmaking Act* (Chapter 265); or
  (viii) the *Excise (Beer) Act* (Chapter 106); or
  (ix) the *Inflammable Liquid Act* (Chapter 311); or
  (x) any provincial law relating to the sale of alcohol; or
(e) it operates at a low level of productivity, and includes a mobile trader, but does not include a business which—
  (i) provides professional services;[15] or
  (ii) acts as an agent of a business which is not an informal business; or
  (iii) is liable to pay tax under the law."

12 Section 3(3) provides that "The Administering Authority may make laws, not inconsistent with this Act, for the implementation of this Act" and thus allows the Administering Authority to make laws either reducing or expanding the list of "informal businesses" or changing the requirements that such businesses need to fulfill. See below for definition of "Administering Authority". Note that there is a limit on the extent to which an Administering Authority may vary the requirements set out in the Informal Sector Development and Control Act 2004.

13 Special provision is made for "mobile traders": see Informal Sector Development and Control Act 2004, s 9.

14 It seems that "and" was meant to be inserted here, otherwise the definition of an "informal business" would be much wider than was intended, and incidentally, more difficult to identify.

15 Thus lawyers and accountants, for example, cannot establish their business in a declared area and claim the benefits given by the Informal Sector Development and Control Act 2004. There is no specific definition of "professional services" in the Act or in the Interpretation Act (Ch 2). However, Double Taxation Agreements usually define the term for purposes of the Agreements. The Double Taxation Agreement between Canada and Papua New Guinea for example, in article 14.2, provides: "The term professional services includes especially independent scientific, literary, artistic, educational or teaching activities as well as the independent activities of physicians, lawyers, engineers, architects, dentists and accountants."

An Administering Authority,[16] may declare, in either general or specific terms, areas in which informal businesses may be conducted.[17] The Act provides for inspectors to visit these areas to ensure that businesses are operating within the terms of the Act, and in particular, to ensure that necessary sanitary conditions are maintained and, that a business is not likely to cause danger to public health or public safety. For example, s 8(2) inter alia provides that an informal business may only be operated:

- where it is not hazardous to health and safety; and
- where it will not cause unreasonable obstruction to motor traffic or pedestrians; and
- where it will not cause environmental harm (as that term is defined in s 2 of the Environment Act 2000); and
- where it will not cause substantial annoyance to neighbours or persons within the vicinity of the place at which the informal business is operated.

The Act also sets out minimum standards for the sale of food,[18] live animals,[19] betelnut,[20] second-hand clothing and second-hand goods,[21] and for the manufacture of goods and provision of services.[22]

In regard to payment of fees or obtaining licences, s 17 of the Informal Sector Development and Control Act 2004 provides that, with the exception of the requirement to pay fees "in respect of the use of a market", a person operating an informal business is not required to:

- obtain any licence, permit or authority required under any Act specified in the Schedule;[23] or
- pay any fee in respect of such licence, permit or authority; or
- pay any fee under this Act.

16 Administering Authorities are: in the National Capital District – the National Capital District Commission, in an area outside the National Capital District for which there is a Local-level Government – that Local-level Government, and in an area outside the National Capital District for which there is no Local-level Government – the Provincial Government of the province in which the area is situated: Informal Sector Development and Control Act 2004, s 3.

17 The Administering Authority must, before the declaration, consult with relevant ward committees, the Police Force or relevant Government agencies responsible for public health, physical planning and building: Informal Sector Development and Control Act 2004, s 3(1).

18 Informal Sector Development and Control Act 2004, ss 10–12.

19 Informal Sector Development and Control Act 2004, s 13.

20 Informal Sector Development and Control Act 2004, s 14.

21 Informal Sector Development and Control Act 2004, s 15.

22 Informal Sector Development and Control Act 2004, s 16.

23 The Acts specified in the Schedule are: Associations Incorporation Act (Ch 142), Building Act (Ch 301), Business Groups Incorporation Act (Ch 144), Industrial Safety, Health and Welfare Act (Ch 175), Food Sanitation Act 1991, Land Act 1996, Land Groups Incorporation Act (Ch 174), Packaging Act (Ch 285), Physical Planning Act 1989, Second-hand Dealers Act (Ch 322), Trading Act (Ch 324), Public Health Act (Ch 226).

Furthermore, all of the Acts specified in the Schedule[24] are specifically stated no longer to "apply to and in respect of an informal business", except to the extent specified in the Informal Sector Development and Control Act 2004.

It is an offence to carry on business in PNG unless personal names are used, or a business name is first registered under the Business Names Act (Ch 145).[25] This Act continues to apply to informal businesses.[26] So if the sole proprietor or partnership[27] operating as an informal business agree on a name that does not include their names, this name must be registered under the provisions of the Business Names Act (Ch 145); otherwise they may find themselves being charged for committing a breach of one or more of the provisions of the Business Names Act (Ch 145).

Section 3 of the Business Names Act (Ch 145) provides:

> A person who, alone or in association with other persons, carries on business in the country under a business name is guilty of an offence, unless –
>
> (a) the business name consists of the name of that person and the name of each other person (if any) in association with whom that person is carrying on business, without any addition; or
>
> (b) the business name is registered under this Act in relation to that person and each other person (if any) in association with whom that person is carrying on business . . .

Undesirable names cannot be registered,[28] and once registered, the business name needs to be renewed every three years.[29] Once the business name is registered, the name must be used. In addition, the business name must be displayed conspicuously on the outside of every place at which business is carried out under that name.[30] The business name must also appear on the business letterhead, publications, official notices and other business documents used by the business.[31] The certificate of registration also needs to be displayed

24 See note 23 above.

25 This applies not only to sole proprietors, but also to partnerships and companies. If a company trades in a name other than its registered company name, this name must be registered as a business name. See Tashjian, P C, *Business Organisations in Papua New Guinea* (Law Book Co, Sydney, 1989), Ch 4. The main policy behind the Business Names Act (Ch 145) is to ensure that people would be able to find out who are the owners of a business.

26 The Business Names Act (Ch 145) is not one of the 12 Acts set out in the Schedule to the Informal Sector Development and Control Act 2004 that are stated *not* to apply to "informal businesses".

27 Consisting of no more than five persons: see Informal Sector Development and Control Act 2004, s 2 (definition of "informal business").

28 Business Names Act (Ch 145), s 10. No criteria for deciding on undesirable names has been issued. However it is suggested that some parts of the gazettal notice in respect of undesirable company names offer a guideline for application of this Section. Cf footnote 28, above.

29 Business Names Act (Ch 145), s 12.

30 Business Names Act (Ch 145), s 21(b).

31 Business Names Act (Ch 145), s 21(a).

prominently at the business premises. The Act defines "business" and "carry on business" as well as providing for situations where a person shall be regarded as "carrying on business" for the purposes of the Business Names Act (Ch 145).[32]

Section 6 of the Business Names Act (Ch 145) provides that: "Notwithstanding this Act, a contravention of or failure to comply with a provision of this Act does not operate to avoid an agreement, transaction, act or matter."

Businesses conducted as sole proprietors are usually small, since the owner will usually not have a lot of finances to deploy and banks and other financial institutions will not be willing to advance loans without some form of security.[33] On the other hand, when a company is formed, there will usually be several shareholders and the payment for the shares will often be such as to form a sizeable, if not large, cash reserve to carry on the business.

One major disadvantage of sole proprietorship is that not being a separate legal entity from the individual, he or she is responsible for all the debts and other obligations incurred. And there is no limit to such liability. So, depending on the extent of the business, the sole trader may become liable to pay creditors millions of kina if he or she incurs debts of this magnitude. If the business does not have sufficient assets to satisfy the repayment of these monies, the creditors may have recourse to the sole trader's personal assets to repay the loans. This may mean that the sole trader becomes insolvent or bankrupt.[34] The family car and home may have to be sold to satisfy repayment of the loans.

Additionally, when the sole trader dies, the sole proprietorship comes to an end. Unlike a company, it does not have perpetual succession until it is deregistered. Although the sole trader may pass on the goodwill[35] of the

32 There are National Court cases interpreting the words "carrying on business" for the purposes of the Investment Promotion Act 1992. These judgments will be helpful in interpreting the words "carry on business" in the Business Names Act (Ch 145). See *Investment Promotion Authority v Niugini Scrap Corporation Pty Ltd* (2001) N2104; *Odata Ltd v Ambusa Copra Oil Mill Ltd* (2001) N2106 and *Spirit Haus Ltd v Robert Marshall* (2004) N2630. Cf *Timothy Lim Kok Chuan v Simon Goh Say Beng* (2004) N2753.

33 The sole trader can mortgage his or her house to fund the business. However, this may not generate much cash to start or continue the business.

34 The person is unable to pay his or her debts. The procedure to regulate this situation is set out in the Insolvency Act (Ch 253). Being an undischarged bankrupt or insolvent prevents the person from taking part in many business or professional activities, including disqualification from occupying several public offices.

35 Goodwill, for legal purposes, is the benefit and advantage of the good name, reputation, and connection of a business. It arises from the reputation and relations formed with customers of the business and the nature of its location. It adds to the value of a business; it may be site, personality, service, price or habit. It is separate from the goods and other property owned by the business.

business as well as the business name (if it has one) to his or her spouse or children, a new sole proprietorship arises, and there may be significant taxation implications involved.

Partnerships[36]

Whenever two or more people enter into a contract to carry on a business to make profits, then a partnership is formed. There are no other underlying law or statutory requirements for the formation of partnerships. Although many partnerships are reduced to writing, so as to cater for all the business relations between the parties, and to set out how the partnership should operate, the establishment of a partnership can be oral or by conduct. The intention of the parties is the most important factor. If two people agree to grow vegetables, build a store from which the vegetables are sold, and employ people to work in the shop, despite the fact that they have merely verbally or orally agreed on this, a partnership arises at law.

The main disadvantage of a partnership is that it does not create a separate legal entity: all the partners, unless they agree otherwise, remain personally responsible for all the debts incurred by them during the life of the partnership.

In the past, the law provided that the maximum number of partners was 20, unless special permission was obtained to increase this number.[37] Since the Companies Act 1997, this limitation no longer applies, and there is therefore no limit to the maximum number of persons or entities[38] that may now form a partnership. Partnerships will also have to register their business name, unless they trade under their individual names (John Henao and Lucy Sebea). There is no restriction on the types of business that may be formed and operated as partnerships. However, liability will be joint and several as far as outsiders are concerned. This means that although any business may be carried on as a partnership, they are most common amongst lawyers, accountants, architects and other professionals such as engineers and doctors. A partner includes a legal entity, so it is possible to have a partnership between a human being and a company.

36 See below at Chapter 15 for more detailed treatment of partnerships. See also Tashjian, P C, *Business Organisations in Papua New Guinea* (Law Book Co, Sydney, 1989), Ch 3.

37 If the number of partners was more than 20, the members had to be incorporated under the Companies Act (Ch 146) or another Act. The limit was 50 where the Minister considered that the profession or calling, the subject of the partnership, was one that was "not customarily carried on in the country by a corporation": Companies Act (Ch 146) (Repealed), s 16(2). It would appear that the main reason for the rule is that because of the fiduciary nature of partnership, it can work properly only where the number of partners is small enough to allow them to repose trust and confidence in each other.

38 Partnerships may consist of legal (e.g. a company) and natural persons.

Up to five persons may be partners of a "small business" and as such they would therefore be subject to the provisions of the Informal Sector Development and Control Act 2004 and to any other laws passed in relation to a declared small business area.[39] The Partnership Act (Ch 148) would apply to such a business unless the provisions are inconsistent with the provisions of the Informal Sector Development and Control Act 2004. The Partnership Act (Ch 148) would apply terms and conditions to the agreement that the partners have failed to agree on beforehand either orally or in their partnership contract.

The main benefit of a partnership is that it is easy to create, maintain and dissolve. It does not have the formalities and costs that arise on the formation and running of a company under the Companies Act 1997. There is no need to publish partnership accounts nor have them audited. On the other hand, however, the absence of a separate legal entity means that the partners remain personally responsible for the debts incurred by the partnership. The convergence of unlimited liability and agency means that a partner may be bound by the actions of a fellow-partner, although he or she may not have specially approved the action of that partner.

Usually, a partnership interest cannot be transferred. The absence of perpetual succession in partnerships may thus cause problems: the death, bankruptcy, retirement or admission of a new partner means that the partnership is dissolved when these events occur, and a new partnership created, unless the partners agree otherwise.

Joint ventures

A partnership must also be distinguished from a joint venture. Joint ventures are usually short term arrangements that are entered into to achieve a particular object, whereas partnerships are usually long term arrangements.[40] They have the benefit, like partnerships of being easy and cheap to create, maintain and dissolve. The benefit of a joint venture from the parties' perspective, is that the joint venturers are not jointly and severally liable for the debts incurred by the joint venturer. As such one joint venturer can control the extent to which the other joint venturers incur liabilities on his or her behalf.

Because a joint venture is not incorporated, it suffers from the same disadvantages of a partnership, such as the absence of limited liability and perpetual succession.

39 If there are more than five partners, the partnership would not constitute a "small business" for the purposes of the Informal Sector Development and Control Act 2004.

40 The court sometimes finds it very difficult to distinguish between a partnership and a joint venture: see *Canny Gabriel Castle Jackson Advertising Pty Ltd v Volume Sales (Finance) Pty Ltd* (1974) 131 CLR 321. Before the Companies Act 1997, joint ventures were limited to not more than 20 persons: see above note 37.

Trusts[41]

A trust (sometimes called a trading trust) exists where one person is under an obligation to hold or invest property on behalf of another person. The formalities are minimal: usually just a written document by the settlor (the person setting up the trust) that the trustee should hold the property on behalf of the beneficiary, i.e., the person who benefits from the trust. The trustee holds the legal estate in the property and the beneficiary has the beneficial or equitable ownership of the property. Beneficial ownership allows the beneficiary to enjoy the property or the proceeds arising from the use or investment of the property. There are a wide variety of trusts depending on the intention of the settlor. There is thus a great deal of flexibility to cater for different types of business. This is not a significant advantage over companies as different types of companies may be created for different situations by setting out the requirements in the constitution of the company.

Although a trust can be created without great expense or formality, unlike the case with a company, the establishment of a trust does not create a separate legal entity. The trustee, not the beneficiary, is the one who can enter into contracts and hold property. The trustee becomes personally liable for any debts and obligations incurred by the trust, and this places the trustee in an uncertain position, especially where the trust is a trading trust.[42] If the business is not risky and perpetual succession not an issue, a joint venture may be used.

Again, a trust may be terminated without much difficulty, depending on the terms of the trust, whereas dissolving (deregistering or liquidating) a company involves a lot of formality, unless the company has paid off all its debts and follows the quicker deregistration procedure. One of the important considerations is that of tax. Seeing that the beneficiary has a beneficial interest in the trust property, whereas in a company, the person only owns shares in the company, and not the company property itself, the beneficiary may be taxed on this property.

Ownership of shares gives the shareholder a say in the running of the business, unless the extent of share ownership is so large as to water down significantly this benefit. However, a beneficiary under a trust will usually have very little power to determine how a trust is carried out. The trustee is the legal owner and this normally gives him or her enormous powers or direction and control, even if this power must be exercised in a fiduciary manner.

41 For the development and role of equity and the trust concept in Papua New Guinea, see James, R W, *Challenges of Equity in Developing the Underlying Law* (Faculty of Law, University of Papua New Guinea, Waigani, 1996).

42 This liability is usually passed on to the beneficiaries where the trustee requires to be indemnified by the beneficiaries, and if the trust does not have sufficient assets, creditors may get access to the assets of the beneficiaries owing to their right to be subrogated (i.e., have access) to the trustee's right to the beneficiary's property.

Advantages and disadvantages of unincorporated businesses[43]

A disadvantage of sole proprietorship is that the sole trader remains personally responsible for all the debts incurred during the operation of the business. Persons who are owed money will be able to recover their debts by suing the individual, and if that person does not have sufficient cash or money in the bank to satisfy the debt, the creditor may ask the court to order that the property of the sole trader be sold so that the sole trader will have sufficient money to repay the money owed to the creditor.

Sole ownership may be easily started and terminated. The greatest advantage of being a sole trader is that the person may set up and stop the business without too much difficulty. There are no reporting and other requirements during the existence of the business. When the person dies, then that business also dies, as there is no perpetual succession. It may be taken over by a relative: in this case, however, it is a matter of a *new* sole trader being established. Although the new sole trader may take over the business assets by virtue of the rules of succession,[44] the new sole trader will not normally be liable for the debts incurred by the deceased sole trader.

The biggest disadvantage of incorporation as a company in particular, are the formalities required. There are several requirements that have to be fulfilled prior to incorporation and, once the company is formed, there are many reporting requirements. These are significantly increased if the company is listed on the Port Moresby Stock Exchange (POMSoX).[45] They involve much time and effort and can be quite costly. These expenses include the direct cost of professional assistance in preparing documents, filing fees, audit and accountancy fees, and the indirect costs during the life of the company. Furthermore, it should be borne in mind that once the company has ceased trading, it should be wound up (liquidated) or deregistered. Unless this is done, the company will still be regarded as operating, with all the attendant obligations. In addition, once incorporated, as we shall see, the board of directors are the ones to decide whether to bring or defend proceedings. As such, a shareholder may be at the mercy of the directors who do not agree with the shareholder's views.

43 For the advantages and disadvantages of co-operatives, see Tashjian, P C, *Business Organisations in Papua New Guinea* (Law Book Co, Sydney, 1989), pp 205–206, 209–210. For the advantages and disadvantages of partnership compared to a company registered under the Companies Act 1997, see Beck, A and Borrowdale, A, *Papua New Guinea Companies and Securities Law Guide* (CCH Australia Ltd, Sydney, 1999), pp 7–9.

44 The deceased sole trader may make a will giving away the business assets, or the law relating to intestate succession may set out who should inherit certain property belonging to the deceased. For an overview of the law relating to wills and succession, see *Re James Allan Sannga* [1983] PNGLR 142.

45 For the requirements, see Beck, A and Borrowdale, A, *Papua New Guinea Companies and Securities Law Guide* (CCH Australia Ltd, Sydney, 1999), Ch 7.

Incorporated groups

Incorporated business groups

As is noted in Chapter 17 dealing with business groups,[46] these entities were established on the eve of PNG's Independence to allow for "greater participation by local people in the national economy by the establishment by them of group business and other economic enterprises".[47] The Business Groups Incorporation Act (Ch 144) provides for the "incorporation of certain customary and similar groups", and confers on them, as corporations, power (including ancillary powers) to:[48]

(i) conduct business enterprises; and
(ii) borrow money; and
(iii) acquire, hold, dispose of and manage land.

These organisations are therefore unique and are essentially regulated by the customary law of the relevant group establishing the business group.

All the advantages of an incorporated group are enjoyed by a business group, subject to two major limitations: they are prevented by the Business Groups Incorporation Act (Ch 144) (i) from acquiring, holding or disposing of customary land,[49] and (ii) from raising funds from the public.

Another limiting factor is that there must be some relationship between the members of a business group, even if it is merely one determined by locality of residence. The Act provides that the Registrar may incorporate "a customary group of persons" as a business group.[50] The Act does not define who constitute a customary group. Although the Registrar is given a wide discretion as to who he or she considers to be such a group, registration must be refused if the Registrar is satisfied that "the group characteristics are so temporary, evanescent or doubtful that the group does not have a

46 See also Tashjian, P C, *Business Organisations in Papua New Guinea* (Law Book Co, Sydney, 1989), Part IV.

47 Business Groups Incorporation Act (Ch 144), s 1.

48 A business group cannot: (a) borrow money from the public; or (b) make any invitation to the public – (i) to deposit money with; or (ii) lend money to, the group. Business Groups Incorporation Act (Ch 144), s 18(3).

49 It would appear that the business group cannot only not purchase customary land, but cannot acquire any rights in such land, even of a limited kind, such as rights in the nature of leases and licences or other *sui generis* customary rights. The opinion to the contrary effect by Tashjian, supra, (at p 194) is therefore questionable: "A business group cannot acquire or hold customary land but may engage in business which involves the use of customary land, that is, the group may lease the land and conduct a business on the leased premises"; see also statement at p 200 about attempts to circumvent the Act by the customary owners incorporating themselves as a land group and as a business group, with the land group then leasing the land to the business group.

50 Business Groups Incorporation Act (Ch 144), s 11(1).

corporate nature".[51] The Registrar can incorporate sub-groups and groups that include persons who are not members of the "primary customary group" provided that "those persons regard themselves, and are regarded by the others, as bound by the relevant customs of the primary customary group".[52]

The Registrar *may* refuse incorporation if he is satisfied that:[53]

- the group is not a customary group and has no real connexion with such a group; or
- the group contains persons who are not members of the customary group applying for incorporation; or
- the group contains members who are not natural persons; or
- some other form of incorporation or of organisation under some other Act would be more appropriate and effective.

The above limitations mean that the incorporated business group structure cannot be used generally to bring together individuals and businesses from different parts of the country to form an economic unit. This is a significant disadvantage.[54]

There are several other reasons which would militate against the common use of business groups as a vehicle for businesses. The application of custom introduces an element of uncertainty which banks and other lending institutions regard as a negative factor. Also the fact that the liability of members of the management committee for debts incurred by the business group is unlimited may prevent persons from taking on this responsibility.

A major benefit of the Act is that it allows for the establishment of a separate entity, and limited liability protection for members of the group. Business groups are also easier to incorporate than a company, and the reporting requirements are significantly less than for companies. None of the provisions of the Companies Act 1997 applies to incorporated business groups. The accounting and record-keeping requirements of business groups are very basic: bank accounts must be kept, certain receipts must be given, and an annual statement of assets and liabilities must be filed with the Registrar of Business Groups.[55]

As we noted earlier in respect of the Informal Sector Development and Control Act 2004, the government has instituted changes to allow for

51 Business Groups Incorporation Act (Ch 144), s 11(4).

52 Business Groups Incorporation Act (Ch 144), s 11(3). For example, persons regarded as part of the group through marriage.

53 Business Groups Incorporation Act (Ch 144), s 11(5).

54 See further on this, below at pp 716–719. See also Mugambwa, J, "Incorporated Business Group: An Alternative Business Group Association for the Ordinary People" (1990) 103:3 *South Africa Law Journal* 454, 462–464.

55 Business Groups Incorporation Act (Ch 144), ss 21–23.

"informal businesses" to operate without unnecessary restrictions. In fact, it was considered that even the provisions of the Business Groups Incorporation Act (Ch 144) should not be made applicable to "informal businesses" operating under the Informal Sector Development and Control Act 2004, and that Act is set out in the Schedule as one of the Acts that does not apply to "informal businesses".

Incorporated land groups[56]

The Land Groups Incorporation Act (Ch 147) was one of several Acts enacted in the early 1970s to allow Papua New Guineans to participate in the cash economy by using customary land as a vehicle for development and setting up structures to ensure that banks and other institutions could safely deal with the land groups without fear that the groups were not the true owners of the land. The long title to the Act provides that it is an Act:

(a) to recognize the corporate nature of customary groups; and
(b) to allow them to hold, manage and deal with land in their customary names, and for related purposes.

The purposes as set out in s 1:

1. Purposes of this Act.

The purposes of this Act are to encourage
(a) greater participation by local people in the national economy by the use of the land; and
(b) better use of such land; and
(c) greater certainty of title; and
(d) the better and more effectual settlement of certain disputes, by –
(e) the legal recognition of the corporate status of certain customary and similar groups, and the conferring on them, as corporations, of power to acquire, hold, dispose of and manage land, and of ancillary powers; and
(f) the encouragement of the self-resolution of disputes within such groups.

Although the Act states that one of its purposes is to provide for "greater certainty of title", this is not done through the "registration of customary land" as such, but is an incidental effect of registering the group. By doing so it is

56 Power, A (ed), *Land Group Incorporation* Part 1: Village and Legal Guides, Supporting Documentation (AusAID, Port Moresby, 1999); Tashjian, P C, *Business Organisations in Papua New Guinea* (Law Book Co, Sydney, 1989), Part IV.

hoped that land disputes will be reduced and the ownership of the incorporated land group recognised. However, despite the incorporation of a group in respect of an area of land, it is still possible for another clan or group to claim ownership of the customary land, and to be so recognised by a land court or the National Court.[57]

Part III.5 of the Act, headed "Effect of Recognition", deals with the status and powers of incorporated land groups. It is not clear how extensive the powers of the land group are. On the one hand, s 11, dealing with the "status" of such groups, seems to grant very wide powers indeed. Apart from being a corporation, having perpetual succession, and being able to sue and be sued in its corporate name, the section states that "for the purpose of the more effective exercise and performance of its powers and functions, [the incorporated land group] may do and suffer *all things* that a corporation may do or suffer".[58] However, s 13, dealing with the "powers" of such groups provides that:

> (1) The powers of an incorporated land group –
> (a) relate only to land and its use and management, and to associated matters; and
> (b) shall be regulated and exercised in accordance with, and subject to any conditions or limitations imposed by, its constitution and any relevant custom; and
> (c) shall be exercised in the manner specified by its constitution or any relevant custom, or otherwise by law.
> (2) Subject to Subsections (1) and (3), an incorporated land group may –
> (a) acquire, hold and dispose of customary land and rights in or in respect of customary land, in the manner (if any) and to the extent (if any) allowed by custom; and
> (b) acquire, hold and dispose of other land and rights in or in respect of other land; and
> (c) use and manage the land, or enter into agreements for the use or management of it; and

57 The statement by Tashjian, supra, (at p 178) that "The Land Groups Incorporation Act was yet another attempt to register customary landholdings thereby creating greater certainty of title (ownership)" is wrong, as are the following statements: "Because land ownership is such a sensitive and volatile issue in Papua New Guinea there has been little registration of customary land [correct] and very few land group registrations [incorrect]" (p 187); "The major disadvantage for the land group is the restriction of its activities to customary land only" (p 187); "Due to the sensitive nature of land matters in Papua New Guinea, it is difficult to get a land group registered" (p 188). The statement (at p 194) that an incorporated land group is "really a single purpose corporation" that is "formed for the use of land and cannot engage in business that does not *directly* concern land" is also incorrect. The concern with land may be "indirect" or incidental, and yet the group may be considered to engage in that business.

58 Land Groups Incorporation Act (Ch 147), s 11(1)(d).

(d) borrow money or accept property on credit for the purposes of the preceding provisions of this subsection; and
(e) distribute any product of the land or any profits arising out of the use or management of it, and has any other powers necessary or convenient for the exercise of those powers.[59]

(3) No right or interest in or in relation to land that is given by an incorporated land group to a person who is a member of the group is registrable under any law relating to the registration of land or of interests in land.

This Act was part of a package of four Acts to establish the plantation redistribution scheme under which alienated land was to be restored to their former owners and the land registered and managed under that Act.[60] The Act provided for incorporated land groups to hold and manage both alienated and customary land.[61] One drawback of the Act was that the incorporated land groups were limited to conducting business relating to land. They could not for example, operate a PMV business or operate "trade stores".

The accounting and record-keeping requirements of land groups are non-existent: there is no requirement to keep bank accounts, issue receipts or to file annual statements or returns to the Registrar of Incorporated Land Groups. Another major benefit of the Land Groups Incorporation Act (Ch 147) is that it allows for the establishment of a separate entity, and limited liability protection for the governing authority ("committee or other controlling body" of the land group) as well as the members of the group.[62] Land groups are easier to incorporate than companies, and the reporting requirements are significantly lesser. None of the provisions of the Companies Act 1997 applies to incorporated land groups. Of great significance, is the fact that landowners cannot lose their customary land under foreclosure or similar processes.

59 The statement by Tashjian that "land groups are not given power to borrow money or to conduct business as are the business groups" (at p 179) is erroneous.

60 For discussion of the operation of the scheme, see Eaton, P, "Melanesian Land Reform: The Plantation Acquisition Scheme" (1980) 8 *Melanesian Law Journal* 134–142. There was nothing to prevent plantations being "redistributed" to ordinary companies whose make up included the descendants of the original owners of the land. It was not possible for customary land to be returned to a business group.

61 As noted above, a statement by Tashjian to the contrary is incorrect.

62 Section 17 provides that "Unless the constitution or any relevant custom provides otherwise, the liability of a member of an incorporated land group on the winding-up of the group is limited to the amount of his interest in the property of the group, plus any amount owing by him to the group." Section 19 safeguards customary land owned by the incorporated land group by providing that: "Subject to any other law regulating the matter, on the dissolution of an incorporated land group under this Act any customary land owned by the group reverts to the persons who would be the customary owners if the group had never been recognized under this Act."

There are other benefits to using the land group structure as a business vehicle. Incorporated land groups can also apply to the government for the grant of state leases, or purchase existing state leases. The Land (Tenure Conversion) Act 1963 was amended in 1987 to allow tenure-converted customary land to be registered in the name of a business group or an incorporated land group.[63] The definition of "citizen" was extended to cover these two entities. However, individuals could continue to apply for tenure conversion in keeping with the Act's original intention of individualising tenure of land, and the Act also recognised that unincorporated groups claiming ownership of customary land (e.g., "a customary kinship group", a "customary descent group" or "a customary local group or community") could apply for the converted customary land to be registered in its name. The effect of the conversion order was that the customary land ceased to be customary land and ceased "in all respects to be subject to or regulated by custom": it became freehold land (a fee simple).[64]

More recently, the Land Groups Incorporation Act (Ch 147) has been utilised to incorporate clans and other land-holding groups in oil-rich areas in the Southern Highlands province in order to facilitate the payment of royalties and also to allow for customary owners to enter into Forest Management Agreements over customary land.[65]

The Land Groups Incorporation Act (Ch 174) is not applicable to "informal businesses" operating under the Informal Sector Development and Control Act 2004.

Another advantage is that a land group is considered to be a "citizen" for several purposes, allowing them to get significant benefits which are intended to be given only to citizens.[66]

Co-operatives

The law relating to co-operatives is covered in detail in Chapter 16 below.[67] Like business groups and land groups, co-operatives are meant to encourage and facilitate the participation of Papua New Guineans, mainly in rural areas, in the modern national economy. Unlike the law relating to business groups and land groups, the law relating to co-operatives is quite complex.

63 Section 4 of the Land (Tenure Conversion) Act 1963 was repealed and replaced by the Land (Tenure Conversion) (Amendment) Act 1987 (No. 38 of 1987), s 1.

64 The effect of *In the Land and Goods of Doa Minch* [1973] PNGLR 558 and *Re James Allan Sannga* [1983] PNGLR 142 is that, in spite of the supposed effect of the conversion order, custom continues to govern intestate succession to such land.

65 Forestry Act 1991, s 57. The *Land Disputes Settlement Act* (Ch 45) does not apply to land owned by a land group (s 3).

66 See for example, the Coffee Industry Corporation (Statutory Functions and Powers) Act 1991, and the Licensing of Heavy Vehicles Act (Ch 367).

67 See also Tashjian, P C, *Business Organisations in Papua New Guinea* (Law Book Co, Sydney, 1989), Ch 18.

However, unlike such groups, co-operatives may have a much wider membership including persons who are not related and who are not subject to the same customary law. The advantages of companies formed under the Companies Act 1997 is that a single individual may form and operate a company. Co-operatives, however, need at least seven members and three directors. Again whereas companies may consist of Papua New Guineans and non-citizens and there is no limit on the ownership (distribution) of shares in the company, only citizens may be members of co-operatives and no one member may own more than one-fifth of the business. Co-operatives also have stringent rules relating to the distribution of profits: no profits may be distributed without the permission of the Registrar and 20 per cent of all profits earned must be put into a special reserve account. There are no such limitations with companies formed under the Companies Act 1997. Because of these limitations, the co-operative has not been regarded as an important vehicle to engage Papua New Guineans into business. Although neglected by government for some time, more recently, because of pressure from international agencies, the government is now trying to resurrect interest in this form of business organisation.[68]

Savings and loans societies

Savings and loans societies are not profit-motivated institutions, but are more like co-operative banking societies. Because this text is concerned with commercial organisations, only passing mention shall be made of such societies.[69] The members of the society deposit their funds into a common pool which is used to make loans to members in need of financial assistance. The society charges interest on these loans and the interest payments are passed on as interest on the deposits of members. A society may collect deposits and make loans only to members of the society. In order to make loans beyond members' savings, societies may borrow and invest.[70] Other powers of such societies include the power to:

- deposit money in a bank;
- raise money on loan, subject to the approval of the Registrar, for the objects of the society and mortgage or pledge its property as security for the loan;

68 See Chapter 16 below.

69 In other countries, savings and loans societies are often referred to as credit unions. For a more detailed account see Tashjian, P C, *Business Organisations in Papua New Guinea* (Law Book Co, Sydney, 1989), Part VI and Boston, D O, "The Savings and Loans Society of Papua New Guinea: Some Aspects of its Structure and Functions" (1975) 3 *Melanesian Law Journal* 326–345. Note that, since the publication of these texts, the Savings and Loans Societies (Amendment) Act 1995 (No. 24 of 1995) has made significant amendments to the Savings and Loan Societies Act (Ch 141).

70 Savings and Loan Societies Act (Ch 141), s 15.

- invest funds in securities of or guaranteed by the State, or in other prescribed securities;
- invest funds in any institution, subject to the approval of the Registrar; insure its loans, funds or property against loss;
- hold, buy, lease, sell, surrender, exchange, mortgage or otherwise deal in property.

Savings and loans societies are essentially single-purpose corporations. They are established to collect and manage savings in order to make loans to their members, and they may not engage in any other business: they must confine their activities to the savings and loan business.

Section 10(1) of the Act provides that "a minimum of 500 persons"[71] or "such other number as is determined by the Registrar" who are qualified to form a savings and loan society may apply for registration as a savings and loan society. On incorporation under the Act, the society becomes a separate legal entity. It:[72]

(a) has perpetual succession; and
(b) must have a seal; and
(c) has power –
  - to hold property; and
  - to enter into contracts; and
  - to institute and defend actions, suits and legal proceedings; and
  - to do all things necessary or convenient for the purposes of its constitution.

In addition, a key feature is that the members' liability is limited. Section 14 of the Act provides that:

> The liability of a member of a society is limited to the amount of outstanding loan and interest thereon less savings and interest thereon credited to the account of the member.

One of the drawbacks is that not everyone can join a savings and loans society. Section 19(1) provides that:

> The membership of a society shall be limited to a group of persons having a common bond of occupation, association or interest or to groups of persons residing within a well-defined community or area.

The record of savings and loans societies in PNG is a sorry one. As Tashjian noted:[73]

71 Until the law was changed in 1995, it used to be a group of 20 or more.
72 Savings and Loan Societies Act (Ch 141), s 2.
73 Tashjian, P C, *Business Organisations in Papua New Guinea* (Law Book Co, Sydney, 1989), p 271; see also pp 275–276.

> Misappropriations . . . and poor management have been the biggest problem areas for many societies. These problems often arise because essentially what we have is non-bankers performing banking functions. Many of the misappropriations and losses are due to negligence and ignorance of financial matters. Many of the loans that go unpaid were made without proper consideration.

Associations[74]

Where a group of persons come together to carry out social or non-profit activities, they may operate as unincorporated groups or organisations. This, however, exposes the members to unlimited liability. They will be personally responsible jointly for the debts and other liabilities that the committee of the organisation incurs on their behalf. If, however, the group incorporates as an "incorporated association" under the provisions of the Associations Incorporation Act (Ch 142), they are protected from personal liability. The association as a separate entity is solely responsible for its obligations and if it does not have sufficient funds to meet these, the creditor loses out: the creditor cannot obtain redress from the members of the association.

The Associations Incorporation Act (C 142) defines an "association" to mean an "association, society, club, institution, Christian mission or other body in the country". Associations do not normally distribute their profits but use them to advance the cause or interest for which it was formed. As Tashjian notes:[75]

> Although an organisation has a non-profit structure, it is still a business organisation. These organisations are in business to make money, as are partnerships and companies. However, they do not, and cannot, distribute the money to their members. Any money made by an association must be used for the benefit of the members by applying it toward promoting the association's stated objectives, for example, the development of better schools, the building of a new club house, the technical training of members, health care, and the like.

The Associations Incorporation Act (C 142) allows the group to incorporate and operate simply and inexpensively. Although it is possible to incorporate a company under the Companies Act 1997 to achieve the same goals, this is

74 Given that this text is concerned with "commercial law", this type of organisation is not dealt with in any depth. For a more detailed treatment of this area, see Tashjian, P C, *Business Organisations in Papua New Guinea* (Law Book Co, Sydney, 1989), Part V. The Act has not changed since the publication of this text and the date of publication of this book. Only the provisions regarding fees has been changed in respect of the Associations Incorporation Regulation (Ch 142).

75 Tashjian, P C, *Business Organisations in Papua New Guinea* (Law Book Co, Sydney, 1989), p 218.

complex and the reporting requirements too onerous. Before the enactment of the Associations Incorporation Act (C 142), non-profit organisations who sought protection of its members from personal liability would set up a trust,[76] incorporate as a company, or petition Parliament to set up a special Act to govern its affairs.[77] The Associations Incorporation Act (C 142) allows for the incorporation of a group without the complex burdens of the Companies Act 1997, or the need to petition government for a special Act, and also obviates the problems of dealing with an intermediary trustee.

The only types of associations that may be registered under the Associations Incorporation Act (C 142) are those that do not distribute their profits to members, but rather apply the profits towards its goals.[78] As such, registered associations are not a good vehicle for carrying on commercial business. Another benefit is that incorporated organisations pay no tax or a reduced tax.

Section 20 of the Associations Incorporation Act (C 142) sets out the general powers of incorporated associations:

Subject to the Act, and to any special restrictions or prohibitions in its rules or trust deed, and without prejudice to any other powers contained in its rules or trust deed or implied by law, an incorporated association has power, by virtue of the Act:

- to act as trustee for any other association which has the prescribed qualifications for incorporation; and
- to accept and hold on trust any property that is given to the association subject to any trust, and to carry out any such trust; and
- to invest its moneys in or on any security in which trustees are for the time being authorised by law to invest trust funds; and
- to open and operate on bank accounts; and
- to borrow money on such terms and in such manner and on such security (if any) as the association thinks proper, for the purpose of carrying out its objects and purposes; and
- to secure the repayment of money so raised or borrowed, or the payment of a debt or liability of the association, by giving a mortgage, charge or security on or over all or any of the property of the association.

76 See above, p 182. The property of the association would be held by the trustee on their behalf. However they would not be liable. The trustee would be liable, and this could be a problem.

77 Many religious organisations were set up and managed by or under such Acts: see the Revised Laws of Papua New Guinea from Chapter 1002 onwards (Assemblies of God in Australia (New Guinea) Mission Act (Ch 1002)). As recently as 2003, two such Acts of Parliament were passed: Catholic Diocese of Aitape Act 2003 and Catholic Diocese of Aitape Health Services Act 2003.

78 Political parties have been registered as incorporated associations. Social and sporting clubs, museums, religious bodies, private schools and other charitable institutions also use this structure.

Because an incorporated association is a legal entity, separate from its members, the fact that members resign or die does not affect its status. It still continues, and may be terminated only by following the procedures set out in the Associations Incorporation Act (C 142) (cancellation or winding up) and after the necessary action taken by the Registrar. Associations must continue to have the non-profit or community purpose. If they cease to do so, the Registrar of Associations may cancel their incorporation.

The Committee is the governing body of the association. It has the power to enter into contracts and engage in business on behalf of the association.

Members of an incorporated association are not personally liable for the debts and liabilities incurred by the association unless they specifically agree to this or the rules of the association so state. To show outsiders that this is the case, the association must put "Incorporated" or "Inc" after its name to warn people who deal with the association that the members have limited liability. Members of associations do not have shares and are not entitled to the payment of dividends. Like shareholders however, they have voting rights and other privileges.[79]

Associations have perpetual succession and will continue to exist until the Registrar of Associations (i.e. the Registrar of Companies) cancels their registration (because the association is not operating properly or has lost its non-profit status or community purpose) or they are wound up (liquidated). Associations may be either voluntarily or involuntarily wound up. The association may be wound up for example, because it has ceased to operate as an association, it is unable to pay its debts as and when they fall due, or where the National Court thinks that it is just and equitable to do so. Most of the provisions of the Companies Act 1997 relating to the winding up or liquidation of companies apply to the winding up of associations.[80]

Statutory authorities or statutory bodies[81]

There is nothing to prevent the Independent State of Papua New Guinea from establishing a corporation. These entities are usually referred to as

79 This includes returning the money in the event that the association is wound up.

80 See s 31 of the Associations Incorporation Act (C 142). See Chapter 14 dealing with the liquidation of companies. Note, however, that the Companies Act 1997 no longer provides for the liquidation of unregistered companies as the Companies Act (Ch 146) used to so provide in Part XI.5 (Winding-up of Unregistered Companies). The Companies Act (Ch 146) was expressly repealed by s 440 of the Companies Act 1997, without that Act or Regulations made thereunder making any transitional provisions regarding the winding up of incorporated associations. It is therefore quite difficult to decide what provisions would now apply to the winding up of registered associations. It may be that the National and Supreme Courts will utilise their "inherent" powers under s 155(4) of the Constitution to make "such . . . orders as are necessary to do justice in the circumstances of a particular case".

81 Mugambwa, J, "Control of Statutory Corporations in Papua New Guinea" [1987] *LAWASIA* 138–151.

statutory bodies or statutory corporations or bodies corporate. The qualification "statutory" means that they owe their existence to an Act of the National Parliament,[82] which usually sets out the composition of the Board to manage the corporation, as well as the purposes and powers of the organisation. There are many such bodies. Some examples, as well as the governing legislation are:

- National Housing Corporation (National Housing Corporation Act 1990).
- PANGTEL – Papua New Guinea Telecommunications Authority (Telecommunications Act 1996).
- Niugini Insurance Corporation (Niugini Insurance Corporation Insurance Corporation Act (Ch 366)).
- Post and Telecommunication Corporation (Postal Services Act 1996).

Most of these statutory corporations are of a public nature,[83] and some are more of a private nature.[84] The establishing legislation usually provides that the corporation:

- is a corporation with perpetual succession;
- shall have a seal;
- may acquire, hold and dispose of property; and
- may sue or be sued in its corporate name.

Corporations sole

The law in PNG makes provision for corporations sole. In effect, the law provides that a person for the time being holding a certain office is to be regarded as a corporation sole.[85] This allows for continuity: whenever the person holding the office dies or retires, the person who succeeds him or her automatically becomes the corporation sole and is able to transact business just like his or her predecessor did. Unlike the position in England, where corporations sole arise both at common law and by statute, corporations sole in PNG arise only as a result of statutes.

82 A "'statutory corporation' means a corporation established by a statutory provision": Interpretation Act (Ch 2), s 7A(1).

83 Loans and Assistance (International Agencies) Act (Ch 132), s 10B.

84 See for example, the Coffee Industry Corporation.

85 See for example, the Forsayth Prize Fund Trust Act (Ch 164), s 2, which provides that the Secretary for Education is a corporation by the name of the Forsayth Prize Fund Trust with power to manage and control the property of the Forsayth Prize Fund Trust. See also the Roman Catholic Archdiocese of Rabaul Act (Ch 1012), which provides that the Roman Catholic Archbishop of Rabaul is a corporation sole.

Several statutes governing Christian missionary organisations provide for the Head of the Mission to be a corporation sole, having:

- perpetual succession;
- a seal;
- power to acquire, hold, manage, transfer, mortgage, or otherwise deal with property of any kind; and
- the power to sue and be sued in its corporate name.

The Custodian for Trust Land and the Public Curator are two "general" corporations sole with important and varied functions. Following the defeat of the Germans in the First World War, all enemy property in the former territory of German New Guinea, with the exception of mission property, was vested by statute in the Custodian of Expropriated Property with a view to its eventual sale to citizens of the Allied and associated countries.[86] The law continues to provide that the Custodian, now renamed the Custodian for Trust Land, is a corporation sole and has capacity in that name:[87]

- to sue and be sued; and
- with the written consent of the Minister for Lands, to take, purchase, hold, sell, lease or otherwise deal with estates or interests in land.

The Public Curator has several functions, with many of them being specified in the Public Curator Act (Ch 81). They mostly relate to trusts and the administration of testate and intestate estates.[88]

The important thing to note about corporations sole in PNG, is that their functions do not usually include the running of businesses, and as such, more detailed consideration is outside the compass of this text.

Companies

Historical introduction

In the division of powers between the national, provincial and local-level governments, the law relating to corporations or companies is exclusively within the jurisdiction of the National Parliament. Provincial governments and local-level governments may not make laws relating to corporations

86 The proceeds of sale was placed in a War Compensation Fund to defray the expense of the Allied forces in prosecuting the war.

87 Land Registration Act (Ch 191), s 166.

88 The property of a deceased person initially vests in the Public Curator until probate or administration is granted to an executor or administrator, see Wills, Probate and Administration Act (Ch 291), s 44.

or companies.[89] Section 40(1) of the Organic Law on Provincial Governments and Local-level Governments specifies that each arm of government (National Government, provincial governments and local-level governments) shall have specific powers, and that the powers that are not so specified shall be assumed to remain with the National Government.[90] In specifying the powers granted to provincial and local-level governments, ss 42 and 44 of the Organic Law on Provincial Governments and Local-level Governments, do not mention powers governing corporations or companies. As such, only the National Parliament may enact legislation dealing with corporations or companies.[91] Both before Independence, and subsequently, PNG has had only national legislation relating to corporations or companies.[92]

In 1997 there was a major change to company law in PNG. Up till then, PNG had based its company law on that of Australia.[93] In 1997, however, the National Parliament enacted the Companies Act 1997 which was modelled, almost entirely,[94] on the Companies Act 1993 of New Zealand; an Act which it has been said, sought to "provide in full for the formation, termination, and regulation of the affairs of companies", and in doing so was intended to "do away with most of the case law on companies, revising

89 Bougainville (North Solomons') Province has recently (2005) been granted extensive autonomy and the National Constitution was amended by adding, *inter alia*, s 290(2)(k), which states that "corporation law" is one of the "functions and powers available to the Bougainville Government in and in relation to Bougainville". In this respect, the province of Bougainville differs from all other provinces in Papua New Guinea. Section 296(1) of the National Constitution provides that: "National laws relating to the functions and powers available to the Bougainville Government shall continue to apply until replaced by Bougainville laws." Up to the date of publication of this text, this power has not been exercised.

90 Section 41(1) of the Organic Law on Provincial Governments and Local-level Governments also provides that: "A law-making power that is not specified in Section 42 or 44 remains with the National Parliament."

91 As we have already noted above at note 89, Bougainville forms an exception to this rule because of the recent grant of more extensive powers to that provincial government. Despite the lack of power in provincial and local-level governments to pass laws dealing with corporations or companies, s 87(1)(e) of the Organic Law on Provincial Governments and Local-level governments provides that a local-level government has power to impose a "corporation tax". The Consolidated Revenue Fund includes "corporate taxes".

92 For an overview of these laws see Deklin, A, "Company Law in Papua New Guinea" in Tomasic, R (ed), *Company Law in East Asia* (Aldershot, Hants, England; Brookfield, Vt: Ashgate, Dartmouth, 1999), Ch 15; Kimuli, M A, Amankwah, H A and Mugambwa, J T, *Introduction to the Law of Business Associations in Papua New Guinea* (2nd ed, Pacific Law Press, Hobart, 1990); and Tashjian, P C, *Business Organisations in Papua New Guinea* (Law Book Co, Sydney, 1989). See also earlier editions of CCH's *PNG Companies Act*.

93 The culmination of this was the Companies Act (Ch 146), enacted in 1963, with several subsequent amendments.

94 There are a few areas where Australian provisions were adopted in a modified form, and there are some original (i.e. locally devised) provisions.

some of the most deep-seated concepts in the subject".[95] The Companies Act 1997, instead of "acting as a statutory overlay of common law like earlier companies legislation, was intended primarily to be a code".[96] The New Zealand Law Commission Report which eventually led to the passing of the Companies Act 1993 (New Zealand) stated:[97]

> In the conduct of the review, we have been aware that the need to simplify expression and content of company law is itself a major goal for reform. So too is the need to make company law more accessible and usable by collecting together in the statute the main rules. The [Companies Act 1955 (New Zealand)], besides being complex and dense in form, contains only part of the law relating to company regulation. Some of the major company rules are not contained in legislation at all but have to be discerned from the case law, which in many important respects is difficult and unclear.
>
> We have worked on the principle that those needing to know what their rights and obligations are should not be driven immediately to seek legal advice. The Companies Act should be the statement of first recourse. Directors and shareholders and not simply their professional expert advisers should be able to use it.

Despite these lofty aims, it is still not possible to limit oneself to reading the Companies Act 1997 (and the related regulations, the Companies Regulation 1998) to discover the company law of PNG: it is still necessary to refer to concepts of the underlying law and decisions of Papua New Guinean and foreign courts in order to understand fundamental company law principles.[98]

As Deklin points out in relation to earlier company legislation in PNG, the Companies Act (Ch 146) "was merely the adoption of the Australian model with some adaptations necessitated by PNG circumstances".[99] It can be said that the Companies Act 1997 is merely the adoption of the New Zealand model with some adaptations necessitated by PNG circumstances. A company law developed peculiarly with PNG conditions in mind still awaits another day.[100]

95 Wishart, D, *Company Law in Context* (Oxford University Press, Auckland, 1994), p 31. As we shall see, this attempt may not have been as successful as had been hoped for.

96 Watson, S, Gunasekara, G, Gedye, M, van Roy, Y, Ross, M, Longdin, L, Sims, A and Brown, L, *The Law of Business Organisations* (4th ed, Palatine Press, Auckland, 2003), p 94.

97 New Zealand Law Commission, *Company Law: Reform and Restatement*, Law Commission, Report No 9 (Law Commission, Wellington, New Zealand 1989), paras 122–123.

98 See for example, the discussion in Chapter 9 (Directors' Duties) in relation to the question whether the Companies Act 1997 sets out a code in respect of directors' duties.

99 Deklin, A, "Company Law in Papua New Guinea", in Tomasic, R (ed), *Company Law in East Asia* (Aldershot, Hants, England; Brookfield, Vt: Ashgate, Dartmouth, 1999), p 571.

100 This will include reform of the law relating to business groups, land groups, co-operatives etc.

The extensive adoption of concepts and provisions from the New Zealand Companies Act 1993 raises questions concerning the continued binding effect of English cases relating to companies[101] and of decisions of the courts within the New Zealand court structure.[102] The long title to the New Zealand Act (which sets out the purposes of the Act) provides that it is:

> An Act to reform the law relating to companies, and, in particular –
>
> (a) To reaffirm the value of the company as a means of achieving economic and social benefits through the aggregation of capital for productive purposes, the spreading of economic risk, and the taking of business risks; and
> (b) To provide basic and adaptable requirements for the incorporation, organisation, and operation of companies; and
> (c) To define the relationships between companies and their directors, shareholders, and creditors; and
> (d) To encourage efficient and responsible management of companies by allowing directors a wide discretion in matters of business judgment while at the same time providing protection for shareholders and creditors against the abuse of management power; and
> (e) To provide straightforward and fair procedures for realising and distributing the assets of insolvent companies.

Despite the fact that the drafters did not reproduce this long title in the Companies Act 1997,[103] it is argued that because of such an extensive verbatim reproduction of the New Zealand provisions, the purposes set out in

101 Schedule 2.2(1) of the *Constitution*, provides that, subject to certain preconditions, "the principles and rules of common law and equity in England immediately before Independence Day" [i.e., 16 September 1975], are adopted as part of the "underlying law". The law governing the adoption of the common law and equity has become more problematic since the enactment of the Underlying Law Act 2000 without the express repeal of the Customs Recognition Act (Ch 19). For a recent and comprehensive analysis of the situation, see Zorn, J G and Corrin Care, J, "Everything Old is New Again: The Underlying Law Act of Papua New Guinea" [2002] *LAWASIA Journal* 61–97. Note also that s 48(1) of the Constitution of the Autonomous Region of Bougainville which came into operation in 2005 provides that "the underlying law of Papua New Guinea as at the date of the coming into operation of this Constitution shall be the underlying law of the Autonomous Region of Bougainville".

102 The final appellate court for New Zealand was until recently, the Judicial Committee of the Privy Council. The Supreme Court Act 2003 established the Supreme Court of New Zealand as a new final court of appeal comprising New Zealand judges. It replaced the Judicial Committee of the Privy Council as the final court of appeal of New Zealand and came into being on 1 January 2004. Only a few cases relating to company law and the interpretation of the Companies Act 1993 were taken to the Privy Council on appeal.

103 The long title of the Companies Act 1997 merely states: "Being an Act to reform the law relating to companies and to repeal the Companies Act (Chapter 146) and for related purposes."

the long title to the Companies Act 1993 (NZ) set out above are just as relevant to the determination of company law cases in PNG: the National and Supreme Courts should use them wherever appropriate to assist in the interpretation of most provisions of the Companies Act 1997.[104]

Types of corporations

Some corporations are constituted without the assistance of statute. The customary clan or tribe or other traditional entity exists without any legislation creating or sustaining it. It can sue and be sued as a whole, without the individuals comprising it being liable or having rights in their own name. Deklin points out that PNG customary law "does recognize the corporate entity of various social groups, such as the tribe, although it did not develop the structure of that entity in as elaborate a way as the introduced company law does".[105] He stated:[106]

> One common aspect of this customary law is that it recognizes tribes, extended families and lineages as corporate entities separate from their members. Thus, ownership of land is vested in the tribe which then grants licences to individual members to use various portions of land to meet their daily needs through activities such as gardening.

Deklin contends that this "provides the justification for the use of the introduced company law rather than the customary law by commercial groups".[107]

104 Tompkins, Hon Justice, "Directing the Directors: The Duties of Directors under the Companies Act 1993" (1994) 2 *Waikato Law Review* 13 at 18 stated that "[a]ny consideration of the enacted directors' duties should commence with the long title to the 1993 Act, to which I suspect reference will frequently be made in submissions directed to the purpose or object of any particular provision". See also at pp 27 and 39. Usually, the long title is referred to where there is some ambiguity in the substantive provisions. For a decision of the Supreme Court where Bredmeyer J referred to the long title to assist in interpreting an Act, see *The State v Danny Sunu* [1983] PNGLR 396 at 403–404: "To interpret a statute I am entitled to refer to its objectives and I may look at the short and long title to assist in that task . . . The long title is not determinative of the meaning of any sections of an Act but it is, as I have said, a good guide to its objectives."

105 Deklin, A, "Company Law in Papua New Guinea", in Tomasic, R (ed), *Company Law in East Asia* (Aldershot, Hants, England; Brookfield, Vt: Ashgate, Dartmouth, 1999), p 570. See also Tavua, I F, "Clan—a commercial legal corporation?", (1971) 1(2) *Melanesian Law Journal* 71–72.

106 Deklin, A, "Company Law in Papua New Guinea", in Tomasic, R (ed), *Company Law in East Asia* (Aldershot, Hants, England; Brookfield, Vt: Ashgate, Dartmouth, 1999), p 568. Modern statutory law has attempted to recognise this traditional corporate principle: see, for example, the Business Groups Incorporation Act (Ch 144) and the Land Groups Incorporation Act (Ch 147).

107 Deklin, A, "Company Law in Papua New Guinea", in Tomasic, R (ed), *Company Law in East Asia* (Aldershot, Hants, England; Brookfield, Vt: Ashgate, Dartmouth, 1999), p 570.

Most corporations in PNG, however, are the creature of statute, either directly created by the Act of Parliament itself or created following a process prescribed in an Act. Examples of corporations created directly by an Act of the Parliament are:

(i) Coffee Industry Corporation;
(ii) National Broadcasting Corporation;
(iii) Independent Public Business Corporation of Papua New Guinea;
(iv) Insurance Corporation;
(v) Investment Corporation;
(vi) Kwato Church Corporation;
(vii) National Housing Corporation;
(viii) Oil Palm Industry Corporation;
(ix) Small Business Development Corporation.

With regard to legislation laying down procedures for the creation of corporations, there are several such Acts. Some of the Acts create specific types of corporations which have limited or specialised functions. For example, the Land Groups Act 1974[108] was passed to incorporate land groups. These corporations were given specific powers by the Act, and certain powers were withheld. For example, an incorporated land group does not have power to engage in general business unrelated to land, e.g., as a Public Motor Vehicle (PMV) operator. On the other hand, although a business group incorporated under the Business Groups Incorporation Act 1974[109] may engage in many types of businesses, but cannot own and deal with customary land, like an incorporated land group. In contrast to these two Acts, the Companies Act 1997 provides for general corporations (or companies) that may carry out any type of business.

Legislation governing corporations does not usually make a distinction between citizen and non-citizen corporations. However, in at least one instance, such a distinction is made. The Organic Law on the Integrity of Political Parties and Candidates 2003, s 2, defines a "non-citizen corporation" as a business enterprise or corporation or an organisation, corporate or non-corporate, that is profit-making or non-profit-making, and that was:

(a) originally incorporated, registered or formed in a foreign country; or
(b) where it is originally incorporated, registered or formed in Papua New Guinea –
    (i) whose membership or controlling body is largely non-citizens; or
    (ii) of which more than 25% of its equity or the balance of voting power or the management is in the control of non-citizens.

108 Land Groups Incorporation Act (Ch 147).
109 Business Groups Incorporation Act (Ch 144).

Types of companies

Before the Companies Act 1997, the law recognised five different types of companies based on members' liability:[110]

(i) companies limited by shares;
(ii) companies limited by guarantee;
(iii) companies limited both by shares and by guarantee;
(iv) unlimited companies (with and without share capital); and
(v) no-liability companies.

All of these companies could be public companies, and all except companies limited by guarantee and no-liability companies could be proprietary companies.[111] A public company had to have a minimum of five members,[112] whereas a proprietary company had to have not fewer than two and not more than 50 members.[113]

In addition to this, "Division 4 status" could attach to any of these five different types of companies.[114] In the words of Deklin:

> Division 4 status relieves companies of the payment of some of the fees payable under the [Companies Act (Ch 146)], and also from compliance

110 The first three types of companies were classified as "limited (liability) companies". It was possible to convert a company from one type to another by following the procedure set out in the Companies Act (Ch 146). See Deklin, A, "Company Law in Papua New Guinea", in Tomasic, R (ed) *Company Law in East Asia* (Aldershot, Hants, England; Brookfield, Vt: Ashgate, Dartmouth, 1999), pp 573–578, and Kimuli, M A, Amankwah, H A and Mugambwa, J T, *Introduction to the Law of Business Associations in Papua New Guinea* (2nd ed, Pacific Law Press, Hobart, 1990), Ch 2.

111 The essential difference between public and proprietary companies were: in the case of a proprietary company, the minimum number of shareholders could be two, whereas in the case of public companies, this was five.

112 There was no upper limit, i.e., maximum number of shareholders allowed.

113 As we shall see, since the Companies Act 1997, it is possible to have "one man" companies: where one person owns all the shares in and is the sole director of a company. See below, pp 210, 228. See s 16 of the Companies Act (Ch 146) for the other requirements for proprietary companies. Section 1(1) defined a public company as "a company other than a proprietary company". The section also defined a "proprietary company". See s 16 of the Act, which set out the requirements. These included: it could not be a company limited by guarantee or guarantee and shares or a no-liability company; the memorandum or articles could not restrict the right of its shareholders to transfer its shares; the constitution had to limit the number of shareholders to 50; prohibit any invitation to the public to subscribe for shares in, or debentures of, the company; prohibit any invitation to the public to deposit money with the company for fixed periods or payable at call, whether or not interest was payable on the amount.

114 Under Division 4, Part XII of the Companies Act (Ch 146). See Kimuli, M A, Amankwah, H A and Mugambwa, J T, *Introduction to the Law of Business Associations in Papua New Guinea* (2nd edn, Pacific Law Press, Hobart, 1990), pp 15–16; Deklin, A, "Company Law in Papua New Guinea", in Tomasic, R (ed), *Company Law in East Asia* (Aldershot, Hants, England; Brookfield, Vt: Ashgate, Dartmouth, 1999), p 575.

> with some of the more complex and onerous provisions of the Act. Division 4 status was introduced in response to the criticisms that the [Companies Act (Ch 146)], as it then stood, was too complex and expensive to operate under and that it imposed onerous obligations on local businesses. It was, therefore, not conducive to the growth and expansion of indigenous enterprises."[115]

Division 4 status was a special status given to companies whose membership consisted of local persons[116] or institutions[117] or a combination of them, or the membership of which was substantially composed of local persons by local persons.[118] Any type of company that could have been incorporated under the Companies Act (Ch 146) could apply to the Registrar of Companies for Division 4 status.

The essence of Division 4 status was that companies having that status were:

> relieved from payment of some of the fees and from compliance with some of the more complex and onerous provisions of the Companies Act (Ch 146). The substitute provisions were invariably simpler and less demanding.[119] Division 4 status was introduced in response to criticism that the Companies Act (Ch 146) was too complex, too expensive to operate under, and imposed very onerous obligations on local businessmen, and was therefore not "conducive to the growth and expansion of indigenous enterprises".[120]

The situation has been greatly simplified since the enactment of the Companies Act 1997. All companies now have to have shares,[121] and only two types of companies may now exist: limited and unlimited liability companies.[122] All companies incorporated under or recognised by the Companies Act 1997 are presumed to be limited liability companies unless

115 Deklin, A, "Company Law in Papua New Guinea", in Tomasic, R (ed), *Company Law in East Asia* (Aldershot, Hants, England; Brookfield, Vt: Ashgate, Dartmouth, 1999), p 575.

116 Because of the operation of the national Constitution, by 1980, this requirement encompassed "citizens", whether automatic or naturalised. Originally, only "automatic citizens" were considered to be local persons.

117 For example, business groups, land groups, local-level government councils, local-level government authorities and statutory corporations (Companies Act (Ch 146), s 369(1)).

118 Companies Act (Ch 146), s 369.

119 For a detailed analysis of Division 4 status, see Irwin, P L, "Incorporation Laws in Papua New Guinea" (Unpublished LlM thesis, Melbourne University, 1981), pp 31–47.

120 Kimuli, M A, Amankwah, H A and Mugambwa, J T, *Introduction to the Law of Business Associations in Papua New Guinea* (2nd edn, Pacific Law Press, Hobart, 1990), p 14.

121 Companies Act 1997, s 11(b). It is no longer possible to have companies limited by guarantee or companies limited by shares and guarantee. It is also no longer possible to have no-liability companies following the enactment of the Companies Act 1997.

122 Companies Act 1997, s 11(c). Technically, it is the shareholding that is either limited or unlimited. It is theoretically possible for a company to have different types of shares, some conferring limited and some unlimited liability.

the company has a constitution that provides otherwise.[123] So if a company is to be an unlimited company, it must adopt a constitution and expressly state in it that the shares of the company are unlimited. In an unlimited company, the shareholders will be fully liable for all the debts of the company where it is or becomes insolvent. The company is in effect an incorporated partnership.[124] Although it is usual to speak of "limited liability companies", it is strictly speaking the liability of the shareholders which is limited. The company is fully liable for all the obligations it incurs, whereas the liability of the shareholders is limited to what is imposed by the Companies Act 1997 or the company's constitution.[125] Given this, it is possible to have different shares in a company, some of which impose limited liability, and others which impose greater or unlimited liability.[126] This makes it even more difficult to refer to limited and unlimited companies, rather than to shares having limited or unlimited liability.

The Companies Act 1997 also abolished the distinction between private ("proprietary") companies and public companies, with all companies being governed by the same Act. However, other legislation imposes additional requirements for companies that are listed on the Port Moresby Stock Exchange (POMSoX) and issue securities to the general public.[127]

Despite the changes in the law, in practice there will still continue to be a distinction between private (proprietary) companies and public companies. The members of small "closely held" private companies will usually adopt a constitution which will make it similar to the old proprietary companies, especially relating to disclosure and reporting.

The Companies Act 1997 no longer recognises special types of companies (other than exempt companies and overseas companies) or companies set up for special purposes. It is left to the incorporators or shareholders at a later date to adopt a constitution that sets out, as far as the Act allows them, special rules relating to the company.[128]

123 Companies Act 1997, s 79(2). Note that although the company may change the liability of its members, even converting the shares from limited to unlimited liability, the consent of existing shareholders is necessary: see s 48 and s 83.

124 For partnership liability, see Chapter 15. We have noted at note 37 that there is little reason to have unlimited shares except where the law requires such companies, e.g., in the accountancy profession, where its members are required to be liable without limitation.

125 Usually, the value or cost of the shares issued to that person.

126 Companies Act 1997, s 79.

127 See the Listing Rules of the Port Moresby Stock Exchange (POMSoX) and the Securities Act 1997 and the Securities Regulation 1999. The policy behind the securities legislation is to protect the investing public. This is achieved by the legislation providing that securities (e.g., shares or debentures) may not be offered to the public unless the company first registers and make available to investors, a comprehensive disclosure document, known as a prospectus. For a discussion of this area of the law, see Beck, A and Borrowdale, A, *Papua New Guinea Companies and Securities Law Guide* (CCH Australia Ltd, Sydney, 1999), Ch 7.

128 See the discussion below on "exempt companies".

A company must also have a name,[129] and at least one director.[130] If it has only one director he or she must be "ordinarily resident" in PNG; if there are more than one director, then only one director need be so resident.[131] Before the company can be incorporated it must have a registered office, an address for service and, it seems, a postal address.[132]

Exempt companies

It is possible for incorporators to achieve a similar situation to what could be achieved by incorporating a proprietary or "closely held" company. This is done through the adoption of a constitution which sets out similar rules as those that used to apply to proprietary companies. Furthermore, the Companies Act 1997 allows for "exempt companies" to be registered. This means that such companies will be subject to less onerous reporting requirements.[133] An exempt company is one that did not have, during a relevant accounting period:

- total assets of more than K5 million;
- more than 25 shareholders; or
- more than 100 employees.

If the company satisfies only two of the above three requirements, it can still be an exempt company if all of the shareholders agree not to appoint an auditor for the relevant accounting period. Furthermore, a subsidiary of an exempt company is itself an exempt company.

Overseas companies

The other type of special company is the overseas company carrying on business in PNG. The Companies Act 1997 defines an overseas company as "a body corporate that is incorporated outside of Papua New Guinea".[134] The Companies Act 1997 does not regulate overseas companies to the same extent as companies that are incorporated in PNG.

If an overseas company carries on business in PNG, it is required to register under the Companies Act 1997 and it then becomes subject to various obligations imposed by that Act,[135] in particular those relating to service of

129 This is considered in more detail below, at p 213.
130 Companies Act 1997, s 11(d).
131 Companies Act 1997, s 128(2).
132 Companies Act 1997, s 13(2). For the requirement of a postal address, see Companies Act 1997, Schedule 6.
133 Companies Act 1997, s 171.
134 Companies Act 1997, s 2(1). Part XX (Overseas Companies) of the Companies Act 1997 is the part of the Act that particularly applies to overseas companies.
135 The other important legislation applying to overseas companies carrying on business in Papua New Guinea is the Investment Promotion Act 1992 and the Investment Promotion Regulation 1992.

documents, filing of financial statements and liquidation of certain assets of the company.

The term "carrying on business" is not precisely defined in the Companies Act 1997. The question whether a company is carrying on business in PNG is one of fact, and s 382 of the Companies Act 1997 sets out certain activities which will amount to carrying on business.[136] These are:

1. establishing or using a share transfer office or a share registration office in the country; or
2. administering, renting, managing, or otherwise dealing with property in the country as an owner, agent, legal personal representative, or trustee, whether by a servant or agent or otherwise; or
3. maintaining an agent, employee, or officer for the purpose of soliciting or procuring or entering into orders, arrangements, agreements, or contracts (whether conditional or not), whether or not the agent, employee, or officer is continuously resident in the country; or
4. maintaining an office, agency, or branch (however described), whether or not the office, agency, or branch is also used for one of those purposes by another enterprise; or
5. making an application for, or being issued, any permit, licence, lease or authority issued for commercial purposes by the State or by:
   (i) the National Government; or
   (ii) a provincial government or any other level of government; or
   (iii) a unit, department, agency or instrumentality of the state or of a provincial government; or
   (iv) any body, authority or instrumentality established by the state or under an Act;

Section 382(b) of the Companies Act 1997 provides that an overseas company does not carry on business in PNG merely because, in the country, it:

- is or becomes a party to a legal proceeding or settles a legal proceeding or a claim or dispute; or
- holds meetings of its directors or shareholders or carries on other activities concerning its internal affairs; or
- maintains a bank account; or
- effects a sale of property through an independent contractor; or

136 See *Brinks Incorporated and Brinks Air Courier Australia Pty Ltd v Brinks Pty Ltd* (1997) N1567 for a consideration of the term "carrying on business" as defined in the repealed Companies Act (Ch 146), s 355. For consideration of the meaning of that term in s 3(1) of the Investment Promotion Act 1992, see *Investment Promotion Authority v Niugini Scrap Corporation Pty Ltd* (2001) N2104; *Odata Ltd v Ambusa Copra Oil Mill Ltd* (2001) N2106; and *Spirit Haus Ltd v Robert Marshall* (2004) N2630. These cases will be helpful in discovering the meaning of the term as used in the Companies Act 1997.

- solicits or procures an order that becomes a binding contract only if the order is accepted outside the country; or
- creates evidence of a debt or creates a charge on property; or
- secures or collects any of its debts or enforces its rights in relation to securities relating to those debts; or
- conducts an isolated transaction that is completed within a period of one month, not being one of a number of similar transactions repeated from time to time; or
- invests its funds or holds property.

Registration

An overseas company that carries on business in PNG is required to apply for registration under Part XX of the Companies Act 1997 within one month of commencing the carrying on of business.[137] Although s 385 of the Companies Act 1997 provides that a failure by an overseas company to register under the Act does not affect the validity or enforceability of any transaction entered into by the overseas company, the validity of the contract may, however, be affected by failure of the overseas company to comply with the provisions (including registration provisions) of the Investment Promotion Act 1992.[138] In some cases, an overseas company that is not carrying on business in PNG may apply for registration in order to protect its name.[139]

The obligations placed on registered overseas companies are to:

- file financial statements[140] and annual returns[141] in PNG;
- ensure that its full name, and the name of the country where it was incorporated, are clearly stated in written communications sent by, or on behalf of, the company and documents issued or signed by, or on behalf of, the company that evidence or create a legal obligation of the company;
- notify the Registrar of Companies of a change of name,[142] a change in constitution,[143] a change in the directors, or in the names or residential addresses of the directors,[144] a change in the address of the place of

137 Companies Act 1997, s 383(1). Separate provision is made for companies that carried on business in PNG before the commencement of the Companies Act 1997: see particularly s 383(2).

138 If an overseas company fails to register as required by the Companies Act 1997, both it and every director and person in default is guilty of an offence and liable to a penalty of up to K10,000: Companies Act 1997, s 383(3).

139 Companies Act 1997, s 384(1). Cf *Brinks Incorporated and Brinks Air Courier Australia Pty Ltd v Brinks Pty Ltd* (1997) N1567.

140 Companies Act 1997, s 390.

141 Companies Act 1997, s 391.

142 Companies Act 1997, s 388(2).

143 Companies Act 1997, s 389(1)(a).

144 Companies Act 1997, s 389(1)(b).

business or principal place of business,[145] a change in any person, or the address of any person, authorised to accept service in the country of documents on behalf of the overseas company or who is responsible for submitting to the Registrar documents required under the Companies Act 1997,[146] and also a notice of intention to cease carrying on business in PNG,[147] and where it has been liquidated, dissolved or deregistered or ceases to be a corporate body in its place of incorporation.[148]

Liquidation of overseas companies

Section 393 of the Companies Act 1997 provides for the liquidation of the assets located in PNG of overseas companies. This is a limited form of liquidation, as the existence of the company is not affected. The only thing that happens is that on the completion of the liquidation process, the company will cease to carry on business in PNG and it will be removed from the overseas register. An application must be made to the National Court. The liquidation is carried out in accordance with Part XVIII, subject to the modifications and exclusions set out in Schedule 12.

Division 4 status

Division 4 status no longer exists under the Companies Act 1997. Despite this, persons registering companies still have some flexibility and certain privileges are given to companies that would have been entitled to Division 4 status under the repealed Companies Act (Ch 146). Companies may adopt a constitution and set out therein different types of rules that will apply and thereby limit the types of activities the company may engage in and how it may go about doing business. Furthermore, although the Companies Act 1997 does not make specific provision for "Division 4 status" companies, the Act does provide for "exempt companies" (where reporting and audit requirements are reduced), and gives the Registrar of Companies the power to reduce or waive fees and other requirements in respect of such companies. For example, if the company is an exempt company under s 412(2) of the Companies Act 1997 this may be done if:

(a) every shareholder is one of the following:
  (i) a citizen of the country who is ordinarily resident in the country;
  (ii) a company to which this section applies;
  (iii) a business group incorporated under the *Business Groups Incorporation Act* (Chapter 144);

145 Companies Act 1997, s 389(1)(c).
146 Companies Act 1997, s 389(1)(d).
147 Companies Act 1997, s 392(1).
148 Companies Act 1997, s 392(2).

(iv) the State or a statutory authority or instrumentality of the State; and

(b) every director is a citizen of the country who is ordinarily resident in the country.

Incorporating companies

Registration of new companies

It is possible for an individual to apply to the Registrar of Companies to incorporate a company. It is, alternatively, possible for that person to buy a "shelf company" from a firm of lawyers or accountants who have already gone through the process. In such a case, the shares in the shelf-company will be transferred to the "purchaser". The new owner may then decide to operate the shelf company according to its current rules. On the other hand, the purchaser may decide to change the name, as well as some of the rules governing the company, so as to make it conform more closely to what he or she wants to use the company for. In such a case, if the shelf-company did not already have one, the purchaser would draw up and register a constitution for the shelf-company, which sets out these purposes.

Part II (ss 11 to 16) of the Companies Act 1997 deals with incorporation of companies. Section 12 provides that: "Any person may, either alone or together with another person, apply for registration of a company under this Act, despite the contrary in any other Act." The any person may either be a natural person (over the age of 18 years of age) or a legal person (like another company or corporation). So a company may apply to incorporate another company.

Section 11 of the Companies Act 1997 sets out the "essential requirements" for a company. It provides that a company shall have:

- a name; and
- one or more shares; and
- one or more shareholders, having limited or unlimited liability for the obligations of the company; and
- one or more directors.[149]

Because the shareholder and director do not have to be different persons, it is possible to have a one person company (i.e., a single person with one share who is both a director and shareholder).

The first step to be taken by persons intending to form a company is to select a name for the company and apply to the Registrar of Companies for the

149 At least one director of the company must be "ordinarily resident" in PNG, both at the time of first registration and throughout the life of the company: Companies Act 1997, s 128(2).

reservation of that name.[150] Once the Registrar has approved and reserved the name, an application may be made for registration of the company.

The application must be in the prescribed form and made to the Registrar of Companies.[151] It must be accompanied by certain documents. These include:[152]

- a document in the prescribed form signed by every person named as a director, containing his consent to being a director and a certificate that he or she is not disqualified from being appointed or holding office as a director of a company;
- a document in the prescribed form signed by any person named as a secretary, containing his consent to being the secretary;[153]
- a document in the prescribed form signed by every person named as a shareholder, or by an agent of that person authorised in writing, containing his consent to being a shareholder and to taking the class and number of shares specified in the document; where the document has been signed by an agent, the instrument authorising the agent to sign it must also accompany the application for registration;
- a notice from the Registrar of Companies reserving a name for the proposed company;[154]
- where the proposed company is to have a constitution, a certified copy of the company's constitution.[155]

The information given to the Registrar must include:[156]

- the number of persons named as directors of the proposed company;
- the number of persons (if any) named as secretaries of the proposed company;
- the postal address of the proposed company;
- the registered office of the proposed company;[157]
- the address for service of the proposed company.[158]

150 Companies Act 1997, s 21.
151 Companies Regulation 1998, Form 1.—Application for registration of a company.
152 Companies Act 1997, s 13(1).
153 As we shall see, it is not essential for a company to have a company secretary.
154 The first thing one has to do is to apply to the Registrar of Companies to reserve a name for the company. This must precede the application to incorporate the company. See below at p 213 (Company Name) for reserving a company name.
155 See s 9 of the Companies Regulation 1998 for method of certification.
156 Companies Act 1997, s 13(2). This information is provided for in Form 1.
157 The registered office must be identifiable and easily accessible: Companies Act 1997, s 161(2). It does not have to be the company's main place of business, and will usually be the office of the company's accountant or lawyer.
158 Companies Act 1997, s 167.

Soon after receiving a properly completed application, the Registrar must register the application and issue a certificate of incorporation in the prescribed form. Provided that the application has been properly completed, the Registrar should normally register them.[159]

A certificate of incorporation of a company is conclusive evidence that all the requirements of the Companies Act 1997 as to registration have been complied with and on and from the date of incorporation stated in the certificate, the company is incorporated under the Act.[160] From the date of incorporation, the company is a legal entity in its own right separate from its shareholders and continues in existence until it is removed from the companies' register.[161] It may commence business immediately after it has been registered.[162]

Re-registration of existing companies

The Companies Act 1997 substantially reformed company law in PNG, and it was decided that rather than merely applying the reformed law to existing companies, all companies should be re-registered under the Companies Act 1997. Existing companies could do so voluntarily within a period of grace, following which all companies not re-registered by then, would be compulsorily and automatically re-registered on a fixed date. The reason for re-registration was because, although many of the reforms could easily be applied to companies, the reforms as to capital and constitutional structure were too fundamental to be applied to all existing companies without a procedure being implemented allowing those who would be prejudiced to have their complaints heard and rectified.[163]

The provisions for re-registration allowed the board of directors to apply for re-registration. The application was to be accompanied by evidence that a "registration proposal" had been approved by special resolution of each class of members (shareholders) (i.e., 75 per cent of the shareholders in meetings of members who have the same interests in common), and the directors had to certify that the registration proposal was not unfairly prejudicial to and did not unfairly discriminate against any member of the company. The re-registration could include a new constitution for the company to be registered which allowed the shareholders in the company the chance to reorganise the constitution of the company to suit themselves, given the newly enacted provisions of the Companies Act 1997.

159 Companies Act 1997, s 14. Companies Regulation 1998, Form 5. – Certificate of incorporation. See s 396 of the Companies Act 1997 for reasons why the Registrar may reject the application for incorporation.

160 Companies Act 1997, s 15.

161 Companies Act 1997, s 16.

162 The first meeting of shareholders must be held within 18 months of registration: Companies Act 1997, s 101(2).

163 Wishart, D, *Company Law in Context* (Oxford University Press, Auckland, 1994), p 101.

If no application for an existing company to re-register was made, an existing company was deemed to be reregistered on 2 September 1998.[164] The company was "deemed, on and from the day that is six months after the commencement of this Act, to be registered as a company under Part II on the terms and conditions set out in Schedule 14[165] as supplemented or modified by any Regulations made under Section 439".

These companies would not have a constitution and would be governed solely by the provisions of the Companies Act 1997, on the terms and conditions set out in Schedule 14 as supplemented or modified by any Regulations made under s 439 (of which there were none), until such time, if ever, a constitution is adopted. A shareholder who considered that the deemed registration of an existing company was prejudicial to them could apply to the Court "within one year of the deemed registration"[166] for an order requiring the directors of the company at the time of deemed registration to pay such compensation to the member as is fair and reasonable, having regard to: (a) the extent of the loss or damage suffered by the member as a result of the deemed registration; and (b) the extent to which the directors are responsible for the failure of the company to submit an application for registration to the Registrar.[167]

Section 444(1) provided that the registration or deemed registration of an existing company as a company under the Companies Act 1997 did not:

- create a new legal entity; or
- prejudice or affect the identity of the body corporate constituted by the company or its continuity as a legal entity; or
- affect the property, rights, or obligations of the company; or
- affect proceedings by or against the company.

Company name

A company cannot be registered without a name,[168] and choosing a name for the company is one of the first things that must be done. The Registrar of Companies must first approve the name before an application can be made to incorporate the company. The incorporators must therefore first apply to the Registrar to reserve a company name.[169] Any name may be reserved

164 Companies Act 1997, s 443. The company was deemed to be re-registered "on and from the day that is six months after the commencement of this Act". (The Act commenced on 2 March 1998: see National Gazette G23 of 2 March 1998.)

165 *Inter alia*, the memorandum and articles of the company ceased to have effect and the company is governed by the provisions of the Companies Act 1997. The persons holding office as directors of the company immediately before the company was deemed to be registered were the directors of the company as at 2 September 1998.

166 Before 2 September 1999.

167 Companies Act 1997, s 443(2).

168 Companies Act 1997, s 11(a).

169 Companies Act 1997, s 21.

provided that it does not confuse the public or a section of the public, is not offensive, and is not forbidden by law. A name can have great commercial and prestige value, and some companies will go to great lengths to make sure that other companies do not register similar names which will have an adverse impact on the company's name and goodwill. If they fail to prevent the Registrar from registering a particular name, they may bring an action using the underlying law concept of the tort of passing off.[170] It might also be the case that a statutory organisation may try to prevent a company from using certain words in its name or for its product.[171]

Section 22(3) of the Companies Act 1997 provides that except with the consent of the Minister, a company shall not be registered by a name that is, in the opinion of the Registrar of companies: (a) undesirable;[172] (b) misleading, deceptive or offensive;[173] or (c) a name, or a name of a kind, that the Minister has directed the Registrar not to accept for registration. Section 22(1) of the Companies Act (Ch 146) provided that, except with the consent of the Minister, a company shall not be registered by a name that is, in the opinion of the Registrar, "undesirable or is a name or a name of a kind, that the Minister has directed the Registrar not to accept for registration".[174] In a notice published in National Gazette G49 of 17 June 1993, the Minister, pursuant to s 22(1) of the repealed Companies Act (Ch 146) directed the Registrar not to accept for registration, without his consent generally or in a particular case, any of the following names:

170 In *Brinks Incorporated and Brinks Air Courier Australia Pty Ltd v Brinks Pty Ltd* (1997) N1567, the National Court held that the tort of passing off formed part of the underlying law of PNG. Reference to the action of passing off in the Trade Marks Act (Ch 385) (s 59) is added proof that the legislature recognised that the tort of passing off formed a part of the underlying law of Papua New Guinea. Cf Trade Marks Act (Ch 385) s 106(5), however. See also *CBS Inc v Ranu Investments Pty Ltd* [1978] PNGLR 66, where the judge considered that the action of passing off was "a novel one in Papua New Guinea" and stated: "To what extent this type of law will be developed in Papua New Guinea and indeed to what extent it is appropriate to the circumstances of this country will no doubt be a matter for the trial judge in this action to decide."

171 See the case of *Arabicas Pty Ltd v Coffee Industry Corporation Pty Ltd* [1998] PNGLR 19, where the Coffee Industry Corporation Pty Ltd tried (unsuccessfully) to impose a condition on Arabicas Pty Ltd that it was not to sell locally or export any coffee purporting to be "organically" or "naturally" grown and processed.

172 See for example, *South Pacific Airlines of New Zealand Ltd v Registrar of Companies* [1964] NZLR 1. The Registrar of Companies has wide powers to disapprove of the use of names, including names that might mislead or deceive a section of the public, as well as names that are offensive. In *South Pacific Airlines of New Zealand Ltd v Registrar of Companies*, the court held that the following types of names were offensive: any name of an obscene nature; any name that might give particular offence to a friendly state, section of the community, or any particular religion; and any name that would offend public policy.

173 See *George v Registrar of Companies* [1981] 2 NZLR 237; (1981) 1 NZCLC para 95-054.

174 Section 22(2) of the Companies Act (Ch 146) (repealed) provided that the Minister "shall cause a direction given by him" under s 22(1) to be published in the National Gazette.

(1) Names suggesting connexion with members of the Royal family or Royal patronage, e.g., names which include the words "Royal", "King", "Queen", or "Crown".
(2) Names suggesting connexion with the Crown, the Commonwealth of Nations, the Government of the Independent State of Papua New Guinea or of any other part of the Queen's dominions, possessions or territories, e.g., names which include the words "Commonwealth", "Federal", "State", "Empire" or "Imperial".
(3) Names suggesting connexion with the government of a foreign country or with the United Nations.
(4) Names suggesting connexion with a Government Department, Authority or Instrumentality or a municipal or other local Authority including, without limitation, names which include the following words or any words of like import:—"Authority", "Council", "Development Project".
(5) Names containing the following words or any words of like import:—"Trust", "Trustee", "Chamber of Commerce", "Chamber of Manufactures", "Chartered", "Stock Exchange", "Guarantee", "Co-operative", "Building Society", "Starr Bowkett", "Bank", "Banker", "Banking", "Savings".
(6) Names suggesting connexion with ex-servicemen's organisations or that its members are totally or partially incapacitated, e.g., names which include the words "Anzac", "Ex-servicemen", "Returned Soldier", "Blind", or "Blinded".
(7) Names that are misleading as to the nature, objects or purposes of the company or in any other manner.
(8) Names that are blasphemous or likely to be offensive to members of the public.
(9) Names that are likely to be confused with or mistaken for the name of an existing company, business group, land group, foreign company, registered association, firm, co-operative society or friendly society or a business name.
(10) Names that are likely to be confused with or mistaken for the name reserved by or on behalf of a company, a foreign company, a proposed company, or a company which it is proposed to register as a foreign company.
(11) Names in any language which bear a meaning in English which will, or is likely to, fall into any of the preceding categories.

Despite the repeal of the Companies Act (Ch 146), this direction still continues to apply to the reservation of names under the Companies Act 1997.[175]

175 Section 22(2) of the Companies Act (Ch 146) (repealed), provided that the Minister "shall cause a direction given by him" under s 22(1) to be published in the National Gazette. However, there is no such requirement in the Companies Act 1997 in relation to the ministerial direction under that Act. The Registrar of Companies therefore continues to treat the Companies Act (Ch 146) direction as a direction under s 22(3)(c) of the Companies Act 1997.

Except in the case of unlimited companies, the name of a company must end with the word "Ltd".[176] Section 22(2) provides that a company shall not be registered by a name (a) the use of which would contravene any law;[177] or (b) that is identical or almost identical to the name of another company;[178] or (c) that is identical or almost identical to a name that the Registrar has already reserved and that is still available for registration.

Once the incorporator has decided on a name for the company, he or she must apply in the prescribed form[179] to the Registrar to reserve that name.[180] Once the Registrar has reserved the name, he will advise the applicant that the name is available for use within three months of the date of the notice, unless the reservation is sooner revoked.[181] If an application for incorporation is not made within the three-month period, a further application to reserve the name will have to be made. If the Registrar refuses to reserve the name, the applicant may appeal to the National Court within one month after the date of notification of the Registrar's decision, or within such further time as the court may allow.[182]

176 Companies Act 1997, s 22(1).

177 Any "law" here means, it is suggested, any "enactment". See *Re Bank of New Zealand* [1997] 2 NZLR 239, (1996) 7 NZCLC 261,251. See also *Flight Centre (New Zealand) Ltd v Registrar of Companies* (1994) 7 NZCLC 260,612 and *New Zealand Conference of Seventh-Day Adventists v Registrar of Companies* [1997] 1 NZLR 751; (1997) 8 NZCLC 261,269. See for example, Civil Aviation Act 2000 , s 7(1); International Organizations (Privileges and Immunities) Act (Ch 87), s 9; United Nations and Specialized Agencies (Privileges and Immunities) Act (Ch 88), s 9; Banks and Financial Institutions Act 2000, s 63, s 64; National Institute of Standards and Industrial Technology Act 1993, s 60; Scout Association of Papua New Guinea Incorporation Act (Ch 1032), s 11; Superannuation (General Provisions) Act 2000, s 116; Telecommunications Act 1996, s 197. For example, the Registrar will refuse to register a company with the name "bank" unless the consent of the Bank of Papua New Guinea is first obtained. So for example the Papalain Bank of Bougainville Ltd would not normally be registered.

178 Note that the section does not prevent "similar" names from being reserved. See *Flight Centre (New Zealand) Ltd v Registrar of Companies* (1994) 7 NZCLC 260,612. In *Stanley-Hunt Earthmovers Ltd v Registrar of Companies* (1997) 8 NZCLC 261,403 Tompkins J allowed an appeal against the Registrar of Companies' refusal to order Stanley-Hunt Earthmovers (1996) Ltd to change its name. The learned judge held that "Stanley-Hunt Earthmovers Ltd" and "Stanley-Hunt Earthmovers (1996) Ltd" were almost identical. The judge rejected the Registrar's view that the year marker sufficiently distinguished the names, and was of the view that the name Stanley-Hunt was particularly distinctive and Earthmovers described the nature of its activity and that the names were almost identical. He was of the view that if the keywords and the order in which they appear make them virtually indistinguishable from one another, then the names would be "almost identical".

179 Companies Regulation 1998, Form 6.—Application for reservation of a company name.

180 Companies Act 1997, s 23(1).

181 Companies Act 1997, s 23(3).

182 Companies Act 1997, s 408(1).

It is also possible for a company to apply to the National Court to prevent the Registrar from reserving a name for a company that is too similar to its own name, where the Registrar decides that he will not refuse to reserve the name because it is misleading or deceptive.[183] Some applicants may apply for a name that is intended to mislead the public, in that they seek to represent their business as that belonging to another company.[184] Apart from bringing an action under the Companies Act 1997, a company seeking to protect the name of its business may bring an action of "passing off" and obtain an injunction as well as an account for loss of profits and damages for loss of goodwill.[185] The recent enactment of the Independent Consumer and Competition Commission Act 2002 also provides protection where the use of a similar and confusing company name causes loss to an established business.[186]

In *Flight Centre (New Zealand) Ltd v Registrar of Companies*,[187] Blanchard J rejected an argument that s 22 of the New Zealand Companies Act 1993 applied to a breach of the Fair Trading Act 1986 (NZ), as that Act fell within the definition of an enactment.[188] If the court had accepted that argument, it would have meant that if a name was misleading or deceptive under the Fair Trading Act 1986 (NZ), it would have been unnecessary for a company to go to court for a remedy, but instead could ask the Registrar to direct the offending company to change its name because it contravened s 22 of the Companies Act 1993 (NZ). Blanchard J rejected this argument, regarding the removal of "undesirable" as a ground for refusal of consent under the Act. It is unclear whether this decision will be followed in New Zealand. Although the result of *Flight Centre (New Zealand) Ltd v Registrar of Companies* is in keeping with the tenor of the New Zealand Act to reduce the Registrar's powers of inquiry, the provisions relating to names in the Companies Act 1997 differs markedly from its New Zealand counterpart. The Registrar under the PNG Companies Act 1997 is given more powers of inquiry that his New Zealand counterpart. In addition, the word "undesirable" has been retained in the PNG Companies Act 1997. So, although in New Zealand it is clear that "for the subsection to apply and the Registrar to have

183 See *Taylor Bros Ltd v Taylors Group Ltd* [1988] 2 NZLR 1, also reported as *Taylors Textile Services Auckland Ltd v Taylor Bros Ltd* (1988) 2 NZBLC 103,032; (1988) 2 TCLR 447.

184 *Tussaud v Tussaud* (1890) 44 Ch D 678.

185 See for example, *Brinks Incorporated and Brinks Air Courier Australia Pty Ltd v Brinks Pty Ltd* (1997) N1567.

186 See particularly, Independent Consumer and Competition Commission Act 2002, Part VI.

187 (1994) 7 NZCLC 260,612. See also *New Zealand Conference of Seventh-Day Adventists v Registrar of Companies* [1997] 1 NZLR 751, (1997) 8 NZCLC 261,269, where Fisher J reviewed the issue and came to a similar conclusion to that of Blanchard J.

188 The local equivalent of the Fair Trading Act 1986 (NZ) is the Independent Consumer and Competition Commission Act 2002.

the power to order a company to change its name, the name must contravene an enactment which deals specifically with company names", this is not the position in PNG.

Change of name

A company may decide at a later date to change its name. In addition, the Registrar of Companies may decide that the company ought to change its name, or the National Court may require the company to change its name.[189] The company may initiate the action only after it has been approved by a special resolution of shareholders.[190]

Where the Registrar believes on reasonable grounds that the name under which a company is registered should not have been allowed, the Registrar may serve written notice on the company to change its name by a date specified in the notice, being a date not less than one month after the date on which the notice is served.[191] As Beck and Borrowdale point out, the use of the words "should not have been allowed" seem to refer to the name reservation process and as such, events occurring subsequent to the reservation "can therefore not be relevant".[192]

A change of name takes effect from the date stated on the certificate; however, it does not affect the identity of the company, nor any existing rights or obligations, or legal proceedings by or against the company.[193]

Use of company name

A company must ensure that its name is clearly stated in (a) every written communication sent by, or on behalf of, the company, and (b) every document issued or signed by, or on behalf of, the company that evidences or creates a legal obligation of the company.[194] Failure to comply with these requirements leads to serious consequences. Both the company and every director commits an offence,[195] and every person who issues or signs a document which incorrectly states the name of the company, is personally liable where the document evidences or creates a legal obligation which the company fails to fulfil.[196]

189 See *Taylor Bros Ltd v Taylors Group Ltd* [1988] 2 NZLR 1, also reported as *Taylors Textile Services Auckland Ltd v Taylor Bros Ltd* (1988) 2 NZBLC 103,032; (1988) 2 TCLR 447.

190 Companies Act 1997, s 24(1)(c).

191 Companies Act 1997, s 25(1).

192 Beck, A and Borrowdale, A, *Papua New Guinea Companies and Securities Law Guide* (CCH Australia Ltd, Sydney, 1999), para 205.

193 Companies Act 1997, s 24(4).

194 Companies Act 1997, s 26(1).

195 Companies Act 1997, s 26(5).

196 It is clear that *oral* contracts are not caught by the provisions of s 26: see *RJ Hayes Ltd v Innes-Jones* (1990) 5 NZBLC 66,183.

As Beck and Borrowdale point out, one of the most common misstatements of company names is the omission of the word "Limited" or "Ltd". In such cases the courts easily hold that individuals become liable for the "company's" obligations.[197] The Companies Act 1997 now provides two defences to persons faced with such claims. They will not be liable if they can prove that:[198]

- the other party was aware that it was the company incurring the obligation; or
- it would not be just or equitable to hold them liable.

As Beck and Borrowdale go on to point out, the first of these defences is clear. With regard to the second defence, it will be a question of balancing the equities: "In a situation where both parties have acted in good faith, and there was no indication that the negotiations were on behalf of the company, it would generally be hard to show why the individual should not be liable".[199]

Constitution

Before the Companies Act 1997, a company usually had articles of association and a memorandum of association.[200] These in effect formed the constitution of the company. The memorandum defined the nature of the company,[201] and the articles of association set out the rules governing the internal management of the company.[202] Following the enactment of the Companies Act 1997, many of the rules that were catered for in these two documents are set out in the Act. Furthermore, a company may in some cases vary these rules or adopt additional rules and make provision for this in a constitution.[203]

197 Beck, A and Borrowdale, A, *Papua New Guinea Companies and Securities Law Guide* (CCII Australia Ltd, Sydney, 1999), para 206. See also *Hutt Valley Energy Board v Hayman* (1988) 4 NZCLC 64,244; *National Bank of New Zealand Ltd v Culturi* (1992) 6 NZCLC 68,114; and *Carpet Mill Products (Wellington) Ltd v Williams* (1989) 4 NZCLC 65,330.

198 Section 26(2)(c) and (d) set out defences available to these persons.

199 Beck, A and Borrowdale, A, *Papua New Guinea Companies and Securities Law Guide* (CCII Australia Ltd, Sydney, 1999), para 206.

200 Every company was required to have its own memorandum; in some cases companies were not required to have their own articles. They could adopt model articles set out in the companies legislation.

201 For example, it would set out such matters as: the company's name, the share capital if any, the members' liability.

202 It covered such matters as now meeting were to be convened and conducted, the division of powers between the board of directors and the company in general meeting, how directors were to be appointed, how shares were to be transferred and how dividends were to be declared.

203 In this respect, the constitution replaces the memorandum and articles of association.

A company is not required to have a constitution.[204] If a company does not adopt a constitution, the company, the board, each director, and each shareholder of the company will have the rights, powers, duties, and obligations set out in the Companies Act 1997 itself.[205] In many cases, the rules set out in the Act are sufficient for the company to operate. In some cases however, it may be necessary to set out special rules that will meet the requirements of the shareholders (owners), as the requirements set out in the Companies Act 1997 may be inappropriate.[206] For example, the shareholders of a small company may decide that certain management decisions should be approved of beforehand by the shareholders, and to impose restrictions on the transfer of shares by giving existing shareholders a right of first refusal before shares are offered to outsiders (preemptive rights). On the other hand, the shareholders of larger companies may want to create greater obligations or rights than those afforded by the Companies Act 1997 (for example capital alterations such as share buybacks). These changes may be made by adopting a constitution containing such provisions. If the shareholders decide to have a constitution,[207] it becomes a binding agreement ("contract") between the company and each shareholder, and between each of the shareholders.[208] However, only those provisions which are allowed by the Companies Act 1997 will operate. There are some provisions of the Companies Act 1997 that cannot be changed.[209]

A company may register a constitution with its incorporation documents,[210] or it may adopt a constitution at a later stage: it may change the constitution at any time. Because of its importance, adoption, alteration and revocation of the constitution requires a special resolution of the shareholders.[211] Notice of the adoption, alteration or revocation of a constitution must be given by the board to the Registrar of Companies within one month of the adoption, alteration or revocation.[212] The constitution may contain "matters contemplated by [the Companies Act 1997] for inclusion in the constitution of a company; and such other matters as the company wishes to include in its constitution".

204 Companies Act 1997, s 27.
205 Companies Act 1997, s 29.
206 It should be noted that some provisions of the Companies Act 1997 cannot be changed, even if set out in a constitution.
207 It may be possible to accommodate these needs by means of a shareholders' agreement.
208 Companies Act 1997, s 32.
209 To the extent that the provisions of the constitution are inconsistent with the provisions of the Companies Act 1997, the constitutional provisions will be invalid and of no effect.
210 Companies Act 1997, s 13(1)(f).
211 Companies Act 1997, s 33(2). Section 2(1) of the Companies Act 1997 defines a "special resolution" as "a resolution approved by a majority of 75% or, where a higher majority is required by the constitution, that higher majority, of the votes of those shareholders entitled to vote and voting on the question".
212 Companies Act 1997, s 33(3).

The constitution must be consistent with the Companies Act 1997, since it has no effect to the extent that it contravenes, or is inconsistent with, that Act or any other Act.[213] Provided it is consistent, a company may set out additional rules in its constitution,[214] and in such a case, the company, the board, each director, and each shareholder of the company will have the rights, powers, duties, and obligations set out in the Companies Act 1997 except to the extent that they are lawfully negated or modified by the constitution of the company.[215] The company may have either a short or long form constitution.[216] In the former case, the constitution merely sets out the modifications to the rights, powers, duties, and obligations in the Companies Act 1997 and additional rules. In the case of a long form constitution, all the rules in the Companies Act 1997, as well as additional rules are set out in the constitution.

Rights and obligations conferred by constitution

A company cannot undertake certain acts unless it has a constitution that authorises them. These relate to capital and include:

- acquiring its own shares;[217]
- issuing redeemable shares;[218]
- having two share registers;[219]
- taking out insurance and entering into indemnities for directors.[220]

If it is intended that the shareholders have unlimited liability, this must be stated in a constitution.[221] Any restrictions on capacity must also be included in the constitution.

Companies may either extend or restrict certain rights given by sections of the Companies Act 1997. These include:

- the right of the board of directors to change the name of the company;[222]
- the right to transfer shares;[223]
- the requirement that shareholders pass ordinary resolutions for matters that affect shareholders;[224]

213 Companies Act 1997, s 32(2).
214 Companies Act 1997, s 32(2).
215 Companies Act 1997, s 28.
216 For examples of these types of constitution, see the website of the Papua New Guinea Institute of Directors: www.id.org.pg.
217 Companies Act 1997, s 57(1).
218 Companies Act 1997, s 59.
219 Companies Act 1997, s 68(2).
220 Companies Act 1997, s 140.
221 Companies Act 1997, s 79.
222 Companies Act 1997, s 24(1)(c).
223 Companies Act 1997, s 65(1).
224 Companies Act 1997, s 87.

- the right to include provisions that limit the right of the board and directors;[225]
- the right to restrict remuneration of directors; and[226]
- the power to issue shares instead of dividends.[227]

There are some provisions of the Companies Act 1997 which are mandatory, which companies have no power to alter. These include the requirements that the company must:

- have at least one shareholder, one director and a name;[228]
- pass a special resolution when changing the constitution, approving a major transaction or amalgamation or going into liquidation;[229]
- pass the solvency test before making a distribution.[230]

The mandatory provisions are found throughout the Companies Act 1997 and have little in common except that their alteration might adversely affect the rights of either minority shareholders or creditors of the company.[231]

Alteration of the constitution

According to the underlying law, before the enactment of the Companies Act 1997, as long as they acted *bona fide* for the company as a whole, a majority of shareholders could act as they please in running the business of a company.[232] This has been changed by the Companies Act 1997: the Act has modified majority rights so as to protect minorities. Apart from the major transaction provision (discussed below), there are limits on the majority's power to alter or revoke the constitution. First, if the alteration involves a variation of class rights, a special procedure must be followed: a special resolution agreeing to the proposed changes will be required by each interest group involved.[233] Changes to such shareholder rights as the right to distribution, voting rights, pre-emptive rights and the right to have procedures set out in the Companies Act 1997 and the constitution followed, would require the consent of the affected interest group. Second, if the alteration

225 Companies Act 1997, s 109.
226 Companies Act 1997, s 139.
227 Companies Act 1997, s 52.
228 Companies Act 1997, s 11. If the company has only one director, he or she must be ordinarily resident in PNG. If more than one director, at least one of the directors must be ordinarily resident in PNG.
229 Companies Act 1997, s 88.
230 Companies Act 1997, s 50.
231 Watson, S, Gunasekara, G, Gedye, M, van Roy, Y, Ross, M, Longdin, L, Sims, A and Brown, L, *The Law of Business Organisations* (4th edn, Palatine Press, Auckland, 2003), p 173.
232 *Greenhalgh v Arderne Cinemas Ltd* [1951] Ch 286.
233 Companies Act 1997, s 98. Interest group is defined in s 97.

to the constitution affects a shareholder's liability to the company, it is treated as a distribution, and the procedures required for a distribution would have to be complied with.[234] Third, if the alteration imposes or removes a restriction on the activities of the company, shareholders who consistently oppose the change will have buyout rights.[235] If it affects the rights attaching to shares, the owners of those shares will have buyout rights.[236]

As we noted above, a constitution may be altered by a special resolution. This is usually 75 per cent of the voting shares in the company at a meeting of the company.[237] Alternatively, the procedure set out in s 103 of the Companies Act 1997 may be used.[238]

If the National Court considers that the affairs of the company have or will be carried out in an oppressive, unfairly discriminatory, or unfairly prejudicial manner, under s 152(2)(d) of the Companies Act 1997, the court may alter the company's constitution. The court may also alter the constitution where it is "not practicable to alter the constitution of the company using the procedure set out in [the Companies Act 1997] or in the constitution itself", i.e., the company cannot follow the procedures set out in the Companies Act 1997 or in its constitution.[239]

If the alteration to the constitution is inconsistent with the Companies Act 1997 or causes a breach of duty by a director, a shareholder may apply to the National Court for an alteration to the constitution to be revoked.[240]

A company may be prevented from engaging in conduct that contravenes its constitution. This may be done either following an application for an injunction,[241] or by means of a derivative action.[242] In some situations it is necessary for the company or for its directors or a director to take action required by the constitution. The court may make such orders requiring a director or board of directors of the company to take any action that is required to be taken by the constitution of the company or the Companies Act 1997 "if it is satisfied it is just and equitable to do so".[243]

234 Companies Act 1997, s 55.
235 Companies Act 1997, s 91.
236 Companies Act 1997, s 99.
237 The company's constitution may specify that more than 75 per cent of votes is required for a special resolution of the company. In effect the constitution may require unanimous approval before a constitution may be altered.
238 Companies Act 1997, s 34.
239 Companies Act 1997, s 35.
240 Companies Act 1997, ss 142 and 149.
241 Companies Act 1997, s 142.
242 Companies Act 1997, s 143. See Chapter 10 (Shareholder Remedies) for discussion relating to derivative actions.
243 Companies Act 1997, ss 148 and 150.

Dealings before incorporation

The persons who form a company are called promoters, and they have special duties. They are in a fiduciary relationship with the company and, accordingly, they must act in the interest of the company, not in their own interests. They must disclose any pre-incorporation contracts they made on behalf of the company and account for any secret profits that they derive from setting up the company.

When a company is formed to take over an existing business, it will usually be necessary for the promoters of the company to enter into a contract with the owner of that business to ensure that the company has a right to compel the transfer of any property and to run the business. The promoters will enter into what is known as a "pre-incorporation contract".

The underlying law presented many impediments to the enforcement of pre-incorporation contracts, based mainly on the problem of an agent contracting for a non-existent principal.[244] These matters are now comprehensively dealt with in Part X Division 2 of the Companies Act 1997, and there is no longer any need to have recourse to the underlying law. In fact s 157(5) of the Companies Act 1997 states that: "Notwithstanding any law, where a pre-incorporation contract has not been ratified by a company, or validated by the Court under Section 159, the company may not enforce it or take the benefit of it." This provision should be interpreted as providing that the provisions in the Companies Act 1997 dealing with pre-incorporation contracts, exhaustively set out the law relating to these types of contact.

The Companies Act 1997 permits a contract to be made before a company is incorporated either by "a person on behalf of a company before and in contemplation of its incorporation" or by "a company before its incorporation".[245] The Act permits these pre-incorporation contracts to be ratified within such period as may be specified in the contract, or where no period is specified, then within one month after the incorporation of the company.[246] A pre-incorporation contract may be ratified by a company in the same manner as a contract may be entered into on behalf of a company under s 155.[247] If this is done, the contract is as valid and enforceable as if the company had been a party to the contract when it was made.[248]

The person who made the pre-incorporation contract may be liable in certain situations. First, the contract must have been ratified by the company and a party must have instituted court proceedings against the company for breach of the contract. The court may then (of its own motion, or upon

244 For a discussion of these, see Bucknill, M R, "Pre-incorporation Contracts" (1986) 12 *New Zealand Universities Law Review* 27.

245 Companies Act 1997, s 157(1).

246 Companies Act 1997, s 157(2).

247 Companies Act 1997, s 157(4).

248 Companies Act 1997, s 157(3).

application of the company or the party who instituted the proceedings) order the person who made the contract on behalf of the company to pay damages or the court may grant other relief as it considers "just and equitable", against the person who contracted on behalf of the company. This award may be in addition to or in substitution for any order which may be made against the company.[249]

Where the company does not become incorporated within the time specified in the contract or within a reasonable time if no such time limit is set, or it fails to ratify the contract after it has been incorporated and within the time stated in the contract or a reasonable time if no date is fixed, the person who made the contract on behalf of the company will be personally liable "unless a contrary intention is expressed in the contract".[250] The amount of damages recoverable from him or her will be "the same as the amount of damages that would be recoverable in an action against the company for damages for breach by the company of the unperformed obligations under the contract if the contract had been ratified and cancelled".[251] The person will not be liable, however, if after its incorporation, the company "enters into a contract in the same terms as, or in substitution for, a pre-incorporation contract".[252]

A party to a pre-incorporation contract that a company fails to ratify may apply to the National Court for relief.[253] The court may make any of the following orders:

- an order directing the company to return property, whether real or personal, acquired under the contract to that party;
- any other relief in favour of that party relating to that property;
- an order validating the contract whether in whole or in part.

Section 159(2) of the Companies Act 1997 further provides that the National Court may, "where it considers it just and equitable to do so", make any order or grant any relief it thinks fit against the company or person who contracted on its behalf, and may do so whether or not one of the above listed orders has been made.

249 Companies Act 1997, s 160.
250 Companies Act 1997, s 158(1).
251 Companies Act 1997, s 158(2).
252 Companies Act 1997, s 158(3).
253 Companies Act 1997, s 159. It should be noted that if the pre-incorporation contract is worded in such a way that the contractor on behalf of the company will be personally liable where the company does not ratify the contract or does not ratify it in time, the contract may be enforced against this person without having recourse to the Division of the Companies Act 1997 dealing with pre-incorporation contracts.

Chapter 8

Capacity and Structure of Companies

One of the fundamental features of company law is the concept of corporate personality: in law a company is a legal entity distinct from its shareholders and officers. This chapter discusses this concept and the exceptional situations in which the law ignores the separate personality of a company and focuses on the actual persons responsible for the act in issue.

Capacity of companies[1]

In the early development of company law, there were certain things that companies were not permitted to do because the constitution governing them did not give them such powers. If they attempted to do those acts, the acts were held to be *ultra vires* (void and of no effect). This lack of capacity often caused problems: outside third parties who negotiated in good faith with the company would later find out that they could not enforce the contract because it was invalid.[2] Over the years, the law has been reformed to allow companies to have greater capacity and to protect outsiders. The Companies Act 1997 now provides that a company has full legal capacity: "full capacity to carry on or undertake any business or activity, do any act, or enter into any transaction" subject to the Companies Act 1997 and to any other law.[3] No act of a company and no transfer of property to or by a company is invalid merely because the company did not have the capacity, the right, or the power to do the act or to transfer or take a transfer of the property.[4]

Section 17(2) provides that the constitution of a company may contain a provision relating to the capacity, rights, powers or privileges of the company only where the provision restricts the capacity of the company or those rights, powers and privileges. However, this restriction will not affect outsiders (or third parties, as they are sometimes called). Members of the company

1 Company capacity is also dealt with in Chapter 11 – Corporate Liability.
2 See *AGC (Pacific) Ltd v Woo International Pty Ltd* [1992] PNGLR 100 for a discussion of *ultra vires* transactions before the commencement of the Companies Act 1997.
3 Companies Act 1997, s 17.
4 Companies Act 1997, s 18(1).

may, however, take action to obtain an injunction before the company carries out the action,[5] or to prevent further breaches of the constitution.

The fact that an act is not, or would not be, in the best interests of a company does not affect the capacity of the company to do the act.[6] In some cases where the company does not have capacity to perform certain actions (major transactions) or has capacity only by following certain procedures, the law may treat the transaction differently depending on who is trying to enforce it. The transaction may be treated as valid as far as outsiders are concerned,[7] whereas as far as members or shareholders are concerned, it will be considered to be invalid.

Structure of companies

Despite the fact that a company is a separate legal entity, in reality, some companies may be closely related to each other. Some companies are vertically integrated.[8] At the top of the pyramid is the holding or parent company which holds all or the majority of shares in subsidiary companies. Furthermore, there may be cross-shareholding so that subsidiary companies in the group may own shares in each other or with the parent company. In this way it is very difficult to see that the companies are independent entities, as far as making commercial and other decisions are concerned. Nevertheless, as far as the law is concerned, each of these companies is a separate and distinct entity. In dealing with these companies, the courts are torn between applying the technical legal position, and looking behind the corporate veil to expose the commercial and economic "realities" of the situation.[9]

Characteristics of companies

Company is separate legal entity, distinct from its members and controllers

In *Ome Ome Forests Ltd v Ray Cheong*,[10] Kandakasi J stated in regard to arguments of a defendant, who had some legal training:

> Those arguments in my view fly in the face of his legal education and knowledge and understanding of the attributes of an incorporated company. One of the things a student in company law first learns and

5 Companies Act 1997, s 142.
6 Companies Act 1997, s 18(3).
7 The transaction may, however, be set aside where the outsider "has, or ought to have, by virtue of his position with or relationship to the company, knowledge" that the transaction was beyond the powers of the company: Companies Act 1997, s 19(1).
8 See *WorkCover Authority of NSW v Placer (PNG) Exploration Ltd* (2006) N3003 as an example of this.
9 See *Industrial Equity Ltd v Blackburn* (1977) 137 CLR 567 and *Walker v Wimborne* (1976) 137 CLR 1, where the High Court of Australia was torn between these two principles.
10 (2002) N2289.

cannot easily forget is the separate legal personality of a company distinct from its shareholders going by the well known authority in *Salomon v Salomon & Co Ltd* [1897] AC 22.

Once a company has been registered under the Companies Act 1997, it becomes a separate legal entity, distinct from its shareholders (members) and directors:[11] incorporation allows the assets and obligations of the company to remain separate from the personal assets and obligations of the shareholders and directors, and vice versa.[12] Although the Companies Act 1997 does not expressly say so, the company is given the powers of an individual, and can therefore own property, enter into contracts, and sue and be sued in its own name, just like any natural person.[13] As we noted above, s 17(1) of the Companies Act 1997 provides that a registered company has "full capacity to carry on or undertake any business or activity, do any act, or enter into any transaction". However, in addition, the company has special powers that a corporation has and that a human being does not have: to issue shares and share options, issue debentures and grant floating charges, and to give security by charging uncalled capital.

Although a company will usually have several shareholders and directors (who together constitute the board of directors of the company), it is possible for a company to have only one shareholder and also one director, who may be the single shareholder.[14] The Companies Act 1997 nowhere states that the single shareholder must be the director; however, s 108(2) states that: "In this Act, the terms 'board' and 'board of directors', in relation to a company, mean…where the company has only one director, that director." So unless another director is appointed, the sole shareholder (who is not a director) will be the company's director as well as its board of directors for the purposes of the Companies Act 1997. It also follows from s 128(2)

11 Companies Act 1997, s 16: "A company is a legal entity in its own right separate from its shareholders and continues in existence until it is removed from the register." Although the plural ("shareholders") is used here and in most provisions of the Companies Act 1997, the Companies Act 1997 allows a single person (whether natural or legal) to form a company. That "person" will be the only shareholder and director. Most companies have more than one shareholder and director. Cf Companies Act 1997, s 362(6) and s 42, which refer to a "sole shareholder" and a "shareholder" of a company respectively.

12 The separate legal identity of the company means that a holding company and its subsidiary have separate legal identities, separated by a "corporate veil".

13 Of course, there will be things that a company cannot do because of its inherent nature: e.g., marry, make a will, be guilty of rape. Even in respect of this last category, it is theoretically possible that a corporate entity may be found guilty of rape, if the provisions, for example, stated that the company would be liable if it adopted a corporate culture that encouraged or allowed rape to occur.

14 Section 362(6) of the Companies Act 1997 makes reference to a "sole shareholder". Cf Companies Act 1997, s 108(2) and s 179(1)(b); the latter subsection refers to the situation "where the company has only one director".

that if the company's sole shareholder is also its sole director, that person must be resident in PNG, and from s 129(1) and (3) that the single shareholder-director must be a "natural person".[15] It is therefore possible for a person to be the sole shareholder and director of a company, to constitute the company's board of directors, and to be an employee of the company. As the company is a separate entity, it can employ its directors and members,[16] and provide these persons with such benefits as workers' compensation.

The company's debts and liabilities are separate and distinct from those of the persons who control the company, namely, its shareholders and directors. Separate legal personality together with limited liability means that a "shareholder is not liable for an obligation of the company by reason only of being a shareholder".[17] The shareholder's liability is normally confined to any unpaid amount on his or her shares. Once these amounts are fully paid, the shareholder will not normally incur any further liability. As we shall see, however, in some cases the courts have "lifted" or "pierced" the "corporate veil" to make the shareholders or directors of a company liable for the debts or obligations of the company. In some cases, the courts will also lift the corporate veil to allow the shareholders of a company to obtain benefits.[18]

As we noted above, s 16 of the Companies Act 1997 provides that a company "is a legal entity in its own right separate from its shareholders and continues in existence until it is removed from the register". This merely reinforced the rule laid down in the leading and famous case of *Salomon v Salomon & Co Ltd*.[19]

Mr Salomon ran a leather and boot manufacturing business as a sole trader under the name of "A Salomon & Co". He had carried on business for over 30 years and had built up a successful enterprise. Salomon had several children, including four grown up sons and a daughter, and all of his sons worked in the business with him as employees. He decided to incorporate his business and formed a limited liability company called "A Salomon & Co

15 Section 129(3) of the Companies Act 1997 provides that: "A person that is not a natural person cannot be a director of a company." It is therefore not possible for a company to establish a subsidiary company of which it is the sole shareholder, to be the subsidiary's director. This also applies to two or more companies establishing a subsidiary company.

16 Even if there is only one shareholder who is the only director, the "company" may employ the "shareholder-director" as an employee: see *Lee v Lee's Air Farming Ltd* [1961] AC 12.

17 Companies Act 1997, s 79(1).

18 As we will see later when discussing directors' liability in Chapter 9 (Directors Liability), directors may become liable to third parties for their actions when managing the company. Section 79(2) provides: "Except where the constitution of a company provides that the liability of the shareholders of the company is unlimited, the liability of a shareholder to the company is limited to any liability expressly provided for in this Act or in the constitution of the company."

19 [1897] AC 22.

Pty Ltd". The Companies Act 1862 (UK) that was in force at the time required seven subscribers to the memorandum of association (equivalent to a company constitution) and his wife and each of their five grown-up children purchased one share each. Salomon and his two eldest sons were appointed directors. Salomon controlled the running of the company as a result of an agreement between them that all the other shareholders would be nominees, i.e., they would vote at meetings in accordance with the wishes of Salomon.

The company paid Salomon part of the purchase price for the business immediately on transfer of his business to the company by issuing shares in the company. It also agreed to pay him the remainder of the price over time. This agreement for future payment was secured by the company giving Salomon a floating charge over the company's assets.[20] The effect of the floating charge was that it gave Salomon priority over unsecured creditors: the company's assets had to be used to pay out Salomon in full before they could be used to pay the unsecured creditors. (The same rules of priority would apply to any assignee of the charge.)

When the company's business failed, the assets of the company were not sufficient to pay all the creditors. So Salomon, having a company charge giving him or any assignee priority to repayment, would be entitled to be paid before unsecured creditors. This, however, would only take place if the floating charge was valid. The creditors argued that Salomon should not be paid in priority, because the degree of control he exercised over the company was such that the company should be treated as his agent or trustee. If the company was Salomon's agent or trustee, Salomon would be required to indemnify[21] the company for the debts that it incurred.

The court of first instance and the Court of Appeal held that the company was either the agent or the trustee of Salomon and, as such, Salomon did not have priority to payment; that he was in fact required to indemnify the company for the debts that it had incurred. On appeal to the House of Lords, it was held that Salomon was neither agent nor trustee of the company, and this despite the amount of control that he exercised over the company. The company was in fact a separate entity operating the business. Therefore, the floating charge given to Salomon was valid, and he was entitled to be paid in priority to unsecured creditors of the company. The fact that after repayment in full to Salomon, the company would not have any or sufficient funds to pay back the unsecured creditors for their loans, could not affect the right of Salomon to repayment of his secured loan.

20 For more details on company charges, see Chapter 12 (Shares and Company Financing).

21 To indemnify means to make good a loss which a person has suffered in consequence of the act or default of another.

The case of *Lee v Lee's Air Farming Ltd*,[22] illustrates more graphically the effect of the separate personality of a company. Lee had established (promoted) a company to conduct his business of aerial top dressing.[23] The company's share capital consisted of 3,000 £1 shares: of these, 2,999 were allotted to Lee, with the remaining £1 share held by his solicitor. The company was in effect a one-person company, with Lee exercising full control. Lee was the sole beneficial shareholder and, by the company's articles of association, its sole governing director. He was also employed at a salary as chief pilot of the company. Lee was killed in a flying accident whilst working for the company. His wife sued the company set up by her husband under the Workers' Compensation Act 1922 of New Zealand, alleging that her husband was a "worker" employed by the company for the purposes of the Workers' Compensation Act 1922. The insurance company refused to pay, arguing that Lee and the company were, in fact, one and the same, and that Lee could not therefore be classified as an employee when he was also in total control of the company as its governing director. This line of argument found favour with the New Zealand courts; however on appeal to the Privy Council, the Judicial Committee ruled in favour of the plaintiff. The Privy Council reaffirmed the importance of the separate entity doctrine, holding that the company was a separate legal entity from Lee, and it was therefore possible for Lee to act in two or more capacities at the same time: as promoter, as majority shareholder, as governing director, as agent for, and as an employee of the company. It was therefore possible for Lee as director to give directions to himself as an employee of the company.

Company has capacity to sue and be sued, and company's right of action does not belong to its shareholders

A company may sue and be sued by its own members. This arises from the separate personality of companies. There is, however, another related rule which flows from the separate entity doctrine, and that is, that a company's right of action does not belong to its shareholders. Seeing that a company is a separate legal entity, it is the proper plaintiff or defendant in court proceedings brought by and against it. According to this rule, the proper plaintiff in an action alleging a wrong done to the company by the directors, by a majority of shareholders or by outsiders, is the company itself. The board of directors, who are given the responsibility of running the company, is the body that will decide if and when to bring or defend proceedings in the company's name. As we will see later,[24] however, this can sometimes work

22 [1961] AC 12.
23 A covering of fertiliser spread on soil without being ploughed under. In this case, the top dressing is done by using a plane.
24 See Chapter 10 (Shareholder Remedies).

to the detriment of members who are treated unfairly by the directors. In such cases the law allows shareholders to bring actions against the company, either in their own names or as representatives of the company (derivative actions).

The rule in *Foss v Harbottle*[25] established that where a right of action is vested in a company, the company and the company alone is the proper plaintiff. The rule is a consequence of the separate legal entity doctrine. The rights of the company belong to the company, not to the shareholders. They only have rights in shares in the company, which may or may not allow them to compel the company to bring the action. So the proper plaintiff in an action in respect of a wrong alleged to have been done to a company is the company: in order to redress a wrong done to a company or to recover moneys or damages alleged to be due to a company, the actions should prima facie be brought by the company itself. Because of the separate entity doctrine, no wrong is done, at least directly, to the shareholder. The rule is not limited to shareholders: it applies equally to directors. So if the directors cause the injury, as the directors owe their duties to the company alone, and not to its members or shareholders, it is up to the company to bring proceedings against the director.[26]

Company's property does not belong to its shareholders

It is quite clear that the property owned by a company does not belong to the shareholders or to the directors. It belongs to the company itself. Thus, if a company fails to insure the property, the shareholder cannot claim that he or she has an insurable interest in the property.

In *Macaura v Northern Assurance Co Ltd*,[27] Macaura owned land with timber standing on it. He sold the land and timber to a company that he formed and, in return, received fully paid up shares as compensation for the transfer. The company carried on the business of felling and milling timber. Macaura had insured the timber against loss by fire *in his own name*; however, he did not transfer the insurance policy to the company nor did the company take out a new policy on the timber. A fire destroyed all the timber that had been felled. It was held that the company could not benefit from the insurance taken out by Macaura. When Macaura made a claim his insurers refused to pay, arguing that he had no insurable interest in the timber: only persons with a legal or equitable interest in property were regarded as having an insurable interest. The House of Lords agreed that the insurers

25 (1843) 2 Hare 461 [67 ER 189]; *AGC (Pacific) Ltd v Woo International Pty Ltd* [1992] PNGLR 100; *Ome Ome Forests Ltd v Ray Cheong* (2002) N2289; *The State v Graham Yotchi Wyborn* (2005) N2847.

26 Exceptions to the rule in *Foss v Harbottle* (1843) 2 Hare 461 are more in the nature of qualifications, especially where a member brings an action against the company for infringement of personal rights.

27 [1925] AC 619.

were not liable. Only Macaura's company, as owner of the legal and equitable interest in the timber, had an insurable interest in it. The shareholders had no insurable interest in the company's property. They owned only the shares in the company.

Ability to enter into contracts and acquire, hold and dispose of property

One of the powers which naturally flows from the company being a separate entity, is that it can decide on whether to enter into contracts, and whether to purchase or sell property. The contracts and transfers of land or other property (e.g. chattels like cars and machinery) will be in the name of the company, as such. There are normally no limits as to the types of contract that the company may enter into. In respect of land, however, there are certain limitations. A company may not, for example, purchase or otherwise acquire customary land. Nor may a company apply for the tenure conversion of customary land. If the company has freehold land, it must apply for that land to be converted into substitute leases. The main reasons for these limitations, is that the company is not regarded as a citizen, and in cases where corporate entities are given special privileges in relation to land, it is usually limited to incorporated business groups or incorporated land groups, which are made up of citizens.[28]

Some legislation make a distinction between "national enterprises" and "foreign enterprises" and place greater controls or prohibitions on the types of activity that the foreign enterprises may carry out.[29]

Section 56(1) of the Constitution provides that only citizens may acquire freehold land. Section 56(2)(c) provides that an Act of the Parliament may "define the corporations that are to be regarded as citizens" for the purpose of subsection (1). The Land (Ownership of Freeholds) Act (Ch 359) is the Act which does this. Section 15 sets out the corporations that are to be regarded as citizens for the purposes of s 56(1)(b) of the Constitution. These are:

- the state;
- other governmental bodies within the meaning of Schedule 1.2(1) of the Constitution that are corporations;
- local government councils and local government authorities;
- incorporated land groups within the meaning of the Land Groups Incorporation Act;

28 Land (Tenure Conversion) Act 1963, ss 4 and 7.

29 See Organic Law on the Integrity of Political Parties and Candidates 2003 which makes a distinction between a "non-citizen corporation" and other corporations. See also the Fisheries Management Regulation 2000. Section 3(1) of the Investment Promotion Act 1992, is the main provision that determines the character of the enterprise.

- business groups within the meaning of the Business Groups Incorporation Act; and
- any other corporations that are declared by Act to be corporations that are to be regarded as citizens for the purposes of s 56(1)(b) of the Constitution.[30]

Perpetual succession

Once a company is formed, it continues in existence until it is deregistered.[31] Even if all of the shareholders die, the company continues to exist. Perpetual succession also allows for the continuity of the company despite the fact that there is disagreement between shareholders. A shareholder will usually be able to sell his or her shares, either to the remaining shareholders or to outsiders. As we have seen with partnerships, the falling out between partners will usually lead to the dissolution of the partnership.

Related to this is the ability of shareholders to transfer their shares to outsiders and also to members of their family in succession. Unless the company's constitution otherwise provides, a shareholder may sell or otherwise dispose of his or her shares at any time. When the shareholder dies, the shares owned by that person will be transferred to those who are entitled to them under the will of the testator or because of the rules of intestate succession.

Common seal

Section 75(1)(a) of the Companies Act 1997 implies that all companies need to have a common seal. The section provides that "every company shall, within one month after the issue, or registration of a transfer, of shares in the company, as the case may be, send to every holder of those shares a share certificate signed under the common seal [etc.]". Given that all companies, whether limited or unlimited, must have shares, it means that to comply with s 75, all companies must have a common seal.[32]

Limited liability

Limited liability means that a member or investor in a company is not liable for more than the amount they invest, i.e., than the value of their shares. It is also said that, once a company has been registered, a corporate veil arises between it and its shareholders, directors, employees and anyone else having a direct relationship with the company. This corporate veil

30 No later Acts have declared other corporations to be citizens for the purpose of s 56(1)(b) of the Constitution.

31 Companies Act 1997, s 16.

32 See also s 155(1)(a) of the Companies Act 1997, which refers to a company's "common seal".

should not be lifted to expose these individuals to liability or other legal actions which have been incurred by the company, even if the shareholders or directors were the organs through which the action took place. These twin principles of limited liability and the veil of incorporation play an important role in the functioning of companies.

In respect of a company limited by shares, a member's liability is limited to any unpaid amount on his or her shares.[33] Once the shares are fully paid for, the shareholder cannot be called upon to pay any further moneys to the company. If, however, the shareholder had paid only part of the value of the share (e.g. 50 toea for every share that was worth K1 each), he or she will remain liable to pay the remaining 50 toea multiplied by the number of shares issued to him or her, either to the company when it is a going concern, or if the company is being wound up, to the liquidator.[34] Section 79(2) of the Companies Act 1997 in particular provides:

> (2) Except where the constitution of a company provides that the liability of the shareholders of the company is unlimited, the liability of a shareholder to the company is limited to any liability expressly provided for in this Act or in the constitution of the company.

Persons dealing with companies limited by shares are warned about this limited liability by the need for the company to use the words "Limited" or the abbreviation "Ltd" when the limited liability company's name is used.[35]

It has been said that limited liability is a fundamental principle of corporate law.[36] Despite this assertion, however, the law in some jurisdictions recognises "no liability" companies and unlimited liability corporations. In addition, in almost all jurisdictions, the law allows limited liability to be disregarded in some circumstances so that claims may be brought against directors or creditors for payment of debts incurred by the limited liability company.

With regard to an unlimited company,[37] or no liability company on the other hand, the members of the company are prima facie[38] jointly and

33 Companies are usually referred to as "limited liability companies". However, it is not the company's liability that is limited, but its shareholders'. The company remains fully liable for all debts that it lawfully incurs.

34 Part VI, Division 2 of the Companies Act 1997 deals with liability of shareholders.

35 Companies Act 1997, s 26(3). Cf s 82. Creditors may circumvent the limited liability of the company by insisting on a personal guarantee from the shareholder(s) for the company's debts. This will usually be the case where the company is closely held, e.g. a company whose shares are owned exclusively by a husband and wife.

36 Easterbrook, F H and Fischel, D R, "Limited Liability and the Corporation" (1985) 52 *University of Chicago Law Review* 89.

37 The repealed Companies Act (Ch 146) defined an "unlimited company" as "a company formed on the principle of having no limit placed on the liability of its members".

38 Contracts with certain creditors may vary this principle by, for example, providing limitations on liability.

severally[39] liable for the company's debts without limitation upon a winding up. Because of this extensive liability, unlimited companies are not used in the commercial area, but are used primarily by professional associations where its members are required to be liable without limitation.[40]

Flexibility

Because the persons who incorporate a company may adopt a constitution that suits their needs, this makes the company structure very flexible indeed.[41] Usually, this is done by attaching different rights to different classes of shares. Shares in companies, particularly companies listed on the Port Moresby Stock Exchange, allows a shareholder to sell his or her shares allowing for a flexible investment.

Finance

It is usually easier for companies than for other business organisations to obtain finance from banks and other financial institutions. The continuity provided by perpetual succession allows for long-term financial arrangements. Apart from guarantees provided by members of small companies, the lenders are able to secure repayment by taking out fixed and floating charges against the company's assets.

Floating charges, which are unique to companies, allow a company to continue to deal with the assets the subject of the charge. It means that the business will continue until such time as the floating charge crystallises. Crystallisation occurs when one of the terms of the charge that allows for this happens. The charge thereupon becomes fixed, and the assets subject to the charge can no longer be dealt with by the company without the permission of the lender (chargor).[42]

Lifting the corporate veil

Introduction

It has been said that limited liability is a fundamental principle of company law.[43] Limited liability means that a member or investor in a company is

39 This means that one shareholder may be sued for the entire debt owed by the company. However, that shareholder may then recover (or try to recover) money from the other shareholders so that all shareholders share equally in the debt or expenses (i.e., the shareholder has a right to contribution) from the other shareholders.
40 Accountants Act 1996, s 71.
41 There are some provisions of the Companies Act 1997 that cannot be altered by adopting different provisions in the company's constitution.
42 For a more detailed discussion of this topic, see Chapter 12 (Shares and Company Financing).
43 Easterbrook, F H and Fischel, D R, "Limited Liability and the Corporation" (1985) 52 *University of Chicago Law Review* 89.

not liable for more than the amount they invest, i.e. than the value of their shares. It is also said that once a company has been registered, a corporate veil arises between it and its shareholders, directors, employees and anyone else having a direct relationship with the company, for example creditors of the company. This corporate veil should not be lifted to expose these individuals to liability or other legal actions which have been incurred by the company: even if the shareholders or directors were responsible for these actions. These twin principles of limited liability and the veil of incorporation thus play an important role in the functioning of companies.

As we noted above, once a company is incorporated, it is a separate legal entity. The courts should recognise this when determining the rights of the company and the rights of its members. The separate legal entity doctrine means that members of the company cannot be made responsible for the acts of the company and the company cannot be made responsible for the acts of its members.

In *Salomon v Salomon & Co Ltd*, Lord Macnaghten said:[44]

> The company is at law a different person altogether from the subscribers to the memorandum; and, though it may be that after incorporation the business is precisely the same as it was before, and the same persons are managers, and the same hands receive the profits, the company is not in law the agent of the subscribers or trustee for them. Nor are the subscribers as members liable, in any shape or form, except to the extent and in the manner provided by the Act.

Sometimes, a strict application of the separate legal entity principle can lead to absurd or unjust consequences. It can have an adverse effect on various people, including creditors, shareholders of related companies and victims of corporate torts. The legislature and the courts have struggled with the question of whether the separate legal entity concept should be disregarded and, if so, what should be the basis or bases for such decisions. The practice of disregarding the separate legal entity of a company is commonly referred to as "lifting the corporate veil" or "piercing the corporate veil". In doing so, shareholders may be made personally liable for the company's acts, two or more related companies may be treated as one, or the company may be treated as a sham or façade. The corporate veil thus not only separates individuals from the companies they control, but it also separates subsidiaries from holding companies.

Bases for lifting the corporate veil: good and bad effects

It is generally agreed that the principles of incorporation and limited liability (and the accompanying raising of the corporate veil) have been

44 [1897] AC 22 at 51.

"an incalculable boon to western commerce and ultimately to world prosperity".[45] In *Metal Manufacturers Ltd v Lewis*, Kirby P said:[46]

> There is no doubt that the separation of the corporation from the entrepreneurs behind it provided the 'essential impulse' to the most remarkable economic development of the last 200 years. Although those dealing with a corporation would sometimes suffer upon its insolvency and liquidation, a social judgment was made that their losses were the price occasionally to be borne, where the protective mechanisms of company law had earlier failed, upon the basis that the general immunity of directors, as of investors, from liability for the debts of the corporation promoted the innovation, investment and risk-taking by the corporation essential to economic progress.

Despite the undoubted advantages, the separate legal entity principle has also been the means of avoiding personal liability that would otherwise arise. It has been abused by individuals to evade debts incurred by a company controlled by them for which they ought to be personally responsible if the company fails to repay.

The separate legal entity principle by itself would allow a holding company to carry out speculative or risky transactions through a wholly owned subsidiary, and to avoid liability if the speculation does not succeed. In such a case the principle would allow the holding company to liquidate the wholly owned subsidiary on the ground of insolvency. This would allow the parent or holding company to "escape unscathed"[47] and the creditors of the subsidiary to suffer loss, even if the group as a whole was solvent, and may have many assets.

Despite the problem raised by Lord Halsbury LC in *Salomon's case*[48] of giving effect to the separate entity principle, and also fashioning rules to cater for situations where the corporate veil should be lifted ("a very singular contradiction"), the legislatures and courts have since then, done so on many occasions. They have done so, *inter alia*, to ensure that companies do not gain unfair advantages by hiding behind the corporate veil and to ensure that deserving creditors get paid.

45 Whincup, M "'Inequitable Incorporation': The Abuse of a Privilege" (1981) 2 *The Company Lawyer* 158.

46 (1988) 13 NSWLR 315 at 317.

47 See Schmitthoff, C, "The Wholly Owned and the Controlled Subsidiary" [1978] *Journal of Business Law* 218 at 221.

48 "Either the limited company was a legal entity or it was not. If it was, the business belonged to it and not to Mr Salomon. If it was not, there was no person and no thing to be an agent at all; and it is impossible to say at the same time that there is a company and there is not": *Salomon v Salomon & Co Ltd* [1897] AC 22 at 31.

The principle of a company being a "separate legal personality" is enshrined in s 16 of the Companies Act 1997 which provides that: "A company is a legal entity in its own right separate from its shareholders . . ."

Statutory provisions have introduced significant exceptions or modifications to the separate entity principle. There are several statutory provisions where the separate legal entity principle has been disregarded. In addition to this, the courts, applying the underlying law, have advanced several reasons for disregarding the same. There are not many PNG cases where the matter has come before the courts for consideration, and so reference will sometimes be made to the position in England, New Zealand and Australia with a view to seeing if they could offer some guidance to judges in PNG faced with similar cases in the future. We shall first look at PNG cases explaining the underlying law position, and then to statutory exceptions.

Courts realise that the corporate veil may lead to injustice or other problems. In *Littlewoods Mail Order Stores Ltd v McGregor*,[49] Lord Denning MR stated that:[50]

> The doctrine laid down in *Salomon v Salomon & Co Ltd* [1897] AC 22 has to be watched very carefully. It has often been supposed to cast a veil over the personality of a limited company through which the courts cannot see. But that is not true. The courts can and often do draw aside the veil. They can, and often do, pull off the mask. They look to see what really lies behind.

In *Salomon v Salomon & Co Ltd*,[51] Lord Halsbury stated that "it is impossible to say at the same time that there is a company and there is not". Despite this seemingly categorical statement, within three years of the decision, an English court had held that it was permissible to disregard the corporate legal personality of a company and expose the reality of the situation.[52] Since then, although academics and some judges have struggled to find the basis or bases on which courts will disregard the separate personality of a company,[53] many judges have been content to lift the veil when they consider the facts of the case require it, without bothering too much about the rationale for so doing. It has been said of this area that there is "little evidence of consistency and considerable material for debate",[54] and

49 [1969] 3 All ER 855.

50 [1969] 3 All ER 855 at 860.

51 [1897] AC 22 at 31.

52 *Re Carl Hirth* [1899] 1 QB 612.

53 The process has variously been described as *lifting* the corporate veil, *piercing* the corporate veil, *penetrating* the corporate veil etc. For a consideration of some of the various terms used, see Pickering, M, "The Company as a Separate Legal Entity" (1968) 31 *Modern Law Review* 481 at 481–482. In *Ome Ome Forests Ltd v Ray Cheong* (2002) N2289 Kandakasi J referred to the process as piercing the "corporate shield".

54 Beck, A, "The two sides of the corporate veil", in Farrar, J H (ed), *Contemporary Issues in Company Law* (CCH, Auckland, 1987), p 72.

that the grounds on which the jurisdiction to lift the corporate veil may be exercised "form something of a miscellany".[55] In *Briggs v James Hardie & Co Pty Ltd*,[56] Rogers AJA lamented the fact that "there is no common, unifying principle, which underlies the occasional decision of courts to pierce the corporate veil". Lifting the corporate veil has also been said to be "rare, severe, and unprincipled",[57] with many of the decisions being "irreconcilable and not entirely comprehensible". It has been said that the circumstances in which the courts in common law jurisdictions will lift the corporate veil are "ill-defined and unpredictable".[58]

In analysing when the courts will lift the veil of incorporation, many commentators divide the various instances where the courts have lifted the veil into several distinct categories. However, there is no agreement amongst them as to the type or number of categories, and some cases which seem to be similar, have been placed into different categories. Even the ultimate policy for lifting the veil is elusive, some considering that it ultimately depends on "policy" or "justice".

As a general rule courts are most unwilling to lift the corporate veil, although there is considerable variation within the major common law jurisdictions: American courts are most likely to lift the veil, whereas Australian courts are the most unwilling.[59] The PNG courts have tended to veer towards a willingness to lift the corporate veil.

In formulating guiding principles and particular circumstances when the courts in PNG will lift the corporate veil, the primary question is whether they ought to develop the law without recourse to overseas developments. If it is decided to have recourse to such decisions, the issue then becomes which jurisdiction to look at: there is the choice of England (because of the adoption provisions in the Constitution and in the Underlying Law Act 2000) and New Zealand, on whose Companies Act 1993 the latest Companies Act 1997 was modelled. Australian authorities may also serve as a guide, though there is no compelling reason for this. Decisions from the US, where the courts are more willing to lift the corporate veil than in

55 Grantham, R B and Rickett, C E F, *Company and Securities Law: Commentary and Materials* (Brookers, New Zealand, 2002), p 222.

56 (1989) 16 NSWLR 549 at 567.

57 Easterbrook, F H and Fischel, D R, "Limited Liability and the Corporation" (1985) 52 *University of Chicago Law Review* 89. Smellie J in *Hallam v Ryan* (1990) 5 NZCLC 66,123 at 66,148 stated that it was "notoriously difficult to discern any established approach by the courts to the question of lifting the corporate veil".

58 Whincup, M, "'Inequitable Incorporation' – the Abuse of a Privilege" (1981) 2 *The Company Lawyer* 158 at 159. Earlier editions of LCB Gower's *Principles of Modern Company Law* stated that "Judicial developments have essentially been haphazard and irrational . . . The results in individual cases may be commendable but [the courts' policy] smacks of palm-tree justice rather than the application of legal rules".

59 In between these two extremes, in order of likelihood, are Canada, England and New Zealand.

Australia or New Zealand also compete for application.[60] This raises questions as to the authority of the case law from these jurisdictions.

Although PNG courts are at liberty to decide the underlying law relating to lifting the corporate veil without reference to cases from any other jurisdiction, there are several considerations which point in different directions. The High Court of Australia was, in the pre-Independence period, the ultimate appellate court within the PNG appellate jurisdiction, and its decisions were binding on the pre-Independence Supreme Court and Full Court. Despite a severing of the link at Independence, the judgments of the National and Supreme Courts are still full of references to Australian authorities, and they continue to hold much persuasive authority in PNG courts. On the other hand, the Constitution (Schedule 2.2) provided that, subject to certain conditions, "the principles and rules that formed, immediately before Independence Day, the principles and rules of common law and equity in England are adopted, and shall be applied and enforced, as part of the underlying law". It is now generally believed that these provisions in Schedule 2.2 of the Constitution have been superseded by the Underlying Law Act 2000, which similarly provides that the principles and rules of the common law and equity of England that obtained immediately before 16 September 1975 (i.e., Independence Day) are "sources of the underlying law".[61]

It is also possible that the law of New Zealand relating to lifting the corporate veil may be most relevant in determining what the underlying law rules on this matter are. In at least one case,[62] Kandakasi J applied the common law of New Zealand relating to lifting the corporate veil based on the fact that the Companies Act 1997 was modelled on the New Zealand Companies Act 1993.[63] The matter is made the more difficult to determine

60 The "American approach" may also be looked at with profit. The courts will lift the corporate veil: "If any general rule can be laid down... it is that a corporation will be looked upon as a legal entity as a general rule, and until sufficient reason to the contrary appears but, when the notion of legal entity is used to defeat public convenience, justify wrong, protect fraud, or defend crime, the law will regard the corporation as an association of persons", per Sanborn J in *United States v Milwaukee Refrigerator Transit Co* (1905) 142 Fed 247 at 255, or where it is used to defeat an overriding public policy: *Bangor Punta Operations Inc v Bangor & Aroostook R Co* (1974) 417 US 398. See *Ford's Principles of Corporations Law* (11th edn), para 4.255. For the approach in other, particularly European, jurisdictions, see Ottolenghi, S, "From Peeping Behind the Corporate Veil, to Ignoring it Completely" (1990) 53 *Modern Law Review* 338.

61 See also the Laws Adoption and Adaptation Act (Ch 20) and the Goods Act (Ch 251), s 58(2) for specific application of "rules of the common law of England (including the law merchant)" in respect of contracts for the sale of goods, and the Marine Insurance (Adopted) Act (Ch 258), s 3 ("rules of the common law of England – including the law merchant – apply to contracts of marine insurance)".

62 *Odata Ltd v Ambusa Copra Oil Mill Ltd* (2001) N2106.

63 If one were to take this line of reasoning to its logical conclusion, one can argue that Canadian and US judgments, at least in some situations, are of persuasive value, seeing that the New Zealand Companies Act 1993 is at least partly based on US and Canadian provisions and principles.

because, although there is authority soon after Independence[64] that judges in PNG "will be more inclined to go behind corporate structures than judges in other countries have been prepared to", i.e., they will feel less restrained in lifting the corporate veil than judges in other jurisdictions, the courts have not yet firmly established this line of reasoning. The thinking behind this is that the courts in PNG will develop the law in line with local conditions, and will be more prepared to lift the corporate veil than courts in most overseas jurisdictions (including New Zealand, it would appear).

In *CBS Inc v Ranu Investments Pty Ltd*,[65] Pritchard J said:[66]

> It may well be that the defendant company, despite its paid-up share capital of K2.00, is both wealthy and profitable. However, I do not think that judges have to go around with their eyes shut and the fact is in this country, as has happened elsewhere, many companies have been incorporated with little or no asset backing and have gone into receivership. It is a fact that individual persons have caused companies to be incorporated which have become insolvent only to incorporate another and continue trading, leaving the creditors of their previous company (or companies) lamenting. There has been considerable reverence paid by the Courts of many countries to the concept of a company being a legal person in its own right. In this regard I am somewhat of a heretic and in a newly developing country such as ours, when under the *Constitution* the judges of this Court must develop the rules of the underlying law of this nation in accordance with the principles of natural justice and ensure that such law develops as a coherent system in a manner that is appropriate to the circumstances of the country from time to time, *I believe that judges will be more inclined to go behind corporate structures than judges in other countries have been prepared to*. (Emphasis added.)

Although, on at least two occasions, these sentiments were referred to with apparent approval, they have never been *specifically* approved or adopted. Despite this lack of express approval, it is submitted that the trend of the few cases on lifting the corporate veil decided in PNG is towards more flexibility in lifting the corporate veil. In *Odata Ltd v Ambusa Copra Oil Mill Ltd*,[67] Kandakasi J stated:

> As Pritchard J said in *CBS Inc v Ranu Investments Pty Ltd* [1978] PNGLR 66, judges should not approach the issue with their eyes shut.

64 *CBS Inc v Ranu Investments Pty Ltd* [1978] PNGLR 66 (Pritchard J).
65 [1978] PNGLR 66.
66 [1978] PNGLR 66 at 68.
67 (2001) N2106.

> They should ever be vigilant to detect any possible instance of an attempt at abusing the corporate veil's protect[ion] and make appropriate orders. This is important in a newly developing country such as ours, where there is a Constitutional duty on judges of the National and Supreme Courts to help develop the underlying law for the nation in accordance with the principles of natural justice. The onus is therefore, on a judge to determine in each case whether it is appropriate to lift the corporate veil and help develop the rules with fairness and equity as the main guiding principles. On my part therefore, in full appreciation of that duty, I have already expressed the view that, the principles emerging from a survey of overseas authorities should be the guiding principles in addition to the principles already emerging from the few local cases to date.[68]

Exceptions to the separate entity doctrine

There are several cases where shareholders or officers of the company have been made personally liable for the debts of a company. There have also been situations where the benefits normally given to a company have been given to a shareholder or directors. The same applies in respect of companies within a group where benefits or liabilities of the subsidiary company have been treated as belonging to the parent company and vice versa. Some of these cases depend upon common law underlying law rules relating to when the courts will lift the corporate veil; others, however, are based upon statute. (Statute may either expressly or impliedly refer to situations where the corporate veil should be lifted.) Several provisions of the Companies Act 1997 provide for the corporate veil to be lifted. There are also provisions in other Acts that allow the courts to lift the corporate veil. There are therefore two types of categories where the separate legal personality of a company may be disregarded: the underlying law and statute.

Disregard of the separate entity doctrine according to the underlying law

The corporate veil may come between shareholders and outsiders, between the company and its shareholders, or where several economic entities are joined or one economic entity divided.

In *Kappo No 5 Pty Ltd v Wong*,[69] the Supreme Court referred to the fact that there had been "a lack of judicial unanimity with regard to the general

68 The "principles emerging from a survey of overseas authorities" seem to be those that the judge extracted from the CCH publication, *New Zealand Company Law and Practice*.
69 [1998] PNGLR 544.

principles about the circumstances in which the corporate veil may be lifted". In saying this it was echoing the lament of Rogers AJA in *Briggs v James Hardie & Co Pty Ltd*,[70] referred to earlier, that "there is no principled approach to be derived from the authorities". However, it declined to take up the challenge to lay down definitive rules on the matter. Nor have later cases, with the exception of Kandakasi J in *Odata Ltd v Ambusa Copra Oil Mill Ltd*,[71] attempted to do so. Despite the apparent acceptance by Kandakasi J that it was "not possible and is undesirable to categorise the circumstances in which there can be a departure" from the separate entity doctrine (i.e. to set out rules when the corporate veil may be lifted), he proceeded to lay down a set of principles and circumstances when the courts will lift the corporate veil. This categorisation was later adopted by Salika J in *The State v Graham Yotchi Wyborn*,[72] and Lay J in *WorkCover Authority of NSW v Placer (PNG) Exploration Ltd*.[73]

Despite statements by courts and academics that "there is no common, unifying principle, which underlies the occasional decision of courts to pierce the corporate veil", some commentators have sought to distill rules or principles that bring some order to the area. A common classification attempts to set out the law in England in nine categories where the courts are willing to lift the corporate veil:[74]

1. agency;
2. fraud;
3. group enterprises;
4. trusts;
5. torts;
6. enemy;
7. tax;
8. the Companies Act itself;
9. other legislation.

Instead of adopting the above approach, Kandakasi J in *Odata Ltd v Ambusa Copra Oil Mill Ltd*[75] was content to rely on a statement of the position in New Zealand as set out in a CCH publication, *New Zealand Company Law and Practice*. He considered that these principles were "relevant and appropriate for our jurisdiction in addition to the position already developed (whether by *obiter dicta* or not)" by PNG cases.

70 (1989) 7 ACLC 841.
71 (2001) N2106.
72 (2005) N2847.
73 (2006) N3003.
74 See for example, Farrar, J, *Company Law* (4th edn, Butterworths, London, 1998), p 70. Earlier editions referred to seven categories: torts and other legislation were excluded.
75 (2001) N2106.

He therefore adopted them as "proper principles for consideration on the issue of whether or not the corporate veil should be lifted". From his reading of the relevant sections of the New Zealand CCH text, he considered that "the following position emerges":

- The fundamental starting point is the importance of the doctrine of corporate personality and any suggestion to depart from it should be treated with caution.
- The doctrine is to be applied unless the result is so unsatisfactory that it warrants a departure from it.
- It is not possible and is undesirable to categorise the kind of circumstances in which there can be a departure.
- It is appropriate to depart from the doctrine if a company or its personality is being used as a façade, stratagem or simulacrum in an attempt to circumvent the reality of the situation (*Woolfson v Strathclyde Regional Council* [1978] SC 90 (HL), *Tunstall v Steigmann* [1962] 2 QB 593). There is some difficulty with this because there is some difficulty in determining the true meaning of the word 'façade' and determining whether there was an intention to conceal the true facts which was a test developed by the decision in *Chen v Butterfield* [1996] NZCLC 261,086.
- In a contractual context there is a need for some element of fraud or sharp practice in that party's conduct, or it must otherwise be unconscionable in the sense of equitable fraud to adhere to the doctrine (see *Jones v Lipman* [1962] 1 All ER 442, *Gilford Motor Co Ltd v Horne* [1933] Ch 935).
- The veil will not be lifted to allow for the application of the unanimous assent rule to hold a company liable by the actions of the shareholders acting unanimously.
- It is not sufficient that the mere presence of the corporate veil leads to an inequitable or generally unfair result. The interests of commercial certainty dictate that a strong case is needed to lift the corporate veil (see *Trevor Ivory Ltd v Anderson* (1992) 6 NZCLC 67,611; [1992] 2 NZLR 517).
- The corporate veil may be lifted if doing so is justified in all the circumstances of the case. The case on point is *Creasey v Breachwood Motor Ltd* [1992] BCC 638.
- Where a statute provides either expressly or by implication for a lifting of the corporate veil, it may be lifted.

From the above list, it will be seen that propositions or factors 1 and 3 are general rules or principles (a "fundamental starting point") ("not possible and undesirable to categorise the circumstances in which the corporate veil may be lifted") that show that the doctrine of corporate personality is important, and perhaps impliedly, that the person who wants to establish it, bears the burden of proof (i.e., "any suggestion to depart from it should be treated with caution"). The other propositions (number 2 and numbers 4 to 9, adding up in all to seven circumstances) are situations where the court will lift the corporate veil.

In *WorkCover Authority of NSW v Placer (PNG) Exploration Ltd*,[76] Lay J stated that there was no need for him "to analyze the principles in great detail". He stated, however, that the authorities of *Pinpar Development Pty Ltd v TL Timber Development Pty Ltd*[77] and *Odata Ltd v Ambusa Copra Oil Mill Ltd*[78] established the situations where the court would lift the corporate veil: "generally in a contractual situation there must be some element of sharp practice or fraud" and where the actions of a company were "a mere façade" for another company.

There are two other "situations" that need to be added to Kandakasi J's seven situations, where the court should consider lifting the corporate veil. In *Ome Ome Forests Ltd v Ray Cheong*,[79] Kandakasi J added a situation that he had overlooked in his elucidation of the law in *Odata Ltd v Ambusa Copra Oil Mill Ltd*:[80] that the court may also lift "the corporate shield" where a party attempts to use it in order to avoid criminal prosecution. It also appears that his Honour also overlooked the "agency" exception, although *Odata* was itself a case where the agency exception applied. It is suggested that there is another overarching situation set out in the Constitution,[81] that may also apply: where not to lift the corporate veil would be harsh or oppressive. As such, there are at least ten situations that a court needs to take into account in deciding whether to lift the corporate veil. It should also be noted that these circumstances are not mutually exclusive, so that one set of facts may give rise to two or more situations where a court may lift the corporate veil. Sometimes the facts of the case may cause an underlying law exception and a statutory exception to apply.[82]

After setting out the relevant factors, Kandakasi J continued:

> Our *Companies Act 1997* is similar to the New Zealand Companies Act. Besides, I consider these principles relevant and appropriate for our jurisdiction in addition to the position already developed (whether

76 (2006) N3003.
77 [1999] PNGLR 139.
78 (2001) N2106.
79 (2002) N2289.
80 (2001) N2106.
81 An "expansive view" of s 41 is to the effect that it "should be regarded as of general application" (see for example, *Premdas v The Independent State of Papua New Guinea* [1979] PNGLR 329, per Prentice CJ).
82 See for example, *Neville v Privatization Commission* (2001) N2184.

by *obiter dicta* or not). Hence I adopt them as proper principles for consideration on the issue of whether or not the corporate veil should be lifted.

Harsh or oppressive conduct

The Constitution provides that courts may give relief in situations where to allow matters to stand would be "harsh or oppressive". Section 41 of the Constitution declares to be invalid ("an unlawful act"), *inter alia*, any "harsh or oppressive" acts done under a valid law,[83] and the section can be applied to overturn transactions that were validly entered into.[84] Section 41(1) of the Constitution provides that any act that is done under a valid law but in the particular case: (a) is "harsh or oppressive"; or (b) is not warranted by, or is disproportionate to, the requirements of the particular circumstances or the particular case; or (c) is otherwise not, in the particular circumstances, reasonably justifiable in a democratic society having a proper regard for the rights and dignity of mankind, is an "unlawful act". Most civil law claims have been brought in relation to granting relief against the exercise of the mortgagee's power of sale, and have so far concentrated on s 41(1)(a) and (b), i.e., that the action was "harsh or oppressive" or was not warranted by, or was disproportionate to, the requirements of the particular circumstances or of the particular case.[85] It is argued that s 41 of the Constitution may be used in some situations to lift the corporate veil.

Unfair or inequitable result

In *Neville v Privatization Commission*,[86] Kandakasi J held that the court was entitled to lift the corporate veil where to not do so would lead to "an unfair or inequitable result". That case was concerned with the privatisation of the Papua New Guinea Banking Corporation (PNGBC). The state owned the only share in Finance Pacific, which in turn was the only shareholder of PNGBC. The state-owned share in Finance Pacific was transferred to the Privatization Commission under the provisions of the Privatization

83 For a general consideration of this provision, see Kwa, E L, *Constitutional Law of Papua New Guinea* (Lawbook Co, Sydney, 2001), pp 153–154.

84 See Amankwah, H A, Mugambwa, J T, Muroa, G, *Land Law in Papua New Guinea* (LBC Information Services, Sydney, 2001), pp 181–182.

85 Arguments relating to the meaning of "not, in the particular circumstances, reasonably justifiable in a democratic society having a proper regard for the rights and dignity of mankind" have in the main focused on breaches of constitutional rights: see Chalmers, D, "Human Rights and What is Reasonably Justifiable in a Democratic Society" (1975) 3 *Melanesian Law Journal* 92–102.

86 (2001) N2184.

Act 1999.[87] The Nevilles brought court proceedings against the Privatization Commission (the Commission) to prevent PNGBC from proceeding with a mortgagee sale of the assets of the Nevilles and Coecon Ltd (Coecon), a company all of whose shares were owned by the Nevilles.

The Nevilles and the Commission agreed to a consent order for an injunction preventing PNGBC from proceeding with a mortgagee sale until a court claim for several million Kina by Coecon against the state for breach of contract was completed. (Coecon had obtained judgment against the state, but damages were yet to be assessed.) PNGBC then applied to be joined as a party to the proceedings, arguing that the Commission had no power to consent to the injunction on its behalf. It relied on the principle of separate legal entity upon incorporation under the Companies Act 1997. As such, in deciding whether to dissolve the injunction, Kandakasi J had to consider, *inter alia*, whether he could look behind the corporate veil to determine issues of ownership and control of PNGBC.

Before privatisation occurred, Finance Pacific was at all times owned and controlled by the state. Finance Pacific indirectly owned the entire shareholding in PNGBC. In effect, therefore, PNGBC was owned and controlled by the state, both prior to and following the privatisation of Finance Pacific.

After privatisation of Finance Pacific, the state continued to be the sole owner of PNGBC. Likewise, the Commission was an entity of the state charged with the duty to privatise state entities identified by the government of the day for privatisation. The Commission held the assets of such entities that were in the course of privatisation on behalf of the state pending the state divesting itself of them. In other words, the Commission was the entity created by the Privatization Act 1999 through which the state could divest itself of state-owned businesses. Hence, the Commission was simply an agent of the state for the purposes of transferring the assets of an entity identified for privatisation to new owners.

The Nevilles claimed that the reason why Coecon could not repay its loans to PNGBC on time, thus leading to the appointment of a receiver by PNGBC and attempts to carry out a mortgagee sale, was because of the failure of the state to pay amounts as they fell due under a multi-million Kina contract between the state and Coecon. Coecon had considerable difficulties in obtaining payment from the state because of cash-flow problems of the state, rather than any dispute with the state with regard to liability. As a result of this, Coecon incurred substantial costs in keeping staff and equipment at the project site because of a request by the state to do so, and following assurances by state officers that "funds would soon

87 This Act was passed to allow for the orderly privatisation of state-owned assets. By virtue of s 14(2) of the Privatization Act 1999, a notice in the National Gazette had the effect of vesting the "assets, management, administration and control of the . . . enterprise" in the Commission.

become available" to pay the outstanding debt owed by the state to Coecon. "The receivership was brought about solely by the fact that the payments due in respect of the . . . contract were not made by the State to Coecon."

The Nevilles and the Privatization Commission agreed to the grant of an injunction preventing PNGBC from proceeding with a mortgagee sale of the Nevilles' assets whilst the Nevilles pursued a claim for the recovery of a substantial debt due and owing to them from the state, recovery of which would fully settle all of the debts that were owed to PNGBC. PNGBC had not consented to the injunction and argued that the Privatization Commission had neither the power nor authority to consent to the injunction on its behalf. It relied on the fact that it was a separate legal entity that was incorporated under the Companies Act 1997. On the other hand, the Nevilles and the Privatisation Commission argued that, once the bank was identified for privatization and placed under the control of the Privatisation Commission, even though not yet privatised, it could no longer assert its separate personality. The court held that once PNGBC was placed under the control of the Privatization Commission, it was not entitled to raise its separate legal personality as against the Commission and other parties.

Kandakasi J was of the view that the circumstances dictated a lifting of the corporate veil so that the actions of the Commission could be seen in their proper perspective. He held that: "It appears most unfair for the State through PNGBC to force the Nevilles to the point of bankruptcy and then seek to gain from such conduct."

Kandakasi J further stated:

> Generally the law allows for a lifting of the corporate veil even in situations in which there is no clear statutory or other sources of vesting control in any other entity or an authority. The few cases on this issue in the country to date appear ready to lift the corporate veil *if the control of a company is in somebody else*. (Emphasis added.)

He held that it was "unconscionable" for the state, as the controller of PNGBC through the Commission, to take steps to sell the assets of Coecon. This was particularly so after having brought about Coecon's indebtedness to PNGBC by the state's own failure to make the payments due to Coecon under the construction contract. By not paying Coecon the amounts which were due to it under the construction contract, the state has caused Coecon to fall into arrears with PNGBC. He stated:

> In *Odata Ltd v Ambusa Copra Oil Mill Ltd* (2001) N2106, I also found that, *if the circumstances of the case warrant a lifting of the corporate veil*, then the Court should not hesitate to so order . . . One of the circumstances in which the Courts will always grant injunctions, is where the other party has acted *unconscionably*. (Emphasis added.)

He held that PNGBC was not entitled to raise its separate legal personality once it came under the powers of the Commission pursuant to ss 14 and 1 of the Privatization Act 1999:

> What the State through PNGBC appears to be doing in this case in effect is a departure from the State's duty to protect its people from *unjust deprivation of property or any other unfair conduct*. Even if it was not in breach of any specific law, it would appear to amount to the *State taking an unfair advantage against its own natural and corporate citizens* . . . The circumstances do dictate a lifting of the corporate veil so that the actions of the shareholder can be seen in its proper perspective. This, as noted already, reveals that the sole shareholder and or the ultimate beneficiary of PNGBC is *the State, on which account the Nevilles have suffered serious financial difficulties*. (Emphasis added.)

Agency

The courts will lift the corporate veil when a subsidiary company is considered to be acting as an agent of a holding company. The courts will, in such cases, avoid the commercial reality of the separate entities and treat the group as a single entity. Many of the cases in this area are also relevant to group enterprises.

In *Odata Ltd v Ambusa Copra Oil Mill Ltd*,[88] Kandakasi J acknowledged that agency was a ground for lifting the corporate veil. In doing so he was recognising the fact that where a subsidiary company is found to be acting as an agent of a holding or parent company the courts are more willing to lift the corporate veil, disregard the separate entities comprising the group, and treat the group of companies as a single enterprise.

The main English case dealing with agency as a ground for lifting the corporate veil is *Smith, Stone & Knight Ltd v Birmingham Corporation*.[89] Birmingham Corporation compulsorily acquired premises owned by the plaintiff, Smith, Stone and Knight Ltd. A wholly-owned subsidiary company belonging to the plaintiff conducted a business on the premises. However, the corporation rejected a compensation claim from the plaintiff because it had been an occupier of the land only for a short time. The business had previously been carried on by the plaintiff and the business had never been transferred formally to the subsidiary. Its manager had been appointed by the plaintiff company, it kept no books of its own and it

88 (2001) N2106. The issue of agency was raised but not developed in *Kappo No 5 Pty Ltd v Wong* [1998] PNGLR 544.
89 [1939] 4 All ER 116.

paid no rent. It was successfully argued by the plaintiff that the subsidiary carried on the business as its agent and that, as principal, it was they who should be compensated for the disturbance caused by the compulsory acquisition. The court agreed with this argument and ordered compensation to be paid to the holding company. In deciding whether the subsidiary was the agent of the holding company, Atkinson J set out six requirements, all of which had to be met, before a court could hold that a subsidiary was carrying on the holding company's business.

These requirements (questions) were:

(i) Were the profits treated as the profits of the parent company?
(ii) Were the persons conducting the business appointed by the parent company?
(iii) Was the parent company the head and brain of the trading venture?
(iv) Did the parent company govern the venture, decide what should be done and what capital should be spent on the venture?
(v) Did the parent company make the profit by its skill and direction? and
(vi) Was the parent company in effectual and constant control of the subsidiary company?

In *Odata Ltd v Ambusa Copra Oil Mill Ltd*,[90] Kandakasi J found that the National Provident Fund (NPF) formed Ambusa Copra Oil Ltd (Ambusa) as its subsidiary. The customary landowners provided customary land for a joint venture with NPF for the establishment of a Copra Oil Mill. Their contribution of the land was considered to amount to the value for the purchase of 50 per cent of the shares in Ambusa Copra Oil Mill Ltd. Although NPF owned only half of the shares in Ambusa, it operated Ambusa as if it had ownership of all the shares. It had control of the board and the activities of Ambusa, including the entering into and finalisation of negotiations with Odata for the purchase, construction and operation of a copra oil mill. NPF also signed the contract and terminated it without any input from the customary landowners through their company, Ambusa Ltd. Even when Ambusa (the subsidiary company) was sued by Odata, NPF assumed the carriage and conduct of the defence of Ambusa in the court proceedings.

The elements which led Kandakasi J to hold that an agency relationship had been created between NPF (as principal) and Ambusa (as agent) were:

- The majority of the board of directors of Ambusa came from NPF.
- The two landowner representatives (directors) attended only the first meeting of the board.

90 (2001) N2106. The issue of agency was raised but not developed in *Kappo No 5 Pty Ltd v Wong* [1998] PNGLR 544.

- No landowner was ever involved in the negotiations that led to the contract between Odata and Ambusa.
- A NPF representative conducted the negotiations and signed the contract with Odata in his capacity as executive director of Ambusa, which was a position he held because of his employment with NPF.
- There was no evidence to show that the landowners knew anything about the business they were entering into with NPF; in the absence of any evidence to the contrary it was clear that the landowners did not have the "slightest clue" about the business.
- The landowners had no meaningful say or any part in the running of the affairs of Ambusa.
- Everything was run by NPF from its boardroom by NPF employees.
- Even NPF letterheads were used in communications with Odata.
- The decision to terminate was forced on Ambusa because NPF decided to "pull out" of the joint venture with the landowners.
- In the present case, NPF formed Ambusa as "its subsidiary".
- NPF had control of the board and the activities of Ambusa including:
    - the entering into negotiations with Odata;
    - finalising negotiations with Odata;
    - signing the contract with Odata;
    - eventual termination of the contract with Odata;
    - the carriage and conduct of the defence of Ambusa during the current legal proceedings.

These factors pointed to Ambusa being only an agent of NPF. Ambusa was a sham or "front for NPF for all practical purposes" (the fourth factor in the nine factors listed by Kandakasi J). The above circumstances also made the eighth factor applicable: "The corporate veil may be lifted if doing so is justified in all the circumstances of the case." It was only fair that "the corporate veil should be lifted" to allow NPF to face Odata's claim.

Fairness

In *Jacob Luke v John Ralda*,[91] the parties entered into a contract for the sale of a second-hand bus. Neither party had a clear appreciation of the distinction between a company "owned" by the respondent and the respondent in his personal capacity. The respondent claimed that he entered into a contract with the appellant in his personal capacity. The appellant claimed that the contract was with his company and, therefore, that the proper party to be sued was the company and not him personally. Woods J dismissed an appeal against a decision of the District Court, which lifted the corporate veil and ordered the appellant to be personally liable for breach of warranty of fitness.

91 [1992] PNGLR 549.

The appellant had sold a defective vehicle to the respondent. At no time did the appellant make it known to the respondent that he was acting for a company, which he "owned" and managed. His Honour found that, in the particular circumstances of the case, it was "fair" that the appellant, and not his company, should be made personally liable because he failed to let the respondent know that he was acting for and on behalf of the company. The case can be classified as one in which the court lifted the corporate veil as a matter of fairness.[92] The court applied "principles of an underlying law requiring fair dealings". Woods J stated:

> The District Court lifted the corporate veil on the basis that Jacob Luke was the owner/manager of the company and, therefore, could be sued personally. The District Court seems to be applying *an underlying principle of fairness of transactions in whether a party may have been conscious of dealing with a company or the individual who acted as though he was the company. To the man in the street or, as herein, the village, the defendant appeared to be putting himself out as the company or the legal entity.* The Magistrate seems to have found that the defendant's evidence was so vague that he would be justified in finding that the part reimbursement of the original purchase monies was an admission of some warranty or obligation. (Emphasis added.)

In *Neville v Privatization Commission*[93] (discussed in detail below), the court also held that the circumstances of the case warranted a lifting of the corporate veil as a matter of fairness and equity.

Group enterprises and control

Despite the fact that, in other jurisdictions, the element of control by itself will not lead to the lifting of the corporate veil,[94] in PNG, the element of "control" by the parent company over the subsidiary company is a most important factor in lifting the corporate veil and holding the parent company liable. In *WorkCover Authority of NSW v Placer (PNG) Exploration Ltd*,[95]

92 The seventh circumstance in Kandakasi J's list. The case may also be explained as one of estoppel, where the appellant had acted in such a way as to lead the respondent to believe that the contract was one between him and the appellant, rather than one with his company. The respondent had acted on this representation to his detriment, and the court would not allow the appellant to evade the strict legal position. It should be noted, however, that the court did not make any reference to estoppel.

93 (2001) N2184.

94 See for example, *Bentley Poultry Farm Ltd v Canterbury Poultry Farmers Co-operative Ltd (No 2)* (1989) 4 NZCLC 64,780. See Tennent, D, "Unconscionable Use of Corporate Group Structure" [2004] *New Zealand Law Journal* 411–415 for an analysis of New Zealand cases dealing with this area of the law.

95 (2006) N3003 .

Lay J emphasised the element of control that was necessary before a court would lift the corporate veil where a company within a group of companies sets up a defence based on lifting the corporate veil. In this respect he relied on the judgment of Kapi DCJ in *Pinpar Development Pty Ltd v TL Timber Development Pty Ltd*.[96] In *Pinpar* the defendant (cross-claimant) tried to join a third party to the proceedings on the ground that the third party had financial control over the plaintiff. Although admitting that the plaintiff was a subsidiary of the third party, it was submitted that the third party was "in no way responsible for the management and operations" of the plaintiff in respect of the logging and marketing agreement which formed the basis of the defendant's cross-claim. Kapi DCJ therefore had to consider the extent to which a parent company controlled a subsidiary, and whether this made the parent company liable. The elements that showed control were:

- the alleged parent company and 15 other subsidiary companies had a common insurance cover in respect of logging operations;
- the meetings with regard to the negotiations of the logging and marketing agreement took place in the offices of the parent company;
- the general manager of the subsidiary that was being sued was also a manager of another subsidiary company of the parent company;
- the parent company acted on behalf of the subsidiary that was being sued in respect of workers' compensation for workers employed by the subsidiary;
- the parent company paid royalties in respect of operations by the subsidiary company.

Kapi DCJ said that all these factors pointed to the *possibility* that the parent company was in control of the subsidiary. However, a final ruling on this would be made in the substantive proceedings as a result of evidence called (the current proceedings were of an interlocutory nature to join the parent company as a party to the current proceedings).

After referring to "the fluid state of the law with regard to rights and liabilities of associated companies," Kapi DCJ stated that:

> Having regard to all the authorities, I accept the *principle that a parent company may be liable* for the actions of a subsidiary company provided that the subsidiary company was acting as agent of the parent company. Alternatively, *where the parent company in truth is in control of the subsidiary company and may or may not use the corporate veil for the purposes of fraud, or as a device to evade a contractual or other legal obligations, the parent company may be liable.* (Emphasis added.)

96 [1999] PNGLR 139.

Although there was reference to fraud and device or sham, it would appear that the exercise of "control" by the parent or holding company over the subsidiary company weighed heavily with Kapi DCJ in deciding whether the holding company may be liable for the actions of the subsidiary company.

In *WorkCover Authority of NSW v Placer (PNG) Exploration Ltd*,[97] Lay J distilled out of the cases the principles that the court will lift the corporate veil where there was fraud or where the company was a sham or façade. The crucial question in that case was whether the plaintiff could register a judgment that placed liability on the defendant, where the main defendant in the foreign court proceedings was another subsidiary company owned or controlled by the common parent company. There were several grounds argued by the defendant as to why the judgment should not be registered against it, including the fact that it had not voluntarily submitted to the jurisdiction of the foreign court or tribunal. To counter this argument, the plaintiff argued that the court ought to lift the corporate veil to see that the defendant was one of a group of companies owned by the same parent company, which it was argued, had complete control over both subsidiaries, and that submission to the jurisdiction of the court by one subsidiary of a common parent company, amounted to submission by the other subsidiary. The court rejected this argument on the ground that before this could be done, it had to be shown either that the obtaining of the foreign judgment had been obtained by some fraud or that the companies were separate entities without the parent company exercising control over the defendant.

Lifting corporate veil where party attempts to use it to avoid criminal prosecutions, including contempt proceedings

Can shareholder/director steal from his or her own company?

We have already seen that a company may have a single shareholder who is also the sole director of the company. There is no doubt that a company is separate from its shareholders and directors. However, what if a person who was the only shareholder and director took money from the company? Could he or she be found guilty of stealing this money under the Criminal Code or other legislation? In *R v Roffel*,[98] Roffel had signed company cheques paying for personal purchases. Roffel was one of two directors and shareholders, and sole controller of the company's affairs. He was charged with stealing by dishonestly appropriating corporate funds with the intention

97 (2006) N3003.
98 [1985] VR 511.

to permanently deprive the company of those funds. It was held that as Roffel had authority to sign such cheques for the company, this was a bilateral transaction, the company gifting the money to Roffel. It was not a unilateral act by Roffel to deprive the company of its money and did not therefore constitute stealing.

The majority decision of *R v Roffel* was disapproved by the House of Lords in England in *R v Gomez*,[99] and by the High Court of Australia in *Macleod v R*.[100] The decision of *The State v Graham Yotchi Wyborn*,[101] is also against *R v Roffel*.

The starting point for any consideration of the effect of *R v Roffel* is the case of *Ome Ome Forests Ltd v Ray Cheong*.[102] In that case, his Honour Kandakasi J stated:[103]

> I consider it necessary for the rule of law that that there should be an additional exception to the rule in *Foss v Harbottle* [1843] 2 Hare 461, to include cases in which the corporate shield is raised to avoid criminal prosecutions. This should include contempt of Court proceedings given that it is criminal in nature and is punishable by a penalty or imprisonment or both. This in turn follows on from the fact that companies being only legal persons, they can only act through natural persons or human beings: *AGC (Pacific) Ltd v Woo International Pty Ltd* [1992] PNGLR 100. It would therefore be untenable in my view, for only a company to be prosecuted and punished and allow the actual perpetrators to escape through the corporate veil.

In *The State v Graham Yotchi Wyborn*,[104] Salika J lifted the corporate veil in a criminal case to hold a director of the company in which he held a substantial if not majority shareholding to be liable for the actions of the company itself. In doing so, he relied on several civil law cases dealing with the lifting of the corporate veil[105] and, in particular, adopted the

99 [1993] 1 All ER 1.

100 [2003] HCA 24.

101 (2005) N2847. Cf *Macleod v R* [2003] HCA 24 and McConvill, J and Bagaric, M, "Macleod and the offence of defrauding the company in 'one person business': The divergence between legal principle and logic widens" (2003) 16 *Australian Journal of Corporate Law* 53–64. See also Austin, R P, Ramsay I M, *Ford's Principles of Corporations Law* (12th edn, LexisNexis Butterworths, Australia, 2005), para 4.090.

102 (2002) N2289.

103 (2002) N2289.

104 (2005) N2847. Cf *Macleod v R* [2003] HCA 24 and McConvill, J and Bagaric, M, "Macleod and the offence of defrauding the company in 'one person business': The divergence between legal principle and logic widens" (2003) 16 *Australian Journal of Corporate Law* 53–64.

105 *CBS Inc v Ranu Investments Pty Ltd* [1978] PNGLR 66; *Jacob Luke v John Ralda* [1992] PNGLR 549; *Odata Ltd v Ambusa Copra Oil Mill Ltd* (2001) N2106; *Ome Ome Forests Ltd v Ray Cheong* (2002) N2289; and *Kappo No 5 Pty Ltd v Wong* [1998] PNGLR 544.

governing principles set out by Kandakasi J in *Odata Ltd v Ambusa Copra Oil Mill Ltd.*[106]

The Managing Director of Sikani Engineering Ltd was charged with misappropriation of money belonging to the state, contrary to s 383A(1) of the Criminal Code (Ch 262). He sought to establish a defence based on the corporate veil, claiming that he was not liable because the contract had been made between the state and his company, a separate legal entity: seeing that the money had been transferred to the company, the company, rather than he, should have been charged with misappropriation. That section provides, *inter alia*, that a person who dishonestly applies to his own use or to the use of another person, property belonging to another person, or property belonging to the accused which is in the accused's possession or control (either solely or conjointly with another person) subject to a trust, direction or condition or on account of any other person, is guilty of the crime of misappropriation of property.

Sikani Engineering Ltd won a public tender for the construction of the Daru Town Market with a bid price of K180,000. The contract was a verbal contract and it was agreed that "an advance part payment" of K100,000 would be made to a bank account in the name of Sikani Engineering Ltd. (It is not clear whether this was a special account and whether one of the implied terms was that moneys paid into this account would be used exclusively towards implementation of the construction of the Daru Town Market.) The state claimed that a total of K65,357.29 had been drawn from the account and used for purposes other than the construction of the Daru Town Market. No work was carried out on the construction of the market. According to the evidence, the "owners" of the company seem to have "gone on a spending spree without even starting the job".

The accused argued that he was wrongly named as defendant: that the company Sikani Engineering Ltd was the appropriate defendant because, whatever he did, he did it for and on behalf of the company and Sikani is a separate and distinct legal personality from him, although he is a director, shareholder and the proprietor of the company. The submission is derived from the proposition of law enunciated in the case of *Salomon v Salomon & Co* [1897] AC 22, where it was held that:

> the individual or individuals forming [a] company are separate legal entities, "however complete the control might be one or more of those individuals over the company".

Later on, the court stated:

> Should this court sitting as a Criminal Court apply the same legal principles as in the civil cases relating to the issue of lifting the corporate veil?

106 (2001) N2106.

> As the National Court I am guided and directed by the *Constitution* under Schedule 2.3 to develop the underlying law taking into account the principles of natural justice and to do justice. In this case I am prepared to lift the corporate veil in a criminal case if the evidence warrants me to do it. I am also prepared to lift the veil if any of the 9 factors that Kandakasi J discussed to which I alluded earlier have been satisfied.

The judge was prepared to lift the corporate veil under factors 8[107] and 9[108] of the list set out by Kandakasi J in *Odata*: Salika J held that, in the circumstances, he lifted the corporate veil on the basis that its lifting is *justifiable under the circumstances*. Moreover, he lifted the corporate veil under s 421 of the Companies Act 1997. It is an offence for a company director or shareholder to fraudulently apply company property for his or her own benefit or use. The accused could have been charged under the Companies Act of 1997. Section 421 of the Companies Act 1997 expressly lifts the corporate veil. If the governing law on companies can lift the corporate veil, his Honour held that the corporate veil, by implication, can and should be lifted under the criminal laws.

> ...In this case the almost daily withdrawals of huge sums of money, his inability to properly account for how the monies were spent, and not even starting the project yet wanting the K80,000 to be paid has left a trail for one to come to the conclusion that the accused is not truthful about the usage of the money he and the company were given, this giving justification for the lifting of the corporate veil.
>
> In our opinion, the doctrine that a company is a separate entity and a legal personality is a legal fiction. This is because a company is deemed to have a heart of its own breathing but it does not have a brain, legs and hands and a mouth of its own. The officers, directors and shareholders perform those functions for the company. Section 421 of the Companies Act recognizes those underlying deficiencies of a company and so has put in place a mechanism to ensure that its brains, its legs and hands and its mouth do the right things only or that its body functions according to the will and dictates of the heart and are held accountable.
>
> There are no resolutions of the Board of Directors before the court to show that the accused was acting from the resolutions of the company. Otherwise it could be said that as the accused and his wife are the only shareholders and therefore the only signatories to the company accounts they were the same as the Company.

107 The corporate veil may be lifted if doing so is justified in all the circumstances of the case.
108 Where a statute provides either expressly or by implication for a lifting of the corporate veil, it may be lifted.

> Taking all the circumstances of the case including the lifting of the corporate veil, I am satisfied beyond reasonable doubt of the guilt of the accused. He is the brain, the legs and hands and the mouth of Sikani. I find him guilty of the Counts 1, 2, 3 and 4.

It was suggested that an action should have been brought under s 421 of the Companies Act 1997, rather than lifting the corporate veil under the Criminal Code. Section 421(a) of the Companies Act 1997 provides, *inter alia*, that a director of a company who fraudulently takes or applies property of the company for his or her own use or benefit, or for a use or purpose other than the use or purpose of the company commits an offence, and is liable on conviction to the penalty set out in s 413(4).[109]

Use of company for fraud or as a device to avoid contractual or other legal obligations

The court will strike down transactions arrived at by fraud, or where the parties or one of them use the company as a device to avoid contractual or other legal obligations.

Use of company for fraud

Where a company's structure is used to perpetrate a fraud, the court may lift the corporate veil to expose the fraud.[110] The leading English authority on fraud is the case of *Gilford Motor Co Ltd v Horne*,[111] where a managing director of a company (Gilford Motor Co Ltd) signed an employment contract agreeing not to solicit customers from his employer. However, upon leaving the company's employment, he formed a company to solicit these customers. The English Court of Appeal held that the company was a mere sham to cloak his wrongdoing, and that he as well as the company could be restrained (by way of injunction) from committing a breach of contract either directly himself or indirectly through the company.

This ground for lifting the corporate veil has been held to be applicable in PNG.[112] In *IRC v Hamidian Rad*,[113] Kandakasi J considered that he had

109 In *Ome Ome Forests Ltd v Ray Cheong* (2002) N2289, the corporate veil was lifted to allow for the prosecution against a company official *in the interest of justice in all of the circumstances to do so*. The corporate veil was no protection for a company official in contempt of court in the interest of justice in all of the circumstances.

110 *Re Darby, ex parte Brougham* [1911] 1 KB 95.

111 [1933] Ch 935.

112 See *CBS Inc v Ranu Investments Pty Ltd* [1978] PNGLR 66 and *Odata Ltd v Ambusa Copra Oil Mill Ltd* (2001) N2106.

113 (2002) SC692.

not explicitly referred to this ground in listing the factors allowing the courts to lift the corporate veil: he therefore added this further ground:

> if a corporate veil is raised for the purpose of avoiding legal obligations, such as is the case here [hiding behind a corporate veil for the purpose of avoiding personal tax liability], the corporate veil should be readily lifted to make those responsible meet their legal obligations.

In this case, Hamidian-Rad was charged with not paying sufficient taxes. He argued that his company was liable for taxation, and not him personally. To this argument, Kandakasi J stated:

> Likewise Ikub also played no part in the generation of the income. Ikub was the Respondent as he was the main person behind Ikub and providing services to the State. He was not strictly speaking a mere employee rendering services to Ikub. Instead he was the brain and the arms and legs of Ikub. Without him, Ikub could not have contracted with the State. He was fully maintained which included hotel accommodation by the funds paid to Ikub by the State. In these circumstances I am of the view that he could not hide behind the corporate veil of Ikub for the purposes of avoiding his tax liability.

In *Ome Ome Forests Ltd v Ray Cheong*,[114] following court action between Ome Ome (a landowner company) and two companies that had been engaged in the extraction and marketing of Ome Ome's timber products, the National Court eventually made an order against the two companies to release payments, including royalty payments to the companies.[115] Whilst this order for payment was in force, officers of the two companies continued to make the payments to *the shareholders* of these companies rather than to the company itself. Contempt charges were therefore laid against the relevant officers of both companies, who argued that the original court orders were made against their companies, and that seeing that the companies were registered separate entities, and that they were merely "officers" of the company (in one case a managing director and in another, an operations manager), the company, and not they, ought to be liable for contempt of court.

Kandakasi J held that, seeing that the order was made against the company, it was possible to lift the veil of incorporation to hold the officers in charge of the company liable for contempt of court. His Honour stated:

> Having said all of this, I consider it necessary for the rule of law that there should be an additional exception to the rule in *Foss v*

114 (2002) N2289.

115 The court had earlier ordered these companies to withhold the payment.

Harbottle,[116] to include cases in which the corporate shield is raised to avoid criminal prosecutions. This should include contempt of Court proceedings given that it is criminal in nature and is punishable by a penalty or imprisonment or both. This in turn follows on from the fact that companies being only legal persons, they can only act through natural persons or human beings: *AGC (Pacific) Ltd v Woo International Pty Ltd* [1992] PNGLR 100. It would therefore be untenable in my view, for only a company to be prosecuted and punished and allow the actual perpetrators to escape through the corporate veil.

Use of company as a device to avoid contractual or other legal obligations

In *IRC v Hamidian-Rad*,[117] the Supreme Court, or at least Kandakasi J, held that the corporate veil "should be readily lifted" where it is raised to avoid legal obligations such as tax liabilities. This case illustrates yet another exception to the separate entity doctrine.

Disregard of the separate entity doctrine by statutes

There are several provisions in the Companies Act 1997 that allow the corporate veil to be lifted. There are also several provisions outside that Act that either directly or indirectly allow the courts to lift the veil of incorporation. We shall look at the provisions in the Companies Act 1997 first, and then at other provisions.

Provisions in the Companies Act 1997

The Companies Act 1997 provides for a number of situations where the corporate veil may be lifted (i.e., the separate entity doctrine is entirely disregarded or its application is reduced) in order to provide protection for outsiders dealing with a company. We will discuss only the more important provisions.

Relief from Fees

Section 412 of the Companies Act 1997 provides that the Registrar of Companies may grant relief from the payment of fees by certain companies: companies where every shareholder is a citizen of PNG and who ordinarily reside in the country. In such cases, the Registrar may look behind the corporate veil to see the nationality of the shareholders and to find out whether they were "ordinarily resident"[118] in PNG.

116 [1843] 2 Hare 461.
117 (2002) SC692.
118 See *Robert James Reynolds v Kevin Walcott* [1985] PNGLR 316; *Application of GN and RN* [1985] PNGLR 121; *SCR No 3 of 1984; Kevin Masive v Iambakey Okuk* [1984] PNGLR 390; *Re TK (an Infant)* [1965–66] PNGLR 189; and *Edric Eupo v AGC (Pacific) Ltd* [1971–72] PNGLR 470 for consideration of the terms "resident" and "ordinarily resident".

Insolvent trading

The Companies Act 1997 imposes a positive duty on directors to avoid insolvent trading. The relevant provisions attempt to protect creditors who deal with a company when the company is either insolvent or about to become insolvent. They seek to ensure that a director exercises caution in incurring further debts where the director believes or there are reasonable grounds for believing (and the director is aware of these reasonable grounds or a reasonable person in a like position would be so aware) that the company is insolvent or may soon become insolvent. Any director who fails to prevent insolvent trading is liable to pay compensation to unsecured creditors who have suffered loss or damage as a result of the insolvent trading.[119] A parent or holding company may also be held liable to unsecured creditors of its subsidiary when it allows the subsidiary to continue trading when it is insolvent or may soon become insolvent.[120] Either the liquidator or the creditor may bring proceedings in the National Court to recover, from a director personally, compensation "equal to the amount of loss or damage" suffered by the creditor. In such an action, the court is allowed to impose liability on persons (i.e., directors) who are behind the corporate veil.[121]

Promoters

Sometimes promoters enter into various contracts or arrangements for the company before it is incorporated. Some of these contracts are valid. At common law such contracts were not binding on a company, nor could they be enforced by the company. Sections 157 to 160 of the Companies Act 1997 now govern the situation. The law relating to pre-incorporation contracts is discussed in more detail above.[122] Despite ratification by the company, the promoter may still remain liable. Section 157(3) of the Companies Act 1997 provides that: "A contract that is ratified is as valid and enforceable as if the company had been a party to the contract when it was made." Section 157(5) provides that: "Notwithstanding any law, where a pre-incorporation contract has not been ratified by a company, or validated by the Court under Section 159, the company may not enforce it or take the benefit of it."

Section 160 of the Companies Act 1997 provides that where the pre-incorporation contract has been ratified by the company, the court may make such order for the payment of damages or other relief as the court

119 Companies Act 1997, s 348. For more detailed discussion of this area of the law, see Chapter 9 – Directors' Duties.

120 Companies Act 1997, s 349.

121 It is sometimes argued that the veil of incorporation applies only to "shareholders". However many cases where directors have been held liable or have been allowed to rely on the separate entity doctrine, involve directors.

122 See pp 224–225, above.

considers just and equitable, against a person by whom the contract was made. This relief against the promoter may be in addition to or in substitution for any order that may be made against the company. So even though, on ratification of the contract, the company becomes the main entity against which action should be taken, the courts are still allowed to make the promoter liable in some circumstances. As such, one can argue that the corporate veil is lifted. Alternatively, it could be argued that the promoter continues to be liable, but that some of the liability is transferred to the company. As such it is wrong to categorise this area as one of lifting the corporate veil.

Winding up on just and equitable grounds

Section 152 of the Companies Act 1997 provides that the National Court may put a company into liquidation where it considers that it is just and equitable to do so. In exercising this power, the court has the power to look behind the corporate veil to examine the actions of the controllers (members and directors). This is normally done when the relationship between the shareholders is similar to a partnership and a breakdown in the relationship occurs. In *Ebrahimi v Westbourne Galleries Ltd*,[123] the court disregarded the corporate structure to reveal the failure of the business relationship behind it which had lasted 13 years.[124]

Uncommercial transactions

There are several situations where the courts will look behind the corporate veil in order to reveal the true nature of the transaction with a view to setting it aside. This normally occurs once the company has been put into liquidation.[125] The provision dealing with uncommercial transactions,[126] for example, seeks to prevent directors from receiving preferential treatment over creditors. The liquidator can apply to the court to have the uncommercial transaction declared void. In essence, an uncommercial transaction is one in which a reasonable person in the company's circumstances would not have entered into the transaction, having regard to the benefits and detriments that the transactions give rise to.[127]

Financial assistance

There are certain situations where a company may financially assist a person to acquire shares in the company or in a holding (parent) company.[128]

123 [1973] AC 360.
124 For more detailed discussion of this area, see Chapter 14 (Liquidation).
125 See Part VIII.7 of the Companies Act 1997.
126 Companies Act 1997, s 343.
127 For more detailed discussion of this area, see Chapter 14 (Liquidation).
128 Companies Act 1997, s 63; cf s 64.

Whereas other jurisdictions make a person who is involved in a company's contravention of the financial assistance prohibition liable to a penalty, there is no such provision in PNG.[129] As such, there is no need to look behind the corporate veil to determine this. In other jurisdictions, however, this situation would be a statutory exception to the prohibition not to look behind the corporate veil.

Charges in favour of certain persons

The Companies Act 1997 provides that charges in favour of certain persons are void in certain cases.[130] The courts are allowed to look behind the corporate veil to discover the identity of the lender in order to determine whether the charge is void in the circumstances.

Provisions in other statutes

Apart from the Companies Act 1997, there are other situations where legislation gives benefits or imposes duties on companies, and it is necessary to lift the corporate veil to see if the company is entitled to the benefit or subject to the burden. Some of the more important provisions will now be considered. Emphasis will be given to provisions in the Claims By and Against the State Act 1996 to illustrate how courts carry out this investigation

Other terms in statutes that would invite the court to lift the corporate veil include situations where it must be shown that the company is or is not a: "foreign enterprise",[131] "national enterprise",[132] "foreign investor",[133] "citizen",[134] "non-citizen corporation",[135] "citizen enterprise",[136] "citizen company" or "national company"[137] and a "national tenderer".[138]

129 The Companies (Amendment) Act 1988 (No 16 of 1988), which came into force on 1 January 1989 and amended the Companies Act (Ch 146), continued in force until the Companies Act 1997 commenced, subject to specific rules, prohibited a company from financing dealings in their own shares.

130 Companies Act 1997, s 345.

131 Investment Promotion Act 1992; Forestry Regulation 1998.

132 Investment Promotion Act 1992.

133 Investment Promotion Act 1992.

134 Investment Promotion Act 1992, s 3; Copyright and Neighbouring Rights Act 2000, s 3(6); Fisheries Management Act 1998, s 2; Coffee Industry Corporation (Statutory Functions and Powers) Act 1991, s 2; Land Act 1996, s 2, Land Regulation 1999, s 2(1); Land (Ownership of Freeholds) Act (Ch 359), s 15; Land (Tenure Conversion) Act 1963, s 4; Constitution, s 54(c), s 56; Cf Licensing of Heavy Vehicles Act (Ch 367), s 7(2); Interpretation Act (Ch 2), s 3(1) ("automatic citizen").

135 Organic Law on the Integrity of Political Parties and Candidates 2003.

136 Fisheries Management Regulation 2000, s 1.

137 An earlier version of s 69 of the Income Tax Act 1959.

138 Public Finances (Management) Act 1995, s 2.

Claims by and Against the State Act 1996

The Claims By and Against the State Act 1996 lays down certain rules and procedures that must be followed in claims[139] made by or against "the state". The Act does not define "the state", and questions have been raised as to whether corporations or companies which are owned or controlled by the national government or a provincial or local-level government are included within the meaning of "the state".

After some differences of opinion on the matter among judges in the National Court, the Supreme Court[140] has now firmly established that the term "the state" applies not only to the National Government and its agencies, but also to provincial and local-level governments and their agencies.[141] There have also been different views as to whether corporations and companies are comprehended within the term "the state". The National Government, as well as provincial and local-level governments, has set up corporations and companies incorporated under the Companies Act 1997 to carry out various functions. Some of these corporations (established by legislation) and companies (registered under the Companies Act 1997) have been held to be "the state", and the courts have established various criteria to determine this matter.

One of the more important provisions of the Claims By and Against the State Act 1996 is that there can be no process in the nature of execution or attachment that may be issued against the property or revenue of "the State".[142]

As Kandakasi J pointed out in *Dan Kakaraya v The Ombudsman Commission*,[143] "the corporate veil of companies incorporated under the Companies Act 1997, is not a complete cover". In these types of cases, the

139 The Act covers other proceedings and processes, including suits and applications, and execution and attachment. However, for our purposes, we shall use the term claim to encompass all of these proceedings.

140 In *SCR No 1 of 1998; Reservation Pursuant to s 15 of the Supreme Court Act* (2001) SC672.

141 The National Capital District Commission is also included within the term "the State". In *Otto Napi v NCDC* (2004) N2797, the National Court (David AJ) held that the National Capital District Commission (NCDC) is a body that is similar to a Provincial Government and that the NCDC is included within the term "the State" for the purposes of the Claims By and Against the State Act 1996. In *IBF Investment Ltd v NCDC* (2005) N2842, the National Court (Injia DCJ) came to a similar conclusion without relying on *Otto Napi*. Note that it has recently been held that the national government, provincial governments and the NCDC may waive the immunity granted to them by the Claims By and Against the State Act 1996 and thereby exclude the application of relevant provisions of the Act: see *National Provident Fund Board of Trustees v Southern Highlands Provincial Government* (2006) N3028 (Davani J).

142 Execution, for the purposes of our discussion, means the enforcement of a judgment by a public officer under a writ for the seizure of goods.

143 (2003) N2478.

court can draw back the veil to expose the nature of the company to see whether it is or is not part of the state. It is not yet clear from the cases that the term "the state" includes companies "owned and controlled by governmental bodies" that are set up under the Companies Act 1997.

The most recent case has stated that in making such a determination, there are "six factors" that must be shown in order for corporations or companies to be classified as being part of "the state" for the purposes of the Claims By and Against the State Act 1996.[144] It must be shown that:[145]

1. they are established by the Constitution;
2. they are part of the three-tier structure of government enshrined in the Constitution;
3. like the other tiers of government they are constituted by elected representatives;
4. the National Government exercises some control over provincial governments in political, administrative and financial matters;
5. they fall within the definition of "governmental body" contained in the Constitution;
6. judgment debts are recoverable from monies allocated in their budgetary process.

It is not yet clear whether other National Court judges or the Supreme Court will accept that these six factors must concur for a legal entity, particularly a statutory corporation or a company registered under the Companies Act 1997, to be considered to be "the state".[146] Regardless of this, however, it has to be stated that whenever it is claimed that a corporation or company is to be treated as "the state" for the purposes of the Claims By and Against the State Act 1996, or any other legislation, the court will have to "pierce the corporate veil" to see the nature of the entity, and based on the six factors, or some similar or other set of criteria, decide whether the company, corporation or other legal entity has fulfilled them.

In *Okam Sakarius v Chris Tep*,[147] Salika J held that the Cocoa and Copra Extension Agency, a company established under the precursor of the Companies Act 1997 (Companies Act (Ch 146) (repealed)) and owned by the state,[148]

144 Although the issue arose in relation to a statutory corporation, the judge stated that the same principles applied to companies registered under the Companies Act 1997.

145 *Noami Vicky John v National Housing Corporation* (2005) N2770, per Lay J.

146 Lay J stated that these six criteria were "set out" in the Supreme Court judgment in *SCR No 1 of 1998; Reservation Pursuant to s 15 of the Supreme Court Act* (2001) SC672. *Sed quaere*.

147 (2003) N2355.

148 The agency was a subsidiary company of the Cocoa Board and Copra Marketing Board (later becoming the Kokonas Indastri Koporasen (KIK)), which was a state-owned company, established by the National Executive Council and registered under the repealed Companies Act (Ch 146) as a company limited by guarantee.

was included within the term "the state". This decision has, however, been subjected to mild "criticism". In *Sarakuma Investment Ltd v Peter Merkendi*,[149] Cannings J adverted inferentially to the issue of whether *Okam Sakarius v Chris Tep* was correctly decided, in light of the penultimate (i.e., second but last) paragraph of *SCR No 1 of 1998; Reservation Pursuant to s 15 of the Supreme Court Act*.[150] This failure of Salika J to consider the import of the penultimate paragraph in SCR No 1 of 1998; Reservation Pursuant to s 15 of the Supreme Court Act[151] was a reason why Lay J refused to follow *Okam Sakarius* in *Noami Vicky John v National Housing Corporation*.[152] Although *Noami Vicky John* did not concern companies but a corporation (i.e., the National Housing Corporation), the statement in this regard by Lay J, would apply equally to a company established by the National Government, or a provincial government or local-level government.

In *Noami Vicky John v National Housing Corporation*,[153] Lay J held that the National Housing Corporation did not meet all of the six factors that must be met for an entity to be classified as "the state" for the purposes of the Claims By and Against the State Act 1996, and the corporation could not therefore be classified as "the state". Lay J stated:

> The words I have placed in italics [set out in an earlier paragraph and taken from the judgment of the Supreme Court in *SCR No 1 of 1998; Reservation Pursuant to s 15 of the Supreme Court Act*,[154] namely, '*It is to be remembered that this protection does not apply to assets and finances of developmental enterprises of provincial governments that have independent corporate statuses and operate commercially. They are subject to the ordinary laws as corporate citizens.*'] . . . make it plain that the Supreme Court did not consider that a provincial government

149 (2004) N2629.

150 (2001) SC672. The penultimate paragraph reads: "It is to be remembered that this protection does not apply to assets and finances of developmental enterprises of provincial governments that have independent corporate statuses and operate commercially. They are subject to the ordinary laws as corporate citizens." In *Albert Areng v Gregory Babia* (2005) N2895, Sawong J, in deciding not to follow *Okam Sakarius v Chris Tep* made explicit reference to the fact that Salika J, in holding that the National Housing Corporation was part of "the state", did not take into account the penultimate paragraph of *SCR No 1 of 1998; Reservation Pursuant to s 15 of the Supreme Court Act* (2001) SC672. In *John Napi v Kundiawa General Hospital Board* (2006) N3047, Davani J referred to the fact that there have been several cases decided in PNG where the courts have decided that certain bodies are entities of the state despite the fact that they have been incorporated or are corporations. She included *Okam Sakarius v Chris Tep* in that list without any comment as to whether it was correctly decided.

151 (2001) SC672.

152 (2005) N2770.

153 (2005) N2770.

154 (2001) SC672.

owned entity with separate corporate status set up to operate commercially should be a part of the State. No doubt this is so because, although such entities are mostly capitalized with taxation revenues of the provincial governments, their general income is generated commercially from profits and not from taxation of the people. Their day to day financial decisions are made in the interests of making a profit, contrasted with the decisions of a Government, made through the budgetary process for the welfare of the people. There is therefore not the same justification for protection of the commercial entity's finances. They are also of course not established by the *Constitution*, nor part of the three-tier system of government, there is no direct constitutional control over them by the National Government, and they do not have a budgetary process to set aside a specific sum of public funds for payment of judgment debts.

Having made the above statement, his Honour went on as follows:

> But is it enough, to fulfil the criteria set down by *SCR No 1 of 1998; Reservation Pursuant to s 15 of the Supreme Court Act* (2001) SC672 (Amet CJ, Los J, Sheehan J, Salika J and Sakora J) that the entity meets only 2 of the 6 points set out in that decision? And where else is the trend leading if the Plaintiff is held to be 'the State'? Would such entities as the Agriculture Bank or the Central Bank, the National Gaming Control Board, the Harbours Board, Kokanas Industri Koporesen, the Maritime College and many other statutory bodies and State owned companies also be "the State" as distinct from being 'governmental bodies'? A determination of each would turn on the precise facts of each case, but it is as well to keep in mind that this decision might have a much wider application. A decision in respect of one section of the *Claims By and Against the State Act 1996* will generally be expected to affect the meaning of the term 'the State' in other sections of the Act.

Lay J continued:

> In respect of a number of former government institutions the position is now much clearer than it would have been a few years ago because of the trend to corporatisation of State enterprises and superannuation funds. Applying the 'commercial purposes' exception, mentioned by the Supreme Court (in italics above), to National Government entities, these corporatised entities would now more clearly not be 'the State'.

Lay J further stated:

> I do not follow *Okam Sakarius v Chris Tep* (2003) N2355 nor *Mt Hagen Urban Local Level Government v The National Housing*

Corporation (2004) WS 1194 of 2002 (Unreported and Unnumbered National Court Judgment of Mogish J dated 20 April 2004) because in my view, to meet the test applied by the Supreme Court, it is not enough that an entity is financially dependent on the State and controlled by the State, it must also itself be part of the three-tier structure of constitutional government...I conclude that the National Housing Corporation is a governmental body within the meaning defined in the *Constitution* but that it is not included in the term 'the State' as used in the Act on the tests applied by the Supreme Court in *SCR No 1 of 1998; Reservation Pursuant to s 15 of the Supreme Court Act* (2001) SC672.

Privatization Act 1999

In *Neville v Privatization Commission*,[155] Kandakasi J held that:

> "the protection of the corporate veil or separate legal personality upon registration under the *Companies Act 1997* was lifted by Section 14 of the *Privatization Act 1999*. This was by virtue of s 14(2) of the *Privatization Act 1999*,[156] when Parliament removed and placed in the Commission the assets, management, administration and control of enterprises to be privatised". Section 14(2) of the *Privatization Act 1999* provided that upon declaration in the National Gazette that an enterprise was to be a privatized enterprise, "on and from the date specified in the said notice the assets, management, administration and control of the said enterprise shall vest in the Commission". Assets were defined to include "share and capital" (uncalled or otherwise) in any company.

Could the trustee shareholder (i.e. the Privatization Commission) consent to an injunction? Or could this be done only by the company itself (i.e. the management of PNGBC)? With regard to the separate corporate personality argument, the Privatization Commission submitted that the wording of s 14 of the Privatization Act 1999 specifically vested in the Commission all management and administrative control over the assets of Finance Pacific, which consisted only of PNGBC. Kandakasi J held that when Finance Pacific (which was the only shareholder of PNGBC) was transferred to the Privatization Commission, the management, administration and control of PNGBC automatically passed to the Privatization Commission.

155 (2001) N2184.

156 Companies Act 1997, s 14(2): "The Head of State, acting with, and in accordance with, the advice of the National Executive Council may from time to time by notice in the National Gazette declare that an enterprise is to be a privatized enterprise for the purpose of this Act, and on and from the date specified in the said notice the assets, management, administration and control of the said enterprise shall vest in the Commission."

Kandakasi J held:

> In my view, the protection of the corporate veil or separate legal personality upon registration under the *Companies Act 1997* was lifted by s 14 of the *Privatization Act* 1999. This was by virtue of s 14(2) of the *Privatization Act* 1999, when Parliament removed and placed in the Commission the assets, management, administration and control of enterprises to be privatised . . . In this case, Parliament by specific legislation provided that the Commission is to take control of the management and the assets of the enterprises declared to be privatised.

Audit Act 1989

Section 1(1) of the Audit Act 1989 provides that, unless the contrary intention appears:

> 'Government-owned company' means a company incorporated under the *Companies Act 1997*, a majority of the shares in which are held by, or on behalf of, the State but does not include the company referred to as 'the Company' in the *Mineral Resources Development Company Pty Limited (Privatisation) Act 1996* or any subsidiary of that company.[157]

In determining whether a company is government-owned for the purposes of that Act, the court will have to lift the corporate veil in order to see whether "a majority of the shares . . . are held by, or on behalf of, the State". Again, as in the Claims By and Against the State Act 1996, the Audit Act 1989 does not define "the state", and the cases decided on the meaning of that term in the Claims By and Against the State Act 1996 will be helpful in determining the meaning of the phrase "by, or on behalf of, the State" in the Audit Act 1989.

Income Tax Act 1959

The Income Tax Act 1959 has certain provisions that try to ensure that persons who ought to pay tax, do not avoid their liability (anti-avoidance provisions).[158] In such cases, the court may disregard the corporate structure for the purpose of determining tax liability.[159] In *IRC v Hamidian–Rad*,[160]

157 Section 1(1) also provides: "'Provincial Government-owned company' means a company incorporated under the *Companies Act 1997* a majority of the shares in which are held by, or on behalf of, a Provincial Government or Provincial Governments."

158 See also s 154A of the Income Tax Act 1959 which defines "qualifying corporation" to mean "(c) a corporation incorporated under the *Companies Act 1997* the membership of which comprises none other than a resident who is (i) a citizen (other than a naturalised citizen)".

159 Income Tax Act 1959, ss 4(1), 11, 46.

160 (2002) SC692.

the Supreme Court held that the corporate veil may be lifted if it was used to avoid legal obligations such as one's tax liabilities by having regard to the nature of the activity generating the income and the way in which that is carried out. This would mean that the court will almost of necessity, have to look behind the corporate veil to see the activities of those in control of the company.

Investment Promotion Act 1992

Section 41(1)(a) of the Investment Promotion Act 1992, for example, in part provides that a foreign enterprise which carries on business without an appropriate certificate from the minister is guilty of an offence. Part of the definition of a foreign enterprise is one "which is not a national enterprise or a citizen". The definition of "national enterprise" is:

> "an enterprise more than 50% of which is owned directly or indirectly by a citizen, unless the control exercisable in law or by any agreement between the shareholders, or by agreement between the shareholders or the enterprise and a third party, or in practice, is maintained by a person other than a citizen."

This basically means that unless the enterprise that is charged with an offence contrary to s 41(1)(a) admits that it is a foreign enterprise, a court would need to lift the corporate veil to determine ownership or control, and thus the nature of the enterprise.[161]

Statutory provisions dealing with land

Several statutes give special privileges to citizens.[162] Most of the provisions dealing with land referred to in this section were enacted in the period immediately preceding or soon after Independence.[163] Special privileges in respect of land were given to either citizens or to automatic citizens; and as such, the definition of citizen has sometimes been defined to include corporations or companies that were either owned or controlled by Papua New Guineans (sometimes referred to as "national companies"). In such cases the court would have the power to lift the corporate veil to determine the "nationality" of the corporation or company by looking at its membership.

161 Cf *Investment Promotion Authority v Getrude Marika* [1999] PNGLR 18 and *Investment Promotion Authority v Niugini Scrap Corporation Pty Ltd* (2001) N2104.

162 The Constitution provides for different types of citizenship (automatic citizenship and non-automatic citizenship).

163 See for example, the Lands Acquisition (Development Purposes) Act (Ch 192), which was repealed by the Land Act 1996, s 176 and Schedule 1.

The Aliens (Property) Act (Ch 14) (repealed)[164] specifically prevented aliens (non-citizens) from acquiring land without ministerial permission. In order to find out whether a company was an alien, the court could have looked behind the corporate veil. In *Daimler Co Ltd v Continental Tyre and Rubber Co (Great Britain) Ltd*,[165] the House of Lords held that it was permissible to look behind the company (at the shareholders and those in control of corporate affairs) in order to ascertain if it was an "enemy alien". If the company was an enemy alien, it meant that the contract between the parties was void for illegality, as it was illegal to trade with an enemy alien company during the war. In such a case, the identity or nationality of the directors or shareholders played a major role in determining the alien nature of the corporation itself.[166]

164 The Aliens (Property) Act (Ch 14) was repealed by the Land Act 1996 (No 45 of 1996), s 176 and Schedule 1.

165 [1916] 2 AC 307.

166 See also *Bermuda Cablevision Ltd v Colica Trust Co Ltd* [1998] AC 198, PC.

Chapter 9

Directors' Duties[1]

Introduction

In this chapter we will look at the role that directors and the other main administrative officer (the company secretary) play in the life of a company. We shall first note the different types of officers that a company may employ and who are to be considered to be directors. We shall see what laws govern their appointment and termination as well as any rules laid down by the law as to how the board should meet and decide matters. After summarising the procedural requirements that govern decision-making by directors, we will then consider the law relating to directors' duties. Because there are several ways in which the interests of directors may diverge from those of shareholders, we will need to see how the law provides for the minimisation of these conflicts, and for remedying breaches of the general and more specific duties that are placed on directors. This is an area where the underlying law (both at common law and in equity) provided remedies to prevent directors from engaging in transactions which benefited themselves at the expense of the company.[2] The courts also developed equitable and tortious rules to ensure that directors acted with proper care or diligence in relation to the business operations of the company. More recently, statute, particularly the Companies Act 1997, has laid down similar fiduciary duties and duties of care, diligence and skill. One of the important questions that arises from this is whether Parliament intended these new statutory duties to supersede the underlying law rules, or whether both sets of laws were to operate concurrently. As we shall see, this matter is still one of great uncertainty in PNG, and indeed in New Zealand, from where most of the provisions originated.

1 Austin, R P, Ford, H A J, Ramsay I M, *Company Directors: Principles of Law and Corporate Governance* (LexisNexis Butterworths, Australia, 2005); Rennie, H and Watts, P, *Directors' Duties and Shareholder Rights* (New Zealand Law Society Seminar, Wellington, 1996).

2 For example, a director may try to sell some property that the director owns to the company at a grossly inflated price.

In this chapter we shall look only at the general duties of directors.[3] We will look firstly at the underlying law general duties, and then those duties in the Companies Act 1997, which are set out in ss 112 to 127. These duties are:

- Duty to act in good faith [and] in best interests of company (s 112).
- Duty to comply with the Companies Act 1997 and the company's constitution (s 114).
- Duty to exercise care, diligence, and skill (s 115).
- Duty to prevent company engaging in insolvent trading (s 348).
- Duty to disclose and enter into only fair transactions where the director has a conflict of interest (ss 117–122).
- Duty not to disclose or use company's confidential information except for company purposes (s 123).
- Duty to disclose personal share dealings in the company, and not to engage in insider trading (ss 124–127).

Summary and classification of duties

Directors' duties exist under both the underlying law and statute law. Before the enactment of the Companies Act 1997, the underlying law (common law and equity) spelt out the duties of directors. The Companies Act 1997 now also spells out these duties, in a manner similar to the underlying law. However, the Act did not expressly state what is to be the relationship between these two types of duties. Does the Companies Act 1997 form a code of duties so that from 1997 onwards, directors' duties are to be governed *exclusively* by that Act; or did all or some of the underlying law duties continue to operate?[4] The courts in PNG have not yet resolved these issues: although one judge in a National Court case has stated, *obiter*, that the directors' duties' provisions in the Companies Act 1997 form a code, whilst a decision of a Supreme Court case is to the effect that the underlying law rules, or at least some of them, continue to apply.[5] It is suggested that the better view is that the duties have *not* been codified and that the underlying law will continue to operate not only where there is a gap in the statute law, but, because the statutory duties are stated in very broad terms, the underlying law cases will be useful in interpreting the directors' duties' provisions in the Companies Act 1997.

3 Such specific duties as those relating to reporting and distributions (declaring dividends, etc.) will not be considered.

4 The partial operation of the underlying law duties would mean that these duties would operate to the extent that they were not inconsistent with the statutory duties.

5 According to the doctrine of precedent, Supreme Court decisions are binding on the National Court. For a recent statement of this, see *Kokopo Building and Maintenance Ltd v Department of Police* (2005) SC786. It should be noted that, in both cases, the issue of the codification of directors' duties seems not to have been argued nor adverted to by the judges to be a problem.

Directors' duties can be divided into two broad categories: (1) loyalty and good faith (fiduciary duties); and (2) care, diligence and skill. The underlying law duty of loyalty and good faith can be further subdivided into four more specific duties. They are:

- the duty to act in good faith in the interests of the company;
- the duty to avoid conflicts of interest;
- the duty not to fetter discretions; and
- the duty to use powers only for proper purposes.

As we shall see, some of these duties can be further subdivided into even more specific duties. The statutory duties can also be divided into these two broad groups of duties. However, there is one notable omission. There is no express statutory duty placed on a director to act only for proper purposes. Furthermore, the legislative history of the Companies Act 1997 tends to show that, although the underlying law of PNG formerly recognised this duty, from 1997 onwards, the duty no longer exists under the underlying law and the Companies Act 1997 makes no provision for it.

The statutory duties relating to directors that we shall discuss have been set out above. Most of the directors' general duties are provided for in one Part of the Companies Act 1997.[6] However, the provisions dealing with the duty of directors to prevent the company from engaging in insolvent trading is dealt with elsewhere in the Act.[7]

Who bears the duties?

According to the underlying law, directors and senior executive officers who, like directors, can be regarded as fiduciaries owed various duties to the company. In addition to the underlying law providing for such duties, these officers (directors, executive directors and other senior executive officers) would normally have contracts with their companies that also imposed particular duties on them. Unlike the underlying law, the compass of the statutory provision is more limited in the persons governed by the provisions. The statutory duties apply only to directors. However, s 107 of the Companies Act 1997 defines a director in such wide terms that many officers who would not normally be considered to be directors are caught within the def inition, and therefore owe director's duties.

Section 107(1)(a) defines a director as a person occupying the position of director of the company by whatever name called, and the other provisions

6 Part VIII.—Directors and their Powers and Duties, Division 3 (Directors' Duties) and Division 4 (Transactions Involving Self-Interest).

7 Companies Act 1997, s 348. (Part XVIII.—Liquidations, Division 7.—Recovery in Other Cases.)

of s 107 then expand on this definition and apply it to specific statutory provisions which contain the directors' duties' requirements. The expanded definition of director includes:

- a person who is acting on instructions provided by any person who occupies the position of director;[8]
- any person who is a delegate of the board of directors;[9]
- a person who may instruct directors or their delegates;[10]
- a shareholder in certain circumstances.[11]

Professional advisers, such as lawyers and accountants, will not be directors for the purposes of the Companies Act 1997 unless they are specifically appointed as such,[12] or the circumstances show that they are to be deemed to be directors and thus owe directors' duties to the company.[13]

Nominee directors are appointed for the purpose of representing a particular group, usually a substantial shareholder, such as large companies and banks. The nominee director will owe a duty to the company, but will also owe duties to their nominator. Nominators may be liable as a director under s 107(1) if they are able to influence the nominee when carrying out his or her duties.[14]

Appointment and removal of directors

There are qualifications on who may be appointed and who once validly appointed, may continue to act as directors. To be appointed as a director of a company, a person must satisfy the requirements of s 129 of the Companies Act 1997. The person must:

- be a natural person, not a company;[15]
- consent to the appointment in writing, in the prescribed form, and certify that he or she is not disqualified from being appointed or holding office as a director of a company;[16]

8 Companies Act 1997, s 107(1)(b). This is a type of shadow director.
9 Companies Act 1997, s 107(1)(c).
10 Companies Act 1997, s 107(1)(d).
11 Companies Act 1997, s 107(2) and (3).
12 Companies Act 1997, s 107(5).
13 *Fatupaito v Bates* [2001] 3 NZLR 386.
14 *Ryde Holdings Ltd v Sorenson* [1988] 2 NZLR 157; *Kuwait Asia Bank EC v National Mutual Life Nominees Ltd* [1991] 1 AC 187.
15 Companies Act 1997, s 129(1) and (3). In some jurisdictions, companies can act as directors. See *Re Hydrodam (Corby) Ltd* [1994] 2 BCC 161, [1994] 2 BCLC 180. This was the rule that operated in PNG until 1997. See *Sangara (Holdings) Ltd v Hamac Holdings Ltd (In Liquidation)* [1973] PNGLR 504, where one of the companies was a director.
16 Companies Act 1997, s 130. The prescribed form is Form 15 of the Companies Regulation 1998.

- be over 18 years of age;[17]
- not be a person who is prohibited from being a director or promoter of or being concerned or taking part in the management of a company under ss 425, 426 or 428 of the Companies Act 1997;
- not be a person who is or becomes of unsound mind;[18]
- in relation to any particular company, not be a person who does not comply with any qualifications for directors contained in the constitution of that company.[19]

Section 129(4) provides that a person who is disqualified from being a director but who acts as a director is a director for the purposes of a provision of the Companies Act 1997 that imposes a duty or an obligation on a director of a company.

It should be noted that lawyers, accountants, receivers and other people acting in their professional capacity by giving advice are not directors, so long as they act only in a professional capacity.[20]

A *de facto* director is one who carries out the functions of a director but has not, for some reason, been validly appointed.[21] The term also applies to "shadow" directors who in fact direct a company, but do so by directing those on the board.

Composition of board of directors and senior management

A company's directors and officers are responsible for managing the company's business and affairs. In small companies, particularly small family companies, some or all of the shareholders will usually be involved in the management of the company. However, larger companies will have specialised managers conducting the business of the company. These managers may own only a small proportion of the company's shares; indeed, they may not own any shares at all. A "director" is defined by s 107 of the Companies Act 1997 and, for general purposes, includes "a person occupying the position of director of the company by whatever name called".[22]

There is no limit to the number of directors that a company may have; but it must have at least one.[23] The role of a director or the board of directors is to manage, or supervise the management of, the business and affairs of

17 Companies Act 1997, s 129(2)(a).
18 Companies Act 1997, s 129(2)(c).
19 Companies Act 1997, s 129(2)(d).
20 Companies Act 1997, s 107(5).
21 *Corporate Affairs Commission (NSW) v Drysdale* (1978) 141 CLR 236.
22 Companies Act 1997, s 107(1)(a). It does not include a receiver: s 107(2).
23 Companies Act 1997, s 11(d).

the company.[24] The functions undertaken by directors vary significantly depending on the size and type of company and the role of the director in it. In a small company, the director or directors may truly "manage" the company's business in the sense that they work in the business and make the day-to-day decisions involved in running the company. In larger companies, the directors may assume a more supervisory function, with responsibility for the day-to-day decision-making left to other officers.[25]

A company must have at least one director.[26] At least one director must also be "ordinarily resident" in PNG.[27] In most cases, companies will have two or more directors. The company's board of directors may consist of executive directors and non-executive directors (sometimes referred to as independent directors).[28] An executive director is a person who is both a director and a full-time employee of the company. Non-executive directors are usually independent of management and free from any business or other relationship with the company which could interfere significantly with the exercise of their independent judgment. They are not employees of the company and are not therefore involved in the full-time or day-to-day management of the company. Their involvement with running the company is limited to attending board meetings and meetings of committees of the board to which they have been appointed. They are usually more concerned with policy matters and supervision of the company than with day to day management decisions.

In some companies, alternate directors are also appointed. It will sometime happen that a director may be unable to attend board meetings because of sickness or other commitments. These alternate directors are meant to represent and stand in temporarily for the absent directors.

Usually directors will elect a permanent chairman (chairperson) of the board of directors who will normally chair meetings of the board and sign the minutes. He or she will also chair general meetings of shareholders when such are held. This is the person whom the directors elect to chair their meetings

24 Companies Act 1997, s 109(1).

25 The Companies Act 1997 does not define "officer". Section 1(1) of the repealed Companies Act (Ch 146) defined "officer" to include "a director, secretary or employee of the corporation". Although the Companies Act 1997 refers to "officer" on several occasions, it nowhere defines the term for general purposes. Section 254(1) of the Companies Act 1997 so far as it relates to Part XVII. – Receiverships defines a "director", in relation to a "company" and an "overseas company". Section 345 of the Companies Act 1997 defines "officer" for the purposes of that section to include "in the case of a registered overseas company, an agent of the overseas company".

26 Companies Act 1997, s 128(1).

27 Companies Act 1997, s 128(2).

28 A non-executive director may not in fact be an independent director, in that that person may have substantial shares in the company, and thus be vitally interested in its management, or the person may be employed in some capacity with related or subsidiary companies.

and sign the minutes of the meetings. This person will also usually chair meetings of shareholders. In some companies, particularly small family companies, the shareholders who are usually related to the driving force behind the business may give extensive powers of management of the company to him or her: this director is usually called a "governing director". In such cases, the company will have a constitution which gives the governing director all the powers which in another company would be held by the board of directors; in addition, the constitution might allow the governing director to hold office as long as he or she wants and also give the governing director the power to remove and appoint other directors.

The head of management of the company is the chief executive officer (CEO) (sometimes called the managing director (MD) where that person also sits on the board of directors). The CEO is in charge of the day-to-day management of the company, and will usually be a member of the Board of Directors. In fact, in many cases, especially in larger companies, the directors will delegate many of their functions to the CEO. A company may have other executive officers apart from the CEO. Bigger companies will often have a finance director who will be part of senior management and be responsible for the financial operations of the company (sometimes called a Chief Financial Officer (CFO)), and will usually also be a member of the board of directors and attend meetings of directors. There may also be a Chief Information Officer (CIO).

De facto directors

Section 107(1)(c) of the Companies Act 1997 defines a director to include not only a person appointed to the position of director, but also a person:

- to whom a power or duty of the board has been directly delegated by the board with that person's consent or acquiescence; or
- who exercises the power or duty with the consent or acquiescence of the board.

For the purposes of ss 112 to 127 (inclusive), 344 and 350 of the Companies Act 1997, that person is a director and is often referred to as a *de facto* director. The person has not been appointed as a director, but acts as if this is so. These *de facto* directors will be subject to the specified directors' duties, such as the duty to act in the best interests of the company and to act with reasonable care and skill.[29] An example of a *de facto* director would be a person who has resigned as a director but has continued to play an active role in the company, including negotiating with some of the company's creditors

29 Companies Act 1997, ss 112–127, 334, 350.

or with the Commissioner General of Internal Revenue. Because these are major responsibilities, typically exercised by a director, the person will be held to be a *de facto* director.[30] A person describing himself as a consultant to the company but carrying out tasks typically associated with a director was held to be a *de facto* director in *Mistmorn Pty Ltd (in liq) v Yasseen*.[31] Another example of a *de facto* director is a person whom the shareholders have tried to appoint as a director but whose appointment was not properly made (for example, because there was not a quorum of shareholders at the meeting). If this person acts as a director he or she will be a *de facto* director.

Shadow directors

Section 107(1)(b)(i)–(ii) of the Companies Act 1997 defines a director to include a person not validly appointed as a director but with whose instructions a director or the board of directors may be required to or are accustomed to act. This includes a person not appointed a director but who controls the company from the shadows while attempting to deny that he or she is a director. These persons are called "shadow directors".[32] Shadow directors also include a person who exercises or who is entitled to exercise or who controls or who is entitled to control the exercise of powers which, apart from the constitution of the company, would normally be exercised by the board.[33]

Nominee directors

A nominee director is a person appointed to represent the interests of a particular group or another person on the board of directors. For example, some companies may have a director who is appointed to represent the interests of employees, a particular group of shareholders or a creditor. If the company has borrowed a significant amount of money from a bank, the bank may stipulate as part of the loan that the bank has a right to nominate one of its staff or a professional adviser to represent it on the company's board of directors, and to ensure that the company does not do anything that would jeopardise the repayment of the loan. Nominee directors must act in the interests of the company of which they are a director. *Bennetts v Board*

30 *Deputy Commissioner of Taxation v Austin* (1998) 28 ACSR 565.
31 (1996) 21 ACSR 173.
32 The person is a shadow director for the purpose of only ss 112 to 119 (inclusive), 123 to 127 (inclusive), 344 and 350 of the Companies Act 1997. As to shadow directorships generally, see Hobson, M D, "The Law of Shadow Directorships" (1998) 10 *Bond Law Review* 184.
33 Companies Act 1997, s 107(1)(b)(iii).

of Fire Commissioners of NSW[34] and *Dairy Containers Ltd v NZI Bank Ltd; Dairy Containers Ltd v Auditor-General*:[35] " . . . nominee directors need not necessarily approach company problems with an open mind and they may pursue their appointer's interests provided that, in the event of a conflict, they prefer the interests of the company."[36]

Sometimes shareholders will be treated as directors for certain purposes. The company's constitution may confer powers on the shareholders which would normally be exercised by the board (i.e. "which would otherwise fall to be exercised by the board"). Any shareholder who exercises that power or takes part in deciding whether to exercise the power is deemed to be a director for the purposes of ss 112 to 116 (inclusive).[37] Sometimes a company's constitution may require a director or the board of directors to exercise or refrain from exercising a power in accordance with a decision or direction of shareholders. In such a case, where the shareholder makes a decision on the matter, he or she is deemed to be a director for the purposes of ss 112 to 116.[38]

Appointment of directors

When a new company is registered, or two or more companies are amalgamated, the registration form or amalgamation proposal must state who is or are to be the directors. From the date of registration or the date the amalgamation is effective, each director will hold the office of director until they cease to hold office in accordance with the Companies Act 1997 or the company's constitution.[39]

Subsequent appointments of directors will usually be made by an ordinary resolution of shareholders. However, the company's constitution may specify another method of appointment.[40]

The National Court also has power to appoint directors if there are no directors or the number of directors is less than the quorum required for a meeting of the board, and it is not possible or practicable to appoint new directors in accordance with the company's constitution. A shareholder or creditor of the company may apply to the National Court for such an appointment to be made, and the court will make an appointment where it considers that it is in the interests of the company to do so.[41] The court may make the appointment on such terms and conditions as it sees fit.[42]

34 (1967) 87 WN (Pt 1) (NSW) 307.
35 [1995] 2 NZLR 30.
36 [1995] 2 NZLR 30 at 96.
37 Companies Act 1997, s 107(3) which applies ss 112 to 116.
38 Companies Act 1997, s 107(4) which applies ss 112 to 116.
39 Companies Act 1997, s 131(1).
40 Companies Act 1997, s 131(2).
41 Companies Act 1997, s 132(1).
42 Companies Act 1997, s 132(2).

The shareholders of the company must generally vote for each director individually,[43] although the constitution may alter this requirement. The shareholders have the power to decide how long directors are to remain in office before their appointment needs to be voted on again. The term of office is usually specified in the company's constitution. (In a listed company on the Port Moresby Stock Exchange, no director is able to hold office for more than three years without being re-elected.[44])

Even if the term of a director has not elapsed, a director may resign at any time by giving proper notice to the company. The notice must be in writing and delivered to the address for service of the company. The notice is effective from the time it is received or such later time as is specified in the notice.

Directors may be removed from office either by shareholders of the company convening a meeting to do so, or they may be removed by a court order. A director may be removed from office at any time. Section 134(1) of the Companies Act 1997 requires an ordinary resolution of shareholders passed at a meeting called for that purpose or for purposes that include the removal of the director. The notice of the meeting must state that the purpose or a purpose of the meeting is the removal of the director.[45] Section 134 of the Companies Act 1997 is subject to the constitution of the company. The constitution may be drafted so as to remove the shareholders' right to remove directors, or provide an alternative procedure for removal.

Section 152(1) of the Companies Act 1997 grants to the National Court the power to remove a director where a shareholder, former shareholder or other entitled person establishes that the affairs of a company have been, are being, or are likely to be, conducted in a manner that is, or any act or acts of the company have been, are, or are likely to be, oppressive, unfairly discriminatory, or unfairly prejudicial to him or her. The court must be satisfied that it is "just and equitable" to remove the director under s 152(2)(c) of the Companies Act 1997, which regulates the future conduct of the

43 Companies Act 1997, s 133(1). It is possible for there to be a single resolution for the appointment of two or more persons as directors of the company, provided that an earlier separate resolution to this effect was passed without a vote being cast against it: s 133(1)(b). A resolution moved in contravention of this procedure is void even though the moving of it was not objected to at the time: s 133(2). Two or more directors may be appointed by ballot or poll: s 133(5). The appointment has some effect, however. The person is treated as having been validly appointed for the purposes of third party liability: ss 133(3) and 136 (the acts of a person as a director are valid even though the person's appointment was defective). The invalid appointment does not lead to the automatic reappointment of retiring directors in default of another appointment, where such a provision so provides: s 133(3).

44 Listing Rules of the Port Moresby Stock Exchange, r 21.4. This rule does not apply to the managing director, i.e. the managing director is exempt from the rotation process. However, if there is more than one managing director, only one is entitled not to be subject to re-election.

45 Companies Act 1997, s 134(2).

company's affairs. (Section 426 empowers the National Court to disqualify persons from managing companies.)

If a person is disqualified from holding the office of director, that person automatically ceases to be a director at that time of disqualification.

If a person is convicted of certain types of offences, he or she is automatically disqualified from being a director, or being in any way, whether directly or indirectly, concerned or taking part in the management of a company for a specified period.[46] The disqualifying periods are:

- where the person was sentenced to imprisonment, during the period of imprisonment and during the period of five years after release from prison;[47] or
- during the period of five years after the judgment or the conviction.

The offences which lead to automatic disqualification include:

- conviction on indictment[48] of any offence in connection with the promotion, formation, or management of a company; or
- conviction of an offence under ss 420 to 423 of the Companies Act 1997 or of any crime involving dishonesty, whether within the country or outside the country.[49]

A person is automatically disqualified from being a director if he or she is a bankrupt.[50] Automatic disqualification may also occur because of the mental state of the director. Section 129(2)(c) of the Companies Act 1997 provides that "a person who is or becomes of unsound mind" is disqualified from being appointed or holding office as a director of a company.

While some circumstance lead to automatic disqualification (such as being bankrupt or being convicted of the offences noted above), there are other circumstances where the court has a discretion whether or not to disqualify a person from managing companies. For example, s 426(1)(c) of the Companies

46 Companies Act 1997, s 425(1).

47 During the period of five years, the person may apply to the National Court to grant him or her leave to manage a company: Companies Act 1997, s 426(1). The leave of the court may be given on such terms and conditions as the court thinks fit. A person intending to apply for the leave of the court under this section must submit to the Registrar of Companies not less than one month's notice of that person's intention to apply. The Registrar, and such other persons as the court thinks fit, may attend and be heard at the hearing of the application. See Companies Act 1997, s 425(3) and (4).

48 An indictable offence is a serious offence.

49 The term "crime involving dishonesty" means "a crime involving theft, conversion, robbery, burglary, fraud, receiving stolen property, or forgery": see Companies Act 1997, s 425(5).

50 Companies Act 1997, s 425(1)(c). A person is automatically disqualified from acting as a director of a company if that person is an undischarged bankrupt.

Act 1997 authorises the National Court to restrain from acting as a director a person who has:

- persistently failed to comply with the Companies Act 1997 or, where the company has failed to so comply, persistently failed to take all reasonable steps to obtain such compliance; or
- been guilty of fraud in relation to the company or of a breach of duty to the company or a shareholder; or
- acted in a reckless or incompetent manner in the performance of his or her duties as director.

Under s 426, the court has the power to disqualify a person from acting as a director or promoter for up to ten years.[51]

In addition to the National Court having the power to disqualify persons from managing companies, the Registrar of Companies is also given similar powers. Under s 428 of the Companies Act 1997, the Registrar may prohibit certain persons from managing companies. The section applies to:

- companies that have been put into liquidation because of their inability to pay their debts as they became due in the ordinary course of business;[52]
- companies that ceased to carry on business because of inability to pay its debts as they became due in the ordinary course of business;[53]
- companies where execution has been returned unsatisfied in whole or in part;[54]
- companies in respect of whose property a receiver has been appointed;[55] or
- companies that have entered into a compromise or arrangement with their creditors.[56]

The Registrar of Companies must give the person notice in writing of the prohibition, and such notice must be published in the National Gazette. The Registrar must be satisfied that the person was wholly or partly responsible for the state of affairs set out in s 428(1) (see list above).[57] The order should not

51 For liability where the person continues to act as director after the court order, see Companies Act 1997, s 427.
52 Companies Act 1997, s 428(1)(a).
53 Companies Act 1997, s 428(1)(b).
54 Companies Act 1997, s 428(1)(c). This means that a court order that property of the company be seized by the court's Sheriff and sold to satisfy the debt owed by the company cannot be fully carried out because the company does not have any or sufficient property to satisfy the debt.
55 Companies Act 1997, s 428(1)(d).
56 Companies Act 1997, s 428(1)(e).
57 Companies Act 1997, s 428(4)(a)–(b). Section 428(5) provides that the Registrar shall not make the order unless not less than one month's notice of the fact that the Registrar intends to consider the exercise of it is given to the person and the Registrar considers any representations made by the person.

be made if the person can demonstrate that he or she was not responsible for one or more of the above listed situations on which the Registrar is acting, or it is not just or equitable to make such an order. The order may restrict the person from acting as a director or promoter of a company, or from being concerned or taking part, whether directly or indirectly, in the management of a company for a period not exceeding five years after the date of the notice.[58] The person has a right to appeal against or may seek judicial review of the decision of the Registrar.[59] The consequences of a failure to obey an order of the Registrar are quite serious. Such a person is personally liable to a liquidator for every unpaid debt incurred by the company and to every creditor of the company for a debt incurred by the company to that creditor while the person was acting as a director while disqualified to do so.[60]

Proceedings of the board of directors

The constitution of the company can specify some or all of the procedures governing the meetings of the board of directors. In the absence of any rules in the constitution or a relevant statute,[61] or where the constitution does not provide for rules similar to those set out in the rules that apply to meetings of directors are contained in Schedule 4 of the Companies Act 1997, the rules set out in Schedule 4, to the extent not provided for, apply.

A director or (unusually) an employee may call a board meeting by giving no less than two days' notice to the other members of the board.[62] This notice must include the date, time and place of the meeting, and the matters to be discussed at the meeting.[63] A quorum for a meeting of the board is a majority of the directors.[64] The board, which is constituted without a quorum of directors, cannot make decisions and transact business.[65] Decisions at board meetings are made unanimously by all directors present at the meeting or by the majority of those directors present.[66] Unless specified in the constitution, the chairperson does not have a casting vote,[67] and every director has only one vote.[68] There is a presumption that a director present at the meeting has

58 Companies Act 1997, s 428(6). It would appear that for the notice to be effective the period imposed by the Registrar must be stated in the notice, and it must not be for a period of five years or less after the date of the notice is signed, not the date of publication of the notice in the National Gazette. See s 428(3).
59 Companies Act 1997, s 428(7). The notice remains in full force and effect pending the determination of the appeal or review, as the case may be.
60 Companies Act 1997, s 429.
61 See for example, *Ricky Mitio v William G Gardner* (2005) N2792.
62 Companies Act 1997, Schedule 4, clauses 2(1), 2(2).
63 Companies Act 1997, Schedule 4, clause 2(2).
64 Companies Act 1997, Schedule 4, clause 4(1).
65 Companies Act 1997, Schedule 4, clause 4(2).
66 Companies Act 1997, Schedule 4, clause 5(3).
67 Companies Act 1997, Schedule 4, clause 5(2).
68 Companies Act 1997, Schedule 4, clause 5(1).

agreed to and voted for the proposed resolution unless he or she expressly dissents or votes against the resolution.[69]

Unless the constitution of the company or other statutory provision provides otherwise, the provisions set out in Schedule 4 of the Companies Act 1997 govern the proceedings of the board of a company, directors can pass resolutions without formally meeting together.[70] These are called circular resolutions.[71] The resolution will be valid and effective if it is "in writing, signed or assented to by all directors then entitled to receive notice of a board meeting".[72] A copy of the resolution must be recorded in the minute book of board proceedings.[73] *Ricky Mitio v William G Gardner*[74] concerned the validity of a circular resolution relating to the dismissal and appointment of a CEO and Chairman of the Board of Directors of the Coffee Industry Corporation Ltd. Davani J held that the dismissals and appointments were invalid because of failure to follow the procedure set out in the Regulatory Statutory Authorities (Appointment to Certain Offices) Act 2004. What is of interest in relation to circular resolutions is the argument advanced by counsel but not dealt with by Davani J that circular resolutions are to deal only with "urgent or trivial matters [that] do not require the expense of a meeting", and that "important issues" such as the removal of the Chief Executive Officer must be done by way of an actual meeting. The learned judge also referred to "procedural irregularities" which "are not invalidated unless the court is of the opinion that the irregularity has caused or may cause substantial injustice which may not otherwise be remedied by order of the court". This reference seems to mean that, even if the provisions of Schedule 4 are not complied with, the court may dispense with such requirements and hold that the circular resolution is valid and effectual.

As was mentioned above, sometimes statute may intervene to provide for board meetings, and for the appointment and termination of board members. With the recent move by government to privatise services currently carried out by government departments or statutory authorities, like electricity and water, companies have been formed and assets transferred to these entities. In some cases, however, the government still continues to exercise a fair degree of control through the appointment and dismissal of senior management. The interplay of company structure and government control was seen recently in the case of *Ricky Mitio v William Gardner*,[75] where the method of termination

69 Companies Act 1997, Schedule 4, clause 5(4).

70 Companies Act 1997, s 138.

71 The National Court considered such a resolution in *Ricky Mitio v William G Gardner* (2005) N2792.

72 Companies Act 1997, Schedule 4, clause 7(1).

73 Companies Act 1997, Schedule 4, clause 7(3). Despite the use of the mandatory "shall" in this provision, it may be that the court will treat breach of this obligation as remediable: see *Ricky Mitio v William G Gardner* (2005) N2792.

74 (2005) N2792.

75 (2005) N2792.

and appointment of the Chairman of the board of directors and the CEO of Coffee Industry Corporation Ltd[76] was at issue. The board of directors of the Coffee Industry Corporation Ltd purported to terminate the employment of Mr Mitio as CEO and appoint an acting CEO by use of a circular resolution.[77] Up until the enactment of the Regulatory Statutory Authorities (Appointment to Certain Offices) Act 2004, the Memorandum and Articles of Association of the Coffee Industry Corporation, in particular Clause 17.6, governed these dismissals and appointments.[78] However, the Regulatory Statutory Authorities (Appointment to Certain Offices) Act 2004 amended the Coffee Industry Corporation (Statutory Functions and Powers) Act 1991 by providing as follows:

> 5. Appointment of Directors of the Coffee Industry Corporation.
> The Coffee Industry Corporation's nominees to the Board of the Corporation, which number of nominees shall not exceed the number of vacancies on the Board, shall be appointed in accordance with the *Regulatory Statutory Authorities (Appointment to Certain Offices) Act 2004*.

In addition, Schedule 1 of the Regulatory Statutory Authorities (Appointment to Certain Offices) Act 2004 provided that the Coffee Industry Corporation Ltd was a Regulatory Statutory Authority.

Part III of the Regulatory Statutory Authorities (Appointment to Certain Offices) Act 2004 set out the procedure for the revocation of appointment of Chief Executive Officers of regulatory statutory authorities. In effect, it required an investigation into the conduct, activities or performance of the CEO giving rise to the reason for dismissal. This report together with the board's recommendations were then to be forwarded to the Public Services Commission, which would make a decision on the matter, and send its recommendation to the National Executive Council for approval.[79] Section 9 governed the making of an acting appointment of a CEO, and this had not been complied with.

76 The Coffee Industry Corporation is the Coffee Industry Corporation Limited, a corporation limited by guarantee incorporated under the Companies Act (Ch 146).

77 The Companies Act 1997, s 138 and Schedule 4.7(1) make provision for the board of directors to make decisions by a circular resolution, instead of having to convene a board meeting. The section provides that: "A resolution in writing, signed or assented to by all directors then entitled to receive notice of a board meeting, is as valid and effective as if it had been passed at a meeting of the board duly convened and held."

78 Clause 17.6 provided that: "A resolution in writing signed by all members for the time being of the Board in Papua New Guinea (not being less that the number required to constitute a quorum) shall be as valid and effectual as if it had been passed at a meeting of the Board duly convened and constituted."

79 Regulatory Statutory Authorities (Appointment to Certain Offices) Act 2004, s 7.

The court held that the extensive procedures for selection, appointment and dismissal of CEOs set out in the Regulatory Statutory Authorities (Appointment to Certain Offices) Act 2004 now applied to the CEO of the Coffee Industry Corporation Ltd.

The effect of s 3(2) of the Regulatory Statutory Authorities (Appointment to Certain Offices) Act 2004 is, *inter alia*, that once a company or other entity becomes a regulatory statutory authority, the Act or other instrument of incorporation under which the regulatory statutory authority was established is to be read subject to Part VIIA (Regulatory Statutory Authorities) of the Constitution and the Regulatory Statutory Authorities (Appointment to Certain Offices) Act 2004. From then onwards, any appointment, suspension and dismissal of the CEO and the appointment of a non *ex officio* member of the board of the company or entity, was as specified in Part VIIA (Regulatory Statutory Authorities) of the Constitution and the Regulatory Statutory Authorities (Appointment to Certain Offices) Act 2004.

The court held that:

> Section 208B(1)(a) [of the Constitution] states that all appointments shall be made by the Head of State, acting with and in accordance with the advice of the National Executive Council (NEC) given after considering recommendations from the relevant Minister acting on the advice of the relevant Board in accordance with the recommendations from the Public Services Commission, following procedures prescribed by an Act of Parliament. The Act of Parliament in this case is the *Regulatory Statutory Authorities (Appointment to Certain Offices) Act 2004*. The provisions to be read together are Part II of that Act which consists of ss. 4, 5, and 6.

Davani J held that: "Clause 17.6 should not be read on its own as an ordinary company constitution where the norm is that the will of a general meeting is expressed by the passing of the resolutions." The Coffee Industry Corporation Ltd was not "an ordinary company" but had a "unique nature". The Constitution and the Regulatory Statutory Authorities (Appointment to Certain Offices) Act 2004 laid down special procedures for the appointment, suspension and termination of CEOs of special agencies, called regulatory statutory authorities. "In this case none of the procedures were complied with." The court had no difficulty in holding that the purported revocation of the appointment of the plaintiff as CEO was "invalid and of no effect".

So, in this age of technology, it is not necessary for company board of directors' meetings to be held in one physical location with all directors assembled together. The Companies Act 1997 acknowledges modern technology by allowing valid board meetings to be held with directors in different locations, using the current technology available. Once the parties participate in the meeting and can simultaneously hear each other, that is all that is required.

So telephone conference calls as well as audio-video conferencing are sufficient to allow for meetings of a board meeting to be held.[80]

Company secretary[81]

It is not necessary for a company to have a secretary.[82] If, however, the company decides to have such an officer, he or she must be a natural person who is "ordinarily resident" in PNG.[83] The Companies Act 1997 does not require the secretary to have any special skills or qualifications.

Where a company has a company secretary, he or she is the administrative head of the company and may be described otherwise, such as "corporate counsel" or "general counsel" or "chief administrative officer". The powers and functions of the company secretary may vary greatly from one company to another, but are usually quite extensive. The functions may include the following:[84]

- Providing advice to directors and executive officers in relation to the requirements of the Companies Act 1997 and other related laws, regulations, and the company's constitution.
- Reviewing developments in corporate governance and advising and assisting the directors with respect to their duties and responsibilities and compliance with their personal obligations under company law and, if applicable, Stock Exchange requirements.
- Organising company board meetings and general meetings of the company, including preparation of meeting agendas and attending and minuting the meetings and ensuring that correct procedures are followed.
- Advising the board and individual directors on corporate governance principles and plans, the implementation of corporate governance programs and matters affecting the company's constitution.
- Carrying out the instructions of the board, assisting in the implementation of corporate strategies and giving practical effect to the board's decisions.
- Monitoring and ensuring compliance with relevant legal requirements, particularly under the Companies Act 1997.
- Ensuring that the company complies with its constitution, and making sure that amendments to it are made in accordance with correct procedures.

80 Companies Act 1997, Schedule 4, clause 3(b).
81 Part X, Division 6 of the Companies Act 1997 deals with company secretaries.
82 Companies Act 1997, s 169(1).
83 Companies Act 1997, s 169(2). The Companies Act 1997 does not define the term. Several other statutes use the concept of ordinarily resident; however there are no PNG judgments which consider the normal meaning of the term "ordinarily resident".
84 See the following websites for lists of functions normally carried out by company secretaries: www.icsa.org.uk and www.csnz.org.

- Ensuring that the company's share register, company records and accounting records, including the company's register of charges, are properly maintained.
- Filing information with the Registrar of Companies to report certain changes regarding the company or to comply with requirements for periodic filing. This will include changes in the directors of the company, in particular, changes to a director's name or residential address, removal from office in accordance with the Companies Act 1997 or the company's constitution, and new appointments, resignations and deaths. In particular sending the annual return of the company to the Registrar.
- Co-ordinating the publication and distribution of the company's annual report and accounts and interim statement in consultation with the company's internal and external advisers and, in particular, preparing the directors' report.
- Maintaining the company's register of members, dealing with transfers and other matters affecting shareholdings.
- Ensuring the safe custody and proper use of the company seal.
- Liaising with shareholders and a range of other external parties including auditors, lawyers and tax advisers.
- If the company is listed on the Port Moresby Stock Exchange (POMSoX), ensuring that the company meets stock exchange requirements, especially those set out in the Listing Rules.
- Acting as the chief administrative officer of the company, which can include the roles of office manager, public officer, accountant, financial adviser and controller and public relations officer.

A company secretary has only such rights, powers, and duties in relation to the company as are given to him or her by the Companies Act 1997 or by the constitution (if the company has one) or by the board of directors of the company.[85] The board of directors is responsible for appointing the company secretary,[86] and the board needs to ensure that notification of the details concerning the secretary are sent to the Registrar of Companies.[87] Other than this, the Companies Act 1997 does not lay down the company secretary's "rights, powers, and duties in relation to the company" in any great detail,[88] as

85 Companies Act 1997, s 169(4).

86 Companies Act 1997, s 170(1). If there is a vacancy in the appointment of a company secretary, the deputy secretary if there is one, or "a person authorised generally or specifically for the purpose by the board of the company" may carry out the functions of the secretary: Companies Act 1997, s 169(3).

87 Companies Act 1997, s 170(3).

88 The Companies Act 1997 (Schedule 6) provides that the company secretary has the power to make a declaration of solvency in a company's annual return. However, this may be done by a director.

it is anticipated that this will usually be done either by the company's constitution, or by directives issued by the board of directors from time to time.

The board will usually spell out the powers and responsibilities of the company secretary in a document or in the contract of employment. However, outsiders may assume that, as an agent of the company, the company secretary has the usual authority of a person in that position.[89]

The Companies Act 1997 does not specify who has the power to dismiss the company secretary; though this is most probably within the ambit of the board's management powers. A secretary may normally resign on reasonable notice to the board of directors.[90]

In the past, company secretaries did not have a very high status and authority in the company. The company secretary was considered to be a mere servant: "his position is to do as he is told."[91] This is, however, no longer so. Today, the courts recognise that the company secretary occupies a much more important position as chief administrative officer of the company with extensive duties and responsibilities, and therefore powers.[92] The office of secretary, particularly in large companies, is now regarded as a position of importance with significant responsibilities and influence. In *Panorama Developments (Guildford) Ltd v Fidelis Furnishing Fabrics Ltd*,[93] Salmon LJ described the secretary as the chief administrative officer, and a company secretary is now seen as having customary authority to bind the company to certain contracts with outsiders, contracts connected with the administration of the company. It should be noted, however, that the company secretary is not in a fiduciary relationship with the company, and cannot therefore be subject to the strict

89 Companies Act 1997, s 19(1)(c)(ii). Note that, although the board of directors may delegate unusual powers to the company secretary, there are some directors' powers that cannot be delegated: see Schedule 3 of the Companies Act 1997.

90 In *Northside Developments Pty Ltd v Registrar-General* (1990) 170 CLR 146 it was held that resignation notified to a *de facto* managing director without authority to accept it was invalid.

91 *Barnett, Hoares & Co v South London Tramways Co* (1887) 18 QBD 815 at 817, per Lord Esher MR.

92 *Panorama Developments (Guildford) Ltd v Fidelis Furnishing Fabrics Ltd* [1971] 2 QB 711 at 716–717, per Lord Denning MR.

93 [1971] 2 QB 711. In *Paul Torato v Sir Tei Abal* [1987] PNGLR 403, Bredmeyer J stated that the company secretary " . . . may be authorised by the directors to enter into certain types of contracts e.g. of a certain type or up to a certain amount. Over and above his actual authority the company secretary has an ostensible authority to do certain things on behalf of the company, e.g. to sign contracts connected with the administrative side of the company's affairs such as employing staff, and hiring cars: see *Panorama Developments (Guildford) Ltd v Fidelis Furnishing Fabrics Ltd* [1971] 2 QB 711, CA. The courts have ruled that a company secretary has no authority, for example, to call a meeting of the company without a resolution of the directors, or to issue a writ in the company's name. But in respect of such a matter, any act done by a secretary beyond his authority may be ratified by the directors: see *Australian Corporate Affairs Reporter* vol. 1 (CCH) para 6–910."

duties imposed on directors.[94] Despite the fact that he or she is not a fiduciary, the company secretary:

- owes the company duties of good faith and loyalty;[95]
- must avoid a conflict of interest and duty;
- must not misuse company information; and
- must exercise reasonable care, skill and diligence in carrying out his or her duties and responsibilities.

In exceptional cases, for example when the board of directors delegates a broad power to him or her, or the company secretary occupies the position of a director, a company secretary may be treated as a director under s 107 of the Companies Act 1997 and, as such, certain of the directors' duties provision will apply.

Directors' right to company information

In order to carry out their tasks properly, every director has a statutory right to access company information.[96] A director is entitled to inspect the records[97] of the company on giving reasonable notice of his or her intention to do so. In such a case, the director is entitled to see the records in written form, without charge and at a reasonable time specified by the director.[98]

Situations may, however, arise where it would not be in the company's interests for a director to inspect its records, or the proposed inspection may be for a purpose that is not properly connected with the director's duties.[99] In such cases the company may apply to the National Court for an order directing that the records should not be made available for inspection or an order limiting the inspection of them in any manner that the court thinks fit.[100]

Delegation of authority by board

Apart from being responsible for managing the company, the board of directors are responsible for directing and supervising the management. Section 111 of the Companies Act 1997 provides that, unless the Companies Act 1997 or the company's constitution prevents or restricts it, the board of directors has full powers to delegate its powers to either a committee of directors, a single director, an employee of the company, "or any other

94 *New Zealand Couriers Ltd v Sutton* (1982) 1 NZCLC 95–045.
95 *Schilling v Kidd Garrett Ltd* [1977] 1 NZLR 243.
96 Companies Act 1997, s 166.
97 "Records" are defined in s 164(1) of the Companies Act 1997.
98 Companies Act 1997, s 166(1).
99 For example, the director may intend to breach a director's duty and the company information may assist him or her in the breach of that duty.
100 Companies Act 1997, s 166(2).

person".[101] As the subsection notes, the company's constitution may restrict the board's ability to delegate and the board may not delegate any of its powers specified in Schedule 3 of the Companies Act 1997.

As we noted above, the company's constitution may prohibit the board of directors from delegating certain powers, or set restrictions to this power. The Companies Act 1997 also sets out certain powers that the board cannot delegate. These are:

- the issue and cost of shares other than on registration and amalgamation;[102]
- authorisation of distributions, including dividends;[103]
- the issue of shares instead of dividends;[104]
- shareholder discounts;[105]
- offers to acquire shares;[106]
- provision of financial assistance;[107]
- transfer of shares;[108]
- change of registered office;[109]
- change of address for service;[110]
- approval of amalgamation proposal;[111]
- short form amalgamation.[112]

It is common for large public companies to have a number of board committees, including an audit committee and a remuneration committee. The audit committee would deal with matters relating to audit, legislative compliance and risk management, and would review internal and external audit processes and ensure that appropriate accounting policies and procedures are implemented by the company. A remuneration committee would decide the terms of appointment, levels of remuneration, and performance measures for the senior executives of the company, including the chief executive officer (CEO). Apart from delegation to committees, the board of directors will also usually delegate powers to individuals, chief amongst these being the CEO.[113]

101 Companies Act 1997, s 111(1). See Schedule 3 of the Companies Act 1997 for a list of directors' powers that cannot be delegated. See below.
102 Companies Act 1997, s 43 and s 47.
103 Companies Act 1997, s 50.
104 Companies Act 1997, s 52.
105 Companies Act 1997, s 53.
106 Companies Act 1997, s 57.
107 Companies Act 1997, s 63.
108 Companies Act 1997, s 65(4).
109 Companies Act 1997, s 162.
110 Companies Act 1997, s 168.
111 Companies Act 1997, s 234.
112 Companies Act 1997, s 235.
113 As we noted above, the CEO (or managing director) is responsible for the day-to-day management of the company and reports to the board of directors on matters relating to the management and operations of the company.

Where a director is considering matters that are beyond his or her competence, they should seek out professional or expert advice from reliable competent employees, professional advisers and experts, and other directors. Section 116(1) of the Companies Act 1997 authorises a director, when exercising powers or performing duties as a director, to rely on information or advice[114] provided by an employee of the company whom the directors believe on reasonable grounds to be reliable and competent in relation to the matters concerned, or a professional adviser or expert in relation to matters which the director believes on reasonable grounds to be within the person's professional or expert competence, and any other director or committee of directors upon which the director did not serve in relation to matters within the director's or committee's designated authority. Section 116(2) provides that the right to rely on the information or advice depends on the director acting in good faith, making proper inquiries where it is appropriate to do so (i.e., the need for inquiry is indicated by the circumstances), and having no knowledge that such reliance is unwarranted. A sensible director, aware that he or she did not have any or sufficient expertise on a particular matter, could therefore avoid liability under s 115 by obtaining the advice of an expert.

Under s 111(2) of the Companies Act 1997, if the board of directors[115] delegates a power that is delegable, the board will continue to be responsible for the delegate's exercise of that power as if it had exercised the power itself. However, the board will not be liable if it:[116]

- believed on reasonable grounds at all times before the exercise of the power that the delegate would exercise the power properly (i.e., in conformity with the duties imposed on directors of the company by the Companies Act 1997 and the company's constitution); and
- has monitored, by means of reasonable methods properly used, the exercise of the power by the delegate.

It does not seem to be necessary that the board believed on reasonable grounds in good faith and after making proper inquiry that the delegate was reliable and competent.

The division of powers between the board and the shareholders as a group is effected by the Companies Act 1997 and the constitution, if the company has one.[117] For example, the constitution may limit the powers of the board of directors to manage the company. In *Decade Holdings Ltd v*

114 This advice or information can be in the form of reports, statements, financial data and other information prepared or supplied or professional or expert advice given.

115 The section seems to apply only to delegations by the board of directors, and not to where a single director delegates his or her powers.

116 Companies Act 1997, s 111(2).

117 As we noted in Chapter 7 (Introduction to Company Law), a company does not have to have a constitution.

RKC Zeitler,[118] three shareholders who held 50 per cent of the shares in the company signed a resolution prepared in accordance with the constitution removing Zeitler as a director. Zeitler argued that although the resolution complied with the constitution, it did not comply with s 156 of the Companies Act 1993 (NZ),[119] which provided that a director of the company may be removed from office by ordinary resolution passed at a meeting called for the purpose or for purposes that include the removal of the director. (The notice of the meeting expressly referred to the fact that one of the purposes, or the purpose, of the meeting was the removal of the director.) The Master noted that the provision was stated to be expressly subject to the constitution of the company, and in this case, the constitution established its own procedures for removal of directors and this overrode the procedure set out in s 156. Zeitler was therefore properly removed as a director.

The rules and regulations prescribed by the Companies Act 1997 and the constitution have been devised to protect or be for the benefit of the shareholders, its creditors and indeed the general public. As Raine J pointed out in *Secretary for Law v New Guinea Development Corporation Ltd*:[120]

> The fact of the matter is that the directors of a company are in a position of trust qua the shareholders and if money is subscribed by shareholders there must be some discipline, and there must be some means whereby the Government, through its officers, is able to give protection to shareholders. As we all know this has not prevented many company swindles all over the world, but at least disciplinary provisions provide some sanctions, they put some brake upon careless or dishonest management. It might well be that in a developing country such as this regard should be paid to the less sophisticated atmosphere in which companies operate. But this is a matter for the Legislature and whatever amendments are deemed appropriate I have no doubt that a wise Legislature would impose some sort of Government control over the activities of directors and those managing companies.

The rules protect the members and creditors of the company against inattentive, incompetent, insensitive and dishonest directors and officers, ensure discipline in the management of companies and benefit the general public by insisting on disclosure of relevant information. The importance of these rules and regulations and the procedures laid down is evidenced by the fact that non-compliance may invalidate the directors' and officers' actions or lead to criminal prosecution and legal sanctions.[121]

118 (1998) 8 NZCLC 261,778.
119 The equivalent provision to s 134 of the Companies Act 1997.
120 *Secretary for Law v New Guinea Development Corporation Ltd* [1975] PNGLR 179 at 183.
121 Kimuli, M A, Amankwah, H A and Mugambwa, J T, *Introduction to the Law of Business Associations in Papua New Guinea* (2nd edn, Pacific Law Press, Hobart, 1990), p 98.

As Watson points out:[122]

> If a company is likened to a small democratic nation, then its directors are its government. Once elected and in control, the directors have almost total power over the operation of the company until they are removed. Minority shareholders may be able to have directors appointed to the board but, as in a democracy, those in opposition to the majority have little true power. As with a democratic government, directors are answerable to the shareholders, but historically often the actions complained of by the shareholders have already taken place before the directors can be removed. To stretch the analogy further directors, like a ruling party, are responsible for the day-to-day management and administration, as well as determining the future direction of the company.

The relationship between the board of directors and the shareholders of a company has been further clarified with the enactment of the Companies Act 1997. Before then, the matter was governed by the Companies Act (Ch 146) and the underlying law.

The division of powers between the directors and shareholders was governed by the articles of association of the company. If the directors exceeded their powers, the shareholders could validate their actions retrospectively.[123]

The Companies Act 1997 has given greater powers of management and control to directors, but has correspondingly increased their obligations to shareholders. Shareholders have increased statutory rights against directors, although many of the rights and remedies to enforce them have restated the common law position. By extending the definition of director, a far more diverse group will become subject to the duties and corresponding liability attaching to the role of director.

The leading case was *Automatic Self-Cleansing Filter Syndicate Co Ltd v Cunninghame*.[124] The articles of association provided that the directors had the power of general management of the company and to deal with the company's assets. The company (i.e. shareholders in general meeting) instructed the directors to sell the business of the company to a particular buyer. The directors refused, considering that such a sale was not in the best interests of the company. The English Court of Appeal held that once the shareholders had delegated the power to the directors they could not interfere with that power by passing a resolution dealing with that particular power.

According to the underlying law, the power of the company to perform its functions lay with the shareholders. Once the shareholders had delegated

122 Watson, S M, "Directors' Duties in New Zealand" [1998] *Journal of Business Law* 495.
123 *Bamford v Bamford* [1970] Ch 212.
124 [1906] 2 Ch 34.

a particular power to the directors, a meeting of shareholders could not exercise that power.[125]

The underlying law position on the relationship between shareholders and directors was modified by the Companies Act 1997. Section 109 of the Companies Act 1997 states that the business and affairs of a company shall be managed by, or be under the direction or supervision of, the board of the company, and that the board has all the powers necessary for managing, and for directing and supervising the management of, the business and affairs of the company. This is subject to any modifications, exceptions, or limitations contained in the Companies Act 1997 or in the company's constitution (if it has one).[126] Although these powers given to directors are very wide, they are still subject to limits imposed by specific provisions in the Companies Act 1997, and in particular by the requirement that directors obtain the consent of shareholders before entering into "major transactions".[127]

Directors have the power to enter into contracts with third parties that bind the company. This is so even though the person may not have been properly appointed as a director or may have actually ceased being a director, or that a properly appointed director has not been formally delegated power to deal with the third party.[128]

Do the directors' duties provisions constitute a code?

There are differing opinions amongst judges in PNG and others as to whether the directors' duties provisions set out in the Companies Act 1997 constitute a code or not.[129] The same is the position in New Zealand.

125 See also *John Shaw & Sons (Salford) Ltd v Shaw* [1935] 2 KB 113; *Black White & Grey Cabs Ltd v Fox* [1969] NZLR 824.

126 Companies Act 1997, s 109(3).

127 For "major transactions" see s 109 of the Companies Act 1997.

128 Companies Act 1997, ss 19(1) and 136.

129 Beck and Borrowdale seem to consider that the directors' duties provision in the PNG Companies Act 1997 form a code (Beck, A and Borrowdale, A, *Papua New Guinea Companies and Securities Law Guide* (CCH Australia Ltd, Sydney, 1999), para 309). Although referring enigmatically to the imposition of a "further separate fiduciary duty" (i.e. the duty to act for a proper purpose) on directors developed since the late 1960s, without stating whether this duty applies in PNG, they go on to state: "The 1997 Act now comprehensively restates the duties of directors and modifies them in important respects." This seems to be a mere restatement of the relevant text in their New Zealand book (Beck, A and Borrowdale, A, *Guidebook to New Zealand Companies and Securities Law* (7th edn, CCH New Zealand Ltd, Auckland, 2002, para 309), on which the PNG text is based without any analysis of the point. *The Company Director: A short guide to being a Company Director in PNG* (1st edn, Deloitte Touche Tohmatsu, PNG Institute of Directors, Port Moresby, 2003) at p 8 states that: "The Companies Act 1997 (the Act) is the key legislation on directors' duties. It *codifies* the common law and updates prior statutes setting forth the responsibilities of directors." (Emphasis added.)

Kandakasi J in *Spirit Haus Ltd v Robert Marshall*[130] stated (*obiter*) that the directors' duties provisions in the Companies Act 1997 formed a code. After referring to the fact that "[i]t is settled [underlying] law that, directors of companies owe a fiduciary duty to the companies they are directors of", he opined that "Division 3 of Part VIII, ss. 112 to 127 of the Companies Act 1997 *codify these principles* and deal specifically with the duties of directors of companies". (Emphasis added.)

In *Sabatica Pty Ltd v Battle Mountain Canada Ltd*,[131] however, the Supreme Court (comprising Amet CJ, Kapi DCJ and Los J) appeared to consider that despite the enactment of the Companies Act 1997, and the statutory directors' duties set out in that Act, the "common law claim based on negligence" against directors was still available, despite similar duties being imposed by the Companies Act 1997. As such, Division 3 of Part VIII of the Companies Act 1997 did not codify these principles.

This issue is yet to be decided in New Zealand. There is no definitive case law on this issue,[132] and commentators have given varying opinions.[133] The situation is also more complicated in New Zealand in that there was an original provision in the Companies Bill which showed that at least as far as directors' duties were concerned, even if not the remedies that could be obtained for breach of such, the Act was not meant to form a code on these matters. Some commentators consider the removal of clause 116 of the Companies Bill (which expressly preserved the common law relating to directors' duties where not inconsistent with the statutory duties) during its passage through Parliament signified that the Companies Act 1993 (NZ) was intended to be a code.

130 (2004) N2630.

131 (2003) SC709.

132 In *Manukau City Council v Lawson*, unreported, Morris J, 21 May 1999, HC Auckland CP210/SW99, it was suggested that the directors' duties provisions in the New Zealand Companies Act 1993 formed a code. See also *Taurus Transport v Taylor* (unreported) Master Thomson, 22 May 2000, High Court, Napier CP33/99.

133 Walker, G, Reid, T, Hanrahan, P, Ramsay, I and Stapledon, G, *Commercial Applications of Company Law in New Zealand* (CCH New Zealand Ltd, Auckland, 2002), para 1203; Farrar, J, *Corporate Governance in Australia and New Zealand* (South Melbourne, Vic: Oxford University Press, 2001), p 102, 109; *Laws of New Zealand: Volume 6: Companies* (Wellington, Butterworths, 1997), para 3–4; Morison's *Company and Securities Law* (Butterworths, Wellington, 2000), para 24.1; Rennie, R A and Watts, P, *Directors' Duties and Shareholder Rights* (New Zealand Law Society Seminar, 1996); Fitzsimons, P, "New Zealand Company Law" in Tomasic, R (ed), *Company Law in East Asia* (Aldershot, Hants, England; Brookfield, Vt: Ashgate, Dartmouth, 1999), Ch 16, p 605; Fitzsimons, P, "Corporate Governance and the Courts in New Zealand", Australasian Corporate Law Teachers' Association Conference, University of Melbourne, 18 February 1997, p 22–23; Wishart, D, *Company Law in Context* (Oxford University Press, Auckland, 1994) p 251; Grantham, R B and Rickett, C E F, *Company and Securities Law: Commentary and Materials* (Brookers, New Zealand, 2002), p 470; Harris, B, "Fiduciary Duties of Directors under the Companies Act 1993" [1994] *New Zealand Law Journal* 242 at 245.

Despite the uncertainty on this issue in New Zealand, it is suggested that the best statement of the position in that jurisdiction is as follows:[134]

> ...although there is considerable uncertainty as to whether the [Companies Act 1993] purports to be a code, due principally to the ambiguous legislative history, it is unlikely that this is so. It is inconceivable, given the breadth with which the duties are stated, that it was intended that resort could not be had to the common law in interpreting and applying the Act. This, coupled with the fact that the Act's coverage in respect of duties is incomplete (it does not provide for the company's remedies for breach), suggests that the common law has not been replaced other than where it is inconsistent with the Act.

It is suggested that this is also the position in PNG; the Supreme Court decision in *Sabalica Pty Ltd v Battle Mountain Canada Ltd*[135] supports this view, even if the matter may not have been fully argued before the court. We will therefore consider the underlying law relating to directors' duties (unless there are more specific arguments that can be made to show that the law has been altered – proper purposes duty) and also the statutory duties applying to directors by virtue of specific provisions of the Act. Furthermore, even if it transpires that the directors' duties provisions in the Companies Act 1997 form a code, the cases dealing with the underlying law duties will help to interpret the meaning of these provisions, and as such, consideration of them will be of benefit.

Underlying law duty of loyalty and good faith (directors' fiduciary duties)[136]

Underlying law duty to act bona fide in the interest of the company

Directors must act in what they consider to be the best interests of the company. The test is primarily subjective: in the words of Lord Greene MR in *Re Smith and Fawcett Ltd*:[137]

> ...[Directors] must exercise their discretion bona fide in what they consider–not what the court may consider – is in the interest of the company, and not for any collateral purpose . . .

134 Grantham, R, "Contracting with Companies: Rule of Law or Business Rules?" (1996) 17 *New Zealand Universities Law Review* 39 at 63.

135 (2003) SC709.

136 For the provision dealing with the duty of good faith, see Companies Act 1997, s 112.

137 [1942] Ch 304 at 306. This statement of the directors' duty was adopted by Kandakasi J in *Spirit Haus Ltd v Robert Marshall* (2004) N2630.

In *Spirit Haus Ltd v Robert Marshall*,[138] Kandakasi J stated:

> The conduct of company directors are governed by law. It is settled law that, directors of companies owe a fiduciary duty to the companies they are directors of. This duty extends to even a 'nominee', 'alternate' or a 'puppet' director. Paramount in that duty is the duty to exercise their powers *bona fide* for the benefit of the company to the exclusion of those responsible for their appointment, consistently with the well-accepted principle that, a company is a separate legal personality. Lord Greene MR made that clear in *Re Smith and Fawcett Ltd* [1942] Ch 304; 1 All ER 542 in these terms:
>
>> '... [Directors] must exercise their discretion bona fide in what they consider—not what the court may consider—is in the interest of the company, and not for any collateral purpose . . .'
>
> This imports an obligation on the directors of companies not to place themselves in a position where the exercise of their powers for the company's benefit is in any way fettered. More specifically, this means that the directors must not place themselves in a position where their duties and personal interests may conflict.

There are several aspects to this duty. The first is the duty to act bona fide, sometimes referred to as the duty to act as an honest person of business would be expected to act. This means that directors should put the interest of the company ahead of their own or someone else's interest or, put more strongly, directors must not, therefore, promote their own or some other party's interests ahead of that of the company.[139]

Another aspect of the duty requires the director to act "in the interests of the company as a whole". This will always mean that the directors must consider the interests of the company's shareholders, in fact a hypothetical individual shareholder.[140] It is not only current shareholders, but future ones as well.[141] They must also take into consideration the interest of creditors when the company is insolvent or is nearing insolvency.[142] The test is an objective one.

Underlying law duty to avoid conflict of interests[143]

Directors are in a fiduciary relationship with the company and as such are under a duty to put the interest of the company before their own where

138 (2004) N2630.
139 *Mills v Mills* (1938) 60 CLR 150; *Re W & M Roith Ltd* [1967] 1 WLR 432.
140 *Greenhalgh v Arderne Cinemas Ltd* [1951] 1 Ch 286.
141 *Darvall v North Sydney Brick and Tile Co Ltd* (1987) 16 NSWLR 212.
142 *Kinsela v Russell Kinsela Pty Ltd (in liq)* (1986) 4 NSWLR 722.
143 This duty is sometimes referred to as a duty to avoid conflict of duties, or conflict of interest and duty.

there is a conflict. Because of the temptation to put their interests first, judges and Parliament have developed principles to ensure that if there is such a conflict, the directors ought to put their duty to the company ahead of their own interest. Although several commentators considered that the duties imposed on directors by the Companies Act 1993 (NZ) were too onerous and would have the undesired effect of stifling business enterprise, it has been stated that since the enactment of the New Zealand Act, there has been no discernable reduction in the number of companies in operation and that the decisions of the courts so far, have been largely consistent with the Act's objective of encouraging "efficient and responsible management of companies by allowing directors a wide discretion in matters of business judgment while at the same time providing protection for shareholders and creditors against the abuse of management power".[144]

In *Spirit Haus Ltd v Robert Marshall*,[145] Kandakasi J stated:

> Where a director is in a position of possible conflict of interest, he is required to disclose the nature of his interest to his fellow directors. Additionally, if the matter in which a director has an interest is significant, he is required to have that disclosed in the directors' report. Further, unless the articles or the constitution of the company otherwise provides, a director may not vote or participate in the decision concerning the matter in which he has an interest. The accepted practice is for him to disclose his interest and disqualify [himself] from participation in the deliberations on the matter he has an interest in.

After citing ss 112 to 127 of the Companies Act 1997, his Honour concluded:

> The legislation could not be any clearer than the words it employs to identify the possible conflict situations. In any case, it is clear that all other relationships and situations are covered as long as they come within the test of "otherwise directly or indirectly materially interested in the transaction". The provisions of subsection (2) deal with the giving of security by the company to third parties, which have no connection with a director.
>
> Section 118 provides as to the manner in which a director should disclose his interest. It provides that as soon as a director becomes aware

144 Watson, S, Gunasekara, G, Gedye, M, van Roy, Y, Ross, M, Longdin, L, Sims, A and Brown, L, *The Law of Business Organisations* (4th edn, Palatine Press, Auckland, 2003), para 12.00, referring to the Companies Act 1993, long title. Note that although the Companies Act 1997 did not reproduce the long title of the New Zealand Companies Act 1993, the fact that the PNG Act so closely follows the New Zealand Act means that the local Act must have similar purposes.

145 (2004) N2630.

> of the fact that he is interested in a transaction or proposed transaction with the company, he must cause to be entered in the company's interests register and where the company has more than one director disclose that to the board of the company. That discloser must include the full monetary value if known or if it cannot be quantified, the nature and extent of that interest.
>
> These requirements are very serious matters. That seriousness is highlighted by the fact that s 112(5) and s 118(4) make it an offence for a director to breach his or her fiduciary or duty of care and the duty to disclose a situation of conflict of interest, respectively. These offences attract penalties respectively of K200,000.00, or a term of imprisonment up to five years or both and a penalty of K10,000.00. This is by virtue of s 413(4) and (2) respectively.

The company may place in its constitution a provision which permits a director to have interests in a contract with the company.[146] In the absence of such express provisions, there seems to be only one way to enable the company to overlook the breach of duty. This is for the director to make a full disclosure to the members of the company and to have the contract entered into ratified by the company in general meeting.[147] The better view is that the board of directors acting on their own cannot ratify the contract.[148]

Relief by the company

Members of a company may relax a duty owed by the directors by a vote at a general meeting of the company. This can be done by a simple majority and the approval may be made either before the action of the directors,[149] or after the breach has occurred.[150] There are some limitations on this power, however. No approval may be given where the action of the directors constitute a fraud on the minority shareholders,[151] to condone a breach of duty that would otherwise be illegal, such as a misappropriation of company property,[152] or where the interests of creditors has supervened and their interest would be prejudiced by the approval.

There are some limitations to this power to approve a director's action in general meeting. It cannot operate if it would constitute a fraud on the minority shareholders. It may also not operate to condone a breach of duty which is also

146 *Re Automotive & General Industries Ltd* [1975] VR 454.
147 *George A Bond & Co v Bond* (1929) 30 SR (NSW) 15.
148 Cf *Queensland Mines Ltd v Hudson* (1978) 52 ALJR 399, where the Privy Council held that the approval of the board of directors was sufficient.
149 *Winthrop Investments Ltd v Winns Ltd* [1975] 2 NSWLR 666.
150 *Bamford v Bamford* [1970] Ch 212.
151 *Ngurli v McCann* (1953) 90 CLR 425.
152 *Cook v Deeks* [1916] 1 AC 554.

otherwise an illegal act, such as a misappropriation of the company's resources. Furthermore, it is not possible for the shareholders to approve a breach of duty if the interests of creditors are prejudiced.[153]

Fiduciary duties of directors

It has been stated that equity (i.e. the underlying law) recognises three conceptually distinct principal fiduciary rules:[154]

- company directors must not, in any matter falling within the scope of their service, have a personal interest or inconsistent engagement with a third party, except with the company's fully informed consent (*the conflict rule*);
- company directors must not misuse their position for their own or a third party's advantage, except with the company's fully informed consent, and therefore they must account to the company for any gain which they make in connection with their fiduciary office (*the profit rule*);
- company directors must not misappropriate the company's property or corporate opportunities for their own or a third party's benefit (*the misappropriation rule*).

The conflict rule

The conflict rule has been formulated in various ways, some very strict, and others less so. The strict formulation states that a person "... is not allowed to put himself in a position where his interest and duty conflict".[155] This would mean, however, that a director would not be allowed to hold shares in the company and would create many problems when the director occupies board positions in competing companies. The tendency of modern courts is therefore to move from a strict formulation to a more practical approach. The courts now refer to the fact that there must be a "real sensible possibility",[156] "significant possibility",[157] or "a real and substantial possibility"[158] of conflict.[159] The most obvious situation where this conflict arises is where

153 *Kinsela v Russell Kinsela Pty Ltd (in liq)* (1986) 4 NSWLR 722.
154 Austin, R P, Ramsay I M, *Ford's Principles of Corporations Law* (12th edn, LexisNexis Butterworths, Australia, 2005), para 9.020.
155 *Bray v Ford* [1896] AC 44 at 51, per Lord Herschell.
156 *Phipps v Boardman* [1967] 2 AC 46 at 124, per Lord Upjohn.
157 *Chan v Zacharia* (1984) 154 CLR 178 at 199, per Deane J.
158 *Hospital Products Ltd v United States Surgical Corporation* (1984) 156 CLR 41 at 103, per Jason J.
159 The relaxation of the strictness of the formulation of the rule was noted by Wilson J in *Alan Arthur Morris v PNG Associated Industries Ltd* (1980) N260(L) at para 3.34.

the director enters into a transaction, directly or indirectly, to which the company is party.

The underlying law conflict rule states that directors or senior executive officers of companies must not place themselves in a position where there is an actual or substantial possibility of a conflict between their personal interest and their duty to act in the interests of the company, unless the permission of the company is obtained.[160] It is not any possible conflict which results in the common law rule applying. There must be an actual conflict or a substantial possibility of conflict.

Because directors occupy a fiduciary position in relation to their company, they are not allowed to put themselves into a position where their duties to the company conflict with their personal interest. This has long been the common law position in England and has been adopted as part of the underlying law.[161] The most common situation where the underlying law conflict rule applies to a director is where the director is involved in transactions with the company. The director may not enter into a contract to sell property to the company or buy property from the company. In the case of a contract to sell property to the company, there is a conflict between the director's personal interest (to obtain the highest price possible for the property) and the director's duty to act in the interests of the company (to ensure that the company buys the property at the lowest price possible). In the case of a purchase of property from the company, the reverse applies. The principle applies both to direct dealings with the company, and cases where the director is indirectly involved, for example where he or she has an interest in a partnership or company which deals with the company. This was the position in *Aberdeen Railway Co Ltd v Blaikie Bros*.[162]

Aberdeen Railway Co entered into a contract to purchase office furniture from a partnership which conducted business under the name Blaikie Bros. Blaikie, who was a director and chairman of Aberdeen Railway, did not tell the other directors that he was the managing partner in Blaikie Bros. The court held that the director had breached his duty to not place himself in a position where his personal interest conflicted with his duty to the company. The court stated that the conflict was that the director's personal interest

160 *Boardman v Phipps* [1967] 2 AC 46. The permission may be obtained either beforehand or afterwards (by ratification).

161 See *Alan Arthur Morris v PNG Associated Industries Ltd* (1980) N260(L). In that case Wilson J noted that the plaintiff "discharged such fiduciary duty as he owed to the defendant company when he declared his interest and did not participate in the discussion in relation to the resolutions at all. The deed was tabled at a board meeting and the matter was open for discussion under the chairmanship of an independent person. Everything was in the deed and in the resolutions, and there was no concealment of any material fact, misuse of confidential information or the like. The other directors were put on notice 'to scrutinise the terms of the deed, knowing the interest of one of their body'".

162 (1854) 1 Macq 461, [1843–60] All ER Rep 249.

was to have Blaikie Bros sell the equipment to Aberdeen Railway at the highest price possible. However, the director's duty to act in the interests of Aberdeen Railway imposed on the director the duty of obtaining the equipment at the lowest possible price. As a result of the breach of duty by the director, the court held that Aberdeen Railway was entitled to have the contract with Blaikie Bros set aside, and this despite the fact that the price that it paid for the furniture was fair.

In such cases the courts will therefore not enter into any discussion as to whether the transaction was a good or bad one for the company.[163]

The profit rule

A director may not use company property either for the director's personal benefit, or for the benefit of any other person, without the authority of the company. Many of the situations where directors breach this duty is where they apply the company's property to themselves personally, to a company in which they have an interest, or in favour of their family or relatives. Directors are prevented from taking remuneration or other benefits from the company unless (i) authorised by law, (ii) authorised by the company's constitution, or (iii) with the fully informed consent of the company in general meeting.

The misappropriation rule (secret profits)

The misappropriation rule builds on the underlying law conflict rule, and provides that directors must not take corporate property, information or opportunities (referred to generally as secret profits), without the permission of the company. Where a director takes corporate property, information or opportunities without the permission of the company, he or she places personal interest over the duty to act in the interests of the company. It is usually quite clear what is corporate property or information. Difficulties sometimes arise, however, in defining what is a corporate opportunity, particularly one that "belongs" to the company. The courts have held that a corporate opportunity is a business opportunity which the company is considering or one in which the company might reasonably be expected to be interested, given the type of business that the company is engaged in or carrying on.

The English common law (including equity) which forms a source of the underlying law of PNG, applies this rule strictly.[164] It is so applied as a warning to directors that they should not engage in similar conduct. Although judges in PNG are free to depart from the adopted English common law, it is suggested that they will follow this principle as a prophylactic, as

163 Cf *Phipps v Boardman* [1967] 2 AC 46, where the action of the "trustee" benefited the trust.

164 The rule is not as strictly applied in US jurisdictions, particularly the state of Delaware: see Kershaw, D, "Lost in Translation: Corporate Opportunities in Comparative Perspective" (2005) 25 *Oxford Journal of Legal Studies* 603–627.

a warning to directors that if they engage in this type of conduct, any benefits that they gain will be stripped from them and given to the company.

The most obvious example of the misappropriation rule is where the underlying law prevents a director from accepting a bribe or other personal benefit to ensure that the company acts in a certain way or to influence the board of directors to vote for a particular course of conduct.[165]

What if the company cannot take the opportunity?

We have seen that a director must not take a business opportunity which the company is currently considering or in which it might reasonably be expected to be interested, given its current line of business. What if the company is unable to take up the opportunity because, for example, it does not have the financial resources? In these circumstances, is a director of the company able to take up the opportunity without there being a breach of duty? The English courts have applied the rule strictly in these circumstances to still decide there is a breach of duty. In short, it does not matter that the company is not able to exploit the corporate opportunity. A director who takes up such opportunities will be made to account for any profits derived thereby.[166]

In *Regal (Hastings) Ltd v Gulliver*,[167] the directors of Regal (Hastings) Ltd, which owned a cinema, decided to lease two additional cinemas with a view to selling the three cinemas as a single enterprise. Regal formed a subsidiary company (Hastings Amalgamated Cinemas Ltd) to acquire the leases. After negotiations it became necessary for the subsidiary to have a paid-up capital of £5,000: the landlord of the two cinemas insisting that this was necessary. Regal could provide only £2,000 for the purchase of shares in Hastings Amalgamated Cinemas Ltd. To provide the extra capital required, four of the directors, together with the company solicitor and persons nominated by the chairman, subscribed for shares in the subsidiary company to the value of the remaining £3,000. Later, there was a sale of all the shares held in the two companies. The owners of the shares in the subsidiary made a substantial profit from this sale. The new directors of Regal (Hastings) Ltd then caused the company to bring an action against the former directors to recover the profits they had made from the sale of the shares in the subsidiary. Although it was found that the directors and the other parties had not acted dishonestly, the House of Lords held that the directors had made a gain by virtue of their position as directors and that this gain had not been authorised

165 *Boston Deep Sea Fishing & Ice Co v Ansell* (1883) 39 Ch D 339; *Furs Ltd v Tomkies* (1936) 54 CLR 583.

166 See also *Holden v Architectural Finishes Ltd* [1997] 3 NZLR 143, (1996) 7 NZCLC 260,976; *Thorrington v McCann* (1998) 8 NZCLC 261,564.

167 [1942] 1 All ER 378.

by the company. The House of Lords held that the directors "having obtained these shares by reason and only by reason of the fact that they were directors and in the course of the execution of that office" were accountable to Regal (Hastings) Ltd for the profits. The fact that the directors were acting in good faith, and that there would have been no profit for Regal (Hastings) Ltd to claim but for the actions of the directors were considered by the House of Lords to be irrelevant.

The decision in *Regal (Hastings) Ltd v Gulliver* has been criticised on several grounds, including the fact that the new owner of Regal (Hastings) Ltd and Hastings Amalgamated Cinemas Ltd, by proving a breach of duty by the four directors of Regal (Hastings) Ltd, was able to obtain a windfall profit. Although the new owner had paid what was a fair price for the shares of both companies, by establishing a breach of duty by the four directors, the profits made by the four directors had to be paid to Regal which was to the financial benefit of the new owner. The old shareholders of Regal did not receive any of these profits even though they were shareholders at the time the directors breached their duties.[168]

Can a director resign to take up a corporate opportunity?

A director cannot exploit a corporate opportunity where the resignation "may fairly be said to have been prompted or influenced by a wish to acquire for himself the opportunity sought by the company, or where it was in his position with the company rather than a fresh initiative that led him to the opportunity which he later acquired".[169]

Where a director resigns from a company to take up a corporate opportunity, the courts have held that the director will breach his or her duty by taking up the opportunity without the permission of the company where:

- the resignation was prompted or influenced by a desire to acquire the opportunity sought by the company; or
- it was the director's position with the company rather than a new initiative that led the director to the opportunity which the director later acquired.[170]

In *Industrial Development Consultants Ltd v Cooley*,[171] Cooley was appointed as managing director of Industrial Development Consultants Ltd (IDC), without a service agreement. While he was in that position, a public authority requested him to design a building for them, and made it clear that

168 For a recent strict application of this principle, see the English case of *Bhullar v Bhullar* [2003] EWCA Civ 424.
169 *Canadian Aero Service Ltd v O'Malley* (1973) 40 DLR (3d) 371 at 382.
170 *Canadian Aero Service Ltd v O'Malley* (1973) 40 DLR (3d) 371 at 382.
171 [1972] 2 All ER 162. See also *Canadian Aero Service Ltd v O'Malley* (1973) 40 DLR (3d) 371.

it would not grant the agreement to IDC. Cooley then pretended to be ill to secure his release from the company and carried out the agreement with IDC for his own benefit. It was held that Cooley was liable for the profits he had made because they were acquired as a result of his position and it was immaterial that the opportunity could not have been taken up by IDC.

The position is different where a director has made full disclosure to the company and it has declined an opportunity. This is clear from the decisions in *Queensland Mines Ltd v Hudson*[172] and *Peso Silver Mines Ltd v Cropper*.[173]

Underlying law duty to use powers for proper purposes[174]

In several common law jurisdictions, the law explicitly requires a director to exercise his or her powers for a proper purpose. In some jurisdictions this duty is regulated by the common law;[175] in others the duty has been set out in a statutory provision.[176] In New Zealand, the duty has been encapsulated in s 133 of the Companies Act 1993, which specifically requires that directors exercise their powers "for a proper purpose". This was done, despite the recommendation of the New Zealand Law Commission not to include a proper purpose provision in the Act, mainly because the Commission feared that this would limit the exercise of a director's duty to exercise his or her powers in good faith.[177]

172 (1978) 52 ALJR 399. In this case the disclosure was made to the Board of Directors and not the company in general meeting; nevertheless the Privy Council held that the disclosure was sufficient. It is doubtful whether the courts in PNG will follow this decision.

173 (1966) 58 DLR (2d) 1.

174 Grantham, R B, "The powers of company directors and the proper purposes doctrine" (1994–1995) 5 *King's College Law Journal* 16.

175 The matter is still governed by the common law in the UK, though there has been discussion about codifying it. The doctrine is recognised in Principle 1 of the statement of directors' duties proposed in the Draft Clauses, in that there is an obligation to act in accordance with the company's constitution and to exercise those powers "for a proper purpose": *Modernising Company Law – Draft Clauses*, Cm 5553-II, July 2002, Sch 2, para 1. The UK Company Law Review (CLR) produced in 2001 thought that it should be left open for judicial development whether the proper purposes rules should be grounded solely in an interpretation of the company's constitution, and the proposed statement appears to do so: *Company Law Review, Completing the Structure* (URN 00/1335, November 2000), para 3.14. See Davies, P L, *Gower and Davies' Principles of Modern Company Law* (7th edn, Sweet & Maxwell, London, 2003), p 387.

176 This duty is now specifically provided for in s 181(1)(b) of the Corporations Act 2001 (Aus).

177 *Company Law: Reform and Restatement* (Report No 9, Law Commission, New Zealand, 1989), paras 507-8. The Commission recommended against the inclusion of a separate duty to act for a proper purpose. The Commission believed that by reformulating the director's duty of loyalty to require "reasonable belief" that the action was in the interests of the company, a separate duty to act for a proper purpose was unnecessary. It did not consider that by excluding a specific reference to "proper purpose" from the statute,

Some commentators regard the proper purpose test as redundant and logically presupposed by the duty to act in good faith for the benefit of the company,[178] and it has been rejected as a separate duty in at least one jurisdiction: the "improper purpose" test, as a requirement distinct from subjective good faith, has been rejected in British Columbia: *Teck Corporation Ltd v Millar*.[179]

It is unlikely that the current law of PNG imposes a duty on directors to exercise their powers for a proper purpose. Although the underlying law did at one stage recognise such a duty,[180] it can be argued that the law on this matter was changed in 1997, when a deliberate decision was made not to include a provision similar to s 133 of the New Zealand Companies Act 1993 in the PNG Companies Act 1997. This showed that the drafters and legislators did not deem it appropriate to cater for this duty:[181] the failure to put the duty into statutory form constituting an implied repeal of the

the "common law" on directors' duties would be altered. Section 133 was included during the drafting stage, because of the views of the Department of Justice. The New Zealand Law Commission considered that by addressing the main problem areas of modern company law directly (e.g., minority shareholder remedies, and restrictions on share issues), some of the current common law rules developed to avoid apparent injustices, such as the concept of "proper purposes" could be "safely set aside". It considered that this area involved "great uncertainty in the absence of identifiable limits to the powers of companies and directors" and as such there was no need to specify such a duty in the Act: New Zealand Law Commission, *Company Law: Reform and Restatement, Law Commission* (Report No 9, New Zealand, 1989), xxiii. It considered that its draft provision dealing with class rights and minority remedies would obviate the need for resort to the doctrine of directors acting only for "proper purposes". (The new legislation would provide protection in the most common "proper purpose" cases, i.e., those concerning the issue of shares and the refusal to permit the transfer of shares.) The attempt by the Law Commission to omit the proper purpose duty from the New Zealand Companies Act 1993 was "defeated by the Justice Department": see Farrar, J, *Corporate Governance in Australia and New Zealand* (Oxford University Press, South Melbourne, Vic, 2001), p 108.

178 See, for example, Fridman, S, "An Analysis of the Proper Purpose Rule" (1998) 10 *Bond Law Review* 164–183. See Nolan, R C, "The Proper Purpose Doctrine and Company Directors" in Rider, B A K (ed), *The Realm of Company Law* (Kluwer International, London, 1998) for a defence of a separate rule. As Professor John Farrar notes (*Corporate Governance in Australia and New Zealand*, Oxford University Press, South Melbourne, Vic, 2001, p108) "Although there is some overlap in the cases [dealing with proper purpose doctrine and the duty to act in good faith for the benefit of the company] there is not complete identity."

179 (1973) 33 DLR (3d) 288.

180 See *North Solomons Provincial Government v Bougainville Development Corporation Ltd* [1988] PNGLR 247.

181 We shall see below that an argument can be mounted for the continued application of this duty after 1997 and in the light of this, some consideration is given to the nature and effect of this duty.

underlying law proper purposes duty. The argument against directors of companies registered under the Companies Act 1997 having a duty to act for proper purposes is based on the following line of reasoning:

- there is no specific statutory provision (either in the Companies Act 1997 or elsewhere) requiring directors to exercise their powers "for a proper purpose";
- the decision to leave out the proper purpose duty provision from the Companies Act 1997 was based on the fact that its inclusion in the New Zealand legislation was controversial with some commentators being of the opinion that of all the provisions relating to directors' duties "this is likely to be the most troublesome";[182]
- the provisions on directors' duties in the Companies Act 1997 constitute a code, and as such, it is not possible to draw on the underlying law (i.e. common law) "proper purpose" doctrine.[183]

If it is not accepted that the directors' duties provisions constitute a code, it could still be argued that the fact that the PNG Parliament "rejected" including this duty as a specific duty in the Companies Act 1997 constituted a rejection of the concept of a director being under an obligation to exercise his or her powers for a proper purpose. As such, it amounted to an implied rejection or repeal of any underlying law proper purpose duty.

If the provisions do not form a code, it is possible that this power may exist as part of the underlying law: as such it is necessary to give the matter further consideration.

The common law doctrine of proper purposes

Because of the difficulty of proving that a director had not acted *bona fide* in the best interests of the company, the courts in some jurisdictions, from the 1960s onwards, began to develop a separate requirement that directors had to use their powers for the purpose for which they were conferred. *Hogg v Cramphorn Ltd*[184] is an early case illustrating this duty. The Articles of Association of the company gave the directors power to allot shares "on such terms and conditions as the directors think fit". In order to defeat a takeover bid that the directors believed in good faith was not in the

182 Tompkins, Hon Justice, "Directing the Directors: The Duties of Directors under the Companies Act 1993" (1994) 2 *Waikato Law Review* 13 at 20. "The 1993 reform package was subjected to trenchant and justified criticism for the lack of clarity in relation to directors' duties, not least in relation to the mystical 'proper purpose' requirement (s133)": Hodder, J, "Whither the Companies Act?" [1997] *New Zealand Law Journal* 97 at 99.

183 See above at pp 297–299 for discussion on whether the directors' duties provisions constitute a code.

184 [1966] 3 All ER 420.

company's best interests, the directors created an employee trust and allotted shares (which had weighted voting rights) to the trustees, who were supporters of the directors' views on the proposed takeover. The effect of this was to give enough voting power in the shareholders' meeting to defeat the takeover bid. Those making the takeover bid challenged the validity of the allotment. Although the directors were able to meet the subjective bona fide test in that they honestly believed that the creation of the trust and the issue of the shares were in the best interest of the company as a whole, the court had to assess whether the power of the directors to issue shares had been exercised for a proper purpose. The court held that this was an objective test, and as the power to issue shares is not for the purpose of defeating a takeover bid, the directors were in breach of their duty. As such, the case illustrates the fact that the proper purpose rule is not concerned with good faith. A director may act *bona fide* in what he or she believes to be the best interests of the company and still exercise a power for an improper purpose, and thus breach this duty. If a director is acting outside of powers, it will be irrelevant to show that he or she was acting in the best interests of the company.

In deciding whether a fiduciary has improperly exercised a power conferred on him or her, the court carries out two tests. It:[185]

(i) ascertains as a matter of law the purposes for which the power may or may not be exercised; and
(ii) determines as a matter of fact the purpose for which the power was exercised in the instant case and whether that purpose is within the category of permissible purposes.

The test of whether any power of a director is exercised for a proper purpose is an objective one. Thus the exercise of a power for an improper purpose will still be invalid, even if the motives of the directors are bona fide or altruistic. Even if directors have acted honestly in what they believe to be for the benefit of the company, they may nevertheless be liable if they have exercised their powers for a different purpose than that for which the powers were conferred upon them.[186]

Most of the cases where the proper purposes duty has been raised concern the power of directors to issue shares, and particularly in relation to takeover bids where the directors are trying to prevent a hostile takeover. As we have seen, the power to issue shares is governed by s 43(1) of the Companies Act 1997, which provides that, subject to the Act and the constitution of the company, "the board of a company may authorise the issue of shares at any

185 *Howard Smith Ltd v Ampol Petroleum Ltd* [1974] AC 821 at 835.

186 *Whitehouse v Carlton Hotel Pty Ltd* (1987) 162 CLR 285: "the exercise of a power for an ulterior or impermissible purpose is bad notwithstanding that the motives of the donee of the power in so exercising it are substantially altruistic."

time, to any person, and in any number it thinks fit". The main question is what type of actions may directors of a target company take to frustrate or prevent a takeover bid.

The main reason why a company issues shares is to raise capital for the company, and Directors are usually given the power to issue shares for this reason. However, it may issue shares for other proper purposes, including as consideration for the purchase of property and to remunerate employees of the company.[187] In relation to the power to issue shares, the courts have held that it is permissible to exercise the power to:

- raise capital when required;[188]
- ensure the financial stability of the company, even if there is no immediate need for the capital, for example, by entering into a joint venture with another company by issuing shares to that company where this ensures long-term stability for the company issuing the shares;[189]
- take advantage of a genuine commercial opportunity;[190] and
- distribute reserves of profits by way of bonus shares.[191]

Although the Privy Council in *Howard Smith Ltd v Ampol Petroleum Ltd* stated that it was not possible to set out in advance the limits of the power to issue shares, directors may not exercise the power to issue shares to:

- act in accordance with self-interest – for example, to preserve their control of the company;[192] or
- destroy an existing majority block of shares, or otherwise manipulate voting power.[193]

Shares have been held to have been issued for improper purposes where the shares were issued for the purpose of:

- diluting the shareholding of a shareholder;[194]
- entrenching control of the company in certain shareholders by issuing them more shares;[195]

187 Issuing shares to employees under an employee share plan provides a financial incentive to the employees to work in the interests of the company.
188 *Howard Smith Ltd v Ampol Petroleum Ltd* [1974] AC 821.
189 *Harlowe's Nominees Pty Ltd v Woodside (Lakes Entrance) Oil Co NL* (1968) 121 CLR 483.
190 *Pine Vale Investments Ltd v McDonnell and East Ltd* (1983) 1 ACLC 1294, *Winthrop Investments Ltd v Winns Ltd* [1975] 2 NSWLR 666.
191 *Mills v Mills* (1938) 60 CLR 150.
192 *Ngurli Ltd v McCann* (1953) 90 CLR 425.
193 *Howard Smith Ltd v Ampol Petroleum Ltd* [1974] AC 821; *Whitehouse v Carlton Hotel Pty Ltd* (1987) 162 CLR 285.
194 *Kokotovich Constructions Pty Ltd v Wallington* (1995) 17 ACSR 478.
195 *Whitehouse v Carlton Hotel Pty Ltd* (1987) 162 CLR 285.

- attempting to reduce to a minority position, a shareholder or shareholders who hold a majority of the voting power;[196] and
- directors maintaining control of the company.[197]

A share issue can be made to take advantage of a commercial opportunity even if it has the effect of defeating a takeover;[198] a share issue can also be used to distribute profits by way of bonus shares.[199]

The question whether a director has used his or her power for a proper purpose is the second issue that must be dealt with in analysing the proper purposes' duty. This is a question of considering the facts to establish the reason why the power was exercised and then establishing if that purpose was within the permissible purposes or the impermissible purposes. The onus of showing that a power has been misused lies on the person who claims that the power has been misused, and it must be shown on a balance of probabilities.[200] Courts are usually reluctant to interfere in the internal management of a company unless improper purposes are clearly demonstrated.

For example, in *Howard Smith Ltd v Ampol Petroleum Ltd*[201] the question was whether the share issue was used to raise capital or to assist a group in gaining control of the company. The case involved a takeover battle between Howard Smith and Ampol Petroleum for a shipbuilding company called RW Miller. The directors of RW Miller wished to facilitate Howard Smith's takeover bid, because it intended to pay shareholders more for their shares. Once it became known that Ampol (acting together with another company, Bulkships Ltd, which together had a majority shareholding), intended to block Howard Smith's bid, the directors of RW Miller issued further shares to Howard Smith, reducing Ampol's stake in the company and thereby their power to reject the Howard Smith bid. RW Miller needed about $10 million to finance tankers under construction and the board of directors decided to issue 4.5 million shares at $2.30 each to Howard Smith to obtain this finance. The directors claimed that the main reason for the share issue was to raise capital. Ampol challenged the allotment. The court concluded that although the directors were not motivated by any purpose of personal gain or advantage or any desire to retain their position on the board, the substantial purpose for issuing the shares was not to satisfy any need for capital but to destroy the majority holding of Ampol and Bulkships in order to allow the favoured bidder (Howard Smith) to defeat the rival bidder who had held the majority of shares. The directors had therefore breached their duty to act for proper purposes.

196 *Howard Smith Ltd v Ampol Petroleum Ltd* [1974] AC 821.
197 *Hogg v Cramphorn Ltd* [1967] Ch 254.
198 *Pine Vale Investments Ltd v McDonnell and East Ltd* (1983) 1 ACLC 1294.
199 *Mills v Mills* (1938) 60 CLR 150.
200 [1974] AC 821.
201 *Australian Metropolitan Life Assurance Co Ltd v Ure* (1923) 33 CLR 199 at 206 and 219.

In *Advance Bank of Australia Ltd v FAI Insurances Australia Ltd*,[202] directors of a company used the company's funds to promote the re-election of several of the directors. The court held that this was an improper purpose and a breach of directors' duty.

The case of *Permanent Building Society (in liq) v Wheeler*[203] is another example where the directors exercised their power of management for improper purposes. The board of a building society caused the society to purchase land at an over-value. The purpose of the transaction was to provide the vendor with money to purchase the business of another company in which the majority of the society's directors had personal interests. The case is also important as an illustration of the point that a director may be in breach of the director's duty even though he or she is not involved in a particular transaction. One of the directors who had not participated in the negotiations was held to have acted for an improper purpose because he knew of the improper purpose of the other directors and failed to prevent the transaction from proceeding. The court ordered the directors to compensate the society for its losses.

Directors must also exercise their discretion to refuse to register transfers of shares in the interests of the company and not for improper purposes. In *Australian Metropolitan Life Assurance Co Ltd v Ure*,[204] Isaacs J considered that if directors acted honestly upon business considerations such as whether the transferee was insolvent or a person whose business reputation would damage the reputation of the company if they were to become directors, the directors would be acting within their power. However, if they take into account irrelevant considerations, the court would direct the transfer to proceed. An example of an irrelevant consideration may be the race or ethnicity or sex of the purchaser.

In cases involving the issue of whether directors were motivated by improper purposes, the court will endeavour to find out the intention or motives of the directors. Finding out what motivated an action is always a difficult exercise, and the problem is made the more so when the court is analysing the intention of several directors to come to the dominant intention.

Problems may arise where there are mixed or multiple purposes. What of the situation where a company issues shares to raise capital and also to defeat a takeover bid?

In *Harlowe's Nominees Pty Ltd v Woodside (Lakes Entrance) Oil Co NL*,[205] Harlowe was trying to take over Woodside. Woodside allotted nine million shares to a third company. Harlowe sought a declaration that the

202 (1987) 9 NSWLR 464.

203 (1994) 14 ACSR 109. In *Bishopsgate Investment Management Ltd (in liq) v Maxwell (No 2)* [1994] 1 All ER 261, a director was held to have used his powers for an improper purpose where he gave away the company's assets to a family company.

204 (1923) 33 CLR 199.

205 (1968) 121 CLR 483.

allotment to the third company was invalid on the grounds that the board of Woodside used their powers otherwise than bona fide in the interests of Woodside as a whole. The directors of Woodside knew of the takeover but stated that the allotment was made with the object of ensuring the financial stability of Woodside, which was exploring for oil and gas and so needed finance. It was held on the facts that the company needed to have large sums at its disposal for exploration work to enable it to programme its activities without fear that the required money would not be forthcoming. The agreement with the third company achieved this without prejudice to existing shareholders.

Another issue that often needs to be addressed is whether the improper purpose needs to be the sole purpose for the exercise of the power to be invalid? Earlier cases in Australia stated that an exercise of a power will be invalid only if the impermissible purpose or a combination of impermissible purposes can be seen to have been dominant.[206] More recently, however, the approach is that regardless of whether the impermissible purpose is the dominant one, or only one of a number of significant objects, the exercise will be invalidated if the impermissible purpose was causative, in the sense that, but for that purpose, "the power would not have been exercised."[207] Under this second "but for" test, it has been suggested that this also requires the impermissible purpose to be a significantly contributing cause.[208]

Did the proper purpose doctrine form part of the underlying law of Papua New Guinea before 1997?

In *North Solomons Provincial Government v Bougainville Development Corporation Ltd*[209] the Supreme Court referred to the case of *Howard Smith Ltd v Ampol Petroleum Ltd*,[210] noting that it concerned the issue of directors acting for "an improper purpose". Although the court did not expressly state that the doctrine formed part of the underlying law of PNG, it is clearly implicit from the judgment that this was so. The court was not directly concerned with the substantive law relating to "proper purpose' but a procedural issue relating to joinder of the directors as defendants and whether an interlocutory injunction should be reinstated against the directors pending trial, restraining them from processing the shares that were alleged to have been issued in breach of their duty not to act for improper purposes.

206 *Ngurli Ltd v McCann* (1953) 90 CLR 425 at 445; *Mills v Mills* (1938) 60 CLR 150 at 165.
207 *Whitehouse v Carlton Hotel Pty Ltd* (1987) 162 CLR 285 at 249.
208 *Kokotovich Constructions Pty Ltd v Wallington* (1995) 17 ACSR 478.
209 [1988] PNGLR 247.
210 [1974] 1 All ER 1126.

In response to the plaintiffs' arguments that the respondents had acted for impermissible purposes in issuing the shares, the respondent contended that the allotment was made for a proper purpose, namely, the company's need for capital, and not for any improper purpose such as to benefit the defendant directors and their families, or to strengthen the votes controlled by the defendant directors because the provincial government had given notice that it wanted them dismissed. The Supreme Court, however, considered that "these arguments, which may well be of substance, go to the merits of the case and should be properly left for the trial". Despite this, the court held that: "Where there was a *prima facie* case that the allotment of shares was unlawful and for an improper purpose, it was appropriate that an interlocutory injunction restraining any processing of the shares so issued be made." As such, it endorsed the view that the doctrine of proper purpose was part of the underlying law. It concluded:[211]

> We consider that there was no good reason why the injunction should have been dissolved and we see good reason why it should be reinstated or continued. On the material before us the plaintiff has [established] a *prima facie* case that the allotment of shares was unlawful and for an improper purpose. The directors were under attack, the Provincial Government – query its powers 'directed them to be removed', the directors issued 700,000 shares below value, inter alia, to their own companies, and to the detriment of other shareholders including the plaintiff, the North Solomons Royalty Trust and the Catholic Church which together owned about 70 per cent of the shares in the company.

Does the proper purpose doctrine form part of the underlying law today?

We noted at the beginning of this section that the circumstances surrounding the enactment of the Companies Act 1997 tend to show that the drafters of the Act intended to abolish the proper purposes doctrine.[212] The essential question is whether the Companies Act 1997 abrogated the underlying law duty of directors to act for proper purposes. There is certainly no provision in the Act specifically abrogating or repealing the rule, and there are principles of statutory interpretation that favour the continuing validity of the rule. Courts will construe with strictness statutes which entail a deprivation of

211 [1988] PNGLR 247 at 253.

212 It is possible for the courts to make use of extrinsic materials (such as the second reading speech of the Minister in Parliament and perhaps even the drafting notes of the drafters who were recruited from New Zealand) in order to discover the intention of Parliament. See *Minister for Lands v Frame* [1980] PNGLR 433; *The State v Danny Sunu* [1983] PNGLR 396; *Rundle v MVIT* [1988] PNGLR 20; *Graeme Rundle v MVIT* [1987] PNGLR 44; cf *SCR No 2 of 1995; Reference by Western Highlands Provincial Executive* (1995) SC486 for discussion of the law on this matter.

common law rights,[213] and it could be argued that removal of the proper purposes duty takes away rights from shareholders. If one were to examine the legislative history of the Companies Act 1993 (NZ) on which the Companies Act 1997 is closely modelled, one could strongly argue that the "failure" of the drafters to include a provision similar to s 133 together with the recommendation of the New Zealand Law Commission means that the PNG Parliament did not intend the underlying law duty of directors to exercise their powers for proper purposes to operate (or more correctly to operate any longer) in PNG. This view would be further strengthened if Kandakasi J is indeed correct, that the Directors' Duties provisions in the Companies Act 1997 form a code.[214] It should also be noted that the Law Commission's exclusion of the proper purpose rule was made in the context of the Commission's recommendation that the duty to act in the interests of the company be tested according to what a reasonable director would believe to be the interests of the company. In the event, the test of reasonableness was not introduced into the "best interests" duty, and the proper purpose rule was retained in the New Zealand Act.[215] In the case of the PNG Act, the test of reasonableness was not introduced into the "best interests" duty. As such, if the National Court were to hold that the proper purposes duty did not apply in PNG, the situation would be different from that in New Zealand. If the drafters had intended to eliminate the proper purposes duty, they should have reverted to the Law Commission's draft provision that required a test of reasonableness in the "best interests" duty to make up for this "failure" to enact a proper purposes duty. It could therefore be argued that the failure to accommodate the reasonableness test in the best interests duty means that the proper purposes duty has not been eliminated by silence on that issue.

Duty not to fetter discretions

Boards of directors are granted, whether by the Companies Act 1997[216] or a company's constitution,[217] a great deal of discretion in carrying out

213 See *Safe Lavao v The Independent State of PNG (Re Kerema Town and Airstrip Land)* [1978] PNGLR 15 and *The Waterboard v National Capital District Interim Commission* (1990) N868, per Brown J quoting from the judgment of Mason J in *American Dairy (Qld) Pty Ltd v Blue Rio* (1981) 56 ALJR 47 at 49: "the general rule is that the court will construe a statute in conformity with the common law and will not attribute to it an intention to alter common law principles unless such an intention is manifested according to the true construction of the statute".

214 *Spirit Haus Ltd v Robert Marshall* (2004) N2630.

215 Borrowdale, A, *Duties and Responsibilities of Directors and Company Secretaries in New Zealand* (3rd edn, CCH New Zealand, Auckland, 2003), para 612.

216 Companies Act 1997, ss 111, 107(1)(c). Schedule 3 contains a list of directors' powers that cannot be delegated.

217 If a company adopts a constitution, it will usually permit delegation to the managing director and to committees of the board. One can have a committee comprised of one person.

their powers. Because they hold these powers for the company, they cannot fetter their future discretion when exercising these powers in the future, at least not without the consent of the company in general meeting. Thus, directors cannot validly contract (either with one another or with a third party) as to how they will vote at future board meetings. However, if a director has bona fide entered into an agreement on behalf of the company, he or she can, in the contract, validly agree to take such further action at board meetings as are necessary to ensure that the company carries out the contract.[218]

We have earlier noted the position of "nominee directors", where a person has been appointed as a director to act as a delegate for a particular group of shareholders. Nominee directors may find it difficult both to fulfil their duty to the company and to act as the nominee of a shareholder or other group. The courts have not yet ruled on how these directors are to balance these competing interests.[219] In Australia, for example, the law seems to be that a nominee director may have dual loyalties; however, in the event of a conflict of interests, the director's foremost duty is to the company of which he or she is a director. In *Scottish Co-operative Wholesale Society Ltd v Meyer*,[220] Scottish Co-operative Wholesale Society (Scottish Co-operative) formed a subsidiary company Scottish Textile & Manufacturing Ltd (Scottish Textile) to manufacture synthetic cloth (rayon material). Scottish Co-operative formed Scottish Textile because it could not obtain a licence without the experience of the petitioners, Meyer and Lucas, who were the minority shareholders and directors of Scottish Textile. Scottish Co-operative owned the majority shares in Scottish Textile and appointed three of its directors as nominees on the board of Scottish Textile. Scottish Co-operative supplied Scottish Textile with the materials that it needed to conduct its business. However, when a licence was no longer required owing to the lifting of licensing control, Scottish Co-operative established a new department to compete with Scottish Textile: it diverted the materials that it used to supply to Scottish Textile to this department, and refused to supply that company with the cloth it needed except at non-competitive prices. This severely affected the profitability of Scottish Textile. Although the three Scottish Co-operative nominees on the board of Scottish Textile

The normal types of committees for large companies are: (i) an executive committee with power to act for the board between board meetings; (ii) an audit committee; (iii) a finance committee; (iv) a remuneration committee; (v) a nomination committee; (vi) a risk committee; (vii) a planning committee; (viii) a public affairs committee; and (ix) a superannuation committee. Specific committees can also be set up: for example, a due diligence committee to conduct the inquiries necessary for a prospectus. As delegation does not imply a reduction of a power, the board may continue to act despite the delegation.

218 *Thorby v Goldberg* (1964) 112 CLR 597.

219 See Austin, R P, Ford, H A J, Ramsay I M, *Company Directors: Principles of Law and Corporate Governance* (LexisNexis Butterworths, Australia, 2005), Ch 14 (Common Directorships and Nominee Directors).

220 [1959] AC 324.

were aware of Scottish Co-operative's policy, they did nothing to remedy the situation. The House of Lords held that this action amounted to oppression under the English equivalent of s 152 of the Companies Act 1997 as the three nominee directors had acted contrary to the interests of the company as a whole. The court ordered the majority to buy out the shares of the minority.[221]

The Companies Act 1997 contains provisions relating to the duty of a director with common competing board membership.

Section 112(2) provides that a director of a company that is a wholly owned subsidiary may, when exercising powers or performing duties as a director, where expressly permitted to do so by the constitution of the company, act in a manner which he or she believes is in the best interests of that company's holding company even though it may not be in the best interests of the company. Section 112(3) provides that a director of a company that is a subsidiary, but not a wholly owned subsidiary may, when exercising powers or performing duties as a director, where expressly permitted to do so by the constitution of the company and with the prior agreement of the shareholders, other than its holding company, act in a manner which he or she believes is in the best interests of that company's holding company or another company within the same group of companies even though it may not be in the best interests of the company. Finally, s 112(4) stipulates that a director of a company incorporated to carry out a joint venture between the shareholders may, when exercising powers or performing duties as a director in connection with the carrying out of the joint venture, where expressly permitted to do so by the constitution of the company, act in a manner which he or she believes is in the best interests of a shareholder or shareholders, even though it may not be in the best interests of the company.

Underlying law duty of care, diligence and skill

In addition to having a fiduciary duty of loyalty and good faith to the company, the directors also owe it a duty of care, diligence and skill. These duties originally flowed from the underlying law, and as a result of contract in some cases. The Companies Act 1997 also makes provision for this duty.

In earlier cases, the duty was cast at a lower level. In *Re City Equitable Fire Insurance Co Ltd*,[222] Romer J held that the degree of skill required was that which might reasonably be expected from a person of the director's knowledge and experience. The learned judge further held that a director

221 In *Re Broadcasting Station 2GB Pty Ltd* [1964–65] NSWR 1648, it was held that merely voting in accordance with the interests of a controlling shareholder did not amount to oppression under the Australian equivalent of s 152 of the Companies Act 1997. See also *Bennetts v Board of Fire Commissioners of NSW* (1967) 87 WN (Pt 1) (NSW) 307. Cf *Levin v Clark* [1962] NSWR 686.

222 *Re City Equitable Fire Insurance Co Ltd* [1925] Ch 407.

need not give continuous attention to his or her company, and that a director is properly entitled to leave certain matters to other officials of the company and to rely on them to perform their duties.

In *Daniels v AWA Ltd*,[223] the New South Wales Court of Appeal held that a common law duty of care existed in addition to an equitable duty. In *Sabatica Pty Ltd v Battle Mountain Canada Ltd*, the Supreme Court seems to have held that the underlying law duty comprises both an equitable duty of care and a common law duty (for negligence).[224]

In maintaining this duty, the director must be familiar with the company and monitor the activities of the company as well as anyone placed in a management position by them. As far as the degree of skill required is concerned, it is clear that a director need not have the skills required by those professing a specialised skill. However, where they lack a particular skill, they ought to ensure that they are informed about and monitor those who are delegated responsibility in that area. If a director possesses specialised knowledge then it should be used. In overseas jurisdictions, particularly Australian, the collapse of companies leaving many unsecured creditors with substantial losses had led to a cry for a higher standard of care. In *Commonwealth Bank of Australia v Friedrich*,[225] Tadgell J stated:

> As the complexity of commerce has gradually intensified (for better or for worse) the community has of necessity come to expect more than formerly from directors whose task it is to govern the affairs of companies to which large sums of money are committed by way of equity capital or loan. In response, the parliaments and the courts have found it necessary in legislation and litigation to refer to the demands made on directors in more exacting terms than formerly; and the standard of capability required of them has correspondingly increased. In particular, the stage has been reached when a director is expected to be capable of understanding his company's affairs to the extent of actually reaching a reasonably informed opinion of its financial capacity.

In reaching decisions, directors in some instances ought to rely on advice of others, particularly senior executives in the firm and professional advisers like accountants and lawyers.

223 *Daniels (formerly practising as Deloitte Haskins & Sells) v Anderson; Hooke v Daniels (formerly practising as Deloitte Haskins & Sells); Daniels (formerly practising as Deloitte Haskins & Sells) v AWA Ltd* (1995) 13 ACLC 614; (1995) 16 ACSR 607. See also *Permanent Building Society (in liq) v Wheeler* (1994) 14 ACSR 109.

224 (2003) SC709.

225 (1991) 5 ACSR 115 at 126.

To whom are the duties owed?

Historically, directors owed their duties to the company. Under the Companies Act 1997, there will be certain situations where directors owe duties to individual shareholders as well. This does not mean that directors, when they make decisions, can ignore the interests of others (for example, creditors). Directors should have regard to the interests of people with whom the company deals. However, in most situations the duties will be owed to the company which means that it is the company which must enforce breaches of these duties.

The Companies Act 1997 makes it clear what statutory duties are owed to the company.[226] There are duties to:

- act in good faith and in the best interests of the company;[227]
- exercise care;[228] and
- not disclose, make use of or act on company information.[229]

Duties may be owed to an individual shareholder

The Companies Act 1997 stipulates certain duties which are owed to shareholders.[230] These may also be duties owed to the company, and include such duties as to:

- supervise the share register;[231]
- disclose interests;[232] and
- disclose share dealings.[233]

A shareholder or former shareholder may bring an action against a director for breach of a duty owed to him or her as a shareholder. Prior to the enactment of the Companies Act 1997, there were limited circumstances in which a director could be held to owe a duty to an individual shareholder. A leading case which considered this was *Coleman v Myers*.[234] The company was a small private company in which most of the shareholders were relatives and held the shares either individually or in trusts. The respondents were the managing director and chairman. They were also directors of a wine and spirit company which was half-owned by the family company, the value of the half-share being approximately $5 million. There were also property holdings

226 Companies Act 1997, s 147(3)(d)–(f).
227 Companies Act 1997, s 112.
228 Companies Act 1997, s 115.
229 Companies Act 1997, s 123.
230 Companies Act 1997, s 147(3)(a)–(c).
231 Companies Act 1997, s 70.
232 Companies Act 1997, s 118.
233 Companies Act 1997, s 126.
234 [1977] 2 NZLR 225.

as part of the wines and spirits asset portfolio. The respondents devised a plan which allowed them to acquire all the shares in the family company for $4.80 per share, payment for the shares to be made out of the company's assets. The major shareholders were family trusts of which one of the respondents was a trustee. The takeover offer was made by way of a separate company owned by one of the respondents. The appellants in the action were minority shareholders. The plan was carried out and the respondent purchased all the shares and paid for them by selling some of the company's property holdings. These resources were made available to the respondent by temporary loans from the company, followed by capital dividends. The minority shareholders brought an action alleging fraud, breach of fiduciary duty, negligence and breach of the Companies Act 1955. The court held that a duty was owed to the shareholders. The duties arose from the family character of the business; the position of the respondents in the company; the degree of inside knowledge and the manner in which the takeover was executed.

If the facts in *Coleman v Myers* were to be considered by a court today, it is likely that it would find a statutory duty owed to the shareholders. The duty would stem from the obligation of directors under the Companies Act 1997 to disclose their share acquisitions.[235] In Australia, it has also been held that directors will owe a duty to an individual shareholder where special facts exist. In *Brunninghausen v Glavanics*,[236] the court decided that the director owed a duty to a shareholder because the director was in a position of particular advantage in relation to the shareholder and special circumstances (confidential negotiations to sell the business of the company) allowed the director to exploit the shareholders.

Duties may be owed to creditors

Section 348 of the Companies Act 1997 casts a duty on company directors to prevent their company from engaging in insolvent trading, and this duty is owed to creditors as well as shareholders.

Directors' statutory duties

Section 114 duty (duty to comply with the Companies Act 1997 *and the company's constitution)*

In addition to the duties set out in the duties section of the Companies Act 1997 (Part VIII, Divisions 3 and 4), other sections of the Act impose additional obligations on directors. Furthermore, the company may set out extra directors' duties in its constitution. Section 114(1) specifically provides

235 Section 127 requires directors of closely held companies to trade shares at "fair value" or pay damages for the offence.
236 (1999) 46 NSWLR 538.

that a director "shall not act, or agree to the company acting, in a manner that contravenes [the Companies Act 1997] or the constitution of the company". So a director must comply with the Companies Act 1997 and with the company's constitution, and must ensure that the company also complies with the Act and constitution. Section 114(2) states that a director who acts in contravention of s 114(1) commits an offence and is liable on conviction to a penalty of a fine not exceeding K200,000 or imprisonment for a term not exceeding five years, or both. So the director must not only not act, but ensure that the company also does not act in breach of the provisions of the Companies Act 1997. The equivalent provision in New Zealand has not yet been tested in the courts and commentators wonder how broadly the provision will be interpreted. It has been stated that on the face of it, breaches of provisions such as s 215, which make it a requirement that the Board ensure that an Annual Return is filed every year, will make directors not only potentially criminally liable under s 143 but also civilly liable through a civil derivative action under s 143 to the company itself.

It has been stated that although the section refers only to a contravention of "the Companies Act 1997", a director should not cause the company to act illegally through contravention of any statute generally, since this is to act for an improper purpose and is likely not to be in the best interests of the company.[237]

It has also been argued that, construed literally, the reference to the act of a director ("shall not act, or agree to the company acting") in contravention of the Companies Act 1997 or the constitution, the section may be thought to apply only where the director performs some positive act which is in contravention of the Act or constitution. However, it is suggested that the section applies also to a failure by a director to act, where this is in contravention of the Act or constitution. The omission to perform some duty or obligation in breach of the Act or constitution falls within the phrase. (It is suggested that the word "act", as used in the Companies Act 1997, includes an omission or failure to act, and this despite the fact that some sections of the Act provide specifically for an "act or omission"; cf Schedule 1.2 of the Constitution.) The Companies Act 1997 imposes many statutory responsibilities on directors. Failure to discharge any such responsibility is an offence, and ss 413 to 416 describe the penalties which attach. The effect of s 114(1) is that failure to discharge any such responsibility is also a breach of the duty to comply with the Act. For example, under s 188(1), the board must cause accounting records to be kept. Failure to do so constitutes a breach of s 114(1) and, while this is not expressed in the Act, must be actionable at the instance of the company. In other words, not only does failure to

237 Borrowdale, A, *Duties and Responsibilities of Directors and Company Secretaries in New Zealand* (3rd edn, CCH New Zealand, Auckland, 2003), para 613. Cf above at p 316 the discussion on whether the "proper purpose" duty continues to apply in PNG.

cause accounting records to be kept constitute a criminal offence, it exposes the directors to personal civil liability for breach of s 114(1).[238]

The case of *Alan Arthur Morris v PNG Associated Industries Ltd*[239] illustrates the consequences of failure of directors to comply with the Companies Act (then the Companies Act (Ch 146) (repealed)) and the constitution of the company. The defendant company at two meetings of the board of directors and two general meetings purported to dismiss the plaintiff from the position of managing/executive director and remove him from directorship of the company. Under the service agreement, the plaintiff's employment as managing/executive director could only be terminated by the board of directors if, at any time during his appointment, the plaintiff had been guilty of any grave misconduct which was prejudicial to the interests of the company. Under the articles of association, the plaintiff could be removed from directorship only by a resolution of the general meeting.

At the first "meeting" of the directors, four of the directors of the company simply walked into the boardroom, which formed part of the plaintiff's office and purported to hold a board meeting at which the plaintiff's employment as managing/executive director was terminated. No notice of the meeting had been given to any director and accordingly not all directors were present. Neither a director nor a company secretary upon the request of a director, as required by the articles, convened the meeting, and no chairman was appointed. In relation to the second "meeting" of the directors, the court noted, *inter alia*, that the request to the secretary to convene the "meeting" was made, contrary to the articles, by a person who had ceased to be a director of the company, and that the chairman of the "meeting" was not a director of the company. The court had no difficulty in finding that these so-called directors' "meetings" and the decisions made at them to terminate the plaintiff's employment as managing/executive director were invalid.

In regard to the "general meetings" of the company, at which the decision was purportedly made to remove the plaintiff from directorship, the court noted that notices of the meetings had not been given to all members of the company, contrary to the articles and s 145(4) of the repealed Companies Act (Ch 146). Even such notices as were given were shorter than required by the articles and consent to such shorter notices were, contrary to s 145(3)(b), given by persons who were, at the time, not members of the company. Additionally, special notice was not given as required by s 127 of the Companies Act (Ch 146) (repealed). Again, the court had no difficulty in holding that the "meetings" and the purported removal of the plaintiff from directorship of the company were invalid.

The court held that the defendant company through its organ (the board of directors), because of the flagrant breaches of the company's constitution

238 Borrowdale, A, *Duties and Responsibilities of Directors and Company Secretaries in New Zealand* (3rd edn, CCH New Zealand, Auckland, 2003), para 613.

239 (1980) N260(L).

(articles of association) and the Companies Act (Companies Act (Ch 146) (repealed)), did not validly terminate the plaintiff's employment as managing/executive director or remove him from his position as director. Damages were accordingly awarded for wrongful dismissal.

In *Sangara (Holdings) Ltd v Hamac Holdings Ltd (In Liquidation)*,[240] a deed evidencing the sale of shares by the respondent company to the appellant company was declared invalid because the respondent company's seal had not been affixed onto the deed in the manner required by the articles of association (the constitution). Similarly, in *Sandy Creek Gold Sluicing Ltd v McEachern*,[241] meetings of the board of directors of the second appellant company and the resolutions passed at those meetings were held invalid because of the failure to comply with the requirements of the articles of association, the then equivalent of the company's constitution.

Section 112 duty (duty to act in good faith and in the best interests of the company)

Section 112(1) of the Companies Act 1997 provides that "a director of a company, when exercising powers or performing duties, shall act in good faith and in what the director believes to be the best interests of the company". To act in good faith, means to act honestly.[242] The test is a subjective test. This means that the director must act as he or she thinks will be in the best interests of the company, not what some reasonable director would have considered to have been in the company's best interests.[243]

The courts in PNG are yet to rule on the meaning of this section. However, there are a few things that we may speculate on. It seems that in using the term 'best interests" the drafters of the Act did not mean to use a different test than that under the common law.

Although there is doubt as to the extent to which a director may be liable where he or she honestly believed that their action was in the interest of the company, it seems that the former interpretation should be accepted. In *Marchesi v Barnes*,[244] Gowans J suggested that the section would not be breached where a director by conscious and deliberate conduct, took a course of action which was not in the best interests of the company.

240 [1973] PNGLR 504.
241 [1965–66] PNGLR 169.
242 Some provisions refer to the duty as a duty to act "honestly and in good faith with a view to the best interests of the corporation".
243 The New Zealand Law Commission in its draft statute recommended an objective test. Directors would have had to believe on reasonable grounds that they were acting in the best interests of the company. One would have expected the drafters of the Companies Act 1997 to have reverted to this objective test once the duty to use powers for proper purposes was not included as an express provision in the Act.
244 [1970] VR 434.

In *Australian Growth Resources Corporation Pty Ltd v Van Reesema*,[245] however, King J thought that it was possible for a director to breach an equivalent section even though the director was acting in what he honestly believed was the best interests of the company.

Another question that arises is what constitutes the company's interests, indeed best interests. A company has several stakeholders: shareholders, company as a commercial group separate from its shareholders (an enterprise), other companies within a group of companies, creditors, employees and others.

The courts have held that the interests of the company are not the same as what a majority of the shareholders want. The courts have held that the directors must act in the interests of the company "as a whole".[246] The directors must balance the interests of the majority and minority shareholders, realising that in most cases, the interests of the company will equate with the wishes of the majority of its shareholders.

There are conflicting decisions on whether the interests of the company can include the interests of the company as a commercial entity separate from its shareholders. Some cases have held that it cannot be done,[247] whereas other courts have decided that it can be done.[248]

When the company is clearly solvent, the directors are required to make decisions which are in the interests of the company's shareholders. However, when the company is insolvent or verging on insolvency, the situation is quite different. In such situations, the interests of the company become those of its creditors rather than its shareholders.[249] The directors owe a duty to the creditors so that they would not be allowed, for example, to divest the company of assets so they are not available to pay the debts of the company's creditors. This duty may apply not only to existing creditors, but prospective creditors.[250] In such situations, the court will allow creditors to bring an action against the directors to prevent them from disposing of the company's assets.[251]

245 (1988) 13 ACLR 261.

246 *Greenhalgh v Arderne Cinemas Ltd* [1951] 1 Ch 286 at 291.

247 *Greenhalgh v Arderne Cinemas Ltd* [1951] 1 Ch 286.

248 *Ngurli Ltd v McCann* (1953) 90 CLR 425 at 438.

249 *Nicholson v Permakraft (NZ) Ltd* [1985] 1 NZLR 242; *Gray v Wilson* (1988) 8 NZCLC 261,530; *Hilton International Ltd (in liq) v Hilton* [1989] 1 NZLR 442; *Walker v Wimborne* (1976) 137 CLR 1; *Kinsela v Russell Kinsela Pty Ltd (in liq)* (1986) 4 NSWLR 722. See also 369413 *Alberta Ltd v Pocklington* (2000) 194 DLR (4th) 109 (Alta CA); *Canbook Distribution Corporation v Borins* (1999) 45 OR (3d) 565; *Private Equity Management Co v Vianet Technologies Inc* (2000) 48 OR (3d) 294; cf *Peoples Department Stores Inc (Trustees of) v Wise)* 224 DLR (4th) 509. See Thomson, D, "Directors, Creditors and Insolvency: A Duty not to Oppress" (2000) 58 *University of Toronto Faculty of Law Review* 31 for the position in Canada.

250 *Fernyhough v Rankin Nominees Ltd* (1998) 8 NZCLC 261, 623.

251 The creditor will have standing under s 350 of the Companies Act 1997.

Sections 117–127 duties (duty regarding transactions Involving self-interest – disclosure and self-dealing rules)

Conflict of interest (ss 117–122)

Sections 117–122 cover the duty to disclose and enter into only fair transactions where the director has a conflict of interest. The Companies Act 1997 requires the interest of all directors in proposed transactions of the company to be noted in a register. Once this is done, the director is allowed to engage in conduct in relation to those interests that would otherwise be considered to be in breach of the director's fiduciary duties. Directors are deemed to be interested in a transaction to which the company is a party in the following circumstances:

- where the director is a party to, or will or may derive a material financial benefit from, the transaction;[252]
- where the director has a material financial interest in another party to the transaction;[253]
- where the director is a director, officer, or trustee of another party to, or person who will or may derive a material financial benefit from, the transaction;[254]
- where the director is the parent, child, or spouse of another party to, or person who will or may derive a material financial benefit from, the transaction;[255]
- where the director is otherwise directly or indirectly materially interested in the transaction.[256]

A director of a company is considered not to be interested in a transaction where the director gives a guarantee in respect of loans made to the company.[257]

If a director is considered to be interested in a transaction, he or she has a duty "forthwith" to make a disclosure to the Board of Directors and cause the interest to be registered in the interests register.[258] Where the company has more than one director, the director with the interest must disclose to the Board the nature and monetary value of the interest if it can be quantified, and if this is not possible, the "nature and extent of that interest".[259]

252 Companies Act 1997, s 117(1)(a).
253 Companies Act 1997, s 117(1)(b).
254 Companies Act 1997, s 117(1)(c). There are certain qualifications to this rule.
255 Companies Act 1997, s 117(1)(d).
256 Companies Act 1997, s 117(1)(e).
257 Companies Act 1997, s 117(2).
258 Companies Act 1997, s 118(1).
259 Companies Act 1997, s 118(1)(a) and (b).

Unless the company's constitution provides otherwise, a director of a company who is interested in a transaction entered into, or to be entered into, by the company, may:[260]

- attend a meeting of directors at which a matter relating to the transaction arises and be included among the directors present at the meeting for the purpose of a quorum;
- vote on a matter relating to the transaction;
- sign a document relating to the transaction on behalf of the company;
- do any other thing in his capacity as a director in relation to the transaction.

It is not necessary for the disclosure procedure to be carried out where "all the shareholders of a company agree to, or concur in, any action which has been taken or is to be taken by the company" in respect of the proposed transaction where a director has a personal interest.[261]

As a general rule, failure by a director to comply with these requirements does not affect the validity of a transaction entered into by the company or the director.[262] However, the company may avoid the transaction in such situations. To do so, it must disclose the offending transaction to its shareholders as well as its intention to not to be bound by the transaction.[263] Avoidance or cancellation of the transaction is only possible, however, where the company did not receive "fair value under it".[264] Section 119(4) provides that where a transaction is entered into by a company in good faith in the ordinary course of its business and on usual terms and conditions, the company is presumed to receive fair value under the transaction.[265]

If a transaction is set aside, the interests of third parties are protected. If the property was acquired from anyone other than the company, for valuable consideration, and without knowledge of the circumstances of the offending transaction, the third party has a right to retain the property even if the offending transaction is set aside.[266]

Use of company information (s 123)

Section 123 covers the duty not to disclose or use company's confidential information except for company purposes. A fiduciary is not entitled to misuse information belonging to the company for their own purposes. This information

260 Companies Act 1997, s 122.
261 Companies Act 1997, ss 89(1) and 89(2)(f) and Schedule 1(f).
262 Companies Act 1997, s 118(2). However, the director commits an offence: see Companies Act 1997, s 118(4).
263 Companies Act 1997, s 119(1).
264 Companies Act 1997, s 119(2).
265 Other provisions in s 119 set out the onus of proof and assumptions that may be made in respect of such transactions.
266 Companies Act 1997, s 120.

relating to sensitive business conduct is confidential, and the directors are under a duty not to use or to disclose this information. Not only can they not disclose, but they may not use this information for their personal gain. The Companies Act 1997 supplements the underlying law rules relating to confidentiality of company information by making specific provisions as to when such information may be made use of or revealed.[267] In some situations, the director will resign the directorship and establish a business in competition with the company. For the information to be covered by s 123, it must be information that "would not otherwise be available" to the director but for the fact that he or she was a director. The director must not "disclose that information to any person" or "make use of or act on the information" except for the purposes of the company or as required by law.[268] The director may, however, disclose or use the confidential information if they are authorised by the board to do so beforehand, and it will not or is unlikely to prejudice the company.[269] In this case, particulars of the circumstances surrounding the disclosure must be entered in the interests register of the company.[270]

In some cases, a major shareholder or creditor may have a right to nominate a nominee director to the Board of Directors of a company. This director will represent the nominator's interests and expected to report back on the operations of the company. In those situations, the Companies Act 1997 allows disclosure of information by the nominee provided that the name of the person to whom the information is disclosed is entered on the interests register. In such cases, the board has power to prohibit disclosure by the nominee director.[271]

Disclosure of share dealing by directors (s 124–127)[272]

Because of their familiarity with the operations of the company, directors are in a good position to know the true value of the shares in the company.

267 See Harris, B, "Fiduciary Duties of Directors under the Companies Act 1993" [1994] *New Zealand Law Journal* 242, 245 for a consideration of the equivalent sections in the Companies Act 1993 (New Zealand).

268 Companies Act 1997, s 123(1)(a) and (b). For a consideration of the equivalent section of the New Zealand Companies Act 1993, see *Frykberg v Heaven and Ballymore Advertising Ltd* (unreported) 17 July 2002, M7602/02, HC Auckland (Heath J).

269 Companies Act 1997, s 123(3)(b) and (c). Disclosure of the relevant interest in the interests register is also an exception: see Companies Act 1997, s 118 (disclosure of interest).

270 Companies Act 1997, s 123(3)(a).

271 Companies Act 1997, s 123(2).

272 See Beck, A and Borrowdale, A, *Guidebook to New Zealand Companies and Securities Law* (7th edn, CCH New Zealand Ltd, Auckland, 2002), para 308. See also Watson, S and Gunasekara, G, "Shareholder Buy-Outs: New Problems for Directors of Unlisted Companies" (2001) 7 *New Zealand Business Law Quarterly* 265; Watson, S, "Coleman v Myers under the 1993 Act" (1995) 1 *New Zealand Business Law Quarterly* 335; Harris, B, "Fiduciary Duties of Directors under the Companies Act 1993" [1994] *New Zealand Law Journal* 242.

This advantage may lead them to use this knowledge to their advantage in selling and buying shares in the company. The underlying law rule was that a director did not owe any fiduciary duty to purchasers of shares in the company.[273] They therefore did not need to divulge any information that they had obtained that was relevant to the price of the shares. The underlying law has been modified by the Companies Act 1997 by making provision for certain disclosures to be made and restrictions on share dealing.

Unlike under the New Zealand Companies Act 1993, the PNG Companies Act 1997 does not require a director to make an initial disclosure to the Board of Directors of a "relevant interest" in shares upon the company first being registered under the Act. However, thereafter, whenever a director "acquires or disposes of a relevant interest[274] in shares issued by the company" he or she must disclose the number and class of shares in which the relevant interest is held, the nature of the interest, the consideration paid or received and the date of the acquisition or disposition.[275] These details must be entered in the interests register.[276]

A director with inside information who proposes to deal in the shares or securities of the company or a related company must make sure that the consideration is:

- not less than the fair value of the shares or securities, where these are acquired by the director;[277] or
- not more than the fair value of the shares and securities, where these are disposed of by the director.[278]

Inside information is information which a director has in his or her capacity as a director or employee of the company or a related company, not otherwise available to him or her, and which is material to an assessment of the value of the shares or securities. If a director has inside information, it does not matter whether the director discloses this information to the other party to the transaction or not. Nor does it matter that the other party has, or has access to, the confidential information. The director needs to acquire or sell the shares or securities at their fair value.[279] Fair value is determined on the basis of all

273 *Percival v Wright* [1902] 2 Ch 421. In some circumstances, the court could hold that a fiduciary duty arose from the particular circumstances surrounding the transaction: *Coleman v Myers* [1977] 2 NZLR 225, SC; 2 NZLR 298, NZCA.

274 The term "relevant interest" is very broadly defined in s 124(1), and includes the beneficial ownership of shares and the right to exercise or control voting rights attached to shares.

275 Companies Act 1997, s 126(1)(a).

276 Companies Act 1997, s 126(1)(b).

277 Companies Act 1997, s 127(1)(a).

278 Companies Act 1997, s 127(1)(b).

279 Thexton v Thexton [2001] 1 NZLR 237, (2001) 9 NZCLC 262,432, NZHC; Thexton v Thexton [2002] 1 NZLR 780, (2002) 9 NZCLC 262,777, NZCA.

information known to the director or publicly available at the time.[280] When a director dealing in shares fails to ensure that the consideration reflects the fair value, the director is liable to pay to the purchaser or seller of the shares, as the case may be, the difference between the consideration paid or received and their fair value.[281]

Section 115 duty (statutory duty of care, diligence, and skill)

The duty of a director to exercise care can arise from a number of sources. These are:

- a contract between the director and the company;[282]
- the underlying law;
- section 115 of the Companies Act 1997.

Section 115, which states the extent of the duty of care, diligence, and skill owed by the director, does not specifically preserve the underlying law (common law and equity) but, as we have already noted earlier in the chapter, the better view is that the underlying law duty survives the Companies Act 1997.

Section 115(1) states:[283]

> (1) A director of a company, when exercising powers or performing duties as a director, shall exercise the care, diligence, and skill that a reasonable director would exercise in the same circumstances taking into account, but without limitation –
> (a) the nature of the company; and
> (b) the nature of the decision; and
> (c) the position of the director and the nature of the responsibilities undertaken by him.

Whether a director has breached the statutory duty of care is determined by considering the nature of the company and the decision, and also the position of the director and responsibilities being undertaken. Section 115(1) of the Companies Act 1997 requires that when a director is "exercising powers or performing duties as a director" that he or she exercise the degree of care, diligence and skill that "a reasonable director" not a "reasonable person" would

280 Companies Act 1997, s 127(2).
281 Companies Act 1997, s 127(4), (5).
282 A duty of care can arise from a contract between an executive director and the company. A term of the contract might be that the executive director must exercise the care, diligence and skill expected of a person who occupies the position in question.
283 Subsection (2) states that: "A director who acts in contravention of this section commits an offence and is liable on conviction to the penalty set out in Section 413(4)."

exercise in the "same circumstances". The section makes it clear that the standard of care and diligence required is an objective one, based on the competence of a reasonable director: that of a "reasonable director" in a like position to the particular director. Thus, in determining the reasonableness of the behaviour of the director, one would have to take into account matters such as the size and nature of the company, the composition of the company board, and the state of the company's financial affairs.

In Australia, courts have held that there is no significant difference between the statutory duty of care and the common law duty of care in terms of the standards to be applied. This means that a director who has breached the statutory duty of care will also have breached the duty of care which arises under the law of negligence and also the duty of care which arises in equity.[284] In New Zealand, the position is less clear. It has been suggested that the Companies Act 1993 (NZ) imposes more stringent obligations on directors than previously existed.[285] Prior to the Act coming into force, gross negligence by a director was almost always required for the duty of care to be breached.[286]

It is submitted that, because of s 115(1), the standard of care is now one of ordinary negligence: the standard of the reasonably competent director. The Companies Act 1997 does not impose a higher standard of skill on directors who hold relevant professional qualifications: the extra knowledge and abilities of the professional executive director do not mean there is a higher duty of care specifically imposed on them.[287] However, because the court will take account of "the position of the director and the nature of the responsibilities undertaken by him", if the director is appointed to undertake a particular task, the director may be liable if he or she does not have the requisite skills to fulfil that task.[288] A director with a lesser level of skill and experience must, on the exercise of his or her power, still reach the level of the reasonable director.[289]

As discussed earlier, the issue whether the Companies Act 1997, abrogates the directors' common law duty of skill and care is yet to be determined.

284 Although the standard of care will not vary according to the source of the duty in Australia, there is an important difference in relation to remedies.

285 Beck, A and Borrowdale, A, *Papua New Guinea Companies and Securities Law Guide* (CCH Australia Ltd, Sydney, 1999), para 315.

286 In *Re City Equitable Fire Insurance Co Ltd* [1925] Ch 407, the court held that a director would not be liable unless guilty of gross or culpable negligence. This was further supported by the Privy Council in *Kuwait Asia Bank EC v National Mutual Life Nominees Ltd* [1991] 1 AC 187.

287 See, however, *Dorchester Finance Co Ltd v Stebbing* [1989] BCLC 498 (decided 1977). See also the recent decision of Austin J in *ASIC v Rich* [2003] NSWSC 85.

288 See for example, *ASIC v Rich* [2003] NSWSC 85, where a non-executive director, who was, however, chairman of the board, was considered to have a higher level of responsibility that other non-executive directors.

289 It has been suggested, with reference to corresponding provisions of the Companies Act 1993 (NZ), that in effect the statutory duty is not greatly different from that of the underlying law espoused in *Re City Equitable Fire Insurance Co Ltd,* supra; see Watson, S, Gunasekara, G, Gedye, M, van Roy, Y, Ross, M, Longdin, L, Sims, A and Brown, L, *The Law of Business Organisations* (4th edn, Palatine Press, Auckland, 2003), para 12.04.

In *Sabatica Pty Ltd v Battle Mountain Canada Ltd*,[290] the Supreme Court (comprising Amet CJ, Kapi DCJ and Los J) appeared to consider that, despite the enactment of the Companies Act 1997, the "common law claim based on negligence" was still available. (Directors are subject to a common law duty to exercise reasonable care and skill in addition to any contractual law duty or statutory obligations.) The court pointed out:

> This duty is generally owed to the company, and an individual shareholder cannot ordinarily sue in his own right. The basis of the prohibition on a shareholder suing is that where a director acts negligently the loss suffered is usually that of the company (see *Prudential Assurance Co Ltd v Newman Industries Ltd (No 2)* [1982] 1 Ch 204 at pages 222–223).
>
> However, where the company has not suffered any loss through the directors breach, or has no cause of action, or where a shareholder has suffered a separate and distinct loss, then the shareholder may have a separate cause of action in its own right (see *Johnson v Gore Wood & Co* [2002] 2 Ch 1; *Chen v Karandonis* [2002] NSWCA 412).

It therefore seems that, without the matter being fully discussed, the Supreme Court in *Sabatica Pty Ltd v Battle Mountain Canada Ltd*[291] considered that the underlying law claims based on common law and equitable negligence still continue to operate alongside the statutory duties of skill and care imposed by the Companies Act 1997. As such the directors' duties provisions do not constitute a code. Perhaps the part of the judgment where this is most clearly demonstrated is where the court referred to *Ford* (with apparent approval), where it was stated that:

> It is now clear that directors are subject to a common law duty to exercise reasonable care and skill in addition to any contractual law duty or statutory obligations.[292]

Section 115(2) of the Companies Act 1997 provides that a director who acts in contravention of s 115(1) commits an offence and is liable on conviction to the penalty set out in s 413(4).

Unlike the position in Australia and in some American jurisdictions, the Companies Act 1997 does not contain a statutory business judgment rule. This rule is aimed at encouraging entrepreneurship amongst directors by providing a defence for actions in relation to claims of breach of duty of

290 (2003) SC709.

291 (2003) SC709.

292 Austin, R P, Ramsay I M, *Ford's Principles of Corporations Law* (12th edn, LexisNexis Butterworths, Australia, 2005), para 8.320. The current edition states: "It is now clear that directors are subject to a common law duty to exercise reasonable care and skill in addition to any contractual, equitable or statutory obligations." It should be noted, however, that whereas s 185 of the Corporations Act 2001 (Australia) provides that the statutory provisions dealing with directors' liability for care and diligence etc. are in addition to, *inter alia*, the common law and equitable rules, there is no similar equivalent in the Companies Act 1997.

care, diligence and skill. This only operates, though, if the conditions in the subsection are fulfilled. The rule provides that a director or other officer who makes a business judgment is assumed to have made it with the requisite degree of skill and diligence if the director or other officer:

- makes the judgment in good faith and for a proper purpose;
- has no material personal interest in the matter;
- informs themselves as they believe is reasonably appropriate; and
- rationally believes the judgment is in the best interest of the corporation.

If the director is to be relieved of this breach, the members of the company will need to give their approval to the breach, either before it occurs or subsequently.[293]

Section 348 duty (duty to prevent company engaging in insolvent trading)

Apart from the failure to reproduce the New Zealand provisions dealing with a director's duty to act for proper purposes ("exercise a power for a proper purpose"),[294] there are two other specific provisions of the Companies Act 1993 (NZ) dealing with directors' duties that were not reproduced in the PNG Companies Act 1997: ss 135 (reckless trading) and 136 (duty not to let the company incur obligations that cannot be performed).

Section 135 of the Companies Act 1993 (NZ) provides that a director of a company must not: (a) agree to the business of the company being carried on in a manner likely to create a substantial risk of serious loss to the company's creditors; or (b) cause or allow the business of the company to be carried on in a manner likely to create a substantial risk of serious loss to the company's creditors. Section 136 provides that: "A director of a company must not agree to the company incurring an obligation unless the director believes at that time on reasonable grounds that the company will be able to perform the obligation when it is required to do so."[295]

There is no exact equivalent to ss 135 and 136 in the Companies Act 1997. However, there is a provision which performs the same functions as these provisions and which, it is argued, obviated the need for the relevant New Zealand sections to be reproduced. Section 348 of the Companies Act 1997 casts a duty on company directors to prevent their company from engaging in insolvent trading. And although this provision is not reproduced in the Part and Division of the Companies Act 1997 dealing with directors' duties, it

293 See pp 302–303.

294 Companies Act 1997, s 133.

295 See Ross, M, *Corporate Reconstructions: Strategies for Directors* (CCH New Zealand, Auckland, 1999), Ch 5 and Walker, G, Reid, T, Hanrahan, P, Ramsay, I and Stapledon, G, *Commercial Applications of Company Law in New Zealand* (CCH New Zealand Ltd, Auckland, 2002), Ch 13 for an analysis of these provisions.

could easily have been; in other words, the fact that it is reproduced elsewhere in the Act does not prevent it from being dealt with here.

A director is under a duty to prevent the company incurring debts if there are reasonable grounds for believing that it is insolvent[296]: the director has a duty to prevent insolvent trading. Subject to raising defences, contravening directors are liable to pay compensation to the person who suffers loss or damage, of an amount equal to the loss or damage suffered by unsecured creditors in relation to the debt so incurred because of the company's insolvency. Unlike in some other jurisdictions (see for example the Corporations Act 2001 (Aus), s 588G(3)), the PNG provisions governing failure to prevent insolvent trading do not result in directors being liable for a civil penalty order or a criminal offence.

The reason for the provision is to discourage directors from improvidently committing the company to obligations to pay money as a debt when they have reasonable grounds for supposing that the company is, or will upon incurring the debt in question, become insolvent.[297]

Who is liable?

The duty to prevent insolvent trading applies to a person who was a director at the time when the company incurs the relevant debt (Companies Act 1997, s 348(1)). The duty is imposed on directors only, because they control the overall management of the company and have the ultimate power to prevent debts being incurred. Because of the wide definition of director for the purposes of s 348,[298] persons not formally appointed as directors who act as either *de facto* or shadow directors are also subject to the duty. It should also be noted that for the person to be liable, he or she must have been a director *at the time when* the company incurred the relevant debt.

It is not clear whether alternate directors may be liable under s 348. It would seem that, before they could be liable, it would have to be shown that they were acting as directors when the company engaged in insolvent trading.[299]

Incurring a debt

In order to establish a contravention of s 348 of the Companies Act 1997 the claimant must establish that the company incurred a debt. A debt is an obligation by one person to pay a sum of money to another.[300] A debt is incurred when a company "so acts to expose itself contractually to an obligation to

296 Companies Act 1997, s 348.
297 *Hawkins v Bank of China* (1992) 26 NSWLR 562 at 577, per Kirby P.
298 Companies Act 1997, ss 2(1) and 107. See discussion of *de facto* and shadow directors at p 280.
299 Cf *Playcorp Pty Ltd v Shaw* (1993) 10 ACSR 212 and *Standard Chartered Bank of Australia Ltd v Antico* (1995) 38 NSWLR 290.
300 *Powell v Fryer* [2001] SASC 59.

make a future payment of a sum of money".[301] In many cases the company will contract with the supplier to provide goods or services on credit terms: in such cases the debt is the obligation to pay the purchase price at the agreed time for payment. A debt is also incurred if a company borrows money from a bank or other lender,[302] or leases business premises from a landlord. The expression "incurs a debt" also covers situations that do not necessarily involve contracts under which a company exposes itself to an obligation to make a future payment of a sum of money as a debt. For example, in *Powell v Fryer*,[303] it was held that the term debt included statutory obligations to pay taxes, assessed penalties for non-payment of taxes, statutory levies for workers' compensation insurance and assessed penalties for non-payment of such levies.

In *Hawkins v Bank of China*,[304] the New South Wales Court of Appeal noted that the expression "incurs a debt" was capable of a number of meanings and the appropriate meaning depended on the context and the statutory purposes of the legislation. It was held that the word "debt" included a contingent debt such as a guarantee and the word "incurs" included "the undertaking of an engagement to pay a sum of money at a future time, even if the engagement is conditional and the amount involved is uncertain". Seeing that these interpretations best advance the purpose of the legislation, which has a similar purpose in Australia, it is suggested that a PNG court would follow *Hawkins v Bank of China*.

In *Jelin Pty Ltd v Johnson*,[305] it was held that a "debt" included a claim for an ascertained amount but did not include unliquidated claims such as damages for fraudulent misrepresentation. However, in *Hawkins v Bank of China*,[306] Gleeson CJ left open the possibility that incurring a debt included incurring a liability for unliquidated damages.

In Australia, s 588(1A) of the Corporations Act 2001 gives an expanded meaning to the expression "incurs a debt". It is not clear whether PNG courts would read into the local term this expanded meaning.[307]

When is the debt incurred?

It is important to ascertain the time when a debt is incurred, because s 348 requires proof that the company was unable to satisfy the solvency test

301 *Hawkins v Bank of China* (1992) 26 NSWLR 562.
302 *Commonwealth Bank of Australia v Friedrich* (1991) 5 ACSR 115.
303 [2001] SASC 59.
304 (1992) 26 NSWLR 562.
305 (1987) 5 ACLC 463.
306 (1992) 26 NSWLR 562.
307 According to s 588(1A) of the Corporations Act 2001 (Australia), paying a dividend, making a reduction of share capital, buying back shares, issuing and redeeming redeemable preference shares that are redeemable at the company's option, financially assisting a person to acquire shares, and entering into an uncommercial transaction are transactions that are deemed to be incurring a debt.

at the time the debt was incurred or that by incurring the debt the company thereby became unable to satisfy the solvency test.

There is no definite rule for working out when a debt is incurred. The time varies from case to case. In *Hawkins v Bank of China*,[308] Gleeson CJ held that a debt is incurred when, by its conduct or operations, the company has necessarily subjected itself to a conditional, but unavoidable, obligation to pay a sum of money at a future time. In that case a company guaranteed a pre-existing debt that had been made to other companies in the same group or to the bank of China. At the time of the guarantee the borrowing companies were unable to pay their loans because they were insolvent. It was held that the guarantor company incurred a debt to the bank when the guarantee was executed because after that date the company's obligation to the bank and the guarantee was unavoidable by any action of its own.

Insolvency

The company must either be insolvent at the time that the relevant debt(s) is incurred, or must be pushed by the debt(s) into insolvency, for s 348 to apply. Another limitation is that s 348 can be invoked only where the company has been placed into liquidation (s 348(2)(b)).[309] This means that only a liquidator or particular creditor may bring proceedings under the section. However, it is suggested that a shareholder, director or other entitled person will be able to sue for an injunction under s 142 to restrain a director who proposes to act in contravention of s 348.

Extent of participation: agreeing to company incurring or permitting company to incur a debt

Section 348 imposes liability on a director when he or she "agrees to the company incurring a debt *or permits the company* to incur" a debt. The term "permits" is wide enough to allow for the reasoning in Australian cases where directors have been held liable for insolvent trading, even though they did not have actual knowledge of the business of the company, but were content to abdicate their responsibilities to more active members of the board. This is well illustrated in the case of *Morley v Statewide Tobacco Services Ltd*.[310] Mrs Morley was the widow of the founder of a company which ran kiosks for the sale of various goods, including cigarettes and other tobacco supplies made by the respondent. At all times Mrs Morley was a director and shareholder, but never took any part in the management of the company. When her husband died, her son took over management of the business; however, he gave her very little information

308 (1992) 26 NSWLR 562. See also *Leigh-Mardon Pty Ltd v Wawn* (1995) 17 ACSR 741.
309 The subparagraph refers to the person to whom the debt is owed having "suffered loss or damage in relation to the debt because of the liquidation of the company".
310 [1993] 1 VR 423.

about the business, which she believed to be operating profitably. One of the issues that arose in the case was whether Mrs Morley could set up a defence to liability that the debt was incurred without her express or implied consent or authority. It was not disputed that Mrs Morley had no actual knowledge of the particular debt in question, but it was argued that by appointing her son manager of the business, she impliedly authorised or consented to the debts which he caused to be incurred by the company in carrying out his management functions. The Supreme Court of Victoria accepted this. Authority or consent could be found even though it did not relate to specific debts but merely to the general incurring of debts.

Although there is no provision in the PNG sections similar to the Australian provision which refers to "failing to prevent the company from incurring the debt" (s 588G(2)), it is submitted that the term "permits the company to incur a debt" would lead to a ruling similar to that made in *Morley v Statewide Tobacco Services Ltd.*

Onus of proof

The onus of establishing the elements of s 348 lies on the person seeking to make the director liable, the standard of proof being the balance of probabilities. Expert opinion evidence by an accountant or financial analyst as to whether the company met the solvency test at the time when the debt was incurred would be admissible, provided that the opinion is based on the expert's specialised knowledge.[311] The standard of proof to be attained by a director to establish a statutory defence is the balance of probabilities.[312]

Defences

The only defences available to a director against whom action is brought under s 348 is to prove that the company satisfied the solvency test at time of incurring the debt or that the director had reasonable grounds for believing that the company would satisfy the solvency test. No other defences such as those listed in s 588H of the Corporations Act 2001 (Australia) (delegation and reliance on information supplied by others; not taking part in management of company at time because of illness or some other good reason and taking all reasonable steps to prevent the company from incurring debt) are available to the director.

Consequences of contravention

The Companies Act 1997 does not provide for criminal liability for insolvent trading. Compare the position in New Zealand and Australia,[313] for example. The only relief available is a civil claim for compensation.

311 *Quick v Stoland Pty Ltd* (1998) 157 ALR 615.
312 *Metropolitan Fire Systems Pty Ltd v Miller* (1997) 23 ACSR 699.
313 Corporations Act 2001 (Aus), s 588G(3).

Compensation

Section 348 of the Companies Act 1997 does not provide any guidance on how to resolve the competing claims of liquidator-initiated and creditor-initiated actions or proceedings. What is to be done where a creditor brings an action against the directors first? If he or she recovers any compensation, is that held on behalf of all the creditors, or is the claimant entitled to retain the full sum? The PNG provisions do not supply any guidance on this question.

Section 348 permits both the liquidator and creditors to bring actions against directors for insolvent trading. The section does not establish an order of precedence, and if both the liquidator and a creditor bring an action under the section simultaneously, it would appear that provided that the liquidator's claim includes a claim on behalf of the creditor, the court ought to stay the action of the creditor. This is because if the creditor's claim is pursued, any moneys recovered by the creditor would be available only to him or her. This would offend the notion of equal sharing in insolvency.

Any creditor may bring an action under s 348, not just those whose debts were incurred when the company was unable to satisfy the solvency test, or on the incurring of whose debt, the company thereby became unable to satisfy the solvency test. Creditors of the company before this time have standing to bring an action against the directors for insolvent trading. (*Sed quaere*: by referring to the person to whom "*the* debt" is owed, rather than "a debt" is owed.)

Compensation is measured by loss or damage to the creditor to whom the debt is owed.

Court relief

In other jurisdictions, legislative provisions specifically provide that a court may relieve a person, either wholly or partly, from a liability for contravention of the insolvent trading provision if it appears that the person acted honestly and having regard to all the circumstances of the case ought fairly to be excused.[314] There is no similar provision in the Companies Act 1997, nor in any other law such as the National or Supreme Court Acts or Constitution that would enable a PNG court to give such relief, and it is unlikely that the courts will develop the underlying law to provide such relief.

To whom are directors' duties owed?

The duties of directors are owed to the company itself. With regard to consideration of interests, the general rule is expressed in terms that directors or other officers who owe duties, owe such duties to the members of the company as a whole.[315] This obviously includes the shareholders as a group. There is no duty owed to the general public, nor to the company's employees.[316] However, directors

314 Corporations Act 2001 (Aus), s 1317S(2).
315 *Greenhalgh v Arderne Cinemas Ltd* [1951] Ch 286.
316 *Parke v Daily News Ltd* [1962] Ch 927.

and other officers do not normally owe any duties to creditors.[317] In some situations, however, a duty to take account of the interests of creditors will arise. This is so particularly where the company is insolvent or in financial difficulties. In *Walker v Wimborne*,[318] the liquidator of Asiatic Electric Pty Ltd sought to recover damages from the directors for breach of duty. The directors of Asiatic were also directors of related companies, which were administered as a group. The directors moved funds between different companies in the group to meet debts as they arose. It was held by the High Court that it was the duty of the directors of Asiatic to consult its interests and its interests alone when deciding whether payments should be made to other companies and the creditors were prejudiced by the movement of funds between companies. Therefore, the directors had breached their duties.

Remedies for breach of duties

The remedies that may be obtained for breach of directors' duties are varied. In some cases the Companies Act 1997 expressly provides that breach of such a duty will amount to a criminal offence. In most cases, however, the person complaining of the breach will be more interested in obtaining civil law remedies. These would include:

1. *Compensatory damages*. If a company has suffered a loss as a result of breach of director's duties, the company may claim compensation under the underlying law. The amount of compensation will be the amount that would put the company back in the position it would have been in if the breach had not occurred. All directors who committed the breach are jointly and severally liable.
2. *An account of profits*. Where the company has not suffered any loss due to the breach of directors' duty, it may still be able to claim any profits made by the directors which result from their breach of duty.
3. *A claim to trace and recover property*. Because directors are fiduciaries, the principles of equity allow the courts to trace company property that has been misappropriated or misapplied. The company can recover property from the directors and from any third party who is not an innocent purchaser.
4. *Rescission of contract*. In some cases, the company may be able to terminate the contract entered into by the director in breach of his or her fiduciary duty.
5. *Dismissal*. A breach of duty by the director will often amount to a breach of the contract of his or her contract of employment and entitle the company to dismiss the director.

317 *Spies v The Queen* (2000) 18 ACLC 727.
318 (1976) 137 CLR 1.

Chapter 10

Shareholder remedies

Introduction

In this chapter, we discuss the range of remedies which are available to individual shareholders. These remedies will be available not only when a director has broken one of the directors' duties, but also where the action of the company or others has wronged the shareholder. The action may have been oppressive, or may have unfairly discriminated against or unfairly prejudiced the shareholder. The Companies Act 1997 introduced new remedies to enable the shareholder to vindicate his or her rights. However, as we shall see, it is still possible that the shareholder may have remedies still available according to the underlying law.

Overview of remedies

Three types of actions or remedies were available to a shareholder according to the underlying law:

- A *personal action*, where the personal rights of the shareholder are interfered with. This would include an action against the company where the company refused to record the shareholder's vote at a meeting, or where the company declared a dividend, but then refused to pay it to the shareholder. Seeking to enforce a personal right of the shareholder (for example, the right to vote) where the directors or majority shareholders are attempting to take away this right.
- A *representative action* would be available where one member sued on behalf of all others who have suffered the same wrong. This is a collective personal action.
- A *derivative action*. In this situation, the wrong is done to the company, and an individual shareholder sues on behalf of the company because wrongdoers are in control of the company and are preventing it from suing in its own name.

Personal action

Section 147(1) of the Companies Act 1997 provides that a current or former shareholder may bring an action *against a director* for breach of a duty owed to him as a shareholder. Section 149 further provides that a shareholder[1] of a company may bring an action *against the company* for breach of a duty *owed by the company* to him as a shareholder. The underlying law restricted these actions to wrongs that infringed the personal rights of the shareholder as an individual, as opposed to his or her rights as one of the shareholders of the company. The main concern was to prevent floodgates being opened. It was difficult to determine which wrongs infringed the personal rights of shareholders, as the underlying law did not lay down a clear test on the matter. In this regard the Companies Act 1997 has improved the position, because it lists certain directors' duties in particular sections of the Act as being "duties owed to shareholders" and others as "duties owed to the company and not to shareholders".

The breaches by directors that will not be grounds for personal actions are:

- duty of directors to act in good faith and in the best interests of the company;[2]
- director's duty of care;[3]
- use of company information.[4]

The following directors' duties are stated to be owed to shareholders as individuals and will therefore be grounds for personal actions:

- to supervise the share register;[5]
- to disclose interest;[6]
- to disclose share dealings.[7]

The three duties listed immediately above do not form an exhaustive list. Section 147(3) provides that the express statement that these duties owed to shareholders does not limit subsection (1), so that other directors' duties set out in the Act or forming part of the underlying law may be considered to be "owed to shareholders". For example, it is suggested that the provision

1 It is interesting to note that whereas s 147(1) explicitly refers to both a "shareholder" and a "former shareholder", s 149 does not make this distinction. It is therefore arguable that the remedy set out in s 149 is available only to "current shareholders". *Sed quaere*. It is likely that the court will interpret the word "shareholder" in s 149 expansively to include both types of shareholder.
2 Companies Act 1997, s 147(3)(d), s 112.
3 Companies Act 1997, s 147(3)(e), s 115.
4 Companies Act 1997, s 147(3)(f), s 123.
5 Companies Act 1997, s 147(3)(a), s 70.
6 Companies Act 1997, s 147(3)(b), s 118
7 Companies Act 1997, s 147(3)(c), s 126.

dealing with insolvent trading is a personal action,[8] as is the duty to exercise a power for a proper purpose, should this underlying law directors' duty still continue to exist in PNG following the enactment of the Companies Act 1997.[9]

It is also possible for shareholders to bring personal actions against the company for breaches of duties owed to them by the company.[10] These duties are not spelt out in the Companies Act 1997, but would include failure by the company to pay a dividend to a shareholder.[11]

Section 147(2) of the Companies Act 1997 provides that a personal action may not be brought "to recover any loss in the form of a reduction in the value of shares in the company or a failure of the shares to increase in value by reason only of a loss suffered, or a gain forgone, by the company". It would seem that, despite s 147(2), it is still possible for a personal action to recover for consequential diminution in the value of shares where this arises from a separate duty owed to shareholders arising independently of the relationship between the shareholder and the company. In *Johnson v Gore Wood & Co (No 1)*,[12] the House of Lords held that a shareholder could recover for losses suffered personally when the loss suffered by the shareholder was separate and distinct from the loss suffered by the company.

Representative action

A representative action is a collective personal action. Section 151 of the Companies Act 1997 now deals with such actions. Where a shareholder of a company brings proceedings against the company or a director, and other shareholders have the same or substantially the same interest in relation to the subject matter of the proceedings, the court may appoint that shareholder to represent all or some of the shareholders having the same or substantially the same interest.[13]

Derivative action

A derivative action is an action brought by one shareholder on behalf of the company for a wrong done to the company by the directors. Such actions arose because of the underlying law rule in *Foss v Harbottle*,[14] where a

8 Cf *Companies Act 1993* (NZ), s 169(3)(f), which provides that reckless trading (s 135) is a duty owed by directors specifically to shareholders as individuals.
9 See discussion in on directors' duties in Chapter 9.
10 Companies Act 1997, s 149.
11 Cf *Wood v Odessa Waterworks Co Ltd* (1889) 42 Ch D 636 (shareholders have a right to have a dividend paid in cash if the Articles of Associations so state).
12 [2002] 2 AC 1.
13 *Kuwait Asia Bank EC v National Mutual Life Nominees Ltd* [1991] 1 AC 187 is an example of a representative action.
14 (1843) 2 Hare 461, 67 ER 189.

wrong is done to the company, the company and not an individual shareholder is the proper plaintiff. In that case the Victoria Park company was formed to acquire land. A parcel of land that had been purchased by Thomas Harbottle was resold to the company. The park was opened and, soon thereafter, difficulties arose between the shareholders. Richard Foss and Edward Turton, on behalf of themselves and other shareholders, brought an action against Harbottle alleging that he had sold his land to the company at an inflated price causing the company to make a loss. The judge held that the action must fail. The majority of shareholders could have ratified the act complained of in a meeting of shareholders, and the proper course of action was for the plaintiffs to have obtained the authority of the shareholders in general meeting to bring an action in the name of the company. The result of *Foss v Harbottle* is that:

- in order to redress a wrong done to the company, the action should prima facie be brought by the company itself;[15]
- if the action complained of is something which in substance the majority of the company are entitled to do, or if something has been done irregularly which the majority of the company are entitled to do regularly, or something is done illegally which the majority of the company are entitled to do legally, there can be no use in having litigation about it, the ultimate end of which is only that a meeting has to be called, and then ultimately the majority gets its wishes.[16]

The rule in *Foss v Harbottle* therefore prevents fruitless litigation where the majority can overturn the court decision by a simple majority vote. If the majority could do this in all situations, it would mean that the majority who are wrongdoers will be able to run the company for their own purposes. However, there are certain breaches of directors' duties or wrongs done by the company that cannot be ratified (validated) or in respect of which directors can be released from personal liability. The ratification must be done "in the same manner in which the power may be exercised".

The question is to determine what types of wrongs or breaches of directors' duties cannot be validly ratified by shareholders. The Companies Act 1997 allows certain actions of directors to be ratified by shareholders.[17] The Act limits this to "the purported exercise by a director or the board of a company of a power vested in the shareholders or any other person". This means, for example, that if the action taken by the directors should have been carried

15 *Burland v Earle* [1902] AC 83 at 93, per Lord Davey.

16 *MacDougall v Gardiner* (1875) 1 ChD 13 at 25, per Mellish J. See *Bamford v Bamford* [1968] 2 All ER 655, where a breach of director's duty relating to the proper purpose doctrine was validly ratified by the shareholders.

17 Companies Act 1997, s 154(1).

out only after the approval of shareholders with 75 per cent of the voting power in the company, the action will be validated only if shareholders holding 75 per cent of the shares later vote in favour of the action at a meeting of the company.[18] If the exercise of the power is validly ratified, it is thereafter "deemed to be, and always to have been, a proper and valid exercise of that power".[19]

Unlike the position in New Zealand, where the common law right to ratification survives the Companies Act 1993, it does not appear that the underlying law rules relating to ratification continue to apply following the enactment of the Companies Act 1997.[20]

Why are the remedies needed?

There are many actions of directors and the majority shareholders which can harm minority shareholders. For example, we saw that the majority shareholders may:

- amend the company's constitution in a way which disadvantages the minority (for example, the constitution may contain a provision giving a class of minority shareholders a right to appoint their own director and the majority endeavours to delete this provision from the constitution); or
- vote to approve the sale of assets of the company to themselves at a price which is below the market value of the assets.

Actions of directors may also harm minority shareholders. For example, the directors may:

- pay themselves excessive remuneration and, at the same time, refuse to have the company pay dividends to shareholders;
- divert business opportunities away from the company to themselves so that the company and its shareholders suffer financial harm; or
- issue shares in the company to themselves with the objective of becoming majority shareholders and reducing the proportion of shares held by other shareholders.

Minority shareholders who are disadvantaged by actions of majority shareholders or directors may elect to sell their shares. However, this is not

18 An example would be directors entering into a "major transaction" without obtaining a special resolution of the shareholders as required by s 110 of the Companies Act 1997.

19 Companies Act 1997, s 154(2).

20 Section 177(4) of the Companies Act 1993 (NZ) expressly provides: "Nothing in this section limits or affects any rule of law relating to the ratification or approval by the shareholders or any other person of any act or omission of a director or the board of a company." It can be strongly argued that the failure of the drafters of the Companies Act 1997 to carry over this provision shows that the underlying law rules no longer apply.

always possible. While this may be possible in a company which has its shares listed on the stock exchange and there is a liquid market for those shares, most companies do not have a liquid market for their shares. It is common for small companies to have a provision in their constitutions limiting the right of shareholders to sell their shares. This is because the shareholders of those companies want control over who become shareholders. A restriction often found in the constitutions of these companies is one which requires a shareholder to obtain the permission of directors prior to the shareholder selling his or her shares. This means that minority shareholders who are disadvantaged by the actions of directors or the majority shareholders may be unable to sell their shares. In these circumstances, the legal remedies available to the minority shareholder are very important.

Difference between the shareholder's derivative action and other remedies

One of the remedies we examine in this chapter is the shareholder's derivative action. A derivative action is a legal action which should be brought by the company – for example, where there is a breach of a common law duty. We have seen that this duty is owed to the company, and therefore it is the company which should bring legal proceedings for breach of the duty. Where the company does not bring the legal proceedings, we will see that in some circumstances the court allows an individual shareholder to bring a derivative action on behalf of the company. The shareholder's legal action *derives from* the company's legal action.

There is an important difference between:

- a shareholder's derivative action; and
- the shareholder's statutory remedies and the shareholder's personal action.

Although the derivative action is brought by a shareholder, it is based on a legal action which the company has (for example, a breach of duty owed to the company). This means that if the derivative action is successful and the director is ordered by the court to pay compensation, the compensation is paid to the company and not to the individual shareholder.[21] This is because it is the company which has the right to bring the legal action and, although the court has allowed an individual shareholder to bring the legal action, the shareholder is bringing the action on behalf of the company. Whereas the shareholder who brings the successful legal action will not directly receive the compensation which the director is ordered to pay, the shareholder will benefit indirectly because the compensation is paid to the company.

21 The court has power to order that any compensation obtained be paid to the applicant shareholder: see Companies Act 1997, s 145(d).

In relation to the statutory remedies of shareholders and the personal action available to shareholders, these legal actions are brought in a personal capacity because the shareholder has a personal right or is affected individually. The shareholder does not bring the legal action on behalf of the company. This means that if the individual shareholder is successful in the legal action, it is the shareholder who directly receives the benefit of any order made by the court.

Shareholder's statutory remedies

Overview

In this section, we discuss the statutory remedies available to shareholders. The remedies are:

- oppression remedy;[22]
- putting the company into liquidation because it is just and equitable to do so;[23] and
- granting an injunction to prevent a contravention of the Companies Act 1997 or the company's constitution.

We also discuss the statutory right which a shareholder has to apply to the court for an order allowing the shareholder to inspect the books of the company. This will be very helpful in obtaining evidence which may help the shareholder in bringing an action in the National Court.

The oppression remedy

The oppression remedy is contained in s 152 of the Companies Act 1997. Section 152 authorises the National Court to provide a remedy where the court finds that: the company's affairs, or any act or acts of the company has been, or is being, or is likely to be conducted in a manner that is oppressive to, unfairly discriminatory against or unfairly prejudicial to, a shareholder, former shareholder or other entitled person, whether in that capacity or any other capacity.

Types of companies the remedy can apply to

Although the oppression remedy applies to all types of companies, including listed companies, it will normally be used in relation to small companies which

22 Companies Act 1997, s 152.
23 Companies Act 1997, s 291(3)(d).

have few shareholders.[24] In these tightly held companies, the persons seeking the remedy will usually be unable to continue a workable relationship with the other shareholders.

There are several reasons for this. First, shareholders in these companies may have more at risk than just the capital they have invested. They may frequently be involved in the management of the company. A dispute among shareholders may result in majority shareholders terminating the employment of a minority shareholder who is an officer of the company, thereby depriving the shareholder of remuneration. The oppression remedy might here assist the minority shareholder.

Secondly, oppressed shareholders in small companies will usually be "locked-in" to the company, in that they might not be able to sell their shares. Minority shareholders in a listed company which has a liquid market for its shares may readily sell their shares. However, this is not the case for closely held companies because these companies generally have a restriction on the right of shareholders to sell their shares. An oppressed minority shareholder who is "locked in" to the company will then rely on the oppression remedy.

Who can apply?

An oppression action under s 152 of the Companies Act 1997 may be brought by:

- a current shareholder;[25]
- a former shareholder;[26] or
- any other entitled person.[27]

24 The oppression remedy has been used in respect of listed companies to challenge the actions of directors that have involved a breach of duty. The remedy may also be useful in respect of a joint-venture company, even where the joint venture involves a large scale business operation. In such cases the investors who may be incorporated establish a venture where each of the joint venturers contribute equity, expertise, rights or goods or services. They are usually closely held and without public listing, and there is a possibility that a party may be "locked-in", unfairly treated or "squeezed-out" (i.e., left out of the decision-making process) etc.

25 It is unclear whether the applicant must be registered as a member or whether an equitable interest as an unregistered transferee is sufficient. It would appear, following the definition of shareholder in s 78 of the Companies Act 1997, which sets out two situations where persons "entitled" to have their name entered in the share register, and based on the *expressio unius est exclusio alterius* principle, that all other cases where the applicant has an equitable interest will not qualify to allow those persons to be applicants under s 152 of the Companies Act 1997. Cf *Niord Pty Ltd v Adelaide Petroleum NL* (1990) 8 ACLC 684 and *Re Independent Quarries Pty Ltd* (1993) 12 ACSR 188.

26 It may be that if the shareholder's name is removed from the register pursuant to some power in the constitution, before seeking relief under s 152 of the Companies Act 1997, the shareholder must first apply for correction of the register under s 71 of the Act: see *Re M Dalley & Co Pty Ltd* (1968) 120 CLR 603.

27 An "entitled person" means a shareholder or a person upon whom the constitution confers any of the rights and powers of a shareholder (Companies Act 1997, s 2(1)).

The above classification will include a personal representative of any of the above-listed persons (i.e., a person to whom a share in the company has been transmitted by will or as a result of intestacy, respectively called an executor or administrator) and a person to whom shares of any of those persons have passed by operation of law (for example, because of bankruptcy, where the shares will pass to the trustee in bankruptcy).[28] These persons do not have to be registered as a member in order to bring an action pursuant to s 152 of the Companies Act 1997.

The person bringing the action may be a former shareholder whose interests may have been prejudiced prior to the transfer of his or her shares. Although the section does not specifically say so, it would appear that a former shareholder may make use of s 152 *only if* the application relates to the circumstances in which they ceased to be a shareholder.

There is some uncertainty whether a controlling or majority shareholder in a company can be an applicant under s 152. In *Re Polyresins Pty Ltd*,[29] Chesterman J of the Supreme Court of Queensland held that the remedy is available *only to* minority shareholders. However, it has been questioned whether this is not "an unduly narrow" interpretation of the oppression remedy, and there are other more recent authorities where the courts have held that a majority shareholder may make use of the oppression remedy.[30]

Affairs and acts of the company

Actions under s 152 can be brought if the "affairs of the company" have been, are being, or are likely to be, conducted in a manner that is, or is likely to be, oppressive, unfairly discriminatory or unfairly prejudicial. Apart from this, the section also covers "any act or acts of the company" that have been, are or are likely to be oppressive, unfairly discriminatory or unfairly prejudicial.[31]

The rights of entitled persons will include the right to vote at a company meeting, the right to receive a dividend and the right to participate in the distribution of surplus assets of the company.

28 Companies Act 1997, s 141.

29 (1998) 28 ACSR 671.

30 See Austin, R P, Ramsay I M, *Ford's Principles of Corporations Law* (12th edn, LexisNexis Butterworths, Australia, 2005), para 11.440. In some parts of this chapter, applicants for a s 152 oppression remedy are sometimes referred to as "minority shareholders". It should be noted, however, that the remedy may be available to *any shareholder* who can show that they have suffered oppression or been unfairly treated within the terms of the section.

31 In Australia, the equivalent provision in the Corporations Act 2001 (s 232(c)) refers also to "a resolution, or a proposed resolution, of members or a class of members of a company" that is oppressive to, unfairly prejudicial to, or unfairly discriminatory against, shareholders. Apart from applying to oppressive or unfair conduct, the provision would apply where the conduct is "contrary to the interests of the members as a whole" (s 232(d)). The Australian provision make it clear that "omissions by or on behalf of the company" are also included (s 232(b)), whereas the Companies Act 1997 does not expressly refer to "omissions". Other provisions in the Companies Act 1997 expressly refer to "acts or omissions": see for example, ss 139(3), 140, 283(6) and 376(1). Despite this and the *expressio unius est*

Although the Companies Act 1997 does not define the term "affairs of the company",[32] the section is broad enough to capture most of a company's activities. Each case will depend on its own facts, and it is likely that the courts will adopt a liberal approach when interpreting "affairs of the company . . . conducted":[33] "the concept of affairs of a corporation is very wide indeed".[34]

The directors will need to be acting in the company's affairs and not in their personal capacity to be in breach of s 152. The conduct complained of may affect the applicant in their capacity as a shareholder or an entitled person, or in any other capacity. Thus, a remedy can be sought under s 152 even though the applicant is complaining of conduct such as removal as a director or employee of the company. An isolated act, if serious enough, can lead to relief.[35]

Section 152 provides a remedy against any person involved in the affairs of the company. This includes the directors, majority shareholders, substantial shareholders as well as the company itself.[36] The National Court may make an order under the section requiring "the company *or any other person*" to pay compensation etc.

There are several cases where a member of a particular company in a corporate group has sought a remedy under provisions equivalent to s 152 where the oppressive or unfair conduct occurred in other companies in the group. The Act defines and refers to "related companies", especially in respect of the derivative action. The matter is yet to be settled whether the conduct of subsidiaries can be classified as conduct in the "affairs" of the parent company. Authorities are tending to the view that the conduct of subsidiaries can constitute conduct in the "affairs" of the parent company.[37]

exclusio alterius argument that can be based on it, it is suggested that an "omission" may come within the meaning of "affairs" or "act" of the company within s 152 of the Companies Act 1997. In *Sabatica Pty Ltd v Battle Mountain Canada Ltd* (2003) SC709, the main complaint of the applicant related to an omission on the part of the company or its directors ("The allegations are that they did not allow proper consideration of (or give effect to) proposals which would have seen NML's assets distributed to its shareholders"). Yet the Supreme Court did not consider that this meant that the application was outside of the provisions of s 152 of the Companies Act 1997: the omission constituted a cause of action. See *Sanford v Sanford Courier Service Pty Ltd* (1986) 10 ACLR 549 (relief where a company with sufficient profits persistently refuses to pay dividends). Cf *Re Smith and Fawcett Ltd* [1942] Ch 304 and *Re Empire Building Ltd* [1973] 1 NZLR 214.

32 Cf s 53 of the Corporations Act 2001 (Aus), which defines "affairs of a body corporate".

33 *Vujnovich v Vujnovich* [1988] 2 NZLR 129 (NZHC); [1988] 2 NZLR 129 (NZCA).

34 *Australian Securities Commission v Lucas* (1992) 7 ACSR 676 at 677, per Drummond J.

35 *Re Norvabron Pty Ltd* (No 2) (1986) 5 ACLC 184; *Wayde v New South Wales Rugby League Ltd* (1985) 180 CLR 459.

36 In *Sabatica Pty Ltd v Battle Mountain Canada Ltd* (2003) SC709, the Supreme Court stated: "We accept the submission by counsel for the Appellant that the Respondents did not have to be cast as 'directors' to be liable under s 152 of the Companies Act 1997. The claim may be brought against 'any person' who breaches the section."

37 See *Morgan v 45 Flers Avenue Pty Ltd* (1987) 5 ACLC 222 and contrast with *Re Norvabron Pty Ltd (No 2)* (1986) 5 ACLC 184 and the recent English Court of Appeal

The Companies Act 1997 focuses on the affairs being conducted in a manner that is oppressive, and it outlines certain forms of conduct that will amount to prejudicial conduct. All the shareholder will have to prove, to obtain some relief, is that one of the categories of conduct, activities or action outlined in s 152(4) has occurred. If the company wishes to claim that it has not acted in a prejudicial manner, it will need to appeal to the court's discretion. These types of conduct – any one of which is described as a failure to comply with sections of the Act – are:

- pre-emptive rights to the issue of shares;[38]
- consideration for which shares are issued;[39]
- dividends;[40]
- company purchasing or otherwise acquiring its own shares;[41]
- provision of financial assistance by a company to acquire its own shares;[42]
- alteration of shareholder rights;[43] and
- major transactions.[44]

What tests do the courts apply in oppression cases?

Where it is alleged that directors have acted oppressively or unfairly, the approach to be applied is that stated by the New Zealand Court of Appeal in *Thomas v HW Thomas Ltd*,[45] which has been adopted by the PNG Supreme Court in the case of *Sabatica Pty Ltd v Battle Mountain Canada Ltd*.[46] Is the decision made by the director a decision which results in an unjust detriment to the interests of a shareholder or shareholders of the company? If so, the director has acted in breach of s 152 of the Companies Act 1997.[47]

The expressions "oppressive", "unfairly discriminatory" and "unfairly prejudicial" are not defined in the Companies Act 1997, but the three expressions are seen as overlapping and assist in explaining each other. Richardson J, in *Thomas v HW Thomas Ltd*,[48] thought that the expression

decision in *Re Citybranch Group Ltd v Rackind* [2004] EWCA Civ 815, [2004] 4 All ER 735. The latter cases is also an illustration of an omission constituting affairs of the "company".

38 Companies Act 1997, s 45.
39 Companies Act 1997, s 47.
40 Companies Act 1997, s 51.
41 Companies Act 1997, s 57.
42 Companies Act 1997, s 63.
43 Companies Act 1997, s 98.
44 Companies Act 1997, s 110.
45 [1984] 1 NZLR 686.
46 (2003) SC709.
47 *Latimer Holdings Ltd and Powell v SEA Holdings New Zealand Ltd* [2004] NZCA 226.
48 [1984] 1 NZLR 686. See Wishart, D A, "Fairness in Company Law" (1990) 4 *Canterbury Law Review* 284–301 for a treatment of the word "fairness" in this provision.

is a compound expression.[49] The terms were not distinct alternatives to be considered separately in watertight compartments and that the statutory concern was directed to instances or courses of conduct amounting to an unjust detriment to the interests of a member or members of the company. There could be cases where relief could be given without the applicant having to show invasion of his or her own rights or demonstrating a lack of probity of want of good faith towards him or her.[50]

In *Sabatica Pty Ltd v Battle Mountain Canada Ltd*,[51] the Supreme Court of Papua New Guinea referred with approval, to the interpretation of those terms in s 209 of the repealed Companies Act 1955 (NZ) by the New Zealand Court of Appeal in *Thomas v HW Thomas Ltd*:[52]

> While the New Zealand legislation has significant variations, the use of the words "oppressive, unfairly discriminatory or unfairly prejudicial" is common. In *Thomas v HW Thomas Ltd* [1984] 1 NZLR 686 at 693 Richardson J said:
>
> > 'In employing the words "oppressive, unfairly discriminatory or unfairly prejudicial" Parliament has afforded petitioners a wider base on which to found a complaint. Taking the ordinary dictionary definition of the words from the *Shorter Oxford English Dictionary*: oppressive is "unjustly burdensome"; unfair is "not fair or equitable; unjust"; discriminate is "to make or constitute a difference in or between; to differentiate"; and prejudicial, "causing prejudice, detrimental, damaging (to rights, interests, etc.)". I do not read the subsection as referring to three distinct alternatives which are to be considered separately in watertight compartments. The three expressions overlap, each in a sense helps to explain the other, and read together they reflect the underlying concern of the subsection that conduct of the company which is unjustly detrimental to any member of the company whatever form it takes and whether it adversely affects all members alike or discriminates against some only is a legitimate foundation for a complaint under s 209. The statutory concern is directed to instances or courses of conduct amounting to an unjust detriment to the interests of a member or members of the company. It follows that it is not necessary for a complainant to point to any actual irregularity or to an invasion of his legal rights

49 Or "composite whole", to use the words of the New South Wales Supreme Court in *Morgan v 45 Flers Avenue Pty Ltd* (1987) 5 ACLC 222 in interpreting the Australian counterpart provision.

50 Austin, R P, Ramsay I M, *Ford's Principles of Corporations Law* (12th edn, LexisNexis Butterworths, Australia, 2005), para 11.450.

51 (2003) SC709.

52 [1984] 1 NZLR 686 at 693.

> or to a lack of probity or want of good faith towards him on the part of those in control of the company.'
>
> This passage is helpful in indicating the nature of the cause of action under s 152 of the Companies Act 1997 and we would adopt it.

Despite the repeal and replacement of s 209 by ss 174 and 175 of the Companies Act 1993 (NZ), the New Zealand Court of Appeal considers that the interpretation of these terms ("oppressive, unfairly discriminatory or unfairly prejudicial") laid down in *Thomas v HW Thomas Ltd* still continues to apply.[53]

It is not necessary for the applicant to show a lack of probity or good faith on the part of the directors or the majority shareholders, i.e., that the directors acted dishonestly or with the intention of oppressing the shareholder. It is the effect of the actions of the directors or majority shareholders which is important. The test is an objective one: whether a reasonable director would see the conduct as oppressive or unfair.[54]

The shareholders of a company may have different expectations, which the court must balance. However, the court is reluctant to assume the role of management of the company. *Thomas v HW Thomas Ltd* provides an example of such a situation.

It is possible for actions of directors to discriminate against certain shareholders and yet this will not always be a breach of s 152. In order to prove a breach of s 152, there must be oppression or unfair prejudice or unfair discrimination against a shareholder or shareholders. The directors may act to the prejudice of a shareholder but they may act in good faith to advance the objects of the company. An example is provided by the Australian case of *Wayde v New South Wales Rugby League Ltd*.[55]

The New South Wales Rugby League Ltd is a company which administers the rugby league competition in New South Wales. Its shareholders are various rugby league clubs. The league's constitution states that it has the objective of promoting the best interests of rugby league and the constitution also authorises the board of directors of the company to decide which clubs can participate in the League's competitions. The board of directors of the league decided that one club, Western Suburbs (Wests), should not participate in the competition. Did the actions of the directors breach the Australian equivalent to s 152 of the Companies Act 1997 and oppress or unfairly discriminate against a shareholder (Wests)? The actions of the directors certainly discriminated against Wests. The club would be unable to participate in the rugby league competition. However, the court decided that this did not breach the

53 *Latimer Holdings Ltd and Powell v SEA Holdings New Zealand Ltd* [2004] NZCA 226.

54 *Re Noble & Sons Ltd* [1983] BCLC 273; *Wayde v New South Wales Rugby League Ltd* (1985) 180 CLR 459.

55 (1985) 180 CLR 459.

s 152 equivalent. The actions of the directors may have caused discrimination, but they were not unfair. The directors were obliged to promote the best interests of the game and this included solving the difficulty presented by a competition which occupied too long a period of the year. The solution of the directors, which involved reducing the number of clubs playing in the competition, was a reasonable decision and did not breach the s 152 equivalent.

Examples of oppressive and unfair conduct

We now outline some of the circumstances which shareholders have alleged constitute oppression or unfair conduct.

DIVERSION OF BUSINESS OR CORPORATE OPPORTUNITIES

In the chapter dealing with directors' duties, we saw that directors breach their fiduciary duties if they divert corporate opportunities to themselves or their associates. Section 152 provides a remedy for minority shareholders in such circumstances. Where a director of a company or the majority shareholders of a company divert business opportunities to themselves or to other companies which they control, but in which the minority shareholder bringing the oppression action has no interest, this will constitute oppression.[56]

In *Scottish Co-operative Wholesale Society Ltd v Meyer*,[57] a company was formed for the purpose of purchasing yarn (thread which is spun) and producing cloth. Two individuals who possessed licences for the purchase of yarn owned 49 per cent of the shares in the company. The other 51 per cent of the shares in the company were held by a company called the Scottish Co-op Wholesale Society Ltd. The company had five directors, comprising of the two individual shareholders and three directors nominated by the society. The arrangement was that the individual shareholders obtained supplies of yarn as they had the licence for its purchase and the cloth was woven at the society's mill. The cloth was then sold to the company, which marketed and sold the cloth. There was a dispute between the two individual shareholders and the society, and this resulted in the society no longer providing supplies of cloth to the company. The society began obtaining its own supplies of yarn from suppliers other than the two individual shareholders of the company. The society believed that the company no longer had a useful purpose, and the majority directors of the company who were appointed by the society allowed the company's business to decline. The two individual shareholders brought a legal action alleging that the affairs of the company

56 See also *Re Bright Pine Mills Pty Ltd* [1969] VR 1002; *Fexuto Pty Ltd v Bosnjak Holdings Pty Ltd* [2001] NSWCA 97.
57 [1959] AC 324.

were being conducted in an oppressive manner in that business opportunities were being diverted away from the company to its parent company – the society. The court held that there was oppression and the society was ordered to purchase the shares of the two individual shareholders at a price decided by the court.

IMPROPER EXCLUSION FROM MANAGEMENT

A common allegation in oppression cases is that the minority shareholder has been excluded from participating in the management of the company. If the minority shareholder has a reasonable expectation of continued participation in management, the removal of the minority shareholder will be oppressive.[58] This will usually be the case where the company is formed to operate as a family business, with family members having an expectation of participating in the management of the family business.

In *Hogg v Dymock*,[59] a company was established to operate an historic prison in Fremantle in Western Australia as a tourist heritage attraction. The plaintiff held a 50 per cent share in the company and was the executive director. The defendants were a husband and wife, who held the other 50 per cent share jointly and who were also directors. There was a disagreement between the plaintiff and the defendants, leading to the two defendants voting at a directors' meeting to dismiss the plaintiff and appoint themselves as managing directors. The plaintiff alleged that she had been oppressed by the two defendants. The court found that the company had been established on the basis that the plaintiff and defendants would effectively be partners in the company and share equally in the day-to-day conduct of the business as well as in the management of it at the level of directors. There had been a common expectation of continuing involvement by the plaintiff so that her dismissal by the other directors was oppressive.

UNFAIRLY RESTRICTING DIVIDENDS OR DIVERSION OF PROFITS

The shareholders of a company may have a disagreement about the amount of dividends the company should pay to its shareholders. We saw in *Thomas v HW Thomas Ltd*[60] that, just because a minority shareholder wants higher dividends, the decision of the directors of the company to adopt a conservative financial policy and not pay high dividends is not oppressive where this policy is agreed to by the other shareholders.[61] However, if the majority shareholders

58 *Fexuto Pty Ltd v Bosnjak Holdings Pty Ltd* [2001] NSWCA 97; *GFS Management Services Pty Ltd v Ground and Foundation Supports Pty* Ltd [2001] WASC 143.

59 (1993) 11 ACSR 14.

60 [1984] 1 NZLR 686.

61 *Thomas v HW Thomas Ltd* [1984] 1 NZLR 686.

or directors deliberately pay low dividends or no dividends and this is part of a plan to prefer their own interests (for example, by paying themselves excessive remuneration in the form of high directors' fees, housing and car allowances and retirement benefits out of the profits that could otherwise be paid as dividends), then this can constitute oppression.[62]

OPPRESSIVE CONDUCT OF BOARD MEETINGS

Where board meetings of a company are conducted in an unfair manner, this can constitute oppression. The case of *John J Starr (Real Estate) Pty Ltd v Robert R Andrew (A'asia) Pty Ltd*[63] illustrates this. A company was established to conduct the business of franchising real estate agencies. The plaintiff held 22 per cent of the shares of the company and was also a franchisee of the company (that is, he conducted a real estate franchise). The defendant and his wife held 63 per cent of the shares of the company. The plaintiff alleged that the board meetings of the company were conducted in an oppressive manner. It was alleged that the defendant, who was managing director:

- refused to provide the board with proper budgets;
- would bring forward significant matters which concerned the interests of the franchisees, some of whom were represented on the board, without sufficient notice;
- restricted the speaking time available to directors at board meetings when significant matters needed to be discussed; and
- made major decisions without reference to the board of directors.

The court held that the way in which the board meetings were conducted was oppressive.[64]

AUTOCRATIC EXERCISE OF POWER BY A DIRECTOR

Where a governing director exercises power in an autocratic manner at the expense of the majority of shareholders, this can constitute oppression.

In *B W Broughton v Longview Products Ltd*,[65] a family company operated a poultry farm. The father was the governing director, and his two sons were both directors and majority shareholders. The relationship between the father and his two sons became strained, so the father dismissed the two sons as

62 *Re Waitikiri Links Ltd* (1989) 4 NZCLC 64,922; *Sanford v Sanford Courier Service Pty Ltd* (1986) 10 ACLR 549; *Shamsallah Holdings Pty Ltd v CBD Refrigeration and Airconditioning Services Pty Ltd* [2001] WASC 8. Cf *Morgan v 45 Flers Avenue Pty Ltd* (1987) 5 ACLC 222; *Dosike Pty Ltd v Johnson* (1996) 22 ACSR 752.

63 (1991) 6 ACSR 63.

64 *John J Starr (Real Estate) Pty Ltd v Robert R Andrew (A'asia) Pty Ltd* (1991) 6 ACSR 63.

65 (1989) 3 BCR 395.

directors and appointed his wife as a director. The court held that the actions were oppressive but were not sufficient to support a winding-up order.

ISSUING SHARES IN CIRCUMSTANCES WHERE THE MAIN PURPOSE IS TO REDUCE A SHAREHOLDER'S OWNERSHIP INTEREST IN THE COMPANY

Where the majority shareholders or the directors issue more shares in the company and the main purpose is to reduce the proportionate holding of a particular shareholder of the company, this can constitute oppression.

In *Kokotovich Constructions Pty Ltd v Wallington*[66] a company had only two shareholders (W and K) who were in a *de facto* relationship. K had a "governing director's share" which had special voting rights. The relationship between W and K broke down, and K, by using his governing director's share, removed W as director and secretary of the company and also issued additional shares to himself and shareholders of his family. The court found that the purpose of the issue of shares by K was to reduce W's ownership interest in the company and this was oppressive.

FAILURE OF DIRECTORS TO ACT IN THE INTERESTS OF THE COMPANY[67]

Breaches of duty by directors can constitute oppression. The following is a summary of the facts of two related cases (*Re Spargos Mining NL*[68] and *Jenkins v Enterprise Gold Mines NL*[69]). In both cases, the plaintiff was a minority shareholder of the companies.

Spargos Mining and Enterprise Gold Mine were taken over by the Independent Resources Ltd (IRL) group of companies. The boards of both Spargos and Enterprise were controlled by representatives of IRL. Both Spargos and Enterprise had substantial assets at the time of their acquisition by IRL. The plaintiff in both cases alleged that there had been a series of transactions where the funds of both Spargos and Enterprise were channelled out of the two companies either to IRL or to its related companies. Some of the transactions, including the following, were almost entirely devoid of any commercial benefit to the company, and in many cases, significant conflict of interests by the directors:

- Enterprise providing a loan to an IRL company which was never repaid and for which the IRL company provided no security.
- Spargos acquiring shares of another company within the IRL group.

66 (1995) 17 ACSR 478.

67 See also *Re Overton Holdings Pty Ltd* (1984) 2 ACLC 777; *Dynasty Pty Ltd v Coombs* (1995) 13 ACLC 1290.

68 (1990) 3 ACSR 1.

69 (1992) 6 ACSR 539.

The shares were acquired at a price which was three times their market value and the court found that at the time of the purchase the company whose shares were bought by Spargos was operating at a substantial loss and by the time of the court proceedings, the company was insolvent.

- Spargos purchasing 600,000 preference shares in IRL at a price of $A5 per share with the objective of providing funds to IRL. By the time of the court proceedings, the shares were worthless. The court found that the terms of the investment in the shares was such that Spargos received no benefit and the purpose was solely to provide cash to IRL. The shares did not provide any guarantee of regular cash income by way of dividend, and the court found that the prospect of any dividends was remote. Another term of the shares was that they could be redeemed only by IRL and not by Spargos, so that Spargos was effectively locked into the investment.

The court held that these actions of the directors of both Spargos and Enterprise constituted oppression. The directors of Spargos and Enterprise had failed to act in the interests of those companies. Instead, they had breached their duties by acting in the interests of IRL and other companies in the IRL group.

IMPROPER SHARE ISSUE

We have seen in the chapter on directors' duties[70] that directors breach their fiduciary duties if they issue shares for improper purposes. If directors who breached their duty are also majority shareholders, they will act oppressively or unfairly if, as shareholders, they vote to ratify their improper actions.[71]

Remedies where there is oppression

Section 152 of the Companies Act 1997 allows the court to choose from a wide range of remedies where the court finds that there has been oppression or unfair conduct and it is just and equitable to make an order. The remedies under s 152 include the following orders:

- *That the company or any other person acquire the shareholder's shares.*[72] A share buy-out is the most common remedy sought by minority shareholders and ordered by the courts in Australia under the Corporations Act 2001 and in New Zealand under the Companies Act 1993, where there is oppression,[73] and it is very likely that this will be the position in

70 Chapter 9.

71 *Hannes v MJH Pty Ltd* (1992) 7 ACSR 8; *Re Dalkeith Investments Pty Ltd* (1984) 9 ACLR 247.

72 Companies Act 1997, s 152(2)(a). See Taylor, L, "Minority Buy-Out Rights in the Companies Act 1993" (1997) 6 *Canterbury Law Review* 539–563.

73 See for example, *Re Federated Fashions (NZ) Ltd* (1981) 1 NZCLC ¶95-011 and *Cornes v Kawerau Hotel (1994) Ltd* (1999) 8 NZCLC 261,815.

PNG. It allows an oppressed minority shareholder to sell his or her shares at a price which the court determines to be fair; in determining a valuation, the court has a wide discretion.[74] The court can order the company or "any other person" to buy the shares of the oppressed shareholder.

- *That the company or any other person pays compensation to "a person".*[75] This remedy may be appropriate where a shareholder sold shares at an undervalue.[76] The shareholder may have acted on the misleading advice of the company.
- *Regulating the conduct of the company's affairs in the future.*[77] This could include the replacement of the directors, and the authorisation of legal action. It could also include an order that a director not participate in the management of the company.[78] In *Re Spargos Mining NL*, the court ordered the removal of two directors and appointed other people as directors who were independent of the controlling shareholders. The court also ordered the new board to investigate a number of transactions the company had made in the past for the purpose of deciding whether there should be further legal action against the directors.[79]
- *Altering or adding to the company's constitution (if it has one), or ordering the company to adopt a constitution (if it does not have one).*[80] It may be necessary to alter a company's constitution in certain situations where the future affairs of a company are regulated. In *Re Spargos Mining NL*, the court ordered the deletion of certain provisions of the company's constitution which allowed the directors of the company to appoint additional directors. In *Hannes v MJH Pty Ltd*[81] the court ordered that the company's constitution be changed to remove Hannes' absolute control over the voting at shareholders' meetings by giving the other shareholders a right to appoint their representative to the board. Other changes to the constitution gave the other shareholders a role in relation to the alteration of the constitution and determining the director's remuneration as

74 *Re Bagot Well Pastoral Co Pty Ltd* (1992) 9 ACSR 129.
75 Companies Act 1997, s 152(2)(b).
76 *Cotterall v Fidelity Life Assurance Co Ltd* (1987) 3 NZCLC 100,054.
77 Companies Act 1997, s 152(2)(c).
78 *Re HR Harmer Ltd* [1958] 3 All ER 689.
79 See also *Re Overton Holdings Pty Ltd* (1984) 2 ACLC 777, where the court granted an order authorising a member to institute legal proceedings on behalf of the company, in effect, a derivative action.
80 Companies Act 1997, s 152(2)(d). It should be noted that s 152(2) does not give the court the express power to order that the company adopt a constitution. Despite this, it is suggested that the National Court does have this power, as the list of powers in s 152(2) is not an exhaustive list. Section 152(2) provides that the court may make "such order as it thinks fit, including, *without limiting the generality of this subsection*, an order . . . (d) altering or adding to the company's constitution . . .".
81 (1992) 7 ACSR 8.

well as advance notice of further issues of shares. Any alteration made by the court has the same effect as if it had been made by the shareholders and it will be binding.[82] Furthermore, the company cannot make any changes to the alterations to the constitution made by the court unless the court order allows for this or unless a fresh application is made seeking the court's approval.[83]

- *Appointing a receiver and manager of the company.*[84] A receiver is a person appointed to control property of the company until court proceedings are concluded.[85] This is a remedy of last resort. In *Jenkins v Enterprise Gold Mines NL*[86] the Full Court of the Supreme Court of Western Australia ordered the appointment of a receiver and manager with powers to investigate transactions involving apparent breaches of directors' fiduciary duties and where necessary to institute court proceedings against the directors.
- *Directing the rectification of the records of the company.*[87] For the purposes of this remedy, the "records" of the company are those which fall within the definition of records in s 164 of the Companies Act 1997. The remedy will be awarded to correct an error and where it does not override the rights of other shareholders.[88]
- *Putting the company into liquidation.*[89] This remedy (winding up) would rarely be awarded where the company is a solvent going concern, as an alternative remedy would usually be more beneficial for shareholders. The courts have stressed that this is a remedy of last resort.[90] The only occasion when such a remedy has been awarded in New Zealand was where there had been a complete breakdown of relations in a family company that turned a financially sound company into one worth very little.[91]
- *Setting aside action taken by the company or the board which is in breach of the Companies Act 1997 or the constitution of the company.*[92]

82 Companies Act 1997, s 153(2). It is suggested that if the National Court, in exercising its powers under s 152, orders a company to *adopt* a constitution, it can impose conditions and limitations similar to those set out in s 153.
83 Companies Act 1997, s 153(1).
84 Companies Act 1997, s 152(2)(e). Although the provision merely refers to "receiver", the wide and unlimited powers of s 152(2) allows for the appointment of a manager. Section 254(1) of the Companies Act 1997 provides that in Part XVII which deals with receiverships: "receiver means a receiver, or a manager, or a receiver and manager in respect of any property . . ."
85 See Chapter 13 for a full discussion.
86 (1992) 6 ACSR 539.
87 Companies Act 1997, s 152(2)(f).
88 *Nicholls v Parkview Projects Ltd* (1999) 8 NZCLC 262,016.
89 Companies Act 1997, s 152(2)(g).
90 *Cornes v Kawerau Hotel* (1994) *Ltd* (1999) 8 NZCLC 261,815.
91 *Vujnovich v Vujnovich* [1989] 3 NZLR 513 (PCNZ).
92 Companies Act 1997, s 152(2)(h).

Putting the company into liquidation as a shareholder's remedy

The most common reason a company is put into liquidation is because it is unable to pay its debts.[93] The shareholders of the company may also choose to put the company into voluntary liquidation because, for example, they believe the company no longer serves any useful purpose. This is called a shareholders' voluntary liquidation.

In some circumstances, a shareholder can apply to the court to compulsorily liquidate the company. The company does not have to be insolvent. A shareholder of a company can apply to have the company put into liquidation where:

- it is just and equitable to do so;[94]
- the company or the board has persistently or seriously failed to comply with the Companies Act 1997;[95] or
- the company does not comply with s 10 (essential requirements of a company).[96]

Relationship with the oppression remedy

Usually, a minority shareholder who brings an action to put the company into liquidation for one of the reasons stated above also brings an oppression action under s 152 of the Companies Act 1997. The reason for this is that the courts are reluctant to put into liquidation a company which is solvent and which has a future. Other remedies may be more appropriate. For example, it might be appropriate for the court to order other shareholders to buy the shares of the minority shareholder. However, this cannot be done under s 291 because the only remedy available to the court is that of putting the company into liquidation. The court can choose from a wide range of remedies under the oppression remedy in s 152. It is desirable for a minority shareholder who wants to have the company put into liquidation to also bring an oppression action in case the court believes that there is a more appropriate remedy than putting the company into liquidation.

The just and equitable ground

The National Court can order a company to be put into liquidation under s 291 if it finds that it is just and equitable to do so.[97] The situations where

93 (See Chapter 14 – Liquidation).
94 Companies Act 1997, s 291(3)(d).
95 Companies Act 1997, s 291(3)(b).
96 Companies Act 1997, s 291(3)(c).
97 Companies Act 1997, s 291(3)(d).

courts have put companies into liquidation because it is just and equitable to do so include:

- breakdown of mutual trust and confidence;
- fraud or misconduct;
- failure of substratum;
- deadlock;
- directors acting in their own interests;
- oppressive, unfairly discriminatory, or unfairly prejudicial conduct or acts; and
- it is in the public interest for the company to be wound up.

This area of the law is considered in detail in Chapter 14 (Liquidation).

Statutory injunction

An injunction is an order of the court requiring a person to do something (mandatory injunction or injunction to force action),[98] or to stop doing something (prohibitory injunction or injunction to restrain action). Section 142 of the Companies Act 1997, empowers the National Court to grant both types of injunction:[99]

(a) restraining a person who is engaging in or proposes to engage in conduct that is or would contravene the constitution of the company or the Companies Act 1997 from engaging in that conduct; or
(b) requiring a person who has refused or failed, is refusing or failing, or is proposing to refuse or fail, to do an act or thing that he is required to do by the constitution of the company or the Companies Act 1997 to do that act or thing.[100]

This section differs from its New Zealand counterpart in several important respects. Whereas under s 164 of the Companies Act 1993 (NZ), the New Zealand court may seek to restrain "a company that, or a director of a company who, proposes to engage in conduct" that would infringe the Companies Act 1993 or the company's constitution, the National Court can issue an injunction against a broader range of "persons" but not, it seems, against a company. The section refers to "a person".[101] In addition, whereas the New Zealand section refers to the company or directors who "proposes to

98 This is similar to the order of specific performance.
99 The court's power is discretionary.
100 The wording of s 142(1)(b) is so strong that the heading to s 142 should have been entitled "Injunctions and Specific Performance" instead of merely "Injunctions".
101 It is possible to argue that "person" in s 142 is wide enough to include a company. A company is a legal, as opposed to natural, person.

engage in conduct" that would contravene the Act or constitution, the Companies Act 1997 refers to restraining a person who is "engaging in or proposes to engage in conduct". It also goes further than the New Zealand legislation in requiring a person who has refused or failed, is refusing or failing, or is proposing to refuse or fail, to do an act or thing that he or she is required to do. In this respect the Act emphasises that mandatory injunctions are covered by s 142. The order made under s 142(1)(b) is, therefore, similar to an order for specific performance.

An injunction can be a useful remedy where there is continuing conduct which contravenes the Companies Act 1997 or the constitution of the company. For example, a director may be breaching a duty to the company by continuing to take company funds. The court can grant an injunction preventing the director from doing this. There can be later court proceedings for recovery of the funds. Another example is where a director has property which belongs to the company and the director is about to sell that property. The court can grant an injunction preventing the director from selling the property.

Where the National Court has power to grant an injunction under s 142, it also has power to order "such consequential relief as it thinks fit".[102]

Who can apply?

An injunction under s 142 can be applied for by:[103]

- the company; or
- a director or shareholder of the company; or
- an entitled person;[104] or
- the Registrar of Companies.

A "shareholder of the company" and an "entitled person" will include a personal representative[105] of the shareholder or entitled person and a person to whom shares of any of those persons have passed by operation of law.[106]

102 Companies Act 1997, s 142(3).

103 Companies Act 1997, s 142(2). The Corporations Act 2001 (Aus) allows a wider set of applicants, including "a person whose interests have been, are or would be affected by the conduct", and in some cases a creditor. See *Broken Hill Proprietary Co Pty Ltd v Bell Resources Ltd* (1984) 2 ACLC 157 and *Airpeak Pty Ltd v Jetstream Aircraft Ltd* (1997) 23 ACSR 715 for decisions to the effect that these provisions should be given a liberal interpretation in favour of those seeking injunctive relief. In some cases the Australian provisions shift the onus of proof to the company once the applicant alleges a breach of the Corporations Act 2001 (Aus).

104 For definition of "entitled person" see Companies Act 1997, s 2(1): it includes "a person upon whom the constitution confers any of the rights and powers of a shareholder".

105 Section 2(1) of the Companies Act 1997 defines "personal representative" in relation to a person to mean "the executor, administrator, or trustee of the estate of that person".

106 Companies Act 1997, s 141. This would include a trustee in bankruptcy.

What is a contravention of the Act or the constitution?

Section 142 covers actual or proposed conduct and the injunction is therefore preventative. It cannot be used "in relation to conduct or a course of conduct that has been completed".[107] If a shareholder wishes to claim a remedy for acts which have already occurred then such a claim cannot be brought under s 142. Other remedies will have to be used.[108] Examples of conduct supporting the granting of an injunction may include the restraint of directors from:

- holding a proposed meeting;[109]
- passing a proposed resolution;
- executing a proposed transaction, e.g., sale of property.

Interim Injunctions[110]

The court may, at any time before the final determination of an application for an injunction under s 142(1) of the Companies Act 1997 is made, "make, as an interim order, any order that it is empowered to make under that subsection".[111] Thus, the court may make an interim injunction, pending the final hearing, for example, so as to preserve property or the *status quo*. This means that the applicant may speedily obtain an order with the merits of the case to be decided upon at a later hearing.

Undertaking as to damages

The plaintiff will usually be required to give an undertaking as to damages, should the defendant sustain any by reason of the court making the interim injunction. Usually, the plaintiff will sign a document undertaking to pay damages if he or she loses the case on substantive merits. Sometimes, this will be accompanied by the payment into court of monies which provides adequate security for the undertaking as to damages. Other types of security may be ordered.

107 Section 142(4) of the Companies Act 1997 expressly so provides, and it is also implicit in s 142(1)(a). It should be contrasted with s 1324 of the Corporations Act 2001 (Aus), which allows an injunction to be granted where a "person has engaged . . . in conduct that constituted" a contravention of the Act etc. That Act also governs a wider sphere of activities, including aiding, abetting, counselling, inducing or otherwise assisting in the contravention of the Corporations Act 2001.

108 For example, either statutory remedies (s 143, s 149, s 152), or underlying law remedies.

109 *Cue Energy Resources Ltd v Browse Petroleum Pty Ltd* (2001) 9 NZCLC 262,526.

110 The underlying law principles governing the grant of an interim injunction are set out in *Norah Mairi v Alkan Tololo (No 1)* [1976] PNGLR 59; *Employers Federation of Papua New Guinea v Papua New Guinea Waterside Workers and Seamen's Union* (1982) N393; *Markscal Ltd v MRDC* [1996] PNGLR 419; *AGK Pacific (NG) Ltd v Anderson* (2000) N2062; *Golobadana No 35 Ltd v Bank of South Pacific Ltd* (2002) N2309.

111 Companies Act 1997, s 142(5).

The New Zealand Companies Act 1993 is silent on the issue of the court granting an injunction subject to an undertaking as to damages. In some cases where a defendant would suffer damages if an injunction were wrongly awarded against him, and it may be difficult for that person to later recover those damages against the applicant for the injunction, the court is sometimes prepared to grant an injunction only if the applicant gives an undertaking as to damages.[112] This undertaking will usually take the form of a document signed by the applicant and filed in court. However, sometimes it may be necessary for the applicant to give a security, either in the form or a bond or the deposit of money with the court or as directed by the court. This security can be used by the defendant in assisting him or her to recover costs, should the applicant lose the case and not afford to pay costs and damages. In applications for interlocutory or interim injunctions, it is usual for the application to provide an undertaking as to damages or provide adequate security for an undertaking as to damages, should the defendant sustain any by reason of the order: this is usually required as a condition for the grant of an injunction.

Section 142(6) provides that where the court grants an interim injunction, it "shall not require the applicant, as a condition of granting an interim injunction, to give any undertakings as to damages".[113]

Statutory right to information and to inspect records of the company

A shareholder of a company may believe that the directors are not giving sufficient information about the management and operations of the company to

112 See *Gobe Hongu Ltd v The National Executive Council* (1999) N1920 and *National Housing Corporation v Yama Security Services Pty Ltd* (2000) N1985, where Sevua J stated that "the usual undertaking as to damages is a condition precedent to the granting of an interlocutory injunction". In *Pama Anio v Aho Baliki* (2002) N2267, Davani J said that the fact that the plaintiff had not given such an undertaking affected her decision not to grant interlocutory injunction. However, in *Kurt Reimann v George Skell* (2001) N2093, Kandakasi J stated that an undertaking as to damages before the grant of interlocutory orders is not a strict one. Instead, it is within the discretion of the court to determine whether such an undertaking should be given.

113 Cf Independent Consumer and Competition Commission Act 2002, s 100; Securities Act 1997, ss 143(3), 144(7); Telecommunications Act 1996, s 178(4). It is submitted that the National Court should also not require undertakings as to fees and expenses of the court action. Although these are not expressly mentioned in the section, the fact that the legislature mentioned the greater (issue of damages), it must have intended to include the lesser. The New Zealand counterpart provisions do not contain a subsection similar to subsection (6). Cf s 1324(8) of the Corporations Act 2001 (Aus), on which this subsection may have been based. Note, however, that it is only where the application is made by ASIC that the court may not order an undertaking (from ASIC "or any other person") as to damages. It is also interesting to note s 1324(10) of the same Act empowering the court, where an application is made for an injunction, to grant damages in addition to or in substitution for the grant of an injunction. There is no such provision in the Companies Act 1997. Cf Securities Act 1997, s 144(8) and Bank of Papua New Guinea v Resources and Investment Finance Ltd (2002) N2284.

its shareholders. The National Court may award a remedy for the shareholder to access information held by the company and to inspect company records.[114]

Right to information

Under s 219 of the Companies Act 1997 a shareholder may at any time make a written request to the company for information held by the company. The request must specify the information sought in sufficient detail to enable it to be identified.[115]

Within one month of receiving such a request, the company must:[116]

- provide the information; or
- agree to provide the information within a specified period, either free of cost or at a reasonable cost;[117] or
- refuse to provide the information, specifying the reasons for its refusal.

There may be several legitimate reasons why the company may want to refuse to provide the information, and the Companies Act 1997 does not attempt to set these out. It does, however, provide some examples of situations where such refusal would be legitimate:[118]

- where the disclosure of the information would or would be likely to prejudice the commercial position of the company, of any other person, whether or not that person supplied the information to the company; or
- the request for information is frivolous or vexatious.

If the company requires the shareholder to pay a charge for the information, the shareholder may withdraw the request, and is deemed to have done so unless, within one month of receiving notification of the charge, the shareholder informs the company:[119]

- that the shareholder will pay the charge; or
- that the shareholder considers the charge to be unreasonable.

The National Court may, on the application of the shareholder, make an order requiring the company to supply the information if it is satisfied that:

114 Company records are defined in s 164 to include the interests register of the company, financial statements and the minutes of all meetings.
115 Companies Act 1997, s 219(2).
116 Companies Act 1997, s 219(3).
117 If the company decides to charge the shareholder for the information, it must not only specify the cost, but explain how the charge goes towards meeting the cost of providing the information.
118 Companies Act 1997, s 219(4).
119 Companies Act 1997, s 219(5).

- the company does not have sufficient reason to refuse to supply the information; or
- the company has sufficient reason to refuse to supply the information but that other reasons exist that outweigh the refusal.[120]

The court may, on the application of the shareholder, make an order requiring the company to supply the information within such time or on payment of such charge as the court thinks fit, if it is satisfied that:

- the period specified for providing the information is unreasonable; or
- the charge set by the company is unreasonable.[121]

Where the court makes an order for the company to supply the information, it may specify the use that may be made of the information and the persons to whom it may be disclosed.[122]

Right to inspect company records (Investigation of company records)

Under s 220 of the Companies Act 1997, on the application of a shareholder or creditor, the National Court may appoint a suitable person "to inspect and to make copies of, or take extracts from, the records[123] or other documents[124] of the company, or such of the records or documents of the company as are specified in the order". The person who is appointed must act under the direction of the court and report to the court, which may make such order in relation to the disclosure and use that may be made of the records and information obtained as it thinks fit.[125] When making an order under s 220, the court must be satisfied that the applicant is acting in "good faith" and that the inspection is for a "proper purpose", and that the person who will be making the inspection is qualified in accordance with s 193.[126]

The Companies Act 1997 does not provide any guidance on what constitutes a "proper purpose". Some assistance in interpreting the meaning of "good

120 Companies Act 1997, s 219(7).
121 Companies Act 1997, s 219(6).
122 Companies Act 1997, s 219(8).
123 Records are defined in s 164 of the Companies Act 1997.
124 Documents are defined in s 2(1) of the Companies Act 1997.
125 The court may make such ancillary orders as it thinks fit, including an order that the accounts of the company be audited by the person appointed to carry out the inspection: Companies Act 1997, s 220(1).
126 The person must be registered as a Registered Company Auditor under the Accountants Act 1996, and must not be: (a) a director or employee of the company; (b) a person who is a partner, or in the employment, of a director or employee of the company; (c) a liquidator or a person who is a receiver in respect of the property of the company; (d) a body corporate; (e) a person who, by virtue of para (a) or (b), may not be appointed or act as auditor of a related company.

faith" and "proper purpose" may be gained from Australian cases considering s 247A(1) of the Corporations Act 2001 (Cth)) under which the court may authorise a person to inspect books of a company only if it is satisfied that the applicant is "acting in good faith and that the inspection is to be made for a proper purpose".[127]

Examples of an independent proper purpose is where the inspection is for the purpose of pursuing a reasonable suspicion that directors have breached their duties,[128] and where the constitution of the company contains a pre-emption provision and inspection is sought to assist a shareholder to obtain an opinion on the value of the shareholding.[129] An example of lack of proper purpose is where a shareholder is motivated by a wish to obtain confidential information for the benefit of one of the company's competitors,[130] or to facilitate a take-over bid.[131]

The reasonable costs of the inspection are to be met by the company unless the court orders otherwise, which it will usually do if the appointment of the inspector turns out to be unnecessary.[132]

As Beck and Borrowdale point out, s 220, as a remedy, "seems to have little attraction for the ordinary shareholder seeking to redress a grievance", given the other remedies available to shareholders, and will probably be more useful to creditors "as they do not have other remedies under the [Companies Act 1997] while the company is solvent".[133]

Shareholder's personal action

Overview

In addition to statutory remedies, a shareholder may have a personal right of action.

What are "personal rights"?

A shareholder may be given a personal right:

- as part of an express contract between the shareholder and the other shareholders or between the shareholder and the company which is outside the provisions of the company's constitution (if it has one); or
- by statute or the underlying law.

127 Later authorities have treated both terms as expressing a composite notion.
128 *Humes Ltd v Unity APA Ltd* (No 1) [1987] VR 467.
129 *Tinios v French Caledonia Travel Services Pty Ltd* (1994) 13 ACSR 658.
130 *Knightswood Nominees Pty Ltd v Sherwin Pastoral Co Ltd* (1989) 7 ACLC 536.
131 *Garina Pty Ltd v Action Holdings Ltd* (1989) 7 ACLC 962.
132 Companies Act 1997, s 220(6). See *Re Maketu Contractors (1964) Ltd; Forster v Maketu Contractors* (1964) Ltd (1992) 6 NZCLC 68,199.
133 Beck, A and Borrowdale, A, *Papua New Guinea Companies and Securities Law Guide* (CCH Australia Ltd, Sydney, 1999), para 1022.

In addition, the shareholder has a statutory right to enforce the constitution as the constitution is binding as between the company and each shareholder and between each shareholder.[134]

Where an action of the directors or other shareholders affects the personal right of a shareholder, the shareholder has a personal action to enforce the right.

Express contract

A shareholder may be a party to an express contract (that is, a written contract) with other shareholders, or party to an express contract with the company. For example, the contract may state that the shareholder has an automatic right to appoint a nominee or representative as director of the company. The contract might also say that in certain matters to be decided by all shareholders the individual shareholder has additional rights. If an attempt is made to take away these personal rights without the consent of the shareholder, the shareholder is able to bring legal action to enforce the contract. It should be noted that this right exists outside company law and is based on contract law.

In PNG, an "entitled person" may have a contract with the company.[135] An "entitled person" is any person who may be granted shareholder-type rights and powers by the company's constitution. For example, an entitled person may be a creditor of the company.

Contractual effect on the constitution

As we have already discussed in Chapter 8, a company's internal management may be governed by a constitution, the mandatory and replaceable rules in the Companies Act 1997, or a combination of both. A company's constitution (if it has one) and any replaceable rules that apply to the company are binding as if they constitute a contract. The constitution (if a company has one) and any mandatory and replaceable rules that apply to the company have the effect of a contract between:

- the company and each shareholder;
- the company and each director; and
- a shareholder and every other shareholder.

The constitution may give personal rights to shareholders. For example, in a small family company which has a constitution, a provision of the constitution will often state that a shareholder cannot sell his or her shares:

- without the approval of the directors; or
- without offering them for sale to other shareholders before offering them to any person who is not a shareholder of the company.

134 Companies Act 1997, s 32(1).
135 Companies Act 1997, s 2.

If a shareholder attempts to sell his or her shares without complying with the restriction in the constitution, another shareholder (for example, a shareholder who would like to buy the shares) has a personal right to enforce the provision of the constitution.

Personal right given by statute or the underlying law

Under s 147, the Companies Act 1997 confers a personal right on shareholders to bring an action against directors of the company for a breach of duty owed to the shareholders. The duties owed to shareholders are duties to:

- supervise the share register;[136]
- disclose interests;[137] and
- disclose share dealings.[138]

Section 147(3) makes it clear that there are certain duties which will not give rise to a personal action by a shareholder against directors of the company. These are duties owed to the company and are the duties to:

- act in good faith and in the best interests of the company;[139]
- exercise care;[140] and
- use company information appropriately.[141]

The list of duties owed to shareholders is not limited to those prescribed in s 147 and may extend to additional duties owed by directors to shareholders. For example, it might include the statutory duty of directors to prevent insolvent trading,[142] and the underlying law duty to exercise powers for a proper purpose.[143] For example, a restriction on the directors of a company dealing in shares with the inside information outlined in s 149 may be extended to a duty designed to protect shareholders' interests. The company's constitution may make it clear that directors will owe duties to shareholders. If such duties are contained in the company's constitution, they must not conflict with the Companies Act 1997.

It will always be a matter of interpretation as to whether a duty contained in the Companies Act 1997 or the company's constitution is a duty owed to shareholders giving rise to an action under s 147.

136 Companies Act 1997, s 70.
137 Companies Act 1997, s 118.
138 Companies Act 1997, s 126.
139 Companies Act 1997, s 112.
140 Companies Act 1997, s 115.
141 Companies Act 1997, s 123.
142 Companies Act 1997, s 348.
143 As to whether this duty exists, see Chapter 9 (Directors' Duties).

Under s 147(2), a shareholder is unable to bring an action against a director simply because the shares held by the shareholder have not increased in value.[144]

Under s 148 of the Companies Act 1997, a shareholder may apply to the court requiring a director to comply with the Companies Act 1997 or the company's constitution. The court will make an order if it considers it just and equitable to do so.

A shareholder is also able to bring an action against the company for breach of any duty owed to him or her as a shareholder. These may be duties which exist outside the Companies Act 1997 and the company's constitution. The Companies Act 1997 does not specify the types of duty which may be included in this type of action, but once again it will have to be a duty that relates to the company–shareholder relationship. An example may be the failure of a company to pay dividends which it has declared.

A shareholder may have personal rights according to the underlying law. Some examples are:

- the right to notices of meetings which provide adequate information about matters that will be discussed at the meeting;[145] and
- the shareholder's right to vote at meetings unless the constitution of the company takes away that right;[146] and
- the proper purpose duty.[147]

Under the Companies Act 1997, these rights may now be supported by the Act and may be achieved through the shareholder's derivative action.

Shareholder's derivative action

What is a "derivative action"?

A legal action is derivative when the person who brings the action relies not on a cause of action which belongs to them personally, but on a cause of action belonging to someone else. When we use the phrase "derivative action" in company law, it means an action brought by a shareholder or director based on a cause of action which the company has, rather than a cause of action belonging to the shareholder.

In the case of the shareholder's statutory remedies and the shareholders' personal action, these actions are brought in a personal capacity because the shareholder has a personal right or is affected personally. The derivative action

144 *Prudential Assurance Co Ltd v Newman Industries Ltd (No 2)* [1982] Ch 204.
145 *Kaye v Croydon Tramways Co* [1898] 1 Ch 358.
146 *Pender v Lushington* (1877) 6 Ch D 70.
147 As to whether this duty exists, see Chapter 9 (Directors' Duties).

is brought by a shareholder, but is based on a legal action which the company has (for example, a breach of duty owed to the company). If the derivative action is successful and the defendant is ordered by the court to pay compensation, the compensation is usually paid to the company and not to the individual shareholder.[148] This is because it is the company which has the right to bring the legal action.

The statutory derivative action[149]

Section 143 of the Companies Act 1997 provides for a statutory derivative action. The section confers standing on directors and shareholders to apply to the National Court for leave to bring proceedings, or intervene in proceedings that have already been started by someone else, for the purpose of continuing, defending or discontinuing those proceedings.

It is not clear from the Companies Act 1997 whether s 143 abolished the underlying law derivative action (which was fraught with uncertainty and procedural problems) or whether this action continues to be available to shareholders.[150] Section 143(6) seems to state that the "Companies Act 1997 has put in place a statutory derivative action which has entirely superseded the common [i.e., underlying] law procedure".[151] In *Hetherington v Carpenter*,[152] the New Zealand Court of Appeal held that the equivalent section in the New Zealand Companies Act 1993, did not apply to overseas companies, but that the common law rules continued to operate in such cases.

148 But see s 145(d) of the Companies Act 1997.

149 See Taylor, L, "The Derivative Action in the Companies Act 1993", in Borrowdale, A, Rowe, D and Taylor, L (eds), *Company Law Writings: A New Zealand Collection* (Centre for Commercial and Corporate Law Inc., School of Law, University of Canterbury, 2002), pp 245–262; Fitzsimons, P, "Statutory Derivative Actions in New Zealand" (1996) 14 *Company and Securities Law Journal* 184–190; Fitzsimons, P, "The Companies Act 1993: a new approach to shareholder litigation in New Zealand" (1998) 18 *The Company Lawyer* 306–312; Watson, S M and Morgan, O, "A Matter of Balance: The Statutory Derivative Action in New Zealand" (1998) 19 *The Company Lawyer* 236; Borrowdale, A, "The Statutory Derivative Action" [2000] *New Zealand Law Journal* 409–410.

150 New Zealand Law Commission, *Company Law: Reform and Restatement* (Law Commission, Report No 9, Law Commission, Wellington, New Zealand 1989); New Zealand Law Commission, *Company Law Reform: Transition and Revision*, Report No 16, Law Commission, Wellington, New Zealand, 1990), para 568: "Any shareholder, with the leave of the Court, may bring a derivative action to remedy a wrong done to the company (section 127). This provision, which is modelled on the Canadian reforms, does away with the rule in *Foss v Harbottle* while preserving, through Court supervision, protection against abuse."

151 Beck, A and Borrowdale, A, *Papua New Guinea Companies and Securities Law Guide* (CCH Australia Ltd, Sydney, 1999), para 1008.

152 (1997) 8 NZCLC 261,290 (NZCA). See also Campbell, N, "Does the Companies Act codify remedies?" [2001] *Company and Securities Law Bulletin* 53.

Leave required

A derivative action cannot be taken as of right. It depends on the applicant first obtaining leave of the court to bring the action.[153] The court may grant leave only if the company or a related company does not intend to bring, diligently continue or defend, or discontinue the proceedings, as the case may be,[154] or it is in the interests of the company or related company that the conduct of the proceedings should not be left to the determination of the directors or the shareholders as a whole.[155]

The permission of the court is needed because, as we have seen, where a duty is owed to the company, the rule is that the company should enforce that duty. There are several good reasons for this rule:

- if each shareholder of a company was allowed to bring a legal action in relation to a wrong done to the company, there would be the possibility of hundreds of legal actions which would make it difficult to conduct efficient litigation, and would impose significant burdens on the courts; and
- the company can usually be expected to be in a better position to decide whether to bring legal action for a wrong done to it, rather than rely on an individual shareholder to bring the action.

While the rule has these advantages, it can have a significant disadvantage. Where the directors, who it is alleged have breached their duties to the company, are also a majority of the board, it is hardly likely that these directors will have the company commence legal action against them for breach of duty. A rule which provides that it is only the company which can bring legal action for breaches of duties owed to the company can, therefore, disadvantage the company and its shareholders. Consequently, Parliament has enacted the statutory derivative action contained in s 143 of the Companies Act 1997.

The rule which specified that the company is the proper plaintiff for the enforcement of duties owed to it developed from a case called *Foss v Harbottle*.[156] However, realising that breaches of duty may not be enforced where the alleged wrongdoers are directors who are a majority of the board, the courts subsequently developed several exceptions to the proper plaintiff rule in *Foss v Harbottle*, the major exception being the common law derivative action.[157]

153 Companies Act 1997, s 143(1).
154 Companies Act 1997, s 143(3)(a).
155 Companies Act 1997, s 143(3)(b).
156 (1843) 2 Hare 461, 67 ER 189.
157 The case of *Pangia Constructions Pty Ltd v Papua New Guinea Banking Corporation* [1996] PNGLR 1 shows that the National Court recognised that the derivative action formed part of the underlying law shortly before the enactment of the Companies Act 1997.

Who can apply?

Section 143(1) of the Companies Act 1997 states that the following persons may apply to the National Court for permission to bring a statutory derivative action:

- a shareholder of the company;[158] or
- a director of the company.

It should be noted that that the Companies Act 1997 restricts the persons who may apply. Neither former shareholders[159] nor former directors are expressly referred to and therefore they have no standing to sue using the statutory derivative action.[160] It is also unclear whether a shareholder of a company who is not a member of a related company may initiate or intervene in proceedings on behalf of the related company.

Notice of the application will need to be served on the company.[161] The company:

- may appear and be heard: and
- must inform the court "whether or not it intends to bring, continue, defend, or discontinue the proceedings, as the case may be".[162]

What are the criteria used by the court in granting leave?

Where the National Court is considering whether or not to grant leave and allow a person (the applicant) to bring a derivative action, there is a preliminary hurdle to be overcome: the court may grant leave *only if* it is satisfied that:

- the company does not intend to bring proceedings, diligently continue, defend or discontinue existing proceedings;[163] or

158 Also included is the personal representative of a shareholder and a person to whom the shareholder's shares have passed by operation of law: Companies Act 1997, s 141.

159 Seeing that other sections (e.g., s 152) expressly refer to former shareholders, it is suggested that the court cannot extend the meaning of shareholder in s 143(1) to include former shareholders. The same argument applies in respect of "other entitled persons".

160 Several sections of the Companies Act 1997 expressly refer to "former directors": See ss 139, 140, 212, 311, 322, 348, 376.

161 Companies Act 1997, s 143(4).

162 Companies Act 1997, s 143(5).

163 Companies Act 1997, s 143(3)(a). The burden is on the company to satisfy the court of its intentions in respect of the proceedings. *Quaere* the importance of shareholder ratification of directors' breaches of duty. See Taylor, L, "Ratification and the Statutory Derivative Action in the Companies Act 1993" (1998) 16 *Company and Securities Law*

- it is in the interests of the company that the conduct of the proceedings should not be left to the directors or the determination of the shareholders as a whole.[164]

Although these two grounds are necessary conditions, they are not sufficient conditions. Satisfying the National Court on these two grounds is only the first hurdle that an applicant must overcome. Once the court is satisfied, the applicant needs to go further and satisfy the court on all of the following issues.

The shareholder or director will have to show good reason for bringing the proceeding. The court has a discretion whether or not to grant leave and will take into consideration a number of factors when assessing the application. These factors *include* the following:[165]

- the likelihood of success of the proceedings;[166] and
- the costs of the proceedings in relation to the relief likely to be obtained;[167] and
- any action already taken by the company or related company to obtain relief;[168] and
- the interests of the company or related company in having the proceedings commenced, continued, defended or discontinued, as the case may be.[169]

The application of s 143 criteria has been considered in several New Zealand cases. In the first case to be considered, *Vrij v Boyle*,[170] the New Zealand High Court stated that, when considering applications under statutory provisions in New Zealand similar to s 143, the test that should be adopted is whether the "prudent business person" in the conduct of his or her own

Journal 221–225. Note that the New Zealand Companies Act 1993 does not have an equivalent to s 177(4) of the Companies Act 1997. Cf Companies Act 1997, s 143(3)(b).

164 Companies Act 1997, s 143(3)(b). The burden of proving this is on the applicant.

165 Companies Act 1997, s 143(2). This is not an exhaustive list. A factor that the court may take into account is whether another action or remedy is more appropriate: e.g., under s 152 or a liquidation proceeding: *Techflow (NZ) Ltd v Techflow Pty Ltd* (1996) 7 NZCLC 261,138.

166 Companies Act 1997, s 143(2)(a).

167 Companies Act 1997, s 143(2)(b). See *Techflow (NZ) Ltd v Techflow Pty Ltd* (1996) 7 NZCLC 261,138.

168 Companies Act 1997, s 143(2)(c).

169 Companies Act 1997, s 143(2)(d).

170 [1995] 3 NZLR 763. See Fitzsimons, P, "Derivative Actions, Small Companies and Partnerships: The Case of *Vrij v Boyle*" (1995) *Companies and Securities Law Bulletin* 128; Fitzsimons, P, "Statutory Derivative Actions in New Zealand" (1996) 14 *Company and Securities Law Journal* 184–190, Fitzsimons, P, "The Companies Act 1993: a new approach to shareholder litigation in New Zealand" (1998) 18 *The Company Lawyer* 306–12, Watson, S M and Morgan, O, "A Matter of Balance: The Statutory Derivative Action in New Zealand" (1998) 19 *The Company Lawyer* 236.

affairs, would bring such proceedings.[171] Factors would include such matters as the amount at stake, the apparent strength of the claim, the likely costs and the prospect of executing any judgment.[172]

Power of the court where derivative action allowed

Once the National Court decides to grant leave for the bringing of a derivative action, it has extensive powers to supervise and control the proceedings. Section 145 provides that the court "may, at any time, make *any* order it thinks fit in relation to proceedings". Without limiting the type of orders that the court may make, the sections set out some of these powers:

- authorise "the shareholder or any other person"[173] to control the conduct of the proceedings;[174]
- give directions for the conduct of the proceedings;[175]
- make an order requiring the company or the directors to provide information or assistance in relation to the proceedings;[176] and
- make an order that the proceeds of the action be paid, in whole or in part, to both[177] former and present shareholders instead of to the company.[178]

Permission to discontinue or settle proceedings

Section 146 of the Companies Act 1997 provides that a derivative action (including proceedings in respect of which the court grants a director or

171 For a criticism of this test, see Borrowdale, A, "The Statutory Derivative Action" [2000] *New Zealand Law Journal* 409.

172 See also *Techflow (NZ) Ltd v Techflow Pty Ltd* (1996) 7 NZCLC 261,138; *AIDC Ltd v ANZ Banking Group New Zealand Ltd* (1996) 13 BCSLR 194; *Frykberg v Heaven and Ballymore Advertising Ltd* (unreported) 17 July 2002, M7602/02, HC Auckland; *Thorrington v McCann* (1998) 8 NZCLC 261,564; *McKay v PHC Holdings Ltd* (1998) 8 NZCLC 261,603; *Re Russley Hotel & Villas Ltd; Mattison v Gough* (2000) 8 NZCLC 262,399; *Grieve v Coromandel Kauri Company Ltd* (unreported) 21 May 2002, HC Hamilton.

173 The phrase "any other person" would include a director applicant, the company itself or any other person who may have brought the original proceedings in which the applicant sought to intervene.

174 Companies Act 1997, s 145(a).

175 Companies Act 1997, s 145(b).

176 Companies Act 1997, s 145(c).

177 It seems that it is not possible for the court to make an order that *either* the former *or* the present shareholders should be paid *instead of the company*. This seems a strange provision, unless the court will read the word "and" to mean "or", or better still, "and/or"

178 Companies Act 1997, s 145(d). Note that although both shareholders and directors have standing to apply for leave to bring a derivative action, the section *specifically* refers only to shareholders: it is still possible that the court may direct the payment of compensation under this provision to directors as well.

shareholder permission to intervene) cannot be settled, compromised or discontinued without the permission of the court. Once a derivative action has been allowed, several people, including the company, have an interest in it, and it would be unfair if the applicant can decide whether to terminate the action. This section is therefore designed to prevent collusion between the applicant and the defendants which might benefit the applicant but not be in the best interests of other interested parties, including the shareholders and the company. The section would prevent the applicant from being bought-off by the company, or it might prevent directors making a payment to the applicant in order to persuade him or her to discontinue the legal proceedings on behalf of the company.[179]

Power of the court to make orders regarding costs

Section 144 of the Companies Act 1997 gives the court a broad power, on the application of a shareholder or director, to make an order that "the whole or part of the reasonable costs" relating to the action,[180] be met by the company. This is fair where the court accepts that the applicant is bringing the action on behalf of the company, and where, normally, the amount ordered to be paid by a defendant in the proceedings will be paid to the company or the related company.[181] The application for costs can be made at any time after the court has granted leave to bring the action. The reason for this is that the company will be paying for the proceedings to continue.[182] The court can order costs "on the application of the shareholder or director to whom leave *was* granted under Section 143 to bring or intervene in the proceedings". The emphasis on "leave was granted" (i.e., leave having been granted) tends to show that an order about the company's costs cannot be made under s 144 until after the leave to bring the proceedings has been granted by the court. It is suggested that the order for costs can be made *before* the applicant has actually taken steps to bring on the company's behalf the proceedings the court has allowed him or her to institute in its name and for its benefit.[183]

179 Walker, G, Reid, T, Hanrahan, P, Ramsay, I and Stapledon, G, *Commercial Applications of Company Law in New Zealand* (CCH New Zealand Ltd, Auckland, 2002), para 1713.

180 Including the costs relating to the bringing of the action or intervening in existing proceedings, and any costs relating to any settlement, compromise or discontinuance of it that has been approved by the court.

181 Different considerations may apply where the court makes an order directing that any amount ordered to be paid by a defendant in the proceedings shall be paid, in whole or part, to former and present shareholders of the company or related company instead of to the company or the related company. See Companies Act 1997, s 145(d).

182 *MacFarlane v Barlow* (1997) 8 NZCLC 261,470.

183 Cf *Charlton v Baber* [2003] NSWSC 745.

The wording of the section would appear to establish a presumption for the payment of costs by the company. It is only where the court "considers that it would be unjust or inequitable for the company to bear those costs" that the applicant or some party other than the company ought to bear all or part of the costs. The burden of proof as to whether it is unjust or inequitable (not unreasonable) for the company to bear any or all of the costs is on the company.[184]

184 The applicant will therefore not have the onus of adducing evidence as to the company's ability to pay the costs of the proposed derivative action as at the time that leave is sought: Cf *Swansson v RA Pratt Properties Pty Ltd* [2002] NSWSC 583.

Chapter 11

Corporate Liability

Introduction

This chapter is concerned with how companies enter into contracts and assume other legal obligations, and particularly how individuals may make the company liable under a contract, sale, or other legal transaction. It is also concerned with the tortious and criminal liability of companies. In some cases the company will incur direct obligations based on the "organic theory" which identifies individuals who are the "directing mind and will of the company". When these people act, their knowledge and intentions are attributed to the company itself. So, for example, the knowledge of the Managing Director may be attributed to the company so as to make it guilty of an offence involving *mens rea*. In other cases, the company may act indirectly through agents. (In practice, outsiders rarely deal with the board of directors or the members in general meeting: most dealings are with the company's agents or employees.) In all cases the question is whether the organ or person has the company's authority to do the act in question. That authority may be actual or apparent.

In deciding whether to hold that an agent binds the company, the law tries to balance two competing interests.[1] On the one hand it tries to promote business dealings and convenience by reducing the need for the general public to make inquiries regarding the authority of a person every time a transaction is entered into. On the other hand, the law tries to protect innocent shareholders and creditors of companies by requiring some inquiry. If those dealing with companies were always protected, and did not have to make inquiries, this could allow those purporting to act for the company to engage in fraud at the expense of creditors and shareholders. In trying to balance these two competing interests, the law tends to favour protecting those who deal with the company and allow for the efficient operation of business.[2]

1 See Chapter 5, which deals with agency generally. The law concerning agents making a company liable is a specialised aspect of this general law of agency.

2 See in particular, the comments of Sakora AJ in *AGC (Pacific) Ltd v Woo International Pty Ltd* [1992] PNGLR 100 at 103.

The Companies Act 1997, the underlying law, and sometimes the company's constitution provide "rules of attribution" to help in determining the liability of a company, given the fact that it has no brains and no hands to act, but must act directly or indirectly through human agents. The answer is usually determined by the element of control exercised by the person who did the act for or on behalf of the company. However this is not always the case, as the surrounding circumstances may demand that the company be made liable even before then.[3]

As Sakora AJ stated in *AGC (Pacific) Ltd v Woo International Pty Ltd.*[4]

> "That a company is capable of suing and is liable to be sued in its corporate name is not merely an administrative convenience; it follows logically from the concept of separate legal entity and principles of agency. Thus civil liability and criminal responsibility of the company arise from a myriad of situations through the acts and omissions of its servants and agents.
>
> But not every act or omission or default can give rise to legal consequences or responsibilities, nor every servant or agent can commit the company or incur liability. It all depends on the circumstances surrounding the act or omission in question, the nature of the act or omission, the relative position of the agent or servant in the hierarchy of the corporation and what they are and are not empowered to do. Thus, putting it another way, not every servant of the company is a 'responsible officer'; the mind of some employees is not the mind of the company."

Corporate liability for civil wrongs

A company is capable of suing and being sued

Companies can be liable for civil (including tortious) wrongs in the same way as individuals.[5] In some cases the company will be sued directly based

3 For example, in *Meridian Global Funds Management Asia Ltd v Securities Commission* [1995] 2 AC 500 a company was held to have knowledge of a substantial security interest as soon as it had been acquired by its employee acting within his authority. The Privy Council held that the purpose of the securities legislation warranted that disclosure take place quickly, and it would have been inappropriate to hold that knowledge was acquired later when it was disclosed to senior management. Rather than considering whether the person in the company was the "directing mind and will" of the company, the Privy Council considered that the rules of attribution were to be discovered by looking at the legislation to determine who should be responsible. It may be that the legislation would require someone low in the hierarchy of the company to be held liable. See the case of *Bromley and Manton Pty Ltd v Eremas Andrew* [1978] PNGLR 498 where the court took into account the purpose of the legislation in order to decide whether the branch manager's actions should make the company liable.

4 [1992] PNGLR 100 at 107.

5 Civil wrongs (mainly torts) are usually remedied by the award of compensation or damages. Torts include trespass, negligence, nuisance and defamation.

on the organic theory of liability. In others, the company will be vicariously (indirectly) liable, like any other employer, for the torts of its servants[6] or agents[7] even where liability is dependent on proof of *mens rea*, fraud or malice. In tort, the general rule is that the company is liable according to the underlying law doctrine of vicarious liability, for the acts of its employees committed in the course of their employment and within their authority. The victim of the tort can recover damages from the employee personally, as the employee is directly liable, and from the company indirectly, as it is vicariously liable. (In the case of contracts with companies, where the liability of the company is based on agency rules, the agent does not usually become liable on the contract nor can he or she normally gain any benefit from the contract.[8])

The case of *Lennard's Carrying Co Ltd v Asiatic Petroleum Co Ltd*[9] illustrates the organic theory of liability. The company owned a ship which carried oil the property of Asiatic Petroleum. Because of its unseaworthy state, it caught fire and its cargo was destroyed. The question was whether the company could invoke the protection of s 502 of the Merchant Shipping Act (UK) to relieve it from liability. That section provided that the owner of certain ships was not liable for loss or damage "happening without his actual fault or privity" in certain circumstances, including loss of goods through fire on board the ship. The question was whether what happened took place without the "actual fault or privity of the owners of the ship".

Lennard's Carrying Co Ltd sought to avoid liability by claiming that the loss arose not from its default, but from the default of Mr Lennard. The House of Lords rejected this argument, holding that Mr Lennard, who was a director of the company knew or ought to have known about the ship's seaworthiness, as he took an active part in the management of the ship: as such the court considered that he was "the active spirit" in the appellant company who were the owners of the ship. The court therefore held that Mr Lennard's action was "the very action of the company itself", and as such, the company was liable.[10]

6 Most of the cases of vicarious liability in Papua New Guinea deal with the vicarious liability of the Independent State of Papua New Guinea as employer, particularly of policemen conducting illegal raids on villages following tribal fights.
7 *Lloyd v Grace, Smith & Co* [1912] AC 716.
8 The major exception is where the contract purports to be made on behalf of an unformed company, and more generally, where the agent has not disclosed to the third party that he or she is acting on behalf of a principal: see Chapter 5 (Agency Law in Papua New Guinea).
9 [1915] AC 705.
10 The directing mind and will need not be a director: see *The Lady Gwendolen* [1965] P 294 and *HL Bolton (Engineering) Co Ltd v TJ Graham & Sons Ltd* [1957] 1 QB 159.

In giving judgment in *Lennard's Carrying Co Ltd v Asiatic Petroleum Co Ltd* Viscount Haldane LC stated:[11]

> Now, my Lords, did what happened take place without the actual fault or privity of the owners of the ship who were the appellants? My Lords, a corporation is an abstraction. It has no mind of its own any more than it has a body of its own; its active and directing will must consequently be sought in the person of somebody who for some purposes may be called an agent, but who is really the directing mind and will of the corporation, the very ego and centre of the personality of the corporation. That person may be under the direction of the shareholders in general meeting; that person may be the board of directors itself, or it may be, and in some companies it is so, that that person has an authority co-ordinate with the board of directors given to him under the articles of association, and is appointed by the general meeting of the company, and can only be removed by the general meeting of the company.

In *HL Bolton (Engineering) Co Ltd v TJ Graham & Sons Ltd*,[12] the English Court of Appeal compared a corporation to a human body, describing those who control what a company does (and who therefore are the directing mind and will of a company) as the brain of an individual. Denning LJ rejected the argument that only actions arising from a meeting of a company's board of directors can form the intention of a company. He accepted that the intention of a company can be derived from its officers and agents, in some instances depending on the nature of the matter under consideration and the relative position within the company. Lord Justice Denning observed:[13]

> A company may in many ways be likened to a human body. It has a brain and nerve centre which controls what it does. It also has hands which hold the tools and act in accordance with directions from the centre. Some of the people in the company are mere servants and agents who are nothing more than hands to do the work and cannot be said to represent the mind or will. Others are directors and managers who represent the directing mind and will of the company, and control what it does. The state of mind of these managers is the state of mind of the company and is treated by the law as such.

The Managing Director or Chief Executive Officer or other senior manager would usually be held to be the "mind and will" or the company, whereas

11 [1915] AC 705 at 713.
12 [1957] 1 QB 159.
13 [1957] 1 QB 159 at 172.

more junior employees would be merely the "hands" of the company acting at the direction of others. Whether or not the intention and actions of the directors or senior managers, employees or agents is that of the company "depends on the nature of the matter under consideration, the relative position of the officer or agent and other relevant factors and the circumstances of the case".[14]

In *AGC (Pacific) Ltd v Woo International Pty Ltd*, Sakora AJ stated the general liability of a company as follows:[15]

> The point is further illustrated by looking closely at one of the essential attributes or characteristics of a company as a corporate entity or body. And this is its capacity to sue and liability to be sued: s 18(4) of the *Companies Act* (Ch 146). When a wrong is done to the company, the company is the proper plaintiff to maintain, in its own name, an action for redress. Members, as such, have generally no standing to sue on behalf of the company. Similarly, if a company commits a wrong or incurs a liability in the course of its operations, it (and not the members or officials) is the proper defendant. This is sometimes referred to as the 'proper plaintiff' rule or the rule in *Foss v Harbottle* (1843) 2 Hare 461; Ch 12 LJ 319. And the wrong obviously is the wrong (liability) committed by the officers and employees of the company. That a company is capable of suing and is liable to be sued in its corporate name is not merely an administrative convenience; it follows logically from the concept of separate legal entity and principles of agency. Thus civil liability and criminal responsibility of the company arise from a myriad of situations through the acts and omissions of its servants and agents.

Lennard's Carrying Co Ltd v Asiatic Petroleum Co Ltd[16] illustrates the situation where the company is *primarily* liable for the tort, where the organic theory attributes the intention and actions of the agent or employee to that of the company itself. The company can also be liable for torts vicariously. Under this principle, the company is *indirectly* liable for the acts of its employees carried out during the course of their employment.[17] Because the purpose of the doctrine is to allocate to the company the risks which its activities generate, the courts have been unwilling to confine the scope of

14 [1957] 1 QB 159 at 173.
15 [1992] PNGLR 100 at 107.
16 [1915] AC 705.
17 Sometimes referred to as "scope of employment". Examples of vicarious liability include: *Roka Coffee Estate Pty Ltd v Largo Gerebi* [1973] PNGLR 486; *Kolta Development Pty Ltd v PNG Defence Force* (1996) N1470; *Dalin More v The Independent State of Papua New Guinea* [1998] PNGLR 290; and *Peter Aigilo v The Independent State of Papua New Guinea* (2001) N2102 An employee may be acting beyond his or her authority but still be within the scope of employment for the purposes of vicarious liability.

the company's vicarious liability to those actions actually authorised by the company. So a company does not escape vicarious liability because the agent or employee has done an act that he or she has been prohibited from doing, or even because he has deliberately done an act for his own benefit, which has prejudiced the company.[18] This lead to the distinction between doing an unauthorised act (no vicarious liability) to doing an authorised act in an unauthorised manner (vicarious liability).[19] The courts in England have been moving away from this distinction to imposing liability when there was a sufficiently close connection between the wrongful acts of the agents or employees and the activities which those persons were employed to carry out.[20] The fact that the wrongful acts were clearly unauthorised and not for the employer's benefit would not prevent the imposition of liability, if this test was satisfied.[21] This will extend to cases where the employee or agent was engaged in fraudulent conduct.[22] In this case the employee's actions make the company liable without the need to impute any intention to the company. Unlike the organic theory discussed above, where the company is sued for the vicarious liability of its employees, the seniority of the employee is generally irrelevant in making the company liable.[23]

Corporate liability for crimes

Companies may also be liable for committing crimes.[24] Usually, the statute imposing sanctions will specifically state that the company is liable. This may be done by defining a "person" to include a company. However, even in the absence of such specific provision, the company may still be liable. Companies have been expressly made subject to fines and monetary penalties.[25] Section 3(1) of the Interpretation Act (Ch 2) provides that: "In any statutory provision . . . 'person' includes (a) a corporation sole; and (b) a body politic or corporate; and (c) the holder (whether substantive or

18 *Lloyd v Grace, Smith & Co* [1912] AC 716.
19 See *David Wari Kofowei v Augustine Siviri* [1983] PNGLR 449.
20 *Lister v Hesley Hall Ltd* [2001] 2 All ER 769; *Dubai Aluminium Co Ltd v Salaam* [2002] UKHL 48.
21 See Davies, P L, *Gower and Davies' Principles of Modern Company Law* (7th edn, Sweet & Maxwell, London, 2003), p 166.
22 *Armagas Ltd v Mundogas SA (The Ocean Frost)* [1986] AC 717.
23 It should be noted that where an individual employee commits such an act, he or she will also be personally liable.
24 The law of criminal wrongs is generally concerned with punishment rather than compensation.
25 Examples of monetary penalties: ss 45H(2), 45R(2), 46AE(2) and 46BD(2) of the Income Tax Act 1959 (a sum not exceeding double the amount of tax that, in the opinion of the court, was avoided or attempted to be avoided).

other) of an office in his capacity as the holder of that office." So, in the absence of any indication in a statute restricting criminal liability to natural persons, there is a presumption that the provision will apply to a company. The indication may be either express or implied.[26] Sometimes, where a company is potentially liable, the provision converts the term of imprisonment to a higher fine.[27] An instance of an implied indication that a company cannot commit a particular crime is where the only possible punishment is imprisonment or capital punishment, i.e. the death penalty.

Even where the legislation expressly provides that the company is to be liable, a company cannot act except through human agency. In such cases the question will be when is the intention (*mens rea*) and action (*actus reus*) of the individual in question to be considered to be that of the company? The courts have laid it down that in some cases the intention and actions of persons representing the company shall be treated as those of the company itself, i.e. attributed to the company. These rules of attribution, first applied in civil cases,[28] were extended to criminal cases. In *Tesco Supermarkets Ltd v Nattrass*, Lord Reid stated:[29]

> A corporation . . . must act through living persons, though not always one or the same person. The person who acts is not speaking or acting for the company. He is acting as the company and his mind which directs his acts is the mind of the company. There is no question of the company being vicariously liable. He is not acting as a servant, representative, agent or delegate. He is an embodiment of the company. If it is a guilty mind then the guilt is the guilt of the company. It must be a question of law whether, once the facts have been ascertained, a person in doing particular things is to be regarded as the company or merely as the company's servant or agent.

In addition to committing a crime directly, companies may be vicariously liable, i.e., the company is liable for a crime committed by one of its officers,

26 Section 19(1) of the Interpretation Act (Ch 2) provides that: "A reference in a statutory provision to an offence punishable on indictment or summary conviction shall be deemed to apply to a corporation as well as to a natural person."

27 See Income Tax Act 1959, ss 357(11) and 361(7) (a fine of not less than K500 and not exceeding K5,000 or imprisonment for a period not exceeding six months, or where the person is a company, a fine of not less than K1,000 and not exceeding K50,000).

28 See for example, *Lennard's Carrying Co Ltd v Asiatic Petroleum Co Ltd* [1915] AC 705.

29 [1972] AC 153 at 170. In *Meridian Global Funds Management Asia Ltd v Securities Commission* [1995] 2 AC 500, the Privy Council questioned the basis of liability set out in the *Tesco* case, emphasising that in all cases, it is essentially a matter of statutory interpretation which person is to be treated as the controller of the company for the purposes of liability. It may be that a relatively junior employee, in no way the "directing mind and will of the corporation" could found the liability of the company. The courts in England have not been willing to extend the *Meridian* approach to the common law crime of manslaughter by gross negligence: see *Re Attorney-General's Reference (No 2 of 1999)* [2000] QB 796.

employees or agents. This depends on construing the relevant legislation to see if Parliament intended the employer (in this case the company) to be liable for the act or omission of the employee, manager or other agent.[30]

In *Heduru Transport Pty Ltd v Gairo Vegoli*[31] and *Bromley and Manton Pty Ltd v Eremas Andrew*,[32] if these offences were those of strict liability, liability would be primary (or direct) and not vicarious. In such cases unlike absolute liability offences where the statute reveals an intent that guilt shall be predicated upon the automatic breach of the statutory prohibition, in cases of strict liability, liability arises on the establishment of the *actus reus*, subject to the defence of due diligence. In *mens rea* offences, criminal responsibility of corporations arises from the attribution to the corporation of the acts of its employees and agents on the basis of the doctrine of the directing mind (organic theory) or identification.

Where crimes are defined in a statute, the statute will often say that companies are included in any reference to a "person" doing something. In all cases, a company cannot commit a particular crime if imprisonment is the only possible punishment. In some jurisdictions, the only punishment for murder is imprisonment (or even capital punishment), and so a company could not be convicted of murder in those places. However, in many jurisdictions it is now possible for a company to commit manslaughter – hence the expression "corporate manslaughter". Sometimes, a statute will say that, where a company is involved, any term of imprisonment is to be converted to a fine.

As with torts, companies can sometimes commit a crime vicariously. However, the courts are very reluctant to use vicarious liability as a basis for crime. In relation to statutory offences, it is a matter of looking at the statute and determining whether Parliament intended that an employer (whether a company or other entity) could be liable for an act or omission of an employee. The essential question is as at what point in the hierarchy of a company is the fault of a person employed in the organisation to be treated as the fault of *the company itself*? This will differ depending on the circumstances of the case. Identification of particular individuals within a corporate structure as directing minds of that company is a question of mixed fact and law.[33]

It is accepted as a general principle that there are two broad classes of crimes for which a company *cannot* be held liable:

- those which by their very nature cannot be committed by an artificial legal person (e.g., bigamy, perjury, driving a motor vehicle);

30 *Mousell Bros Ltd v London and North Western Railway Co* [1917] 2 KB 836 at 845–846 and *R v Australasian Films Ltd* (1921) 29 CLR 195.

31 (1977) N99.

32 [1978] PNGLR 498.

33 *Tesco Supermarkets Ltd v Nattrass* [1972] AC 153 at 170, per Lord Reid.

- those for which the punishment is such that sentence cannot be passed on a company (e.g., if the sentence is mandatory imprisonment or the death penalty).

The statutory definition of a crime may show that a company cannot commit the crime. In *R v Murray Wright Ltd*,[34] a company carrying on the business of a chemist gave the wrong medication which resulted in death of the customer. The company was charged with homicide and the matter was decided as a matter of statutory interpretation under the Crimes Act 1961 (New Zealand), which defined the offence of homicide as "the killing of a human being by another". The Crimes Act 1961 did not define "another", and the question was whether it meant another human being, or just another person, including a legal person like a company. The New Zealand Court of Appeal held that it meant another human being, and that a company could not therefore be guilty of manslaughter.[35]

Attribution of fault by statute

In some cases the statute itself may specifically provide for the attribution of fault to the company as a result of the intention of actions of its employees. In other cases where this is not specifically done, the court has to determine whether this is so from the context of the provision in the legislation. Section 102 of the Independent Consumer and Competition Commission Act 2002 provides an example of where the statute provides that the state of mind or the conduct or actions of persons associated with the company may be attributed to the company, thus making the company liable:

> (1) Where, in proceedings under this Division in respect of any conduct engaged in by a body corporate, being conduct in relation to which any of the provisions of this Part applies, it is necessary to establish the state of mind of the body corporate, it is sufficient to show that a director, employee or agent of the body corporate, acting within the scope of his actual or apparent authority, had that state of mind.
>
> (2) Any conduct engaged in on behalf of a body corporate –
>
> (a) by a director, employee or agent of the body corporate, acting within the scope of his actual or apparent authority; or
>
> (b) by any other person at the direction or with the consent or agreement (whether express or implied) of a director, employee

34 [1970] NZLR 476.

35 It is possible for legislation to make new offences of corporate murder and manslaughter. In several countries, including England, corporate manslaughter is already an offence.

> or agent of the body corporate, given within the scope of the actual or apparent authority of the director, employee or agent, is deemed, for the purposes of this Part, to have been engaged in also by the body corporate.[36]

If the offence is one of strict or absolute liability, intent or *mens rea* is unnecessary. In *Bromley and Manton Pty Ltd v Eremas Andrew*,[37] the court had to consider the liability of the company to prosecution for acts of its employees. Section 62 of the Prices Regulation Act 1949, made it an offence, *inter alia*, for any person to fail to comply with the provisions of any order made under that Act or with any requirement made under any such order. A Prices Order was made under the Act, fixing maximum retail prices for a number of commodities and requiring that these retail prices be displayed in various ways. The appellant company was charged with and convicted of 29 offences in contravention of s 62 of the Prices Regulation Act 1949, and it appeared that the particular store manager where the offences occurred had been served with warning notices prior to the charges being laid and had been fully instructed in relation to marking prices on goods displayed for sale in order to comply with the Prices Order. The appellant appealed against the convictions on the ground that s 23 of the Criminal Code had been incorrectly applied.

Pritchard J held that the requirement to display prices under the Prices Regulation Act 1949 was an absolute one, and that s 23 of the Criminal Code was not available to the appellant company because:

- the Prices Regulation Act 1949, being a law for the protection of the people, s 109(4) of the Constitution requires that s 23 of the Criminal Code cannot be used to evade prosecution on the basis that the company's "corporate mind" is elsewhere or alternatively because it had instructed its employees to display prices;
- where the company has delegated the responsibility of the conduct of its business to an employee, the "will" of that employee is the "will" of the company; and
- knowing the law to have been broken by its employee through receipt of the warning notices, it permitted that situation to continue, and the offences could not be said to have occurred "independently of the will" of the appellant.

The appellant company was therefore convicted of failing to display the maximum retail prices of specified goods in accordance with an order made under the Prices Regulation Act 1949.

36 See also Securities Act 1997, s 138(1) and (2).
37 [1978] PNGLR 498.

Pritchard J adopted the words of Atkin J in *Mousell Bros Ltd v London and North-Western Railway Co* [1917] 2 KB 836:

> I think that the authorities . . . make it plain that while prima facie a principal is not to be made criminally responsible for the acts of his servants, yet the Legislature may prohibit an act or enforce a duty in such words as to make the prohibition or the duty absolute; in which case the principal is liable if the act is in fact done by his servants. To ascertain whether a particular Act of Parliament has that effect or not regard must be had to the object of the statute, the words used, the nature of the duty laid down, the person upon whom it is imposed, the person by whom it would in ordinary circumstances be performed, and the person upon whom the penalty is imposed.

The courts do not usually make use of vicarious liability to impose liability on companies for criminal offences. However, in *Heduru Transport Pty Ltd v Gairo Vegoli*,[38] Frost CJ convicted the company as it was held to be vicariously liable for a criminal offence committed by one of its employees. The company had been found guilty of dumping a quantity of rubbish on a public road contrary to s 5(1) of the Police Offences (Rubbish Dumping) Act 1969, which provided, *inter alia*, that: "A person shall not dump . . . rubbish . . . within sight of any public road . . . otherwise than within or on an authorised refuse depot." A magistrate convicted the appellant company upon a charge that it dumped a quantity of rubbish on a public road, and the company appealed on the ground that it was only the driver who was employed by the appellant company: the four men standing on the truck shovelling the rubbish out of the truck onto the road were employed by the government to which the truck had been hired. A driver, employed and paid by the appellant company, was supplied with each truck. The trucks were hired for the carriage of stores and no member of the company told the driver to dump rubbish on that day. The company argued that seeing that it was not its servants who had dumped the rubbish when the vehicles were out on loan, that it was not therefore directly or indirectly responsible. The case therefore raised the question of the circumstances in which a company is vicariously liable for an offence committed by an employee.

The principal issue, as the magistrate saw it, was whether the persons responsible for dumping the rubbish on 16 October 1976 were the servants of the appellant company at the relevant time. It was held that the driver of the truck remained an employee of the Company, even though the truck had been hired out to the government; he had the control of the truck. The court held that having regard to the subject matter of the Act, the offence fell within the category of "public welfare offences" or "criminal nuisances", for

38 (1977) N99.

which the test was one of strict or absolute liability, without proof of any criminal intent on the part of the persons involved: this absolute liability was necessary if the law was to be effectively enforced. The court held that the company was for the purposes of the criminal law vicariously responsible for the act of the driver even though he was not instructed to perform the act, and the company had no knowledge of it. The prohibition or the duty was absolute, so that the company was liable, even if it had no knowledge of the acts of its servants.

Frost CJ, relying on *HL Bolton (Engineering) Co Ltd v TJ Graham & Sons Ltd*[39] and *Tesco Supermarkets Ltd v Nattrass*,[40] opined that a company may be directly rather than vicariously liable because of the acts or omissions of a responsible officer who, on the facts, is shown to represent the "directing mind and will of the company, and controls what it does". However, he considered that it was quite clear that the principle expounded in those cases could not apply to the facts of the case before him: because of his lowly position, the truck driver "plainly cannot be regarded as the company", i.e., the "directing mind and will of the company".

However, just as the common law requirement of a guilty mind has been dispensed with in the case of absolute offences, it is possible for the application of s 23 also to be excluded. It could be done by an express provision of the statute creating the offence. The operation of s 23 cannot be excluded merely by the objects of the statute creating the offence. The section should not be held to be excluded in relation to a statutory offence unless a statute uses clear and unequivocal language to that effect.

The issue is whether s 23 of the Code has been excluded by necessary implication having regard to the subject matter and objects of the statute.

To see if absolute liability arises, one had to "ascertain whether a particular Act of Parliament has that effect or not regard must be had to the object of the statute, the words used, the nature of the duty laid down, the person upon whom it is imposed, the person by whom it would in ordinary circumstances be performed, and the person upon whom the penalty is imposed".[41]

Turning to the object of the Police Offences (Rubbish Dumping) Act 1969, as required under the PNG Constitution clearly the statute is not one of "a truly criminal character", but rather directed against dumping as a public nuisance or pollution of town and countryside. The types of case in which these defences could be set up seem to be so unusual that it is consistent with the legislative intention that the prohibition should be absolute, in order that fewer persons responsible for a contravention should be allowed to escape.

39 [1957] 1 QB 159 at 172, per Lord Denning MR.
40 [1972] AC 153 at 170–171, per Lord Reid.
41 *Mousell Bros Ltd v London and North Western Railway Co* [1917] 2 KB 836.

Frost CJ considered that the business of a road carrier in the course of which trucks may be used for dumping is peculiarly one in which there is room for the employer to take measures, by supervision, inspection and exhorting of drivers, which will promote the observance of the obligation not to dump rubbish in a prohibited place.

Frost CJ held that as a matter of statutory construction, and to ensure the attainment of the objects of the statute, he would thus uphold the submission of counsel for the respondent that there is an implied exclusion of s 23 of the Criminal Code. Accordingly, the Act creates an absolute offence, and "it is no defence that the act of dumping was committed by a servant on behalf of the appellant without the knowledge of the company".

As the government merely told the driver what to do, that is to get rid of the rubbish, the appellant retained the authority to control the manner in which he carried out his work, and thus the driver remained for the purposes of vicarious liability the employee of the company, and was at the relevant time acting in the course of his employment. Section 7 of the Criminal Code provided that a person who enables, aids, counsels or procures any other person to commit the offence, is deemed to have taken part in committing the offence. The driver was thus guilty of the offence.

In the end the company was found not guilty because s 23 of the Acts Interpretation (Interim Provisions) Act 1975 could not lead to strict or absolute liability. The company could only be found guilty if it was aware of the actions of its employee; it could not be deemed to have committed the offence.

In *Hedura*, the court also held that criminal responsibility is to be determined, not by the common law doctrine of *mens rea* or the requirement of a "guilty mind" of some kind, but under Part I, Division 5 of the Criminal Code. Frost CJ held that the freedom from criminal responsibility set out in Division 5 can only be destroyed "by express enactment by clear and unequivocal language showing that Parliament intended to destroy that freedom".[42] A corporation is a person as defined in the Interpretation Act (Ch 2) and so, for the purposes of Division 5, like a natural person, is not criminally liable or responsible for an act which occurs independently of its will (Criminal Code (Ch 295), s 23), including an act done by a servant in violation of his or her instructions.

It is the Criminal Code to which recourse must first be had, whenever the issue of criminal responsibility is raised. Further, as the driver did not himself dump the rubbish the provisions of the Interpretation (Interim Provisions) Act 1975, s 23, which deals with the modes of participation in an offence, are also basic to the case.

42 *Sebulon Wat v Peter Kari (No 2)* [1975] PNGLR 339.

Corporate liability for contracts[43]

Company contracts and dispositions

One of the powers which a company has is to enter into contracts. Because the company has no mind or will of its own, it must rely on the board of directors to enter into such contracts, either directly or indirectly through the appointment of agents. Companies enter into a variety of contracts on a daily basis and they can enter into such contracts in two ways: directly, by the company itself through the board of directors entering into the contract, often using its common seal; or indirectly, through an agent. Contracts are not normally entered into directly with a company's board of directors, unless the company is very small or the transaction is very large. Rather, an employee of the company, usually one of the executive officers, such as the managing director, would enter into the contract on behalf of the company as its agent. The question then arises as to the authority of the agent who enters into the contract. Can the outsider assume that the board of directors has authorised that person to bind the company, and that the board has placed no limitations on the authority of that person. In most such situations no problems arise. The company will have the power to enter into the contract through its board of directors and usually the board of directors will have the power to, and often does, delegate the authority to enter into the contract to the particular agent. In some cases, however, problems arise as to the capacity of the company to enter into a contract or whether or not the power to enter into the contract has been validly delegated by the board to the particular agent and the extent of that delegation. The question is whether the actions of the supposed agent can be attributed to the company. This area is vitally connected with the law of agency. There are many cases where an "agent" purports to make a contract with an outsider (third person) who acts in good faith, and it turns out that the agent lacked authority from the principal to make the contract or the agent exceeded the authority given by the principal. As Ford notes, these problems "are difficult enough when the principal is an individual. But the difficulty is compounded when the principal is an inanimate company".[44]

Gower and Davies summarise the principles that are applicable to this area as follows:[45]

43 For a consideration of the law in Australia, see Chapple, L and Lipton, P, *Corporate Authority and Dealings with Officers and Agents* (CCH Australia Ltd and Centre for Corporate Law and Securities Regulation, Melbourne, 2002).

44 Austin, R P, Ramsay I M, *Ford's Principles of Corporations Law* (12th edn, LexisNexis Butterworths, Australia, 2005), para 12.010.

45 Davies, P L, *Gower and Davies' Principles of Modern Company Law* (7th edn, Sweet & Maxwell, London, 2003), p 129.

(i) A principal is bound by the transactions on his behalf by his agents or employees if the latter acted within either:
   (a) the actual scope of the authority conferred upon them by their principal prior to the transaction or by subsequent ratification:[46] or
   (b) the apparent (or ostensible) scope of their authority.[47]

(ii) A principal, *qua* employer, may also be vicariously liable in tort for acts of his employees or agents which, though not authorised, are nevertheless within the scope of their employment but, in general, is not criminally liable for their acts.[48]

The law governing this area was significantly changed by the Companies Act 1997,[49] and it is worthwhile to consider the matter both before and after the changes were made. It is also important to note that although the company may not have assented to the transaction at the time it was entered into, it is possible that the company may have subsequently validated or ratified the transaction.[50]

In deciding whether a contract with a company is valid, it is necessary to discover (i) whether the company had the capacity to enter into the contract, and (ii) whether the individual(s) acting for the company had the authority to do so.

46 Actual authority may be conferred expressly or impliedly. Authority to perform acts which are reasonably incidental to the proper performance of an agent's duties will be implied unless expressly excluded and an agent who, on previous occasions, has been allowed to exceed the actual authority originally conferred upon him may thereby have acquired actual authority to continue so to act. Ratification of a contract entered into by an agent in excess of his authority enables the principal to sue the other party if the agent had disclosed that he was acting for an identifiable principal.

47 This consists of: (i) the authority which a person in his position and in the type of business concerned can reasonably be expected to have, and (ii) the authority which the particular agent has been held out by the principal as having unless, in either case, the other party knows or ought to have known that the agent was not actually authorised. The liability of the principal in both cases rests on estoppel; but in case (ii) the principal cannot be estopped unless the other party knows that the agent is acting as agent whereas in case (i) the other party may believe the agent to be the proprietor of the business and the principal, having allowed him to appear as such, is estopped from denying his power so to act: see *Watteau v Fenwick* [1893] 1 QB 346 It is suggested that the case of *Lae Cordial Factory Pty Ltd v Dang Bros Pty Ltd* (1978) N176 is explicable in the light of *Watteau v Fenwick*.

48 Unless he or she has initiated, or participated in, the crime.

49 A person dealing with the company may prevent the company from relying on one or more of the assertions set out in s 19 of the Companies Act 1997 unless he or she knew or ought to have known that the assertion was incorrect.

50 See *Michael Yai Pupu v Tourism Development Corporation* (2002) N2258 discussed below at pp 468–473 (ratification).

Capacity of the company to contract before the Companies Act 1997

Where a contract was entered into before the commencement of the Companies Act 1997, its validity depended on whether the company had the capacity to enter into such a contract. This depended on whether the transaction was within the powers of the company set out in its constitution. The law was that the powers of the company were limited to those set out in its constitution. If the power was not given, then the company did not have capacity, and any purported contract in the area was null and void (invalid) under the underlying law doctrine of *ultra vires*.[51] It was therefore vital for persons dealing with companies to enquire into whether the company had the capacity (according to the objects clauses in its constitution) to enter into the planned transaction.[52] The consequences of lack of corporate capacity were very serious, as it meant that the outsider could not enforce the contract against the company.[53] However, even before 1997, amendments to the Companies Act (Ch 146) had whittled down the effect of the consequences of *ultra vires*, so that it did not pose a serious threat any longer.[54]

51 *Ultra vires* is a Latin term used especially by lawyers to refer to acts beyond (*ultra*) the legal powers (*vires*) of those who have purported to undertake them. The doctrine applies to a wide variety of situations (see e.g., *Kuya Kehi v Kelu Theodore* [1978] PNGLR 217 – whether Regulations were *ultra vires* the enabling Act), including to corporations that have been granted limited powers: see for example, *Sylvanus Gorio v National Parks Board* [1982] PNGLR 364, where Bredmeyer J held that the defendant did not have power to sell a house to a staff member at a price grossly below its real valuation, because the governing legislation did not grant the Board such powers. For an analysis of the doctrine of *ultra vires* in relation to companies before it was abolished in England, see Gower, L C B, *Gower's Principles of Modern Company Law* (4th edn, Stevens, London, 1979), Ch 8, and supplement to the 4th edn, 1981. The common law of England relating to *ultra vires* as it stood immediately before 16 September 1975 was adopted by Schedule 2 of the Constitution as part of the underlying law. See now The Underlying Law Act 2000, in particular s 3(1)(b).

52 There had been some attempt to reform the vitiating effect of the *ultra vires* doctrine by amendment to the Companies Act (Ch 146) (repealed), s 36 and s 37. However, *ultra vires* was still a problematic area that outsiders dealing with companies had to be aware of. For a discussion of *ultra vires* after the enactment of amendments on *ultra vires* by amendments to the Companies Act (Ch 146) (repealed) but before the Companies Act 1997 was enacted, see the judgment of Sakora AJ in *AGC (Pacific) Ltd v Woo International Pty Ltd* [1992] PNGLR 100 at 104–105 and *Hawkesbury Development Co Ltd v Landmark Finance Pty Ltd* [1969] 2 NSWR 782.

53 The seriousness of the breach as far as third parties were concerned, was lessened by the operation of restitutionary principles: it may have been possible to recover money outside of the contract under the law of restitution or quasi-contract. See for example, *The State v Keboki Business Group Inc and Morobe Provinsel Gavman* [1985] PNGLR 369 and *Fly River Provincial Government v Pioneer Health Services Ltd* (2003) SC705.

54 See Kimuli, M A, Amankwah, H A and Mugambwa, J T, *Introduction to the Law of Business Associations in Papua New Guinea* (2nd edn, Pacific Law Press, Hobart, 1990), pp 24–27 for an analysis of the law relating to corporate capacity before the commencement of the Companies Act 1997.

The Companies Act 1997 merely completed the reform which had been started earlier. Section 37 of the Companies Act (Ch 146) had provided that all companies had the power to make donations for patriotic or for charitable purposes, despite what was provided in the company's constitution,[55] and that except so far as was expressly excluded or modified by the company's memorandum or articles, every company had the powers that were set out in Schedule 2 of the Companies Act (Ch 146).[56] Section 37(1) of the Companies Act (Ch 146) then went on to provide that:

> No act of a company (including the entering into of an agreement by the company), and no conveyance or transfer of property, whether real or personal, to or by a company, is invalid by reason only of the fact that the company was without capacity or power to do the act or to execute or take the conveyance or transfer.[57]

Sakora AJ stated the effect of s 37 of the Companies Act (Ch 146) (repealed) in *AGC (Pacific) Ltd v Woo International Pty Ltd*:[58]

> In more recent times it became increasingly apparent, more particularly in Australia (and, by extension, Papua New Guinea through the operation of somewhat similar legislative schemes), that the combined effect of the two doctrines [of constructive notice and *ultra vires*] was to create quite unrealistic, unwieldly and unpredictable situations. Much time and trouble, not to mention money, would be saved, and better justice would be done, if the rigidity inherent in these two doctrines were removed or relaxed somewhat. The result of this in this jurisdiction has been the modifications or alterations made to the *ultra vires* doctrine in our legislation, whereby the doctrine no longer has the same far-reaching effects upon a company's acts and transactions as it had before. The often very lengthy objects clause is no longer mandatory (except, and understandably so, with corporations involved in mining and charitable activities). But there is no limit to the number of objects for which a company may be incorporated, thereby allowing companies to enlarge their powers and activities: see s 36 *Companies Act* (Ch 146). This in turn renders the nullifying effect of the *ultra vires* doctrine less likely. Section 37 of the *Companies Act* drives home the message by virtually removing the nullifying effect of the doctrine. In considering a New South Wales provision similar to our s 37 in the case of *Hawkesbury*

55 Companies Act (Ch 146), s 36(a).

56 Companies Act (Ch 146), s 36(b). Schedule 2 set out a host of additional objects and powers for the company.

57 Section 37(2) set out certain situations where *ultra vires* could be relied on, including actions by members against the company to prevent it from entering into transactions that were outside of its powers.

58 [1992] PNGLR 100 at 105.

Development Co Ltd v Landmark Finance Pty Ltd [1969] 2 NSWLR 782, Street J said (at pp 795–796) that the provision:

> '. . . strikes down the absolute effect of the *ultra vires* doctrine. An *ultra vires* transaction is no longer a complete nullity, incapable of being recognised as a transaction at all. On the contrary, it is a transaction which, in general terms, is not invalid by reason only of the fact that the company was without the capacity or power to enter into the transaction.'

Although a chartered corporation was presumed to have full capacity, similar to an adult person, at common law, legal capacity of a registered company was limited by the purposes for which it was established. It was vested with only those powers that were necessary to carry out its purposes. The statutory requirement of a memorandum of association setting out the objects of a company was taken to be an exhaustive statement of the extent of the company's capacity.[59] Although several attempts were made by drafters and the courts to circumvent the *ultra vires* rule and allow companies the widest possible powers,[60] and despite later amendments made to the Companies Act (Ch 146), the law was still in an unsatisfactory state before the enactment of the Companies Act 1997.

Capacity of the company to contract after the Companies Act 1997

The devices to circumvent the *ultra vires* doctrine, meant that it no longer served to protect members of creditors of the company, and instead became a nuisance to the company and a trap for unwary third parties. The Companies Act 1997 therefore completely abolished the underlying law doctrine of *ultra vires*.[61] Following the enactment of the Companies Act

59 In *Ashbury Railway Carriage and Iron Co v Riche* (1875) LR 7 HL 653 at 670, Lord Cairns LC opined that the memorandum of association "states affirmatively the ambit and extent of vitality and power which by law are given to the corporation, and it states, if it is necessary so to state, negatively, that nothing shall be done beyond that ambit, and that no attempt shall be made to use the corporate life for any other purpose than that which is so specified".

60 See in particular *Cotman v Brougham* [1918] AC 514 Draftsmen set out a very wide range of objects and powers, stated that each object or power was independent of each other, and thus not limited by the business that the company normally carried on, and at the end of the powers and objects inserted an independent provision stating that the company had the power "to carry on any other trade or business whatsoever which can, in the opinion of the board of directors, be advantageously carried on by the company in connection with or ancillary to any of the above businesses or the general business of the company . . .".

61 In doing so, it adopted the New Zealand provisions, and followed the lead of other Commonwealth jurisdictions, including Australia, Canada and the UK. It should be

1997, it is now possible for companies to enter into any type of contracts, even if those types of contract are restricted by the company's constitution. The important sections are ss 17 to 20. Section 17(1) provides in effect that a company (both within and outside PNG) has "full capacity to carry on or undertake any business activity, do any act, or enter into any transaction". Section 18(1) then goes on to provide that no act of a company and no transfer of property to or by a company is invalid "merely because the company did not have the capacity, the right, or the power to do the act or to transfer or take a transfer of the property". The effect of this provision is that even if the company's constitution provides that it has no power to enter into the contract, the contract will in fact be valid *as far as outsiders* are concerned. Section 18(3) provides that the fact that an act is not, or would not be, in the best interests of the company does not affect the capacity of the company to do the act.[62]

Sections 19 and 20 further provide:

> 19. Dealings between company and other persons.
>
> (1) A company, or a guarantor of an obligation of a company may not assert against a person dealing with the company or with a person who has acquired property, rights, or interests from the company that –
> (a) this Act or the constitution of the company has not been complied with; or
> (b) a person named as a director of the company in the most recent notice received by the Registrar under Section 137 –
> (i) is not a director of a company; or
> (ii) has not been duly appointed; or

noted that, although the Companies Act 1997 empowers registered companies to enter into contracts that are outside its powers, the Act does not apply to statutory corporations. The powers of these corporations are still governed and are often limited by their constituting statute. See *Sylvanus Gorio v National Parks Board* [1982] PNGLR 364; *Andrew Wag v Mount Hagen Town Authority* [1996] PNGLR 385; *Panga Coffee Factory Pty Ltd v Coffee Industry Corporation Ltd* (1999) SC619; *Patterson v NCDC* (2001) N2145; *Bernard Nuri v Kaipel Du* (2003) N2315; *The Independent State of Papua New Guinea v Barclay Brothers (PNG) Ltd* (1992) (unreported and unnumbered Supreme Court judgment delivered on 31 December 2002); *Fly River Provincial Government v Pioneer Health Services Ltd* (2003) SC705; *Papua New Guinea Forest Authority v Concord Pacific Ltd (No 2)* (2003) N2465. In *Patterson v NCDC* (2001) N2145 Kandakasi J stated: " . . . where a contract is entered into contrary to the provisions of a relevant and applying legislation, there is no discretion whether to enforce it or not. It is simply void and unenforceable." Cf Mugambwa, J, "Control of Statutory Corporations in Papua New Guinea" [1987] *LAWASIA Journal* 138 at 147–148.

62 Members of a company which intends to act outside of its powers may apply to the National Court for an injunction to prevent it from doing so: Companies Act 1997, s 142.

(iii) does not have authority to exercise a power which a director of a company carrying on business of the kind carried on by the company customarily has authority to exercise; or

(c) a person held out by the company as a director, employee, or agent of the company –

(i) has not been duly appointed; or

(ii) does not have authority to exercise a power which a director, employee, or agent of a company carrying on business of the kind carried on by the company customarily has authority to exercise; or

(d) a person held out by the company as a director, employee, or agent of the company with authority to exercise a power which a director, employee, or agent of a company carrying on business of the kind carried on by the company does not customarily have authority to exercise, does not have authority to exercise that power; or

(e) a document issued on behalf of a company by a director, employee, or agent of the company with actual or usual authority to issue the document is not valid or not genuine, unless the person has, or ought to have, by virtue of his position with or relationship to the company, knowledge of the matters referred to in any of Paragraphs (a), (b), (c), (d), or (e), as the case may be.

(2) Subsection (1) applies even though a person of the kind referred to in any of Paragraphs (b) to (e) (inclusive) of that subsection acts fraudulently or forges a document that appears to have been signed on behalf of the company, unless the person dealing with the company or with a person who has acquired property, rights, or interests from the company has actual knowledge of the fraud or forgery.

20. No constructive notice.

A person is not affected by, or deemed to have notice or knowledge of the contents of, the constitution of, or any other document relating to, a company merely because the constitution or document is –

(a) registered on the register; or

(b) available for inspection at an office of the company.

Grantham and Rickett have stated that the equivalent New Zealand provisions:[63]

> confer on all companies the widest possible powers and prohibit any challenge to any act of the company, or transfer of property to or from the

63 Grantham, R B and Rickett, C E F, *Company and Securities Law: Commentary and Materials* (Brookers, New Zealand, 2002), p 266. As the authors go on to note: "Such

company, on the ground that the company lacked legal capacity. While, for the purposes of regulating the internal rights of the directors and shareholders, the creators of the company may include limitations on the company's capacity, these limitations are now of no effect against those dealing with the company, even if the latter are aware of the limitations.

Contracting directly with the company

The rules governing the way in which a company may enter into contracts and incur other obligations are now set out in s 155 of the Companies Act 1997.

A company may contract directly with third parties.[64] This is usually done by the board of directors. Section 109 of the Companies Act 1997 provides that: "The business and affairs of a company shall be managed by, or under the direction or supervision of, the board of the company."[65]

The underlying law required a company that wanted to contract *directly* with another person or entity, to do so by affixing its common seal to the document in accordance with any requirements, if any, in its constitution.[66] This method of contracting is still available after the enactment of the Companies Act 1997. A company must still have a common seal to perform the statutory requirements of s 75(1). However, it need not use the common seal for direct contracts, unless the law requires that a seal be used. This is so if the law requires that the contract or other obligation to be by deed if carried out by a natural person. Given that there are no provisions in the law of PNG requiring that any obligations be done by deed, use of the company's seal may be limited to s 75 requirements. Use of the seal in other situations would therefore be optional. Seeing that the Companies Act 1997 does not lay down any requirements as to when a company uses its seal (for example the attesting signature of two directors as witnesses), unless the company's constitution sets out other requirements, a company may enter into a dealing merely by affixing its seal to the document. There is no need for any attestation.

In *Northside Developments Pty Ltd v Registrar-General*, Mason CJ stated the effect of affixing a company seal:[67]

> The affixing of the seal to an instrument makes the instrument that of the company itself; the affixing of the seal is in that sense a corporate

knowledge may, however, lead to the avoidance of the transaction on the ground that the company's directors lacked *authority* to carry out the transaction. This analysis does not amount to an allegation of incapacity." (Emphasis added.)

64 *Richardson v Landecker* (1950) 50 SR (NSW) 250; *MYT Engineering Pty Ltd v Mulcon Pty Ltd* [1999] HCA 24.

65 See Companies Act 1997, s 108 for definition of board of directors.

66 *AR Wright & Son Ltd v Romford Borough Council* [1957] 1 QB 431.

67 (1990) 170 CLR 146 at 160. In *AGC (Pacific) Ltd v Woo International Pty Ltd* [1992] PNGLR 100 at 107, Sakora AJ stated: "In the case of corporate bodies, express statutory

> act, having effect similar to a signature by an individual . . . Thus, it may be said that a contract executed under the common seal evidences the assent of the corporation itself and such a contract is to be distinguished from one made by a director or officer on behalf of the company, that being a contract made by an agent on behalf of the company as [a] principal.

As Asprey JA in *195 Crown Street Pty Ltd v Hoare*[68] stated:

> . . . the execution of a document by a company . . . resembles the execution of a document by a natural person who cannot write except through the medium of someone else who signs the disabled person's name at his request and direction. An authorized signatory of a company's document when acting . . . is the company's amanuensis.

The traditional way in which a company would make a contract with an outside third party was by fixing its common seal to the document in accordance with its constitution.[69] The common seal as such represented the formal "signature" of the company. Certain sections and the Schedules of the repealed Companies Act (Ch 146), referred to a company's common seal in such terms as to make it compulsory for a company to have one.[70] The Companies Act 1997, no longer specifically requires a company to have a common seal. Despite this, however, there is at least one provision which of necessity requires a company to have a common seal. Section 75(1)(a) of the Companies Act 1997 provides that "every company shall, within one month after the issue, or registration of a transfer, of shares in the company, as the case may be, send to every holder of those shares a share certificate signed under the common seal of the company . . .". Given the fact that all companies must have shares, all companies must therefore have a "common seal" so as to comply with this subsection which, it is submitted, is mandatory.[71] It is suggested that it is because of s 75(1) rather than

provisions equate signature by officials of the corporation with the signature of the corporation itself . . . a signature in accordance with provisions of the [Companies Act] was a personal signature of the company."

68 [1969] 1 NSWR 193 at 201–202.

69 A common seal is merely a rubber stamp which sets out the company's name, usually having the words "Common Seal" inscribed on it. The company's constitution would normally require two or more directors or a director and the company secretary to sign their names next to the common seal.

70 See in particular, Companies Act (Ch 146), ss 18(4), 38, 101(2) and (3), 120, 149(5) and 253(2)(d).

71 Section 119 of the Standing Orders of the National Parliament (Ch 1) provides that: "Petitions of corporations aggregate shall be made under their common seal." A company is not required by this section to have a common seal. However, if a company wanted to make a petition to the National Parliament, it would need to adopt a common seal beforehand.

s 155(1)(a), that a company is required to have a common seal.[72] The fact that a company must have a seal does not automatically mean that it must use the seal to execute contracts or other documents.

The position in PNG can be contrasted with the position in New Zealand where it has been said that the Companies Act 1993 (NZ) "makes it clear that the use of a seal is additional to, and not a substitute for, any legal requirements".[73] In PNG the Companies Act 1997 expressly provides for the use of "the common seal of the company".[74]

Section 155(1)(a) provides that where the law requires a deed to be executed by a natural person in order for a contract or other obligation to arise, the company's common seal *must* be used ("entered into on behalf of the company in writing signed under the common seal of the company").[75] Because of the requirement that where the law requires a contract to be executed by deed, then a deed has to be used, most companies will continue to have a common seal. In making this requirement, the Companies Act 1997 makes it almost mandatory for a company to have a common seal and to use it in certain defined transactions.[76] As stated above, although the general law has many references to obligations being imposed by deeds, there are no provisions which expressly require a deed to be used in order for the transaction (including transactions involving land) to be valid.[77] Hence, it is not absolutely necessary for a company to have or to use a seal. In some cases, however, a deed is drawn up rather than an instrument in writing, as the parties to it consider that this lends added authority to it as a legal document.

72 Beck, A and Borrowdale, A, *Papua New Guinea Companies and Securities Law Guide* (CCH Australia Ltd, Sydney, 1999), para 406 suggest that although the Companies Act 1997 "does not specifically require a company to have a seal", s 155(1)(a) lays down the use of a seal as a prerequisite for executing a deed, and that because of this, it "therefore seems that a company must have a common seal".

73 Beck, A and Borrowdale, A, *Guidebook to New Zealand Companies and Securities Law* (7th edn, CCH New Zealand Ltd, Auckland, 2002), para 406.

74 Companies Act 1997, s 155(1)(a).

75 Although s 155(1)(a) provides that the obligation "*may* be entered into . . . in writing signed under the common seal of the company", s 155(2) of the Companies Act 1997 provides that a company may, if its constitution so authorises, have for use in any place outside the country an official seal, which shall be a facsimile of the common seal of the company with the addition on its face of the name of every place where it is to be used, and the person affixing any such official seal shall certify on the instrument to which it is affixed the date on which and the place at which it is affixed.

76 It is not clear what these defined transactions are. In the past, before the Torrens land registration system was introduced, instruments concerning land transactions were required to be under seal in order to create of transfer legal estates or interests. Since the enactment of Torrens registration legislation, this is no longer required. Powers of attorney may be required to be by deed.

77 This is the case even in transactions involving land.

With one exception, the Companies Act 1997 does not set out any formal requirements for the execution of a document bearing the company's seal.[78] If the company's constitution sets this out, it must be followed if the company will need to rely on it.[79] If the company does not have a constitution or if the constitution does not contain such requirements, it is suggested that there need not be any attestation to the fixing of the seal.[80]

The constitution of the company may impose *additional* requirements. It may, for example, require that whenever the common seal is used, that a certain number of directors, or a director and the company secretary, sign it.

In the case of *Tonolei Development Corporation Ltd v Lucas Waka, Minister for Forests*,[81] the National Court had to consider the effect of additional requirements for execution under a common seal imposed by the company's constitution.[82] The issue was whether Tonolei Development Corporation Ltd (Tonolei) accepted an offer of a grant of a timber permit over certain land made by the Minister for Forests on behalf of the Government of Papua New Guinea before the offer was revoked. The

78 Section 156(1) of the Companies Act 1997 provides that: "Subject to its constitution, a company may, by an instrument in writing executed in accordance with Section 155(1)(a), appoint a person as its attorney either generally or in relation to a specified matter." Cf Companies Act (Ch 146) (repealed), s 38. Cf s 127 of the Corporations Act 2001 (Aus), which provides that where a company has a common seal, it may execute a document by having two directors or a director and a secretary witness the fixing of the seal.

79 As we will see later, a third party may rely on a defective document and the company may not assert that the constitution has not been complied with: Companies Act 1997, s 19(1)(a).

80 This may cause evidentiary problems. However, provided that the use of the seal was authorised by the board of directors, the affixing of the common seal is by itself sufficient formality. In *Waghi Security Services Pty Ltd v John Tembon and Western Highlands Provincial Government In Suspension* [1994] PNGLR 138, Woods J refused to accept a written unstamped document as evidence of the contract because it was not properly executed by the company or by the Provincial Government. He stated that: "The same would go for the execution by the Plaintiff Company, there is no common seal affixed and properly certified by the signatures of two proper officers of the Company." (It is not clear from the judgment whether the constitution of Waghi Security Service Pty Ltd required the fixing of a common seal and certification by two proper officers of the company in order for it to be valid, or whether Woods J was laying down a rule of the underlying law that this is the normal requirement, unless the company's constitution states otherwise.)

81 (1983) N404(L). See Srivastava, D K "Case Note: *Tonolei Development Corporation Ltd v Lucas Waka* (1983) Unreported N404L (Contract—Acceptance of an offer by post)" (1982) 10 *Melanesian Law Journal* 175–180; and Roebuck, D, Srivastava, D K, Nonggorr, J, *The Context of Contract in Papua New Guinea* (University of Papua New Guinea Press, Waigani, 1984), pp 141–144 for an analysis of the case concentrating on the issue of the mode of accepting an offer.

82 Counsel for the Minister specifically refrained from accepting an invitation from the judge to discuss whether any of the documentary material could amount to a deed.

underlying law rule relating to contracts, is that an offer may be revoked at any time before it is accepted by the offeree. The issue was therefore whether Tonolei accepted the Minister's offer before it was revoked.

On 26 July 1982, the then Minister for Forests Mr Joseph Aoae made an offer (set out on four pages and described as an "interim permit") to grant a timber permit to Tonolei subject to its acceptance of the conditions outlined in the offer. On 30 July Tonolei's formal acceptance of the offer was typed on p 4 of the interim permit and signed by Mr Mamatau as Chairman of the Board of Directors "on behalf [of]" Tonolei. This formal acceptance together with a covering letter of the same date signed by Mr Kughuka as Deputy Chairman of the company and stating "we now enclose our acceptance of the terms and conditions set out in the Timber Permit" were placed in an envelope and left on the desk in a room in the Department of Forests' headquarters occupied by the secretaries (a steno-secretary and the personal secretary) of the Minister for Forests. This was done on the morning of 2 August 1982. At 1.00 o'clock that afternoon, Mr Somare was elected Prime Minister, thus terminating Mr Aoae's occupation of the Ministry. Subsequently, on 6 August, Mr Lucas Waka was appointed Minister for Forests.

The Secretary of the Department of Forests and a number of other officers within the department did not approve of Mr Aoae's issuance of the "interim permit" to Tonolei and persuaded the new Minister (Mr Waka) to withdraw the offer. On 11 August 1982, the Minister purported to withdraw the offer dated 26 July 1982 by telex and by a written revocation.

Two articles of the company's constitution provided for the method of contracting. Article 114 of the Articles of Association provided that "all other contracts and instruments entered into by the company in the ordinary course of business shall be signed by any 2 directors or by such other person or persons as the directors shall from time to time appoint".[83]

In coming to the conclusion that the revocation or withdrawal of the offer was too late, his Honour Pratt J stated:

> By the ordinary law of contract of course any person duly authorised may make a binding contract . . . There is no direct evidence that any particular person was specifically appointed to sign 'on behalf of' or for the company. There is ample evidence that the Chairman was acting at all times with the approval of at least the majority of the directors and there is no evidence either explicit or implicit that any of the directors disagreed with the terms and conditions set out by the Minister . . . It must be remembered that in some instances the Chairman of Directors

83 Article 98 provided that: "Until otherwise determined after the first meeting of directors, two directors with one of such directors being the Chairman of directors or the Managing Director, shall be a quorum."

has been equated with the vastly more powerful office of Managing Director (see e.g. Gower's *Company Law* 2nd ed, p 147). Although there was no specific resolution nominating the Chairman to sign for the company he was involved in all of the discussions, he attended several times upon the Minister or the Forestry officers in Port Moresby and at the all important meeting to discuss the developments which was held by the directors and shareholders on Block 7 after the return of the directors from the July meeting with the Minister. In addition the letter of acceptance and the acceptance endorsed on page 4 were drawn up by Mr Bolger on the express instructions of the three directors Mino, Kughuka and Mamatau. It seems obvious to me that these three directors at least clearly agreed that one of their members should sign the acceptance. It is even more obvious that when Mr Kughuka wrote his letter of 30 July 1982 he knew of and approved Mr Mamatau's signature on the offer. In his letter, Mr Kughuka says: "we enclose our acceptance". *It seems to me therefore that in placing his signature on the acceptance, Mr Mamatau was certainly authorised to do so for and on behalf of the company*. (Emphasis added.)

Even if I were wrong in holding that there was a compliance with the final part of Article 114 I am still of the view that *the acceptance was signed by two directors*. It is highly desirable that when two signatures are required, they appear together on the one document. That is not to say however that the court may not refer to several documents which must be read together. The wording used by Mr Kughuka [in the covering letter] expresses the clear consensus with the action taken by Mr Mamatau in placing his signature to an acceptance of the terms and conditions set forth by the Minister on 26 July . . . *By reading the acceptance endorsed on the Minister's offer together with the letter signed by the Deputy Chairman together I have no difficulty in finding that the acceptance is in fact signed by two directors*. (Emphasis added.)

Mr Mullumby for the State has placed some emphasis on the words "on behalf of" used in the acceptance endorsed on the offer, and although I have gained some assistance from his authority: *Newborne v Sensolid (Great Britain) Ltd* [1954] 1 QB 45, I cannot agree that the use of this harmless formula makes Mr Kughuka a mere agent for the company. In one sense all directors are agents for the company . . . for a company cannot act without agents. But a director is more than an agent – he contributes to the mind as well as to the locomotion of the company as a corporate body. The term "on behalf of" in the present context really means "for and on behalf of". To construe the term in a manner which would restrict the intention of the other two directors to giving approval to an act by the Chairman of the Board on a basis equal to some junior official acting as a mere agent and nothing else would fly in the face of common sense and business practice.

Tonolei had therefore accepted the offer in terms of the requirements of its constitution. The remaining question was whether this acceptance had been communicated to the Minister for Forests before the offer was withdrawn on 11 August 1982. The court held that, on the morning of 2 August 1982, there was a proper communication of the acceptance to the Minister for Forests: the acceptance taking place when the documents were delivered to the Minister. Pratt J stated:

> According to the 'ordinary usage of mankind' one would be forgiven for thinking that delivery of a written acceptance onto the table, if not even into the actual hands, of the Minister's personal secretary would be adequate delivery to the Minister himself. I would have thought that such delivery was both reasonable and as perfect as the law would require in the far from perfect business world.

The court therefore held that on 2 August 1982, a proper and binding agreement (contract) for the grant of a timber permit came into existence between Tonolei and the Minister for Forests on behalf of the Independent State of Papua New Guinea over the area of land described in, and in accordance with, the terms and conditions laid down in the Minister's letter of 26 July 1982.

Although the constitution may impose *additional* requirements, as we have seen in the *Tonolei* case, it cannot dispense with the need for a seal where the general law requires it, nor allow for an agreement to be made orally, where the general law requires this to be done by an instrument in writing.

While the additional requirements set out in the constitution are binding on the company by virtue of s 32(1) of the Companies Act 1997, the company cannot rely on failure to comply with the requirements as a ground to invalidate the contract, unless the person with whom the company was dealing "has, or ought to have, by virtue of his position with or relationship to the company, knowledge" of the failure of the company to comply with the constitutional requirements.[84]

So, for example, if in the *Tonolei* case the court had held that the signature of the two directors had to be on the same document, and Tonolei was arguing that it was not bound by the contract with the state (Minister for Forests), the court would not allow Tonolei to assert that the constitution of the company has not been complied with unless the Minister for Forests was aware of this failure to comply, or ought to have, by virtue of his position with or relationship to Tonolei, knowledge of the failure.

Where a transaction would have to be in writing when entered into by a natural person, in order to be valid and enforceable, a person acting with

84 Companies Act 1997, s 19(1).

the company's express or implied authority may enter into the transaction on behalf of the company in writing.[85] Where a transaction if entered into by a natural person, is not, by law, required to be in writing, a person acting with the company's express or implied authority may enter into the transaction, either orally or in writing.[86]

Under ideal conditions, a contract entered into directly with the company will need two resolutions of the board: firstly a resolution that the company enter into a particular transaction (substantive authority), and secondly, a resolution authorising the execution of the relevant documents by the company's amanuensis, for example, a director and the company secretary (formal authority). However, most contracts do not live up to this ideal, and these two types of authorisation will have to be "discovered" from all the facts surrounding the transaction.

The company can also enter into an agreement *directly* through an attorney who has been properly appointed to carry out a particular transaction ("in relation to a specified matter"), or transactions generally. For this to happen, the person must be appointed by deed, i.e. by the company using its common seal.[87] In this case, the Companies Act 1997 regards the contract as one being entered into directly with the company, rather than one being entered into by the attorney as the "agent" of the company, and the company is bound provided that the attorney has acted "in accordance with the instrument", i.e., the deed.

Section 19 of the Companies Act 1997 assists an outsider where the company claims that it has not directly contracted with him or her. The section allows the outsider or third party to prevent the company from saying that the Companies Act 1997 or the company's constitution was not followed, or that the person who is shown to have been appointed as a director of the company, was not in fact properly appointed.

85 Companies Act 1997, s 155(1)(b). It is suggested that this writing may be either a deed or any other writing which does not bear the company's common seal. The requirement of writing would be found in other legislation, for example, Part I.1 of the Frauds and Limitations Act 1988, which, as a general rule (to which there are several exceptions) requires that the creation and transfer of estates and interests in land be in writing or evidenced by writing. See also the Hire-purchase Act (Ch 252), Part II, which by reference to the need of a hire-purchase agreement to be "signed", impliedly shows that hire-purchase agreements must be "in writing". There is no reason why this writing may not be a deed, i.e., a writing signed under the common seal of the company. Cf Companies Act 1997, s 155(1)(a). Note in relation to s 155(1)(c) that there is a specific reference to "in writing or orally" and based on the maxim *expressio unius est exclusio alterius*, no deed may be used.

86 Companies Act 1997, s 155(1)(c). It is suggested that this writing may a deed, even though the subparagraph mentions only "by writing or orally".

87 Companies Act 1997, s 156(1). The constitution may either prevent this method of contracting or set out additional requirements that must be complied with.

In *Olympic Stationery Pty Ltd v Niugini Steel Corporation Pty Ltd*,[88] Salika J considered the validity of a contract between the parties for the sale of land. The defendant argued that it was not bound by the lease, as the director and secretary of the company had not been authorised by the board of directors to enter into the contract. The defendant company's articles of association stated that the common seal: "must be used only by the authority of the Directors or of a Committee of Directors authorised by the Directors in that behalf; and must be accompanied by the signature of a Director and shall be countersigned by the Secretary or a Second Director or by some other persons appointed by the Directors for that purpose."

The defendants had denied knowledge and existence of the contract of sale. It submitted that there was no contract binding on it because of the way in which the purported execution took place. It submitted that Mr Kurt Fieldman and Mr Joshua Kuruvilla were not authorised by the board of directors to enter into such a contract and furthermore it submitted that Mr Fieldman was no longer director of it and that Mr Kuruvilla was never the Company Secretary. The defendant pleaded the Statutes of Frauds and of Limitations Act (Ch 330), ss 2(1)(a) and 4. It argued that those provisions deal with situations where the vendor of an interest in land is a company (as in this case) and not a natural person. There are two ways by which a vendor company can "sign" so as to comply with ss 2 and 4 of the Statutes of Frauds and of Limitations Act (Ch 330).[89] The first is by duly fixing the Company seal on a document and the second is pursuant to s 38 of the Companies Act (Ch 146) (repealed).

The Companies Act is silent as to how companies should fix their common seals to documents but it is a matter which is dealt with by the company's articles of association. In this case the defendant company articles of association say that the common seal:

(a) must be used only by the authority of the Directors or of a Committee of Directors authorised by the Director in that behalf; and
(b) must be accompanied by the signature of a Director and shall be counter signed by the Secretary or a Second Director or by some other persons appointed by the Directors for that purpose.

The defendant thus argues that because Mr Fieldman and Mr Kuruvilla were not either directors or secretaries or specially appointed persons they could not execute the document on behalf of it. It submits that the company seal is not duly affixed to the contract of sale.

88 (1995) N1313.
89 See now Frauds and Limitations Act 1988.

In relation to the second means of compliance, s 38 states:

> 38. Form of contracts, etc.
>
> (1) Contracts on behalf of a company may be made as follows: –
>
> (a) a contract that, if made between private persons, would be by law required to be in writing under seal may be made on behalf of the company in writing under the common seal of the company; and
> (b) a contract that, if made between private persons, would be by law required to be in writing signed by the parties to be charged with it may be made on behalf of the company in writing signed by a person acting under its express or implied authority; and
> (c) a contract that, if made between private persons, would by law be valid although made by parol only and not reduced into writing may be made by parol on behalf of the company by a person acting under its express or implied authority, and any contract so made is effectual in law and binds the company and its successors and all other parties to it and may be varied or discharged in the manner in which it is authorized to be made.

The first point the defendant argues is that it says the contract of sale cannot be construed as a document which is purported to be executed by natural persons on behalf of the defendant company. It says that the execution clause was drafted for execution by a Director and Secretary of the defendant company signing as witnesses to the affixing of the common seal and not for execution of the document by individuals on behalf of the defendant. It argues that the only function of the Director and Secretary in such execution is to record by signature, the attestation to the sealing of the instrument but *it is by the sealing of the instrument that the document is executed.* The defendant thus argues that the Contract of Sale cannot be construed to be an example of the defendant company executing an agreement pursuant to s 38 of the Companies Act.

The second point the defendant argues is that s 2 and s 4 of the Frauds and Limitations Act 1988 requires lawful authorisation of agents in writing for the supposition of interest in land to be evidenced by writing of an agent and not the principal. The defendant argues that there was no such written, lawful authorisation of Mr Fieldman and Mr Kuruvilla to enter the contract. The defendant argues that in any event the two officers who purported to execute the contract on behalf of the defendant were acting without the authority of the defendant company.

> The defendant also argue that in appointing a Director or a Secretary, a company is bound by any action taken by the Director or Secretary in accordance with express authority conferred by the shareholders or directors of the company. They also submit that a company is bound by any action taken by a Director or Secretary which is incidental to their position. *This is called implied authority*. A company can also be bound by action taken by a Director or a Secretary where that company holds out that person as having such authority. *That is called 'ostensible authority'*. [Emphasis added.]
>
> The defendant argues that it did not do anything which could be construed as holding out Mr Fieldman or Mr Kuruvilla as having ostensible authority to execute the contract of sale. It argues that the document was not to be executed under authority but by the Company itself under seal.

Salika J concluded:

> In my view the fact that Mr Fieldman and Mr Kuruvilla held themselves out as a Director and a Company Secretary was a matter of internal management of the company and should have been attended to by the Directors. As far as the plaintiff is concerned he is a third party interested in buying land from them. It is not the plaintiffs business to sort out the management deficiency of the defendant company.
>
> The defendant has relied on an extract that it produced to the court showing the affairs of the company as at 28 June 1985. There is no further evidence of the state of affairs of the company between 1985 and 1992. I could not accept that the position of the defendant company was the same between 1985 to 1992. To my mind that extract is of no evidentiary value to the Court.

It is suggested that the assertions that may be made are cumulative.[90] So a third party may not be able to prevent the company from asserting one of the grounds set out in s 19. This will not, however, prevent the third party from relying on another ground. So for example, the company may be able to assert that the company's constitution was not complied with, yet it may not be able to assert that the document was not duly sealed.[91]

Unlike Australian provisions which prevents assertions being made only against the company that they are not correct, in PNG it applies against the

90 This means that a person dealing with the company may make use of more than one of the "assumptions" to make the company liable. There is no express provision in the Companies Act 1997 which states that the provisions are cumulative.

91 Cf *Bank of New Zealand v Fiberi Pty Ltd* (1994) 12 ACLC 48 at 58; *Brick and Pipe Industries Ltd v Occidental Life Nominees Pty Ltd* [1992] 2 VLR 279.

company *and also* to assertions by "a guarantor of an obligation of a company". So neither party may prevent an assertion being made against them. Where the assertion of non-compliance with the Act or the company's constitution or any of the other situations set out in subsection 19(1) of the Companies Act 1997, is made by a third party, the statutory provisions do not apply,[92] and the underlying law rule in *Turquand*'s case applies.

It is not necessary for the third party to make any assumption in order to prevent the company from making an assertion.[93]

Contracting indirectly with the company through agents

In the same way that a natural person may appoint an agent to enter into agreements on his or her behalf,[94] a company may also appoint agents to contract on its behalf. Agents may be given two types of authority: actual authority or apparent authority (sometimes called "ostensible authority" or authority by estoppel). Actual authority may exist either where there is express actual authority or implied actual authority.

Agency may arise by express or implied agreement, or without agreement under the doctrines of apparent (ostensible) and usual authority. Agency may also arise *ex post facto* by ratification.

The authority may be implied from conduct or from the relationship between the company and the person acting on the company's behalf. Incidental implied authority from appointment to a position within the company.

Actual authority

Actual authority can be either "express" actual authority, or "implied" actual authority.[95] Where the company (the principal) says verbally or in writing that an agent can act for the company the agent has express actual authority. Usually, this will be done by the board of directors passing a resolution in appropriate form either at a meeting of directors, or in the form of a circulating resolution signed by all of them and complying with s 138 of the Companies Act 1997 and Schedule 4.7(1).[96] However, the law also recognises that actual authority can arise from statements made by the principal (company) or from the principal's conduct. This type of authority

92 Cf *Australian Capital Television Pty Ltd v Minister for Transport and Communications* (1989) 86 ALR 119.

93 *Lyford v Media Portfolio Ltd* (1989) 7 ACLC 271 at 281.

94 See Chapter 5 (Agency).

95 Legislation may also require that in respect of certain transactions, the appointment of the agent be in writing: see for example, Frauds and Limitations Act 1988, s 2(1)(a)(i)(b).

96 Cf *Ricky Mitio v William Gardner* (2005) N2792.

arising from circumstances or from conduct is referred to as implied actual authority.[97] It is possible for there to be an overlap between implied actual authority and apparent (ostensible) authority. The same set of circumstances can give rise to both types of authority.

Express actual authority

Lord Justice Diplock, in *Freeman and Lockyer v Buckhurst Park Properties (Mangal) Ltd*, described express actual authority as follows:[98]

> An 'actual' authority is a legal relationship between principal and agent created by a consensual agreement to which they alone are parties. Its scope is to be ascertained by applying ordinary principles of construction of contracts, including any proper implications from the express words used, the usages of the trade, or the course of business between the parties. To this agreement the contractor is a stranger; he may be totally ignorant of the existence of any authority on the part of the agent. Nevertheless, if the agent does enter into a contract pursuant to the 'actual' authority, it does create contractual rights and liabilities between the principal and the contractor . . .

Express actual authority arises in two ways: from provisions of the Companies Act 1997 or the company's constitution, or by the board of directors delegating its power. Section 109(1) states that the business and affairs of a company shall be managed by, or under the direction or supervision of, the board of directors of the company, and the board is given "all the powers necessary for managing, and for directing and supervising the management of, the business and affairs of the company".[99] When the board exercises these powers, it is doing so as an organ of the company, or as the company itself, rather than as an agent of the company.[100]

Implied actual authority

A board of directors is permitted by the Companies Act 1997 to delegate most of its functions.[101] The board may appoint a chief executive officer (CEO) and delegate powers to that person either in his or her contract or

97 In this case, no contractual relationship between the agent and the outsider arises. The agent is merely the amanuensis of conduit for the agreement.

98 [1964] 2 QB 480 at 502.

99 Companies Act 1997, s 109(2).

100 *Automatic Self-Cleansing Filter Syndicate Co Ltd v Cunninghame* [1906] 2 Ch 34; *Meridian Global Funds Management Asia Ltd v Securities Commission* [1995] 2 AC 500.

101 Companies Act 1997, s 111 Powers that may not be delegated are listed in Schedule 3.

otherwise.[102] This express actual authority may for example, include the power to enter into contracts not exceeding K100,000.

Fridman states that usual or customary authority (he does not differentiate between the two) is "the authority which an agent in the trade, business, profession, or place in which the particular agent is being employed would usually, normally, or customarily possess, unless something was expressly said by the principal to contradict it".[103]

Implied actual authority is inferred from the conduct of the parties, particularly the principal, and the circumstances of the particular case.

Implied actual authority may arise from things that the principal says and does. Thus, appointing someone to a certain position, or acquiescing in the person doing certain things, may confer on that person implied actual authority to do those things.[104]

Where the company appoints a person as the CEO or managing director, that person will usually be given express powers by the company (the board).[105] However, even where there have not been such delegations, the courts have held that appointing a person to such a position involves the grant of implied actual authority "to do all such things as fall within the usual scope of that office".[106] The usual scope of authority of a CEO's powers will depend on what is the customary or usual authority for a CEO of a similar company (in both size and type of business). The courts have said that a CEO's usual functions include dealing with everyday matters, supervising the daily running of the company, supervising other senior managers and generally being in charge of the company's business.[107] The engagement of employees will usually be within the usual authority of a CEO. On the other hand, the CEO's usual functions do not include entering into a transaction that cannot be called an ordinary trading transaction, or selling the company's business.[108]

102 Cf *Ricky Mitio v William Gardner* (2005) N2792 as an example of a case where at least some of the powers to be delegated to the CEO were spelt out in the company's constitution (Clause 16.1(b)). It is also possible that the employment contract may specify the powers of the CEO or they could be contained in an ordinary document.

103 Fridman, G H L, *The Law of Agency* (7th edn, London: Butterworths, 1996), pp 63–64. It should be noted that the Companies Act 1997, s 19 refers to both *customary* authority ("customarily has authority") and *usual* authority, and does not appear to make a distinction between them. Usual authority is used in contradistinction to *actual* authority.

104 See *Lae Cordial Factory Pty Ltd v Dang Bros Pty Ltd* (1978) N176, discussed p 413, below.

105 See *Ricky Mitio v William Gardner* (2005) N2792.

106 *Hely-Hutchinson v Brayhead Ltd* [1968] 1 QB 549 It may be possible to construe the case of *AGC (Pacific) Ltd v Woo International Pty Ltd* [1992] PNGLR 100 under this heading. See below.

107 *Entwells Pty Ltd v National and General Insurance Co Ltd* (1991) 5 ACSR 424 at 427.

108 *Corpers (No 664) Pty Ltd v NZI Securities Australia Ltd* (1989) ASC ¶55-714.

The implied actual authority of other senior executive officers will depend on what type of functions are usually delegated to them. For example, a senior human resources manager in a large company may have implied actual authority to employ and terminate the appointments of certain types of employees.

Directors, however, usually act as a whole, as the board. When a director acts on his or her own authority, he or she cannot *usually* bind the company.[109] The chairperson of the board of directors is in a similar position: he or she will not usually have power to bind the company.[110]

Apart from appointing someone to a position in the company which carries with it certain powers, other types of conduct by the company (board of directors) can lead to an implied delegation of actual power to that person. For example, it might be that the company has allowed a certain person, whether a board member or not, to act as if he were the CEO, and enter into contracts that such a CEO would normally have the power to enter into. In such a case, the court may hold that that person has the powers of a CEO. This was the position in *Hely-Hutchinson v Brayhead Ltd.*[111] In that case, the chairman of the board of directors of Brayhead was held to have implied actual authority to enter into transactions in the company's ordinary course of business as a result of a previous course of dealing in which he entered into a number of contracts on behalf of the company without the knowledge or permission of the board, and merely reported back to the board at the next convenient meeting after executing the contract. He acted as a *de facto* managing director.

The case of *Lae Cordial Factory Pty Ltd v Dang Bros Pty Ltd*[112] illustrates the situation of a person being given implied actual authority to bind the company from the conduct of the company (through its managing director Mr Davis, who had authority to give such permission).[113] In that case,

109 *Northside Developments Pty Ltd v Registrar-General* (1990) 170 CLR 146 at 204; *Hely-Hutchinson v Brayhead Ltd* [1968] 1 QB 549 at 583–584; *Brick and Pipe Industries Ltd v Occidental Life Nominees Pty Ltd* [1992] 2 VR 279 Note, however, *Olympic Stationery Pty Ltd v Niugini Steel Corporation Pty Ltd* (1995) N1313.

110 *Hely-Hutchinson v Brayhead Ltd* [1968] 1 QB 549. See Nock, RS, (1967) 30 *Modern Law Review* 705.

111 [1968] 1 QB 549 *Brick and Pipe Industries Ltd v Occidental Life Nominees Pty Ltd* [1992] 2 VR 279.

112 (1978) N176 Roebuck, D, Srivastava, D K, Nonggorr, J, *The Context of Contract in Papua New Guinea* (University of Papua New Guinea Press, Waigani, 1984), p 149 treats this case as one of "ostensible authority" claiming that: "The facts showed that the defendant [Lae Cordial Factory Pty Ltd or Mr Davis] held out the tenant [Mr Blackwell] as its agent." See *Gartner v Beaton* [1993] 2 Lloyd's Reports 369; *Lease Management Services Ltd v Purnell Secretarial Services Ltd* [1994] CCLR 127. See also Tettenborn, A, "Agents, Business Owners and Estoppel" [1998] *Cambridge Law Journal* 274.

113 The circumstances which give rise to inferring an implied actual grant of authority may also provide the basis for holding that the agent was given apparent or ostensible authority.

Lae Cordial (the appellant) under the direction of its part owner and managing director Mr Davis used to manufacture soft drinks from premises in Lae. Mr Davis then leased the business (the premises as well as the soft drink manufacturing equipment) to Mr Blackwell, and went to Port Moresby, leaving the company "in existence, at the place where it had always been and in the possession and under the *de facto* control in its day to day operation of Blackwell". Blackwell continued to operate the business in a similar fashion to the way in which the company operated under Mr Davis. The respondent (Dang) sued the appellant for breach of contract, for non-payment for the goods sold and delivered. The appellant denied having ordered or received the goods. The main argument advanced by the appellant was that the magistrate in the court below was wrong in law in finding that the appellant held Mr Blackwell out to be its agent and that even if it were estopped from denying this the respondent was put on inquiry by Blackwell's actions that something was amiss and did nothing about it; i.e., they were put on due inquiry and failed to investigate the matter.[114]

The court held that Lae Cordial. "being a legal person in its own right continued to have its legal existence at the factory premises right throughout the period over which [the] events took place". It further held that "in fact *actual authority was to be implied* from the conduct of Davis in letting Blackwell take possession of the company premises and equipment in the way he did". (Emphasis added.) Moreover, the court stated:

> Whichever way one looks at it [Mr Davis] left this company in existence, at the place where it had always been and in the possession and under the *de facto* control in its day to day operation of Blackwell. Whatever Mr Davis may have intended the legal consequences of his action to have been, and whatever else was contained in the mysterious agreement which was never produced, except for the customers Davis did tell that Blackwell had taken over (assuming he did), to the world at large the company continued to exist and carry on business at the place it always had, and in fact it was under the control of Blackwell, who Mr Davis himself had let into possession knowing full well he was going to continue on in precisely the same business the company had always been engaged in. *I can imagine no clearer case of holding out by Davis that Blackwell had the control of the company, despite his subsequent protestations that this was not so.* (Emphasis added.)

See Diplock LJ in *Freeman and Lockyer (a Firm) v Buckhurst Park Properties (Mangal) Ltd* [1964] 2 QB 480. It is suggested that this case straddles these two areas of authority.

114 The case also raised the issue of whether Dang was estopped from relying on the company holding out Blackwell to be its agent, as it had been put on inquiry by circumstances surrounding the payment that "something was wrong" and ought to have made further inquires. The judge rejected this argument.

For acquiescence, the principal must "know of and acquiesce" in the agent's professing to act on its behalf to become bound by the profession.

The case seems to come close to *Watteau v Fenwick*,[115] a case of "implied" or "usual" authority, which, although having some defenders,[116] has been heavily criticised by academics,[117] and not followed in some jurisdictions.[118] The principal was undisclosed and the agent did something which a person in his position would normally do, i.e., order sugar for the manufacture of "soft drinks".

It may be similarly argued that Dang is a similar type of case. In neither case was the principal disclosed and there was no holding out by the principal. Accordingly, it is submitted that it should not be classified as a case concerning apparent or ostensible authority. Nor should it be thought of as one of implied authority. The agent was endowed with all the normal powers of a principal, i.e. to do everything which was usual in the trade, business or profession that was in question.

Pritchard J concluded that:

> By utter neglect of his responsibilities as Managing Director of the appellant company Mr Davis was the author of its misfortune. He had those responsibilities and responsibilities on behalf of the company to the public who dealt with it. The public is entitled to be protected against people who meddle with corporations in this fashion.

In other cases where the agent makes a representation that he has the necessary authority from his or her principal. However, as the High Court of Australia pointed out in *Crabtree-Vickers Pty Ltd v Australian Direct Mail Advertising & Addressing Co Pty Ltd* there must be some antecedent act on the part of the principal for this conclusion to be made. There must have been a previous course of dealing or the company must have placed the agent in a position or allowed him to remain in such a position from which it can be inferred that his actual representation of authority in himself is in fact correct. The High Court of Australia stated that:[119]

> There are circumstances where the actual representation of authority may be made by the agent but in such cases it will be found that the

115 [1893] 1 QB 346. This case is discussed in Chapter 5 which deals with agency.

116 See for example, Stoljar, S J, *The Law of Agency: Its History and Present Principles* (Sweet & Maxwell, London, 1961), pp 55–59; Powell, R, *The Law of Agency* (2nd edn, Pitman, London, 1961), pp 75–78. It has been argued that *Watteau v Fenwick* is "an excellent example of a pure estoppel by conduct". See also the similar case of *Kinahan & Co Ltd v Parry* [1910] 2 KB 389 (reversed on appeal on the ground that no agency existed, [1911] 1 KB 459).

117 [1893] 1 QB 346.

118 Fridman (p 72) states that it is of "very dubious authority".

119 (1975) 133 CLR 72 at 78.

> relevant representation is made by the principal (or by the person to whom the principal has given actual authority) either by a previous course of dealing or by putting the agent in a position or by allowing him to act in a position from which it can be inferred that his actual representation of authority in himself is in fact correct. It is therefore always necessary to look at the conduct of the principal (or the person to whom he has actually delegated authority).

Implied actual authority of officers of company

Managing Director and CEO

A managing director, or chief executive officer, being in charge of supervising the daily running of the company, supervising the other managers and generally being in charge of the business, has a significant amount of implied actual authority arising from that position.[120] Although the powers of the managing director will be set out in his or her employment contract, the underlying law will spell out such powers if the contract is silent on a matter. The law is that "when a board of directors appoint one of their number to be managing director . . . [t]hey thereby impliedly authorise him to do all such things as fall within the usual scope of that office".[121] A managing director has power to engage others to provide services for the company,[122] and may authorise others to make contracts on behalf of the company of the kind that the managing director could make.[123] He or she may pledge the company's credit and give security over the company's property in the course of normal trading activities However, borrowing or granting security for a borrowing in respect of a transaction outside the company's normal day-to-day business would not be part of the implied authority of a managing director.[124] The courts in Australia have been chary about recognising any implied authority in a managing director where this involves acts or instructions against the backdrop of insolvency, reasoning that in such cases, the company board of directors is the organ that should deal with such matters.[125]

120 *Entwells Pty Ltd v National and General Insurance Co Ltd* (1991) 5 ACSR 424.

121 *Hely-Hutchinson v Brayhead Ltd* [1968] 1 QB 549 at 583, per Lord Denning MR.

122 *Freeman and Lockyer (a Firm) v Buckhurst Park Properties (Mangal) Ltd* [1964] 2 QB 480.

123 *Crabtree-Vickers Pty Ltd v Australian Direct Mail Advertising and Addressing Co Pty Ltd* (1975) 133 CLR 72.

124 *Biggerstaff v Rowan's Wharf Ltd* [1896] 2 Ch 93; *Re Tummon Investments Pty Ltd (in liq)* (1993) 11 ACSR 637; *Capper's Pty Ltd v L & M Newman Pty Ltd* [1960] NSWR 143.

125 Dal Pont, G E, *Law of Agency* (Chatswood, NSW: Butterworths, 2001), para 8.32. See *Nece Pty Ltd v Ritek Incorporation* (1997) 24 ACSR 38.

Other executive directors

Other executive directors will usually have a significant degree of actual or apparent authority. However, if the descriptions of their posts suggest particular areas of responsibility (e.g. "Finance Director", "Sales Director" etc.), they cannot be assumed to have authority outside of those areas.

Individual director

Where a company has several directors, the law does not permit a single director or even a group of them to have usual authority to bind the company.[126] To bind the company, the directors must decide the matter in a directors' meeting or by circular resolution or expressly delegate powers to the individual director. It may be that, in recent times, it has become usual for such directors to be given authority to sign company cheques or attest the fixing of the company's common seal. However, it is not clear whether this is yet considered to be usual authority. In *Sangara (Holdings) Ltd v Hamac Holdings Ltd (In Liquidation)*,[127] the pre-Independence Full Court held that the sale of a substantial portion of a company's assets by a single director would be one of the class of unusual contracts, and so outside the director's ostensible (i.e., implied actual) authority. Where, however, a company has a single shareholder/director, that director will have all the powers of a board of directors, including the power to sell all the company's assets.

Chairman of the board of directors

Where there are several directors, one of them is usually appointed a chairman of the board. The person may be the managing director or a non-executive director. The function of the chairman is to preside over board meetings and general meetings and to ensure that company meetings are properly conducted. The chairman's usual functions do not include making or terminating contracts on behalf of the company,[128] and it has been stated that the chairman has no more authority to bind the company than has any other director acting alone.[129] It is not uncommon for the board of directors to allow one of their number to assume the position of managing director, even though he has never been appointed to that position, and in these circumstances the court has treated him as if he were the managing director.[130]

126 *Northside Developments Pty Ltd v Registrar-General* (1990) 170 CLR 146 at 205; *Brick and Pipe Industries Ltd v Occidental Life Nominees Pty Ltd* [1992] 2 VR 279 at 361.
127 [1973] PNGLR 504 at 5, per Frost J.
128 *Hughes v NM Superannuation Board Pty Ltd* (1993) 29 NSWLR 653.
129 *Hely-Hutchinson v Brayhead Ltd* [1968] 1 QB 549.
130 *Biggerstaff v Rowan's Wharf Ltd* [1896] 2 Ch 93; *Clay Hill Brick Co v Rawlings* [1938] 4 All ER 100; *Freeman and Lockyer (a Firm) v Buckhurst Park Properties (Mangal) Ltd* [1964] 2 QB 480.

Some decisions have even suggested that a non-executive chairman of the board has, as such, individual authority equating with that of a managing director.[131] But it is suggested that this assumption goes too far.

Managers

In the past, when a third party dealt with an officer or employee of the company below the position of managing director, the courts have been reluctant to recognise an implied actual or apparent authority, even in the case of a manager.[132] The courts overseas are now showing a more lenient view, and PNG decisions have recognised that branch managers do have some authority to bind the company in everyday transactions, including leasing land and approving loan applications.[133]

Company secretary

Unlike the New Zealand Companies Act 1993 (NZ), the Companies Act 1997 makes explicit provision for the appointment and the rights, powers and duties of a company secretary. Section 169(4) of the Companies Act 1997 provides that: "A secretary of a company shall have only such rights, powers, and duties in relation to the company as are given to him by this Act or by the constitution or board of the company." In the absence of explicit conferral of power by the company's constitution or the board of directors, the question arises as to the implied actual authority of such an officer. Normally, the secretary will be responsible for the record-keeping within the company, and the preparation and keeping of minutes of

131 *BTH v Federated European Bank* [1932] 2 KB 176; *Clay Hill Brick Co v Rawlings* [1938] 4 All ER 100. In *Tonolei Development Corporation Ltd v Lucas Waka, Minister for Forests* (1983) N404(L), Pratt J implied that the Chairman has a great deal of authority: "It must be remembered that in some instances the Chairman of Directors has been equated with the vastly more powerful office of Managing Director . . . But a director is more than an agent–he contributes to the mind as well as to the locomotion of the company as a corporate body." In *AGC (Pacific) Ltd v Woo International Pty Ltd* [1992] PNGLR 100 at 108, Sakora AJ stated: "Directors and other officers have obviously a greater ostensible [*quaere*, implied actual] authority than the more humble lowly employees." (It is suggested that, although the learned judge referred to the authority as "ostensible", it was "implied actual authority" that was being considered.)

132 *Houghton (JC) & Co v Nothard, Lowe and Wills Ltd* [1927] 1 KB 246 (affirmed on other grounds in *Houghton (JC) & Co v Nothard, Lowe & Wills Ltd* [1928] AC 1); *Kreditbank Cassel GmbH v Schenkers* [1927] 1 KB 826; *South London Greyhound Racecourses Ltd v Wake* [1931] 1 Ch 496. See also the observations of Willmer LJ in *Freeman and Lockyer (a Firm) v Buckhurst Park Properties (Mangal) Ltd* [1964] 2 QB 480 at 494.

133 See *Jay Mingo Pty Ltd v Steamships Trading Pty Ltd* [1995] PNGLR 129 and *Steven Naki v AGC (Pacific) Ltd* (2005) N2782, discussed below, p 431.

meetings.[134] Although older cases treat the company secretary as little more than a clerk, more recent authorities have given such officers more important roles. In *Panorama Developments (Guildford) Ltd v Fidelis Furnishing Fabrics Ltd*,[135] the company secretary fraudulently hired cars as secretary of Fidelis from Panorama who conducted the business of hiring prestige cars. Fidelis refused to pay for the cars arguing that the company secretary did not have power to enter into such contracts. The English Court of Appeal rejected this argument holding that the powers of a company secretary had increased to such an extent that he or she had the usual authority to sign contracts connected with the administrative side of a company's affairs. However, despite this recognition of the increased powers of a company secretary, he or she does not have implied actual authority to manage the company, including the power to borrow money on behalf of the company[136] and to institute legal proceedings in the name of the company.[137] Nor does the company secretary have power to settle such proceedings instituted by or against the company.

In *Paul Torato v Sir Tei Abal*,[138] the issue that the learned judge had to deal with was whether a company secretary could give instructions on behalf of a company to a lawyer representing the company in court proceedings brought against it, instructing him to settle the proceedings on behalf of the company. The company secretary had not been given any express authority to instruct counsel to consent to the order on behalf of the company. Bredmeyer J in discussing the power of a company secretary to bind a company stated:[139]

> The power of the company secretary to bind the company in dealings with outsiders is a matter of agency, the secretary being one of the agents capable of binding the company in certain circumstances. In this regard the secretary may be authorised by the directors to enter into certain types of contracts e.g. of a certain type or up to a certain amount. Over and above his actual authority the company secretary has an ostensible authority to do certain things on behalf of the company, e.g. to sign contracts connected with the administrative side of the company's affairs such as employing staff, and hiring cars: see *Panorama Developments (Guildford) Ltd v Fidelis Furnishing Fabrics Ltd* [1971] 2 QB 711 (CA). The courts have ruled that a company secretary has no

134 For a more detailed treatment of the powers and duties of company secretaries, see Chapter 9 (Directors' Duties).
135 [1971] 2 QB 711.
136 *Re Tummon Investments Pty Ltd (in liq)* (1993) 11 ACSR 637 (where the company secretary was also a director).
137 *Club Flotilla (Pacific Palms) Ltd v Isherwood* (1987) 12 ACLR 387.
138 [1987] PNGLR 403.
139 [1987] PNGLR 403 at 415.

> authority, for example, to call a meeting of the company without a resolution of the directors, or to issue a writ in the company's name. But in respect of such a matter, any act done by a secretary beyond his authority may be ratified by the directors: see vol 1 *Australian Corporate Affairs Reporter* (CCH) par 6–910.

Bredmeyer J held that the matters contained in the consent order to settle the court proceedings were "of great importance to the company involving a large payment not of its profits but of its capital, the appointment of three new directors, changing the articles of association and the signatories to the bank account". The company secretary had not been given express instructions by the company (and the judge seems to have required a formal "resolution of the board of directors" rather than just the agreement otherwise of all the directors). So had there been no other action by the company, it is more than probable that the court would have set aside the consent order. However, he considered that the directors at two extraordinary general meetings of the company held at a later date had "acquiesced in, and ratified, the order and hence the secretary's actions". As such, the company was bound by the consent order to settle the court proceedings.

Other employees

Almost every employee of a trading company has apparent authority to bind the company in some transactions, though this may be very limited. Men and women behind the counter in a departmental store have apparent authority to sell the goods on display for cash and at the marked prices. However, whether employees have more authority will usually depend on apparent than actual authority; so that there must have been a holding out by the company or someone more senior who has been delegated this authority, as having authority to carry out the particular transaction.

Authority implied from acquiescence

It is possible for a board of directors to allow an individual to carry out several transactions of the same kind so that a reasonable person would come to the conclusion that the person has the consent of the board to generally enter into similar agreements in the future. In such cases, the agent would be said to have implied actual authority by acquiescence.[140] Not only would acquiescence have to be shown, but the consent of the board of directors among each other and to the agent would have to be shown from actual words or conduct.

140 *Brick and Pipe Industries Ltd v Occidental Life Nominees Pty Ltd* [1992] 2 VR 279.

Usual or customary authority

Usual authority (sometimes referred to as customary authority),[141] is the authority that an agent has because he or she has been appointed to act for the principal in a particular trade, business, profession, office or place, and the authority that goes with acting in such a setting or place.[142] It is suggested that this type of authority is merely a type of apparent or ostensible authority and is not a separate type of authority.[143] *Bowstead and Reynolds on Agency* points out that the burden of proving the existence of a custom or usage is a heavy one, and the plaintiff must show that the alleged custom is: (i) reasonable; (ii) universally accepted by the particular trade or profession or at a particular place; (iii) certain; (iv) not unlawful; and (v) not inconsistent with the express or implied terms of the contract.[144]

Apparent or ostensible authority

An agent may have apparent or ostensible authority to enter into agreements on behalf of the company. For this to happen, there must be a holding out or representation by someone with actual (express or implied) authority on which the other person (outsider) relied to the extent of altering their position, usually by entering into the contract.

The company, or a person with actual authority from the company to do so, must make a representation to the outsider third party that the agent has authority to enter into the type of contract in question. The representation may be either by words or by conduct. Acquiescence by the board in a person acting as the CEO may constitute a holding out. The representation must be made by someone with actual authority: either the board, or for example a CEO who has actual authority.[145] It does not have to be express

141 The Companies Act 1997, s 19 refers to the authority that an officer or agent of a company "customarily has authority to exercise" and "does not customarily have authority to exercise".

142 Fridman, G H L, *The Law of Agency* (7th edn, London: Butterworths, 1996), pp 63–64 and 69–76; Reynolds, F M B, *Bowstead and Reynolds on Agency* (17th edn, Sweet & Maxwell, London, 2001), para 3-006 and 3-030 ff.

143 See Reynolds, F M B, *Bowstead and Reynolds on Agency* (17th edn, Sweet & Maxwell, London, 2001), para 3-006. *Watteau v Fenwick* [1893] 1 QB 346 is the main case in this area of the law.

144 Reynolds, F M B, *Bowstead and Reynolds on Agency* (17th edn, Sweet & Maxwell, London, 2001), para 3-032.

145 *Freeman and Lockyer (a Firm) v Buckhurst Park Properties (Mangal) Ltd* [1964] 2 QB 480 at 504–505, per Diplock LJ; *Hely-Hutchinson v Brayhead Ltd* [1968] 1 QB 549 at 593, per Lord Pearson; *Crabtree-Vickers Pty Ltd v Australian Direct Mail Advertising and Addressing Co Pty Ltd* (1975) 133 CLR 72; *Clayton Robard Management Ltd v Siu* (1988) 6 ACLC 57 at 777, per McLelland AJA; *National Australia Bank v Sparrow Green Pty Ltd* (1999) 17 ACLC 1665. This part of the rule was adopted by the Supreme Court in *Rainbow Holdings Pty Ltd v Central Province Forest Industries Pty Ltd* [1983]

actual authority. Provided that the person making the representation has sufficient implied actual authority, he or she may make the representation. The conduct that may give rise to implied actual authority can also amount to a representation for the purpose of apparent authority; and so the same set of facts may give rise to both implied actual authority and ostensible authority.[146] The last requirement is that the outsider must be induced by the representation to enter into the contract: the outsider must rely on the representation. In the above situations, the company is estopped from denying that the agent had authority.[147] Where the third party either knows that no actual authority was given, or if a reasonable person in his or her position would have had doubts as to whether the "agent" had the authority to enter into the transaction, there can be no contract between the company and the third party.[148]

It is also important to note that the effect of ostensible authority is negative: the principal is prevented from denying that the agent has authority to enter into the transaction, but it cannot rely on that ostensible authority to enforce the contract. Only if the company ratifies the contract will it be able to enforce it.[149] Apparent authority is also sometimes referred to as "constructive" authority, because it is imposed by law, rather than created by agreement between the principal and agent.[150] The court will estop the company from denying the officer's authority. The statutory provisions dealing with this area are also framed as procedural rather than substantive. The company is not allowed to "assert", i.e., the company is estopped from denying the agent's or officer's authority, from saying that it is not bound because the relevant officer or agent did not have authority to enter into the dealing.

PNGLR 34 at 38. See below. It has been stated that it is anomalous that a company is bound by a contract entered into by a *de facto* managing director but is not bound by a representation of the *de facto* managing director that someone else has apparent authority: Lipton, P and Herzberg, A, *Understanding Company Law* (12th edn, Lawbook Co, 2004), p 119. In New Zealand, the Court of Appeal has disapproved of this requirement: see *Cromwell Corporation Ltd v Sofrana Immobilier (NZ) Ltd* (1992) 6 NZCLC 67, 997. See also *First Energy (UK) Ltd v Hungarian International Bank Ltd* [1993] 2 Lloyd's Rep 194, [1993] BCLC 1409, [1993] BCC 533. Fisher is of the view that: "Apparent authority to underpin an agent's representation concerning his or her own authority is too remote to justify attributing the agent's act to the principal. Coupling appearances to appearances does not create certainty or promote predictability in this branch of the law." Fisher, S, *Agency Law* (Butterworths, Sydney, 2000), p 77. See also [1983] *Journal of Business Law* 409.

146 It is not uncommon for judges to use these terms interchangeably, and to refer to implied actual authority as ostensible authority. However, the two concepts are distinct.

147 Apparent authority is one aspect of the doctrine of estoppel (agency by estoppel): *Rama Corporation Ltd v Proved Tin and General Investments Ltd* [1952] 2 QB 147 at 148–149.

148 *Rama Corporation Ltd v Proved Tin and General Investments Ltd* [1952] 2 QB 147 at 150. See also *Overbrooke Estates Ltd v Glencombe Properties Ltd* [1973] 3 All ER 511.

149 For ratification, see below at pp 468–473.

150 See Fisher, S, *Agency Law* (Butterworths, Sydney, 2000), p 29.

In *Freeman and Lockyer v Buckhurst Park Properties (Mangal) Ltd*,[151] one of the directors of the company was permitted by the others to act as managing director, even though he had never been formally appointed as such. Acting in the customary manner of a managing director, he engaged a firm of architects on behalf of the company. The court held that the company was bound by the contract, as it had held out the director as a managing director, and the plaintiff had acted on that representation. He had apparent authority to employ the architects, because this was within the customary authority of a managing director. Because the plaintiffs had relied on the apparent authority of the managing director, they did not have to examine the company's constitution or inquire whether the managing director had been properly appointed. The representation that the director had authority to engage the firm of architects arose because the board of directors failed to prevent him from acting as if he were the company's managing director.[152]

Freeman and Lockyer v Buckhurst Park Properties (Mangal) Ltd[153] was followed in the case of *Rainbow Holdings Pty Ltd v Central Province Forest Industries Pty Ltd*,[154] where it was held that the appellant company (Rainbow Holdings) was bound because the person who executed the contract on its behalf had apparent or ostensible authority to do so.

One of the assets that the provisional liquidator of Central Province Forest Industries had for sale, was a number of timber logs which were stockpiled on a beach. In a letter dated 7 February 1980 to the provisional liquidator, the managing director of Rainbow Holdings (Mr Davis) made an offer to purchase the logs. Mr Davis concluded the letter of offer as follows: "Should you require clarification of our offer, please contact Mr Gordon Smith [solicitor] of Russell Hay's office, telephone 212066 with whom negotiations may be conducted." On the same day, Mr Gordon Smith of Russell Hay, the firm of solicitors, got in touch with the liquidator's office and advised that he acted for the defendant. He confirmed his instructions to act for the defendant in a letter to the liquidator written soon afterwards: "We act on behalf of Rainbow Holdings Pty Ltd in respect of the above matter", i.e., the purchase of the logs. There was no further contact between the provisional liquidator and Mr Davis. Correspondence, however, continued between the provisional liquidator and the solicitors for Rainbow Holdings in subsequent months, the solicitors referring to Rainbow Holdings as "our client". The position of the solicitors appears not to have changed. Following further negotiations between the solicitors

151 [1964] 2 QB 480.

152 Cf *Crabtree-Vickers Pty Ltd v Australian Direct Mail Advertising and Addressing Co Pty Ltd* (1975) 133 CLR 72, where there was not sufficient representation by the board of directors that the agent had apparent authority.

153 [1964] 2 QB 480.

154 [1983] PNGLR 34.

and the provisional liquidator, the contract price for the logs was renegotiated, given the fact that the condition of the logs had deteriorated in the meantime, because of their exposure on the beach, and a formal contract, for a lower price than that contained in Mr Davis's initial letter of offer, was eventually signed by the liquidator and by the solicitors for the Rainbow Holdings on behalf of their client: the acceptance of the offer was signed by Mr Smith as – "Solicitor for Rainbow Holdings Pty Ltd".

On appeal against an award of damages for breach of contract, Rainbow Holdings submitted that there was no binding contract between the parties as it was signed on its behalf by a person without actual, implied or ostensible authority; nor had Rainbow Holdings ratified the agreement.[155] Rainbow Holdings alleged that the solicitor had no actual authority to enter into the contract on behalf of Rainbow Holdings, and a reasonable person would not consider that such authority had been given.

The Supreme Court held that whilst there was no evidence at the trial that there was an "actual" authority between principal and agent, there was sufficient evidence to show "apparent" or "ostensible" authority. The Supreme Court found that there was "a strong holding out" by Rainbow Holdings in the initial letter of offer of Mr Davis dated 7 February 1980 that the firm of solicitors was its agent. Nor was there anything done at a later date to suggest to the provisional liquidator that the negotiating position had changed in any way. In the circumstances, there was nothing to put the provisional liquidator on inquiry as to the lack of authority of the firm of solicitors. The court found that Mr Davis was aware of the negotiations and held that ratification was not a prerequisite before the agreement became binding.

The Supreme Court held that the concluding words of Mr Davis's letter of 7 February 1980 advising the provisional liquidator that Mr Gordon Smith of Russell Hay's office would negotiate the sale on behalf of the company were "a strong holding out" by the managing director of Rainbow Holdings, Mr Davis (who had express or implied actual authority of the company to do so), that Mr Smith and the firm of solicitors was the company's agent to conclude the contract. Whilst there was no evidence at the trial that there was an "actual" authority (whether express of implied) *between principal and agent*, there was sufficient evidence to show "apparent" or "ostensible" authority. The court, following *Freeman and Lockyer v Buckhurst Park Properties (Mangal) Ltd*,[156] held that for apparent or ostensible authority to arise, it must be shown:[157]

1. that a representation that the agent had authority to enter on behalf of the company into a contract of the kind sought to be enforced was made to the contractor;

155 For the requirements of ratification, see Chapter 5 (Agency), and below at p 468.
156 [1964] 2 QB 480 at 505–506.
157 [1983] PNGLR 34 at 37–38.

2. that such representation was made by a person or persons who had 'actual' authority to manage the business of the company either generally or in respect of those matters to which the contract relates;[158]
3. that he (the contractor) was induced by such representation to enter into the contract, that is, that he in fact relied upon it;[159] and
4. that under its memorandum or articles of association the company was not deprived of the capacity either to enter into a contract of the kind sought to be enforced or to delegate authority to enter into a contract of that kind to the agent.[160]

The representation from the company can be express. However, it will usually be implied, for example, from a course of dealing, or from placing the agent in such a position that it is reasonable for third parties to assume that he has the principal's authority to make the contract of the kind in question.

The issue of apparent or ostensible authority also arose in the case of *AGC (Pacific) Ltd v Woo International Pty Ltd*,[161] where Sakora AJ followed the decisions of *Freeman and Lockyer v Buckhurst Park Properties*

158 In New Zealand, the Court of Appeal has disapproved of this requirement: see *Cromwell Corporation Ltd v Sofrana Immobilier (NZ) Ltd* (1992) 6 NZCLC 67,997. Note, however, that the rule continues to apply in Australia: *Crabtree-Vickers Pty Ltd v Australian Direct Mail Advertising and Addressing Co Pty Ltd* (1975) 133 CLR 72. The latter case held that a representation of authority cannot be made by a person who has only apparent authority. See note 123 supra.

159 It is submitted that this does not mean that the person must act to their detriment; but they must have at least altered their position based on the representation. See *Arctic Shipping Co Ltd v Mobilia AB (The Tatra)* [1990] 2 Lloyd's Rep 51 at 59, per Gatehouse J: "the only 'detriment' that has to be shown . . . is the entering into the contract by the party relying on that authority." Cf *Rama Corporation Ltd v Proved Tin and General Investments Ltd* [1952] 2 QB 147 at 150, per Slade J. The third party outsider is not allowed to say that he relied on the representation if he knew that it was untrue, i.e., that the "agent" did not have the authority which he or she claimed to have: *Bloomenthal v Ford* [1897] AC 156. See Reynolds, F M B, *Bowstead and Reynolds on Agency* (17th edn, Sweet & Maxwell, London, 2001), para 8-026 The reason for entering into the dealing need not be the sole cause of the third party entering into the dealing: *Tsangaris v Graymark Investments Pty Ltd* (1968) 82 FLR 269 at 282, per Maurice J. However, if the third party was induced to enter into the transaction for some reason other than the representation, the company will not be estopped from denying that the purported agent did not have ostensible authority: *Ruben v Great Fingall Consolidated* [1906] AC 439 at 446, per Lord Davey.

160 This requirement is no longer necessary because of the effect of ss 17 to 20 of the Companies Act 1997. In fact, it was not necessary at the time when the judgment in *Rainbow Holdings Pty Ltd v Central Province Forest Industries Pty Ltd* [1983] PNGLR 34 was delivered: see Companies Act (Ch 146), ss 36 and 37.

161 [1992] PNGLR 100. See Kimuli, M, "Authority to Bind a Company in Contract – AGC (Pacific) Ltd v Woo International Pty Ltd (Unreported, 1992) N1061" (1992) 20 *Melanesian Law Journal* 147–154.

(Mangal) Ltd[162] *and Rainbow Holdings Pty Ltd v Central Province Forest Industries Pty Ltd*[163] in the case before him.[164]

The question that arose for decision was whether the respondent company (Woo International) was liable as guarantor for a debt incurred under a commercial lease agreement[165] for a motor vehicle entered into between the appellant finance company (AGC) and another company, Southwind Marine (PNG) Pty Ltd (Southwind) of which a Mr Leo Woo was a director. Woo International, of which Mr Woo was the managing director, had executed the guarantor's agreement which had been duly evidenced by the affixing of the common seal of the company and the signing of the agreement by Mr Woo and another officer of the company. Southwind defaulted in its lease obligations and AGC repossessed and sold the vehicle, incurring a loss once repayments and the sale price were taken into account. AGC sent a letter of demand to Woo International pursuant to the guarantee for immediate payment of the outstanding sum to make good the loss. Woo International having failed to comply with the demand notice, AGC brought an action in the District Court against Woo International to recover the money. In its defence, whilst not disputing the facts of the agreement and the subsequent default by Southwind, Woo International contended that although the guarantee was executed by Mr Woo as the managing director and another officer of the company, they did so without the authority of the company's board of directors, and as such, the guarantee was invalid.[166] The judgment of Sakora AJ in this case is interesting for the general observations made on the law and policy issues relating to companies and agency. Of more immediate interest, however, are his observations in regard to apparent or ostensible authority. Sakora AJ stated:[167]

> The law as enunciated by the cases cited above [*Rainbow Holdings Pty Ltd v Central Province Forest Industries Pty Ltd* [1983] PNGLR 34 and *Freeman and Lockyer (a Firm) v Buckhurst Park Properties (Mangal) Ltd* [1964] 1 All ER 630] recognises an exceptionally wide doctrine of

162 [1964] 2 QB 480 at 505–506.
163 [1983] PNGLR 34.
164 "I adopt and apply the law as declared in these cases to this appeal": *AGC (Pacific) Ltd v Woo International Pty Ltd* [1992] PNGLR 100 at 106.
165 Also known as a finance lease agreement. Under this type of agreement, the lessor, usually a finance company, purchases goods and then leases them to the lessee for a rental payable during the period of the lease. The lessee obtains exclusive possession and use of the goods, but does not own them or have an option to purchase them at the end of the period. However, the lessor will usually be willing, at the end of the lease period, to sell the goods to the lessee at the residual value. This type of agreement offers the lessee tax advantages over credit purchases.
166 It was also contended that Mr Woo had acted in breach of the Companies Act (Ch 146) (repealed), s 139.
167 [1992] PNGLR 100 at 106–108.

agency and vicarious liability in instances such as the present: LCB Gower, *The Principles of Modern Company Law*, 3rd ed (1969). When a natural person could be bound by the acts of his agents, so could a corporation. Thus, by the very nature and composition of a corporate entity, the courts have elected to treat the acts of certain company officials as those of the company itself . . .

But not every act or omission or default can give rise to legal consequences or responsibilities, nor every servant or agent can commit the company or incur liability. It all depends on the circumstances surrounding the act or omission in question, the nature of the act or omission, the relative position of the agent or servant in the hierarchy of the corporation and what they are and are not empowered to do. Thus, putting it another way, not every servant of the company is a 'responsible officer'; the mind of some employees is not the mind of the company . . .

And in relation to contractual obligations arising out of the acts or actions of the employees or officers of the company, the liability arises out of the operation of the doctrine of ostensible (or apparent) authority. The learned editors of the *CCH Reporter* have stated (2,220) that:

'The authority of a person to bind his company depends on what would usually be done by a person in his position. Thus, any person having dealings with an officer or other servant of the company should be confident that the type of transaction is one which would normally fall within the ordinary scope of the authority of such officer.'

Directors and other officers have obviously a greater ostensible authority than the more humble lowly employees. Ostensible authority is important in most matters involving third parties because the rule in *Royal British Bank v Turquand* (1856) 6 E & B 327; 119 ER 886 relieves outsiders from inquiring into the internal management of a company. HAJ Ford, in his *Principles of Company Law*, 3rd ed (1981) says (p 518) that a company will be bound by the act of a person to whom it has given apparent or ostensible authority even though that person may not have actual authority to bind the company. Thus 'responsible' officers of the company have the apparent authority to bind the company by contract. Actual authority is a matter between an officer and his company. His ostensible authority is of more significance to an outsider, a third party.

Sakora AJ held that *Woo International* was liable under the contract of guarantee, because its managing director and the other company officer who signed the guarantee, and witnessed the fixation of the company's seal on the document, although they may not have had actual authority of the company to do so, had ostensible authority to do so.[168]

168 Sakora AJ stated at 108: "In the end I rule that the appellant has properly invoked the principles contained in *Turquand's case* [*Royal British Bank v Turquand* (1856) 6 E & B

There appear to be several grounds on which the learned judge came to this conclusion: based on agency, and also on the organic theory. The head-note to case in the Papua New Guinea Law Reports sets out these holdings as follows:[169]

> Held
>
> 1. Where a person dealing with a company acts in good faith and with no notice or reasonable grounds of suspicion of irregularity or impropriety, he is not affected by any actual irregularity or impropriety in a matter of internal regulation. That is, a third party dealing with a company is not bound to ensure that the internal regulations, derived, *inter alia*, from the articles of association, have in fact been complied with as regards the exercise and delegation of authority in the company. A third party need not go further: he need not ensure that the rules of internal management – sometimes referred to as the rules of "indoor management" have been observed. *Royal British Bank v Turquand* (1856) 6 E & B 327; (1856) 119 ER 886 and *Sangara (Holdings) Ltd v Hamac Holdings Ltd (In Liquidation)* [1973] PNGLR 504 applied.[170]
>
> 2. Lack or absence of authority can, of course, arise during the course of employment where what the officer of the company did (or omitted to do) is something which can only be done by the general meeting or it is something that is entirely outside the powers of the company. The directors and other executives appointed by the members of the company are the people who plan the company's business and run it. The directors may then exercise the powers vested in them through a managing director or managers or agents and officials of the company (see s 18(4) of the *Companies Act*).
>
> In the circumstances of this case, the managing director and the company official had implied or ostensible authority. *Rainbow Holdings Pty Ltd v Central Province Forest Industries Pty Ltd* [1983] PNGLR 34 and *Freeman and Lockyer v Buckhurst Park Properties (Mangal) Ltd* [1964] 1 All ER 630 adopted and applied.[171]

327; 119 ER 886] and the 'indoor management' rule. The respondent company is thus liable under the guarantee agreement to make good the appellant company's losses." The case is further discussed below under the heading of the indoor management rule (or rule in *Turquand*'s case).

169 [1992] PNGLR 100 at 101–102.

170 This rule known as the indoor management rule or the rule in *Turquand*'s case is discussed below.

171 Although the judge does refer to cases dealing with ostensible authority, he did not deal with the requirements set out in those cases and apply them to the facts of the case. If anything, it seems that the authority of the managing director and other responsible company officer arose because of the implied actual authority of the managing director to enter into contracts of guarantee.

3. Directors and managers represent the directing mind and will of the company and, hence, control what the company does.

"The state of mind of these managers is the state of mind of the company and is treated by law as such: *HL Bolton (Engineering) Co Ltd v TJ Graham and Sons Ltd* [1956] 3 All ER 624 . . . [The] Directors and other officers have obviously a greater ostensible authority than the more humble lowly employees. Ostensible authority is important in most matters involving third parties because the rule in Turquand's case relieves outsiders from inquiring into the internal management of a company . . . a company will be bound by the act of a person to whom it has given apparent or ostensible authority even though that person may not have actual authority to bind the company. Thus 'responsible' officers of the company have the apparent authority to bind the company by contract.

4. Accordingly, the respondent company is liable under the guarantee agreement to indemnify the loss suffered by the appellant . . ."

The principles of agency set out in the case of *Michael Yai Pupu v Tourism Development Corporation*,[172] although dealing with the liability of a statutory corporation for the actions of its servants or agents, are clearly applicable to a registered company. The plaintiff claimed the cost of goods (artefacts) supplied to the defendant corporation following a purported order for them by one of the defendant's senior managers (Mr Stalin Jawa). The plaintiff who had conducted an arts and craft business, but was in the process of closing it down and selling stock, entered into negotiations with Mr Jawa for their sale to the corporation. The agreement was partly in writing and partly verbal. After referring to several English cases, including *Hely-Hutchinson v Brayhead Ltd*[173] and *Freeman and Lockyer (a firm) v Buckhurst Park Properties (Mangal) Ltd*,[174] Gavara-Nanu J concluded that a valid contract had been reached between the plaintiff and the defendant. He held that Mr Jawa had either actual or ostensible authority to enter into the contract on behalf of the corporation.[175]

> Mr Jawa's discussions with the plaintiff which preceded the stock take and the sale of the artifacts at the Village Arts shop, were made in his capacity as a manager, and on behalf of the defendant; and were made in the course of his duties and within the scope of his authority. He had

172 (2002) N2258.
173 [1968] 1 QB 549.
174 [1964] 2 QB 480.
175 Gavara-Nanu J also held that, even if Mr Jawa did not have authority to enter into the contract on behalf of the corporation, the agreement to purchase the artefacts was subsequently ratified by the Corporation, and was therefore binding on them.

> both actual and ostensible authority to enter into such transactions with the plaintiff, which were binding on the defendant. The actual authority is implicit in the conduct of the parties and the circumstances of the case.

He continued:

> The defendant had clearly held Mr Jawa out as having authority to hold discussions with the plaintiff and to do other acts, [and] on its behalf to buy the artefacts. Therefore, the contractual transactions emanating from those discussions and actions, were at least within the scope of Mr Jawa's ostensible authority. The defendant is thus, by principles of equity, estopped from disputing the validity and the binding effect of such transactions on it.
>
> In the circumstances, the plaintiff was even entitled to assume that the defendant had agreed to buy his artifacts based on the representations made by Mr Jawa. There is another reason – the fact the defendant had sat back and said nothing to stop the stock take which took about two weeks to complete and then the subsequent transfer of the artifacts to the shed where they were sold for the defendant, means that, by its silence and inaction, the defendant had acquiesced in the transactions.

The defendant's senior managers including Mr Jawa were fully aware of the artifacts been transferred to the Village Arts shop in the shed. It seems that Gavara-Nanu J was of opinion that Mr Jawa could hold himself out as having authority to conclude the purchase of the artefacts. The plaintiff relied upon the "representations made to him by Mr Jawa and other employees of the defendant". He concluded that:

> The company is considered to have made the representation, or caused it to be made or at any rate to be responsible for it. Accordingly, as against the other contracting party, who has altered his position in reliance on the representation, the company is estopped from denying the truth of the representation.

In *Jay Mingo Pty Ltd v Steamships Trading Pty Ltd*,[176] Sevua J held that a Branch Manager (Mr Mane) of a national company (Steamships, the respondents) had apparent or ostensible authority to bind the company in executing a lease of land from Steamships to Jay Mingo Pty Ltd. The lease was for a term (i.e. period) of three years; however, after only 16 months of the term had expired, Steamships attempted to recover possession of the premises.[177] Steamships argued that Mr Mane did not have authority to

176 [1995] PNGLR 129.

177 Under normal circumstances, the lessor (Steamships) could recover possession of the leased premises only if the lessee was in breach of one or more of the terms of the lease,

sign the lease: and that the only person who could do so, was its managing director. The National Court rejected this argument. Although the court came close to holding that Mr Mane had express or implied actual authority to sign the lease, Sevua J was satisfied to hold that Mr Mane had apparent or ostensible authority to sign the lease on behalf of Steamships. There was no reference to any direct holding out by Steamships or its managing director or other more senior official of Steamships that Mr Mane had authority. It seems that the court was content to hold that by allowing Mr Mane to occupy the position of "Branch Manager" in a company like Steamships, this amounted to a holding out that Mr Mane had authority to enter into leases for the company:[178]

> In my view, Dickson Mane, as Branch Manager of the defendant, had implied authority (if not expressed) to deal with this matter in the manner he did. He was the branch manager, so he must have possessed some kind of authority to deal with the defendant's properties in Lae. I consider he had authority to execute the lease on behalf of the defendant . . .
>
> I consider that, at the material time, Mr Mane had authority to sign on behalf of the defendant. After all, he was the defendant's branch manager; therefore, in a position to execute the agreement on behalf of the defendant . . . Dickson Mane had ostensible authority to sign on behalf of the defendant.[179]

In *Steven Naki v AGC (Pacific) Ltd*,[180] Cannings J also had to consider, *inter alia*, the apparent or ostensible authority of a branch manager to enter

or the lease was invalid from the start. It was this latter argument that Steamships relied on in the court proceedings.

178 Apart from holding that Steamships was bound by the actions of its agent in signing the lease, the court also held that Steamships was estopped by its actions from claiming that the lease did not exist. See, in particular, [1995] PNGLR 129 at 134. Although not argued, like *Michael Yai Pupu v Tourism Development Corporation* (2002) N2258, the facts of the case also raise the issue of ratification: As Sevua J stated at 131 and 132, that Steamships "had enjoyed a handsome monthly rental for 16 months . . . It knew that this lease was in existence".

179 [1995] PNGLR 129 at 132–133. See also *British Bank of the Middle East v Sun Life Assurance Co of Canada (UK) Ltd* [1983] 2 Lloyd's Rep 9, where the only holding out by the defendant to the third party was to invest its employee with the title "branch manager", which enabled that person to so describe himself in correspondence on which the third party relied. In such a case, the only representation on which the third party can reasonably rely is the representation that the person in question has the powers normally or usually enjoyed by a branch manager. The only relevant inquiry therefore is as to the powers normally enjoyed by branch managers in general. (Dal Pont, G E, *Law of Agency* (Butterworths, Chatswood, NSW, 2001, p 532.)

180 (2005) N2782.

into a chattel mortgage contract on behalf of his principal, AGC (Pacific) Ltd, a finance company. AGC which had offices in Port Moresby, Lae, Mt Hagen and Kokopo, financed the purchase of a truck by the plaintiff. The plaintiff alleged that the agreement was unlawfully terminated and sought damages from AGC. One of the defences mounted by AGC was that its agent, the branch manager in Kokopo (Mr Fangau), did not have authority to sign a release letter permitting the truck dealer to deliver the truck to the plaintiff, and that as a result, no contract between AGC and the plaintiff came into existence. (The branch manager was alleged to have signed the release letter without authority and in clear breach of AGC's internal procedures.) Cannings J in holding that there was a contract which AGC breached stated:

> However, I do not consider that the breach of AGC's internal procedures has any bearing on the legal relationship between AGC and the plaintiff. Mr Fangau at that time was a branch manager. The negotiations with the plaintiff had been going on in his geographical domain and were within his control. A reasonable person with knowledge of the actions that he took and the documents that he signed would conclude that he had authority to do what he did. He certainly had apparent or ostensible authority. An agent can bind their principal by entering into a contract on behalf of the principal, if he or she acts within the scope of their apparent or ostensible authority – even if they lack actual authority. (*Rainbow Holdings Pty Ltd v Central Province Forest Industries Pty Ltd* [1983] PNGLR 34, Supreme Court, Pratt J, Bredmeyer J, McDermott J.) The same principles apply, with even more force, where a senior employee – a branch manager – acts within his apparent or ostensible authority on behalf of his employer and signs a document in the name of his superior officer.

Although Cannings J specifically referred to *Rainbow Holdings Pty Ltd v Central Province Forest Industries Pty Ltd*,[181] as authority for the law dealing with apparent or ostensible authority, he did not specifically deal with how the representation that the agent branch manager had authority to enter on behalf of the company into a contract of the kind sought to be enforced was made to the plaintiff, Mr Naki; nor with the second requirement set out in *Rainbow Holdings Pty Ltd v Central Province Forest Industries Pty Ltd*: that the representation must be made by a person or persons who had "actual" authority to manage the business of the company either generally or in respect of those matters to which the contract relates: i.e., that the person had express or implied actual authority to

181 [1983] PNGLR 34.

make the representation. Given the facts of the case, it seems best to explain this decision as a case dealing with the implied actual authority of a branch manager of a national company. However, Cannings J specifically stated:

> I find that the fact that [the branch manager] Mr Fangau *acted without actual authority*, in breach of standard procedures, is of no consequence. For the same reason, the other many breaches of AGC's internal procedures which occurred in this case have no legal consequences.

It seems that, like the *Jay Mingo* case, the decision can be best explained as one dealing with apparent authority where the company, by allowing a person to occupy the position of branch manager, holds that person out as capable of effecting contracts that a reasonable person would expect such managers to do.

In *Tian Chen Ltd v The Tower Ltd (No 1)*,[182] Kandakasi J had to consider the law of apparent or usual authority, in particular, whether a real estate agent had apparent authority to bind the landlord. During the course of the judgment, his Honour stated the law in such a way as to imply that the agent himself may make a representation that he or she has authority to do an act.[183] He stated:

> It is settled law under the doctrines of apparent and usual authority that a principal is liable on the contracts made by his agent although the principal has not authorised his agent to make them: see *Summers v Solomon* (1857) 7 E & B 879; *Pole v Leask* (1863) 33 LJ Ch 155. In such a situation one need only be satisfied that *a representation of authority has been made in fact by the agent* as having the authority to act for its principal and that the representation has been made to a third party who has relied on the representation without knowing any lack of authority in the agent: see *Summers v Solomon* (1857) 7 E & B 879; *Panorama Developments (Guildford) Ltd v Fidelis Furnishing Fabrics Ltd* [1971] 2 QB 711; *Chapleo v Brunswick PBS* (1881) 6 QBD 686; *Grammar Corporation v Provetine and General Investments Ltd* [1952] QB 147; *Freeman and Lockyer v Buckhurst Properties (Mangal) Ltd* [1964] 2 QB 480; *Jacobs v Morris* [1902] 1 Ch 816 and

182 (2002) N2313.

183 In *Bernard Nuri v Kaipel Du* (2003) N2315, Kandakasi J referred to this statement with approval. Other PNG decisions, where similar statements have been made or implied, include: *Michael Yai Pupu v Tourism Development Corporation* (2002) N2258; and *AGC (Pacific) Ltd v Woo International Pty Ltd* [1992] PNGLR 100. For discussion on the topic "Representation by agent does not establish authority" see Dal Pont, G E, *Law of Agency* (Butterworths, Chatswood, NSW, 2001), pp 532–535. See also Fridman, G H L, "The Self-Authorising Agent" (1983) 13 *Manitoba Law Journal* 1.

> *Overbrooke Estates Ltd v Glencombe Properties Ltd* [1974] 1 WLR 1335. Also see for a detailed discussion of these principles GH Treitel, *The Law of Contract*, 5th ed, Stevens & Sons, London, 1979, pp 530. (Emphasis added.)

It is suggested that despite this clear statement to the contrary, an officer or agent of a company cannot confer apparent or ostensible authority on himself or herself by representing that he or she has authority.[184] As Lord Pearson stated in *Hely-Hutchinson v Brayhead Ltd*:[185]

> There is, however, an awkward question arising in such cases [as to] how the representation which creates the ostensible authority is made by the principal to the outside contractor. There is this difficulty. I agree entirely with what Diplock LJ said [in *Freeman and Lockyer v Buckhurst Properties (Mangal) Ltd* [1964] 2 QB 480 at 506] that such representation has to be made by a person or persons having actual authority to manage the business. Be it supposed for convenience that such persons are the board of directors. Now there is not usually any direct communication in such cases between the board of directors and the outside contractor. *The actual communication is made immediately and directly, whether it be express or implied, by the agent to the outside contractor.* It is, therefore, necessary in order to make a case of ostensible authority to show in some way that *such communication which is made directly by the agent* is made ultimately by the responsible parties, the board of directors. That may be shown by inference from the conduct of the board of directors in the particular case by, for instance, placing the agent in a position where he can hold himself out as their agent and acquiescing in his activities, so that it can be said that they have in effect caused the representation to be made. They are responsible for it and, in the contemplation of law, they are to be taken to have made the representation to the outside contractor.

As Dal Pont points out, an assertion of authority by an agent that is in some way instigated or permitted by the principal, or made in circumstances in which the principal put the agent in a position where the agent appears to

184 *Armagas Ltd v Mundogas SA (The Ocean Frost)* [1986] AC 717. In Treitel, G H, *The Law of Contract* (11th edn, Thomson/Sweet & Maxwell, London, 2003), p 713, the author specifically adverts to the fact that apparent (i.e. ostensible) authority "*can only arise out of a representation made by the principal*: *it cannot arise out of a representation* made by some other person or out of one *made by the agent himself*". (Emphasis added.) Treitel gives several authorities for this proposition, including *Armagas Ltd v Mundogas SA*. See also *New Zealand Tenancy Bonds Ltd v Mooney* [1986] 1 NZLR 280 at 283 and *Savill v Chase Holdings (Wellington) Ltd* [1989] 1 NZLR 257 at 305.

185 [1967] 3 All ER 98 at 108.

be authorised to make it, can create ostensible authority.[186] It is well established that an agent cannot by his or her own acts confer upon himself or herself ostensible authority, but ostensible authority may arise where the agent has had a course of dealing with a particular contractor and the principal has acquiesced in this course of dealing and honoured transactions arising out of it.

It is not enough for a third party to show that he or she relied on the agent's representation of the authority from the principal; what must be shown is that he or she relied on the representation of the principal that the agent had the necessary authority.[187] However, an agent's assertion of authority does have some probative value. In *Crabtree-Vickers Pty Ltd v Australian Direct Mail Advertising & Addressing Co Pty Ltd*, the High Court of Australia explained the impact of such an assertion as follows:[188]

> There are circumstances where the actual representation of authority may be made by the agent but in such cases it will be found that the relevant representation is made by the principal (or by the person to whom the principal has given actual authority) either by a previous course of dealing or by putting the agent in a position or by allowing him to act in a position from which it can be inferred that his actual representation of authority in himself is in fact correct. It is therefore always necessary to look at the conduct of the principal (or the person to whom he has actually delegated authority).

Where an agent is acting within the usual authority of a person in his or her position, the third party will normally not be expected to inquire as to the details of his authority unless the transaction is abnormal or there are other circumstances giving rise to suspicion. If there are suspicious circumstances or abnormalities, then the third party should "make such inquiries as ought reasonably to be made" to ensure that the authority is sufficient to bind the principal.

In *Armagas v Mundogas*, Lord Keith of Kinkel explained the nature of ostensible authority thus:[189]

> Ostensible authority comes about where the principal, by words or conduct, has represented that the agent has the requisite actual authority, and the party dealing with the agent has entered into a contract with him in reliance on that representation. The principal in these circumstances is estopped from denying that actual authority existed.

186 Dal Pont, G E, *Law of Agency* (Butterworths, Chatswood, NSW, 2001), p 534.
187 *Savill v Chase Holdings (Wellington) Ltd* [1989] 1 NZLR 257 at 305, per McMullin J.
188 (1975) 133 CLR 72 at 78, per Gibbs, Mason and Jacobs JJ.
189 [1986] 1 AC 717 at 777B.

> In the commonly encountered case, the ostensible authority is general in character, arising when the principal has placed the agent in a position which in the outside world is generally regarded as carrying authority to enter into transactions of the kind in question ... Ostensible general authority can, however, never arise where the contractor knows that the agent's authority is limited so as to exclude entering into transactions of the type in question, and so cannot have relied on any contrary representation by the principal ...

A third party cannot rely upon the ostensible authority of an agent if he or she knows that the agent has no authority to enter into the type of transaction in question.[190] Similarly, an agent cannot rely upon ostensible authority where he or she was put on enquiry by the facts of the transaction, and such an enquiry would have shown that there was no authority.[191]

The Rule in Turquand's *case or the indoor management rule*

The underlying law agency rules relating to companies are supplemented by a special company law rule known as the "indoor management rule" or the rule in *Turquand*'s case,[192] which in turn has been supplemented by statutory provisions.[193] The indoor management rule states that, while persons dealing with a company are taken to have constructive notice of the contents of the company's public documents,[194] they do not have to go further and ensure that the company's internal proceedings were properly carried out. In fact, the outsider can assume that these proceedings were properly carried out. The courts thus developed a qualification to the rule that actual or constructive notice of the company's constitution might prevent reliance on the doctrine of ostensible authority. This rule thus assists in proving that a company gave authority, whether implied actual authority or apparent (ostensible) authority. It gives rise to an irrebuttable presumption preventing the company from resiling from a contact on the ground that formation of the contract was irregular and the person acting on behalf of the company had no authorisation to do so. "It is a rule designed for the protection

190 Ibid.

191 *Houghton v Nothard, Lowe & Wills* [1927] 1 KB 246 at 261.

192 Following the name of the case where the rule was clearly stated: *Royal British Bank v Turquand* (1856) 6 El & B1 327, 119 ER 886. The rule existed before this case, and this together with the statutory modifications brought about by s 19 of the Companies Act 1997 has led to the rule being referred to most often in this chapter as "the indoor management rule".

193 Companies Act 1997, s 19. The effect of this section is dealt with below at p 448.

194 This doctrine of constructive notice has now been changed: see Companies Act 1997, s 20.

of those who are entitled to assume, just because they cannot know, that the person with whom they deal has the authority which he claims."[195] Because the rule is based on procedural convenience for outsiders who cannot gain access to company documents to verify if procedural requirements have been met, a company cannot rely on the rule.[196]

In *Royal British Bank v Turquand*,[197] the deed of settlement (i.e., the equivalent to the constitution) of a company, empowered the board of directors to borrow money provided that this was first authorised by an ordinary resolution of a general meeting of shareholders. The company borrowed money from a bank on the authority of two of its directors who authenticated the proper use of the company's common seal. The company later claimed that it did not have to repay the money to the bank as no resolution of the kind required had been passed at a general meeting. The company refused to repay the loan and argued that the bank had constructive notice of the constitution and should have been aware of the lack of authority. The court held that the bank did not need to inquire into whether such a resolution had in fact been passed. The company was bound to the bank because the passing of the resolution was a matter internal to the company and the bank could infer that the necessary ordinary resolution had been passed. Jervis CJ said that a third party reading the company's deed of settlement would discover:

> "not a prohibition on borrowing, but a permission to do so under certain conditions. Finding that the authority might have been made complete by a resolution, he would have a right to infer the fact of a resolution authorising that which on the fact of the document appeared to be legitimately done."

The rule in *Turquand*'s case protects the outsider where, for example, there is an irregularity concerning the proper holding of a meeting. A quorum may not have been present, inadequate notice may have been given or a voting irregularity may have occurred. The rule also operates in situations where the common seal is not affixed in accordance with the constitution or

195 Frost J in *Sangara (Holdings) Ltd v Hamac Holdings Ltd (In Liquidation)* [1973] PNGLR 504, quoting Lord Simonds in *Morris v Kanssen* [1946] AC 459 at 474. Judges have come to different conclusions for the basis of the rule: see in particular the differing views of judges of the High Court of Australia in *Northside Developments Pty Ltd v Registrar-General* (1990) 170 CLR 146.

196 *Hughes v NM Superannuation Board Pty Ltd* (1993) 29 NSWLR 653. In *Morris v Kanssen* [1946] AC 459, a director was not allowed to rely on the rule in *Turquand*'s case. Cf *Hely-Hutchinson v Brayhead Ltd* [1968] 1 QB 549.

197 (1856) 6 E & B 327, 119 ER 886.

the board is not properly constituted. In these cases, an outsider can assume the constitution has been complied with and hold the company liable.[198]

The types of procedural matters that the rule in *Turquand*'s case applies to include the conduct of meetings of the company and the fixing of the common seal to documents. For example, the board may not have been properly constituted, a quorum may not have been present, inadequate notice may have been given or a voting irregularity may have occurred. The common seal may also not have been affixed in accordance with the constitution.[199] The effect of failure to comply with these formalities did not make the contract void; it merely made it not binding on the company unless the company ratified it.[200]

In *Mahony v East Holyford Mining Co*,[201] a bank honoured the company's cheques, signed by two of the three named directors, after having received from the company's secretary a copy of a board resolution giving cheque-signing powers to the three directors, to which their signatures had been appended. Unfortunately, neither "secretary" nor "directors" had been properly appointed. However, the bank successfully resisted an action for repayment of the money. Provided that nothing appeared which was contrary to the articles of association, the bank was entitled to assume that the directors had been properly appointed.[202]

We discussed the case of *AGC (Pacific) Ltd v Woo International Pty Ltd*,[203] when dealing with the apparent or ostensible authority of agents of companies. The case is of importance also in respect of the issue of the

198 Lipton, P and Herzberg, A, *Understanding Company Law* (12th edn, Lawbook Co, Sydney, 2004), p 115.

199 Chapple, L and Lipton, P, *Corporate Authority and Dealings with Officers and Agents* (CCH Australia Ltd and Centre for Corporate Law and Securities Regulation, Melbourne, 2002), p 19.

200 Below, we deal with ratification. It would have to be approved by the organ that had actual or ostensible authority to approve the transaction on behalf of the company, or by an ordinary or special resolution of the shareholders: *Grant v United Kingdom Switchback Railway Co* (1888) 40 Ch D 135.

201 (1875) LR 7 HL 869.

202 Section 136 of the Companies Act 1997 now provides that "acts of a person as a director are valid even though (a) the person's appointment was defective; or (b) the person is not qualified for appointment". This statutory protection is only partial, as it was held by the House of Lords in *Morris v Kanssen* [1946] AC 459 that a similar section applies only where there has been a defective appointment, and not where there has been "no appointment" at all. See also *Re New Cedas Engineering Co Ltd* (1975) [1994] 1 BCLC 797. The distinction between "no appointment" and a "defective appointment" is sometimes difficult to make.

203 [1992] PNGLR 100.

indoor management rule and the issue of putting on inquiry. Sakora AJ stated:[204]

> It has been accepted in this jurisdiction that where a person dealing with a company acts in good faith and with no notice or reasonable grounds for suspicion of irregularity or impropriety, he is not affected by any actual irregularity or impropriety in a matter of internal regulation: *Sangara (Holdings) Ltd v Hamac Holdings Ltd (In Liquidation)* [1973] PNGLR 504. This proposition is sometimes referred to as the rule in *Turquand*'s case: *Royal British Bank v Turquand* (1856) 6 E & B 327; 119 ER 886. The substance of this rule is that a third party dealing with the company is not bound to ensure that the internal regulations (derived from, *inter alia*, the articles of association) have in fact been complied with as regards the exercise and delegation of authority in the company . . .
>
> It should be remembered that a third party has no means of knowing whether an ordinary resolution has been passed by the company. He can read the memorandum and study the *vires*, and inspect the registration of charges, or discover whether a special or extraordinary resolution has been passed. He can read the articles of association and obtain particulars of the directors. But he cannot know, unless he has been told, whether an ordinary resolution such as was required in *Turquand*'s case has been passed by a general meeting. The loan there was clearly within the powers of the company. The company, therefore, had the necessary capacity. And it was also clear that the directors had the necessary authority. A third party need go no further: he need not make sure that the rules of internal management – sometimes referred to as the rules of 'indoor management' – have been observed.
>
> If the principal places secret restrictions on the apparent authority of his agent, they do not affect the third party: the third party need not take steps to ensure that there are no such restrictions, for this would make the carrying on of business a practical impossibility.

As we noted above, Sakora AJ held that the managing director and officer of Woo International, in placing the company's common seal on the guarantee, and authenticating its fixing by placing their signatures next to the seal, had apparent or ostensible authority to do so. He came to this conclusion based on the combination of apparent authority together with the indoor management rule.

Other aspects of the "indoor management rule" have been set out in *Sangara (Holdings) Ltd v Hamac Holdings Ltd (In Liquidation)*.[205] In that

204 [1992] PNGLR 100 at 104.

205 [1973] PNGLR 504. The Full Court upheld the pre-Independence Supreme Court decision of Ollerenshaw J in *Hamac Holdings Ltd v Sangara (Holdings) Ltd* (1969) No 531.

case, Sangara alleged that by a deed executed by the parties, it had bought Hamac Holdings' shares in Morobe Hotels. The transaction had been negotiated by a Mr Fox, who was not only Sangara's agent, but also regarded as a director of Hamac Holdings. (In fact, Fox did not have the required shareholding qualification for appointment to that office.) Fox signed and sealed the deed on behalf of Hamac Holdings. The execution of the deed was not authorised by a resolution of the directors of Hamac Holdings nor witnessed (countersigned) by them as Hamac Holdings' constitution required. Nor was the agreement approved by its shareholders in general meeting. Fox also purported to execute a second deed for the purchase of bonus shares in Sangara. Hamac Holdings argued that the deeds were invalid because the execution was done without proper authority and in breach of its constitution (i.e., its articles of association). The Full Court of the Supreme Court held that Hamac Holdings was not bound by the deeds. They were signed without proper authorisation by Hamac Holdings, and Fox's knowledge of the lack of authorisation was imputed to his principal, Sangara, and the deed was therefore void.

In giving one of the judgments of the Full Court, Frost J stated:[206]

> Thus, in this case, the directors of the appellant are deemed to have knowledge of the provisions of arts 74, 102(a) and 107, supra, and the effect of such provisions, but these irregularities could not be discovered from the public documents of the company. Under these circumstances the rule in *Turquand*'s case (*Royal British Bank v Turquand* (1856) 6 El & Bl 327; 119 ER 886), may enable the appellant to bind the respondent to the contract.
>
> The so-called rule in *Turquand*'s case (*Royal British Bank v Turquand* (1856) 6 El & Bl 327; 119 ER 886) is I think correctly stated in *Halsbury's Laws of England*: 'But persons contracting with a company and dealing in good faith may assume that acts within its constitution and powers have been properly and duly performed and are not bound to enquire whether acts of internal management have been regular' . . . [I leave aside the question what in the application of the rule is the meaning of 'good faith'] . . . It is a rule designed for the protection of those who are entitled to assume, just because they cannot know, that the person with whom they deal has the authority which he claims. This is clearly shown by the fact that the rule cannot be invoked if the condition is no longer satisfied, that is, if he who would invoke it is put

An appeal to the High Court of Australia from the Full Court decision was dismissed for want of prosecution. See Roebuck, D, Srivastava, D K, Nonggorr, J, *The Context of Contract in Papua New Guinea* (University of Papua New Guinea Press, Waigani, 1984), pp 147–148 for discussion of the case.

206 [1973] PNGLR 504 at 538–539.

> upon his inquiry. He cannot presume in his own favour that things are rightly done if inquiry that he ought to make would tell him that they were wrongly done. *Morris v Kanssen* [1946] AC 459, per Lord Simonds at 474–475.

There are several exceptions to the rule in *Turquand*'s case. First, for an outsider to be able to rely on it, he or she must have acted in good faith, and must not have had actual or constructive knowledge to the contrary,[207] and must not have been put on inquiry as to the irregularity.[208] In *Sangara (Holdings) Ltd v Hamac Holdings Ltd (In Liquidation)* Frost J stated in relation to the good faith (*bona fides*) requirement:[209]

> No argument was submitted by either counsel on the meaning of 'good faith', nor was any case cited in which, although it was not shown that the persons contracting had knowledge or were put on inquiry, the rule could not be invoked on the ground that there was otherwise lack of good faith on the part of those persons. But the overriding requirement of *bona fides* has been consistently propounded as part of the rule since *Mahony v East Holyford Mining Co* (1875) LR 7 HL 869 (in those terms by Lord Chelmsford at p 892, and as absence of fraud by Lord Hatherley at p 895), and I see no reason for limiting its general meaning, which I take to denote honest dealing (cf. the sale of goods legislation, *Goods Act* 1951, s 5(2)).

Secondly, the outsider is prevented from relying on the indoor management rule and thus holding a company to be bound by a contract purportedly made by its agent, where he or she has "actual knowledge"[210] or "constructive knowledge"[211] that a requirement has not been complied with: that the agent lacked authority or had only limited authority.[212] If the outsider

207 In the past, if the contract was *ultra vires* the powers of the company, the contract was void. Forgeries were also void. Both of these exceptions are no longer applicable because of changes made by the Companies (Amendment) Act, and continued by the Companies Act 1997.

208 *Morris v Kanssen* [1946] AC 459 at 475, per Lord Simonds.

209 [1973] PNGLR 504 at 539.

210 *Howard v Patent Ivory Manufacturing Co* (1888) 38 Ch D 156.

211 In *Sangara (Holdings) Ltd v Hamac Holdings Ltd (In Liquidation)* [1973] PNGLR 504 at 538–539, Frost J referred with approval to the judgment of Lord Simonds in *Morris v Kanssen* [1946] AC 459 at 475, where his Lordship stated that the rule in *Turquand*'s case "cannot be invoked . . . [by the outsider] if he who would invoke it is put upon his inquiry. He cannot presume in his own favour that things are rightly done if inquiry that he ought to make would tell him that they were wrongly done".

212 In the past, an outsider could not assume matters that were inconsistent with public documents, as the doctrine of constructive notice presumed all outsiders to have notice of the contents of public documents: see Chapple, L and Lipton, P, *Corporate Authority and*

actually knew that the agent had not been conferred with authority to enter into the contract to borrow the K100,000, or the outsider deliberately kept his or her eyes shut in order not to discover a suspected irregularity,[213] the actual knowledge exception would apply.

In *Rolled Steel Products (Holdings) Ltd v British Steel Corporation*, Slade LJ said that the rule in *Turquand*'s case was not "an absolute and unqualified rule of law, applicable in all circumstances". He added: " . . . even if persons contracting with a company do not have actual knowledge that an irregularity has occurred, they will be precluded from relying on the rule if the circumstances were such as to put them on inquiry which they failed duly to make."[214]

The outsider will also not be able to rely on the indoor management rule or on the implied actual authority or apparent authority where he or she was "put on inquiry" and failed to make inquiries that would usually or customarily have been made by someone in their position, or that a reasonable person would have made. When dealing with someone other than the board of directors, the third party is not necessarily protected because he or she acted in good faith. If there are suspicious circumstances, he should "make such inquiries as ought reasonably to be made" and he will be protected only if the suspicions of a reasonable person would have been allayed by the answers to his inquires.[215] It is not open to the person relying on the due inquiry exception to argue that if he or she had made the inquiries, it

Dealings with Officers and Agents (CCH Australia Ltd and Centre for Corporate Law and Securities Regulation, Melbourne, 2002), pp 34–36. This exception to the rule has been watered down by s 20 of the Companies Act 1997, which provides that: "A person is not affected by, or deemed to have notice or knowledge of the contents of, the constitution of, or any other document relating to, a company merely because the constitution or document is (a) registered on the register; or (b) available for inspection at an office of the company." The rule in *Turquand*'s case also did not apply where the corporate signature was forged: *Ruben v Great Fingall Consolidated* [1906] AC 439. Section 19(2) of the Companies Act 1997 now overrules the principle that was considered to be stated in that case that a forgery is a nullity and cannot bind a company. (Cf *Uxbridge Permanent Benefit Building Society v Pickard* [1939] 2 KB 248 and *Northside Developments Pty Ltd v Registrar-General* (1990) 170 CLR 146.)

213 In *English and Scottish Mercantile Investment Co Ltd v Brunton* [1892] 2 QB 700 at 707–708, Lord Esher MR stated: "When a man has statements made to him, or has knowledge of facts, which do not expressly tell him of something which is against him, and he abstains from making further inquiry because he knows what the result would be – or, as the phrase is, he 'wilfully shuts his eyes' – then judges are in the habit of telling juries that they may infer that he did know what was against him. It is an inference of fact drawn because you cannot look into a man's mind, but you can infer from his conduct whether he is speaking truly or not when he says that he did not know of particular facts."

214 [1986] 1 Ch 246 at 284.

215 *Underwood (AL) Ltd v Bank of Liverpool* [1924] 1 KB 775; *Houghton (JC) & Co v Nothard, Lowe & Wills Ltd* [1928] AC 1; and *B Liggett (Liverpool) Ltd v Barclay's Bank Ltd* [1928] 1 KB 48.

would not have revealed the defect. As Frost J, relying on *Chapleo v Brunswick Permanent Benefit Building Society*[216] and *Underwood (AL) Ltd v Bank of Liverpool*[217] pointed out in *Sangara (Holdings) Ltd v Hamac Holdings Ltd (In Liquidation)*,[218] "if persons are put on inquiry and do not investigate, they are still debarred, 'though probably if they had inquired they would have learned nothing' ".

The case of *Northside Developments Pty Ltd v Registrar-General*[219] provides a good example of the outsider being put on inquiry. Northside Developments Pty Ltd (Northside) purported to grant a mortgage over its land to Barclays Bank to secure a loan made by Barclays to other companies owned and controlled by Robert Sturgess (the Sturgess companies). The common seal of Northside was fixed to the mortgage document, and it was witnessed by Robert Sturgess as director and by his son, Gerard Sturgess, who purported to sign as the company secretary. However, the board of directors of Northside had not authorised the transaction, they had not delegated their powers to Robert Sturgess and Gerard Sturgess had never been formally appointed as company secretary. In addition, the company derived no benefit from the transaction. When the Sturgess companies defaulted in repaying the loan, Barclays enforced the mortgage (which involved selling Northside's land). Northside brought legal proceedings seeking compensation, on the basis that the mortgage was invalid because it had not been approved or executed by Northside. The High Court of Australia held that the mortgage document was not binding on Northside. In doing so, all the judges held that the "put on inquiry exception" applied and as such, Barclays could not rely on the indoor management rule. Barclays' officers could see that the loan was being made to the Sturgess companies, companies that were unrelated to Northside, and that Northside was taking on a large amount of risk for no apparent benefit. These circumstances should have put Barclays' lending officers on inquiry to satisfy themselves that Northside's entry into the mortgage was properly authorised and that the seal had been properly affixed, i.e., whether Robert and Gerard Sturgess had authority to fix and witness the company's common seal. Barclays Bank ought to have suspected an irregularity and made further inquiries to see if the common seal had been properly affixed, and thus it could not rely on the rule in *Turquand*'s case.

In Australia, the Indoor Management Rule at common law applies to transactions executed prior to 1 January 1984. After 1 January 1984, s 68A of the various states Companies Codes applies, and after 1 January 1991, s 164 of the Corporations Law applies. After 1 July 1998 (as a result of the

216 (1881) 6 QBD 696 at 715, per Brett LJ.
217 [1924] 1 KB 775 at 789, per Bankes LJ.
218 [1973] PNGLR 504 at 545–546.
219 (1990) 170 CLR 146.

changes effected by the Company Law Review Act 1998), s 128(4) of the Corporations Law applied and now provides that: "A person is not entitled to make an assumption in section 129 if at the time of the dealings they knew or suspected that the assumption was incorrect." It is perhaps important to note that the Explanatory Memorandum (para 8.7) makes it abundantly clear that "put on inquiry" is not incorporated into the new provisions: "This objective test is stricter than the current law and makes it clear that the common law 'put on inquiry' test has no application to the statutory provisions." This section is now verbatim with s 128(4) of the Corporations Act 2001. Sections 164–166 of the Corporations Law replicate ss 68A–68D of the Companies Codes. Neither s 68A nor s 164 is to be applied retrospectively. Thus from 1 July 1998, the Australian provisions ceased to refer to limit the knowledge to that gained from "the person's connection or relationship with the company". As such, and because of the significant shift in the wording of the provision, more recent Australian decisions will be of much less value as precedents. The Supreme Court in PNG, apart from developing its own interpretation, will need to rely on New Zealand and Canadian decisions.

The relevant time for testing the knowledge of the person relying on the indoor management rule is at the time of entering into the transaction,[220] and it is important to note that the prevailing view is that the rule cannot benefit the company[221] nor insiders.[222]

In *AGC (Pacific) Ltd v Woo International Pty Ltd*, Sakora AJ stated that "[t]he doctrine of 'constructive notice' has no relevance nor application to this appeal".[223] It had been contended by counsel for Woo International that "a third party cannot take advantage of . . . the rules of ostensible authority and indoor management, if he has actual [sic] constructive notice that the person he is dealing with lacks authority".[224] The rule is even wider than this: the rule in *Turquand*'s case does not apply if the third party outsider is put on inquiry, i.e., if it is shown from the circumstances, that the person *may not have* had authority. And one such situation is where the

220 *Kanssen v Rialto (West End) Ltd* [1944] Ch 346, CA; affirmed on appeal *sub nom Morris v Kanssen* [1946] AC 459.

221 *Hughes v NM Superannuation Board Pty Ltd* (1993) 29 NSWLR 653.

222 In the earlier cases of *Howard v Patent Ivory Manufacturing Co* (1888) 38 Ch D 156 and *Morris v Kanssen* [1946] AC 459, the courts treated directors as always being insiders. In the later case of *Hely-Hutchinson v Brayhead Ltd* [1968] 1 QB 549 at 567–568, Roskill J stated the exclusion more narrowly: a director was an "insider" only if the transaction with the company was so intimately connected with his position as a director as to make it impossible for his not to be treated as knowing of the limitations on the powers of the officers through whom he dealt.

223 [1992] PNGLR 100 at 105.

224 [1992] PNGLR 100 at 104.

transaction is apparently for the personal benefit of the director or officer of the company. However, this argument was given short shrift by the learned judge: "The doctrine of 'constructive notice' has no relevance nor application to this appeal."[225] He stated:[226]

> In my opinion this argument is misconceived and mischievous as it attempts to misapply a proposition of law to a situation neither intended nor envisaged. The doctrine of 'constructive notice', in the context of company law, says that anyone dealing with a company is deemed to have notice of the company's public documents, including the memorandum and thus of its lawful objects. And this doctrine is invariably resorted to in support of arguments based on the doctrine of *ultra vires* and its general nullifying effect.

Sakora AJ stated:[227]

> The doctrine of 'constructive notice' has no relevance nor application to this appeal. The respondent's principal contention is that the managing director and the other officer concerned had no authority to enter into the agreement on behalf of the company. There has been no suggestion here that executing a guarantor agreement with a financial institution such as the appellant company does not come within the specific business activities initially intended by the company to engage in, or some variety of business which the company might conceivably want to turn to in future. The doctrine of *ultra vires* has not been advanced as a nullifying factor, at least in its present restricted extent, for instance, where a transaction can be rendered invalid by the general law or any provision of the *Companies Act* [(Ch146) (repealed)].

He concluded:[228]

> In the end I rule that the appellant has properly invoked the principles contained in *Turquand*'s case and the 'indoor management' rule. The respondent company is thus liable under the guarantee agreement to make good the appellant company's losses.

With respect, it is submitted that Sakora AJ erred when he stated that the doctrine of constructive notice had no relevance or application to this case. It is suggested that it could have had application because, as we have seen,

225 [1992] PNGLR 100 at 105.
226 [1992] PNGLR 100 at 104.
227 [1992] PNGLR 100 at 105.
228 [1992] PNGLR 100 at 108.

the rule in *Turquand's* case does not apply in circumstances where a person dealing with the company was put on inquiry. In this case, the respondent (Woo International) did not benefit from the agreement, Mr Woo having a personal interest in the whole transaction. As such, it is arguable that the appellant was put on inquiry, and could not rely on the indoor management rule set out in *Turquand*'s case. The learned judge rejected this argument:[229]

> Finally, the respondent offered by way of a 'last ditch' argument that it should not be held liable under the guarantee because the principal agreement was for the personal benefit of Mr Woo and not for the company. It was said in this respect that Mr Woo had a personal interest or stake in the lease agreement. This argument has no merit at all. The circumstances surrounding the entering into and the very nature of guarantor agreements are such that a guarantor need not have any direct and immediate benefits from the agreement(s).

Although, as a general rule, it may be correct to state that a guarantor need not have any direct and immediate benefits from the guarantee, in relation to companies giving guarantees, seeing that they do not have the power to make gifts or give personal benefits to directors or members of the company, this reasoning does not apply. Of particular note is the case of *Re Efron's Tie and Knitting Mills Pty Ltd*,[230] where the rule in *Turquand*'s case was held to be inapplicable to a guarantee provided by a director of the guarantor to a bank to secure his personal liability. Cussen ACJ held that, as the guarantee (which was signed under the company's common seal) was provided to secure the director's personal liability, the bank had constructive knowledge that the guarantee was not in the interests of the company and was bound to inquire into the circumstances of its execution. Cussen ACJ said:[231]

> From the guarantee the company directly gained nothing, but might make itself liable to the bank for the advances past and future to Efron in respect of his private account or accounts. It would seem from the evidence that the giving of the guarantee was not in fact in the interests of the company, but in the interests of the bank. I think there was a refraining

229 [1992] PNGLR 100 at 109.
230 [1932] VLR 8.
231 [1932] VLR 8 at 29 A similar case is the Privy Council decision of *EBM Co Ltd v Dominion Bank* [1937] 3 All ER 555, PC, where, although the security appeared regular in form, the circumstances were such as to put the bank on inquiry and to disentitle the bank from relying on a security purportedly given by the company and proffered by three directors in respect of their personal liabilities. See also *Northside Developments Pty Ltd v Registrar-General* (1990) 170 CLR 146.

> from further inquiries, and the manager [of the bank] decided to get what he could and to take the risk of its turning out invalid.

It is possible that if the court had come to the conclusion that the lender was aware that the company was entering into a transaction which appeared to be unrelated to the purposes of its business and from which it appeared to gain no benefit, it would have held that the lender could not rely on the underlying law indoor management rule, as it had been put on inquiry by these circumstances.[232] Where a company's asset is being charged to secure a loan to an unrelated company at the request of a common director without any apparent benefit to the charging company, the lender should be put on inquiry.[233] If it fails to carry out this inquiry or turns a blind eye to it, the court will hold the mortgage or guarantee to be invalid.

In *ACC (Pacific) Ltd v Woo International Pty Ltd*, the respondent argued that, because it did not benefit from the agreement, Mr Woo having a personal interest in the whole transaction, the case was similar to the *Northside Developments Pty Ltd v Registrar-General* case.[234] The defendant being put on inquiry, it could not utilise the indoor management rule, and ought to have known that Mr Woo could not validly contract as the contract was not properly entered into according to the constitution of the company.[235]

> It would seem to me that the respondent's argument denies or attempts to deny the existence and independence (of executive action) of organs of corporate institutions such as managing directors. In the process it is a denial or attempted denial of the principles of the law of agency.

In respect of *AGC (Pacific) Ltd v Woo International Pty Ltd*,[236] Kimuli states that:[237]

> . . . given the fact that a company is only a legal entity, the assumption and trust [that the officer or employee of the company with whom the

232 *Northside Developments Pty Ltd v Registrar-General* (1990) 170 CLR 146. See also *Bank of New Zealand v Fiberi Pty Ltd* (1992) 8 ACSR 790 (Allen J) and *Story v Advance Bank Australia Ltd* (1993) 31 NSWLR 722. Note, however, that the statutory indoor management rules contained in s 19 of the Companies Act 1997 would affect the position now.

233 *Northside Developments Pty Ltd v Registrar-General* (1990) 170 CLR 146.

234 (1990) 170 CLR 146.

235 It is not clear from the report of *AGC (Pacific) Ltd v Woo International Pty Ltd* [1992] PNGLR 100 what company rules were broken by the managing director and company officer in sealing the guarantee. Although there is an assumption that they had breached the company's constitution, no direct evidence on this seems to have been led either at the District Court hearing or on appeal to the National Court.

236 [1992] PNGLR 100.

237 Kimuli, M, "Authority to Bind a Company in Contract – *AGC (Pacific) Ltd v Woo International Pty Ltd* (Unreported, 1992) N1061" (1992) 20 *Melanesian Law Journal* 147 at 154.

> public deal has the authority which he is represented by the company as possessing and that everything is in order as between that officer or employee and his company] *ought to be displaced only in the most exceptional of circumstances*. The principle of ostensible authority and the 'internal management' rule which Sakora AJ applies in *AGC (Pacific)* ensure that our trust and confidence are not misplaced. [Emphasis added.]

It is suggested that the put on inquiry element of the rule in *Turquand's* case ought to have been applied in this case, and that the circumstances were such (i.e., they were most exceptional circumstances) as to have led to the contract of guarantee being held to be invalid.[238]

Statutory provisions and the indoor management rule[239]

The Companies Act 1997 sets out certain provisions that assist outsiders where the company claims that the person apparently acting as its agent, did not have any or sufficient authority, or that the document that is being relied on was not "valid" or "genuine" or that it was a forgery or was obtained by fraudulent means. Although the Companies Act 1997 does not expressly state so, it is established law that persons dealing with a company are entitled to make various assumptions of regulatory compliance in relation to dealings with companies. Correspondingly, the company is not entitled to assert against persons dealing with the company certain matters about the authority of representatives of a company or about documents purportedly issued by or on behalf of the company.[240] There are several issues which need to be settled in respect of these provisions, including the extent to which the outsider may continue to rely on the underlying law agency principles governing dealings involving companies.

238 It is assumed that there were restrictions placed by the respondent company on Mr Woo as managing director to enter into contracts such as the guarantee contract. The appellant did not advance evidence of this, though the argument proceeded on this assumption.

239 See generally, Fridman, G H L, *The Law of Agency* (7th edn, Butterworths, London, 1996), Ch 16.

240 The New Zealand and PNG Companies Acts do not set out the matters as *assumptions* that the outsider third party can make, but rather as *assertions* that a company *cannot* make. Cf ss 128 and 129 of the Corporations Act 2001 (Australia). Several of the provisions are badly drafted. For example, although s 19(1) and (2) refer to "*has*, or ought to have . . . knowledge" and "*has* actual knowledge", the date on which to test this knowledge is the date on which the dealing took place. Ideally, the provisions ought to have been in the past tense: "had, at the time of the dealing." Section 19(1)(e) should have been "issued *by* or on behalf of a company" instead of "issued on behalf of a company", and the placing of the comma in the wrong place in the proviso to s 19(1) makes it unclear what word or words the phrase "by virtue of his position with or relationship to the company" qualified. See note 221 and accompanying text.

As we noted above, an outsider dealing with someone who purports to be the agent of the company may rely on the indoor management rule. According to this rule, the outsider may assume such things like:

- there have been no procedural defects in the appointment of directors;
- a meeting of the board of directors has been properly called and held;
- any board (or general meeting) approval required under the company's constitution or under the Companies Act 1997 has been obtained.[241]

If, for example, the constitution required approval of the board of directors for borrowings of more than K50,000, and the CEO negotiates a loan of K100,000 from the bank without first gaining the approval of the board, the company will not usually be able to set up a defence that it was not bound by the contract because the board had not approved the loan.

The Companies Act 1997 now allows for arguments similar to the indoor management rule to be advanced by third parties. Section 19 of the Companies Act 1997 prevents a company (as well as a guarantor of an obligation of a company)[242] from asserting against an outsider (i.e., "a person dealing with the company or . . . a person who has acquired property, rights, or interests from the company")[243] that:

- the Companies Act 1997 or the company's constitution has not been complied with;[244]

241 *Royal British Bank v Turquand* (1856) 6 El & Bl 327, 119 ER 886; *Northside Developments Pty Ltd v Registrar-General* (1990) 170 CLR 146; *Story v Advance Bank Australia Ltd* (1993) 31 NSWLR 722.

242 See *AGC (Pacific) Ltd v Woo International Pty Ltd* [1992] PNGLR 100 for an example where a guarantor of an obligation of a company tried to evade liability.

243 The "person" dealing with the company who can rely on the statutory provisions may be a natural person or a legal person such as another company, a corporation sole, a "body corporate" (a statutory corporation, corporate government instrumentality, corporate "governmental body") or even a Provincial Government or the Independent State of Papua New Guinea. The state also has the capacity to appoint an agent. In *Pinpar Development Pty Ltd v TL Timber Development Pty Ltd* (1999) N1857, Kapi DCJ stated: "Having regard to all the authorities, I accept the principle that a parent company may be liable for the actions of a subsidiary company provided that the subsidiary company was acting as agent of the parent company." See also *Odata Ltd v Ambusa Copra Oil Mill Ltd* (2001) N2106 and *KL Engineering and Constructions (PNG) Ltd v Damansara Forest Products (PNG) Ltd* (2001) (Unnumbered and Unreported judgment of Gavara-Nanu J dated 22 May 2001). See *Bernard Nuri v Kaipel Du* (2003) N2315 and *Tasita Pty Ltd v Sovereign State of Papua New Guinea* (1991) 34 NSWLR 691 at 698–699, where it was accepted that a Provincial Government and the Independent State of Papua New Guinea may be liable for contracts made by its agents.

244 Companies Act 1997, s 19(1)(a). This is a statutory restatement and expansion of the indoor management rule. Whereas the underlying law prior to the Act related only to the constitution, s 19 extends the rule to non-compliance with the Companies Act 1997 as well.

- a person named as a director of the company in the most recent s 135 notice received by the Registrar of Companies is not a director of the company, was not properly appointed as a director, or that the person lacked the authority to exercise the power which a director of a company carrying on business of the kind carried on by the company (a similar company), would customarily have;[245]
- a person held out by the company as a director, employee or agent was not properly appointed as such or that the person lacked the authority to exercise the power which such a person in a company carrying on business of the kind carried on by the company (a similar company), would customarily have;[246]
- a person held out by the company as a director, employee or agent of the company as having non-customary authority (i.e., power to exercise an unusual authority or authority that a person in such a position does not customarily have), lacked authority to exercise that power; [247]
- a document "issued on behalf of a company" by a director, employee or agent of the company who has "actual or usual authority" to issue the document was not valid or genuine;[248]
- a document entered into by a director, employee or agent of the company was obtained by fraud or is a forgery;[249]
- a director, employee or agent of the company acted fraudulently in the dealing.[250]

The purpose behind these assertions is to protect outsiders who deal in good faith with persons who can reasonably be expected to have authority to act for the company. To a large extent, the statutory assumptions clarify, if not codify,[251] the underlying law agency rules, including the indoor management rule (i.e., the rule in *Turquand*'s case). It is suggested that each of the "assumptions" (or assertions) is separate and discrete. Even if the outsider cannot rely on one of the assumptions, this does not prevent him or

Section 20 provides that a person is not affected by, or deemed to have notice or knowledge of the contents of, the constitution of, or any other document relating to, a company merely because the constitution or document is: (a) registered on the register; or (b) available for inspection at an office of the company.

245 Companies Act 1997, s 19(1)(b).
246 Companies Act 1997, s 19(1)(c).
247 Companies Act 1997, s 19(1)(d).
248 Companies Act 1997, s 19(1)(e). Cf s 19(2), which applies to similar situations.
249 Companies Act 1997, s 19(2). Section 19(2) seems to be an independent section. However, there is some overlap with elements in s 19(1)(e) and significant problems arise in deciding to what extent s 19(2) adds, if anything at all, to the elements in s 19(1)(e).
250 Companies Act 1997, s 19(2).
251 See below. It is suggested that the statutory provisions did not provide a complete code setting out all the situations where a third party can assume that those dealing with him or her on behalf of the company have power to bind the company.

her from relying on another assumption.[252] Although the assumptions are discrete, there is some overlap and the outsider may rely on more than one assumption.[253] It is also suggested that it is not necessary for the outsider to have made one of the assumptions in order to rely on it.[254] The provisions deal with procedural matters. They do not validate the transactions. They merely prevent the company from asserting them, from relying on their invalidity. Where the non-compliance is made by someone other than the company or a guarantor of an obligation of a company, the statutory provisions do not apply; rather the underlying law rules relating to agency and the rule in *Turquand*'s case apply.

It would appear that the statutory assumptions are not a comprehensive code and the underlying law rule in *Turquand*'s case will still operate in those areas not affected by the statutory provisions.[255] Indeed, it may be argued that even where there is overlap with the statutory provisions, the underlying law rules may continue to operate. For example, the rule in *Turquand*'s case should still continue to apply to corporations other than companies. (The statutory provisions apply only to corporations that are companies.)[256] The statutory provisions also do not apply where some

252 Cf *Brick and Pipe Industries Ltd v Occidental Life Nominees Pty Ltd* [1992] 2 VR 279 at 308. In this case, the outsider could not assume compliance with the constitution, as it had actual knowledge of non-compliance; but that did not prevent it from relying on the assumption of due sealing. It seems that if a specific assumption cannot be relied on, the outsider cannot then rely on the more general assumption.

253 Cf *Bank of New Zealand v Fiberi Pty Ltd* (1993) 12 ACLC 48.

254 Cf *Lyford v Media Portfolio Ltd* (1989) 7 ACLC 271 at 280, per Nicholson J: "... it is clear that whether a person has made the assumptions in dealing with a company, is a matter independent of whether an assertion is made by the company in any proceedings in relation to the dealings with the person. Any assertion that the matters the person was entitled to assume were not correct is, subject to the provisions of the section, to be disregarded in such proceedings. The provisions are directed to the assertion and it is enough that such assertion is made. It is the assertion which brings into application the provisions and not proof that assumptions were in fact made."

255 There is nothing in the provisions of s 19 or elsewhere in the Companies Act 1997 to show that the underlying law rule in *Turquand*'s case has been excluded. Gummow J, in *Australian Capital Television Pty Ltd v Minister for Transport and Communications* (1989) 86 ALR 119 at 156, held that corresponding provisions in earlier Australian companies legislation did not codify the common law rules, but were rather an adjustment for the failings of the rule at common law. See also *Barclays Finance Holdings Ltd v Sturgess* (1985) 3 ACLC 662 at 667, per Wood J; Morrison, D, "The Continued Role of the Common Law Indoor Management Rule Due Inquiry Exception" (1996) 12 *Queensland University of Technology Law Journal* 28–40; and Hammond, C, "Section 164(4)(b) of the Corporations Law: 'To Be Put Upon Inquiry or Not to Be Put Upon Inquiry: Is that the Question?' A Problem of Statutory Interpretation" (1998) 16 *Company and Securities Law Journal* 93–102.

256 So, for example, if the facts of *Michael Yai Pupu v Tourism Development Corporation* (2002) N2258 were to recur and a question as to the question of indoor management rule arose, the matter would have to be tested according to the governing statute and the underlying law rules relating to indoor management; not s 19 of the Companies Act 1997.

person other than the company (or a person who has, or purports to have, acquired title to property from the company) asserts that there was an irregularity in an earlier dealing with the company, and it seems that the underlying law indoor management rule will apply in this case.[257] Section 19(1) provides that it is the "company, or a guarantor of an obligation of a company" who may not in respect of any dealing "assert against a person dealing with the company or with a person who has acquired property, rights, or interests from the company". The assertion is in respect of "a person dealing with the company or with a person who has acquired property, rights, or interests from the company".

For the provisions of s 19 to operate, there must have been a "dealing". A dealing, it is submitted, includes a purported dealing.[258] Although the Companies Act 1997 does not define a dealing, it is suggested that it includes a person entering into any transaction with the company, or where he or she is a party to any act to with the company is a party. The person will be considered to be "dealing with the company" where he or she is a party to a transaction (e.g., a contract) or an act (e.g., a payment of money) to which the company is also a party. "Dealing with" does not connote that the third party gives consideration for the transaction with the company, and a person who is the beneficiary of a gratuitous transaction by the company, it is suggested, is one who is "dealing with the company".[259]

The assertions are applicable where the outsider deals with a person who purports to represent the company, or who purports to have acquired title from the company. Unlike similar provisions where the assertions can be made only where there is a proceeding before a court, the provisions in the Companies Act 1997 do not limit the assertions to proceedings in a court or tribunal. These provisions are discussed in detail below.

Compliance with Companies Act 1997 or company's constitution (s 19(1)(a))

Section 19(1)(a) of the Companies Act 1997 prevents a company from asserting against an outsider that the Companies Act 1997 or the company's constitution has not been complied with.[260] The rule in *Turquand*'s case was subject to the doctrine of constructive notice, which has now been abolished by s 20. The outside third party is no longer assumed to be aware of the provisions in the company's constitution. The outsider may rely on the subsection even though the irregularity would have been apparent to the outsider if he or she had read the constitution. For example, if the

257 See *Australian Capital Television Pty Ltd v Minister for Transport and Communications* (1989) 86 ALR 119 at 157.
258 *Story v Advance Bank Australia Ltd* (1993) 31 NSWLR 722.
259 Cf *International Sales and Agencies Ltd v Marcus* [1982] 3 All ER 551 at 560.
260 Cf *Belven Enterprises Pty Ltd v Lydham Ply Ltd* (1996) 14 ACLC 1478.

constitution contains a restriction on the power of the board to borrow in excess of a certain sum, an outsider who has not read the constitution and is therefore unaware of this provision is *not* taken to know of this restriction.[261]

The company, however, may assert that the Companies Act 1997 or its constitution was not complied with, if it can show that at the time of the dealing, the outsider had or ought to have had, by virtue of his or her position with or relationship to the company, knowledge of the breach of the Act or the constitution.[262]

Directors named in s 137 Notice (s 19(1)(b))

Section 19(1)(b) of the Companies Act 1997 prevents a company from asserting against an outsider that a person named as a director of the company in the most recent s 137 notice received by the Registrar of Companies is not a director of the company, was not duly appointed as a director, or he or she lacked the authority that a director of such a company would customarily have.[263] This is a very specific source of public information. It is limited to directors,[264] and limited to directors named in the most recent s 137 notice. In determining the authority that the director would have, the court must consider the authority of directors of similar companies (i.e., consider the powers which a director of a company carrying on business of the kind carried on by the company would customarily have authority to exercise).[265] The authority depends on the particular office held, the type of

261 Cf *Bank of New Zealand v Fiberi Pty Ltd* (1993) 12 ACLC 48.

262 The effect of this is considered at p 459, below.

263 Companies Act 1997, s 19(1)(b). This subsection overcomes the non-appointment or defective appointment of directors in *some* situations.

264 It does not extend to company secretaries or other company officers. It is suggested that this provision should have extended to company secretaries. Unlike the New Zealand Companies Act 1993, the Companies Act 1997 makes specific provision for company secretaries: see ss 169 and 170. Section 170(3) provides that the board of a company must ensure that notice in the prescribed form of: (a) the appointment of a secretary after incorporation of the company; or (b) a change in the secretary of the company; or (c) a change in the name or the address or the postal address of the secretary of the company, is submitted to the Registrar for registration (Form 21.–Notice of appointment or change of Secretaries or particulars of Secretaries). Note, however, that a company secretary would fall within the definition of "employee" for the purposes of s 19(1)(c), (d) and (e).

265 Earlier Australian legislation had reference to a "company carrying on a business of the kind carried on by the company". In 1989 the provisions were recast and the word "similar company" substituted for the above phrase. The Explanatory Memorandum accompanying the bill stated that the new term "similar company" was merely intended to be a plainer version of the former provision. (See Explanatory Memorandum, *Company Law Review Bill 1998*, [8.10]). If this is so, older and more recent Australian provisions looking at the customary authority of directors, employees and agents will be of persuasive value in interpreting this provision.

company and the kind of business it conducts viewed against what is customary or usual in a similar office in a similar company carrying on a similar business. In analysing corresponding Australian provisions, it has been stated that:[266]

> The kind of business carried on by a company may have been a reference to the size of the company and may have allowed for a distinction to be made between tightly-held, small proprietary companies effectively run by one director and listed public companies which usually have large boards which operate in a collegiate manner. The customary authority of a director of a small company may be regarded as broader than the customary authority of an individual director of a large public company.
>
> . . . customary authority is defined according to a number of factors, including the size of the enterprise, the purpose of the company and why it was incorporated. Where a company has a limited purpose of merely holding a particular asset, the customary authority of a managing director may be considerably narrower than would be the case where the company is engaged in regular business. A consideration of the kind of business carried on by a company may also refer to the usual business activities of the company. If a managing director enters into a contract on behalf of the company that falls outside and is unrelated to the usual business activities of the company, then the [assertion may apply].

The outsider may rely on this provision even if he or she was unaware of the information contained in the most recent notice,[267] and it does not matter

266 Chapple, L and Lipton, P, *Corporate Authority and Dealings with Officers and Agents* (CCH Australia Ltd and Centre for Corporate Law and Securities Regulation, Melbourne, 2002), p 76.

267 Note also that the assertion is limited to the names of directors appearing in a s 137 notice (Notice of change of directors). This notice informs the Registrar of Companies of a change in the directors of a company, whether as the result of a director ceasing to hold office or the appointment of a new director. The section does not apply to directors named in the Application for Registration which contains the names of the first directors, nor the names of directors in annual reports or amalgamation proposals. It is suggested that the provision should have been extended to cover persons named as a company secretary or assistant or deputy secretary in a notice to the Registrar of Companies. However, it might be that s 20 of the Companies Act 1997 covers this situation. It provides that a person "is not affected by, or deemed to have notice or knowledge of the contents of, the constitution of, or any other document relating to, a company merely because the constitution or document is (a) registered on the register; or (b) available for inspection at an office of the company". Cf s 136 of the Companies Act 1997, which provides that: "The acts of a person as a director are valid even though (a) the person's appointment was defective; or (b) the person is not qualified for appointment." Cf *Lyford v Commonwealth Bank of Australia* (1995) 130 ALR 267.

whether the persons named as directors have been improperly appointed or not appointed at all. By naming such persons as directors in this document sent to the Registrar of Companies, a company is holding out that those persons are officers occupying the stated position of directors with authority that is customary for such officers to exercise. In this respect, there is overlap between s 19(1)(b) and s 19(1)(c).

The outsider must establish that the director acted within the scope of the customary powers of a director of a similar company: powers customarily exercised by a director of a company carrying on business of the kind carried on by the company.[268]

The company may prevent a person from relying on s 19(1)(b) if it can show that at the time of the dealing, the outsider had or ought to have had, by virtue of his or her position with or relationship to the company, knowledge that the person was not a director, was not duly appointed, or did not have the authority to exercise the powers customarily exercised by a director of a company carrying on business of the kind carried on by the company.[269]

Holding out and customary authority (s 19(1)(c))

This subsection enacts the underlying law rule of apparent or ostensible authority laid down by Diplock LJ in *Freeman and Lockyer v Buckhurst Park Properties (Mangal) Ltd*[270] and adopted in PNG by such cases as *Rainbow Holdings Pty Ltd v Central Province Forest Industries Pty Ltd*[271] and *AGC (Pacific) Ltd v Woo International Pty Ltd.*[272]

Section 19(1)(c) of the Companies Act 1997 prevents a company from asserting against an outsider that a person held out by the company as a director, employee or agent was not properly appointed as such or lacked the authority that such a person would customarily have.[273] The outsider has the onus of showing that the company held out that the person is a director, employee or agent, and that the particular power exercised by that person so held out is within the scope of the powers customarily exercised or performed by a director, employee or agent of a similar company, i.e.,

268 In *Equiticorp Industries Group Ltd (In Statutory Management) v Attorney-General (No 47)* (1996) 7 NZCLC 261,143 (*sub nom Equiticorp Industries Group Ltd (In Statutory Management) v The Crown (Judgment No 47)* [1998] 2 NZLR 481), Smellie J held that acting improvidently and entering into illegal contracts do not fall within the customary authority of directors.

269 The effect of this is considered below at p 459.

270 [1964] 2 QB 480.

271 [1983] PNGLR 34.

272 [1992] PNGLR 100.

273 Companies Act 1997, s 19(1)(c). Director is defined in s 107 of the Companies Act 1997. The Act does not define "employee" or "agent" for general purposes of specifically for s 19.

powers customarily exercised by a director, employee or agent of a company carrying on business of the kind carried on by the company.[274] It is not necessary for the outsider to show that the person has in fact been appointed, and there is no difference between a defective appointment and a non-existent appointment. Provided that the person is so held out by the company, that is sufficient. The holding out must be "by the company", either the board of directors or a person who has actual (as opposed to apparent)[275] authority to manage the business either generally or in respect of those matters to which the contract or agreement relates. The actual authority may be either express or implied actual authority. The subsection does not state that the holding out must be to the person having dealings with the company. It may be a general holding out. Overseas authorities have held that it is not essential, however, for the outsider to rely on the holding out, and it is not clear whether a PNG court will follow these.[276] In *Re Madi Pty Ltd*,[277] the company held out a person as its secretary by naming that person as its secretary in a document lodged with the Australian Securities and Investments Commission. The company was held to be bound by the act of this person even though he had not been appointed at the time of the lodgement. There was no suggestion that the outsider was aware of the information contained in the company's return and so could not be said to have relied on the information contained in it. In this respect s 19(1)(c) is wider than the underlying law agency rules relating to apparent authority. One of these requirements is that the outsider must rely on the representation made by the company. However, this would not be the case if the outsider were to rely on s 19(1)(c) of the Companies Act 1997. The outsider must also establish that the disputed power exercised by the held-out "director, employee, or agent of the company" is within the ambit of

274 Cf *Freeman and Lockyer (a Firm) v Buckhurst Park Properties (Mangal) Ltd* [1964] 2 QB 480 at 505–506 and *Sangara (Holdings) Ltd v Hamac Holdings Ltd (In Liquidation)* [1973] PNGLR 504 at 540, per Frost J and at 550, per Prentice J.

275 It is open to a PNG court to not follow cases like *Crabtree-Vickers Pty Ltd v Australian Direct Mail Advertising and Addressing Co Pty Ltd* (1975) 133 CLR 72, which held that apparent authority in the person holding out is insufficient. Cf *Brick and Pipe Industries Ltd v Occidental Life Nominees Pty Ltd* [1992] 2 VR 279 at 312, where Ormiston J held in respect of similar Australian provisions that a person with apparent authority could hold out. See also *Rainbow Holdings Pty Ltd v Central Province Forest Industries Pty Ltd* [1983] PNGLR 34 for the limitation of the underlying law indoor management rule of apparent authority to representations by those with actual authority only.

276 The underlying law rule, as stated in *Freeman and Lockyer (a Firm) v Buckhurst Park Properties (Mangal) Ltd* [1964] 2 QB 480 and adopted by the Supreme Court in *Rainbow Holdings Pty Ltd v Central Province Forest Industries Pty Ltd* [1983] PNGLR 34, is that the outsider must have been induced by the representation of authority and must in fact have acted on it. It is not clear whether judges will transpose this reasoning to the statutory indoor management rule.

277 (1987) 5 ACLC 847.

those powers customarily exercised or performed by a director, employee, or agent of a similar company. The customary authority will vary, depending on the position of the person in the company or the type of agency that has been established. Although the courts have gone some way in laying down the customary powers of directors, managing directors and company secretaries,[278] the customary powers of other persons will be a question of fact to be determined on a case-by-case basis.[279]

Although this subparagraph does not make specific mention of the fact that the company cannot assert that the person "is not a director of [the] company", it is submitted that this is of no importance.

The company may prevent a person from relying on s 19(1)(c) if it can show that at the time of the dealing, the outsider had or ought to have had, by virtue of his or her position with or relationship to the company, knowledge that the person was not duly appointed a director, employee or agent of the company, or did not have the authority to exercise the powers customarily exercised by a director, employee or agent of a company carrying on business of the kind carried on by the company.[280]

Holding out and non-customary authority (s 19(1)(d))

Section 19(1)(d) of the Companies Act 1997 prevents a company from asserting against an outsider that a person held out by the company as a director, employee or agent of the company as having non-customary (unusual) authority, lacked authority to exercise that power.[281] This assertion seems to be based essentially on the doctrine of estoppel.[282] Although the subparagraph does not make specific mention of the fact that the company cannot assert that the person "is not a director of [the] company" or "has not been duly appointed", it is submitted that this is of no importance.

The company may prevent a person from relying on s 19(1)(d) if it can show that at the time of the dealing, the outsider had or ought to have had,

278 The customary authority of directors, the managing director or CEO as well as the company secretary according to the underlying law would be applicable or at least persuasive when these statutory assertions are being considered.

279 The authority of branch managers of national companies has been considered in the cases of *Jay Mingo Pty Ltd v Steamships Trading Pty Ltd* [1995] PNGLR 129 and *Steven Naki v AGC (Pacific) Ltd* (2005) N2782.

280 The effect of this subsection is considered below at p 459.

281 Companies Act 1997, s 19(1)(d).

282 The provenance of the provision is unknown. Although borrowed from the New Zealand Companies Act 1993, there are no similar provisions in the Canadian or Australian counterparts which formed the basis of most of the provisions, nor did it form part of the recommendations of the New Zealand Law Commission. It seems to have been introduced during the drafting stage of the New Zealand Act, because of the views of the New Zealand Department of Justice.

by virtue of his or her position with or relationship to the company, knowledge that the person did not have the authority to exercise the non-customary powers.[283]

Documents are valid and genuine (s 19(1)(e))

Section 19(1)(e) of the Companies Act 1997 prevents a company from asserting against an outsider that "a document issued on behalf of a company by a director, employee, or agent of the company with actual or usual authority to issue the document is not valid or not genuine".[284] It would seem that the words "usual authority" means implied actual rather than "apparent authority". As such, it is suggested that it is not necessary for the persons signing or witnessing the document issued on behalf of the company to have been held out by the company as the relevant officers or named as such in the company's lodged documents. It is sufficient if the document appears on its face to have been signed, or the fixing of the common seal witnessed, by the director, employee or agent of the company.

A company need not use a seal, except when it issues share certificates.[285] Section 155 provides that a company may use its seal, or enter into an agreement by a document in writing or even orally. Whenever the issue arises, there are two questions: first, the "substantive authority" of the officers (the existence and the scope of the officer's authority to enter into the contract; substantive authority to bind the company), and secondly, "formal authority" of the officer (i.e., the officer's authority to signify, in the proper form, the company's assent; formal authority to affix the seal).[286] Formal authority relates to procedural regularity in ensuring that the company's assent is in proper form. Substantive authority relates to the authority of the officers to exercise corporate power to enter into the transaction.

The Companies Act 1997 does not stipulate any requirements for authenticating the affixing and witnessing of a common seal. As such, any such requirements would be found in the company's constitution, if at all. Some overseas statutory requirements may require the seal to be witnessed by two directors or by a director and the company secretary.

283 The effect of this is considered below at p 459.

284 Companies Act 1997, s 19(1)(e). This wording is taken directly from the Canadian model: see for example, the Ontario Business Corporations Act RSO 1990, c B16: "a document issued by any director, officer or agent of a corporation with actual or usual authority to issue the document is not valid or genuine." Cf Federal Business Corporations Act, RSS 1978, c B-10, as amended, s 18.

285 The only situation where the Companies Act 1997 requires the company to use a common seal is on a share certificate: s 75(1)(a).

286 Cf Ramsay, I, Stapledon, G, Fong, K, "Affixing of the Company Seal and the Effect of the Statutory Assumption in the Corporations Law" (1999) 10 *Journal of Banking and Finance Law and Practice* 38.

The section does not refer to the company signing a document, executing a document or authenticating a document. All mean the same thing: the manifestation of the company's consent. The essential word is "issue".[287] The company's agents must have "usual authority to *issue* the document". In this respect, this subsection can be contrasted with s 19(2) which requires of the forged document or one obtained by fraudulent means that it "*appears* to have been *signed* on behalf of the company". There is no such signing requirement in s 19(1)(e). It merely refers to "a document *issued* on behalf of a company".

Section 19(1)(d) refers to a document issued on behalf of a company "by a director, employee, or agent of the company with actual or usual authority to issue the document". Section 19(2) refers to "a person of the kind referred to in any of Paragraphs (b) to (e) (inclusive) of that subsection" acting fraudulently or forging a document.

The outsider cannot rely on this provision if he or she knew that the signature/seal was a forgery (fraud, forgery, not valid, not genuine) or ought to have known that the signature/seal was a forgery (not valid, not genuine).[288]

Also, the persons referred to in s 19(2) may be wider than those referred to in s 19(1). The person who carries out the fraud or forgery must be "a person of the kind referred to in any of Paragraphs (b) to (e) (inclusive)". Section 19(1)(e) refers to "a director, employee, or agent of the company with actual or usual authority to issue the document".

The company may prevent a person from relying on s 19(1)(e) if it can show that that at the time of the dealing, the outsider had or ought to have had, by virtue of his or her position with or relationship to the company, knowledge that the document was not valid or genuine.[289]

Limitations on statutory assertions

In relation to any dealing[290] with a company, the company can prevent a person who claims to be entitled under s 19(1) from making any one or

287 It is suggested that this term means "purportedly issued" or "appearing to have been issued". Note that dealing includes purported dealing: Cf *Story v Advance Bank Australia Ltd* (1993) 31 NSWLR 722, at 733, per Gleeson CJ. It also further suggested that it covers not only documents issued "on behalf of" but also "for and on behalf of" the company. Nowhere in the Companies Act 1997 is the term "for and on behalf of" used, which would weaken this assumption.

288 Cf *Story v Advance Bank Australia Ltd* (1993) 31 NSWLR 722.

289 The effect of this is considered below at p 459.

290 Note that the assertion is not restricted to "proceedings" in a court. Cf ss 128 and 129 of Corporations Act 2001 (Australia). The singular includes the plural "dealings": Cf *Advance Bank Australia Ltd v Fleetwood Star Pty Ltd* (1992) 7 ACSR 387. Note that dealing includes purported dealing: Cf *Story v Advance Bank Australia Ltd* (1993) 31

more of the assertions in that section, if the case falls within the proviso to s 19(1) of the Companies Act 1997. The provisions of s 19(1) apply unless the outsider knew ("has ... [actual] knowledge")[291] or ought to have known ("ought to have ... [had] knowledge"),[292] "by virtue of his position with or relationship to the company", of the lack of authority or lack of genuineness of the document, as the case may be.[293] (The right to make these assertions is lost when the person knew or ought to have known that the "assumptions" were incorrect.)

Although the section does not explicitly state at what time the knowledge of the person dealing with the company is to be tested, it seems quite clear that the knowledge must be at the time of the dealing, the time the transaction was entered into.[294] It seems from the above to be clear that the outsider cannot make use of s 19(1) provisions if he or she were wilfully blind in the face of facts which obviously would have led to a conclusion that one of the situations described in s 19(1) had occurred, i.e., there had been an exceeding of authority, or a breach of duty or fraud by the officers of the company, or there had been a forgery.

It can be argued that the concept of knowing (having knowledge) is wide enough to encompass the concept of being put on inquiry. Knowledge is not defined in the Companies Act 1997 and is wide enough to cover not only actual, i.e., subjective knowledge, but other degrees of

NSWLR 722 at 733, per Gleeson CJ. Also note that each of the assertions is separate and discrete: *Brick and Pipe Industries Ltd v Occidental Life Nominees Pty Ltd* [1992] 2 VR 279 and although the assertions may overlap, the outsider may rely on more than one assumption/assertion: *Bank of New Zealand v Fiberi Pty Ltd* (1992) 8 ACSR 790, per Allen J.

291 Cf *Brick and Pipe Industries Ltd v Occidental Life Nominees Pty Ltd* [1992] 2 VR 279, where the Victorian Supreme Court indicated that it might be possible to impute to the lender, the actual knowledge of its solicitor; in which case the knowledge of an agent may be taken to be the actual knowledge of the third party.

292 For discussion of "constructive knowledge" generally, see *Westpac Banking Corporation v Savin* (1986) 3 NZCLC 99,713.

293 See Beck, A and Borrowdale, A, *Papua New Guinea Companies and Securities Law Guide* (CCH Australia Ltd, Sydney, 1999), para 409 for discussion of "knowledge" and "ought to have . . . knowledge". See also *Equiticorp Industries Group Ltd (In Statutory Management) v Attorney-General (No 47)* (1996) 7 NZCLC 261,143 (*sub nom Equiticorp Industries Group Ltd (In Statutory Management) v The Crown (Judgment No 47)* [1998] 2 NZLR 481) for a discussion of these phrases. The court held that the words "ought to have knowledge" (ought to know) requires something more than merely being put on inquiry. It depends on what a reasonable person would have known. See also *Paramac Wholesale Ltd v Family Boats Ltd* (1992) 6 NZCLC 67,652.

294 Cf *Kanssen v Rialto (West End) Ltd* [1944] Ch 346, CA; affirmed on appeal *sub nom Morris v Kanssen* [1946] AC 459; *National Australia Bank v Sparrow Green Pty Ltd* (1999) 17 ACLC 1665; and *Perkins v National Australia Bank* (1999) 30 ACSR 256 at 264. The corresponding provisions in the Australian Corporations Act 2001 now state that the knowledge must be tested "at the time of the dealings".

constructive knowledge.[295] However, as has been pointed out, the juxtaposition of both "know" and "ought to know" in the same proviso suggests that only actual knowledge will disentitle the outsider from reliance on the section.[296] However, whereas the neighbouring and related provision in s 19(2) refers to "actual knowledge", the proviso to s 19(1) refers only to "knowledge", thereby indicating that it is not limited to actual subjective knowledge. It could, for example, encompass wilfully shutting one's eyes to the obvious and wilfully failing to make such inquires as a reasonable person would make.

It also seems that the term "ought to know" ("ought to have ... [had] knowledge") is at least as wide as the underlying law concept of being put on inquiry. In *Bank of New Zealand v Fiberi Pty Ltd*,[297] Kirby P thought that the two concepts overlapped, and that the put on inquiry exception had not been ousted by the statutory provisions similar to the proviso to s 19(1) of the Companies Act 1997. The statutory formulation did not amount to a more restrictive test than the common law (i.e., underlying law) test set out in *Northside Developments Pty Ltd v Registrar-General*:[298] the focus was on whether or not, having regard to all of the circumstances, the outsider ought to have known that the assumption as to authority was sufficiently dubious to put him or her on inquiry. He also rejected the argument that it was necessary for there to be a pre-existing and ongoing, relationship between the outsider and the company: the test could apply from the one transaction which was being considered.[299] It can arise from one transaction (cf *Lyford v Media Portfolio Ltd*,[300] per Nicholson J) and the connection or relationship exception does not have to be a close one with the company. On the other hand, Priestley JA (with whom Clarke JA

295 In *Baden Delvaux and Lecuit v Societe Generale pour Favoriser le Developpement du Commerce et de L'Industrie en France SA* [1993] 1 WLR 509, Peter Gibson J set out five different mental states: (i) actual knowledge; (ii) wilfully shutting one's eyes to the obvious; (iii) wilfully and recklessly failing to make such inquiries as an honest and reasonable person would make; (iv) knowledge of circumstances which would indicate the facts to an honest and reasonable person; and (v) knowledge of circumstances which would put an honest person on inquiry.

296 Beck *et al.*, *Morison's Company and Securities Law* (looseleaf, LexisNexis, London, 1994), para 25.33 and Grantham, R, "Contracting with Companies: Rule of Law or Business Rules?" (1996) 17 *New Zealand Universities Law Review* 39 at 54.

297 (1994) 12 ACLC 48. The irregularity in this case was a signature by the director's son purporting to be the company secretary, a position to which he had not been properly appointed.

298 (1990) 170 CLR 146.

299 "Section 68A is not to be seen as a provision which overrides well-established principles and policies of the common law (as recently expressed in *Northside*) unless that result is made plain by the language of the section." See *Sixty-Fourth Throne Pty Ltd v Macquarie Bank Ltd* (1996) 14 ACLC 670.

300 (1989) 7 ACLC 271.

agreed) thought that although there was some overlap with the underlying law concept, the term meant the knowledge that a reasonable person in the particular circumstances would have had. In judging that question much depends on the person's "connection or relationship with the company"[301] (in the case of the Companies Act 1997, "position with or relationship to the company"). Priestley JA stated:[302]

> This seems to me to indicate that a judge considering whether [s 64A(4)(b) – a provision equivalent to the proviso to s 19(1)] applies to the facts of a case is required to look at the person in question, consider the full factual circumstances of that person's connection or relationship with the company in regard to the particular matter in question and then decide whether in those circumstances that person acting reasonably would know the true position about the matter assumed.

In order for the company to assert that the outsider cannot rely on the dealing, it must be proved that the third party acquired the knowledge or at least ought to have acquired the knowledge "by virtue of his position with or relationship to the company".[303] It would seem that the words "by virtue of his position with or relationship to the company" qualify not only the words "ought to have . . . knowledge", but also the phrase "has ... knowledge". If this is so, it could be argued that *actual* knowledge gained from a position other than the third party's "position with or relationship to the company" does not prevent the company from making the assertion. It has been claimed that the provision applies to prevent "true insiders" from making the company liable.[304] The purpose of these provisions is to protect good faith third parties dealing with the company. Its aim is not to alter the internal effect of a directors' decision to act without authority, except in so

301 See also *Story v Advance Bank Australia Ltd* (1993) 31 NSWLR 722. Gleeson CJ held that the "statutory provisions . . . raises a cognate but not identical question". He went on to state: "the exceptions in subsection (4) are themselves expressed in terms which are in some respects different from the common law qualifications to the indoor management rule."

302 *Bank of New Zealand v Fiberi Pty Ltd* (1994) 12 ACLC 48.

303 The New Zealand provision is the same as the PNG provision. It is based on the similar wording in the Ontario *Business Corporations Act* (RSO 1990, c B 16): "position with or relationship to the corporation." The earlier Australian provisions (in the Companies Code 1984 and the Corporations Law 1991) referred to "actual knowledge" and "connection or relationship with the company is such that he ought to know", and by providing for these in separate subparagraphs made it clear that the words "connection or relationship with the company is such that he ought to know" related *only* to the information that the person "ought to know"; not to the person's actual knowledge.

304 Grantham, R, "Contracting with Companies: Rule of Law or Business Rules?" (1996) 17 *New Zealand Universities Law Review* 39 at 53. See note 222.

far as such provisions are needed to protect third parties. The provisions, therefore, do not prevent shareholders from bringing an action to restrain the company from doing an act to which the directors have committed the company in excess of their powers.[305] Such relief cannot be granted if it would impede the fulfilment of the company's legal obligations to the third party. The provision refers to knowledge rather than notice.[306]

The "proviso" to s 19(1) also makes it clear that the actual or constructive knowledge of the third party must be as a result of the third party's position with or relationship to the company.[307] If the third party becomes aware of one of the situations covered by subsections (1)(a) to (e), the company is *not* prevented from making the relevant assertion. The matter is different, however, if the officer of the company in relation to the dealing "acts fraudulently or forges a document that appears to have been signed on behalf of the company". In such a case, the company can make any of the assertions set out in subsections (1)(b) to (e) unless the third party has "actual knowledge of the fraud or forgery".[308] The test is subjective. It is not clear who has the burden of proof in this situation.[309] It would appear that once the company proves that the officer acted fraudulently or

305 The powers of the court to order an injunction are set out in the Companies Act 1997, s 142. Section 142 does not spell out this limitation. Section 18(1) provides that: "No act of a company and no transfer of property to or by a company is invalid merely because the company did not have the capacity, the right, or the *power* to do the act or to transfer or take a transfer of the property." However, s 18(2), *inter alia*, provides that "Subsection (1) does not limit any of Sections 142 . . .". From this, one can argue that the court may grant an injunction to prevent a company from carrying out a dealing which the company has not properly authorised its directors, agents or employees to do. However, it would seem that, given the objective in various sections of the Act to protect good faith third parties, it ought not to grant the injunction once it has determined that the third party dealing with the company did so in good faith, unless it provides some form or "recompense" to this party if it decides to grant the injunction.

306 See Austin, R P, Ramsay I M, *Ford's Principles of Corporations Law* (12th edn, LexisNexis Butterworths, Australia, 2005) at para 13.300 for discussion of knowledge and notice. Note that s 128(4) of the Corporations Act 2001 (Australia) uses different terminology from the Companies Act 1997: "knew or suspected".

307 ". . . unless the person has, or ought to have, *by virtue of his position* with or *relationship to* the company, knowledge of the matters. . .": Companies Act 1997, s 19(1). Cf s 19 of the Ontario Business Corporations Act (RSO 1990, c B 16) for similar wording on which the section was originally based. Cf sections in the former Australian Corporations Acts of 1984 and 1991: see Hammond, C, "Section 164(4)(b) of the Corporations Law: 'To Be Put Upon Inquiry or Not to Be Put Upon Inquiry: Is that the Question?' A Problem of Statutory Interpretation" (1998) 16 *Company and Securities Law Journal* 93–102.

308 Companies Act 1997, s 19(2).

309 In *Toplis & Harding Pty Ltd v Dadi Toka* [1982] PNGLR 321, Woods J, following *Pole v Leask* (1863) 33 LJ Ch 155, held that "if a person deals with another as agent and seeks to charge a third person as principal, the onus is on him to show that the agency exists, that the agent has the authority he assumes to exercise, or that the principal is estopped from disputing it".

the document is a forgery, it would be up to the third party to show that he or she did not have actual knowledge of the fraud or forgery. The burden of proving that a person knew or ought to have known etc. would appear to be on the company.[310] In these situations the company bears the onus of adducing sufficient evidence to support a finding of fact that a person knew or ought to have known that the assumption was correct.[311] The plaintiff bears the onus of establishing both the existence of the agency and the authority of the agent to effect the act giving rise to the entitlement claimed.[312]

The PNG provision follows the New Zealand provision as far as punctuation is concerned. This makes it unclear whether the modifying phrase "by virtue of his position with or relationship to the company" governs both actual knowledge ("has ... knowledge") and constructive knowledge ("ought to have ... knowledge"). In other words, does the modifying phrase apply to the outsider with actual knowledge where he or she did not acquire that knowledge because of his or her position with or relationship to the company? Is that person prevented from stopping the company from asserting any of the matters referred to in any of the paragraphs of s 19(1) of the Companies Act 1997? The New Zealand provision was in turn based on the Canadian provisions. The Canadian equivalents are divided into three sets, none of which is similar to the punctuation adopted by the PNG draftsman. One set has no punctuation at all. For example, the Saskatchewan Business Corporations Act, RSS 1978, c B-10, s 18 provides: "except where the person has or ought to have by virtue of his position with or relationship to the corporation knowledge to the contrary." Some have commas after "have" and "corporation". This includes the Manitoba Corporations Act, RSM 1987, c C225, s 18: "except where the person has or ought to have, by virtue of his position with or relationship to the corporation, knowledge to the contrary."[313] The third set has the comma in, what it is submitted is, the right place. For example, the Alberta Business Corporations Act, RSA 2000, c B-9, s 19 has: "unless the person has, or by virtue of the person's position with or relationship to the corporation ought to have, knowledge of those facts at the relevant time."

The best way to divorce actual knowledge from constructive knowledge that ought to have been gained from a "position with or relationship to the

310 Cf *Brick and Pipe Industries Ltd v Occidental Life Nominees Pty Ltd* [1992] 2 VR 279.

311 Cf *Brick and Pipe Industries Ltd v Occidental Life Nominees Pty Ltd* [1992] 2 VR 279 at 358–359.

312 Dal Pont, G E, *Law of Agency* (Butterworths, Chatswood, NSW, 2001), para 7.4 (p 161).

313 The Manitoba Corporations Act most clearly shows that the modifying phrase covers *both* actual knowledge and constructive knowledge, was avoided.

company" would have been to set out the two types of knowledge in two separate paragraphs.[314] Alternatively, if it was considered necessary to keep all of the words of the proviso together in one sentence, the easiest way to divorce the modifying phrase from the actual knowledge requirement, would have been to break up the sentence with a comma after "has" and another one after "company", i.e., by removing the comma after the word "have" in the current proviso in the Companies Act 1997. This is how the proviso to s 19 of the Companies Act 1997 should have been punctuated to dispel all doubts whether the modifying phrase ("by virtue of the person's position with or relationship to the company") applied only to the words "ought to have" and not also to the word "has". The draftsman ought to have followed the punctuation adopted in the Alberta Business Corporations Act, referred to above. However, it is submitted that the courts are still free to interpret the PNG provisions in line with this more clearly drafted provision, because the additional comma inserted after "has" does not prevent an interpretation similar to the way in which the more precise Alberta provision will be interpreted.

Sometimes a company and the outsider (if a company) have or share common directors. This raises the question of whether the outsider is taken to have the knowledge possessed by its shared directors. It has been held that where a third party outsider and the company share a company director, the third party ought to know of a contravention of the articles and therefore the company will not be bound.[315] This is, however, not the case where the agent is committing a fraud on one of the principals for whom the agent is acting.[316] As Beck and Borrowdale point out,[317] officers of the company, as well as the company's bankers and solicitors might also be expected to have knowledge as a result of their relationship with a company.[318] Sometimes, shareholders may also have constructive knowledge of the matters set out in s 19(1)(a) to (e), thereby preventing the company from asserting that it is not bound by the dealing.

314 This was done in the former s 164(4)(a) and (b) of the Corporations Law of Australia.

315 *Sangara (Holdings) Ltd v Hamac Holdings Ltd (In Liquidation)* [1973] PNGLR 504; *Eastern Petroleum Australia Ltd v Horseshoe Lights Gold Pty Ltd* (1985) 9 ACLR 980. See also *Farrow Finance Co Ltd (in liq) v Farrow Properties Pty Ltd (in liq)* (1997) 16 ACLC 897 at 931; *Linter Group Ltd v Goldberg* (1992) 7 ACSR 580, *Southern Cross Commodities Pty Ltd* (No 2) (1988) 6 ACLC 647. Grantham, R, "Corporate Knowledge: Identification or Attribution?" (1996) 59 *Modern Law Review* 732.

316 *Sangara (Holdings) Ltd v Hamac Holdings Ltd (In Liquidation)* [1973] PNGLR 504.

317 Beck, A and Borrowdale, A, *Papua New Guinea Companies and Securities Law Guide* (CCH Australia Ltd, Sydney, 1999), para 409.

318 Cf *Brick and Pipe Industries Ltd v Occidental Life Nominees Pty Ltd* [1992] 2 VR 279.

Section 20 of the Companies Act 1997 provides:

> A person is not affected by, or deemed to have notice or knowledge of the contents of, the constitution of, or any other document relating to, a company merely because the constitution or document is –
>
> (a) registered on the register; or
> (b) available for inspection at an office of the company.

It is suggested that because of this provision, a third party is not deemed to know of any restriction or qualification in these "public" documents referred to "merely because" the document is registered or available for inspection at an office of the company. In particular, they are not deemed to have notice of the objects or powers of the company stated in the constitution, or of any special resolutions passed by the board of directors of the company in general meeting.

It is important to note that a third party is not affected by, or deemed to have notice or knowledge of the "contents" of specified documents. It is noteworthy that the term "contents" is used in s 20, rather than a reference to knowledge of "limitations" on powers set out in these documents.[319]

Effect of fraud and forgery (s 19(2))

A company may be prevented from making any of the assertions in s 19(1)(b) to (e) even if the director, employee or agent "acts fraudulently" or "forges a document" in connection with the dealings.[320] The document must "appear ... to have been signed on behalf of the company". This covers agreements in writing and also, it is submitted, situations where use of the company seal[321] or attesting signatures are not genuine, but are

319 This term circumvents the supposed difficulties that the term "limitations" would have posed, as it has been argued that not all provisions which govern how a board or executive member or agent or employee is to act will necessarily constitute a limitation. This was particularly so with respect to quorum requirements, i.e., provisions which require a certain number of the directors to be present for a valid board decision: see *Smith v Henniker-Heaton & Co* [2002] BCC 544; upheld on appeal [2002] BCC 768, CA; cf *TCB Ltd v Gray* [1986] 1 Ch 621.

320 For a discussion of the fraud and forgery cases at common law, which may represent the underlying law position in PNG, see *Northside Developments Pty Ltd v Registrar-General* (1990) 170 CLR 146.

321 The section refers only to a "document" that appears to have been "signed" on behalf of the company. It is suggested that this reference should be wide enough to cover deeds, i.e., a document that has the company's common seal fixed to it, i.e., a deed, and this despite the fact that other sections of the Companies Act 1997 refer to "deeds".

forged.[322] Depending on how courts will interpret the modifying phrase ("by virtue of his position with or relationship to the company") in s 19(1) of the Companies Act 1997, this subsection may be unnecessary, in that all cases of fraud or forgery that would come within s 19(2) would already be covered by s 19(1)(e).

If the dealing involves fraud or forgery by an officer or agent of the company, the Companies Act 1997 makes two changes. First, the disentitling knowledge must be *actual* knowledge of the fraud or forgery.

Section 19(2) of the Companies Act 1997 provides that the statutory bars provided for in s 19(1) apply even though the purported director, agent or employee "acts fraudulently or forges a document that appears to have been signed on behalf of the company" unless the outsider "has actual knowledge of the fraud or forgery". In such a case, constructive notice is not sufficient to disentitle the outsider from relying on s 19(1).[323]

If the person dealing with the company or with a person who has acquired property, rights, or interests from the company has only constructive knowledge of the fraud or forgery, the effect of s 19(2) is that the company will not be able to use s 19(2) to assert that it is not bound by the dealing (i.e., the company will be bound by the dealing).[324] Constructive notice is not sufficient to make persons dealing with the company liable. Secondly, it may be that the acquisition of this knowledge need not have arisen because of the outside third party's relationship with the company ("by virtue of his position with or relationship to the company"). Irrespective of how the knowledge arose, if the third party has actual knowledge that the document was obtained by fraud or forgery, the third party cannot argue that the dealing binds the company; the company may set up the defence that the purported agent did not have authority or that the document was a forgery or was fraudulently obtained. It all depends on what is meant by the phrase "a person of the kind referred to in any of Paragraphs (b) to (e)". Does it mean the person as set out in the main

322 *Story v Advance Bank Australia Ltd* (1993) 31 NSWLR 722. Section 19(2) overrules the principle stated in *Ruben v Great Fingall Consolidated* [1906] AC 439 that a forgery is a nullity and cannot bind a company. But cf *Northside Developments Pty Ltd v Registrar-General* (1990) 170 CLR 146 as to whether *Ruben v Great Fingall Consolidated* is an exception to the rule in *Turquand*'s case.

323 Cf *Story v Advance Bank Australia Ltd* (1993) 31 NSWLR 722.

324 It would seem, however, that the company may assert that it is not bound by the forged or fraudulently obtained document under s 19(1)(e) if it can show that the person dealing with the company or with a person who has acquired property, rights, or interests from the company has constructive knowledge of the fraud or forgery. It is not clear what, if anything, s 19(2) adds to s 19(1)(e) as far as the *type* of knowledge is concerned. However, see below for difference as far as the *mode* of acquisition of knowledge is concerned.

subparagraph, without reference to the proviso, or does the proviso qualify who these persons are? It seems as though the proviso does not qualify the types of persons, as subsection (2) already has a qualifying proviso, similar to, but not the same as, the proviso to subsection (1). Also, the fact that persons to whom paragraph (a) refers is not included in the reference in subsection (2) shows that the qualifying proviso in subsection (1) does not apply to define the kind of persons referred to in subsection (2). However, this raises difficulties.

Once the company shows that the officer or agent acted fraudulently or forged the relevant document, the company is not limited to knowledge of the third party gained "by virtue of his position with or relationship to the company"; it can argue that the third party had "actual knowledge" of the fraud or forgery, and it is irrelevant how this knowledge was gained: it could be gained by any means.

The provisions treat "signing" and "issuing" a document as two completely different actions. Section 19(2) refers to a document that has been "*signed on behalf* of the company", whereas s 19(1)(e) refers to a "document *issued on behalf* of a company". Other sections of the Companies Act 1997 use yet another expression: "signed *by or* on behalf of the company".[325]

A company is prohibited from entering into a "major transaction" and any such transaction is void.[326] The Companies Act 1997 does not provide for the effect of a person entering into a major transaction. It would seem that the company would be bound unless the outsider knew or ought to have known it was such a transaction.

Ratification of defective dealings[327]

Earlier in this chapter, we noted that the underlying law of agency is generally applicable to companies, although the law is somewhat more

325 Other provisions of the Companies Act 1997 refer to signing and issuing in different ways: Companies Act 1997, s 260(1) and (2): "every document issued, *by* or on behalf of the company"; Companies Act 1997, s 388(1)(b): "documents issued or signed by, or on behalf of, the company". Cf *Tonolei Development Corporation Ltd v Lucas Waka, Minister for Forests* (1983) N404(L).

326 Companies Act 1997, s 110.

327 For more detailed treatment of ratification, see Chapter 5 on Agency. See also Fisher, S, *Agency Law* (Butterworths, Sydney, 2000), pp 57–70; Dal Pont, G E, *Law of Agency* (Butterworths, Chatswood, NSW, 2001), Ch 5; Reynolds, F M B, *Bowstead and Reynolds on Agency* (17th edn, Sweet & Maxwell, London, 2001) paras 2-047 to 2-093; and Fridman, G H L, *The Law of Agency* (7th edn, Butterworths, London, 1996), Ch 5. Note that, apart from contracts being ratified, a company may ratify a tortious action, e.g., conversion, and sometimes a criminal act. These situations rarely occur and are not dealt with in this section.

complicated given the fact that a company, being inanimate, must act through humans. We also noted that this area of the law has been subjected to significant changes by the Companies Act 1997. In the general law of agency, a "principal" who did not authorise an "agent" to act on his or her behalf before a transaction was entered into, or who did not authorise the agent to carry out the act to the extent that he or she did, may afterwards endorse the actions of the "agent" and validate or adopt the transaction. This action is commonly referred to as ratification. Ratification does not validate the agent's act from the date of ratification; but rather, it relates back and takes effect from the date of the transaction in question. In this respect, ratification is "equivalent to an antecedent authority".[328] The effect of ratification is that it changes an unauthorised act into an authorised act. The Companies Act 1997 allows a company to ratify, and thereby adopt, a defective transaction.[329] However, again the difficulties are compounded where the principal is a company. We will therefore briefly look at the general law of ratification[330] and then consider the situation where the principal is a company.[331]

First, it should be noted that it is possible for an offer made by a third party through an agent to be made conditional on ratification by the principal. In such a case, there is no binding contract until ratification of the agent's acceptance.[332] In most cases, however, agents do not make contracts conditional on the principal ratifying it.

328 *Koenigsblatt v Sweet* [1923] 2 Ch 314 at 325, per Lord Sterndale MR.

329 According to the underlying law, it was not possible for a company to ratify an *ultra vires* contract: *Ashbury Railway Carriage and Iron Co v Riche* (1875) LR 7 HL 653. The earlier abolition of the *ultra vires* doctrine by the *Companies Act* (Ch 146) (repealed), s 37 and its entrenchment by ss 17 and 18 of the Companies Act 1997, have overcome this inability.

330 Ratification is dealt with in more detail in Chapter 5 (Agency).

331 The directors may ratify if they have the power to do so, and a ratification may be implied from part performance made or permitted by the directors: *Reuter v Electric Telegraph Co* (1856) 6 E & B 341. If ratification is beyond the powers of the directors, it may effectively be ratified by the shareholders: *Spackman v Evans* (1868) LR 3 HL 171. This may be done by an ordinary resolution of the shareholders or by an informal meeting; some cases are authority for the proposition that a ratification by the shareholders may be implied if they can be regarded as having acquiesced in such an act with knowledge of the circumstances, even in the absence of a formal meeting: Davies, L, *Gower and Davies' Principles of Modern Company Law* (7th edn, Sweet & Maxwell, London, 2003), pp 437 ff.

332 *Watson v Davies* [1931] 1 Ch 455 In *Rainbow Holdings Pty Ltd v Central Province Forest Industries Pty Ltd* [1983] PNGLR 34, McDermott J referred to the fact that during Mr Davis's examination in chief, it had not been "suggested to him that ratification was a prerequisite before the agreement became binding", and so it was not possible for the appellants to argue that the agent entered into the agreement subject to its ratification by the principal.

In *Michael Yai Pupu v Tourism Development Corporation*,[333] Gavara-Nanu J adopted the threefold test established by Wright J in *Firth v Staines*,[334] where he said:

> To constitute a valid ratification, three conditions must be satisfied: first, the agent whose act is sought to be ratified must have purported to act for the principal; secondly, at the time the act was done, the agent must have had a competent principal;[335] and thirdly, at the time of the ratification the principal must be legally capable of doing the act himself.

At the time of the ratification, the principal must have full knowledge of all the material circumstances in which the act was done. Ratification may be express or implied. Ratification will be implied whenever the conduct of the person in whose name or on whose behalf the act or transaction was done or entered into is such as to amount to clear evidence that he adopts or recognises such act or transaction in whole or in part. It may be implied from the mere acquiescence or inactivity of the principal.[336] It must also take place within a reasonable time, and will not be recognised where it would unfairly prejudice a third party.

In *Johns v Thomason*,[337] the National Court held that the doctrine of ratification formed part of the underlying law of Papua New Guinea. In 1961 the appellant (Mrs Johns) made a short-call loan[338] to Alwin Finance Pty Ltd (Alwin). At the time of the loan, both Mrs Johns and her then husband, Mr Johns, were shareholders and directors of Alwin. In 1971 the company went into liquidation, and a liquidator was appointed. Mrs Johns (in a proof of debt to the liquidator),[339] claimed repayment of the personal loan

333 (2002) N2258.
334 [1897] 2 QB 70 at 75.
335 This requirement has been altered in respect of pre-incorporation contracts: Companies Act 1997, s 157.
336 Reynolds, F M B, *Bowstead and Reynolds on Agency* (17th edn, Sweet & Maxwell, London, 2001) para 2-070.
337 [1976] PNGLR 15.
338 A "short-call loan" is one that can be withdrawn on demand, i.e., without notice.
339 A proof of debt is a written claim by a creditor in a prescribed form containing details of the debt of a bankrupt or a company in liquidation. A creditor claiming out of the company's estate proves the debt by lodging a proof of debt with the liquidator and having it admitted by the liquidator. A proof of debt must usually give particulars of the debt, accord with the prescribed form, identify substantiating documents, and state whether or not the creditor is secured. Under the Companies Act (Ch 146) (repealed), s 55, it was provided that: "Every creditor must prove his debt or claim, unless the Court directs that any creditors or class of creditors be admitted without proof": cf *Re Glyn Wort* (1975) N20 and *Re Civic Constructions Pty Ltd* [1971–72] PNGLR 414. This is no longer required under the Companies Act 1997.

she had made to Alwin together with interest. The liquidator rejected the proof of debt and Mrs Johns appealed to the National Court against the rejection.

The above case, although involving a company, did not deal with the issue where the person who enters into the agreement, purports to do so on behalf of a company, and the company claims that it was made without its authority, and that no later action of the company ratified the contract. In a recent case, however, the National Court extended the doctrine of ratification to statutory corporations, and the case offers some guidance that similar rules are applicable to companies.

In *Michael Yai Pupu v Tourism Development Corporation*,[340] Gavara-Nanu J held that it is possible for a corporation to validate defective transactions, including those that are defective for want of authority from the board of directors or senior executive officers of the corporation. The learned judge held that *Johns v Thomason*,[341] which, as we have noted, held that the common law concept of ratification formed part of the underlying law of PNG, was correctly decided, and that its application ought to be extended to corporations: the doctrine "would be appropriate and applicable in the circumstances of this case". He said:[342]

> Ratification, is a common law doctrine, which was adopted in this jurisdiction by Frost CJ in *Johns v Thomason* [1976] PNGLR 15, where his Honour, held that, the doctrine is applicable and appropriate, pursuant to Schedule 2.2(1) of the *Constitution*, in circumstances whereby, an act which, at the time it was entered into or done by an agent, lacked the authority, express or implied, of a principal, [can] by the subsequent conduct of the principal become ratified, either by clear adoptive acts or by acquiescence equivalent thereto, accompanied by full knowledge of all essential facts by the principal and [be] made as effectively his own as if he had previously authorized it.

Gavara-Nanu J held that even if he was wrong in holding that Mr Jawa (a senior manager of the defendant) had actual or apparent (ostensible) authority from the corporation to enter into the contract with the plaintiff, the transfer of the artefacts to the corporation's premises "with the full knowledge of the defendant"[343] and their subsequent sale and the retention

340 (2002) N2258. Discussed above at p 429.

341 [1976] PNGLR 15.

342 (2002) N2258.

343 It would appear that, by reference to "the defendant", his Honour was referring to the corporations' senior employees or at least to its managing director. The judge did not go into exactly how the ratification was made. At several points, Gavara-Nanu J stated that the contract was ratified "by the defendant". At one stage, in discussing the third of the

of the proceeds of sale by the defendant, was "clear evidence or proof that, the defendant had by such subsequent adoptive acts ratified the negotiations and transactions between its employees or agents and the plaintiff". The defendant had therefore ratified the agreement for the sale of the artefacts made by its agents, and was therefore bound by the contract.

If a person purports to do something on behalf of a company without its actual or apparent authority, and the matter is not governed by s 19 or some other provision of the Companies Act 1997,[344] the company will not usually be bound. However, apart from these provisions, the company may ratify the actions of the purported agent. Ratification, as we have seen above, means that the company has adopted or confirmed the contract or agreement. If it does so, the company will be bound under the rules that apply to agency. The ratification has retrospective effect so that the company is taken to have approved the contract at the time it was entered into. Upon ratification, the company becomes bound by and is entitled to the benefit of the purported contract entered into on its behalf or for its benefit, if the company ratifies the contract within a reasonable time[345] of the unauthorised act.

The company may sign a document to that effect or the directors may pass a resolution ratifying the contract. If the unauthorised act is one that the board of directors had authority to perform, the board can ratify the agreement on behalf of the company by passing a board resolution to that effect[346] or by circular resolution under the Companies Act 1997.[347] If the act of ratifying the agreement is outside of the board's authority, the act will need to be ratified by the unanimous assent of the members in general meeting[348] or by unanimous informal assent (especially where the company has

three conditions that Wright J in *Firth v Staines* [1897] 2 QB 70 at 75 stated must be satisfied to constitute a valid ratification ("at the time of the ratification the principal must be legally capable of doing the act himself"), Gavara-Nanu J noted that "the actions binding the defendant were capable of being done by the defendant *through its employees*" (emphasis added), thereby referring to at least the managing director (chief executive officer of the authority appointed under s 24 of the Tourism Development Corporation Act 1990 (repealed)) and senior managers (e.g., marketing and promotions manager and others appointed under s 26). He stated: "In the circumstances of this case though, it is clear that, Mr Jawa's actions as well as those of other employees, were authorised or deemed to have been authorised by the defendant, [and] the defendant is thus bound by and liable to the plaintiff, for the transactions which emanated from those actions."

344 E.g., Companies Act 1997, ss 54(1)(b), 89, 118(3), 136, 154, 214.

345 *Hughes v NM Superannuation Board Pty Ltd* (1993) 29 NSWLR 653.

346 The company's constitution may require this to be done by an extra-ordinary resolution. Cf *Paul Torato v Sir Tei Abal* [1987] PNGLR 403. Unless the constitution provides otherwise, the resolution must be unanimous.

347 Companies Act 1997, s 138, Schedule 4.7(1).

348 Companies Act 1997, s 89. For this to happen, "*all* the shareholders of a company [must] agree".

few shareholders). Ratification may also be implied from the company's conduct. If, for example, the contract was for the purchase of goods, then payment of the purchase price or use of the goods by the company would constitute evidence that it had ratified the contract.[349]

Section 154 of the Companies Act 1997, deals with ratification of only "certain actions" of the directors or the board of a company. The provision is not extensive and the court ought not to hold that it codifies the law relating to ratification by companies. The equivalent provision in the New Zealand Companies Act 1993 has an additional subsection which, it has been argued, allows for the continuing application of the common law rules relating to ratification.[350] It could therefore be argued that the failure to include this subsection in the Companies Act 1997 means that the PNG provisions were meant to codify the rules relating to ratification and thereby not allow for the continued application of the underlying law relating to ratification.[351] It is suggested, however, that the courts ought not to so hold, given the fact that the section relating to ratification has limited effect, and to hold that it codifies the underlying law of ratification, will leave several situations that ought to be covered by ratification outside of the ambit of its operation.

349 Cf *Michael Yai Pupu v Tourism Development Corporation* (2002) N2258.

350 Section 177(4) of the Companies Act 1993 (New Zealand) provides as follows: "Nothing in this section limits or affects any rule of law relating to the ratification or approval by the shareholders or any other person of any act or omission of a director or the board of a company." Although some commentators state that the effect of this subsection is uncertain ("the intention appears to be that the common law rules relating to ratification of breaches of directors' duties are preserved, although whether this result is achieved is by no means certain": Beck, A and Borrowdale, A, *Guidebook to New Zealand Companies and Securities Law* (7th edn, CCH New Zealand Ltd, Auckland, 2002), para 320) others state the effect in more categorical terms: the "common law right of ratification of breaches by directors clearly survives": Watson, S, Gunasekara, G, Gedye, M, van Roy, Y, Ross, M, Longdin, L, Sims, A and Brown, L, *The Law of Business Organisations* (4th edn, Palatine Press, Auckland, 2003), para 13.05.4.

351 Cf Companies Act 1997, s 157, which deals with ratification of pre-incorporation contracts.

Chapter 12

Shares and Company Financing

Introduction

As we saw in Chapter 10 (Introduction), owning a share in the share capital of a company does not give a member any rights to defined or specific property owned by the company. All that it does is to give a shareholder a general claim against the company.[1] A share is a chose in action, i.e., "personal property,"[2] which confers rights and obligations on the shareholder. Shares entitle the holder to certain rights in the company, such as the right to be paid dividends (a distribution), to attend meetings, to vote on issues affecting the company, and a right to share in any surplus when the company is liquidated, that is, when it is wound up.[3] These rights and duties arise from the underlying law, the company's constitution, and the Companies Act 1997.

The share facilitates distribution among members of financial benefits such as the payment of dividends while the company is operating, and distribution of any surplus on a winding up. It also allows membership rights to be allocated, such as rights to vote at company meetings. So a person with more shares *usually* has more voting rights than a person with less shares. Also certain classes of shares may not have voting rights attached to them, or voting rights only for special purposes. The share also limits the liability of the shareholder: once the share is paid for, this is normally the limit of the liability of the shareholder to contribute towards the expenses of the company. Even if the company runs into debts, a shareholder is under no requirement to pay any further sums to the company. The shareholder's liability is limited to pay for the value of the shares and no more. If the shareholder does this, he or she is usually no longer liable to pay any further money to the company in respect of those shares.

Companies rely on their capital to operate and expand their business. Capital is a term used to describe the money belonging to the company that it may use to finance its business. Capital is divided into equity capital and

1 *Macaura v Northern Assurance Co Ltd* [1925] AC 619.

2 Companies Act 1997, s 36.

3 *Borland's Trustee v Steel Bros & Co Ltd* [1901] 1 Ch 279 at 288.

loan capital. Equity capital is the money derived from the payment for shares by members of the company (shareholders). Loan capital, on the other hand, is money obtained from borrowing money from banks and other financial institutions (lenders), which must at some stage be repaid, usually together with interest. Companies may also use their savings (profits) made in the operation of the business to expand their business.

Before the enactment of the Companies Act 1997, share capital was an important concept. Companies were limited to the amount of shares they could issue. This was called authorised share capital. The issued share capital was the amount of shares *actually* issued. Now, however, since the Companies Act 1997, there is no limit on the number of shares that a company may issue and there is no need for it to have a statement of its authorised share capital.[4]

Shares

Section 37 of the Companies Act 1997 sets out these rights, stating that unless altered by the company's constitution, a share in a company confers on the shareholder:

- the right to one vote on a poll at a meeting of the company on any resolution;
- the right to an equal share in dividends authorised by the board;[5]
- the right to an equal share in the distribution of the surplus assets of the company.[6]

The types of issues that a shareholder may vote on include the power to:[7]

- appoint or remove a director or auditor;
- adopt a constitution;
- alter the company's constitution, where it has one;
- approve a major transaction;[8]
- approve an amalgamation of the company under s 234;
- put the company into liquidation.

4 Companies Act 1997, ss 175, 222(1)(b), 219, Schedule 14.
5 Cf Companies Act 1997, s 51(2).
6 This refers to surplus assets when the company is deregistered or liquidated (wound up). See Chapter 14 (Liquidation).
7 Companies Act 1997, s 37(1)(a).
8 A "major transaction" has the meaning set out in s 110(2) of the Companies Act 1997. In short, it includes an acquisition of, or an agreement to acquire, whether contingent or not, assets the value of which is more than half the value of the assets of the company before the acquisition; or the disposition of, or an agreement to dispose of, whether contingent or not, assets of the company the value of which is more than half the value of the assets of the company before the disposition.

Companies in respect of which shares are issued

Shares are issued for:

- companies limited by shares;
- unlimited liability companies;[9]
- no liability companies;[10]
- companies limited by guarantee.[11]

An unlimited liability company or a company limited by guarantee, does not require a share capital.

Section 16(2) of the Companies Act 1997 states that a company may be:

(a) a company limited by shares; or
(b) a company limited by guarantee; or
(c) a company limited both by shares and by guarantee; or
(d) an unlimited company; or
(e) in the case of a mining company, a no liability company.

The nature of company shares

Initially, a share in a company enabled the shareholder to be treated as the beneficial owner of the property or assets of the company: the company held its assets in trust for the shareholders. However, from the early nineteenth century, the courts began to treat shareholders as having no direct interest in the company's assets. Courts began to define the share in terms of the right to a dividend, to the return of capital on the winding up of a company and to vote. In *Peters' American Delicacy Co Ltd v Heath*,[12] Dixon J described a share in a company as: "Primarily a . . . piece of property conferring rights in relation to distributions of income and of capital." The share is now regarded more as a bundle of rights, and property, and in a large public company, more in the nature of an investment.[13]

It has been argued that a share gives the shareholder an "interest *in* the company".[14] However, this is misleading if it means the shareholder has an interest in the company's property. This is not so until the company is wound up, its debts and liabilities paid and remaining assets transferred to shareholders.

9 Companies Act 1997, ss 11(c), 79(2), 80(3), 81(5)(c), Schedule 14(e) and (f).

10 A "limited company" means a company limited by shares or by guarantee or both by shares and guarantee, but does not include a no liability company;

11 Companies Act 1997, Schedule 14(e) and (f).

12 (1939) 61 CLR 457 at 503–504.

13 *Mellon v Alliance Textiles Ltd* (1987) 3 NZCLC 100,086, per Hardie Boys J at 100,092.

14 See *Borland's Trustee v Steel Bros & Co* [1901] 1 Ch 279 at 288, per Farwell J.

Prima facie, a share carries with it three principal rights: (i) the right to a dividend out of profits, when a dividend is declared; (ii) a right to participate in a distribution of the company's capital on winding up (to a return of capital on a winding up if the company has enough assets after discharging (paying off) its debts); (iii) and perhaps most importantly, a right to participate in decisions taken by the company in general meeting (to attend company meetings and to vote). Rights in a share, however, are determined by the constitution of the company and the particular terms upon which the share was issued. So the presumption can be rebutted or varied and it is possible for a company to issue shares that have no voting rights, or have no rights to participate in a distribution on winding up or that have preferential rights to dividends.

Rights attaching to shares

Section 37 of the Companies Act 1997 provides that, subject to subsection (2), a share in a company confers on the holder:

- the right to one vote on a poll at a meeting of the company on any resolution, including any resolution to:
  - appoint or remove a director or auditor;
  - adopt a constitution;
  - alter the company's constitution, where it has one;
  - approve a major transaction;
  - approve an amalgamation of the company under s 234;
  - put the company into liquidation;
- the right to an equal share in dividends authorised by the board
- the right to an equal share in the distribution of the surplus assets of the company.

Section 37(2) provides that, subject to s 51, the rights specified in subsection (1) may be negated, altered, or added to by the constitution of the company.

Classes of shares and class rights

There is a presumption that the shares of the company carry the same rights and obligations.[15] However, this presumption may be rebutted either by the clear language in the company's constitution or by the particular terms on which the shares are issued, i.e., the resolution of the board authorising the issue of shares. A company may therefore issue shares with different rights and different obligations. The authority to issue different classes of shares is confirmed by s 38 of the Companies Act 1997. That section provides that, subject to the constitution of the company, different classes[16] of shares may be issued

15 *Birch v Cropper* (1889) 14 App Cas 525.

16 Companies Act 1997, s 97(1): "class" means a class of shares having attached to them identical rights, privileges, limitations, and conditions."

in the company. Subsection (2) goes on to provide that, without limiting subsection (1), shares in a company may be redeemable within the meaning of s 59,[17] confer preferential rights to distributions of capital or income,[18] confer special, limited, or conditional voting rights,[19] or not confer voting rights.[20]

The company may decide to issue different classes of shares containing different rights for a variety of reasons. It may enable the company to attract a greater range of investors, as the company can structure its shares to the preferences of a wider range of investors. Different class of shares may be issued to give effect to and reinforce particular constitutional arrangements: for example, shares with no voting rights or with greater voting rights may be issued to allow certain family members or shareholders to enjoy a financial return from the company without necessarily affecting control of the company. (The constitution of the company may provide that the particular class of shares is to carry greater voting rights than other classes of shares.)

Common classifications of shares include:

- ordinary shares;
- preference shares;
- participating preference shares;
- redeemable preference shares;
- converting preference shares;
- deferred or founders' shares;
- cumulative or non-cumulative shares;
- deferred shares.

Ordinary shares

Shares which have ordinary rights and which rank after preference shares are known as "ordinary shares".[21] These are the default shares in a company. In the past, such shares had a nominal or par value, e.g. K1. The Companies Act 1997 now provides that a share shall not have a nominal or par value.[22] The rights which automatically attach to ordinary shares are set out in s 37(1) of the Companies Act 1997:

> (a) the right to one vote on a poll at a meeting of the company on any resolution, including any resolution to–
> (i) appoint or remove a director or auditor; or
> (ii) adopt a constitution; or

17 Companies Act 1997, s 38(2).
18 Companies Act 1997, s 38(2)(b).
19 Companies Act 1997, s 38(2)(c).
20 Companies Act 1997, s 38(2)(d).
21 If a company's shares are not differentiated, they are called ordinary shares. If differentiated, then the other shares are ordinary shares.
22 Companies Act 1997, s 39(1).

(iii) alter the company's constitution, where it has one; or
(iv) approve a major transaction; or
(v) approve an amalgamation of the company under Section 234; or
(vi) put the company into liquidation; and

(b) the right to an equal share in dividends authorised by the board; and
(c) the right to an equal share in the distribution of the surplus assets of the company.

Subsection (1) is subject to subsection 2, which in turn is subject to s 51. The latter section states that the rights specified in s 37(1) "may be negated, altered, or added to by the constitution of the company".

Preference shares

These types of shares arise when one class of holder is not to be paid a dividend in any year unless the holders of a preferred class have been paid a certain minimum dividend in that year. The shares carrying priority to dividend payment are called preference shares and the other types of shares are ordinary shares. The Companies Act 1997 does not define what a preference share is.[23] A preference share is a share that gives its holder some right or preference (e.g., a guaranteed minimum dividend entitlement) not enjoyed by the holder of the share of another type. The rights of preference shares are set out in the constitution of the company, or the instrument(s) creating the preference shares, usually a board resolution, a company resolution or a contract of allotment of shares (or a combination of the three). A series of rights with respect to preference shares which must be set out in the instrument(s) creating the preference shares. These rights include repayment of capital, participation in surplus profits and assets, dividends, voting and priority of payment of capital and dividends. The constitution does not have to set out the rights. It is sufficient if the constitution provided for these to be detailed in some other instrument, such as the resolution issuing the shares.[24] If the company does not have a constitution, the terms of the issue of preference shares should be set out in a special resolution of members of the company.

The rights attaching to preference shares will vary, even within the same company. Most preference shares, however, will give the holder a preferential right to the repayment of dividend. In this regard, preference shares may be cumulative or non-cumulative as to dividend. If the shares are cumulative, the shareholder is entitled to a fixed rate of return regardless of whether profits

23 The repealed Companies Act (Ch 146) expressly referred to preference shares: see ss 63 and 68.
24 *TNT Australia Pty Ltd v Normandy Resources NL* (1989) 7 ACLC 1090.

are made or not. If in one year the entire dividend cannot be paid because the company did not make sufficient profits, the amount which is not paid is carried forward into the following year and must be paid first, before any other dividends are paid. Furthermore, a preference shareholder usually has a right to rank in priority to ordinary shareholders when the company is wound up or liquidated. They have a preferred right to be paid surplus assets. Voting rights attached to preference shares are also limited. In this respect it is almost as if the preference shareholder is a creditor of the company rather than a shareholder. In the past it was held that preference shares were prima facie exhaustive, in that preference shareholders enjoyed only such rights as were expressly stated in the constitution or terms of the issue of the share: the court would not imply rights other than those expressly given in the shares.[25] Section 37 of the Companies Act 1997 seems to have overturned this presumption, especially when compared with the New Zealand equivalent. Section 37(1) states that subject to subsection (2), a share confers on the shareholder certain rights, including the right to an equal share in dividends authorised by the board and the right to an equal share in the distribution of the surplus assets of the company. Subsection (2) then states that "the rights specified in Subsection (1) may be negated, altered, or added to by the constitution of the company". The New Zealand equivalent goes further and provides that not only may the rights be altered by the constitution of the company, but also "in accordance with the terms on which the share is issued" and also under various sections of the Companies Act 1993 (NZ).[26] The mere creation of preferential rights should not automatically make those rights exhaustive.

Furthermore, there is even doubt whether preferential shares may be granted without the company adopting a constitution which expressly confers this power.

Section 43(2) of the Companies Act 1997 provides:

> (1) Where the board authorises the issue of shares which confer rights other than those set out in Section 37(1), or which impose any obligation on the holder, the board shall approve terms of issue which set out the rights and obligations attached to the shares.
>
> (3) Terms of issue approved by the board under Subsection (2):
>
> (a) shall be consistent with the constitution of the company, and to the extent that they are not so consistent are invalid and of no effect; and
>
> (b) are deemed to form part of the constitution, and may be amended in accordance with Section 33.

25 *Re Isle of Thanet Electricity Supply Co Ltd* [1950] Ch 161; *Scottish Insurance Corporation Ltd v Wilsons and Clyde Coal Co Ltd* [1949] AC 462.

26 Companies Act 1993 (New Zealand), ss 41(b), 42, 44, 107(2).

This section reinforces the view that the terms of s 37 will continue to apply to preference shares unless expressly stated otherwise. The courts will not imply that the terms of issue are exhaustive of the rights of such preference shareholders.

Two other types of preference shares are participating preference shares and redeemable preference shares. Participating preference shares allow the shareholder not only to enjoy a right to preferential rights to dividends and repayment on liquidation, but also share in distributions made to ordinary shareholders. Redeemable preference shares are subject to redemption (i.e., being bought out) on a specified date or whenever the company decides to do so.

Deferred or founders shares

Deferred shares are so called because the right to dividends is deferred until dividends of a particular (prescribed) amount (minimum dividend) has been paid to ordinary shareholders. These shares (also called founders' shares) are usually awarded to promoters or founders of a company to reward them for their work in forming the company, and they are an indication of their faith in the profitability of the company.

The Companies Act (Ch 146) (Schedule 4, Part 1) specifically referred to "founders" or "deferred" shares. Although there is no reference at all in the Companies Act 1997 or the Companies Regulation 1998 to "founders" or "deferred" shares, there is nothing to prevent a company from dealing with such shares in a constitution adopted by the company, or in a resolution of the board of directors.

Issue of Shares

A share is normally "issued" when the name of the holder is entered on the share register.[27] And the general rule is that, subject to the Companies Act 1997 and the constitution of the company (if any), the board of a company may authorise the issue of shares at any time, to any person, and in any number it thinks fit.[28]

When a company is first formed, the application will state the number of shares to be issued to each person. Section 42(a) provides that a company must "forthwith after the registration of the company, issue to any person or persons named in the application for registration as a shareholder or

27 Companies Act 1997, s 49(1). This applies to both first shareholders (whose names are on the application to register the company) and later shareholders. The date of issue may be another date if the Registrar of Companies provides so in an applicable exemption given under s 77(1) of the Companies Act 1997.

28 Companies Act 1997, s 43(1).

shareholders, the number of shares specified in the application as being the number of shares to be issued to that person or those persons".

With regard to later shares, prospective shareholders will offer to acquire a certain amount of shares. The board of directors may then accept that offer by authorising the issue of the shares. The shares are then allotted[29] to those persons and the shares will eventually be issued to or registered in their name.

Consideration for the issue or allotment of shares

The consideration for which a share is issued may take any form and may be cash, promissory notes, contracts for future services, real or personal property, or other securities of the company.[30] In respect of share issued following incorporation or amalgamation, the board of directors must comply with certain formalities regarding consideration set out in the Companies Act 1997. Section 47 provides that before the board of a company issues shares it must:

- decide the consideration for which the shares will be issued; and
- resolve that, in its opinion, the consideration for and terms of the issue are fair and reasonable to the company and to all existing shareholders.[31]

The purpose of these requirements is to protect the company from the shares being issued for an inadequate consideration.[32]

Shares must be paid for. Consideration must be valuable consideration at law. As such, a company must receive either cash or assets equivalent in value for shares issued to shareholders.[33] It can be a transfer of particular property or a promise of services to the company. Where payment for shares is consideration other than cash, it must be sufficient consideration according to contract law principles. It must also not be "a mere blind, or clearly colourable or illusory . . .".[34] The issue will usually arise when a company is being wound up and the liquidator alleges that the shares are

29 I.e., set apart or appropriated to a particular person.

30 Companies Act 1997, s 46.

31 The directors who vote in favour of such a resolution must "forthwith" sign a certificate (a) stating the consideration for the issue of the shares, and (b) stating that, in their opinion, the consideration for the issue is fair and reasonable to the company and to all existing shareholders: Companies Act 1997, s 47(2). See note 38 for definition of term "forthwith".

32 This provision supersedes the underlying law rules that shares could not be issued at a discount upon their nominal or par value: *Ooregum Gold Mining Co of India Ltd v Roper* [1892] AC 125; *Re Wragg Ltd* [1897] 1 Ch 796.

33 *Ooregum Gold Mining Co of India Ltd v Roper* [1892] AC 125.

34 *Re White Star Line Ltd* [1938] Ch 458.

not fully paid. Consideration must be money's worth for allotment.[35] However, the courts have taken a permissive attitude to the directors' estimation of the value of non-cash consideration, provided estimation is bona fide.[36] To prevent abuses, s 42(a) of the Companies Act 1997 provides that a company shall forthwith, after the registration of the company, issue to any person or persons named in the application for registration as a shareholder or shareholders, the number of shares specified in the application as being the number of shares to be issued to that person or those persons.

Section 49 provides that, except as otherwise provided in any applicable exemption given by the Registrar of Companies under s 77[37] of the Companies Act 1997, "a share is issued when the name of the holder is entered on the share register".[38]

Pre-emptive rights

Section 45 of the Companies Act 1997 provides for pre-emptive rights. If new classes of shares are created following the establishment of a company, shareholders may find that this erodes their power in the company. Because of this, the Companies Act 1997 gives existing shareholders a right to participate in the new issue of shares in order to help maintain their power. The right to participate (the right of pre-emption) applies when shares issued or proposed to be issued by a company that rank or would rank as to voting or distribution rights, or both, equally with or prior to shares already issued by the company. If this is so, then the board must offer the new shares to the holders of the shares already issued "in a manner and on terms that would, if the offer were accepted, maintain the existing voting or distribution rights, or both, of those holders".[39] The offer must remain open for acceptance for a reasonable time.[40]

Shares may also be altered by "the terms of issue of the share".

35 Companies Act 1997, s 42(a); *Re White Star Line* [1938] 1 All ER 607.
36 *Re Wragg Ltd* [1897] 1 Ch 796.
37 Section 77 of the Companies Act 1997 is very wide, giving the Registrar of Companies, as it does, the power "by notice in writing, and on such terms and conditions as the Registrar thinks fit", power to exempt from any or all of several provisions, including those regarding the issuing of shares, to (a) any company or class of companies, or (b) in respect of any transaction or class of transactions.
38 Note that this differs from when a share is "allotted". Also note that according to the underlying law, the shares of first shareholders was issued to them when the company was registered: *Dalton Time Lock Co v Dalton* (1892) 66 LT 704. Now, unless the Registrar of Companies provides otherwise, first shareholders and subsequent shareholders are issued shares at the same time, i.e., when their names are entered on the share register.
39 Companies Act 1997, s 45(1). The constitution of a company may negate, limit, or modify the requirements of s 45: see s 45(3).
40 Companies Act 1997, s 45(2).

Share options

Section 41 of the Companies Act 1997 provides for contracts for the issue of shares, or share options. Section 41(1) provides that a contract or deed under which a company is or may be required to issue shares whether on the exercise of an option or on the conversion of securities or otherwise is "unlawful and void" unless the board:

- has authorised the issue of the shares under s 43; and
- has complied with s 47 (which requires the board to approve consideration and resolve that, in its opinion, the consideration for and terms of the issue are fair and reasonable to the company and to all existing shareholders).

Usually, the option to purchase the shares must be strictly complied with as regards the time within which it must be exercised and the terms and conditions.

Distributions

The law of distributions, including the payment of dividends, has been completely rewritten. Section 2(1) of the Companies Act 1997 defines a distribution as follows:

> "distribution", in relation to a distribution by a company to a shareholder, means –
> (a) the direct or indirect transfer of money or property, other than the company's own shares, to or for the benefit of the shareholder; or
> (b) the incurring of a debt to or for the benefit of the shareholder, in relation to shares held by that shareholder, and whether by means of a purchase of property, the redemption or other acquisition of shares, a distribution of indebtedness, or by some other means;"

Thus, distributions occur when a company transfers money or other assets to its shareholders before liquidation. Distributions can be in the form of:

- dividends;
- repurchase by the company of its own shares;
- redemption by the company of its own shares;
- provision of financial assistance by the company for the purchase of its own shares.

Before the commencement of the Companies Act 1997, the law dealt with distributions to shareholders in a disorganised way. Capital could be returned to shareholders if the court agreed to this, and the rules relating to what constituted dividends and their payment was difficult to comprehend. The Companies Act 1997 now attempts to bring some order to this jumbled area and deal with the law under one topic called "distributions". The main concern of these rules is to allow for distribution (whether of capital or dividends) only where the company can satisfy the solvency test. The assumption is that the shareholders and creditors of a company will be protected if a distribution can be made and if once made, the company remains solvent. As Beck and Borrowdale point out:[41]

> Before the [Companies Act 1997] came into force, the law dealt with distributions to shareholders in a fragmentary fashion. Capital could be returned to shareholders only by way of a reduction of capital which required an order of the Court. Under the common law numerous rules evolved for the payment of dividends to shareholders. Apart from the common goal of these rules, statutory and common law, to preserve the capital of the company for the protection of creditors and minority shareholders (the so-called capital maintenance doctrine), there was little to connect them.
>
> Under the Companies Act 1997 the various distributions which may be made are subject to a body of rules set out in the statute. The most important of these is the requirement that the solvency test is satisfied before the distribution is made. This is a novel concept borrowed from North American corporate law. It is based on the premise that creditors and shareholders are protected if a distribution can only be made if it leaves the company solvent.

The most common type of distribution continues to be a cash payment to shareholders called dividends. Within the Companies Act 1997, a dividend is described as all distributions except the company acquiring its own shares and a company giving financial assistance. When paying a dividend, unless it is calculated on the amounts paid upon shares or unless certain shareholders have waived their rights to dividends or the constitution specifically provides otherwise, dividends of the same amount must be paid on all shares in a class.[42] The power of the board to pay dividends may, however, be restricted in the constitution.[43]

Before the Companies Act 1997, the rules concerning the payment of dividends were found in the repealed Companies Act (Ch 146) (in particular s 388) and case law. In essence, the law required that dividends could be paid

41 Beck, A and Borrowdale, A, *Papua New Guinea Companies and Securities Law Guide* (CCH Australia Ltd, Sydney, 1999), para 514.
42 Companies Act 1997, s 51.
43 Companies Act 1997, s 50(1).

only out of income or profits, not capital.[44] The New Zealand Law Commission considered that it was essential to reform the "very complicated rules relating to payment of dividends".[45] It considered that the law was unclear, drew artificial distinctions and was generally unsatisfactory, and was of the view that the rules should be replaced by a solvency test such as that adopted in several Canadian or US jurisdictions.[46]

The Companies Act 1997 has made substantial reforms to the rules relating to the payment of dividends, further relaxing the application of the capital maintenance doctrine to dividends. The Act, in essence, provides that, so long as the company is solvent and will remain solvent after the payment of dividends (referred to in the Act as one type of "distribution"), the directors may pay such dividends as they consider appropriate. Directors are therefore no longer restricted to paying dividends out of profits; they may now pay dividends out of capital as well as out of profits.

Section 50(1) of the Companies Act 1997 sets out the basic rule relating to distributions: the board of a company that is satisfied on reasonable grounds that the company will, immediately after the distribution, satisfy the solvency test may, subject to Section 51 and the constitution of the company, authorise a distribution by the company at a time, and of an amount, and to any shareholders it thinks fit. The essential condition is whether the board can satisfy the "solvency test" following the distribution.

The solvency test[47]

The solvency test is set out in the Companies Act 1997 and contains two separate components: "liquidity" and "balance sheet" tests. A company must satisfy both components in order to satisfy the solvency test. The liquidity component (also referred to as "trading solvency") requires a company to be able to pay its debts as they become due in the ordinary[48] course

44 Section 388(2) of the Companies Act (Ch 146) (repealed) provided that: "A dividend is not payable to the shareholders of a company except out of profits or in accordance with Section 62."

45 New Zealand Law Commission, *Company Law: Preliminary Paper No 5 (A Discussion Paper)* (Law Commission, Wellington, New Zealand, 1987), para 87.

46 New Zealand Law Commission, *Company Law: Preliminary Paper No 5 (A Discussion Paper)* (Law Commission, Wellington, New Zealand, 1987), paras 88–91.

47 For an excellent analysis of this area of the law, see Haynes, C I, "The Solvency Test: A New Era in Directorial Responsibility" (1996) 8 *Auckland University Law Review* 125–141. See also Ross, M, *Corporate Reconstructions: Strategies for Directors* (CCH New Zealand, Auckland, 1999), Ch 7; Ross, M, "The Statutory Solvency Test", in Borrowdale, A, Rowe, D and Taylor, L (eds), *Company Law Writings: A New Zealand Collection* (Centre for Commercial and Corporate Law Inc, School of Law, University of Canterbury, 2002), pp 177–202.

48 The New Zealand provision refers to "*normal* course of business". The provision was based on s 6.40(c)(1) of the American Model Business Corporations Act, which uses the

of business.[49] The balance sheet requirement demands that the company's assets must be of greater value than its liabilities, including contingent liabilities.[50] This part of the test refers to "balance sheet solvency". In order to arrive at a decision whether the company has a balance sheet solvency at the date of distribution (i.e., whether the value of a company's assets is greater than the value of its liabilities, including contingent liabilities), the directors are required to have regard to (i.e. they *must* have regard to) two factors:[51]

- the most recent financial statements of the company that comply with s 179; and
- all other circumstances that the directors know or ought to know affect, or may affect, the value of the company's assets and the value of its liabilities, including its contingent liabilities.

In addition, the directors *may* rely on valuations of assets or estimates of liabilities that are reasonable in the circumstances.[52]

The terms "debts" and "liabilities" have specific meanings when used in discussion of the solvency test. Debts *include* fixed preferential returns on shares ranking ahead of those in respect of which a distribution is made (except where that fixed preferential return is expressed in the constitution as being subject to the power of the directors to make distributions), but does not include debts arising by reason of the authorisation.[53] Liabilities *include* the amount that would be required, if the company were to be removed from the register after the distribution, to repay all fixed preferential amounts payable by the company to shareholders, at that time, or on earlier redemption (except where such fixed preferential amounts are expressed in the constitution as being subject to the power of directors to make distributions); but, subject to para (a), does not include dividends payable in the future.[54]

term "*usual* course of business". (See *Model Business Corporation Act* (3rd edn, Revised through 2002, adopted by the Committee on Corporate Laws of the Section of Business Law with support of the American Bar Foundation.) Some analysts found it unusual that the phrase "ordinary course of business" was not adopted in New Zealand, given the fact that there was considerable New Zealand case law on the meaning of that phrase (see, e.g., Haynes, C I, "The Solvency Test: A New Era in Directorial Responsibility" (1996) 8 *Auckland University Law Review* 125 at 130) and this may have led the drafters of the Companies Act 1997 to adopt this phrase.

49 Companies Act 1997, s 4(1)(a).

50 Companies Act 1997, s 4(1)(b). In determining the value of a contingent liability, "account may be taken of (a) the likelihood of the contingency occurring; and (b) any claim that the company is entitled to make and can reasonably expect to be met to reduce or extinguish the contingent liability": Companies Act 1997, s 4(4).

51 Companies Act 1997, s 4(2)(a).

52 Companies Act 1997, s 4(2)(b).

53 Companies Act 1997, s 50(4)(a).

54 Companies Act 1997, s 50(4)(b).

It should be noted that the time at which the solvency test must be satisfied is the time of distribution and not the time of authorising the distribution.[55] If, between the time of authorisation and the time of distribution, the company for some reason ceases to satisfy the test, the distribution should not be made, as it would be invalid. Where, after a distribution is authorised and before it is made, the board ceases to be satisfied on reasonable grounds that the company will, immediately after the distribution is made, satisfy the solvency test, any distribution made by the company is deemed not to have been authorised.[56]

The power to make a distribution is made subject to any contrary terms in the constitution, and to s 51 of the Companies Act 1997, which deals with dividends.

The distribution[57] may be made to shareholders only, and the directors who vote in favour of a distribution must "forthwith sign a certificate stating that, in their opinion, the company will, immediately after the distribution, satisfy the solvency test". They must also state the grounds for that opinion.[58]

A company may recover a distribution made to a shareholder if, immediately after the distribution, it fails to satisfy the solvency test. However, a shareholder may be able to resist recovery if he or she can show:

- the shareholder received the distribution in good faith and without knowledge of the company's failure to satisfy the solvency test; and
- the shareholder has altered his or her position in reliance on the validity of the distribution; and
- it would be unfair to require repayment in full or at all.

If the company cannot recover all or some of the distribution from the shareholder, it may recover the amount from a director personally in any of the following circumstances:

- where the director failed to take reasonable steps to ensure that the proper procedure was followed;[59]
- reasonable grounds for believing that the company would satisfy the solvency test did not exist at the time the relevant resolution was passed, and the director voted in favour of the resolution;[60]

55 *Nelson v Rentown Enterprises Inc* (1992) 96 DLR (4th) 586.
56 Companies Act 1997, s 50(3).
57 Distribution is defined in s 2(1) of the Companies Act 1997 as "the direct or indirect transfer of money or property, other than the company's own shares, to or for the benefit of the shareholder; or the incurring of a debt to or for the benefit of the shareholder, in relation to shares held by that shareholder, and whether by means of a purchase of property, the redemption or other acquisition of shares, a distribution of indebtedness, or by some other means".
58 Companies Act 1997, s 50(2).
59 Companies Act 1997, s 54(2)(a) and (c).
60 Companies Act 1997, s 54(2)(b) and (d).

- where, after the authorisation of the distribution, the board and the director cease to be satisfied on reasonable grounds that the company will, immediately after the distribution is made, satisfy the solvency test, and the director fails to take reasonable steps to prevent the distribution being made;
- where a discount is accepted by a shareholder under a scheme approved or continued by the board and at the time the scheme was approved or the discount was offered, the board ceased to be satisfied on reasonable grounds that the company would satisfy the solvency test, and the director fails to take reasonable steps to prevent the distribution being made.

In all of these circumstances, the court may take into account that the distribution of a lesser amount may not have caused the company to be insolvent, and in effect, give a credit to the director in the amount which could legitimately have been distributed.[61]

The underlying law rules allowed a company to recover from shareholders a dividend which was improperly paid out of capital where the shareholders knew or ought to have known that the payment was improperly made.[62] It seems that the repayment can be ordered even where the improper payment did not cause the company to become insolvent.[63] As such, the underlying law permitted a greater range of recovery. Because the provisions of the Companies Act 1997 dealing with distributions appear to be a code, it is suggested that the underlying law no longer applies and recovery is dependent on the payment leading to breach of the underlying law solvency test.

Section 54 sets out circumstances where the director becomes personally liable when the distribution was improperly made, and recovery from a shareholder cannot be made. In such cases recovery is limited to situations where the company breached the insolvency test. According to the underlying law, however, an action can be brought against the director for not exercising "the care, diligence, and skill that a reasonable director would exercise".[64] The director may be liable where there is no technical breach of the solvency test, but where the director in authorising the payment of a dividend, jeopardises the solvency of the company by the payment.[65] Even if the provisions relating to distributions form a code, there is no reason why an action cannot still be taken against such directors, as the breach is not to one of the sections dealing with distributions, but to a separate provision dealing with directors' duties.[66]

61 Companies Act 1997, s 54(5).
62 *Hilton International Ltd (in liq) v Hilton* [1989] 1 NZLR 442 at 479.
63 *Segenhoe Ltd v Akins* (1990) 8 ACLC 263.
64 Companies Act 1997, s 115.
65 *Hilton International Ltd (in liq) v Hilton* [1989] 1 NZLR 442 at 475.
66 As to whether the directors' duties provisions form a code, see Chapter 9.

Issue of shares instead of dividends

Unless specifically prohibited in the constitution of a company, shares may be issued instead of a dividend. The offer of shares must be made in such proportions that, if all shareholders accept, relative voting and distribution rights will remain the same, and the same offer must be made to all shareholders of a class. Shareholders must be given reasonable opportunity to accept.[67] Before issuing shares in lieu of a dividend, the board must resolve that the terms of the issue are fair and reasonable to the company and all existing shareholders and resolve that the cash value of the dividend is not less than the value of the shares. Directors voting in favour of the resolution must sign a certificate giving details of the consideration for and terms of the issue and state these are fair and reasonable to the company and existing shareholders.[68] Section 50(2) of the Companies Act 1997 provides that the directors who vote in favour of a distribution must forthwith sign a certificate stating that, in their opinion, the company will, immediately after the distribution, satisfy the solvency test and the grounds for that opinion.[69] The directors will also need to comply with all the provisions relating to the issue of shares discussed below.

Shareholder discount schemes

The Companies Act 1997 gives authority for the establishment of shareholder discount schemes. These may be instituted only if the board of directors is satisfied that they are fair and reasonable to the company and shareholders, and available on the same terms to all shareholders of a class.[70] As an alternative procedure, provided the company will continue to pass a solvency test, a discount scheme may be approved by the unanimous agreement of all shareholders.[71]

A scheme cannot be approved or continued if the company does not satisfy the solvency test.[72] A discount which should not have been given may be recovered in the same way as an unauthorised distribution if the board ceases to be satisfied on reasonable grounds that the company would satisfy the solvency test.[73]

67 Companies Act 1997, s 52.
68 Companies Act 1997, s 47.
69 See also Companies Act 1997, s 75(2) and (3).
70 Companies Act 1997, s 53(2).
71 Companies Act 1997, s 89(1) and (2)(a), (b).
72 Companies Act 1997, s 53(3).
73 Companies Act 1997, s 53(4).

Dividend as a debt

According to the underlying law, a final dividend[74] created an immediate debt when it was declared in general meeting,[75] unless there was a statement of a later date for payment, in which cases the debt arose then.[76]

It is suggested that the underlying law rules in these situations continue to operate, so that a shareholder is not entitled to sue for a final dividend until it is authorised by the board or by the shareholders in general meeting (where the constitution or terms of the issue provide for this).

Shares instead of dividends

Subject to the constitution, the board of directors may issue shares to any shareholders who have agreed to accept the issue of shares, wholly or partly, instead of a proposed dividend or proposed future dividends.[77] The company may issue the shares provided that the following prerequisites are fulfilled:[78]

- the right to receive shares, wholly or partly, in lieu of the proposed dividend or proposed future dividends has been offered to all shareholders of the same class on the same terms;
- if all shareholders elected to receive the shares in lieu of the proposed dividend, relative voting or distribution rights, or both, would be maintained;
- the shareholders to whom the right is offered are afforded a reasonable opportunity of accepting it;
- the shares issued to each shareholder are issued on the same terms and subject to the same rights as the shares issued to all shareholders in that class who agree to receive the shares;
- the provisions of s 47 (relating to consideration for the issue of shares) are complied with by the board.

74 The law drew a distinction between the declaration of interim and final dividends. An interim dividend was an estimated or provisional dividend, the declaration of which did not give rise to an enforceable debt: *Marra Developments Ltd v BW Rofe Pty Ltd* [1977] 2 NSWLR 616; *Potel v Inland Revenue Commissioners* [1971] 2 All ER 504. As such, it could be revoked at any time before payment.

75 *Re Severn and Wye and Severn Bridge Railway Co* [1896] 1 Ch 559; *Marra Developments Ltd v BW Rofe Pty Ltd* [1977] 2 NSWLR 616.

76 *Potel v Inland Revenue Commissioners* [1971] 2 All ER 504 at 511.

77 Companies Act 1997, s 52. The transfer of shares instead of a dividend is not a "distribution" for the purposes of the Act: s 2(1) definition "distribution". The solvency test does not therefore have to be satisfied before a distribution of shares instead of dividends.

78 Companies Act 1997, s 52(a) to (e). It would appear that the company's constitution may alter these prerequisites.

Repurchase of shares

The Companies Act 1997 provides much simpler and easier rules relating to the repurchase of shares by a company. The underlying law rule in *Trevor v Whitworth*[79] prevented a company from acquiring its own shares. There were many dangers in allowing this to happen.[80] The Companies Act 1997, in relaxing this rule, has established certain preconditions which must be fulfilled in order to protect against the dangers. There are now *only four* situations[81] where a company may acquire its own shares:

- if the procedure laid down in s 57 of the Companies Act 1997 is followed;
- if the shares are redeemed at the option of the company by following s 60 of the Companies Act 1997;
- if all "entitled persons" have agreed to the acquisition; or[82]
- if a shareholder has exercised his or her minority buy-out rights.[83]

Section 57(1) of the Companies Act 1997 provides that: "A company may agree to purchase[84] or otherwise acquire its own shares where it is authorised to do so by its constitution." Before a company offers or agrees to purchase its own shares, the board must resolve that:[85]

- the acquisition is in the best interests of the company; and
- the terms of the offer or agreement and the consideration to be paid for the shares are fair and reasonable to the company; and
- it is not aware of any information that has not been disclosed to shareholders which is material to an assessment of the value of the shares, and as a result of which the terms of an offer or the consideration offered for shares are unfair to shareholders accepting the offer.

The company's offer to acquire its own shares may be made to all shareholders or only to some. In the case where the offer is made only to some, the relative voting and distribution rights of all the shareholders will be affected. The Companies Act 1997 in this situation, requires the board of

79 (1887) 12 App Cas 409.

80 The dangers were to both creditors and shareholders: see Beck, A and Borrowdale, A, *Papua New Guinea Companies and Securities Law Guide* (CCH Australia Ltd, Sydney, 1999), para 525 for a list of some of these dangers, as well as some benefits.

81 Companies Act 1997, s 56(1): "but not otherwise."

82 Companies Act 1997, s 89(2)(c). The section governs repurchase or redemption of the company's shares and notwithstanding any provision in the company's constitution to the contrary.

83 Companies Act 1997, ss 91–93.

84 A purchase requires the company to also comply with the solvency test.

85 Companies Act 1997, s 57(2).

directors to take into account the interest of those shareholders who are not party to the offer or agreement to acquire, by requiring the board to pass a resolution, in addition to the resolution required by s 57(2), that the offer or entry into the agreement is fair to the shareholders who are not party to the offer or agreement.[86]

A contract with a company providing for the acquisition by the company of its shares is specifically enforceable against the company except to the extent that the company would, after performing the contract, fail to satisfy the solvency test.[87]

Redemption of shares

Whereas repurchase of shares is a usually[88] contractual agreement between the company and the individual, requiring both parties' agreement, redemption occurs where one party (either the company or the shareholder) may unilaterally force the other to purchase or sell the shares. Like repurchase, the shares are paid for, transferred to the company, and cancelled.

Section 59 of the Companies Act 1997 defines when a share is redeemable. For the purposes of the Act, a share is redeemable where the constitution of the company makes provision for the redemption of that share by the company:

- at the option of the company; or
- at the option of the holder of the share; or
- on a date specified in the constitution.

The constitution must also provide for a consideration that is:

- specified in the constitution or elsewhere; or
- to be calculated by reference to a formula; or
- required to be fixed by a suitably qualified person who is not associated with or interested in the company.

Redemption at option of company

A redemption of a share at the option of the company is an acquisition by the company of the share, for the purposes of s 57(2) and (3) and a distribution, for the purposes of s 50.[89] This means that the company's board of directors

86 Companies Act 1997, s 57(3).

87 Companies Act 1997, s 58(1). A company has the burden of proving that after performance of the contract it would be unable to satisfy the solvency test: s 58(2). Section 58(3) deals with the entitlement of the party to be paid generally or when the company is being wound up (liquidated).

88 The exception is the minority buy-out procedure discussed below at p 496.

89 Companies Act 1997, s 60.

must follow the procedure set out above in relation to repurchases, and distributions, in the latter case, particularly relating to the company satisfying the solvency test.

Redemption at option of shareholder

Subject to s 61(1), where a share is redeemable at the option of the holder of the share, and the holder gives proper notice to the company requiring the company to redeem the share:[90]

- the company shall redeem the share on the date specified in the notice, or where no date is specified, on the date of receipt of the notice; and
- the share is deemed to be cancelled on the date of redemption; and
- from the date of redemption the former shareholder ranks as an unsecured creditor of the company for the sum payable on redemption.

"Redemption":

- is not a distribution for the purposes of ss 50 and 51; but
- is deemed to be a distribution for the purposes of s 54(1) and (5).[91]

This essentially means that the formalities relating to the solvency test do not have to be complied with. However, if it later transpires that the company would not have, immediately after the redemption, been able to satisfy the solvency test, the money may be recovered from the shareholder unless he or she:[92]

- received the distribution in good faith and without knowledge of the company's failure to satisfy the solvency test; and
- altered his or her position in reliance on the validity of the redemption; and
- it would be unfair to require repayment in full or at all.

Where, in an action brought against a shareholder for recovery of money paid for a redemption of shares when the company was unable to satisfy the solvency test, the court is satisfied that the company could, by making a distribution of a lesser amount, have satisfied the solvency test, the court may permit the shareholder to retain an amount equal to the value of any payment ("distribution") that could properly have been made.[93]

90 Companies Act 1997, s 61(1).
91 Companies Act 1997, s 61(2).
92 Companies Act 1997, s 54(1).
93 Companies Act 1997, s 54(5).

Redemption on fixed date

Where a share is redeemable on a specified date:[94]

- the company must redeem the share on that date; and
- the share is deemed to be cancelled on that date; and
- from that date the former shareholder ranks as an unsecured creditor of the company for the sum payable on redemption.

Like a redemption at the option of a shareholder, a redemption on a fixed date is not a distribution under ss 50 and 51, but is deemed to be a distribution for the purposes of s 54(1) and (5).[95]

Where a company:

- has issued shares that are redeemable on a specified date; and
- does not redeem those shares by that date,

the company must, immediately[96] after that date, submit a notice in the prescribed form[97] to the Registrar of the number of shares that have not been redeemed.[98]

Financial assistance to purchase own shares

Before the commencement of the Companies Act 1997, the law expressly prohibited a company from giving financial assistance for the purchase of its own shares.[99] The law frowned on this practice because the company got nothing in return for the purchase price and moreover, it was put in peril of the loan not being repaid.[100] The law has been changed by the Companies Act 1997 to allow companies to give financial assistance directly or indirectly for the acquisition of its own shares if certain pre-conditions set out in s 63 are complied with.

94 Companies Act 1997, s 62(1).
95 Companies Act 1997, s 62(2).
96 It may be that the court will decide that immediately has a meaning similar to "forthwith". See note 38, above.
97 Companies Act 1997, s 62(3). Companies Regulation 1998 (Form 12.–Notice of failure to redeem shares on fixed date).
98 Where a company does not comply with subsection (3), every director of the company commits an offence and is liable on conviction to the penalty set out in s 414(2): Companies Act 1997, s 62(4).
99 *Trevor v Whitworth* (1887) 12 App Cas 409.
100 Companies Act (Ch 146), s 69. See also the Companies (Amendment) Act 1988 (No 16 of 1988), which commenced on 1 January 1989.

Before a company gives financial assistance, the board must resolve that:[101]

- giving the assistance is in the interests of the company;
- the terms and conditions on which the assistance is given are fair and reasonable to the company and to any shareholders not receiving that assistance;
- immediately after giving the assistance, the company will satisfy the solvency test.

Apart from financial assistance being direct or indirect, for the purposes of the section, the term "financial assistance":[102]

- includes giving a loan or guarantee, or the provision of security; but
- does not include entering into a transaction (including a loan or guarantee, or the provision of security):
  - in good faith in the ordinary course of business and on usual terms and conditions; or
  - in which the company receives fair value.

Minority buy-out rights

In the past, the articles of association of a company provided a method for the other shareholders to purchase the shares of a dissatisfied shareholder. This remedy provided to the shareholder was not always satisfactory as the market for the shares was small, and the mode of fixing the price was unfavourable to the seller. Now that a company may acquire its own shares, a similar right for shareholders to require the company to acquire the shares of a dissatisfied shareholder have been included in the Companies Act 1997.

Section 91 of the Companies Act 1997 authorises a shareholder to require a company to purchase his or her shares in defined circumstances. The shareholder must be entitled to vote, and must have voted against any of the following circumstances that have been approved by special resolution:

- adoption, alteration or revocation of a constitution which imposes or removes a restriction on the company's activities;[103]
- approving a major transaction;[104]
- approve a change in the company's name;[105]

101 Companies Act 1997, s 63(2). The giving of financial assistance under this section is not a distribution for the purposes of s 50: s 63(3).
102 Companies Act 1997, s 63(4).
103 Companies Act 1997, s 91(a).
104 Companies Act 1997, s 91(c).
105 Companies Act 1997, s 91(a).

- approve an amalgamation of the company under s 234;[106]
- put the company into liquidation.[107]

When a company receives a notice requiring a buy-out, it may:[108]

- agree to the purchase of the shares by the company at the stated price;
- arrange for some other person to agree to purchase the shares;
- apply to the court for an order under s 95 (to apply for an order exempting it from purchasing the shares);
- apply to the court for an order under s 96 (for, *inter alia*, an order exempting the company from purchasing the shares).

The company must nominate the price. If the shareholder disagrees with this price, the shareholder may ask the National Court to appoint an arbitrator to do so.[109]

The company does not have to purchase the shares if it can show that:

- the purchase would be disproportionately damaging to it (s 95(1)(a));
- it cannot reasonably be required to finance the purchase of the shares (s 95(1)(b));
- it would not be just and equitable to require the company the purchase the shares (s 95(1)(c));
- it would result in the company failing to satisfy the solvency test (s 96(2)(a)).

Company financing and registration of charges

Secured or unsecured credit

Creditors lending money or extending credit to companies usually require the company to provide security for their loans. Creditors who take security have a proprietary right over one or more assets of the borrower which, in the event of default, enables them to take the assets and sell them to recover any amounts outstanding on their loans. Unsecured creditors, on the other hand, can only sue for the debt. They have no rights over particular assets of the company.

Corporate finance

Companies get the funds or capital they need to finance their trading operations from various sources. These include the money paid by shareholders for

106 Companies Act 1997, s 91(b).
107 Companies Act 1997, s 91(e).
108 Companies Act 1997, s 91.
109 Companies Act 1997, s 93(5).

shares in the company (share capital or equity finance), money loaned to the company (i.e, raised by way of loans from banks and other financial institutions or through trade credit (debt capital), and internally generated funds, that is, accumulated or retained profits – earnings made by the company from previous trading operations or depreciation allowances on assets. Most companies would rely on all three sources of finance. It will have obtained finance from the issue of shares to shareholders, it would have long-term loans and short-term overdraft facilities of the bank and the reserve of retained earnings to be used for new undertakings or capital works.

Power of companies to borrow money

Most companies can borrow from financial institutions. Section 17(1)(a) of the Companies Act 1997 provides that a company has full capacity to carry on or undertake any business or activity, do any act, or enter into any transaction. It is implied from this that the company may borrow any amount to carry out any type of business. However, this power may be restricted by a provision in any constitution that the company adopts.[110] We shall discuss below in detail the company's power to borrow by issuing debentures and giving security by way of charge over its property.

Share or equity capital

Companies need finance with which to operate. This finance may come either from the sale of shares (equity capital or equity financing) or from borrowing money (through loans or having an overdraft) from financial institutions, like banks. This type of borrowing from lenders is called debt financing or loan capital. It is also possible that, after a limited time of operating, the company generates sufficient profits from its business so that it is able to use this money to ensure that the business continues to run profitably.

There are several reasons why a company may prefer one type of financing to another. Included among these are consideration of whether new shareholders are needed who will reduce the power of existing shareholders, a right to payment of interest, even if the company is not making any profits, the need to pay taxes (loan payment usually being tax deductible whereas equity capital dividends are not tax deductible), and priority of payment of claims (with creditor's claims being repaid before repayment of equity capital.)

Debt capital and share (equity) capital compared

A company has to make a decision as to whether it wants to raise finance though equity financing or debt financing: the question is which is better for

110 Companies Act 1997, s 17(2).

the company and its "owners", i.e., its shareholders and for the company as a going concern. Compared to debt capital, share capital is long-term. There is no obligation on the company to return to shareholders their contribution during the company's life, whereas loan funds must be repaid to shareholders. Shareholders invest funds in exchange for shares in the company, and the funds thus become the property of the company. Share capital is a residual claim on the company's assets and income. This means that the shareholders' claims are met only after all of the prior fixed claims such as those of the debt creditors and employees have been met. On the other hand, however, while the entitlements of debt creditors and employees are fixed, shareholders are entitled to all that remains after the fixed claims have been met.

In addition, share capital carries with it the right to participate in the internal affairs and governance of the company, whereas debt capital does not carry with it such rights. The money borrowed is repayable over a period of time, and once the company has repaid the amount borrowed (generally called the "principal") and interest for the period, they no longer have any interest in the business. A company that has great prospects in the long term may find debt financing more profitable in the longer term. Another aspect that the company needs to consider is that with a sale of shares (equity financing), the money paid to the shareholders as dividends (now called distributions) is not taxable, whereas money paid to a lending institution as interest is a business expense and, as such, can be deducted for tax purposes. With the grant of more shares, it tends to dilute the ownership of existing shareholders, whereas equity financing does not.[111] Loans also have the added attraction that the company will usually be able to pay it off when it is convenient.

Despite these differences, some forms of share capital are functionally closer to debt. Preference shares, for example, may not carry control rights but the return to shareholders may be fixed in much the same way as the return of interest on debt. Preference shareholders' claims may also enjoy priority ranking. On the other hand, some forms of debt capital, particularly long-term debt, have close similarities to share capital. Debt creditors may agree to subordinate their claims to interest to the claims of other creditors, and agree to be repaid only after all other claims have been met.[112] Debt creditors may also stipulate extensive rights of control over the company as part of their loan arrangements. For example, the loan agreement may limit the type of business the company may engage in and also give the creditor representation on the company's board of management.

111 With large financing, it is possible that the lending institution may insist that a person nominated by them should become a director of the borrower (company) so as to ensure that the company operates efficiently so as to generate sufficient income to repay the loan and interest to the lender.

112 See s 361(3) and Companies Act 1997.

Financing a company: debentures and charges

As with a natural person, a company can borrow and give security for a loan. However, unlike a natural person, a company has the power to issue debentures, give a floating charge over the assets of the company, and give security over uncalled capital.

Debentures

The definition of "debenture" is a broad one. It may take a number of forms, such as a mortgage, charge, or secured or unsecured debt. A charge may be either fixed or floating. Section 2(1) of the Companies Act 1997 provides that the term "debenture" includes "debenture stock, bonds, notes, certificates of deposit and convertible notes". However, there is no other provision in the Act that refers to convertible notes, bonds, notes and certificates of deposit. This definition is not a very helpful one and the law leaves it to the underlying law to fill the gap and give further definition to these terms. It is also important to note that the definition is not exhaustive, so that other types of security documents may be included within the concept of a "debenture".

In *Handevel Pty Ltd v Comptroller of Stamps (Vic)*,[113] the court admitted that it is difficult to give "debenture" a precise meaning. However, it noted that:

> . . . it has been generally agreed that the two characteristics of a debenture are, first, that it is issued by a company and, that it acknowledges or creates a debt . . . The debt may be secured on the assets of a company but security in this sense is not an essential characteristic of a debenture . . .

The debenture is a chose in action that includes an undertaking by the company to repay as debt money deposited with or lent to the company. A chose in action may (but need not) include a charge over property of the company to secure repayment of the money. If it does not contain a charge over the company's property, it is an unsecured debenture. This would be very rare. In effect, a debenture is basically any document setting out the terms of a loan to a company.[114]

The terms of the loan covered by the debenture will vary according to the requirements of the company and the lender. A debenture will usually provide for the time for repayment, the interest to be charged and whether any property of the company is to be charged with repayment of the loan.

113 (1985) 157 CLR 177at 195. Affirmed in *Austral Mining Construction Pty Ltd v NZI Capital Corporation Ltd* (1991) 4 ACSR 57.

114 See Beck, A and Borrowdale, A, *Papua New Guinea Companies and Securities Law Guide* (CCH Australia Ltd, Sydney, 1999), para 603.

Although debentures cover both secured and unsecured loans, the general perception is that a debenture covers only *secured* loans.

In all of these cases, the lender becomes a secured creditor. Some of the terms of the loans:

- a trust deed for securing an issue of debentures;
- company may be an issuer of a prospectus which includes debentures;
- charges to secure any issue of debentures;
- a series of debentures containing or giving by reference to any other document a charge;
- deposit of any debentures as security for a debt;
- trustee for debenture holders;
- debenture and debenture stock;
- debenture holder of the company;
- debentures secured by a fixed or a floating charge;
- invitations to the public to lend money to a company are regulated.

Convertible notes or convertible debenture notes

As we noted above, a convertible note is a debenture.[115] Convertible notes or convertible debenture notes may be mandatory, where the company may be able to force the note-holder on a certain date or event, the company may be able to convert them regardless of the wishes of the holder. Alternatively, debenture holders may be converted at the option of the holder.

Debenture stock

Section 226 of the Companies Act 1997 provides for the endorsement of a certificate of registration on "every debenture forming one of a series of debentures, and on every certificate of debenture stock" that the company issues and the payment of which is secured by a registered charge:

- a copy of the certificate of registration; or
- a statement that registration has been effected and the date of such registration.

The requirement above does not apply to a debenture or certificate of debenture stock that the company issues before the charge is registered.[116] The person who fails to comply with s 222(1) is guilty of an offence.[117]

115 See Companies Act 1997, s 2(1).
116 Companies Act 1997, s 226(2).
117 Section 226(3) of the Companies Act 1997 provides that: "A person who knowingly authorises or permits the giving of a debenture or certificate of debenture stock that is not endorsed as required by this section commits an offence and is liable on conviction to the penalty set out in Section 413(1)."

What is a charge?

Debentures may be a charge over the assets of the property owned by the company. The charge may be a specific charge, a floating charge, or a combination of both. A company is empowered to create a charge over its property to secure the repayment of any monies borrowed. It may charge its property such as land and buildings, its undertaking, its uncalled capital and any other assets that it has. Charges may have different meanings. In relation to borrowing, it usually means a security for a debt. It may be either a legal charge or an equitable charge. It can be a legal mortgage, but is more usually an equitable mortgage. The most common securities granted by companies over their assets are fixed and floating charges.

The Companies Act 1997 provides that the company may grant charges over its property (e.g., assets, undertakings), and that certain types of charges will be accorded priority in any dispute that takes place between lenders. So the first question to decide is whether the loan is a charge, and whether it falls within the types of charge that are registrable so that they may rank highly in any dispute between lenders.

Section 2(1) of the Companies Act 1997 provides that for the purposes of that Act, a "charge" "*includes* a right or interest in relation to property owned by a company, by virtue of which a creditor of the company is entitled to claim payment in priority to creditors entitled to be paid under s 361, but does not include a charge under a charging order issued by a court in favour of a judgment creditor.[118] The definition is not exhaustive, in that it merely states those charges that are definitely within the definition. In essence, all charges are equitable interests or securities. The section also defines a "secured creditor", in relation to a company, to mean "a person entitled to a charge on or over property *owned* by that company" (emphasis added). The section further provides that a mortgage "includes a charge on property for securing money or money's worth", and that a charge "includes a mortgage and an agreement to give or execute a charge or mortgage". A charge is a binding liability to pay that relates to a particular asset or assets of the company. Not all charges that a company creates can be registered. Only those that are set out in s 222(4) are capable of registration. This is an *exhaustive* list of eight registrable charges.

Section 453 of the Companies Act 1997 is a transitional provision governing registered or registrable charges under the repealed Companies Act (Companies Act (Ch 146)). In essence, it provides that all charges shall from the date of such registration or deemed registration of the company, or any

118 Section 2(1) of the Companies Act 1997 provides, *inter alia*, that: "'security' means any interest or right to participate in any capital, assets, earnings, royalties, or other property of any person; and includes (a) any interest in or right to be paid money that is, or is to be, deposited with, lent to, or otherwise owing by, any person (whether or not the interest or right is secured by a charge over property."

charges that were or were deemed to be part of and included in the Register of Charges kept by the Registrar of Companies under s 112 of the repealed Act, are deemed to be registered in the Register of Charges maintained by the Registrar under the Companies Act 1997.

Fixed charges

A fixed or specific charge relates to and attaches to fixed or specific property of the company. It will usually be an equitable security. It is not necessary for the property to be owned by the borrowing company or even to be in existence when the charge is given.[119]

Floating charges[120]

Parties cannot, simply by describing a charge as a fixed charge, or as not being a floating charge establish that it is not.[121] In deciding whether a charge is fixed or floating, the courts look at both the intention of the parties as expressed in the charge agreement and the substance of the transaction. The charge will be deemed to be a floating charge:[122]

- if it is over a shifting fund of present and future assets;
- the company is free to carry on its business in the ordinary way and use those assets without the consent of or reference to the chargee.

Lord Macnaghten highlighted the distinction between a fixed charge and floating charge in *Illingworth v Houldsworth*:[123]

> A specific charge, I think, is one that without more fastens on ascertained and definite property or property capable of being ascertained and defined; a floating charge, on the other hand, is ambulatory and shifting in its nature, hovering over and so to speak floating with the property which it is intended to affect until some event occurs or some act is done which causes it to settle and fasten on the subject of the charge within its reach and grasp.

119 *Holroyd v Marshall* (1862) 10 HLC 191, 11 ER 999, [1861–73] All ER Rep 414, HL.

120 Only a company may grant a floating charge, something that a natural person or other type of entity may not do.

121 *Evans v Rival Granite Quarries Ltd* [1910] 2 KB 979 at 993, per Fletcher Moulton LJ.

122 See *United Builders Pty Ltd v Mutual Acceptance Ltd* (1980) 144 CLR 673 and *Perrins v State Bank of Victoria* [1991] 1 VR 749. Often lenders take both a fixed and a floating charge in the same document.

123 [1904] AC 355 at 358. Lord Macnaghten stated in *Governments, Stock and Other Securities Investment Co Ltd v Manila Railway Co Ltd* [1897] AC 81 at 86: "It is of the essence of such a charge that it remains dormant until the undertaking charged ceases to be a going concern, or until the person in whose favour the charge is created intervenes."

Romer LJ made a similar distinction between a fixed and floating charge when he said in *Re Yorkshire Woolcombers Association Ltd*:[124]

> I certainly think that if a charge has the three characteristics that I am about to mention it is a floating charge:
> (1) if it is a charge on a class of assets of a company present and future;
> (2) if that class is one which, in the ordinary course of the business of the company, would be changing from time to time; and
> (3) if you find that by the charge it is contemplated that, until some future step is taken by or on behalf of those interested in the charge, the company may carry on its business in the ordinary way as far as concerns the particular class of assets I am dealing with.

Thus, a borrowing company is free to deal with the assets secured by a floating charge in the ordinary course of its business, and the lender, having only an equitable interest, cannot ordinarily interfere. As Rogers CJ explained in *Fire Nymph Products Ltd v The Heating Centre Pty Ltd*:[125]

> It is of the essence of a floating charge that until its crystallisation, assets, the subject of it, may pass free from the charge . . . In determining the reach of the restrictions on the freedom to deal with assets the subject of the floating charge, it is necessary to remember the purpose of a floating charge. If the charge were wholly fixed, the company could not commercially carry on business.

So, for example, the company may deal with the trading stock and pass on ownership of them to customers. The lender has a valid security over the shifting fund of assets but has no right to interfere in the conduct of the business only so long as the company does not breach any term of the charge and only deals with the charged assets in the ordinary course of its business.[126] A breach may occur where for example the company breaches one of the terms of the loan, or goes out of business.[127] However, as soon as some event occurs to cause the floating charge to become fixed (to "crystallise"), the company can no longer deal with the goods that were subject to the floating charge and which it has in its ownership: from then onwards, except with the express or implied approval of the creditor, the chargee

124 [1903] 2 Ch 284 at 295. This classification of a floating charge was followed in *Re Coslett* [1996] 6 All ER 46.

125 (1988) 14 ACLR 274 at 277.

126 As assets subject to a floating charge can be disposed of in the "ordinary course of business", the meaning of this phrase is important. See *Reynolds Bros (Motors) Pty Ltd v Esanda* Ltd (1983) 1 ACLC 1333. Cf *Fire Nymph Products Ltd v The Heating Centre Pty Ltd* (1992) 10 ACLC 629.

127 *Stein v Saywell* (1969) 121 CLR 529.

cannot deal with the property that is subject to the charge at all, or only with the permission of the chargee.

To sum up, fixed charges attach to specific property; an equitable (fixed) charge may attach to property to be acquired by the company in the future. Until default, a floating charge does not attach to property. On default, the charge "crystallises", and fixes over assets subject to it.

Problems with floating charges[128]

The floating charge is a much less secure security over company assets than a fixed or specific charge. With a fixed charge, the property remains available to the lender, and if it consists of lands and buildings, will usually appreciate in value during the life of the loan, and so be available to fully repay it when it becomes due and payable. With a floating charge, there is no guarantee that the company will have any or sufficient assets covered by the floating charge to repay the loan. In the meantime, the company may have traded unsuccessfully, so that the stock or assets has decreased in amount of value, and thus be unable to fully or even substantially cover the repayment remaining on the loan.

Another problem involving floating charges relates to the development and use of "retention of title" clauses in supply contracts. The seller of the goods to the company stipulates that the goods do not pass to the ownership of the company until payment is made. This may mean that much of the stock used by the company does not belong to it, but to the various suppliers. When a floating charge crystallises, it does not cover these goods, and so the owners may reclaim them from the company. The holder of the floating charge or its appointed receiver will *not* have access to them to sell them and help towards recovery of the loan to the company.

There are other problems with floating charges. Such charges will be defeated by creditors who complete execution, or a landlord who levies distress before the charge crystallises.[129] In addition, certain "preferential" creditors[130] take priority over a floating charge, and this may mean that once the receiver has paid off these creditors, there is not much left for the holder of the floating charge. Despite these limitations however, the floating charge may still be used to secure loans to companies.

128 Is a floating charge a present security? See *Evans v Rival Granite Quarries Ltd* [1910] 2 KB 979, per Buckley LJ. As to which charges are floating, see *United Builders Pty Ltd v Mutual Acceptance Ltd* (1980) 144 CLR 673; *Re Yorkshire Woolcombers Association Ltd* [1903] 2 Ch 284; *Re Florence Land and Public Works Company, ex p Moore* (1878) 10 Ch D 530 at 540.

129 See Companies Act 1997, Division XVIII.2 (Provisions Relating to Prior Execution Process). See Land Act 1996, s 166; Land Registration Act (Ch 191), s 75, Summary Ejectment Act (Ch 202); and Public Health (Sewerage) Regulation (Ch 226), s 197 (Levy and distress).

130 Set out in Companies Act 1997, Schedule 9, clause 7.

Negative pledges

A floating charge is often accompanied by a "negative pledge". A negative pledge is a contractual promise made by the borrower to the lender, usually as a term of a loan agreement, that it will not grant any charge over the charged property in favour of other creditors without the consent of the lender. Alternatively, the promise may be that it will not grant any higher or equally ranking (*pari passu*) charge without the consent of the lender. This agreement may be contained in the charge itself, or in a separate document.

A breach of the negative pledge by the borrowing company will usually lead to a termination of the loan and give the lender the right to demand immediate repayment and give the lender the power to recover damages for the breach. In most cases the lender is concerned with maintaining priority of its charge of the charged property.

If such a pledge is broken, priority of the competing charges will depend on such factors as the nature of the charge, whether and when it was registered, if the lender had notice of the earlier charge, and whether the floating charge contained a negative pledge.[131]

The issue is between two lenders competing for priority. There is also usually a competition between the company and the lenders.

Not all charges have a negative pledge. However, this pledge gives added protection to the lender when the loan takes the form of a floating charge from the company.

There is also the possibility of the priority of the floating charge between the holder of the floating charge and a liquidator when the company goes into liquidation.

Trustee for debenture holders

Because individual debenture holders may not be in a position to protect their interests, it is possible for a "trustee for debenture holders" to be appointed to look after their interest. Section 224(4) of the Companies Act 1997 provides that:

> A reference in this section to the chargee in relation to a charge shall, where the charge is constituted by a debenture and debentures and there is a trustee for debenture holders, be construed as a reference to the trustee for debenture holders.[132]

131 For discussion of the priority of charges, see p 524.
132 See also Companies Act 1997, s 222(6)(a)(iv).

Registration of charges[133]

Registration of charges is important to enforceability of a charge and priority. The registration system is critical to any lender seeking to take security. Section 225 of the Companies Act 1997 provides that the Registrar of Companies must keep a Register of Charges. Certain types of charges created by a company are to be registered in it. The main purpose of the register is to provide a system of alerting lenders to companies who want to lend on the security of certain assets, as to whether the company has already given a charge over those assets. The register also allows an unsecured creditor to establish which assets have been charged and how many creditors will be paid before it is paid. Other provisions determine the priorities of registrable charges against each other.

Charges requiring registration

The Companies Act 1997 defines a charge to include:[134]

> a right or interest in relation to property owned by a company, by virtue of which a creditor of the company is entitled to claim payment in priority to creditors entitled to be paid under Section 361,[135] but does not include a charge under a charging order issued by the National or Supreme Court in favour of a judgment creditor.[136]

133 This is another area of the Companies Act 1997 of PNG where the current New Zealand provisions are of little help in understanding this area of law. There were earlier corresponding provisions in Part IV of the repealed Companies Act 1955 (New Zealand) which were similar to the PNG provisions. However, New Zealand implemented a totally new approach to dealing with charges, including registration of charges, when it passed the Personal Property Securities Act 1999. As such, there are no provisions in the current Companies Act 1993 (New Zealand) that correspond to the charges provisions of the Companies Act 1997. The provisions relating to registration of charges in the Companies Act 1997 are similar to the provisions of the Corporations Act 2001 (Australia), in particular, provisions in Part 2K.2 and Part 2K.3. The Australian cases and commentary considering the provisions in these two Parts are most helpful in understanding the scope of the Registration of Charges provisions in the Companies Act 1997. In addition, some of the relevant provisions in the Companies Act 1997 seem to have been based on the wording of Part V Division 7 of the repealed Companies Act (Ch 146). However, there seem to be no judgments handed down by the National or Supreme Courts of Papua New Guinea considering these repealed provisions. There are also similar provisions in the English Companies Act 1985. See in particular s 396. See also Part IV of the New Zealand Companies Act 1955 and the cases decided thereon.

134 Section 2(1) of the Companies Act 1997 provides that in the Companies Act 1997, "unless the contrary intention appears". Furthermore, the definition of charges in that subsection provides that a "'charge' *includes* a right or interest in relation to property . . ." (emphasis added). This adds up to the fact that the definition of "charges" is not an exclusive or comprehensive definition.

135 Section 361 of the Companies Act 1997 refers to preferential claims.

136 Companies Act 1997, s 2(1).

It should be noted that this is not an exhaustive definition, so that there may be other types of charge that fall within the registration scheme of the Companies Act 1997, but which are not covered by the definition in s 2(1) of that Act. It should also be noted that the registration scheme applies only to charges to which Part XIII of the Companies Act 1997 apply.

Registration requirements

Where a company creates a charge that must be submitted to the Registrar of Companies for registration in line with Part XIII of the Companies Act 1997, the company must submit two documents to the Registrar for registration within two months after the creation of the charge. These two documents are: (i) a notice for registration of the charge in the prescribed form;[137] and (ii) a certified copy of the registrable security document or agreement creating or evidencing the charge.[138]

Where a company creates a series of debentures containing or giving by reference to any other document a charge the benefit of which the debenture holders of that series are entitled to equally, the company must submit to the Registrar for registration within two months after the execution of the document containing the charge or, where there is no such document, after the execution of the first debenture of the series:

- a notice in the prescribed form[139] stating the total amount secured by the whole series, the dates of the resolutions authorising the issue of the series and the date of the document (if any) by which the security is created or defined, a general description of the property charged; and the names of the trustees (if any) for the debenture holders;
- either a certified copy of the document creating or evidencing the charge, or where there is no such document, a copy of the first of the debentures of the series;[140]
- how the charge was created;
- if the charge involved the issue of debentures, the name of the trustee for the debenture holders;

137 Companies Regulation 1998, Form 24 (Notice for registration of charge). A certified copy of the document creating or evidencing the charge must be annexed to this form. It also states that there has been compliance with the Stamp Duties Act (Ch 117).

138 Companies Act 1997, s 222(1). The new replacement provisions in New Zealand, rather than requiring a copy of the entire security document, merely requires brief particulars of the charge, sufficient to identify the debtor, the secured creditor and the assets subject to the charge.

139 Companies Act 1997, s 222(1). Companies Regulation 1998: Form 24 (Notice for registration of charge).

140 Companies Act 1997, s 222(6). It would appear that this provision applies even where the execution is made outside PNG.

- if the charge did not involve the issue of debentures, the name of the chargee.

The particulars that must be included in the documentation registered in the Register of Charges maintained by the Registrar of Companies include:

- date of creation of charge;
- type of charge: fixed, floating or both a fixed and floating charge;
- if the charge is a floating charge, is the creation of subsequent charges restricted or prohibited? (i.e., is there a negative pledge?);
- brief description of liability secured by the charge: where the charge secures a present and prospective liability, or a prospective liability up to a specified maximum amount, details of the prospective liability and the amount specified;
- brief description of the property charged;
- details of person(s) entitled to the charge (chargee);
- issue of a series of debentures;
- date(s) of resolution(s) authorising the issue of the series;
- details of the trustee(s);
- rate of any commission;
- certified copy of the document creating or evidencing the charge must be annexed to form 24;
- statement of compliance with Stamp Duties Act (Ch 117).

The Register of Charges maintained by the Registrar of Companies has important information in it. For example, it may contain information about the charge, including any restrictions such as a negative pledge. Potential lenders are therefore able to find out whether or not the company has already borrowed upon the security of an asset.

Registration of charges in company's Register of Charges

Under the repealed Companies Act (Ch 141),[141] every company had to keep at its registered office, a register of "every instrument creating a charge" and also "a Register of Charges". This requirement is no longer necessary since the Companies Act 1997 came into operation. Despite the fact that a company is no longer under an obligation to keep a Register of Charges, this does not prevent a company from voluntarily keeping such a register. Furthermore, it does not prevent potential lenders from making inquiries of the company as to what registrable and unregistrable charges it has created over its property. The company should be asked to provide a statutory declaration concerning these charges and any other details of indebtedness.

141 Companies Act (Ch 146), s 116 (Copies of charging instruments and Register of Charges).

The bank or other lending institution may make it a precondition for granting a loan that the company make these records available to it for inspection before entering into a lending agreement. The fact that there is a time lag between lodgement for registration and actual registration; it would be a good idea to elicit such information from a company which may have entered into financial transactions just before another lender decides to lend money to the company.

Register of Charges

The Registrar of Companies must keep a register of all the charges entered into by the company and must enter the following information in it:[142]

- in respect of each charge, the time and date on which a charge was entered in the register and of any assignment or variation of it;[143]
- in the case of a charge where the holders of a series of debentures are entitled to the benefit of that charge, the particulars contained in the notice received under s 222(6);[144]
- in the case of any other charge:
    - where the charge is a charge created by the company, the date of its creation;[145]
    - where the charge was a charge existing on property acquired by the company, the date of the acquisition of the property;[146]
    - the amount the charge secures;[147]
    - a description sufficient to identify the property charged;[148]
    - the name of the person entitled to the charge;[149] and
    - the details of any assignment or variation.[150]

On registration of a charge and payment of the fee, the Registrar must issue a certificate in the prescribed form of every registration stating, where applicable, the amount the charge secures and the certificate is conclusive evidence that the requirements as to registration have been complied with. In such situations, the charge is effective even though the charge was filed out of time,[151]

142 Companies Act 1997, s 225(1).
143 Companies Act 1997, s 225(2).
144 Companies Act 1997, s 225(2)(a).
145 Companies Act 1997, s 225(2)(b)(i).
146 Companies Act 1997, s 225(2)(b)(ii).
147 Companies Act 1997, s 225(2)(b)(iii).
148 Companies Act 1997, s 225(2)(b)(iv).
149 Companies Act 1997, s 225(2)(b)(v).
150 Companies Act 1997, s 225(2)(b)(vi).
151 *Re Eric Holmes (Property) Ltd (In Liquidation)* [1965] Ch 1052; *Re CL Nye Ltd* [1971] Ch 442.

and the registered particulars are inaccurate.[152] It might be that a person[153] may challenge the conclusive nature of the certificate for manifest error on the face of the certificate or evidence that it was obtained by fraud.

Section 226 of the Companies Act 1997 provides that a copy of the certificate must be endorsed on all debentures subsequently issued by the company.[154]

Effect of failure to register a charge

Section 222(2) of the Companies Act 1997 provides that where a charge that needs to be registered under the Companies Act 1997, is not in fact registered (submitted for registration) the charge is "so far as it confers any security on the company's property or undertaking . . . void against the liquidator of the company and any creditor of the company".[155] In effect, this means that the lender is no longer a secured creditor, but becomes an unsecured creditor, as the charge has no legal effect. The lender being an unsecured creditor must share equally (*pari passu*) in any proceeds of the company after it has gone into liquidation and has paid off its "secured creditors". There may in fact be no funds available for distribution at this stage. It should be noted, that so long as the company continues to operate, the charge is good between the company and the person holding the charge (i.e., the creditor or mortgagor or someone to whom the charge has been transferred). The unregistered debenture holder could still retain the right to appoint a receiver; however, the receiver's appointment may be challenged by a person with a superior right.

Failure to register does not just make the charge void "against the liquidator of the company and any creditor of the company" so far as any security over the company's property is concerned, but also makes the debtor company liable to a default fine under s 222(13) of the Companies Act 1997. The borrowing company has a duty to ensure that registration is properly carried out. The Act not only imposes a positive duty on the company, but also makes its officers liable to an offence. The section provides that where default is made in complying with s 222, each director of the company commits an

152 Companies Act 1997, s 225(3). As to the conclusiveness of the certificate, see *Re Mechanisations (Eaglescliffe) Ltd* [1966] Ch 20; *National Provincial and Union Bank of England v Charnley* [1924] 1 KB 431.

153 The state may have the *locus standi* to make the challenge: *R v Registrar, ex p Central Bank of India* [1986] QB 1114.

154 Companies Act 1997, s 226(1).

155 Seeing that the section specifically states that the unregistered charge is void against the liquidator and any creditor of the company, it is valid against the company, and as such, an unregistered charge holder may therefore retain its right to appoint a receiver, see *Re Row Dal Constructions Pty Ltd* [1966] VR 249. This is based on the principle of *expressio unius est exclusio alterius*: *PLAR No 1 of 1980* [1980] PNGLR 326.

offence and is liable on conviction to the penalty set out in s 414(1). If a charge or other document required to be registered under Part XIII is registered by some other person "who is interested in a charge or other documents that are required to be registered" under Part XIII (and the person who would gain most is usually the creditor), the interested person is entitled to recover from the company the amount of any fees properly paid by him or her on registration.[156]

Time for registration where property subject to charge is located outside Papua New Guinea

With the exception of a charge on property of an overseas company which is located outside the country,[157] a charge created in PNG which affects property outside the country may be registered under the Companies Act 1997.[158] It does not matter that further proceedings are necessary (e.g., registration in that other country) to make the charge valid or effectual according to the law of the place where the property is situated.[159]

Time for registration where property subject to charge is located in Papua New Guinea

The normal period for registration of a charge is within two months of its creation.[160] Section 222(1) of the Companies Act 1997 provides that the company shall submit a notice for registration of the charge in the prescribed form, and a certified copy of the document creating or evidencing the charge "to the Registrar for registration within two months after the creation of the charge".

It seems quite clear that the requirement is only that the applicants submit or *lodge* the documents to the Registrar for registration within the time limit. The section does not actually require the Registrar to register the documents within the two-month period in order for the charge to be effectively registered for the purposes of Part XIII. If, however, there is any doubt on this matter, it should be resolved in favour of interpreting the section so that all that is required is submission of the documents within the two-month period. As Beck and Borrowdale point out, whilst arguing that

156 Companies Act 1997, s 230.
157 Companies Act 1997, s 221. It is not clear why an exception is made in respect of overseas property of an overseas company.
158 Companies Act 1997, s 222(5).
159 Companies Act 1997, s 222(5).
160 This period may be extended by virtue of s 229 of the Companies Act 1997 itself or, in specific cases, by permission of the Registrar.

a charge is valid if the documents are *received* by the Registrar within the specified time, even if they are registered much later:[161]

> The validity of the company charge should not be compromised by delay in registration on the part of the Registrar. This is consistent with New Zealand authority which has held that in this context 'registration' means delivery to the Registrar for registration, and does not refer to the subsequent entry of the charge in the Register of Charges which the Registrar is required to keep (*First City Corporation Ltd v Downsview Nominees Ltd (No 2)* (1989) 4 NZCLC 65,192). Accordingly, a charge is valid if the documents are received by the Registrar within the specified time.

This interpretation is not consistent with the policy behind the section: to assist lenders, by providing information to assist them in finding out whether any charge affects the property, security over which money will be loaned. However, it is just that a lender should not be penalised if it has done all within its power to register the charge. Section 225(3) provides that: "The Registrar shall issue a certificate in the prescribed form of every registration stating, where applicable, the amount the charge secures and the certificate is conclusive evidence that the requirements as to registration have been complied with."

Extension of time for registration where charge made in Papua New Guinea

Section 228 of the Companies Act 1997 governs the extension of time for registration of a charge, and rectification of the Register of Charges. It provides that a company or "a person interested" in the registration of the charge, may apply to the Registrar of Companies to grant relief, or rectify the Register of Charges or the memorandum of satisfaction and release, as the case may be. The Registrar has power to grant relief where the omission to submit for registration a charge or an assignment or variation of a charge within the time required or that an omission or misstatement of any particular in the Register of Charges or the memorandum of satisfaction and release (referred to in s 228 as a "notice"):

- was accidental or due to inadvertence or to some other sufficient cause;
- is not of a nature to prejudice the position of creditors or shareholders;
- that on other grounds it is just and equitable to grant relief.

161 Beck, A and Borrowdale, A, *Papua New Guinea Companies and Securities Law Guide* (CCH Australia Ltd, Sydney, 1999), para 608.

Section 228(2) of the Companies Act 1997 provides that a person who is dissatisfied with the Registrar's decision may apply to the National Court for relief. If the court is satisfied that an omission to register was accidental or due to inadvertence or to some other sufficient cause, it may extend the time for registration, order the Registrar of Charges to grant relief, or rectify the Register of Charges or notice referred to in s 227 (Registration of satisfaction and release), as the case may be.

Failure to register may be due to dilatoriness or oversight. It may also be due to a misunderstanding of the legal requirements.[162] The fact that a company secretary was incorrectly advised or that there was confusion between solicitor and company secretary as to who was to register the charge, are examples of grounds for extension. However, a mistake of fact is not due to inadvertence and does not excuse a failure to register.[163] It may, however, be possible to argue that this type of mistake is one where "it is just and equitable to grant relief".[164]

It has been held in other jurisdictions that the court is reluctant to interfere with the rights of creditors after winding up has commenced or the company's solvency is in question.[165]

Extension of time for registration where charge made outside Papua New Guinea

Where the document creating or evidencing the charge is executed or made outside PNG, s 229 of the Companies Act 1997 provides that the normal two-month registration period is automatically extended by "one month" or "such further period as the Registrar from time to time allows". The time is therefore automatically extended from two to three months for charges created outside PNG. However, this three-month period can be further extended by the Registrar of Companies to whatever period he or she considers necessary. It does not seem to matter where the property, the subject of the charge, is located.

162 *Sikkema v Kensington & Braham* (1981) 1 NZCLC ¶95-022; *Liquidator of Contemporary Cottages (NZ) Ltd (in liq) v Margin Traders Ltd* (1981) 1 NZCLC ¶95-031; *Borden (UK) Ltd v Scottish Timber Products Ltd* [1979] 3 WLR 672, *Re Bond Worth Ltd* [1979] 3 WLR 629.

163 *CBC v George Hudson Pty Ltd (in liq)* (1973) 47 ALJR 732. Section 410 of the Companies Act 1997 (Liability of Registrar) provides that: "The Registrar or a Deputy Registrar and any person appointed or authorised by the Registrar or employed in the office of the Registrar is not liable to an action or other proceeding for damages for or in relation to an act done or omitted in good faith in performance or purported performance of any function, or in the exercise or purported exercise of any power, conferred or expressed to be conferred by or under [the Companies Act 1997] or the *Securities Act 1997*." Costs of a court action may not be awarded against the Registrar: s 418 of the Companies Act 1997.

164 Companies Act 1997, s 228(1)(b).

165 *JJ Leonard Properties Pty Ltd v Leonard (WA) Pty Ltd* (1988) 6 ACLC 247.

Provisional entry in the Register of Charges

To encourage and facilitate early lodgment of charges, s 225(5) to (8) provides for provisional entry in the Register of Charges. This enables charges to be registered despite the fact that stamp duty may not have yet been paid or the notice is in some respects defective. A Notice for Registration of Charge may be entered in the Register of Charges and marked "provisional" if it contains at least the name of the company that created the charge and the name of the trustee for debenture-holders or the chargee, as the case may be. If the company then provides the further particulars within one month or such further period as the Registrar of Companies allows, these are recorded in the Register and the word "provisional" is deleted. The charge is then deemed to be registered and to have been registered from and including the time and date of the provisional entry.[166] If the company does not provide the required further particulars within the one-month grace period or the further period allowed by the Registrar, the charge is then deemed to have been registered only on the date when the information is entered in the Register of Charges.[167] A charge may also be lodged for provisional entry in the Register where stamp duty has not been paid on the applicable document. In such a case, evidence of payment of stamp duty must be forwarded to the Registrar of Companies within one month.[168] The Registrar may refuse to register a document submitted for registration in any of the following circumstances:[169]

- is not in the prescribed form, if any; or
- does not comply with the Companies Act 1997; or
- contains any matter contrary to law; or where the register is kept wholly or partly by means of a device or facility referred to in Section 395(2) of the Companies Act 1997[170] is not in a form that enables particulars to be entered directly by electronic or other means in the device or facility; or
- has not been properly completed; or
- contains an error, alteration, or erasure; or
- contains material that is not clearly legible; or
- is not accompanied by the prescribed fee.

In that event, the Registrar must request the applicant either to make the appropriate amendments and re-submit the document or submit a fresh document.

166 Companies Act 1997, s 225(9).
167 Companies Act 1997, s 225(8).
168 Companies Act 1997, s 225(7).
169 Companies Act 1997, s 396(2) (Registration of documents).
170 The register may be kept in such manner as the Registrar thinks fit that records or stores information electronically or by other means and that permits the information so recorded or stored to be readily inspected or reproduced in useable form.

Section 396(8) of the Act makes it clear that neither the registration nor the refusal of registration creates a presumption as to the validity of a document. Charges made under the former Companies Act (Ch 146) are now treated as having been registered under the Companies Act 1997.[171]

Where property acquired is subject to existing charge

If a company registered in PNG acquires property that is subject to an existing charge, and the charge is of such a kind that, had the company created the charge after the acquisition of the property, it would have been required to register it under Part XIII of the Companies Act 1997, the company must submit to the Registrar within two months after the date on which the acquisition is completed:[172]

- a notice in the prescribed form
- a certified copy of the document creating or evidencing the charge.

Where the company makes default in registering the charge, each director of the company commits an offence and is liable on conviction to the penalty set out in s 414(1).[173]

Similar rules apply in respect of overseas companies which become registered in PNG, but before registration:

- created a charge that, if the company had created it while it was registered in Papua New Guinea, would have been required to be registered under Part XIII;[174] or
- acquired property that is subject to a charge of any kind that, if the company had created it, would if after the acquisition and while it was registered in Papua New Guinea, have been required to be registered under Part XIII.[175]

It is important that the charge be registered as soon as possible, especially if there are several charges over the same property, as the general order of priority is according to the time and date of registration. The company is under an obligation to register the charge with the Registrar of Charges. However, if the company fails to do so, the lender or creditor may submit

171 Companies Act 1997, s 453.
172 Companies Act 1997, s 223.
173 Note that failure to register does not lead to invalidity of the charge. The section also applies to an overseas company that create charges, or acquire property that is already subject to a charge, before the company becomes registered in PNG.
174 Companies Act 1997, s 223(1)(b).
175 Companies Act 1997, s 223(1)(c).

the charge to the Registrar for registration. This is so as to protect its rights in connection with the order of priority. Lenders are usually advised to do so as a matter of course to ensure protection. Once notice of a registrable charge has been submitted to the Registrar of Companies, any later lenders are deemed to have constructive notice of the information contained in the Register of Charges.[176]

Any express or implied consent given by the holder of a charge that would otherwise be entitled to priority, or any agreement between the chargees varying the priorities of the chargees may vary the priority laid down in s 231 and Schedule 15 of the Companies Act 1997. Agreement between chargees does not need the chargor's (i.e., the company's consent).

Charges to which Part XIII applies

Part XIII of the Companies Act 1997 deals with registration of charges. The general rule is that company charges that are governed by Part XIII of the Companies Act 1997 must be *submitted* to the Registrar of Companies for registration within two months after the creation of the charge.[177]

Section 222(4) lists eight categories of charges (whether legal or equitable) that are registrable. The list is exhaustive and any of the listed charges that are created[178] *must* be submitted for registration in the Register of Charges maintained by the Registrar of Companies to ensure their validity against the liquidator and unsecured creditors.[179] Only those charges specifically mentioned in s 222(4) need to be registered.[180]

176 Companies Act 1997, Schedule 15.4.

177 Some texts, e.g., Beck, A and Borrowdale, A, *Papua New Guinea Companies and Securities Law Guide* (CCH Australia Ltd), Sydney, 1999), para 607, provide that the charge must be "registered" within two months of creation. However, s 222(1) of the Companies Act 1997 refers to the duty to "*submit*" [the charge] to the Registrar for registration" (emphasis added). Another term for submitted is "lodged" for registration. Corresponding provisions in the Companies Act (Ch 146) use the term "lodge" or variants thereof.

178 A charge arising by operation of law, rather than one "where a company creates a charge" is not registrable: *London and Cheshire Insurance Co Ltd v Laplagrene Property Co Ltd* [1971] Ch 499. It is valid without being registered. See also *Waitomo Wools (NZ) Ltd v Nelsons (NZ) Ltd* (1974) 1 NZLR 484.

179 The list of registrable company charges set out in s 222(4) of the Companies Act 1997 are a verbatim reproduction of the list in s 110(3) of the repealed Companies Act (Ch 146). There seem to be no reported or numbered PNG judgments dealing with this section or considering what charges fall outside the provision.

180 Because of the argument that the section means "submitted for registration" rather than "registered", ideally the statement should read "need to be submitted for registration". However, given the fact that the law in this area has not been tested, and given the important consequences of a failure to register, the phrase "submitted for registration" will be used. Highlighting the fact that the chargee should get the documents registered on a failure of the company to do so, the word "registered" is used.

The registrable charges listed in s 222(4) of the Companies Act 1997 are:[181]

- charges (other than charges solely on land) to secure any issue of debentures;[182]
- charges on uncalled share capital of a company;[183]
- charges or assignments created or evidenced by instruments (including instruments creating or evidencing absolute bills of sale or absolute assignments or transfers of book debts[184]) that, if executed by an individual, would be invalid or of limited effect if not registered under the Instruments Act (Ch 254)[185]
- floating charges on the undertaking or property of a company;[186]
- charges on calls made but not paid;[187]
- charges on a ship or aircraft, or on a share in a ship or aircraft;[188]
- charges on goodwill, on a patent or licence under a patent, on a trade mark, or on a copyright or a licence under a copyright;[189]
- charges on the book debts of a company.[190]

The first issue is whether the security is a "charge", and secondly, whether it is a type of charge referred to in s 222(4) of the Companies Act 1997.

Section 221 provides that a "reference in this Part to a company includes a reference to an overseas company to which Part XX applies, but nothing in that Part applies to a charge on property of an overseas company which is located outside the country".

Given the fact that certain charges do not need to be registered, and that a potential lender to a company may not be able to find out the full extent to which the company's property has been burdened, lenders ought as a matter of due course to find out from the borrowing company itself, what charges encumber the company's assets. For instance, fixed charges over partnership assets and commercial contracts do not need to be registered to

181 Detailed commentaries on each of similar categories in the Companies Act 1985, s 396 can be found in Boyle, A J, Sykes, R and Sealy, L S (eds), *Gore–Brown on Companies* (44th edn, Jordan Publishing Ltd, Bristol, 1998), para 18.9; and Pennington, R R, *Company Law* (7th edn, Butterworths, London, 1995), 636–647.

182 Companies Act 1997, s 222(4)(a).

183 Companies Act 1997, s 222(4)(b).

184 For a recent analysis of the nature and creation of book debts, see *National Westminster Bank plc v Spectrum Plus Ltd, Re Spectrum Plus Ltd, sub nom National Westminster Bank plc v Spectrum Plus Ltd* [2005] UKHL 41, [2005] 4 All ER 209, [2005] 2 AC 680, HL.

185 Companies Act 1997, s 222(4)(c).

186 Companies Act 1997, s 222(4)(d).

187 Companies Act 1997, s 222(4)(e).

188 Companies Act 1997, s 222(4)(f).

189 Companies Act 1997, s 222(4)(g).

190 Companies Act 1997, s 222(4)(h).

be valid. In *United Builders Pty Ltd v Mutual Acceptance Ltd*,[191] the company gave a charge over its share in a partnership. This charge was not registered. The court held that it was a fixed charge and therefore not required to be registered under provisions similar to s 222(4) of the Companies Act 1997. The company then gave a later floating charge over its property that was registered. It was held that the registered floating charge was subject to the priority of the earlier created fixed charge, even though the fixed charge was not registered.

We shall briefly discuss each category of charges that must be registered (or at least) submitted to the Registrar of Companies for registration:

CHARGES (EXCEPT CHARGES RELATING ONLY TO LAND) TO SECURE ANY ISSUE OF DEBENTURES

This category seems to cover the issue of a series of debentures.[192] If the charge relates only to land, it does not need registration under s 222(4)(a) of the Companies Act 1997. Sections 26, 28, 33 and 45 of the Land Registration Act (Ch 191) provide for the effect of registration. Charges relating to land do not need to be registered under the Companies Act 1997, because they are registered under the Land Registration Act (Ch 191).

CHARGES ON UNCALLED SHARE CAPITAL OF A COMPANY

Charges on uncalled capital, i.e., shares in the company that have not been fully paid, for must be registered under s 222(4)(b) of the Companies Act 1997.

INSTRUMENTS ACT CHARGES

Section 222(4)(c) of the Companies Act 1997 provides that the following charges must be registered: charges or assignments created or evidenced by instruments that, if executed by an individual, would be invalid or of limited effect if not registered under the Instruments Act (Ch 254). If executed by an individual they would require registration under the Instruments Act (Ch 254). This includes instruments creating or evidencing absolute bills of sale or absolute assignments or transfers of book debts.

Chattel securities by companies are not registrable bills of sale within the Bills of Sales Acts. However, any charge which would have been registrable as a bill of sale by an individual and which is created by a company, must be registered in the Register of Charges.

191 (1980) 144 CLR 673.

192 *Automobile Association (Canterbury) Inc v Australasian Secured Deposits Ltd* [1973] 1 NZLR 417.

Section 1 of the Instruments Act (Ch 254) provides a definition of a "bill of sale" for the purposes of that Act. It "includes":

- a bill of sale;
- an assignment or transfer of chattels;
- a declaration of trusts of chattels without transfer;
- an inventory of chattels with receipt attached; and
- a receipt for purchase money of chattels and any other assurance of chattels;
- a power of attorney, authority or licence to take possession of chattels as security for a debt;
- an agreement by which a legal or equitable right to chattels or to a charge or security over chattels is conferred (whether or not the agreement is intended to be followed by the execution of another instrument).

The definition does not include:

- an assignment for the benefit of the creditors of the person making it;
- a marriage settlement or an agreement for a marriage settlement;
- a transfer or assignment of a ship or vessel required to be registered under the Acts adopted by Schedule 2.6 of, and Part 2 of Schedule 5 to, the Constitution, or a share of any such ship or vessel;
- a transfer of goods in the ordinary course of business of a trade or calling;
- a bill of sale of goods outside the country or at sea;
- a bill of lading, india warrant, warehouse keeper's certificate, warrant or order for the delivery of goods, or any other document used in the ordinary course of business as:
    - proof of the possession or control of chattels;
    - authorising or purporting to authorise, by endorsement or by delivery, the possessor of the document to transfer or receive the chattels represented; or
    - a preferable lien on wool or crops or a stock mortgage;
- a debenture issued by an incorporated or joint-stock company and secured on the capital stock or chattels of the company;
- a hire-purchase agreement.

A bill of sale (s 4(2)) and a lien on yearly crops (s 14) registered under the provisions of the Instruments Act (Ch 254) do not need to be registered under the Companies Act 1997.

FLOATING CHARGES ON THE UNDERTAKING OR PROPERTY OF A COMPANY

It is not clear from the wording of the requirement, but it seems that floating charges referred to in s 231(2)(a) of the Companies Act 1997 refers to floating charges over the whole or only part of the undertaking, property or business of the company. It need not be over the "whole undertaking or all the property of the company".

All floating charges are registrable. This contrasts with fixed charges which are registrable only if they fall within one of the specific headings.

CHARGES ON CALLS MADE BUT NOT PAID

Charges on shares where the shareholder has been asked to pay the outstanding money for the cost of the shares, but payment has yet to be made.

CHARGES ON A SHIP OR AIRCRAFT, OR ON A SHARE IN A SHIP OR AIRCRAFT

This includes mortgages on ships or a share in a ship. Legal mortgages are created in the manner provided for under the Merchant Shipping Act (Ch 242) and registered at the ship's port of registry. Equitable mortgages do not need to comply with this formality.

CHARGES ON GOODWILL, ON A PATENT OR LICENCE UNDER A PATENT, ON A TRADE MARK

Trade mark or service marks and licences to use trade marks or service marks, and on a registered design or a licence to use a registered design will come under s 222(4)(c) of the Companies Act 1997.[193]

CHARGES ON THE BOOK DEBTS OF A COMPANY

A book debt is a debt becoming due to a business entrepreneur in the normal course of carrying on the business as distinct from either a debt due on transactions unconnected with the business or a debt that is merely incidental to the conduct of the business: *Waters v Widdows*.[194] For example, short-term deposits made by an investment company are book debts, whereas similar deposits made by a manufacturing company might not be so classified. The distinction is important because the Companies Act 1997 requires only charges on the book debts of a company to be registered.[195]

In some types of securities, title in the asset remains with, or is vested in, the secured creditor. These types of security arrangements are not registrable under the Companies Act 1997 because if the debtor company did not

193 See *Brinks Incorporated and Brinks Air Courier Australia Pty Ltd v Brinks Pty Ltd* (1997) N1567 for a discussion of trade marks.

194 (1983) 54 ALR 691. See also *Official Receiver v Tailby* (1886) 18 QBD 25.

195 Companies Act 1997, s 222(4)(h).

own the assets, then it could not "create" a charge over them. Examples are assets held by a company pursuant to a lease or a hire purchase agreement. So hire purchase agreements are not charges created by a company and are therefore not registrable under the Companies Act 1997.[196]

Charges that do not need to be registered include:

- charges on personal chattels, including personal chattels that are unascertained or to be acquired are not registrable charges;
- charges on property of an overseas company which is located outside the country;
- charges solely on land to secure any issue of debentures.

The registration requirements are "mandatory", in that the Companies Act 1997 provides that if the charge is governed by Part XIII of the Companies Act 1997, the charge "shall" [i.e., must] be submitted for registration.

If the purpose of the submission for registration of charges is to protect proposed lenders to the company, the list of charges that should be registered should be as complete as possible, and where the Companies Act 1997 does not refer to a charge, those types of omitted charges should be easily discoverable by some other method of investigation. It is arguable that the Companies Act 1997 does not guarantee potential creditors the protection that they can legitimately expect. Bearing in mind the list of charges specified in s 222(4), there are several forms of lending that would escape the list of eight categories. They include:

- a charge on other companies' securities;
- a hire purchase;
- a lease agreement;
- a loan with a reservation of title (*Romalpa*) clause.

Most of the above forms of lending are not charges because true ownership of the assets remains with the lender; it is not transferred to the ownership of the company. Hire purchase agreements created by companies are not "charges" for the purposes of s 222 of the Companies Act 1997, and do not have to be registered.[197] A loan with a reservation of title clause will allow the lender or trade supplier to repossess property to enforce payment of the price. However, it does not fall within the terms of s 222(4) of the Companies Act 1997 and need not be submitted for registration to make it enforceable.

196 *Paintin & Nottingham Ltd v Miller Gale and Winter* [1971] NZLR 164.
197 *Paintin & Nottingham Ltd v Miller Gale and Winter* [1971] NZLR 164.

***Retention of title or* Romalpa *clauses*[198]**

One method of ensuring that payment is made for goods supplied by a creditor to a company is by including a retention of title clause in the agreement.[199] By including this clause in the contract, the creditor retains ownership of the property until the time when full payment has been made, at which time, ownership of title to the goods is transferred to the buyer (in this case, the company). The retention of title clause gives the creditor the power to recover possession of the goods supplied, and not merely be an unsecured creditor for the amount of the purchase price. Although retention of title clauses may be drafted to apply to goods that have already been paid for, the value of such clauses lies in applying to goods on which all or some payment is outstanding.[200]

The use of retention of title clauses are a common practice with sales of trading stock. The clauses are clearly applicable to goods that have been delivered to the purchaser and have not been mixed or altered,[201] and have not left the possession of the purchaser, for example by being sold.[202] In such cases, where the goods have been resold, the creditor may attempt to follow or trace the proceeds of sale and obtain these. This will depend on whether they were resold by the purchaser for the account of the seller.[203] However, it should be noted that a normal retention of title clause is useful only where the goods can be identified. If the goods have been transformed or mixed with other goods, the retention of title clause will fail and the seller will be in the same position as an unsecured creditor: *pari passu* will apply

Such clauses, however, will not be effective if the clause reserves an interest less than full ownership of the goods,[204] or where the goods have been mixed. In such cases, where the purchaser is a company, the seller's interest will amount to a registrable charge which must be registered in accordance with s 222 of the Companies Act 1997.[205]

198 For more detailed analysis of this area of the law, see McCormack, G, "Reservation of Title in England and New Zealand" (1992) 12 *Legal Studies* 195; McCormack, G, *Reservation of Title* (2nd edn, Sweet & Maxwell, London, 1995); Collier, B, *Romalpa Clauses: Reservation of Title in Sale of Goods Transactions* (Law Book Company, Sydney, 1989).

199 The clause is also referred to as a "reservation of title clause" or a "Romalpa clause" after the case that explicitly established this method of security: *Aluminium Industrie Vaassen BV v Romalpa Aluminium Ltd* [1976] 1 WLR 676.

200 *Armour v Thyssen Edelstahlwerke AG* [1991] 2 AC 339.

201 Cf *Pongakawa Sawmill Ltd v New Zealand Forest Products Ltd* [1992] 3 NZLR 304.

202 *AM Bisley Ltd v Gore Engineering & Retail Sales Ltd* (1989) 2 NZBLC 103,595.

203 *Re Andrabell Ltd* [1984] 3 All ER 407, *Tatung (UK) Ltd v Galex Leisure Ltd* (1989) 5 BCC 608.

204 For example, where the agreement passes the equitable title, without the legal title passing. In such cases, the purchaser does not obtain full ownership (i.e., legal and equitable ownership) of the goods. As such, the charge, in order to be valid, must be submitted for registration: *Aluminium Industrie Vaassen BV v Romalpa Aluminium Ltd* [1976] 1 WLR 676.

205 *Re Bond Worth Ltd* [1979] 3 WLR 629.

Priority of company charges

Section 231 and Schedule 15 of the Companies Act 1997 set out some of the rules governing priority of charges; i.e., who should be repaid first. In addition to this, where the Companies Act 1997 does not make provision or adequate provision for priorities of charges, the underlying law rules (i.e., both common law and equitable rules) apply to fill the gap.

Section 231 and Schedule 15 determine priority only where *all* the competing charges are registrable under s 222(4).[206] Priorities between competing unregistrable charges or between unregistrable and registrable charges are therefore determined according to the underlying law. Therefore, the first thing to do in any analysis of which of two or more competing charges takes priority, is to determine which of these two sets of rules apply. This in turn entails a determination of whether all or one or more of the competing charges are registrable under s 222(4). If *all* the competing charges are not registrable, or *at least one of them* is not registrable under the priority rules set out in the Companies Act 1997, then the underlying law rules regarding priority of payment applies. If, however, all of the competing charges or at least one of them is a registrable charge under the Act, the rules set out in the Companies Act 1997 apply. For convenience, we shall first consider the rules under the underlying law and then the rules under Companies Act 1997.

Underlying law priority rules

There are two main rules. The first rule is that where the equities are equal the first in time prevails.[207] So, for example, the charge that was created first has priority unless the equities are not equal. A situation where the equities would not be equal is where the first chargee's conduct has led the second chargee to believe that the property is not encumbered. The second rule is that a person who bona fide purchases for value a legal interest in property takes free of existing equitable interests in that property provided he or she does not have notice of their existence and provided there is no fraud, misrepresentation or gross negligence on his or her part.[208] A bona fide purchaser for value without notice takes the property that is subject to a fixed charge free of the charge. The creditor is obliged to pursue his or her remedies against the company that has disposed of the security in breach of the terms of the charge.

Priorities of registrable charges (priority where all the charges are registrable)

Section 231 and Schedule 15.1 and 15.2 of the Companies Act 1997 govern the priority of registrable charges. As a general rule a charge that has been

206 See above for these type of charges.
207 *Cave v Cave* (1880) 15 Ch D 639; *Rice v Rice* (1853) 2 Drew 73, 61 ER 646.
208 *Pilcher v Rawlins* (1872) 7 Ch App 259.

registered earlier has priority over a subsequently registered charge. Schedule 15.1(1) sets out the general priority rules in relation to registered charges as follows:

A registered charge on property of a company has priority over:

- a subsequent registered charge on the property, *unless* the subsequent registered charge was created before the creation of the prior registered charge *and* the chargee in relation to the subsequent registered [registrable] charge proves that the chargee in relation to the prior registered charge had notice of the subsequent registered [registrable] charge at the time when the prior registered charge was created;[209] and
- an unregistered charge on the property created before the creation of the registered charge, unless the chargee in relation to the unregistered charge proves that the chargee in relation to the registered [registrable] charge had notice of the unregistered [registrable] charge at the time when the registered charge was created; and
- an unregistered charge on the property created after the creation of the registered charge.

Schedule 15.2(2)–(5) illustrates the operation of the priority rules in Schedule 15.1.

Priority rules for registrable charges – Schedule 15.1

	A does not have notice of B	*A has notice of B*
Charge B created prior to registered charge A but registered after it	A has priority	B has priority
Unregistered charge B created prior to registered charge A	A has priority	B has priority
Unregistered charge B created after registered charge A	A has priority	

Subordination of a debt

The above rules apply unless a chargee has consented (expressly or impliedly) to give up priority.[210] For example, debentures may be issued on terms that the debt owing is to be subordinated so that other debts will be repaid before it is repaid. Alternatively, the terms may rank the debt on the

209 Notice may be constructive, for example, where a later chargee learned some facts which would put a reasonable person on enquiry as to whether there was an earlier charge but he or she failed to make enquiries.

210 Companies Act 1997, s 231(2).

same repayment level as the share capital. The holder of a floating charge is deemed to have consented to giving priority to a later fixed charge[211] unless the contract creating the floating charge contains a "negative pledge" and the pledge is registered, and so long as the floating charge does not become a fixed charge on any of the property.[212]

Assignment and variation of a charge

Section 224 of the Companies Act 1997 provides for the assignment and variation of charges. In order to keep the Register of Charges up to date, s 224(1) provides that where a charge is assigned, the new owner (assignee) must notify the Registrar of Companies within two months after he or she becomes the holder of the charge. The assignee must also give copy of the notice to the company. A similar notice to the Registrar is required where there is a variation of the terms of a charge that has the effect of increasing the company's liabilities secured by the charge or prohibiting or restricting the creation of subsequent charges on the subject property.[213]

Satisfaction and release of property from a charge

Where the debt secured by a charge has been paid in whole or in part, or the property charged has been partly or wholly released from the charge, any person who is interested in the charge or the property or undertaking may submit to the Registrar of Companies a prescribed memorandum of satisfaction.[214] The section does not lay down any time limit within which this must be done. If this prescribed memorandum of satisfaction is filed, then the security interest becomes free of the charge, or free of the charge up to the specified amount.

Liquidation and floating charges

The issue of priority of charges may also arise between the chargee of a floating charge and the company's liquidator. Section 347 of the Companies Act 1997 provides that where a company is in liquidation, any

211 It has been held that the parties cannot agree to a floating charge being given precedence over an earlier floating charge, because the two charges would be incompatible. See note 130.
212 See discussion on "negative pledge" at p 526.
213 Section 224(2) of the Companies Act 1997.
214 Companies Act 1997, ss 227, 230, 227(1)(c). (Notice of partial or total satisfaction of registered charge) (Form 31); 227(1)(d) (Notice of release or disposal of charged property (Form 32).) A prescribed memorandum of satisfaction in the Companies Regulation 1998 is yet to be prepared.

floating charge created over its property within six months *before commencement of its liquidation*, is void as against the company's liquidator.[215] However, such a charge is not void against the company's liquidator where:

- it is proved that the company was able to pay its debts as they became due in the ordinary course of business immediately after the charge was created;[216] or
- consideration (in the form of a contemporaneous or future advance), guarantee or supply of property or services to the company) is given at or after the time of creation of the charge.

Conclusion

The law relating to corporate debt capital involves an appreciation of many other areas of law. Outside the domain of the Companies Act 1997 account needs to be taken of principles of property law and equity, particularly in relation to competing interests over property, the role of trustees and the nature of secured transactions. Within the Companies Act 1997, the provisions we have examined in this chapter must be read alongside the chapters dealing with the interests of creditors on winding up of a company, and the regulation of fundraising.

215 Companies Act 1997, s 347(2).
216 Companies Act 1997, s 347(3).

Chapter 13

Receivership

Introduction

When a company becomes insolvent, it should go into external administration. In PNG, there are two main types of external administration: receivership and liquidation (also known as winding up).[1] We will deal with receivership in this chapter and liquidation in the next. Although insolvency is the main reason why companies go into receivership or liquidation, it is possible for these to happen even where a company is solvent. Receivership and liquidation serve two different purposes. Receivership is a way for a secured creditor to try to recover its loan by appointing a person to act on its behalf. Liquidation, on the other hand, involves an independent professional liquidator whose duty it is to sell the company's assets and distribute the proceeds among the company's creditors; the end result is usually the dissolution of the company.

The applicable law

Receivers can be appointed in relation to the assets of a natural person[2] or other type of business organisation, for example, a firm or a business group.[3] In such cases the provisions of the Companies Act 1997 relating to receivership will not apply: either the underlying law, or the underlying law and specific legislation would apply.

1 The other forms of external administration is a voluntary or statutory scheme of arrangement. In other jurisdictions, voluntary administration are also important forms of external administration. In New Zealand there is also provision for statutory management. However, this type of external administration was not adopted by the Companies Act 1997.

2 See for example, Part X (ss 102–104) of the Lawyers Act 1986, which, in certain circumstances, empowers the Council of the PNG Law Society to apply to the National Court for the appointment of a receiver to any property held or recoverable by a lawyer or law firm.

3 One of the entities in respect of whose assets a receiver was appointed in *Elijah Harold v Regina Waim Harro (No 2)* (2004) N2646, was a business group.

Types of receiver

A receiver is a natural person who is appointed to take control of some or all of the company's assets. The receiver will usually be someone who is independent of the company's management, and normally will be an accountant or a lawyer in private practice. According to the underlying law, a receiver had very limited powers: to receive and sell the company's assets, but not to carry on the company's business. To authorise the receiver to carry on the business, this power had to be specifically granted, and it was done by appointing the person as "receiver and manager". Following the commencement of the Companies Act 1997, however, it is no longer necessary to confer such powers, as the appointment of someone as a receiver automatically carries with it the powers of management.[4]

Appointment of receiver

A receiver may be appointed either by a secured creditor who wishes to enforce its security or by the National Court. Most receivers would be appointed by a creditor of the company, pursuant to a contractual power contained in the charge or other security instrument. This will usually be the case because the company has defaulted in its obligations under the charge.

Appointment under deed or agreement (private appointment of a receiver)

Normally, the security instrument will give the secured creditor power to appoint a receiver at any time after the loan secured by the charge becomes payable. This is sometimes referred to as a private appointment, and will usually occur on the happening of an "event of default". Such events or debtor defaults will include non-payment of interest or principal (execution issued against the borrowing company) or when the company ceases to carry on business. If an event of default does not occur, the creditor will not have a right to appoint a receiver;[5] in such a case the debtor company may be entitled to substantial damages, as appointment of a receiver is a drastic remedy and can almost immediately destroy a company's credibility.[6] Where an event

4 Section 254(1) of the Companies Act 1997 defines a receiver as "a receiver, or a manager, or a receiver and manager in respect of any property appointed". In addition, s 264(2)(c) of the Act gives a receiver the power to "*manage* the property in receivership".

5 It may be possible to apply to the court for a receiver to be appointed. However, courts exercise this power very sparingly. See *Rea v Chix Products (California) Ltd* (1986) 3 NZCLC 99,852 and below at 530–534.

6 Watson, S, Gunasekara, G, Gedye, M, van Roy, Y, Ross, M, Longdin, L, Sims, A and Brown, L, *The Law of Business Organisations* (4th edn, Palatine Press, Auckland, 2003), p 387. The creditor has the onus of proving that the appointment was improper.

of default occurs, however, the creditor may immediately appoint a receiver;[7] and the creditor may rely on the event of default which has occurred. He may do this even though at the time of appointing the receiver he was not aware that there had been a real breach, but had relied on some other purported breach which turned out not to have been a real breach.[8]

The method of appointment set out in the charge or other security instrument must be strictly followed. In addition to any requirements contained in the security instrument, s 257(2) of the Companies Act 1997 provides that the appointment must be in writing.[9]

Appointment of a receiver by the National Court

The heading of this section could be headed by the National Court. District Courts and other courts in PNG (e.g., Village Courts, Land Courts, Land Titles Commission, etc.) do not have jurisdiction to appoint a receiver. However, the Supreme Court has power to substitute such orders on an appeal from the National Court and, although it does not have express original jurisdiction to appoint a receiver, it may on appeal substitute. In addition, in its original jurisdiction (constitutional), there is nothing to prevent the court from appointing a receiver. For example, where it orders damages for breach of constitutional rights and it fears that the property of the defendant may be dissipated in order to frustrate the enforcement of the remedy.

The National Court has an inherent power, as well as statutory powers, to appoint persons to be receivers of undertakings and assets of companies.[10] This is acknowledged by the definition of receiver in s 254(1) of the Companies Act 1997, which states that a receiver means a receiver, or a manager, or a receiver and manager in respect of any property appointed "by the Court in the exercise of a power conferred on the Court or in the exercise of its inherent jurisdiction". The National Court's inherent jurisdiction arises from the adoption of the common law and equity of England as part of the underlying law, whereas its statutory jurisdiction arises from several sources. The court's general jurisdiction in this area is established by s 12(1) of the Laws Adoption and Adaptation Act (Ch 20), which authorises the National Court, where "it appears to the Court just or convenient" to appoint "a receiver"[11] by "an interlocutory order . . . either conditionally or on such

7 *DFC Financial Services Ltd v Coffey* [1991] 2 NZLR 513.

8 *McMahon v State Bank of New South Wales* (1990) 8 ACLC 315; *Curragh Developments Ltd (in rec) v Rodewald* (2001) 9 NZCLC 262,639.

9 The fact that the appointment of a receiver is defective, does not automatically mean that the transactions entered into by the receiver are also invalid: see Companies Act 1997, s 256, and below at pp 554–555.

10 Although it is common to refer to a company being placed into or put into receivership, strictly speaking, it is the assets of the company that are placed into receivership.

11 It is submitted that although the section refers only to "receiver" and not "receiver and manager", the word "receiver" would be interpreted to include a "receiver and manager".

terms and conditions as the Court thinks just". Additionally, there are several provisions in various statutes which supplement this power by granting specific power to the National Court to appoint a receiver or a receiver and manager.[12]

The District Court does not have power to appoint a receiver. The District Court, being a creature of statute, must be given specific power in this regard, and there is no provision in the District Courts Act (Ch 40) conferring such power on District Courts.

When will the National Court appoint receivers?[13]

Courts in British Commonwealth jurisdictions have considered that their power to appoint receivers should be exercised only in the most exceptional cases, and as a last resort to preserve property at risk or to facilitate enforcement of a judgment where there is no other means of enforcement.[14] Although at first sight the power to appoint a receiver where "it appears to the Court just or convenient" seems to be quite a wide power, in fact courts have been very reluctant to exercise the power and interfere in the internal affairs of companies and will do so only sparingly and in limited circumstances: they will do so only as a last resort and when the court is satisfied that the existing law and contractual arrangements are such that there are no other means of achieving the desired end. Where there are such

12 The inherent and statutory jurisdiction is reinforced by provisions in the National Court Rules (Ch 38) regulating the procedure and powers of the National Court. The main rules are contained in Order 14, r 9(d) and Order 14, Division 3 – Receivers, rr 17–23.

13 The appointment of a receiver may be interlocutory or final. For example, an appointment of a receiver may be sought to protect an asset which is in danger of being dissipated whilst other legal proceedings are current. (See *CAC (NSW) v Walker* (1987) 5 ACLC 991 at 993.) An appeal to the Supreme Court from an interlocutory judgment of the National Court appointing a receiver may be made without leave of the Supreme Court: Supreme Court Act (Ch 37), s 14(3)(b)(ii).

14 For New Zealand authorities to this effect, see: *Re Tisco Holdings (NZ) Ltd* (unreported, HC, Auckland, M 1322/95, 27 October 1995); *Rea v Chix Products (California) Ltd* (1986) 3 NZCLC 99,852; *Steel v Matatoki International Ltd* (1988) 4 NZCLC 64,710; *Te Runanganui o Ngati Kahungunu Inc v Scott* [1995] 1 NZLR 250; *Re Samco Sargent Consolidated Ltd* (1977) 1 BCR 112; *Bullen v Tourcorp Developments Ltd* (1988) 4 NZCLC 64,661; *Bank of Credit and Commerce International SA v BRS Kumar Bros Ltd* [1994] 1 BCLC 211. For Australian authorities, see: *Duffy v Super Centre Development Corporation Ltd* [1967] 1 NSWR 382; *Bond Brewing Holdings Ltd v National Australia Bank Ltd* (1990) 1 ASCR 445. For an overview of the Australian position, see O'Donovan J, *Company Receivers and Managers* (2nd edn, Law Book Co, Sydney, 1992), especially at pp 6532–6544 where it has been suggested that the courts in Australia will exercise the "just or convenient jurisdiction" in four classes of circumstances: where a security is enforceable; where the security is in jeopardy; where the corporations property is in jeopardy; and in the circumstances described as equitable execution.

dissensions in the governing body of the company that it is impossible to carry on the business with advantage to the parties interested, the court will interfere, but only for a limited time, and to as small an extent as possible. The function of a court appointed receiver is that of a caretaker, rather than a doctor – not to restore the company to profitability, but to preserve those assets of the company upon which its fortunes may depend, and to preserve its potentiality for earning profits in the future.[15]

This seems to also be the position in PNG. The court will be willing to appoint a receiver and manager to preserve property which, but for such appointment, might disappear or be dissipated, and also to ensure the proper administration where there are severe disputes between the directors. In *Gabriel Velegamus v Paul Aisoli*,[16] a shareholder in a landowner development company applied to the National Court for the appointment of a receiver to the assets and undertaking of the company. The company had been formed specifically to exploit the timber resource in a Timber Rights Purchase Area (TRPA). However, ownership of the land subject to the TRPA became subject to "a long and difficult dispute" among "some 40 clans involved", and there was dispute as to who were the rightful representatives of the landowning clans, who had authority to decide who should comprise the board of directors, who constituted the board, and whether there was a legally binding lease/management agreement with a logging company where there were two foreign-owned companies vying for interest in the exploitation of the timber resource. Relations between the shareholders and directors of the company was extremely acrimonious and the judge considered that "the parties are so much at odds that I can see no hope of any satisfactory resolution". There was also evidence before the court that "cut timber was rotting away and decreasing in value", and would continue to do so the longer the company was prevented from exporting the cut logs. In addition, there was evidence that the timber permit had a minimum cut requirement and was liable to forfeiture or non-renewal". He considered that: "If the logs are not sold, then all parties will suffer." The judge (Andrew AJ) considered that under the National Court's inherent jurisdiction, it may appoint a receiver and manager of the undertaking and assets of a company where the property of the company is in jeopardy or where the ownership and/or control of the company is in dispute such that there is no effective management. Given the facts of the case (that the property of the company was in jeopardy and that the management was ineffective), he ordered the appointment of a receiver and manager to all the undertaking and assets of the company.

15 See *Duffy v Super Centre Development Corporation Ltd* [1967] 1 NSWR 382 at 383–384, per Street J.

16 [1988–89] PNGLR 63.

The recent case of *Elijah Harold v Regina Waim Harro (No 2)*[17] is also in line with the above statement of the law, i.e., that the court will exercise its powers of appointing receivers in limited circumstances.

The applicant applied to the National Court for a receiver to be appointed in respect of the property and undertakings of three companies and a business group controlled by her former husband, because of persistent failure to comply with orders for discovery on matters essential to the resolution of a property settlement in court proceedings in which the applicant was a party. She argued that the appointment of a receiver as an officer of the court was the only way in which the court could take control of the proceedings and get relevant evidence relating to the companies and the business group before the court. Manuhu AJ, referring, *inter alia*, to Order 9, r 5 of the National Court Rules, which provided that where a party made default in complying with procedural requirements, "the Court may make such orders as it thinks fit", stated:

> The cumulative effect of these provisions is that the Court has the discretionary authority to appoint a receiver in any appropriate proceeding before it. However, like all exercise of discretion, the exercise of that authority has to be justified. It is therefore necessary to appreciate the types of situations warranting the appointment of a receiver.

He then went on to consider the law relating to court appointed receivers, and concluded that such a receiver should be appointed:

(a) where the appointment is necessary to facilitate execution of property;
(b) where the appointment is necessary for the purpose of safeguarding the property for the benefit of those who may be entitled to it;
(c) where the appointment is necessary to preserve property from some danger which threatens it;
(d) where the appointment is necessary to ascertain whether certain transactions have occurred to defeat matrimonial causes claims;
(e) where the appointment is necessary to enable the Court to expedite a proceeding before it;
(f) where the appointment is necessary to enable the Court to avail itself of relevant evidence;
(g) where the appointment is necessary to enable a company to continue to operate; and
(h) where the appointment appears to the Court to be just and convenient.

17 (2004) N2646.

He considered that the failure of the companies and business group to discover adequately was serious enough to warrant a change of process, and to set up one that would enable the court to take control of the legal proceedings with a view to having it finalised without further delays. This warranted the appointment of a receiver and manager to take control of the property and business of the companies and business group "until the final determination of [the] proceedings . . . or until further order".

Who has standing to apply

Professor O'Donovan lists eight persons who have standing to seek the appointment of a receiver by the court: (1) any "party" who is before the court; (2) a legal mortgagee; (3) an equitable mortgagee; (4) an assignee; (5) a subsequent mortgagee; (6) the defendant corporation; (7) third parties and shareholders, and (8) creditors.[18]

It is not necessary that the applicant have a proprietary interest in the assets subject to the receivership application. As the Full Court of Victoria stated in *Bond Brewing Holdings Ltd v National Australia Bank Ltd*:[19]

> [O]n principle all that need be shown to give rise to the discretion to appoint a receiver . . . is that the applicant has a right which will be protected or enforced by the grant of that remedy and that no adequate remedy at law is available.

The Full Court also considered that, where the company opposed the application, it would be inappropriate to appoint a receiver and manager on the application of an unsecured creditor: *Bond Brewing Holdings Ltd v National Australia Bank Ltd*.[20]

Appointment under the Companies Act 1997 and other statutes

Appointment by the court may also be made pursuant to the Companies Act 1997 and other statutes. Under the Companies Act 1997, for example, a receiver may be appointed under the oppression provisions. There are several statutory provisions which provide for appointment of a receiver or receiver and manager on the occurrence of certain events. Some of these are limited to individuals or partnerships, but some include the appointment to property held by companies.

18 O'Donovan J, *Company Receivers and Managers* (2nd edn, Law Book Co, Sydney, 1992), pp 6561–6563.
19 (1990) 8 ACLC 330 at 345–346.
20 (1990) 8 ACLC 330 at 347ff.

Secion 46(b) of the Organic Law on the Integrity of Political Parties and Candidates, provides that, where the Commission cancels the registration of a political party, it may appoint a receiver to take charge of the property of the party and, for that purpose, obtain all books of account, documents, title deeds and other papers and documents (in hard copy or electronic format) relating to the assets and liabilities of the party.

The effect of the appointment of a statutory manager

The Banks and Financial Institutions Act 2000, Life Insurance Act 2000 and the Superannuation (General Provisions) Act 2000 make provision for the appointment of a "statutory manager" in situations where a bank or life insurance business is in financial trouble. The appointment of a statutory manager affects the appointment and administration of receivers and liquidators. The Banks and Financial Institutions Act 2000 and Life Insurance Act 2000 and the Superannuation (General Provisions) Act 2000 provide that the term "external administrator" includes a receiver and liquidator.

Section 20 of the Married Women's Property Act (Ch 281) provides that the court has in an action or proceeding instituted by a woman or by a next friend on her behalf, power to appoint a receiver to enforce payment of costs of the opposite party out of any property that is subject to a restraint on anticipation, "as to it seems just".

The Mining Development Act (Ch 197), s 9(3) does not say that the person is a receiver, but that: "The person who is in possession under Subsection (2)(a) has and may exercise the powers and authorities of a receiver and manager of the mine and of all other property and assets of the borrower comprised in the mortgage." (Cf Insolvency Act (Ch 253), s 96.)

The Partnership Act (Ch 148), s 24(2)(a) and (b) provides that on the application of a judgment creditor of a partner, a court may make an order charging the partner's interest in the partnership property and profits with payment of the amount of the judgment debt and interest, and by the same or a subsequent order appoint a receiver of his or her share of profits (whether already declared or accruing), and of any other money that may be coming to him or her in respect of the partnership.

Where a company has issued securities that are subject to the Securities Act 1997, the court is given express power, under s 73(3)(f) and s 143(1)(h)(i) and (ii) to appoint a "receiver or manager" of any property the company has given as security (collateral) for the securities, upon the application of the trustee (who are appointed under the Securities Act 1997 to act in the interests of investors).

In relation to, and for the purpose of, acquiring or retaining possession of the property of an insolvent, a trustee is in the same position as if he were *a receiver of that property appointed by the Court in its equitable jurisdiction,* and on application by the trustee, the court may enforce the acquisition or retention of the property as if he were a receiver.

Section 169(2)(a) of the Insolvency Act (Ch 253) provides that, at any time after the presentation of a petition against a debtor, the court may appoint a receiver or manager of the property or business, or any part of the property or business, of the debtor.

Part X (ss 102–104) of the Lawyers Act 1986 empowers the Council of the PNG Law Society to apply to the National Court for the appointment of a receiver to any property held or recoverable by a lawyer or law firm, where various circumstances exist.

According to the underlying law, a court appointed receiver only had such powers as were expressly conferred on him or her by the terms of the court order making the appointment. The Companies Act 1997, however, now provides that the receiver will have full powers of management unless the court otherwise orders.[21] In most cases where the court appoints a receiver, it will be to maintain the *status quo* whilst complicated legal issues that cannot be quickly resolved are litigated. In such cases the receiver's powers will usually be limited to taking custody and control of all or some of the assets of the company to protect them and preserve their value.[22]

Eligibility for appointment: who may be appointed a receiver

The Companies Act 1997, like the New Zealand Companies Act 1993, but unlike the Australian Corporations Act 2001, does not set out any particular qualifications or standards for a receiver.[23] The Act does, however, list persons and organisations who are disqualified from being appointed or acting as receivers, unless the National Court orders otherwise.[24] Some are incompetent to act in any receivership, whereas others are disqualified from acting in particular receiverships because they are too closely related to the parties involved.

Persons who are disqualified from acting in any receivership are:[25]

- a person who is under 18 years of age;
- an undischarged bankrupt;

21 See Companies Act 1997, s 264, in particular, subsection (2)(c).

22 See for example, *Gabriel Velegamus v Paul Aisoli* [1988–89] PNGLR 63.

23 As we shall see, the Companies Act 1997 provides that only Registered Liquidators may be appointed or act as liquidators. Given the significant effect that both appointments can have on creditors, it is suggested that a similar restriction should have been placed on the appointment of receivers.

24 It would seem that the circumstances where the court will do this must be exceptional.

25 Companies Act 1997, s 256(1). Both the person who appoints and the disqualified person who acts as receiver, commit an offence and are liable on conviction to the penalty set out in s 413(2): Companies Act 1997, s 256(3).

- a person who is of unsound mind or otherwise incapable of managing his or her own affairs;
- a person who has been prohibited by the National Court from acting as a receiver or liquidator under ss 286(6) or 334(5) of the Companies Act 1997; or
- a person who is prohibited from promoting, directing or managing a company under the Companies Act (Ch 146) or the Companies Act 1997.
- a mortgagee of the property in receivership.[26]

Persons who are disqualified from acting in particular receiverships are:

- current directors of the debtor company or the secured creditor, and persons who have been directors within two years immediately preceding the commencement of the receivership;
- a current shareholder of the debtor company, or a former shareholder who has disposed of the shareholding within the period of two years preceding the commencement of the receivership;
- a shareholder holding 5 per cent or more of any class of shares issued by the secured creditor, or who had such a holding within the period of two years preceding the commencement of the receivership;
- a person who is disqualified from acting as a receiver by the instrument that confers the power to appoint a receiver.

Section 256(2) provides that a body corporate[27] shall not be appointed or act as a receiver.[28] However, there are other provisions that expressly authorise a body corporate to act as a receiver and the question is how does this provision in the Companies Act 1997 sit with these provisions.

Status of a receiver

A receiver appointed by the court is an officer of the court. As such, the receiver is not the agent of the debtor company or any of its creditors. He or

26 See definition of receiver in s 2 of Receiverships Act 1993 (NZ) and s 254(1) of the Companies Act 1997. The reason why the definition of receiver in s 2 of Receiverships Act 1993 (NZ) excludes "a mortgagee of the property in receivership" is that in New Zealand, Part VIIA of the Property Law Act 1952 contains the rules applicable to such mortgagees.

27 Neither the Companies Act 1997 nor the Interpretation Act (Ch 2) defines "body corporate". It includes companies, "corporation", a corporation sole, a society registered under the Savings and Loans Societies Act (Ch 141), incorporated by statute, "statutory body".

28 An appointment in contravention of this section is a nullity: *Portman Building Society v Gallwey* [1955] 1 All ER 227, and both the person who appoints and the body corporate that acts as receiver, commits an offence and are liable on conviction to the penalty set out in s 413(2): Companies Act 1997, s 256(3).

she acts to protect the interest of all stakeholders in the company. He or she acts as principal and as such is personally liable for all contracts entered into by the debtor company during the course of the receivership.[29] He or she is answerable to the court alone: he or she is not controlled by either the debtor company or its creditors. The receiver must act within the limits of the court order making the appointment and any subsequent court directions, given that the court has a right to review and control the receiver's conduct.

The primary role of a receiver is to act in the interest of the creditor on whose behalf he or she was appointed. He or she will take possession of the assets over which the debtor company has granted security and attempt to repay the secured creditor by either profitably managing the assets or selling them or by doing both. Even though the secured creditor appoints a receiver, in carrying out his or her functions, the receiver will normally be acting as the agent *of the company*, and not of the secured creditor. And this is so even though the receiver is appointed to look after the interests of the creditor, and not those of the company. This aspect of the agency relationship means that the company, and not the appointing creditor, is legally responsible for the acts or omissions of the receiver.

According to the underlying law, a receiver was the agent of the appointing creditor unless the security instrument expressly provided otherwise. Most instruments provided that the receiver was the agent of the debtor company. (The security instrument will usually stipulate that the receiver is the agent of the company.) However, since the enactment of the Companies Act 1997, even if the instrument is silent on this issue, s 257(3) states that a receiver appointed by, or under a power conferred by, a deed or agreement "is the agent of the company unless it is expressly provided otherwise in the deed or agreement or the instrument by or under which the receiver was appointed".[30] Although agent of the company, the receiver does not owe the debtor company the normal fiduciary duties of an agent.[31]

The receiver is appointed to act autonomously within the terms of his or her appointment, and he or she is not subject to directions of the debtor company or the appointing creditor, though the latter usually has a measure of control by stipulating in the security agreement a right to terminate the appointment and appoint a new receiver.

29 It is possible for the court appointed receiver to expressly contract out of personal liability.

30 If the documentation appoints the person to be the agent of the secured creditor (which will be rare), the appointee (who may be described as a receiver" in the documentation" will fall outside the statutory definition of a "receiver" in the Companies Act 1997 (see s 254(1) "receiver" para (c) and (d)) and the provisions dealing with receivership will not apply. In this situation, the appointing creditor will be considered to be a mortgagee in possession acting through an agent.

31 *Gomba Holdings (UK) Ltd v Minories Finance Ltd* [1989] 1 All ER 261 at 263.

As agent of the debtor company, the receiver has no power to bring legal proceedings or take other actions for the company's benefit in his or her own name; any such actions must be commenced in the name of the debtor company.

Effect of appointment of a receiver on debtor company

Effects on management

Where a receiver is appointed, the company remains as a separate personality. However, the appointment does have an important effect on management: *Hawkesbury Development Co Ltd v Landmark Finance Pty Ltd.*[32] The receiver takes control of the assets but cannot dismiss the directors. The scope of the powers remaining with the board depends upon the extent of the powers given to the receiver. The statutory duties of the directors will continue so that they will, for example, need to prepare company accounts and call statutory meetings.

Effects on property

The property of the company does not vest in the receiver on his or her appointment: *Australian Mutual Provident Society v George Myers & Co Ltd (in liq).*[33] The receiver can bring actions in the name of the company to recover assets.

Effects on creditors

A creditor is entitled to seek execution over assets subject to a floating charge at any time prior to crystallisation: *Robson v Smith.*[34] If the charge has crystallised and the execution has not been completed, then the debenture holder or the appointee will have priority: *Evans v Rival Granite Quarries Ltd.*[35]

Effects on lessors

The lessor retains any remedies under the lease, such as ejection for arrears: *Purcell v Public Curator of Queensland.*[36] Unlike liquidators, receivers have no general right to relinquish burdensome property. Similar principles apply to remedies under a chattel lease granted to the company before it was placed in receivership.

32 (1970) 92 WN (NSW) 199.
33 (1931) 47 CLR 65.
34 [1895] 2 Ch 118.
35 [1910] 2 KB 979.
36 (1922) 31 CLR 220.

Effects on contracts of employment

The law makes a distinction where the receiver is the agent of the debenture holder (the appointor) and where he or she is the agent of the company. In the former case, the appointment usually brings about the termination of all the employment contracts.[37] Where the receiver is the agent of the company, the appointment does not automatically terminate employee contracts except where the continuation of the employment contract is inconsistent (as a matter of fact) with the role of the receiver. A contract with a chief executive officer might be an example of such an inconsistency. So in this latter case, the employment contracts of most employees other than the managing director or CEO continue. However, there are two events which can occur soon after the appointment of a receiver which will terminate contracts of employment. First, where the appointment is accompanied by the immediate sale of the company's business, in which case all the employees' contracts of employment are automatically thereupon terminated. In this case the sale rather than the appointment brings about the dismissal – by repudiating the obligation to continue to employ.[38] Secondly, where simultaneously with, or very soon after, the appointment, the receiver enters into new contracts with particular employees which are inconsistent with the continuation of their previous contracts. However, the dismissal results from the new contractual arrangements rather than the appointment itself.[39] In *McEvoy v Incat Tasmania Pty Ltd*,[40] Finkelstein J summed up the law in relation to termination of employment contracts as follows:

> The starting point is to deal with the effect of the appointment of a receiver on a contract of employment. Surprisingly, the law is still in a state of uncertainty. It is generally accepted that the appointment of a receiver by the court terminates the contract: *Reid v Explosives Co Ltd* (1887) 19 QBD 264; *James Miller Holdings Ltd v Graham* (1978) 3 ACLR 604. This view is not, however, universally accepted: e.g. *International Harvester Export Co v International Harvester Australia Ltd* [1983] 1 VR 539; *Sipad Holding DDPO v Popovic* (1995) 14 ACLC 307. The rationale for the predominant view is that a court appointed receiver does not operate the concern on behalf of the company, but adverse to it. Speaking generally, the opposite is true in the case of a privately appointed receiver who is the company's agent. In that event, the rule is that the contract of employment is not terminated: *Foster Clark Ltd's*

37 *Hopley-Dodd v Highfield Motors (Derby) Ltd* [1969] ITR 289.
38 *Re Foster Clark's Ltd's Indenture* [1966] 1 All ER 43.
39 *(Re Mack Trucks (Britain) Ltd* [1967] 1 All ER 977, [1967] 1 WLR 780.
40 [2003] FCA 810 at [6].

Indenture Trusts, Loveland v Horscroft [1966] 1 WLR 125; *Nicoll v Cutts* [1985] BCLC 322. There are several exceptions to this rule, which are discussed in *Griffiths v Secretary of State for Social Services* [1974] QB 468. The exceptions are: (1) Where the appointment is accompanied by the sale of the company's business; (2) Where the receiver enters into a new employment contract which is inconsistent with the employee's old contract; and (3) Where the continuation of the employment contract is inconsistent with the role of the receiver. A contract with a chief executive officer might be an example of such an inconsistency.

Effects on other contracts

A receiver is free to disregard contracts entered into before his or her appointment if the company's reputation is not at stake. However, contracts should be upheld if the failure to observe would have a detrimental effect on the company's goodwill: *Airlines Airspares Ltd v Handley Page Ltd.*[41]

A receiver-manager is appointed as an agent of the company, so the company is liable for damages if a trading contract is disregarded: *George Barker Ltd v Eynon.*[42] Furthermore, he or she takes control subject to all prior equities entered into prior to his or her appointment: *Re Diesels & Components Pty Ltd (receivers and managers appointed).*[43]

Powers of receiver

The powers of a receiver appointed to take control of company property flow from two sources: from the security instrument or court order under which the receiver was appointed, and from the Companies Act 1997.[44] The security instrument or court order are the primary source of the receiver's powers and are supplemented by s 264(2) of the Companies Act 1997, which provides:

> (2) Subject to the deed or agreement or the order of the Court by or under which the appointment was made, a receiver may –

41 [1970] 1 Ch 193.

42 [1974] 1 WLR 462.

43 (1985) 9 ACLR 825.

44 Other Acts confer specific powers on receivers, though not in respect of companies: Organic Law on the Integrity of Political Parties and Candidates, s 46(1)(b), which provides that "Where the registration of a political party is cancelled under this Division the Commission may . . . appoint a receiver to take charge of the property of the party and, for that purpose, obtain all books of account, documents, title deeds and other papers and documents (in hard copy or electronic format) relating to the assets and liabilities of the party" whose registration is cancelled; Lawyers Act 1986, s 103(1).

(a) demand and recover, by action or otherwise, income of the property in receivership; and
(b) issue receipts for income recovered; and
(c) manage the property in receivership; and
(d) insure the property in receivership; and
(e) repair and maintain the property in receivership; and
(f) inspect at any reasonable time documents that relate to the property in receivership and that are in the possession or under the control of the company; and
(g) exercise, on behalf of the company, a right to inspect documents that relate to the property in receivership and that are in the possession or under the control of a person other than the company; and
(h) in a case where the receiver is appointed in respect of all or substantially all of the assets and undertaking of a company, change the registered office or address for service of the company.

The above provision means that the receiver will have all the powers listed in s 264(2) unless the security instrument specifically excludes or restricts them. One important power implied by s 264(2)(c) is to "manage the property in receivership", which means the power to carry on trading. It should be noted that the section does not include expressly a power of sale, so that it would seem that this must be expressly granted in the instrument or court order if the receiver is to have this power. It is therefore advisable for creditors to include in the instrument of charge an express power to sell.

There are various other powers that other sections of the Companies Act 1997 confer on receivers. These include powers to:

- call up unpaid share capital provided that it is covered by the charge created by the security instrument;[45]
- apply to the court for an order authorising the sale of mortgaged property, where the mortgagee refuses consent to the sale;[46]
- require directors of the company in receivership to provide reasonable assistance and to produce and verify financial and other relevant information;[47]
- apply to the court for directions in relation to conducting the receivership;[48]
- continue to act as a receiver where the company goes into liquidation.[49]

45 Companies Act 1997, s 265.
46 Companies Act 1997, s 267.
47 Companies Act 1997, s 262.
48 Companies Act 1997, s 283.
49 Companies Act 1997, s 280.

In a general, receivership (i.e., where the receiver is appointed to take control of all (or nearly all) of the company's property, including its "undertaking" (i.e., its business), the receiver (usually referred to as a "receiver and manager") will normally have power to manage the company's business, as well as power to sell assets and raise cash. In a particular receivership (i.e., where the receiver is appointed to take control of one piece of company property), the receiver will not normally be given power to manage the company's business. Section 264(2)(c) of the Companies Act 1997 provides that a receiver has the power to "manage the property in receivership". Where the receivership is over all or almost all of the company's property, this power will amount to a power to manage the company.

The power of a receiver to manage the business of a company is a useful power where the company may be able to trade its way out of financial difficulties, so that the creditor is repaid out of profits rather than proceeds of sale of assets, and the management of the company is then returned to the directors and company management.

Associated with the power to manage the business of the company is the power to borrow for the purposes of the receivership. Again, like the power of sale, s 264(2) does not specifically deal with a power to borrow. The power will (and should) normally be provided for in the security instrument. However, it may be argued that even if the security instrument is silent on the matter, the power may be implied as being reasonably incidental to the receiver's functions, especially where the receiver continues to carry on the business of the company:

> Generally then, a receiver will have power to take possession of the debtor company's assets, sue in its name, carry on all or part of its business, close down all or part of its business, sell its assets and repay the appointing creditor all principal and interest that is due. Thus the receiver will normally have full control of the debtor company's affairs as the company's directors had prior to the receivership.[50]

Duties of receiver

General

The general duties of a receiver are set out in s 268(1)–(3) of the Companies Act 1997. Theses subsections provide:

> (1) A receiver shall exercise his powers in good faith.
> (2) A receiver shall exercise his powers in a manner he believes on reasonable grounds to be in the best interests of the person in

50 Watson, S, Gunasekara, G, Gedye, M, van Roy, Y, Ross, M, Longdin, L, Sims, A and Brown, L, *The Law of Business Organisations* (4th edn, Palatine Press, Auckland, 2003), p 393.

> whose interests he was appointed [i.e., the appointing secured creditor].

The receiver's primary duty is to act in the interests of the secured creditor. However, s 268(3) also places a secondary duty on the receiver to "exercise his powers with reasonable regard to the interests" of the company and its creditors and those with other claims to or interests in the secured property.

Duty in selling property

A receiver's specific duties in relation to the sale of company property are set out in s 269 of the Companies Act 1997. These duties override the general duties set out in s 268.[51] In exercising a power of sale, the receiver has a duty to the company in receivership and its creditors, sureties[52] and others with an interest in the property "to obtain the best price reasonably obtainable as at the time of sale". It is not possible to cover the various aspects of this duty here.[53] However, the receiver should bear in mind the following considerations:

- although the receiver may choose the time to sell, he or she must ensure that there is adequate advertising before the property is sold;
- give proper consideration to whether items should be sold together or separately;[54]
- engage competent selling agents where necessary;
- plan a sale designed to test the market by public auction, where an auction sale would be usual for the type of property in question;
- ensure that the sale is properly advertised with full information about the features of the property likely to attract buyers;
- allow adequate time for the advertisement to have effect;
- refrain from telling possible buyers a reserve price at auction and details of the amount due to the secured creditor;

51 Companies Act 1997, s 268(5).

52 A surety is a person who makes himself or herself answerable for another's actions. In this context it is best to think of the surety as a person who contracts with the creditor of another person (the debtor) to be responsible for the debtor's debt if the debtor fails to pay. The surety's liability does not arise until the principal debtor has defaulted.

53 For a more detailed consideration of the duties of the receiver when selling company property, see below at pp 546–551 and Croft, C and Johannsson, J, *Mortgagee's Power of Sale* (2nd edn, LexisNexis, 2004). The recent English Court of Appeal decision of *Silven Properties Ltd v Royal Bank of Scotland plc* [2003] EWCA Civ 1409 contains a very useful summary of the receiver's duties.

54 *Champagne Perrier-Jouet SA v HH Finch Ltd* [1982] 3 All ER 713 at 725.

- refrain from selling the property to themselves, their associates or companies or entities in which they have an interest,[55] or if they do, prove that they took reasonable steps to obtain the best price reasonably obtainable at the time of sale.[56]

It has been said that the duty placed on receivers by s 269 ("to obtain the best price reasonably obtainable as at the time of sale") is "no more than a restatement of the common law rule [established in *Cuckmere Brick Co Ltd v Mutual Finance Ltd*][57] that a mortgagee exercising a power of sale must take reasonable precautions to obtain the true market value of the property".[58]

In *Silven Properties Ltd v Royal Bank of Scotland plc*,[59] the claimants mortgaged properties to the bank to secure loans. The bank, pursuant to the mortgages, appointed receivers of the mortgaged properties which were later sold by the bank and receivers. The mortgages, as was usual, provided that the receivers were to be the agents of the mortgagors (i.e., the claimants). The mortgagors sued the bank and the receivers for damages alleging that they had sold the properties at an undervalue. The Court of Appeal was concerned with the receiver's duty of sale in respect of certain properties. In the case of each of these sales it was conceded by the claimants or established by evidence at the trial that the properties were sold at the best price reasonably obtainable at the dates of such sales for the properties in the condition in which they were.

Lightman J, in giving the judgment of the court, set out various propositions relating to the duties of receivers on sale of mortgaged property. However, it was claimed that in respect of these sales the receivers were

55 *Farrar v Farrars Ltd* (1888) 40 Ch D 395.

56 *Tse Kwong Lam v Wong Chit Sen* [1983] 1 WLR 1349 at 1355–1356. Cf *Apple Fields Ltd v Damesh Holdings Ltd* [2003] UKPC 54, [2004] 1 NZLR 721.

57 [1971] 2 All ER 633.

58 Beck, A and Borrowdale, A, *Guidebook to New Zealand Companies and Securities Law* (7th edn, CCH New Zealand Ltd, Auckland, 2002), para 1314. *Cuckmere Brick Co Ltd v Mutual Finance Ltd* [1971] 2 All ER 633 has been applied in several PNG cases, including *Westpac Bank (PNG) Ltd v Henderson* [1990] PNGLR 112; *Australia and New Zealand Banking Group (PNG) Ltd v Kila Wari* (1990) N801; *Walter Perdacher v PNGBC* (1997) N1637; *PNGBC v Pala Aruai* (2002) N2234; *Nogiso Investments Ltd v PNGBC* (2003) N2439; and *Continental Trading Ltd v Dewe Patsy trading as PSB Trade Store* (2004) N2503. Although it may be possible to criticise the judges for applying the "negligence" test instead of the "good faith" test in these decisions, such a criticism cannot apply when a receiver sells "company property", as the Companies Act 1997 specifically authorises the negligence test. For a consideration of the above PNG decisions from the point of view of the mortgagee's duty on sale of land, see Mugambwa, J, "The Mortgagee's Duty on Sale: Australia and New Zealand Banking Group (PNG) Ltd v Kila Wari (Unreported, 1990) N801" (1992) 20 *Melanesian Law Journal* 155–161; Amankwah, H A, Mugambwa, J T, Muroa, G, *Land Law in Papua New Guinea* (LBC Information Services, Sydney, 2001), pp 178–181; Amankwah, H A, Mugambwa, J T, *Land Law and Policy in Papua New Guinea* (2nd edn, Cavendish, London, 2002), pp 226–233.

59 [2003] EWCA Civ 1409.

under a duty not to sell the properties as they were. Instead, they were under a duty before selling, in order to obtain the best price obtainable, to pursue planning applications for the development of the properties and (in the case of two of the properties, which were vacant or partially vacant, but in respect of which there were negotiations for grant of leases) to proceed with the grant of leases, and to defer a sale until these goals were achieved. The issue was whether, as a matter of law, the receivers were under a duty to delay the sale for the purposes suggested by the claimants and were entitled, whether or not it was reasonable for them to do so, to sell the properties without delay as they were.

The effect of s 41 of the constitution on powers and duties of receivers

It has been argued in cases where mortgagees have sold property under the power of sale in the mortgage instrument and the Land Registration Act (Ch 191) that s 41 of the Constitution can apply to overturn the sale.[60] That section declares to be invalid ("an unlawful act") any "harsh or oppressive" acts done under a valid law.[61] Similar arguments that found favour with the courts in holding that the provisions of s 41 could not be invoked in relation to a valid exercise of a mortgagee's power of sale derived from the Land Registration Act (Ch 191) are equally applicable to a valid exercise of a receiver's power of sale derived from s 269 of the Companies Act 1997. It is therefore worth considering if and when the court would exercise its powers under s 41 to overturn such sales.

Section 41(1) of the Constitution provides that any act that is done under a valid law but in the particular case is (a) "harsh or oppressive", or (b) not warranted by, or is disproportionate to, the requirements of the particular circumstances or of the particular case, or (c) otherwise not, in the particular circumstances, reasonably justifiable in a democratic society having a proper regard for the rights and dignity of mankind, is an "unlawful act". Most claims that have been brought in relation to the exercise of the mortgagee's power of sale have so far concentrated on s 41(1)(a) and (b), i.e., that the action was "harsh or oppressive" or was not warranted by, or is disproportionate to, the requirements of the particular circumstances or of the particular case.[62]

60 See Amankwah, H A, Mugambwa, J T, Muroa, G, *Land Law in Papua New Guinea* (LBC Information Services, Sydney, 2001), pp 181–182.

61 For a general consideration of this provision, see Kwa, E L, *Constitutional Law of Papua New Guinea* (Lawbook Co, Sydney, 2001), pp 153–154.

62 Arguments relating to the "not, in the particular circumstances, reasonably justifiable in a democratic society having a proper regard for the rights and dignity of mankind" have in the main focused on breaches of constitutional rights: see Chalmers, D R C, "Human rights and what is reasonably justifiable in a democratic society" (1975) 3 *Melanesian Law Journal* 92–102.

In *Tarere v ANZ Bank*,[63] an important question raised was whether the constitutional protection set out in s 41 was applicable to the mortgagee's power of sale. The defendant bank had sold several properties pursuant to the power of sale allowed in the Land Registration Act (Ch 191). The plaintiffs admitted that the mortgagee "had authority to foreclose [sic] under the terms of the subject mortgages under the relevant provisions of the Land Registration Act (Ch 191)".

There is judicial disagreement as to the scope of s 41. Some judges have held that it applies to all acts, whereas others have sought to limit its application to acts done under a law which restricts one of the constitutional rights.

In *Re Minimum Penalties Legislation*,[64] the majority of the Supreme Court (Kidu CJ, Kapi DCJ and Kaputin J) decided that the section applies to any act done under a valid law and is not limited to an act done under a law which restricts one of the constitutional rights.[65]

Hinchliffe J held that s 41 had no application to the exercise of a mortgagee's power of sale under the Land Registration Act (Ch 191), as s 41 was restricted to the protection of qualified rights as well as to basic and fundamental rights set out in the Constitution. Counsel for the plaintiffs had urged on the court that to adopt the restricted interpretation for s 41 would be "inappropriate to the circumstances of Papua New Guinea". This was rejected by Hinchliffe J:[66]

> I do not agree with that submission. I am of the view that the wider interpretation of s 41 of the Constitution could create confusion and

63 [1988] PNGLR 201.

64 [1984] PNGLR 314.

65 See also *SCR No 5 of 1985; Raz v Matane* [1985] PNGLR 329 and *Independent State of Papua New Guinea v Lohia Sisia* [1987] PNGLR 102.

66 [1988] PNGLR 201 at 205. In *Valentine v Michael Thomas Somare* [1988–89] PNGLR 241 Los J stated: "I do not consider that s 41 of the Constitution is meant to cut down any legitimate act as unlawful for minor indiscretions and acts that cause annoyance to a person. If the courts can use s 41 as a permanent pennant waving at all the decision-making authorities, there may not be any decisions made at all. In this respect, I agree with the cautious remarks by Hinchliffe J in *Tarere v ANZ Bank* [1988] PNGLR 201 at 205. That caution should be highly relevant when it comes to the exercise of powers in relation to the administration of migration and nationality laws." Nevertheless, in *Nowra No 8 Pty Ltd v Kala Swokin, Minister for Lands and The Independent State of Papua New Guinea* [1993] PNGLR 498, despite adverting to the need to exercise caution and pay heed to what Hinchliffe J said in *Tarere v ANZ Bank* [1988] PNGLR 201, "that planning of commercial and other activities would be impossible where acts done under valid laws are frequently declared unlawful under s 41 of the Constitution", the judge held that the forfeiture of a state lease by the Minister for Lands under the Land Act (Ch 185) (repealed), s 46, was harsh and oppressive and thereby invalid. The court may grant relief against forfeiture under s 41 of the Constitution if the act of forfeiture, in the circumstances, is harsh and oppressive.

> uncertainty which is not good for stability. Stability is important in a developing country such as Papua New Guinea. A situation would arise, and probably by now has arisen, where acts have been done which are authorised by law (and having nothing to do with basic rights) only to discover that the acts could be declared unlawful. I agree with Mr O'Regan QC when he said:
>
> > 'Planning commercial and indeed other activities on the basis that there was an ascertainable and settled legal order would be impossible.'
>
> The wider interpretation could create an abuse of the court process and encourage people to take action under s 41 of the Constitution purely as a delaying tactic.

There was a need for certainty in the definition of legal rights.[67]

Some later cases have followed Hinchliffe J in restricting the application of s 41 to infringements of constitutional rights. In *Bank of PNG v Muteng Basa*,[68] the issue of whether s 41 applied to the mortgagee's power to obtain vacant possession of the mortgaged premises[69] was considered by the National Court. The defendant, a former employee of the bank who had secured a staff loan at a concessional interest rate, argued that in seeking vacant possession, the mortgagee "unfairly unreasonably and without due regard to the defendant's livelihood and to his past services to the plaintiff Bank" exercised its mortgagee power of sale. Brown J agreed that s 41 of the Constitution was inapplicable to provide a defence to an action for vacant possession, "since the contractual relationships of the parties do not impinge on a constitutional right". The unfortunate effect his cessation of employment had, his subsequent employment and more recent unemployment

67 Apart from the cases discussed immediately below in the text, see also *Nowra No 8 Pty Ltd v Kala Swokin, Minister for Lands and The Independent State of Papua New Guinea* [1993] PNGLR 498; *Jivetuo v The Independent State of Papua New Guinea* [1984] PNGLR 174; *Amos Bai v Morobe Provincial Government* [1992] PNGLR 150 and *John Kameku v Patilius Gamato* (2004) N2512.

68 [1992] PNGLR 271. See also *Max Umbu v Steamships Ltd* (2004) N2738, where Salika J held in response to allegations that the actions of the mortgagee in trying to evict him after displacing him from employment, refusing to re-employ him and demanding full payment of the loan money, was harsh and oppressive [in exercising its powers to foreclose under the terms of the mortgage did so unfairly, unreasonably and without due regard to the defendant's livelihood and to his past services to the bank] and that by virtue of s 41(1) of the Constitution an unlawful act which is enforceable under s 155(4) and s 23 of the Constitution, that in *Tarere v ANZ Bank* [1988] PNGLR 201 and *Bank of PNG v Muteng Basa* [1992] PNGLR 271 "the Courts held that the provisions of s 41 of the Constitution are inapplicable and not available as the contractual relationships of the parties did not impinge on their Constitutional rights".

69 Under Land Registration Act (Ch 191), s 74(1)(c).

has adversely affected the defendant's ability to both service the loan and seek refinance; his impecunious state did not give rise to a defence.[70] Still liable on loan, his failure to meet the obligations could lead to the legitimate exercise of entry into possession and exercise of any of the other rights of the mortgagee (powers of sale, entry, possession distress and ejectment and all other powers conferred by the Land Registration Act (Ch 191)).

In *PNGBC v Pala Aruai*[71] it would appear that Kandakasi J would allow the application of s 41 of the Constitution to the mortgagee's power of sale, either by allowing the section to operate more widely than just the protection of constitutional rights, or by holding that some exercises of the power of sale would amount to an unjust deprivation of property contrary to s 53 of the Constitution, and thus call for the application of s 41, even if the more restricted interpretation called for by Hinchliffe J in *Tarere v ANZ Bank*,[72] is adopted.

The mortgagee bank sought vacant possession of the first defendant's residential property with a view to exercising its power of sale. That property, together with another property on which it was proposed to construct a hostel, had been mortgaged to the bank to secure a loan to finance the hostel construction costs. The property on which it was proposed to construct the hostel was owned by a company, the second defendant. The first defendant did not dispute the company's indebtedness to the bank. He argued, however, that the bank "failed to either properly manage or sell the hostel property, which could have resulted in a substantial reduction or a complete settlement of the amounts due and owing to the Bank". He therefore argued that the bank was now precluded from enforcing its security over his residential property.

The mortgagee had already obtained vacant possession of the first mortgaged property as a result of non-payment of the loan. The bank entered into possession by appointing a receiver to manage the hostel to generate rental income to pay off the outstanding loan. However, the mortgagor claimed that owing to the negligence of the mortgagee, it had been unlawfully deprived of possession.

Kandakasi J stated:

> In these circumstances, I consider it most unfair and inequitable that the Bank should be allowed to foreclose on the residential property as

70 In *PNGBC v Barra Amevo* [1998] PNGLR 240, Sevua J followed *Bank of PNG v Muteng Basa* and held that the mortgagor's impecuniosity did not preclude the mortgagee bank from exercising its rights under the terms of the mortgage and the statutory rights conferred by the *Land Registration Act* (Ch 191). The plaintiff bank sought vacant possession of the mortgaged property in order to exercise the power of sale. See also *Pama Anio v Aho Baliki* (2002) N2267.

71 (2002) N2234.

72 [1988] PNGLR 201.

> well. If the Bank was allowed to do so, it would in my view amount to an unjust deprivation of property and may even be harsh and oppressive in the particular circumstances of the case. In arriving at that view, I am of course aware of the judgments in the *Bank of PNG v Muteng Basa*[73] and *Tarere v ANZ Bank*.[74] Both of these were judgments of the National Court.
>
> In both of the above cases, they were straightforward mortgagee sales of properties. The properties were the subject for the advancement and creation of the respective mortgages. The mortgagors in both cases fell into arrears and that resulted in the respective banks exercising their respective powers of sale under their respective mortgages. In the first case, the defendant lost his employment and had no means to service his loan to the plaintiff bank. The facts in the second case are silent on the plaintiffs' ability to repay the loan or meet their loan commitments. In both cases the actions were founded on s 41 of the Constitution. The Court in both cases came to the conclusion that where a bank *legitimately exercises its power of sale* under a mortgage, which is in effect an exercise of a contractual right granted to it by a mortgagor, no issue under s 41 of the Constitution arises. *No issues of negligence or more than one mortgage involving more than just one property arose in those cases*. (Emphasis added.)

He found that the bank was negligent in the exercise of its powers to enter into possession, and generally in the steps it took to enforce its security against the hostel, and that raised the question whether the bank's negligence in respect of the first mortgaged property prevented it from enforcing its security against the defendant's residential property. His Honour came to the conclusion, *inter alia*, that a sale of the residential property may be unnecessary and therefore may amount to an unjust deprivation of Mr Aruai's property. It may also amount to harsh and oppressive action not actuated by a genuine desire to recover the principal and the interest due under the mortgage prior to the bank entering into possession of the hostel property. He therefore declined to make a order for vacant possession. He further held that the plaintiff (the bank) was not to foreclose on Allotment 30, Section 22 Hohola, National Capital District (residential property) until it has first instituted proper management and has secured tenants for each of the units at Allotment 22, Section 3 Hohola, National Capital District (the hostel property) or had sold that property at its true and or correct market value and had properly dealt with the proceeds in accordance with

73 [1992] PNGLR 271.
74 [1988] PNGLR 201.

s 68 of the Land Registration Act (Ch 191) and a shortfall had been established, which Mr Aruai was not able to pay within a period of not less than 14 days. Also he held that in applying the proceeds in accordance with the terms of order 1 above, the interest accruing from the date of the plaintiff entering into possession of the hostel property shall be omitted from a calculation of the amounts due and owing under the mortgage on account of the Bank's negligence.

Other duties

Other duties of the receiver include:

- upon accepting appointment, a receiver should take reasonable care to verify the validity and terms of the appointment;[75]
- to ensure that the receiver and any person associated with the receiver do not purchase assets from the debtor company;[76]
- to ensure that the debtor company does not commit criminal offences whilst under his guidance;[77]
- to open a separate bank account for monies received from the receivership;[78]
- to keep proper accounting records;[79]
- to comply with the notice requirements of s 67 of the Land Registration Act (Ch 191) before exercising a power to sell land;[80]
- to give immediate notice of the receivership to the debtor company and to the public;[81]
- to ensure that all documentation states that the receiver has been appointed;[82]
- to keep the money related to the receivership property separate from other money received or controlled by the receiver;[83]
- to keep proper accounting records;[84]

75 *RA Price Securities Ltd v Henderson [1989]* 2 NZLR 257.
76 *Re Tricorp Investments Ltd* (1988) 4 NZCLC 64,620.
77 *Re John Willment (Ashford)* Ltd [1979] 2 All ER 615.
78 This is good practice in view of s 271 of the Companies Act 1997.
79 Companies Act 1997, s 272.
80 See Amankwah, H A, Mugambwa, J T, Muroa, G, *Land Law in Papua New Guinea* (LBC Information Services, Sydney, 2001), pp 177–178.
81 Companies Act 1997, s 259(1).
82 Companies Act 1997, s 260.
83 Companies Act 1997, s 271. Keeping separate bank accounts.
84 Companies Act 1997, s 272.

- to prepare detailed reports for the debtor company and the secured creditor two months after the appointment, after each subsequent six months of the receivership, and when the receivership ends;[85]
- to pay out receivership expenses and preferential creditors ahead of reimbursing the secured creditor;[86]
- to give notice to the Registrar of Companies of offences committed against the company or where the company or any person has been guilty of any negligence, default, breach of duty or trust in relation to the company;[87] and
- to give notice of the end of the receivership.[88]

Notification and reporting functions/requirements

As soon as a receiver is appointed, he or she must, within seven days of appointment:

- give written notice of his or her appointment to the debtor company;[89]
- submit a notice of appointment in the prescribed form to the Registrar of Companies;[90] and
- "give public notice" of the appointment.

Section 3 of the Companies Act 1997 provides that the public notice requirement is fulfilled by publishing notice of the matter in at least one issue of the National Gazette and also "a newspaper circulating throughout the country".[91] The public notice of his or her appointment as a receiver must contain at least:[92]

- the receiver's full name;
- the date of the appointment;
- the receiver's office address;
- a brief description of the property in receivership; and
- where the receiver is an additional or substitute receiver, the notice must state that fact.

85 Companies Act 1997, ss 273 and 274.
86 Companies Act 1997, s 279.
87 Companies Act 1997, s 277.
88 Companies Act 1997, s 278.
89 Companies Act 1997, s 259(1)(a).
90 Companies Act 1997, s 259(1)(c). See Companies Regulation 1998, Form 36 (Notice of appointment of receiver).
91 Companies Act 1997, s 259(1) and s 3.
92 Companies Act 1997, s 259(1)(b) and (2).

Once the receiver has been appointed, every document issued by the company must state that fact.[93] This requirement applies to correspondence, invoices, purchase orders, cheques and any other business document, whether in written, electronic or other format. The requirement is usually satisfied by writing "in receivership" or "receiver appointed" after the company's name on any such documents.

During the receivership, the receiver has to regularly report on the conduct of the receivership. Within two months of his appointment, the receiver must make an initial report. This "first report" must include:[94]

- particulars of the assets comprising the property in receivership;
- particulars of the debts and liabilities to be satisfied from the property in receivership;
- the names and addresses of the creditors with an interest in the property in receivership;
- particulars of any encumbrance over the property in receivership held by any creditor including the date on which it was created;
- particulars of any default by the company in making relevant information available;
- details of the events leading up to the appointment of the receiver, so far as the receiver is aware of them;
- details of property disposed of and any proposals for the disposal of property in receivership;
- details of amounts owing, as at the date of appointment, to any person in whose interests the receiver was appointed;
- details of amounts owing, as at the date of appointment, to creditors of the company having preferential claims;
- details of amounts likely to be available for payment to creditors other than the appointing creditor or preferential creditors; and
- such other information as may be prescribed.

A receiver may omit from the report details of any proposals for disposal of the property in receivership if he or she considers that their inclusion would materially prejudice the exercise of his or her functions.[95]

In addition to the first report, the receiver must produce updated reports every six months, and a final report within two months of the date on

93 Companies Act 1997, s 260(2). Where the receiver has been appointed in respect of only some of a company's assets, only documents issued by the company relating to those assets need to carry the required notification: s 260(1).

94 Companies Act 1997, s 273.

95 Companies Act 1997, s 273(3).

which the receivership ends.[96] The reports must summarise the state of affairs with respect to the property in receivership as at those dates, and the conduct of the receivership, including all amounts received and paid, during the period to which the report relates.[97] These reports must be sent to the debtor company, the appointing creditor (or the National Court in the case of a court appointed receiver) and the Registrar of Companies.[98]

The other reporting requirements for a receiver are:

- a duty to notify the Registrar of Companies of any breaches of the Companies Act 1997, committed by any person, of which the receiver is aware;[99]
- a duty to notify the Registrar of Companies where the receiver considers that a person has been guilty of any negligence, default, breach of duty or trust in relation to the company;[100]
- a duty to notify the Registrar of Companies of the termination of the receivership not later than 14 days after the receivership of a company ceases.[101]

Liability of receiver

Introduction

Receivers can become liable in several ways. They can be guilty of criminal offences subject to specific statutory penalties. They may also be liable for breach of contract, tort or other obligations and may be liable to pay compensation. To avoid these liabilities receivers usually insist on getting an indemnity from the secured creditor who appoints them. Under the indemnity contract, the secured creditor undertakes to reimburse the receiver for liabilities incurred during the receivership, provided it does not involve dishonesty.

Liability arising from invalid appointment

Sometimes there may be a problem with the appointment of a receiver, so that anything the receiver does makes him or her liable. For example, the charge under which the receiver was appointed might be void, or the event which led to the receiver's appointment may not have actually been an event

96 Companies Act 1997, s 274.
97 See Companies Act 1997, s 274(2) for details to be included in report.
98 Companies Act 1997, s 276.
99 Companies Act 1997, s 277(1)(a).
100 Companies Act 1997, s 277(1)(b).
101 Companies Act 1997, s 278.

of default as defined in the instrument of charge. For example, the receiver might be sued for trespass, i.e., using the company's property without the company's permission or other legal right. In such case it is possible for the National Court to excuse the receiver from liability and make the secured creditor liable instead, if the liability is incurred because of a defect in the appointment of the receiver or the document under which he or she was appointed. In such a situation, the receiver must have acted honestly and reasonably, in order to avoid liability. In such a case, it is a receiver's responsibility to satisfy himself or herself as to the validity of his or her appointment and the terms of the debenture and whether an event of default has arisen. If the receiver does not make reasonable efforts to check on these matters, the court may not excuse his or her liability: *RA Price Securities Ltd v Henderson*.[102]

Liability in contract

Contracts generally

When a receiver has been appointed to take control of all, or almost all, of the company's property, he or she will often have to deal with contracts that the company entered into before the receivership started and which have not been completed. The general rule in such cases is that the receiver can continue with these contracts without being personally liable. Subject to the statutory exceptions for wages and rent (see below), the receiver only becomes liable if he or she does something extra to show that he or she assumes personal responsibility on the contract, i.e., he or she adopts the contract. Otherwise, the other contracting party is limited to suing the company and cannot recover damages from the receiver. The appointment of the receiver does not affect the company's liability under its existing contracts. If the company breaks such a contract, the other party may sue the company for damages.[103]

Liability for rent on leases

If a company is leasing property (whether land and personalty, i.e., chattels) and a receiver is then appointed, the receiver can become personally liable for the rent if the company continues to use or occupy the property during the receivership. The receiver will be personally liable if the company is still using, possessing or occupying the property more than 14 days after the

102 [1989] 2 NZLR 257 at 263.
103 If the company is on the verge of winding up, this may not be worth much, as the claim for damages would rank as an unsecured debt.

start of the receivership. In other words, the receiver's personal liability for rent begins 14 days after the date of appointment and ends either when the company ceases to use, possess or occupy the property, or when the receivership terminates. The receiver will not be personally liable for any rent accruing during this 14-day grace period. If the company ceases to use, possess or occupy the property after the 14-day period, the receiver will be personally liable up until such time.[104] Once user has ceased, or the property has been returned, only the company will be liable under the pre-receivership agreement for the breach in respect of the remaining period.

Liability for wages

One statutory exception to the underlying law rule that a receiver is not personally liable for pre-receivership contracts relates to wages and salaries. Section 281(1)(b) of the Companies Act 1997 provides that a receiver will become personally liable for wages and salaries accruing (i.e., payable) under a pre-receivership (i.e., existing) contract of employment unless the receiver gives lawful notice terminating the contract within 14 days of his or her appointment (i.e., notice of termination of the agreement is "lawfully given within 14 days after the date of appointment"). The 14-day grace period allows the receiver the opportunity to investigate the financial viability of the company and to decide whether to trade on or close down the business and to decide which employees, if any, will be required. In *Re Weddel New Zealand Ltd (in rec & liq)*,[105] the New Zealand Court of Appeal held that the requirement that notice be "lawfully" given did not mean that the receiver had to observe contractual notice periods in relevant employment legislation or in specific employment agreements, but he or she merely had to "conform with the relevant statutory and contractual obligations applicable to receivers . . . ". In *Re Weddel New Zealand Ltd (in rec & liq)*, under a collective employment contract the employer was required to give one month's notice of termination of employees' employment contracts. Three days after their appointment, the employer's receivers sent the employees notices of immediate termination of their contracts of employment. The employees sought orders under the New Zealand equivalent to s 281(1)(b) of the Companies Act 1997 that the receivers were personally liable for payment of wages in that the notices of termination were not in accordance with the terms of their employment contracts. The issue was whether the notices of termination were lawfully given under the equivalent of that section. The New Zealand Court of Appeal held that to be lawful the notice of termination had to be in accord with the

104 The receiver will be entitled to an indemnity for the rent of the receivership property. In addition, the National Court may limit or excuse the receiver from liability.

105 [1998] 1 NZLR 30.

New Zealand equivalent to s 281(1)(b) of the Companies Act 1997 and with the terms of appointment of the receiver. The notice did not have to be in accord with the terms of the particular contract of employment. In coming to this conclusion, the court considered various reasons for this construction, including the fact that "from a common sense practical viewpoint the requirement for a receiver to have to terminate or repudiate a contract of employment promptly to avoid incurring personal liability is obvious" and the New Zealand equivalent to s 281(1)(b) of the Companies Act 1997 "can be read as recognising the reality that such a course of action will frequently be taken even if it constitutes a breach as between the company and employee".[106]

If the receiver gives lawful notice within the 14-day period, he or she is not liable for payment of salary or wages, either within the 14-day period or thereafter. However, most receivers would treat the wage bill for this 14-day period as a receivership expense and pay it in priority to a secured creditor.

Contracts entered into during the receivership

According to the underlying law, a receiver was not personally liable for post-receivership contracts unless he or she acknowledged personal liability.[107] This underlying law presumption has been reversed by s 281(1)(a) of the Companies Act 1997. A receiver is personally liable on contracts entered after the commencement of the receivership unless the terms of the contract expressly exclude or limit the personal liability of the receiver. The receiver who keeps trading will therefore usually be liable for goods and services ordered, property leased, and for the payment of wages and salary for staff. The receiver will also be liable for directors' remuneration if he or she "has expressly confirmed" such contracts.[108]

The receiver is entitled to the statutory indemnity out of the receivership property for contracts entered into after his or her appointment and the payment of wages and directors' remuneration. This indemnity and other legitimate receivership expenses take first priority over the secured property. They must therefore be paid before any moneys are paid to the secured creditor.[109]

Liability for negligence

Liability for trespass

Where the appointment of a receiver is invalid, for example because the security agreement is invalid or has not been complied with or the appointment

106 [1998] 1 NZLR 30 at 33.
107 *D Owen & Co v Cronk* [1895] 1 QB 265.
108 Companies Act 1997, s 281(1)(c).
109 A receiver will normally also secure an indemnity from the appointing secured creditor, just in case the secured assets are not sufficient to cover receivership expenses.

document is deficient), the receiver has no right to take possession of the company's assets and is as such a trespasser. As a result, the receiver may become liable for substantial damages in trespass. In these circumstances, s 282 of the Companies Act 1997 empowers the National Court to relieve the receiver from personal liability incurred solely by reason of a defect in the appointment,[110] provided that the receiver "acted honestly and reasonably and ought, in the circumstances, to be excused".[111] Because one of the receiver's first duties is to check the security and appointment documentation to verify the validity of the appointment, a receiver who fails to take reasonable steps in this regard is unlikely to be relieved of liability.

Receiver's indemnity

A receiver is entitled to an indemnity out of the assets of the company for any personal liability incurred under s 281 of the Companies Act 1997,[112] and where the receiver is agent of the debtor company (as will usually be the case), for any other expenditure of liability legitimately incurred during the course of the receivership.[113] This indemnity takes priority over the appointing creditor's security. In most cases, this statutory indemnity is sufficient to ensure that a receiver does not have to meet personal liability with his or her own funds. Nevertheless, most receivers will ensure that they have a contractual indemnity with the appointment creditor. This will be particularly important where the debtor company is hopelessly insolvent and may not have sufficient assets to meet the receiver's indemnity.

Court supervision of receivership

Where the court appoints a receiver, the receiver becomes an officer of the court, and as such is amenable to the supervision of the court. With private appointments of receivers, it is not envisaged that the court will be actively involved in supervision of the receiver. In some circumstances, however, the court may be asked to intervene. These include:

- the receiver may apply to the National Court for directions on the conduct of the receivership under s 283 of the Companies Act 1997;
- the receiver, the debtor company, its creditors, directors, a liquidator or the Registrar of Companies may apply to the National Court to fix the

110 Note that this section does not empower the court to relieve a receiver from liability generally.
111 Companies Act 1997, s 282(1). Where the court orders relief, the receiver's liability is generally transferred to the appointing creditor: see Companies Act 1997, s 282(3).
112 Companies Act 1997, s 281(9) and (10).
113 *RA Price Securities Ltd v Henderson* [1989] 2 NZLR 257 at 262.

level of the receiver's remuneration and to determine the validity of the appointment;[114]

- the court may terminate or limit the receivership if circumstances no longer justify its continuance;[115]
- under s 286 of the Companies Act 1997, the National Court may order a receiver to carry out his or her duties or remove a receiver from office;
- in the event of a serious or persistent breach of duty by a receiver, the National Court may prohibit the receiver from acting as a receiver or liquidator of any company for up to five years.[116] The court also has an inherent jurisdiction to remove a receiver who is not acting in good faith.[117]

Payment of preferential creditors

A company receiver who has been appointed under a floating charge (or a fixed or specific charge that conferred a floating security at the time it was created) is required to pay "preferential creditors" out of the assets that are subject to the floating charge before paying the appointing creditor.[118] The preferential claims are set out in Schedule 9.[119]

Schedule 9 creates a statutory régime for ranking the priority of certain creditors in relation to each other, other unsecured creditors and secured creditors. Although the preferential creditors are not secured creditors, they are paid in priority to ordinary unsecured creditors.

Before paying preferential creditors, the receiver is authorised to reimburse himself or herself for "his expenses and remuneration".[120] The receiver, in addition to giving effect to the statutory preference, must also ensure that where he or she realises any assets over which there are charges ranking higher in priority to the appointing creditor's interest, the prior ranking secured creditors are paid (to the limit of their security) before the appointing creditor. A receiver who fails to pay secured creditors in the proper order of priority may incur personal liability.

Section 279 of the Companies Act 1997 applies only where the company is not in liquidation at the time of a receiver's appointment. If the company has already been put into liquidation at this time, the liquidator is the one

114 Companies Act 1997, s 283(2).
115 Companies Act 1997, s 284(3).
116 Companies Act 1997, s 286(6).
117 *Re Neon Signs (Australasia) Ltd* [1965] VR 125.
118 Companies Act 1997, s 279.
119 Schedule 9 applies to liquidation, but has been modified to suit receivership. See Chapter 14 (Liquidation) for more details on Schedule 9. Note that ss 1 and 7(b) of the Schedule do not apply to a receiver.
120 Companies Act 1997, s 279(2)(a).

who has the obligation to pay preferential creditors under s 360 of the Companies Act 1997.

Preferential creditors are a group of creditors (in particular employees and the government) that for public policy reasons, Parliament has decided should be paid in priority to certain other creditors, including all other unsecured creditors.

In *David Gopalan v Uni Transport Pty Ltd*,[121] the court had to consider whether an award of damages for wrongful dismissal and the notional loss of wages entitled the applicant to preferential payment by receiver and manager. The plaintiff sought an order that such part of the judgment as the court deemed fit, be paid to the plaintiff by the receivers and managers of the defendant as a preferential payment in the receivership. The court, following Australian authorities, held that the damages awarded for wrongful dismissal were not wages but a sum in lieu of the wages the employee would have received had he continued in the employ of the company. As such, the receiver was not under an obligation to pay any part of the plaintiff's damages awarded as a preferential payment. Furthermore, the court held that it was not possible to hold that the receiver's refusal to pay any moneys was a "harsh or oppressive" act in accordance with Section 41 of the Constitution, and as such invalid ("an unlawful act"). The receivers had no discretion in the matter. Their duty was to pay claims which fell within the province of preferential payments. Seeing that the operation of s 41 of the Constitution depends on there being an abuse in the exercise of a discretionary power, the action of the receiver could not be considered "harsh or oppressive".

Effect of liquidation

A receivership may now be begun or continued despite the liquidation of the debtor company.

In considering the impact of liquidation and receivership, it is necessary to bear in mind the position under the underlying law and the position according to the Companies Act 1997, and also the difference between the receiver being appointed to take control of the security or securities and to deal with it or them, on the one hand, and on the other the receiver being appointed with wide powers so that not only can he or she take control and manage the property but also the business or undertaking of the company. In such situations, the receiver becomes the agent of the company. According to the underlying law, the effect of a liquidation on an existing receivership was to automatically terminate any agency vested in the receiver. However, the receiver could continue to deal with the secured

121 [1986] PNGLR 101.

property of a company unhindered by the liquidation unless the court ordered otherwise in the case of the general agency. But the receivership automatically came to an end on liquidation.

This matter is now governed by s 280 of the Companies Act 1997. The position remains the same in respect of the receiver being able to deal with the secured property of the company unhindered by the liquidation; however, the court is given power to order otherwise (s 280(1)). In the case of the general agency of the receiver, this automatically comes to an end on liquidation unless the court authorises continuation (s 280(2)(a)) or the liquidator gives his or her "written consent" (s 280(2)(b)).

Chapter 14

Liquidation

Introduction

Liquidation, or winding up, is usually an essential part of the process by which the life of the company is brought to an end. In this process a liquidator is appointed, the management of the company's affairs is taken out of the directors' hands, its assets are realised by the liquidator, and its debts and liabilities are ascertained and discharged out of the proceeds of realisation. Any surplus of assets then remaining is returned to its members or shareholders. At the end of the process the company is dissolved and its name is removed from the register of companies. The company as a legal entity thereupon ceases to exist.

There are two types of liquidation: (i) voluntary liquidation and (ii) compulsory or court-ordered liquidation. Within these two types are various categories. Most companies are liquidated because they are insolvent, i.e., they are unable to pay their debts as they become due in the ordinary course of business. However, solvent companies are also liquidated. It might be, for example, that the company has ceased to carry on business, but owns valuable assets which the shareholders wish to realise for themselves.

This chapter explains the liquidation process. Most of the rules are set out in the Companies Act 1997, which introduced new rules and procedures relating to winding up, particularly with regard to the statutory demand procedure.[1]

Objectives and principles of liquidation

Although companies may be liquidated even though solvent, many of the objectives and principles relating to liquidation are based on policies relating to insolvency. Corporate insolvency provisions in the Companies Act

1 For an account of the law relating to winding up under the repealed Companies Act (Ch 146), see Kimuli, M A, Amankwah, H A and Mugambwa, J T, *Introduction to the Law of Business Associations in Papua New Guinea* (2nd edn, Pacific Law Press, Hobart, 1990), Ch 13.

1997 have four principal objectives.[2] First, the insolvency régime seeks to effect an orderly termination of the company's affairs and a maximisation of the return to the company's creditors; without state regulation, creditors will compete against each other to get first access to the company's assets, and in the process the superior value of the company as a going concern is lost. Secondly, the insolvency régime seeks to provide a fair system for the ranking of claims against the company. Creditors who have stolen a march on other unsecured creditors by being paid off just before the company became insolvent have to be made to account for the monies which they have unfairly secured. Furthermore, some order of priority is necessary, because all the claims will not usually be able to be satisfied. Claims are ranked according to the *pari passu* principle: all claims of a similar type share proportionally in the company's assets. It is important to stress the words "claims of a similar type". Secured creditors rank ahead of unsecured creditors, and the law, based on public policy grounds, takes account of a range of interests other than creditors, including those of company employees, and gives them preferential claims, i.e., claims that take precedence over the interests of unsecured creditors. Thirdly, an important role in the insolvency régime is the investigation of reasons for the company's failure.[3] The fourth main objective is to restore companies to profitability where possible. Insolvency is a costly procedure, and the minimisation of those costs demands that companies be salvaged wherever possible. Some have argued that insolvency law should not be concerned with the rescue of companies from failure. However, some jurisdictions have procedures to allow claims against the company to be frozen to allow the company time to trade out of its financial difficulties.[4]

2 See Grantham, R B and Rickett, C E F, *Company and Securities Law: Commentary and Materials* (Brookers, New Zealand, 2002), pp 1022–1023.

3 This reason was more apparent in the repealed Companies Act (Ch 146) than in the current Companies Act 1997. Because the state has an interest in promoting the efficient operation of companies, it is interested in finding out the reasons for the company's failure and protecting society from further failures by imposing sanctions on those responsible. See Companies Act (Ch 146), s 179 and Kimuli, M A, Amankwah, H A and Mugambwa, J T, *Introduction to the Law of Business Associations in Papua New Guinea* (2nd edn, supra), p 117.

4 The voluntary administration procedure (UK and Australia) and Chapter 11 Bankruptcy (US) seek to do this. Voluntary administration proposals have been under consideration in New Zealand for several years, but had not reached a finalised state when PNG adopted many of the provisions of the New Zealand Companies Act 1993. The proposals have since advanced considerably: see Merrett, R, 'Insolvency Law Reform in New Zealand – The Draft Insolvency Law Reform Bill' (2004) 12 *Insolvency Law Journal* 194. See also Watson, S, *et al.*, *The Law of Business Organisations* (4th edn, Palatine Press, Auckland, 2003), pp 406–408. The repealed Companies Act (Ch 146) had provisions to allow for the rescue of companies, but these were not carried over or developed in the new Companies Act 1997.

Duration of liquidation

Liquidation commences when a liquidator is appointed,[5] and ends when the liquidator files certain documents with the Registrar of Companies. It may be prematurely terminated before this happens.[6] However, liquidation will normally run its course, and eventually lead to the company being deregistered. After liquidation and before deregistration, the company continues in existence; however, control passes from the directors to the liquidator.

Liquidation is completed when the liquidator submits to the Registrar of Companies certain documents for registration.[7] These documents are:[8]

- the final report and statement of realisation and distribution in respect of the liquidation;
- a statement that:
  - all known assets have been disclaimed, or realised, or distributed without realisation;
  - all proceeds of realisation have been distributed;
  - the company is ready to be removed from the register;
- a statement that a person may apply to the Registrar or the court objecting to the removal of the company from the register under s 370 or s 371.

Voluntary liquidation

Voluntary liquidation is where a company, rather than the National Court, appoints a liquidator. The reasons why it may appoint a liquidator are fixed by the Companies Act 1997. Within this category, there are two types of appointment: (i) appointment by the shareholders by special resolution; and (ii) appointment of a liquidator by the board of directors if an event specified in the company's constitution authorises this.

Liquidation by shareholders

Section 291(2)(a) of the Companies Act 1997 provides that the shareholders of a company may appoint a liquidator by special resolution.[9] Shareholders

5 Companies Act 1997, s 291(4). Under the Companies Act (Ch 146), liquidation commenced when the petition was made to the court for liquidation.

6 The National Court may, at any time after the appointment of a liquidator of a company, if it is satisfied that it is just and equitable to do so, make an order terminating the liquidation of the company. The company thereupon ceases to be in liquidation: Companies Act 1997, ss 300(1) and (6).

7 Companies Act 1997, s 299(a).

8 Companies Act 1997, s 307(1)(a).

9 A special resolution is passed if at least 75 per cent of votes of those shareholders entitled to vote and voting on the question are cast in favour of the resolution. The company's constitution may specify that a higher percentage of votes is required for a special resolution: Companies Act 1997, s 2: "special resolution".

may decide to liquidate a company for a number of reasons. The company may be insolvent (unable to pay its debts) and should not continue in business.[10] The shareholders may also want to put a solvent company into liquidation and distribute the remaining assets to the shareholders. Where the company is solvent, shareholders may use the liquidation process where they are unable, or do not wish, to use the shortcut procedure to remove the company from the Register.[11]

Section 291(2)(a) of the Companies Act 1997 requires that the shareholders who vote on the special resolution must be "shareholders entitled to vote and voting on the question". A shareholder would normally be able to vote on a resolution to put the company into liquidation, because a share in a company, *inter alia*, confers on the holder the right to one vote on a poll at a meeting of the company on any resolution, including any resolution to put the company into liquidation.[12] However, this may be changed ("negated, altered, or added to") by the constitution of the company,[13] or according to the terms on which the share was issued.

It is not necessary for the shareholders to make a declaration of solvency. Indeed, the Act recognises that the shareholders may decide to appoint a liquidator where the company is insolvent.

Liquidation by directors

It is possible, if a company's constitution so provides, for the board of directors to appoint a liquidator.[14] That section provides that a liquidator may be appointed by the board of the company on the occurrence of an event specified in the constitution. It would appear to be unusual for constitutions to specify events the occurrence of which will lead to the directors being able to appoint a liquidator and put the company into liquidation.

As we noted above, it is possible for a company to enter into voluntary liquidation (either by shareholder special resolution or by a resolution of the board of directors, where the constitution allows for this), where it is insolvent. In such a case, there is no need to consult the creditors about the desirability of doing this or as to whom should be appointed as the liquidator. Although the creditors are very much concerned in this type of liquidation, their rights are protected at a later stage. They are given an early opportunity to challenge the appointment of the liquidator and replace him and can call creditors' meetings and serve on a liquidation committee. (These are discussed below.)

10 The directors in particular will be concerned to ensure that they do not become liable for failure to prevent insolvent trading: Companies Act 1997, s 348.
11 Companies Act 1997, s 366 and see p 606 below.
12 Companies Act 1997, s 37(1)(a)(vi).
13 Companies Act 1997, s 37(2).
14 Companies Act 1997, s 291(2)(b).

In the case of an insolvent company being put into liquidation, if the liquidator was appointed by special resolution of shareholders or by the board of directors following powers in the constitution, the liquidator must call a meeting of creditors, which must be held within one month of the liquidator's appointment, for the purpose of deciding whether to appoint another liquidator in place of the liquidator appointed by the shareholders or board of directors.[15]

Where at a meeting of creditors it is resolved to appoint a person as liquidator of the company, in place of the liquidator appointed pursuant to s 291(2)(a) or (b), that person will become, subject to s 330, the liquidator of the company.[16] Section 330 provides that the appointment of a person as liquidator, other than on the order of the court, "is of no effect unless that person has consented in writing to the appointment". It seems that the consent must be prospective (it cannot be retrospective). So if there is a resolution to replace the shareholders' or board of directors' liquidator, the original liquidator will remain the liquidator until the recommended replacement liquidator has signed a written consent to the appointment.

It would seem that if there is no decision to replace the liquidator appointed by the shareholders or board of directors, the appointment of the liquidator is confirmed, and he can only be removed by an application to the National Court.

In the case of a solvent company, provided certain procedural steps are taken before the board or shareholders appointed the liquidator, there is no need for the liquidator to call a s 293 meeting of creditors. These procedural steps are:

- The board of the company must, within one month before the appointment of the liquidator, have resolved that the company would, on the appointment of a liquidator by the board of directors or shareholders, be able to pay its debts as they become due in the ordinary course of business and a copy of the solvency resolution must have been submitted (it seems before the appointment of the liquidator) to the Registrar of Companies for registration.[17]
- the directors who vote in favour of a solvency resolution are required to "forthwith sign a certificate stating that, in their opinion, the company would, on the appointment of the liquidator be able to pay its debts as they become due in the ordinary course of business". The certificate must also contain the grounds for that opinion.[18] Failure by a consenting

15 Companies Act 1997, s 293(1)(a), (4)(a).
16 Companies Act 1997, s 293(6).
17 Companies Act 1997, s 293(8).
18 Companies Act 1997, s 293(9).

director to sign the certificate is an offence involving liability to the penalty set out in s 413(1).[19]

Court ordered liquidation

There are two types of court-ordered liquidation: (i) where the company is insolvent and (ii) on other grounds.

Winding up on grounds other than insolvency

As we noted above, the most frequent cases where a liquidator is appointed are for the winding up of insolvent companies. However, there are cases where solvent companies are also liquidated. The Companies Act 1997 sets out three grounds on which the National Court may order a company to be liquidated where the company is solvent. Although the first two grounds are rather narrow (persistent or serious default and non-compliance with s 11), the other ground (the just and equitable ground) is very wide.[20]

The application for liquidation may be brought by the company, a director, a shareholder or other entitled person, a creditor of the company (including any contingent or prospective creditor), or the Registrar of Companies.[21]

Persistent or serious default

The National Court may appoint a liquidator where "the company or the board has persistently or seriously failed to comply" with the Companies Act 1997.[22] It has been argued that this ground has been carried over from

19 Companies Act 1997, s 293(10).
20 Although the grounds in the repealed Companies Act 1997 seem more restrictive than those set out in s 240 of the repealed Companies Act (Ch 146), it has been argued that this may not in fact be so, as several of the specific grounds in that section (e.g., directors acting in their own interests and suspension of business for a whole year) are encompassed in the "just an equitable ground": see Beck, A & Borrowdale, A, *Papua New Guinea Companies and Securities Law Guide* (CCH Australia Ltd, Sydney, 1999), para 1410. *Sed quaere*, as the Companies Act (Ch 146) also had a separate "just and equitable" ground: s 240(1)(h).
21 Companies Act 1997, s 291(2)(c).
22 Companies Act 1997, s 291(3)(b). Under the repealed Companies Act (Ch 146), s 240(b), a company could be wound up for default in lodging the statutory report or in holding the statutory meeting; only a shareholder was able to petition on this ground: ss 239(2)(b) and 243(4). Section 240(1)(c) also provided that a ground of liquidation arose where "the company does not commence business within a year after its incorporation, or suspends its business for a whole year". Section 240(1)(f) provided another ground: where "directors have acted in the affairs of the company in their own interests rather than in the interests of the members as a whole, or in any other manner that appears to be unfair or unjust to other members".

the repealed Companies Act (Ch 146) and expanded (s 240(1)(f): "directors have acted in the affairs of the company in their own interests rather than in the interests of the members as a whole, or in any other manner that appears to be unfair or unjust to other members") and that "the jurisprudence which developed out of that provision will still be relevant" when considering whether "the company or the board has persistently or seriously failed to comply" with the Companies Act 1997.[23] However, it would seem that this is a new ("additional") ground[24] rather than a carry over from the Companies Act (Ch 146), and it is therefore not clear to what extent the jurisprudence on s 240(1)(f) will be relevant in interpreting this section.

Non-compliance with s 11 of the Companies Act 1997

The National Court may appoint a liquidator where "the company does not comply with Section 11" of the Companies Act 1997.[25] If the company does not meet the requirements of s 11 by having a name, and at least one share, one shareholder and a director, it may be wound up by the court.[26]

Just and equitable ground

The National Court may appoint a liquidator where "it is just and equitable that the company be put into liquidation".[27] The words "just and equitable" are of wide import and give the court wide powers to act. Although the House of Lords in *Ebrahimi v Westbourne Galleries Ltd*[28] counselled against categorising the situations when the just and equitable principle would be applied, many commentators have allocated the cases to several categories, and for convenience of exposition, this approach will be followed. In doing so, it should be noted that some of the cases have been allocated to different categories and the categories are not closed. The situations where the courts have put companies into liquidation on the "just and equitable"

23 Beck, A and Borrowdale, A, *Papua New Guinea Companies and Securities Law Guide*, supra, para 1420. Persistent or serious default in compliance with the Act provided an ultimate sanction in enforcing the provisions of the Act. It was envisaged that it would be invoked only rarely, for example where the board had disregarded statutory provisions designed to protect minority interests .

24 See New Zealand Law Commission *Company Law: Reform and Restatement* (Law Commission Report No 9 New Zealand Law Commission, Wellington, 1989), para 660.

25 Companies Act 1997, s 291(3)(c).

26 Note that the shareholders or directors (if the constitution so allows) may appoint a liquidator in any of these circumstances, without recourse to the court.

27 Companies Act 1997, s 291(3)(d). Cf Companies Act (Ch 146), s 240(1)(h), which contained a similar ground for liquidation.

28 [1973] AC 360, [1972] 2 All ER 492. Cf *Re Commercial Pacific Lumber Exports Pty Ltd* [1971–72] PNGLR 178.

ground include: breakdown in mutual trust and confidence, fraud or misconduct, failure of substratum, deadlock and public policy. It has been said that, despite the various categories, the overall basis for winding up a company on the just and equitable ground is a "justifiable lack of confidence in the conduct and management of the company's affairs".[29]

There is some debate whether, if the applicant's misconduct caused the breakdown of the relationship, and the other shareholders want the company to continue, this should automatically disentitle the applicant from having the company liquidated, or whether the applicant's conduct would only be one of several factors to be taken into account in deciding whether the company should be wound up. It is suggested that the better view is that the applicant's conduct should not automatically disentitle him or her from obtaining a winding up on the just and equitable ground.[30]

BREAKDOWN OF MUTUAL TRUST AND CONFIDENCE

This ground of liquidation is available mainly to minority shareholders. The applicant must prove, *inter alia*, that the company is solvent and that there will be surplus assets for distribution amongst the shareholders, otherwise he or she will have no "tangible interest" in the liquidation.[31] The applicant must also come to court with clean hands.[32]

The "just and equitable" ground enables the court to subject the exercise of legal rights to equitable considerations of a personal character arising between individuals which might make it inequitable to insist on legal rights or to exercise them in a particular way. For example, the members in general meeting have the legal right to remove a director and a director so removed must normally accept the situation. But if, as was the case in *Ebrahimi v Westbourne Galleries Ltd*, a company was formed or continued on the basis of a personal relationship involving mutual confidence and an understanding that all the shareholders would participate in the management of the company's business, the "just and equitable" provision will come to the assistance of a director who was removed in violation of that mutual confidence and understanding, notwithstanding that such removal was an exercise of a legal right. In that case the petition was presented under the equivalent of s 152(2) (g) of the Companies Act 1997. Mr Ebrahimi had been for many years an equal partner with Mr Nazar in a business dealing in Persian carpets. In 1958 it was decided to incorporate the business and Ebrahimi and Nazar, who were also appointed the first directors, each

29 *Loch v John Blackwood Ltd* [1924] AC 783 at 788.
30 *Vujnovich v Vujnovich* [1989] 3 NZLR 513; *Morgan v 45 Flers Avenue Pty Ltd* (1986) 10 ACLR 692.
31 *Re Rica Gold Washing Co Ltd* (1879) 11 Ch D 36.
32 *Ebrahimi v Westbourne Galleries Ltd* [1973] AC 360, [1972] 2 All ER 492.

held 500 shares. Soon afterwards, Nazar's son was made a director and Ebrahimi and Nazar each transferred 100 of their shares to him. Thus, and at all material times thereafter, the Nazars held a majority of the votes in general meeting. The company prospered, and all the profits were distributed in the form of directors' remuneration. No dividends were ever paid. Around 1965, the relationship between Ebrahimi and Nazar began to deteriorate. There was a major disagreement between Ebrahimi and Nazar, and in 1969 Nazar and his son, as majority shareholders, voted at a shareholders' meeting to remove Ebrahimi as director. The Nazars had legal authority to do so because the company's constitution and the Companies Act allowed a majority of shareholders to remove a director from office. Ebrahimi thereafter ceased to play any part in the management of the company's affairs and, since no dividends were paid, he also ceased to participate in the profits.

The House of Lords held that Ebrahimi and Nazar had joined in the formation of the company on the basis that the character of the association, namely, that Ebrahimi was entitled to participate in management, would, as a matter of personal relation and good faith, remain the same; and that, Nazar having in effect repudiated that relationship and the appellant having lost his right to share in the profits and being in that respect at the mercy of the Nazars and being unable to dispose of his interest without their consent, the proper course was to dissolve the association by winding up the company.

The decision of the House of Lords further established that the just and equitable ground may be available even where there has been no fraud or wrongdoing on the part of those in control.

Lastly, where the petitioner is a shareholder, the "just and equitable" ground will not be confined to circumstances affecting him in his capacity as such. Ebrahimi's rights as a shareholder were in no way affected by his removal from directorship, yet he was permitted to rely on the ground.

It should be noted that a company formed on the basis of mutual trust and confidence between its participants may change over time with the admission of new members to such an extent that equitable considerations no longer apply to the company. Changes during the life of a company could also make it subject to the equitable principles. The company need not have been formed on the basis of mutual trust and confidence for equitable considerations to apply.[33]

FRAUD OR MISCONDUCT

The National Court may wind up a company on the just and equitable ground if there has been fraud, misconduct or oppression. This ground has largely been incorporated into s 152 of the Companies Act 1997, which

33 *O'Neill v Phillips* [1999] 1 WLR 1092.

allows a wide range of remedies. Nevertheless, this ground is still available for winding up companies, and courts will order the winding up of companies formed with the purpose of defrauding the investing public.[34]

In *Loch v John Blackwood Ltd*,[34a] the Privy Council ordered a small company to be wound up because the directors showed a lack of probity or fair conduct in managing its affairs. The directors did not provide financial reports to minority shareholders in accordance with law, and audits had also not been conducted in accordance with law. In short, the directors denied information regarding the company's affairs to the minority shareholders. This was done to enable the directors to acquire their shares at below market value.

An applicant will be entitled to a winding up order on the "just and equitable" ground if he can show that he has justifiably lost confidence in the ability of the existing management to conduct the company's affairs in a proper manner. The petitioner's lack of confidence must be grounded in the conduct of the directors or controllers in regard to the company's business, which normally rests upon some lack of probity or some impropriety. Examples of such conduct are cases in which management persists in withholding information from the shareholders to which they are entitled or where those in control treat the business of the company as if it were entirely their own, without regard for minority interest.

FAILURE OF "SUBSTRATUM"

The National Court may wind up a company on the "just and equitable" ground where it ceases to carry on the business for which it was formed. This is referred to as failure of substratum. It can be illustrated by the cases of *Re German Date Coffee Co*[35] and *Re Tivoli Freeholds Ltd*.[36]

In *Re German Date Coffee Co*,[37] the main objects of the company were to acquire and work the German patent for manufacturing coffee from dates. Other ancillary objects followed. The German patent was never granted, but the company acquired a Swedish patent and made coffee. On the application of two of the shareholders that it was "just and equitable" to wind up the company, it was held that as the substratum (main objects) had failed, the company should be wound up. The company had not been formed to make coffee from dates, but to work a particular patent and, as the patent did not exist, the minority were entitled to have the company put into liquidation.

34 *Re Neath Harbour Smelting & Rolling Works* (1886) 2 TLR 336.
34a [1924] AC 783.
35 (1882) 20 Ch D 169.
36 [1972] VR 445.
37 (1882) 20 Ch D 169.

In *Re Tivoli Freeholds Ltd*,[37a] a company was formed to conduct an entertainment business and other associated activities. Its main asset was land upon which theatres were built. The company came under the control of a majority shareholder, Industrial Equity Ltd, which appointed its own nominees to the board of directors of Tivoli Freeholds Ltd. A fire severely damaged the buildings and the theatrical activities ceased. Tivoli Freeholds Ltd then sold the land with the approval of the general meeting. The board resolved to lend the surplus funds thus obtained to Industrial Equity Ltd, repayable at call. These funds were mainly used for corporate raiding: buying shares in other companies at below their asset value and either selling the assets or restructuring the companies and later selling the shares at a profit. A minority shareholder, who with supporters controlled 42 per cent of the company shares, applied to have the company put into liquidation on the grounds of oppression and on the "just and equitable" ground. The court held that it was just and equitable that the company be wound up. This was because the company was engaging in business entirely outside what could fairly be regarded as the general intention and common understanding of the members when they became members. This was so even though the new activities were not outside the scope of the objects clause in its constitution and therefore not *ultra vires*. The members expected the company to continue in the entertainment business and would not have expected it to lend more than 70 per cent of its funds for corporate raiding.

DEADLOCK

If, for example, shares in the company are equally divided between two members who have become irreconcilable with the result that the business of the company can no longer be effectively carried on, a winding up order will be made by the court on the "just and equitable" ground. Deadlock usually arises where the general meeting is unable to pass resolutions because of major disagreements between shareholders. It can also arise where the company has no directors and there are no prospects of any directors being appointed.[38]

In *Re Yenijde Tobacco Co Ltd*,[38a] two tobacco manufacturers, Rothman and Weinberg, formed a company to take over their separate businesses. They were the sole directors and shareholders of the company. The relationship seriously deteriorated. There were allegations of fraud, quarrels over the dismissal of an employee and the terms of employment of another.

37a [1972] VR 445.

38 *CIC Insurance Ltd (prov liq apptd) v Hannan & Co Pty Ltd* (2001) 38 ACSR 245. Note that this would also be a ground for liquidation under s 291(3)(c) of the Companies Act 1997 (see above p 564).

38a [1916] 2 Ch 426.

They refused to speak to each other and communicated through the company secretary. Weinberg applied for liquidation of the company on the just and equitable ground, and this was granted despite the fact that the company was prosperous.

In *Gabriel Velegamus v Paul Aisoli*[39] the National Court appointed a receiver and manager to run the company as a going concern until further orders, where there was a protracted and seemingly intractable dispute over ownership and control of the company. This is the type of situation that would give rise to an application for liquidation on the ground of deadlock or breakdown of mutual trust and confidence, if the dispute would continue for some time without being resolved, or if the directors and shareholders both split into two implacably opposed groups with the result that the business of the company could no longer be carried on.

DIRECTORS ACTING IN OWN INTERESTS

Section 240(1)(f) of the repealed Companies Act (Ch 146) provided that the court may order the winding up of a company "if directors have acted in the affairs of the company in their own interests rather than in the interests of the members as a whole, or in any other manner that appears to be unfair or unjust to other members".[40] Beck and Borrowdale state that this ground, which used to exist under the repealed Companies Act (Ch 146), "is almost certainly subsumed within the 'just and equitable' ground".[41]

Oppressive, unfairly discriminatory, or unfairly prejudicial conduct or acts

Section 152(1) of the Companies Act 1997 provides that a shareholder or former shareholder of a company, or any other entitled person, who considers that the affairs of a company have been, or are being, or are likely to be, conducted in a manner that is, or any act or acts of the company have been, or are, or are likely to be, oppressive, unfairly discriminatory, or unfairly prejudicial to him in that capacity or in any other capacity, may apply to the court for an order under this section (the oppression action or remedy). Section 152(2)(g) then provides that where such an application is made, and the court considers that it is just and equitable to do so, the court may make a variety of orders, including "an order putting the company into liquidation". Even though this ground is not specifically set out in the Companies Act 1997 as a ground for applying for a court appointed liquidator, it

39 [1988–89] PNGLR 63.

40 Cf *Straits Contracting (PNG) Pty Ltd v Branfill Investments Ltd* [1988] PNGLR 239 and *Re Commercial Pacific Lumber Exports Pty Ltd* [1971–72] PNGLR 178.

41 Beck, A and Borrowdale, A, *Guidebook to New Zealand Companies and Securities Law* (7th edn, CCH New Zealand Ltd, Auckland, 2002), para 1422.

should be borne in mind that applications under s 152 may lead to such a remedy.[42] Although this ground is separate from the "just and equitable" ground considered earlier, there is much overlap, especially as the court is given power to award the remedy where it is "just and equitable to do so". However, the just and equitable ground does not have any limitations such as those contained in s 152(1) (oppression remedy) and is therefore wider.[43]

In the public interest for the company to be wound up

It is possible that the Registrar of Companies (and perhaps the Attorney-General[44]) may be allowed to bring an action on the "just and equitable" ground. Overseas cases show that there must be a risk to the public interest by the company being liquidated that demands protection.[45] Public interest consideration would include regular and repeated breaches of the Companies Act 1997, the need for investor protection, and misconduct and mismanagement in the conduct of the business of the company.

The liquidator

The liquidator is an agent of the company who occupies a position which is fiduciary in some respects and is bound by the statutory duties imposed by the Companies Act 1997. As an agent of the company, the liquidator can bind the company without incurring personal liability on the contract.[46] Appropriate standards of skill and care are expected of the liquidator, having regard to the fact that he or she is a professional. As a fiduciary, a liquidator must exercise his or her powers in good faith and not for any improper purpose.[47] The liquidator must avoid situations where his or her obligation to the

42 For a consideration of the effect of s 152 of the Companies Act 1997 see Chapter 13.

43 Because compulsory winding up is a drastic remedy, and judges are reluctant to wind up a company which is solvent and which has a future, a minority shareholder who applies for the appointment of a liquidator for one of the above stated reasons will also usually bring an oppression action under s 152(1) as an alternative ground, as the court may consider that one of the broad range of remedies set out in that provision is more appropriate. If the application is limited to the "just and equitable" ground, and the court refuses the application, it will be dismissed, as the only remedy available is to put the company into liquidation; there are no alternative remedies.

44 Cf Companies Act (Ch 146), Part VII, Division 4, particularly ss 186 and 239(1)(f).

45 See for example, *Australian Securities Commission v AS Nominees Ltd* (1995)18 ACSR 363; *ASIC v Austimber Pty Ltd* (1999) 17 ACLC 893. Cf *Morgan Roche Ltd v Registrar of Companies* (1987) 3 NZCLC 100 189. See also s 124A (and s 122(1)(g)) of the Insolvency Act 1986 (UK): "Where it appears to the Secretary of State . . . that it is expedient in the public interest that a company should be wound up, he may present a petition for it to be wound up if the court thinks it just and equitable for it to be so."

46 *Stead Hazel & Co v Cropper* [1933] 1 KB 840.

47 *Re Burnells Pty Ltd (In Liq)* (1979) 4 ACLR 213.

company conflicts with his or her personal interests,[48] and he or she must not profit from his or her position as liquidator. For example, he or she may not enter into contracts with the company without disclosure and leave of the court,[49] and he or she is not entitled to engage third parties with whom he or she is associated.[50]

The Companies Act 1997 expressly allows a liquidator to appoint an agent "to do anything which the liquidator is unable to do".[51] However, it is suggested that the power to appoint an agent goes further than this and allows for the appointment of an agent to do work which it is unreasonable to expect the liquidator to do personally.[52] However, a liquidator cannot delegate so much of his or her power that it may be said that he or she has "not properly acted as liquidator at all",[53] nor may he or she delegate in matters that require professional judgment. The liquidator must also ensure the agent is appropriately qualified for the task and is given required information.

If more than one liquidator is appointed,[54] then they must act jointly in the liquidation.

The liquidator will hold office until completion of the liquidation,[55] unless he or she resigns beforehand, dies, becomes disqualified or is removed from office by an order of the National Court.[56] The liquidation is completed when the liquidator has filed with the Registrar of Companies a final report, final accounts and a liquidator's final statement in accordance with s 299 of the Companies Act 1997.

The fees and expenses properly incurred by the liquidator in carrying out the duties and exercising the powers of the liquidator and his or her remuneration are payable out of the assets of the company[57] and constitute a preferential debt.[58]

48 See for example, *Re Papua New Guinea Block Co Pty Ltd (in liq)* [1982] PNGLR 28, where the judge, in ordering the removal from office of the liquidator, held, *inter alia*, that "The liquidator and his agent have placed themselves in positions of conflict of interest such as to rob them of the real and apparent independence necessary for the conduct of a proper winding up".

49 *Silkstone & Haigh Moor Coal Co v Edey* [1900] 1 Ch 167.

50 *Commissioner for Corporate Affairs v Harvey* (1979) 4 ACLR 259.

51 Companies Act 1997, Schedule 8(n). Cf *Re Papua New Guinea Block Co Pty Ltd (in liq)* [1982] PNGLR 28.

52 Companies Act 1997, s 310(1).

53 As seems to have been the case in *Re Papua New Guinea Block Co Pty Ltd (in liq)* [1982] PNGLR 28.

54 Companies Act 1997, s 290(2).

55 Companies Act 1997, s 327.

56 Companies Act 1997, s 334(4)(a). See *Re Papua New Guinea Block Co Pty Ltd (in liq)* [1982] PNGLR 28 for the principles upon which the National Court will act to remove liquidators from office. See also *Commissioner for Corporate Affairs v Harvey* (1979) 4 ACLR 259.

57 Companies Act 1997, s 326. See also ss 324 and 325.

58 Companies Act 1997, Schedule 9, s 1.

Appointment

WHO MAY BE APPOINTED A LIQUIDATOR

The Companies Act 1997 tries to ensure that only qualified persons who will act independently and impartially (i.e., without a conflict of interest) are appointed and act as liquidators of companies: "the guiding principle in the appointment of a liquidator is that he must be independent and must be seen to be independent."[59] This is done by first stipulating that only certain qualified types of accountants may act as liquidators.

Only a Registered Liquidator under the Accountants Act 1996 (usually a qualified practising accountant with insolvency experience) may be appointed or act as a liquidator of a company (Companies Act 1997, s 328(1)). Furthermore, only natural persons may be liquidators: individuals rather than companies of firms are registered as Registered Liquidators under the Accountants Act 1996, and s 328(3) of the Companies Act 1997 expressly provides that a "body corporate" shall not be appointed or act as a liquidator.

Some Registered Liquidators may be precluded from being appointed or acting as a liquidator generally or in respect to a particular company because of their association with it, unless they obtain prior approval of the National Court.[60] Section 328(2) provides that a Registered Liquidator shall not be appointed or act as liquidator if he or she:

- is less than 18 years old;[61]
- is a creditor of the company;
- has been a shareholder, director,[62] auditor,[63] or receiver of the company or of a related company in the two years before the liquidation;

59 *Re Papua New Guinea Block Co Pty Ltd (in liq)* [1982] PNGLR 28 at 39 (Miles J), referring to Sir Nigel Bowen in *Stewden Nominees No 4 Pty Ltd* (1975) 1 ACLR 185.

60 In *Re Papua New Guinea Block Co Pty Ltd (in liq)* [1982] PNGLR 28 at 37, Miles J stated: "It is a basic consequence of the appointment of an official liquidator that he acts as an officer of the court. Whilst it may be proper in certain circumstances for such an officer of the court to conduct his professional affairs outside Papua New Guinea as well as within it, it is wholly inappropriate that an official liquidator should be permanently resident outside the jurisdiction of the court."

61 It would seem highly unlikely that a person under the age of 18 could become a Registered Liquidator, and thus qualify as a liquidator of a company. This provision is a carry over from the New Zealand Companies Act 1993 which did not require any specific qualifications or standards for a liquidator. The Act merely specified persons who are disqualified, without court approval, from being appointed or acting as liquidators. A person less than 18 is included in this list. Nevertheless, the provision will disqualify the precocious Registered Liquidator.

62 Note that "officer" is not included in the list of restrictions. So there is nothing to prevent a company secretary or financial officer of a company who is a Registered Liquidator from being appointed as the liquidator of the company. Whether this *ought* to be done is another question.

63 It would seem that leave of the court for the appointment of an auditor of a company as its liquidator will not be readily forthcoming. Auditors can be expected to be closely

- is an undischarged bankrupt;
- is of unsound mind or unable to manage his affairs;
- has been prohibited by the National Court from acting as a receiver or liquidator under ss 286(6) or 334(5) of the Companies Act 1997; or
- is prohibited from promoting, directing or managing a company under the Companies Act (Ch 146) or the Companies Act 1997.

A person who appoints a person or body corporate in breach of the above requirements and any person or body corporate that acts as a liquidator in breach of these requirements commits an offence and is liable to a fine of up to K10,000.00.[64]

It is possible that a person or a Registered Liquidator may begin acting as a liquidator of a company and it is afterwards discovered that the person was disqualified from acting as such.[65] What is the effect of such a discovery? Are the acts of the so-called liquidator valid, voidable or void. A question arises whether the appointment is invalid and its effects, e.g. whether the actions of the liquidator are also invalid. If at some later date it is discovered that the person appointed liquidator of the company was not qualified to be so appointed, his or her acts in relation to the liquidation are treated as valid by s 329 of the Companies Act 1997.[66] It would also seem possible that where the invalidity resulted from a breach of s 328(2), s 329 would validate the past actions of the liquidator and it would seem to be possible for the court to approve (under s 328(2)) that the Registered Liquidator continue to act as liquidator if this course of conduct would be a most just and convenient way of proceeding.

Even if a Registered Liquidator is qualified according to the above requirements to become a liquidator of a company, it is possible that the underlying law may prevent such an appointment. The courts have sought to ensure that liquidators are impartial, i.e. that they "should be independent and should be seen to be independent".[67] The Companies Act 1997 exempts a liquidator from liability where the liquidator has obtained and acted in accordance with a direction of the National Court.[68]

connected to the board of directors, and a liquidator may be required to scrutinise matters that have been directly or indirectly approved by the auditor, and this could lead to a challenge to the liquidator's independence: see *Re Photo Holdings Pty Ltd* (1976) 2 ACLR 117 at 118.

64 Companies Act 1997, s 328(4).

65 See *Re Papua New Guinea Block Co Pty Ltd (in liq)* [1982] PNGLR 28.

66 In *Re Papua New Guinea Block Co Pty Ltd (in liq)* [1982] PNGLR 28, at the time of appointment, the person appointed by the court as liquidator was not an official liquidator as required by the Companies Act 1963 (as the Companies Act (Ch 146) was called before it was included in the Revised Laws). Despite contravention of the Companies Act (Ch 146), all acts of the liquidator were valid.

67 *Stewden Nominees No 4 Pty Ltd* (1975) 1 ACLR 185 at 187.

68 Companies Act 1997, s 332(3).

Interim liquidator

Section 296(1) of the Companies Act 1997 provides that the National Court may appoint an interim liquidator where an application has been made to the court for an order that a company be put into liquidation and the court is satisfied that "it is necessary or expedient for the purpose of maintaining the value of assets owned or managed by the company".

Unless the court otherwise orders, the interim liquidator has the rights and powers of a liquidator to the extent necessary or desirable to maintain the value of assets owned or managed by the company.[69] As such, the interim liquidator is not to undertake the liquidation.

In *Re Commercial Pacific Lumber Exports Pty Ltd*,[70] Kelly J laid down the principles governing the appointment of a "provisional liquidator" under the repealed Companies Act (Ch 146) (then referred to as the Companies Act 1963), and it is submitted that similar consideration will apply to the appointment of an interim liquidator under the Companies Act 1997. He stated:

> Reported cases indicate that as a general rule the court has been prepared to appoint a provisional liquidator in certain defined sets of circumstances. Two such circumstances, neither of which exists in the present case, are where the petition for winding-up has been presented by the company itself and where the petition is unopposed. Two other circumstances in which a provisional liquidator has been appointed and which it is suggested are applicable here are firstly, where the company is insolvent and secondly, where the situation is such that it is desirable to appoint a provisional liquidator to take possession of and to protect the assets of the company . . . The question then is whether the situation is such that even though the petitioners cannot show that the company is insolvent, nevertheless it is desirable that the assets of the company be protected pending the determination of the winding-up petition. The court is being called upon to exercise a discretion and if it seems to it to be proper to do so under the circumstances of any particular case, it will exercise that discretion to appoint a provisional liquidator even though the situation does not fit exactly into any of the categories in which provisional liquidators have been appointed in other cases . . . It has been suggested that it is necessary that the situation should be one of emergency or at least of urgency, but this is not necessarily so . . . Where the case is not one of insolvency or of a petition presented by the company itself or unopposed the test is simply whether the circumstances are such that to use the words of the Lord President in *Levy v Napier* [1962] SC 469, "a holding operation under the control of a provisional liquidator is appropriate".

69 Companies Act 1997, s 296(2).
70 [1971–72] PNGLR 178.

> The present position of this company is that there is a definite cleavage between two interests, each with an equal shareholding in the company and one of which is also a large unsecured creditor. Irrespective of whether, in view of the provisions of the joint venture agreement, he is entitled to do so, Wakim is asserting control of the company to the exclusion of the directors appointed by Coop and indeed has gone so far as to encumber the whole of the company's undertaking. To my mind this clearly creates a situation in which at the suit of Coop at all events with the interest which it has in the company, the company should be placed in the hands of some neutral person and its assets protected pending the determination of the winding-up petition. I consider that such a "holding operation" is certainly appropriate.
>
> I appreciate that certain of the creditors do not wish this step to be taken as they are understandably concerned with their own interests which they consider would be best served by the company continuing as it is without the appointment of a provisional liquidator. However, I do not consider that the views of these creditors should be allowed to prevail when it appears so desirable for the reasons which I have indicated that at this stage there should be an impartial person appointed to take charge of the assets.

The court thought it "desirable that the provisional liquidator should be given the power to carry on business so far as is necessary for the purpose of preserving the business as a going concern".

Court appointment

Who may apply

The Companies Act 1997 sets out a list of those persons or entities who are allowed to make an application to the court for the appointment of a liquidator.[71] Except in very limited circumstances,[72] the court relies upon the appropriate application being made by one of these applicants. Those who have standing to bring an application for liquidation are as follows.

71 Companies Act 1997, s 291(2)(c). Under the former Companies Act (Ch 146), s 239(1), a wider list of applicants could petition for a compulsory winding up.

72 Companies Act 1997, s 152(2)(g). In *Vujnovich* the New Zealand Court of Appeal and the Privy Council ordered a company to be liquidated even though none of the shareholders had requested it: *Vujnovich v Vujnovich* [1988] 2 NZLR 129, NZCA; *Vujnovich v Vujnovich* [1989] 3 NZLR 513, PC NZ. Note that a wider group of applicants than those listed in s 291(2)(c) may make an application under s 152(1) (oppression remedy) which may eventually lead to a winding up order.

COMPANY (BOARD OF DIRECTORS)

A majority of the directors may resolve to apply to the court for the company to be liquidated.

DIRECTOR

Even if a majority of directors decide not to apply to the court for an order liquidating the company, nevertheless a single director is empowered to bring such an application. In this context, "director" includes a person occupying the position of director of a company by whatever name called.[73]

SHAREHOLDER

A shareholder may apply to the court for a winding up order. Section 78 defines "shareholder", for the purposes of the Companies Act 1997, as:

(a) a person whose name is entered in the share register as the holder for the time being of one or more shares in the company (s 78(a)); or
(b) in the case of newly registered companies, where a share register may not yet be compiled, a person named as a shareholder in an application for the registration of a company at the time of registration of the company(s 78(b)); or
(c) in the case of an amalgamation, a person who is entitled under a registered amalgamation proposal to have his name entered in the share register (s 78(a)).

ENTITLED PERSON

Section 291(2)(c) of the Companies Act 1997 provides that an entitled person (other than a shareholder, who comes within the definition of "entitled person" but who is specifically provided for in the section) may apply to the court for an order liquidating the company. In this section, entitled person means "a person upon whom the constitution confers any of the rights and powers of a shareholder".[74] This right in the shareholder cannot be restricted or taken away by the company's constitution,[75] and the right is available to all shareholders, irrespective of how long they have been members of the company.

CREDITOR

A liquidator may be appointed by the National Court on the application of a creditor (including a contingent and prospective creditor).

73 Companies Act 1997, s 107(1)(a). Shadow directors do not have standing under this provision to apply to the court for liquidation of a company.
74 Companies Act 1997, s 2(1).
75 *Re Peveril Gold Mines Ltd* [1898] 1 Ch 122.

Section 290(1) provides that "creditor" means a person who, in a liquidation, would be entitled to claim in accordance with s 351 that a debt is owing to that person by the company. A secured creditor is included in the definition for the purposes of bringing an action for the appointment of a liquidator.

The definition of creditor refers to s 351, which deals with admissible claims. It describes those debts or liabilities which may be admitted as a claim against the company. These debts and liabilities may be: (i) present or future; (ii) certain or contingent; (iii) an ascertained debt or liability or a liability for damages.[76] A person is a creditor, therefore, only if his or her debt is admissible as a claim in the liquidation.

CONTINGENT OR PROSPECTIVE CREDITOR

Contingent and prospective creditors may also apply to the National Court for the appointment of a liquidator. However, in cases where the basis of the application is that the company is unable to pay its debts as they become due in the ordinary course of business, they *must* first obtain the permission (leave) of the court; and the court may give such leave, with or without conditions, only if it is satisfied that a prima facie case has been made out that the company is unable to pay its debts as they become due in the ordinary course of business.[77] Where the ground of the application is other than the company's insolvency (e.g., persistent or serious default in compliance with the Companies Act 1997), a contingent or prospective creditor does not have to obtain the prior permission of the court to bring the application.

The Companies Act 1997 does not define who are contingent or prospective creditors and, as such, the underlying law governs the matter. It is suggested that a contingent creditor is someone to whom the company has an existing obligation, and that as a result of that obligation, the company may or will become liable to pay a sum of money on the happening of a future event or at some future date.[78]

In *Re William Hockley Ltd*,[79] Pennycuick J expressed the view that contingent creditor meant "a person towards whom, under an existing obligation, the company may or will become subject to a present liability on the happening of some future event or at some future date". In *Community*

76 Section 351(2) of the Companies Act 1997 provides that "Fines, monetary penalties, and costs to which Section 356 applies are not claims that may be admitted against a company in liquidation".

77 Companies Act 1997, s 336(5).

78 *Re William Hockley Ltd* [1962] 2 All ER 111; *Community Development Pty Ltd v Engwirda Construction Co* (1969) 120 CLR 455; *Re Austral Group Investment Management Ltd; McHugh v Austral Group Investment Management Ltd* [1993] 2 NZLR 692.

79 [1962] 2 All ER 111.

Development Pty Ltd v Engwirda Construction Co,[80] the High Court of Australia applied the definition of Pennycuick J to a petitioner whose entitlement to payment under an existing building contract with the company was dependent on final certification which had not taken place at the time when the petition to wind up was presented. In that case, the creditor had undertaken certain building work for the company. Under the contract, certificates had to be signed by the architects before payment could be made to the creditor and this had not taken place at the time of the application for winding up.

A prospective creditor has been described as one who is indebted in a sum of money not immediately payable, and one who is owed a debt which will certainly become due in the future. So a person who has commenced separate proceedings against the company for unliquidated damages for breach of trust, if there was a real prospect of that claim succeeding, would be a prospective creditor.[81]

It should be noted that contingent and prospective creditors cannot issue a statutory demand, since such a demand can only be made where the debt is due.[82]

REGISTRAR

The Registrar may apply to the court to liquidate a company on any of the grounds specified in s 291(3) of the Companies Act 1997. The application will usually be triggered following an investigation into the affairs of the company to see if the interests of creditors or shareholders are being imperiled by acts of misfeasance without their knowledge.[83]

CENTRAL BANK

Under the Companies Act (Ch 146),[84] the Central Bank (Bank of Papua New Guinea) had standing to petition for the liquidation of a company carrying on banking business or that was a licensed financial institution, in accordance with s 18 of the Banks and Financial Institutions Act (Ch 137) (repealed). The Central Bank could present a petition to the National Court under s 239 of the Companies Act (Ch 146) for the winding-up of the bank

80 (1969) 120 CLR 455.

81 *Re Austral Group Investment Management Ltd; McHugh v Austral Group Investment Management Ltd* [1993] 2 NZLR 692; *Re PMC Investments Pty Ltd* (1991) 9 ACLC 1,559.

82 See below at p 587.

83 *Australian Securities Commission v AS Nominees Ltd* (1995) 133 ALR 1; *Morgan Roche Ltd v Registrar of Companies* (1987) 3 NZCLC 100,189.

84 Companies Act (Ch 146), s 239(1)(b).

or financial institution where the business was being improperly conducted, including in a manner detrimental to the interests of its depositors or other creditors.[85]

Section 48(1) of the Banks and Financial Institutions Act 2000 provides that the Central Bank has standing to apply to the National Court for an authorised institution (bank or financial institution) to be liquidated under the Companies Act 1997 where it considers that the authorised institution "is insolvent and could not be restored to solvency within a reasonable period". Subsection (2) provides that the winding up is "to be conducted in accordance with the Companies Act 1997 or any other law under which [the] Authorized Institution is incorporated or is taken to be incorporated".

The Principal Legal Adviser (Attorney-General)

The Companies Act 1997 does not expressly grant standing to the Attorney-General (Principal Legal Adviser) to apply for the liquidation of a company. However, s 239(1)(f) of the repealed Companies Act (Ch 146) gave standing to a Principal Legal Adviser (who is not the Attorney-General) to apply for liquidation of a company under s 186. This was in keeping with the significant powers given to Principal Legal Adviser under the Companies Act (Ch 146). The Principal Legal Adviser has no powers under the current Companies Act 1997 and, as such, no longer has standing to apply for a company to be put into liquidation. However, it is possible that the courts may hold that the Attorney-General has power to apply for a company to be wound up on the "just and equitable" ground where it is in the interest of the public that such a company be wound up.[86]

Grounds for court appointment

Section 291(3) of the Companies Act 1997 provides four exclusive[87] grounds on which the National Court may appoint a liquidator. It may do so where it is satisfied that:

- the company is unable to pay its debts as they become due in the ordinary course of business (s 291(3)(a)); or
- the company or the board has persistently or seriously failed to comply with the Companies Act 1997 (s 291(3)(b)); or

85 Companies Act (Ch 146), s 18(1) and (2)(g).

86 For example, the winding up of companies that operate pyramid schemes (e.g. Fast Money schemes).

87 Exclusive in the sense that the grounds may form the basis of the *original* application for liquidation. In addition, on an application under s 152(1) of the Companies Act 1997 (the oppression action or remedy), the court may grant a remedy of winding up.

- the company does not comply with s 11 of the Companies Act 1997 (s 291(3)(c)); or
- it is just and equitable that the company be put into liquidation (s 291(3)(d)).

Even if an application makes out one of the above grounds, the National Court has a discretion whether or not to appoint a liquidator, and this will depend on the facts of the case.[88] For example, the court will usually decline to appoint a liquidator if the majority of the creditors in value oppose such an appointment.[89]

In *Re Sairs Pty Ltd*,[90] Ollerenshaw J held that where a company is unable to pay its debts a petitioning creditor is prima facie entitled to a winding up order. The mere fact that a majority in value of the creditors oppose the petition will not in itself be sufficient reason to refuse the order, although where the opposing majority show some good or substantial reason for their objection, the court may, in its discretion, refuse to make a winding up order. If such reason is established, the court may nevertheless order the winding up if the petitioner shows special circumstances why it would not be just and equitable to give effect to the wishes of the majority. He held that neither the expense of a winding up by an official liquidator nor the fact that the company is involved in proceedings which may ultimately lead to payment in full of its creditors is sufficient reason for refusing to make a winding up order. The fact that the opposing creditors who are also solely entitled to the control of and beneficial interest in the company, whose liquidation is sought, is also a factor to be taken into account.[91]

In *Re Thames Freightlines Ltd (in rec)*,[92] Greig J stated the principles that the court will take into account in exercising its discretion as follows:[93]

- the applicant creditor is entitled *ex debito justitiae* to a liquidation order;

88 *Re Thames Freightlines Ltd* (in rec) (1981) 1 NZCLC ¶95-012.

89 *Mercantile Credits Ltd v Foster Clark (Australia) Ltd* (1964) 112 CLR 169; *Southern World Airlines Ltd v Auckland International Airport Ltd* (1992) 6 NZCLC 67,604. See, however, *Re Sairs Pty Ltd* [1969–70] PNGLR 293, where the pre-Independence Supreme Court ordered liquidation despite opposition from the (assumed) majority in value of the company's unsecured creditors. In this case the opposing creditors were also shareholders and controllers of the company.

90 [1969–70] PNGLR 293.

91 In earlier proceedings (*Re Stol Air Services Pty Ltd* [1967–68] PNGLR 429), the court granted an injunction to stay a winding up petition so as to allow creditors to review a scheme of arrangement to save the company.

92 (1981) 1 NZCLC ¶95-012 at 98,113

93 See Beck, A and Borrowdale, A, *Guidebook to New Zealand Companies and Securities Law*, supra, para 1411.

- the court has an unfettered discretion as to whether such an order should be made;
- the court will have regard to the wishes of the majority of the creditors and is bound to have regard to the value of the debts on each side;
- the fact that the majority of creditors oppose the application is not, in itself, sufficient to compel the court to decline the order;
- it is for the opposing creditors to show that there are reasons for a refusal of the liquidation order;
- the court will have regard to all the circumstances relevant to the company and its operations and, among other things, the reasons against the liquidation, the interests of other creditors and, in particular circumstances, the weight to be attached to the opposition, in whole or in part, of the creditors; and
- the fact that the assets of the debtor company have been mortgaged to an amount equal to, or in excess of, the assets, or that the company has no assets, is not sufficient to justify refusal of the liquidation order.

Winding up on ground of insolvency

Inability to pay debts (insolvency)

Section 291(3)(a) of the Companies Act 1997 provides that the court may appoint a liquidator where it is satisfied that a company is unable to pay its debts as they become due in the ordinary course of business. Usually, it will be a creditor who brings the application to court and he or she will normally rely on one of the four presumptions of insolvency to establish the company's inability to pay its debts. However, the creditor or other applicant need not rely on any of the four presumptions, but may prove the company's inability to pay its debts by other means.[94] The test is one of "commercial" insolvency; the applicant does not have to show that liabilities exceed assets (which is termed "financial" or "balance sheet" insolvency).[95] Commercial insolvency may be shown, for example, by a failure to honour bills of exchange,[96]or by showing a large number of outstanding debts and unsatisfied judgments.[97] In determining whether a company is unable to pay its debts as they become due in the ordinary course of business, the court may take into account the company's contingent or prospective liabilities.[98]

94 Companies Act 1997, s 336(2). *Re Accord Pty Ltd and the Companies Act* (1977) ACLC 29,417; (1977-78) CLC 40-332.
95 *Re Tweeds Garages Ltd* [1962] Ch 406.
96 *Re Federal Land Company* (1889) 15 VLR 135.
97 *Re Tweeds Garages Ltd* [1962] Ch 406.
98 Companies Act 1997, s 336(4).

Although the test is not one of "financial" or "balance sheet" insolvency, the court may nevertheless take into account the fact that liabilities exceed assets in coming to a conclusion that a company is insolvent. The applicant will bear the burden of proving commercial insolvency on a balance of probabilities, and this may be quite difficult, given that much of the information relating to the company's affairs will not be readily available to the applicant. It is much easier to establish one of the presumptions and thereby shift the burden onto the company of proving that it is not insolvent.

In deciding whether the company is solvent (whether it is able to pay its debts as they become due in the ordinary course of business), the court will take account of whether the company can borrow money against its assets etc. It is also possible that the court may decide that access to unsecured borrowings can be taken into account.[99]

Presumed inability to pay debts

To assist the applicant in proving a company's insolvency, the Companies Act 1997 has set out four situations which if established give rise to presumptions that the company is insolvent. A company is presumed to be unable to pay its debts as they become due in the ordinary course of business where:

- the company has failed to comply with a statutory demand (s 335(a)); or
- execution issued against the company in respect of a judgment debt has been returned unsatisfied in whole or in part (s 335(b)); or
- a person entitled to a charge over all or substantially all of the property of the company has appointed a receiver under the instrument creating the charge (s 335(c)); or
- a compromise between a company and its creditors has been put to a vote in accordance with Part XV of the Companies Act 1997, but has not been approved (s 335(d)).

We will now consider each of these presumptions.

Failure to comply with a statutory demand[100]

As we have seen above, a creditor is entitled to apply to the court for the appointment of a liquidator of the company if the company is unable to pay its debts,[101] and the statutory demand procedure is a quick and inexpensive way of establishing that a company is unable to pay its debts. Section 335(a) of the Companies Act 1997 provides that a company is presumed to

99 *Lewis v Doran* [2004] NSWSC 608.

100 For a detailed treatment of this area, see Beck, A, *Corporate Debt: Statutory Demands* (CCH New Zealand Ltd, Auckland, 2004).

101 Companies Act 1997, s 291.

be unable to pay its debts as they become due in the ordinary course of business where the company has failed to comply with a statutory demand.

A statutory demand is a notice given by a creditor to a company to make payment of a debt due to the creditor. If the company fails to comply with the notice, the creditor is entitled to make an application to the National Court to wind up the company.

Although the repealed Companies Act (Ch 146) contained provisions relating to the serving of a demand on the company as a way of showing that the company was insolvent, the procedure and consequences of service of the demand were quite different from the new procedure introduced by the Companies Act 1997.[102]

As Beck points out:

> Because the failure to comply with a statutory demand has significant consequences, a company cannot simply ignore a properly made demand. If the company has no good reason for its failure to pay the debt, it must either front up with the money or risk all the disadvantages of being confronted with an application for liquidation. These include the public advertisement of the application, which may be very damaging to a healthy company.[103]

If the company has a legitimate reason for not paying the debt, the statutory demand procedure affords it an opportunity to put this matter before the National Court and get the demand set aside.

The statutory demand process is relatively straightforward. The creditor serves on the debtor company a statutory demand requiring it to pay the amount due (or to come to an appropriate arrangement) within one month of the date of service. The company may either pay the debt as required or come to an arrangement, or it may, within one month of the date of service of the statutory demand, apply to the National Court to set aside the demand based on one of the grounds set out in the Companies Act 1997. If the company does not pay or get the statutory demand set aside, the creditor is able to apply to the court for the appointment of a liquidator.

Issuing a statutory demand

A statutory demand can only be issued by a creditor to a company in respect of a debt of at least K1,000 that is due.

102 See Companies Act (Ch 146), s 240(2)(a). In particular, if the company failed to pay the demand, it was "deemed to be unable to pay its debts", i.e., an irrebuttable presumption arose. The Act also did not provide clear or comprehensive guidance of how these demands could be "set aside". For a case dealing with the law and procedure under the repealed Companies Act (Ch 146), see *Re Paradise Real Estate* [1994] PNGLR 286.

103 Beck, A, *Corporate Debt: Statutory Demands*, supra, para 103.

There must be a relationship of debtor and creditor between the company and the person making the demand. The creditor must be a creditor of the company. In this respect it is important to have regard to the corporate veil doctrine, because serving a statutory demand on a holding company within a group of companies, when in fact the debt is owed by a subsidiary, will result in an invalid statutory demand. The debt must not only exist, but it must be due for payment (payable). As such, prospective and contingent creditors cannot issue statutory demands.[104] It may only be brought against a company.[105] It is not possible to use the statutory demand to recover debts from a company incorporated overseas ("overseas company"). However, if the overseas company is registered in Papua New Guinea ("foreign company"), the procedure can be used.[106] Certain types of "body corporate" other than companies could be registered under the repealed Act and reregistered under the Companies Act 1997. A statutory demand can be issued in respect of such corporations or bodies corporate.

A claim for damages cannot be the basis of a statutory demand unless the company admits the claim. The debt must be due before the statutory demand can be issued. The time for payment must have arrived. Therefore, where the debt is payable at some future date or on the happening of some event (condition), a statutory demand cannot be used to recover that amount.[107]

There is a minimum amount which must be due. Section 337(2)(a) provides that the debt(s) must be "not less than the prescribed amount". The amount currently prescribed by s 16 of the Companies Regulation 1998 is K1,000.

The Companies Act 1997 makes it easy to comply with the formalities for issuing a statutory demand by setting out a prescribed form which must be used.[108] Failure to use the prescribed form will make the statutory demand invalid.[109]

The statutory demand must inform the company of the various options open to it: the debt, enter into a compromise, compound with the creditor or

104 See p 581 above for discussion of who is a prospective or contingent creditor.

105 Section 2 of the Companies Act 1997 defines a company as a company "registered under Part II and includes an existing company registered under this Act in accordance with Section 442 or deemed to be registered under this Act in accordance with Section 443".

106 Companies Act 1997, s 393.

107 Companies Act 1997, s 337(2)(a). The statutory demand procedure is therefore not available for contingent and prospective debts: *Re Prime Link Removals Ltd* (1987) 3 NZCLC 100,218; *Goldcorp Holdings Ltd v Greedus* (1988) 4 NZCLC 64,342.

108 Companies Act 1997, s 337(2)(b). The prescribed form is set out as Form 42 of the Companies Regulation 1998. This is unlike in New Zealand, where the Companies Act 1993 (NZ) merely requires that the statutory demand be made in writing. Cf Corporations Regulations 2001 (Aus), Form 509H, Second Schedule.

109 It is suggested that a creditor may vary the form, but only slightly; strict compliance is not necessary, provided there is substantial compliance: Section 27(1) of the Interpretation Act (Ch 2) provides that "Substantial compliance with a form contained in a provision is sufficient". Cf *Daewoo Australia Pty Ltd v Suncorp-Metway Pty Ltd* (2000) 18 ACLC 212.

give a charge over its property. If these are omitted, the court will very likely hold that the statutory demand is invalid. Leaving out the phrase "that failure by the company to comply with this demand within one month" would, it is suggested, be a substantial departure from the prescribed form, and lead to it being considered to be invalid. It could be argued that failure to include any of the essential requirements will not necessarily mean that the demand is invalid; that one needs to bring the failure within the statutory grounds for setting aside. However, it should be noted that the Act provides that a statutory demand "shall" be in the prescribed form.

The statutory demand must state the amount due. If no definite amount is stipulated (for example, "the company owes the creditor an amount over K1,000.00"), it would mean that the statutory demand is invalid. The company will not need to apply to set it aside; it merely has to apply for a declaration that it is not a statutory demand. A statement of the wrong amount will not make the demand invalid. It will merely be a possible ground for setting aside. Problems may arise with claiming interest, as it may not be possible to calculate the amount of interest until payment is finally made. It is legitimate to claim interest in the demand, even if not calculated. However, it is best if some indication is given to the company as to how this is to be calculated.[110]

The address of the creditor should be the correct address, especially for service, as it might be difficult for the company to know where to serve any application it might want to make to set the statutory demand aside. One can add to the statutory demand. For example, it is possible to add an address for service which is different from the address of the company.

In order to be valid, the statutory demand must be served on the debtor company.[111] Again, the word used is "shall" be served. It is mandatory. Service should also take place in accordance with the service requirements of the Companies Act 1997.[112] Service by post or fax or, it would seem, email, is acceptable.[113]

110 *Topfelt Pty Ltd v State Bank of New South Wales Ltd* (1993) 12 ACSR 381.
111 Companies Act 1997, s 337(2)(c).
112 Companies Act 1997, ss 432 434 and 436.
113 Note that the company may be able to establish that a statutory demand has not been served in accordance with ss 432, 434 and 436, in which case, unless the court is willing to hold that alternative methods of service are available, s 337(2)(c) would not have been complied with and the statutory demand would be invalid: Companies Act 1997, s 436(2). In such a case, the creditor would not be able to rely on the statutory demand to apply for the appointment of a liquidator, and not only may the company resist such an application, but where an order for liquidation is granted in such circumstances, it may be set aside as a nullity: *Re Samoana Press Co Ltd* (1988) 4 NZCLC 64,119 referred to in Beck, A, *Corporate Debt: Statutory Demands*, supra, para 220. It is suggested that service of a statutory demand is governed by ss 432 and 434 and that the methods referred to are not an exclusive nor mandatory list. Whereas the provisions governing service of documents

The statutory demand must require the company to pay the debt, or enter into a compromise under Part XV, or otherwise compound with the creditor, or give a charge over its property to secure payment of the debt, to the reasonable satisfaction of the creditor, within one month of the date of service, or such longer period as the court may order.[114]

Beck makes a distinction between defective and invalid demands, holding that defective demands do not prevent the creditor from proceeding.[115] Where the statutory demand is invalid, it has no legal effect, and the company may ignore it with impunity.[116]

Responding to a statutory demand

When a company is served with a statutory demand, it can do one of three things: (1) comply with the demand (i.e. pay the debt); (2) ignore the demand; or (3) apply to the National Court to set it aside. The company has a month from the service of the demand to decide what course of action to take, but leaving it that late may cause problems, especially in relation to delay in service. If the company decides to comply with the demand, by making payment, it should ensure that payment is made on time and to the creditor in line with any specific requests that may be included in the statutory demand (e.g. payment by bank draft).[117]

on companies in legal proceedings (ss 431 and 433) expressly state that the methods specified in those sections are the only methods of service by which a document in legal proceedings may be served, there is no similar provision in ss 432 and 434. Based on the *expressio unius est exclusio alterius* principle, it is suggested that ss 432 and 434 are not exclusive codes and that any means or form of service that can be proved to have brought the statutory demand to the actual notice of the company will be valid service. Cf *Emhill Pty Ltd v Bonsoc Pty Ltd* [2004] VSC 322, where it was held that the service of documents provision in the Corporations Act 2001 (Aus) is facultative, and not exclusive and mandatory. Section 432 of the Companies Act 1997 commences "Notwithstanding the provisions of any other Act". So at least other methods of service on companies specified in other Acts continue to be valid: e.g. Income Tax Act 1959, s 354(2)(e) (service on public officer of company), Maintenance Orders Enforcement Act (Ch 279), s 23(2).

114 Companies Act 1997, s 337(2)(d).

115 Beck, A, *Corporate Debt: Statutory Demands*, supra, paras 221–224.

116 There is no reason why, for the sake of certainty, it may not apply to have it set aside, especially where the effect of the non-compliance is not clear; as is the case at the moment where there are no PNG cases and no clear New Zealand authorities on the matter. It is suggested that the only clear case of invalidity is where the statutory demand is for less than K1,000. It should be noted that New Zealand authorities on this area will need to be treated with caution given that the reference to "immaterial" defects and irregularities in s 338(5) tend to the view that material defects and irregularities (even where there is no substantial injustice) will lead to the statutory demand being held to be invalid and of no effect.

117 The company may also comply with the demand either by arriving at a compromise or agreement with the creditor or providing security to the reasonable satisfaction of the creditor: see Beck, A, *Corporate Debt: Statutory Demands*, supra, paras 303–304 for a discussion of this.

The statutory demand must be complied with within one month after service. The Companies Act 1997 does not define "month". However, the Interpretation Act (Ch 2) defines this term to mean calendar month, and Kandakasi J in *Moran Development Corporation Ltd v Akida Investments Ltd* (2003) N2458 appears to have accepted that this was the meaning to be given to the term as used in s 338(2) of the Companies Act 1997. It would seem to follow, for the sake of consistency, that this should also be the meaning given to the word "month" in s 337(2)(d) of the Act.[118]

Although, as we shall see later, the National Court does not have power to extend the time within which an application to set aside a statutory demand may be made, it does have the power, once an application to set aside has been made within time, to extend the *time for compliance* with the demand.[119]

As we have noted above, it is very difficult to tell when a statutory demand will be held to be invalid, and thus of no effect, so that the company can safely ignore it. The only situation where this is clear is where the demand is for less than the prescribed amount (currently K1,000) and not in writing, let alone in keeping with some semblance of the prescribed form. As such, companies that ignore purported demands, without attempting to set them aside, do so at their peril.[120] So the best course of action where the company believes that the demand is invalid, or the amount claimed is not owing, is to apply to the National Court to set the demand aside.

118 In calculating the month within which the payment or other arrangement must be made, the day on which service is effected is excluded, and if the last day of the period is a Sunday or public holiday, the payment or agreement may take place on the day next following that is not a Sunday or public holiday. Payment may therefore have to be made on a Saturday: Interpretation Act (Ch 2), s 11. Cf *Davis v Pitzz* [1988–89] PNGLR 143.

119 Companies Act 1997, ss 337(2)(d), 338(3). It appears that the reference to the extension of time allowed by the National Court in s 337(2)(d), means an application for extension during the hearing of the application to set aside the statutory demand and not a separate application for extension. It would appear to be not possible for a company to make a separate application to the National Court for extension of the time within which to comply with the demand. The New Zealand authorities are divided on whether the application for extension of time must be made within the statutory time period (in the case of Papua New Guinea, one month). See Beck, A, *Corporate Debt: Statutory Demands*, supra, para 306.

120 It will still be possible for the company, if the creditor proceeds to apply for the appointment of a liquidator, to apply for an injunction for a stay of the application or to formally oppose the application for liquidation proceeding, by showing that the company is solvent (able to pay its debts as they become due in the ordinary course of business), and that it has good reason for not paying the creditor. See Beck, A, *Corporate Debt: Statutory Demands*, supra, para 308.

Setting aside a statutory demand

INTRODUCTION

Where a company has a defence against a statutory demand, it will usually apply to set aside the statutory demand. If it fails to do this, it can still challenge the statutory demand in later winding up proceedings. However, the task is more difficult, as the company must prove that it is solvent, i.e. it is able to pay its debts as they become due in the ordinary course of business.

An application to set aside a statutory demand can be made only to the National Court, and it must be made by the company. The court *may*, on the application of the company, set aside a statutory demand.[121] There are strict time limits on applications to set aside statutory demands. The application must be "made" (i.e., filed in the National Court), and served on the creditor,[122] within one month of the date of service of the demand.[123] If it is not filed and served within the time limit, it is a nullity.[124] Because both filing and service must take place within the one-month period, filing should usually occur a long time before the end of the one-month period so as to obviate any difficulties in service.

The National Court, in *Moran Development Corporation Ltd v Akida Investments Ltd*,[125] held that, once the application had been filed within the time limit, it is not necessary that the hearing of the application take place within the one-month time limit. The court could hear the matter at the earliest available opportunity. Kandakasi J held that the phrase "application shall be made" in s 338(2) meant that the application must be filed and served within the time limit. It did not mean that the court hearing on the application must also take place within the time limit.

It was also argued that "month" meant a calendar month. Section 3(1) of the Interpretation Act (Ch 2) states that "in any statutory provision 'month' means a calendar month". Although the judge did not specifically rule on the issue, it would appear from the facts of the case that month means a calendar month. The statutory demand was served on 12 June 2003 and the application to set aside the statutory demand was filed and

121 Companies Act 1997, s 338(1).

122 Where the creditor is a natural person, it must be personally served. Where the creditor is a company, service should be made strictly in accordance with s 431 of the Companies Act 1997, as the courts may construe these provisions strictly: see Beck, A, *Corporate Debt: Statutory Demands*, supra, para 410. See also *Covington Railways Ltd v Uni-Accommodation Ltd* [2001] 1 NZLR 272.

123 Companies Act 1997, s 338(2).

124 *Hartner Trustee Ltd v Colin MacKenzie Plastering Ltd* (2001) 9 NZCLC 262,645. It is unlikely that the court will extend the time for service: see *A v B* (1995) 7 NZCLC 260,905.

125 (2003) N2458.

served on 11 June 2003; and it was held that this was a valid application to set aside.[126]

The court does not have power to extend the time for filing or serving the application.[127] However, once the application has been properly made, the court may extend the time for *compliance* with the statutory demand at the hearing to set it aside (Companies Act 1997, s 338(3)).

The grounds on which a statutory demand may be set aside are unlimited. The Act specifies two grounds and then goes on to provide that the court may set the demand aside on "other grounds".[128]

Section 338(4) provides that the court may grant an application to set aside a statutory demand where it is satisfied that:

- there is a substantial dispute whether or not the debt is owing or is due;[129]
- the company appears to have a counterclaim, set-off, or cross-demand and the amount specified in the demand less the amount of the counterclaim, set-off, or cross-demand is less than the prescribed amount;[130]
- there are "other grounds" on which the demand ought to be set aside.[131]

The onus of proof lies on the applicant. In New Zealand it has been held that where the debt is disputed or the company argues that it has a counterclaim, set-off, or cross-demand, the applicant must show a "fairly arguable basis" on which it is not liable on the statutory demand.[132] It would seem that where the company relies on "other grounds" to set aside the demand, it will have to go beyond merely showing a "fairly arguable" claim.[133]

In *PNG Balsa Co Ltd v New Britain Balsa Co Ltd,*[134] PNG Balsa Co Ltd applied to set aside a statutory demand served on it by the respondent

126 The Oil and Gas Act 1998 actually spells out what a calendar month is. Section 3(1) states that: "In this Act, unless the contrary intention appears 'month' means the period from and including a day in one calendar month to and excluding the corresponding day in the next calendar month and including the last day in the next calendar month if there is no corresponding day."

127 Companies Act 1997, s 338(3).

128 Companies Act 1997, s 338(4)(c).

129 Companies Act 1997, s 338(4)(a).

130 Companies Act 1997, s 338(4)(b).

131 Companies Act 1997, s 338(4)(c).

132 *Forge Holding Ltd v Kearney Finance* (NZ) Ltd, unreported, High Court, Christchurch, M 149/95, 20 June 1995 (Tipping J); *Queen City Residential Ltd v Patterson Co-Partners Architects Ltd* (No 2) (1995) 7 NZCLC 260,936; *Eastgate Real Estate Ltd v Walker* (2001) 15 PRNZ 308; *United Homes (1988) Ltd, United Homes (1994) Ltd v Workman* [2001] 3 NZLR 447; *Ferguson v Tanglewood Forests Ltd* [2003] NZCA 274.

133 See Beck, A, *Corporate Debt: Statutory Demands*, supra, para 412 and *Warren Reid Wholesale Ltd v Custom Fleet (NZ) Ltd*, unreported, High Court, Auckland, M 2089-IM00, 23 August 2001 (Master Kennedy-Grant).

134 (2004) N2520.

company. It claimed that the demand should be set aside as there was a substantial dispute as to whether the debt was owing. The applicant argued that the demand was also not valid as "nowhere does such [statutory demand] or any other statement attempt to properly qualify or itemise the sum claimed in the statutory demand". Lenalia J emphasised that the power given to the court to set aside a statutory demand is a discretionary one. He was satisfied that "the onus is on the applicant to show a fairly arguable basis upon which it is not liable for the amount or amounts set out in the statutory demand". He accepted overseas cases, mostly from New Zealand, which he stated "in my view reflect what is and what is not "a substantial dispute" under s 338(4)(a) of the Companies Act 1997 and he was prepared to adopt them as part of the underlying law:

> [T]he principles set out in the New Zealand cases of *BB Shipping (NZ) Limited*[135]); *Fletcher Homes Limited v BE Ellis and S Baldick;*[136] and *Taxi Trucks Ltd v Nicholson*[137] say that first, to set aside a statutory demand, an application must demonstrate that 'there is arguably a genuine' and substantial dispute. This simply means that there must be some evidence to show that the debtor company owes debts and such debts ought to be adequately itemised. Secondly, mere assertions that there exist a debt or debts are not sufficient. Materials short of proof is required to support the claim that the debt is disputed. Thirdly, where proof has been given that there exist a substantial dispute, the matter should be resolved by other means.[138]

After reviewing the evidence, the judge came to the conclusion that there was "a genuine and substantial dispute" in relation to the amount claimed in the statutory demand, and he ordered that it be set aside. It should be noted that the word "genuine" does not appear in either the New Zealand or Papua New Guinea statutory provision, and one wonders whether it adds anything to the test.[139] It is suggested that it should not be part of the test to determine whether a statutory demand should be set aside on the basis of s 338(4)(a) (substantial dispute ground).

135 Unreported, High Court, Auckland, Civ 2003 404 2626, Master Lang.

136 Unreported, High Court, Auckland, M 471/99, Master Faire.

137 [1989] 2 NZLR 297.

138 See the case of *Queen City Residential Ltd v Patterson Co-Partners Architects Ltd* (No 2) [1995] 3 NZLR 307.

139 It seems that the word "genuine" was adopted from the New Zealand Court of Appeal case of *Taxi Trucks Ltd v Nicholson* [1989] 2 NZLR 297, where it was stated that the applicant "must show a genuine and substantial dispute as to the existence of the debt". However, this case was dealing with statutory demands under the repealed Companies Act 1955 (NZ), which had substantially different provisions to the replacement

OTHER GROUNDS

A demand cannot be set aside only because of a defect or irregularity unless the court considers that substantial injustice would be caused if it were not set aside.[140] In such a case, "defect" *includes* an immaterial misstatement of the amount due to the creditor and an immaterial misdescription of the debt referred to in the demand.[141] Mistakes such as misspellings of name or address of company will not mean that the statutory demand is invalid, unless this leads to substantial injustice.

An order under this section may be made subject to conditions.[142]

Where, on the hearing of an application under s 338, the court is satisfied that there is a debt due by the company to the creditor that is not the subject of a substantial dispute, or is not subject to a counterclaim, set-off, or cross demand (or it would seem, though the section does not state this, it should not be set aside on "other grounds"), the court may:

- order the company to pay the debt within a specified period and that, in default of payment, the creditor may make an application to put the company into liquidation on the ground of insolvency;[143] or
- dismiss the application and forthwith make an order under s 291(3) putting the company into liquidation for insolvency.[144]

SUBSTANTIAL DISPUTE OVER DEBT

The courts have held that it is not right to liquidate a company on the basis of a disputed debt. As the statutory demand procedure provides a speedy method for creditors to put the company into liquidation where it is clear

Companies Act 1993 (NZ), on which the Papua New Guinea Companies Act 1997 is based. See also *Ro Paradise Real Estate* [1994] PNGLR 286, where Kapi J referred to *Processed Sand Pty Ltd v Thiess Contractors Pty Ltd; Breen Holdings Pty Ltd v Thiess Contractors Pty Ltd* (1983) 7 ACLR 956 at 961, where Waddell J stated that ". . . if a notice of demand is given for a sum, part of which is *genuinely disputed on substantial grounds*, an omission on the part of the company to pay any amount in response to the demand will not give rise to a deemed inability to pay its debts". The corresponding Australian provision refers to "genuine dispute" rather than "substantial dispute": see Corporations Act 2001 (Aus), s 459H(1)(a).

140 Companies Act 1997, s 338(5).

141 Companies Act 1997, s 338(6).

142 Companies Act 1997, s 338(7).

143 Companies Act 1997, s 339(1)(a). For the purposes of the hearing of an application to put the company into liquidation pursuant to an order made under s 339(1)(a), the company is presumed to be unable to pay its debts as they become due in the ordinary course of business where it failed to pay the debt within the specified period: Companies Act 1997, s 339(2).

144 Companies Act 1997, s 339(1)(b).

that the company is insolvent, i.e. unable to pay its debts as they become due in the ordinary course of business, it is not a convenient process for resolving substantive genuine disputes.[145] These ought to be resolved by the court in the ordinary way.[146] In *Taxi Trucks Ltd v Nicholson*[147] the New Zealand Court of Appeal stated:

> The applicant must show a genuine and substantial dispute as to the existence of the debt, and that it would be unfair – as it usually would be – to allow that dispute to be resolved by the Companies Court [i.e. in the interlocutory proceedings] rather than by action commenced in the usual way.

Material misstatements of the amount of the debt due could, it seems, amount in itself to a substantial dispute, even if some substantial injustice cannot be shown.[148] Although Beck has pointed out that it is "difficult to imagine how misstatement of the amount of the debt could cause substantial injustice such as to justify setting aside of a demand. In most instances where injustice would be caused relating to quantum, the company would be able to point to an underlying dispute as to the existence of the debt, or at least to part of it",[149] it could be argued that this is possible.

It may be that there will be few cases in which the fact of a discrepancy alone will give rise to substantial injustice.

There is authority to the effect that, in an extreme case, an overstatement in a statutory demand could lead to the demand being set aside. In the usual case, an overstatement would lead to a variation of the demand. However, the National Court may decide to follow certain Australian authorities which have suggested that a demand may be set aside where the amount claimed "has been so grossly inflated as almost exclusively to comprise matters which it should have been obvious from the outset were in genuine

145 It is otherwise if the dispute is a legal dispute. These types of disputes can be resolved in an application to set aside a statutory demand: see *Commissioner of Inland Revenue v Chester Trustee Services Ltd* [2003] 1 NZLR 395. Cf *Re Luabar Logging Pty Ltd* [1988] PNGLR 124, where the National Court had to determine the validity of rents under a lease which had not been subjected to ministerial approval under s 75 of the Land Act (Ch 185). This is an example of a situation where there was a substantial dispute as to whether the debt was owing, based on the legality of the lease. Note, however, that the claim was made as a defence to a petition to wind up the company. This was a creditor's petition for the winding up of a company, on the ground of inability to pay its debts (Companies Act (Ch 145), s 240(1)(e)), the debt relied upon being rent unpaid.

146 See Beck, A, *Corporate Debt: Statutory Demands*, supra, para 413.

147 [1989] 2 NZLR 297 at 299.

148 Cf the corresponding New Zealand provision, where this is not the case: whereas the PNG provision refers to "an *immaterial* misstatement" of the amount due, the New Zealand counterpart refers to "a *material* misstatement" of the amount due.

149 Beck, A, *Corporate Debt: Statutory Demands*, supra, para 414.

dispute between the parties at the time the demand was served",[150] or if the demand has been "drawn with a view to damaging the alleged debtor by wilfully claiming an amount substantially higher than that known to be due or recklessly demanding such a sum".[151]

The size of the discrepancy between the amount demanded and the amount actually due may be relevant to the issue of injustice.[152] If a substantial overstatement was wilfully included in a demand with a view to damaging the debtor company, or the overstatement was substantial and there was a lack of good faith or an abuse of process then the demand could be set aside under the "other grounds" ground.[153]

COMPANY APPEARS TO HAVE AN OFFSETTING CLAIM

Where a company admittedly owes money to a creditor, it may legitimately be reluctant to pay it if the creditor also owes money to the company. The Act therefore makes provision for demands to be set aside in situations where there is mutual indebtedness. The indebtedness may take the form of a counterclaim, a set-off or cross-demand.

The offsetting claim will be relevant only where its amount is enough to reduce the statutory demand below the prescribed amount of K1,000. The company has to show that it appears to have a counterclaim or set-off or cross-demand which satisfies the criteria provided that they are grounds for believing that the counterclaim might reduce the demand bill of the prescribed amount, that is enough to justify setting the demand aside. However, it is very difficult to quantify the offsetting claim, so if there is doubt over whether the amount demanded would fall below the prescribed amount, the application will likely fail.[154]

COUNTERCLAIM[155]

A counterclaim is any legal claim which the company has against the creditor. The term is broad enough to include a set-off. However, because the

150 *First State Computing Pty Ltd v Kyling* (1995) 13 ACLC 939 at 951. See also *Portrait Express (Sales) Pty Ltd v Kodak (Australasia) Pty Ltd* (1996) 14 ACLC 1,095.

151 *Equuscorp Pty Ltd v Perpetual Trustees Pty Ltd* (1998) 16 ACLC 12 at 32.

152 *Besser Industries (NT) Pty Ltd v Steelcon Constructions Pty Ltd* (1995) 13 ACLC 544.

153 See Keay, A R, *McPherson: The Law of Company Liquidation* (4th edn LBC Information Services, Sydney, 1999), p 82, citing *Equuscorp Pty Ltd v Perpetual Trustees Pty Ltd* (1998) 16 ACLC 12 at 28.

154 *Deadline Typesetting Ltd v Fuji Xerox New Zealand Ltd* (2001) 9 NZCLC 262,629. Cf *Datasouth Holdings Ltd v Melco Sales (NZ) Ltd*, unreported, High Court, Christchurch, M 41/96, 17 May 1996 (Master Venning).

155 Before the Companies Act 1997, a counterclaim could not prevent a liquidation from going ahead: *Anglian Sales Ltd v South Pacific Manufacturing Co Ltd* [1984] 2 NZLR 249.

section uses the term "set-off" as well as "counterclaim" this term means a completely unrelated transaction giving rise to the creditor's claim. In earlier cases decided under the New Zealand Companies Act 1993, it was held that there must be a link between a counterclaim and the debt in order to justify setting aside the demand.[156] However, it is unlikely that these cases will be followed in PNG, as Beck states "it is suggested that there is no linkage requirement, and that, in every case where a counterclaim is alleged, the court must exercise its discretion in an appropriate way. This approach was adopted by the court in *Phoenix Organics Ltd v RD2 International Ltd*".[157] A counterclaim could not extinguish the debt altogether.

SET-OFF

A set-off may be legal or equitable. A legal set-off arises where there are liquidated debts owed between the company and the creditor in the same capacity. (A liquidated debt is one which is fixed in monetary terms or is easily calculated.) In such cases, set-off operates automatically to extinguish the debt to the extent of the lesser debt.[158] If the result is that the creditor's debt falls below the prescribed amount, the statutory requirements for a statutory demand will not have been satisfied, and the court must set it aside. A set-off could extinguish the debt altogether.

An equitable set-off arises where the creditor and company have mutual claims which do not qualify for legal set-off, but which are so closely linked that it will be inequitable to decide one without taking the other into account.[159] Although the equitable set-off will not extinguish the debt it will provide strong grounds for setting aside a statutory demand.[160]

CROSS-DEMAND

Although the term "cross-demand" does not have a technical meaning, there are New Zealand cases to the effect that it is wider than a counterclaim or set-off. Beck states that from these cases:

> It appears that what is envisaged is a demand which has not yet progressed to the stage of being a 'claim'. In other words, the company has made a demand for payment of money from the creditor, but has taken

156 *Rennie v Prospect Resources Ltd*, unreported, High Court, Greymouth, M 14/95, 3 November 1995, Tipping J; *Auravale Industries Ltd v Shalimar Knitwear Ltd* (1999) 8 NZCLC 262,074; *Deadline Typesetting Ltd v Fuji Xerox New Zealand Ltd* (2001) 9 NZCLC 262,629

157 (2003) 9 NZCLC 263,386.

158 *Roberts' Family Investments Ltd v Total Fitness Centre (Wellington) Ltd* [1989] 1 NZLR 15.

159 *Grant v NZMC Ltd* [1989] 1 NZLR 8.

160 *New Zealand Factors Ltd v The Farmers Trading Co Ltd* [1992] 3 NZLR 703.

> no further legal action. This is relevant to the application to set aside the demand because it is an indication that the creditor may not be entitled to the full amount it has claimed.[161]

It seems, therefore, that a cross-demand is a potential claim or a possibility of a claim.

Once the court has taken into account these off-setting claims by the company, it will only set the statutory demand aside if the resulting debt is less than the prescribed amount (currently K1,000).

OTHER GROUNDS

Section 338(4)(c) of the Companies Act 1997 provides a catch-all category enabling the National Court to set aside a statutory demand, even where there is no substantial dispute or where the company appears not to have an offsetting claim.[162] Estoppel giving rise to a valid reason to set aside the statutory demand is included within this ground.[163]

The first thing to note is that the fact that a company can show that it is solvent is not a sufficient "other ground" for setting aside a statutory demand.[164] As Beck points out:[165]

> It might be thought that, as the purpose of a demand is to demonstrate the company's inability to pay its debts, a company would be able to have the demand set aside if it could show that it was in fact solvent. This is not, however, one of the statutory grounds for the setting aside of a demand, and therefore it cannot be assumed that the court would set aside a demand simply on the basis that the company can prove that in fact it can pay its debts. The Court of Appeal has observed that even strong evidence as to solvency may not be enough if the company has failed to comply with a demand: *Covington Railways Ltd v Uni-Accommodation Ltd.*[166]
>
> There is method in this approach. It is not enough to be able to pay; the company must also be able to explain why it has not paid the particular creditor. If there is no good reason for non-payment, then the company must take the consequences.

161 Beck, A, *Corporate Debt: Statutory Demands*, supra, para 423.

162 This ground for setting aside statutory demands was considered in *Commissioner of Inland Revenue v Chester Trustee Services Ltd* [2003] 1 NZLR 395.

163 *Cf Mainzeal Property and Construction Ltd v Facility Finance Ltd* [2000] 3 NZLR 594, NZCA.

164 *Covington Railways Ltd v Uni-Accommodation Ltd* [2001] 1 NZLR 272.

165 Beck, A, *Corporate Debt: Statutory Demands*, supra, para 434.

166 (2000) 8 NZCLC 262,374, [2001] 1 NZLR 272, CA.

It might be that the National Court decides that s 338(4)(c) of the Companies Act 1997 would require it to set aside a statutory demand where the debt in dispute is required to be submitted to arbitration.[167]

In hearing an application to set aside a statutory demand, the role of the court is to decide whether or not to set it aside. It is not to resolve any underlying dispute concerning the debt. If the court decides that there is a genuine and substantial dispute regarding the debt, that dispute will have to be adjudicated in other proceedings.[168] The burden of proof is on the applicant who must show why the court should set the statutory demand aside. The standard of proof is the civil standard: on the balance of probabilities. Even if the company is able to establish one of the defences in s 338(4), the court still has a discretion not to set aside the statutory demand.[169] However, this will rarely be done. If the court decides that the statutory demand ought not to be set aside, it will normally make an order that the amount be paid by the company within a certain period, failing which, the creditor will be entitled to apply for liquidation of the company.[170] Section 339(2) of the Companies Act 1997 provides an irrebuttable presumption that for the purposes of the hearing of an application to put the company into liquidation, pursuant to an order made under s 339(1)(a), the company is presumed to be unable to pay its debts as they become due in the ordinary course of business where it failed to pay the debt within the specified period. Furthermore, s 339(1)(b) of the Companies Act 1997 allows the court to dismiss the setting aside application and "forthwith make an order under s 291(3) putting the company into liquidation", something the court will be unlikely to do unless there are very strong reasons for this.[171]

The creditor will have to ensure that no undue pressure is placed on the company to pay the debt, as it may be set aside as a voidable transaction later in the liquidation proceedings, if the company is put into liquidation within two years of the payment, and the payment is considered not to have been made in the ordinary course of business. If the transaction is later set aside, the creditor will then need to prove its debt in the liquidation with the other creditors, and will be unlikely to recover the full amount of the debt.

167 Cf *Ferguson v Tanglewood Forests Ltd* [2003] NZCA 274.

168 Beck, A, *Corporate Debt: Statutory Demands*, supra, para 507.

169 *Alfex Doors & Windows Ltd v Alutech Windows & Doors Ltd* [2001] NZCA 181; *United Homes (1988) Ltd, United Homes (1994) Ltd v Workman* [2001] 3 NZLR 447.

170 Companies Act 1997, s 339(1)(a).

171 See Beck, A, *Corporate Debt: Statutory Demands*, supra, para 511, who argues that in the absence of the company's consent, it is difficult to see how an order could be justified under this provision.

Abuse of statutory demands

As Andrew Beck has cogently argued, the cases dealing with abuse of the statutory demand procedure were decided under a different legislative régime where the protection of the company was not written into the legislation as it is in the Companies Act 1993 (NZ). Consequently, the courts were forced to develop the "law of abuse" to protect companies. This is no longer necessary, as "the legislation has taken over the role of the courts in providing the appropriate protection from abuse".[172] The "other grounds" heading would now include situations where, previously, the court would have set aside the demand based on abuse of process. Such cases would include where the debt was part of a larger transaction or dispute and so could not be properly dealt with separately,[173] or where the application was brought to achieve some tactical advantage in litigation.[174] As Beck points out: "objections to statutory demands must now relate to one of the statutory reasons for setting demands aside. There does not appear to be any continuing scope for independent arguments as to abuse of the procedure."[175]

Stale statutory demands

Once a company has failed to comply with a statutory demand, the creditor must quickly apply to the National Court for an order that a company be put into liquidation, otherwise he or she will not be able to rely on failure of the company to comply with the statutory demand as prima facie evidence that the company is insolvent. The application must be made within one month after the last date for compliance with the demand. Although a company may have been unable to pay its debts as they become due in the ordinary course of business at the time when the demand was served and soon thereafter, fortunes of companies sometimes quickly change for the better. To allow statutory demands which were served a long time ago and remained unsatisfied to continue to be the basis of a presumption of insolvency goes against commercial reality, the need to hedge the stigma of being considered insolvent, and the need for persons to act in a timely manner.[176]

Other grounds of deemed insolvency

Apart from failure to comply with a statutory demand, the Companies Act 1997 provides three other situations where a company will be presumed to

172 Beck, A, *Corporate Debt: Statutory Demands*, supra, para 105.
173 Beck, A, *Corporate Debt: Statutory Demands*, supra, para 429.
174 *Edge Computers Ltd v Colonial Enterprises Ltd* (1996) 9 PRNZ 621.
175 Beck, A, *Corporate Debt: Statutory Demands*, supra, para 105.
176 Companies Act 1997, s 336(1).

be unable to pay its debts as they become due in the ordinary course of business, i.e., insolvent.

EXECUTION RETURNED UNSATISFIED

A company will be presumed to be unable to pay its debts as they become due in the ordinary course of business if execution issued against the company in respect of a judgment debt has been returned wholly or partly unsatisfied.[177] When judgment has been obtained in a court, the judgment creditor is entitled to levy execution in respect of that judgment. This usually means having the sheriff or bailiff go to the debtor's premises in order to seize goods of sufficient value to meet the judgment debt. If there is not sufficient property at the premises to meet the debt, the execution will be returned unsatisfied.[178] It is in such cases, where the debtor company does not have sufficient property to cover the debt, that the court will presume the company to be insolvent.

APPOINTMENT OF A RECEIVER BY SUBSTANTIAL CHARGEE

A company will be presumed to be unable to pay its debts as they become due in the ordinary course of business where a person entitled to a charge over all or substantially all of the property of the company has appointed a receiver under the instrument creating the charge.[179]

COMPROMISE NOT APPROVED

A company will also be presumed to be unable to pay its debts as they become due in the ordinary course of business where a compromise between the company and its creditors has been put to a vote in accordance with Part XV of the Companies Act 1997 but has not been approved.[180]

REBUTTABLE PRESUMPTIONS

It is important to remember that the four presumptions of insolvency that the Companies Act 1997 establishes are just that: presumptions. It is possible for the company, on whose shoulder rests the burden of rebutting the

177 Companies Act 1997, s 335(b). The case of *Re Sairs Pty Ltd* [1969–70] PNGLR 293 is an example of a case where this presumption operated.

178 Cf *Re Sairs Pty Ltd* [1969–70] PNGLR 293, where the petitioner obtained judgment in default of a defence against the respondent and caused to be issued a writ of *fieri facias*, which was returned *nulla bona*.

179 Companies Act 1997, s 335(c).

180 Companies Act 1997, s 335(d).

presumption, to prove, on a balance of probabilities, that it is solvent, i.e., it is able to pay its debts as they become due in the ordinary course of business. As noted above, where a statutory demand has been served on the company, it cannot set aside the statutory demand by adducing evidence that it is solvent. It must attempt to set aside the demand by arguing the grounds set out in s 338. However, if it fails to apply to set the statutory demand aside, or if its application fails, during the substantive hearing for the appointment of a liquidator, it may then adduce evidence of its solvency and thereby seek to prevent the National Court from exercising its discretion to appoint a liquidator. In the three other cases (execution returned unsatisfied, appointment of a receiver by substantial chargee, compromise not approved), the company may also adduce evidence of solvency to rebut the presumption raised.

Effect of commencement of liquidation

Liquidation begins on the date on which the liquidator is appointed,[181] and has the following immediate effects:[182]

- the liquidator obtains custody and control of the company's assets;
- the directors remain in office but cease to have many of their powers, functions and duties;
- unless the liquidator agrees or the court orders otherwise, a person may not commence or continue legal proceedings against the company or in relation to its property;
- unless the liquidator agrees or the court orders otherwise, a person may not exercise or enforce, or continue to exercise or enforce, a right or remedy over or against property of the company;
- a share in the company cannot be transferred, unless the court orders otherwise;
- the rights or liabilities of a shareholder of the company cannot be altered;

181 Companies Act 1997, s 291(4). The law on this matter has been significantly changed. Under the repealed Companies Act (Ch 146), liquidation was deemed to have commenced upon the filing of the petition in the case of a compulsory liquidation, or upon the passing of the relevant resolution in the case of a voluntary liquidation. In *Salvatore Algeri v Patrick Leslie* (2001) N2119, the judge mistakenly stated that: "The all-important time and date for the start of winding up is deemed to be on the filing of the application or petition for winding up; not on the making of the order. And once made, the Court order for a winding up is binding on all shareholders and creditors, as well as on the company itself." Although this used to be a correct statement of the law under the repealed Companies Act (Ch 146), it is no longer so.

182 Companies Act 1997, s 298(1). This is not an exclusive list of the effect of commencement of liquidation.

- a shareholder cannot exercise many of the powers granted under the constitution of the company or the Companies Act 1997;
- the constitution of the company cannot be altered.

DIRECTORS' POWERS

In the majority of cases, companies are wound up because of financial difficulties caused or contributed to by those in control of the business and affairs of the company, namely, the directors. If any remedial action is to be taken, e.g. prosecution for offences committed in relation to the company, recovery of compensation in respect of insolvent trading on the part of the directors, or recovery of damages for misapplication of the company's property, misfeasance or breach of trust, it is essential that the directors be removed from their offices. In this connection it is well settled that, on a winding up, the board of directors of a company becomes *functus officio* and its powers are assumed by the liquidator.

LEGAL PROCEEDINGS

Section 298(1)(c)(i) of the Companies Act 1997 provides that a person shall not commence or continue legal proceedings against the company or in relation to its property unless the liquidator agrees or the court orders otherwise. The effect of the liquidation is to prevent proceedings being commenced without the agreement of the liquidator or the National Court, or where proceedings had been commenced before liquidation, to automatically stay such proceedings. In the words of Pratt J, the effect of a section similar to s 298(1)(c) is that the proceedings come to "a full stop" and the claimant is "not entitled to take any further action in the matter until leave had been obtained".[183] The grounds upon which leave to proceed may be granted include whether there are any circumstances which render it necessary that the action should be continued, or whether the claim with which it is sought to proceed is not one which can be as easily dealt with in the winding up as in any other way. In the *Bishop Shipping* case, for example, the fact that service of the majority of the pleadings prior to winding up had already taken place, and the substantial and difficult legal issues between the parties for trial,[184] caused the judge to grant leave to proceed with the counterclaim.

183 *Bishop Shipping Services Pty Ltd v The MV "Pedro"* [1980] PNGLR 247 at 250.
184 For example, the action had been commenced in the Admiralty jurisdiction for the supply of necessaries, and the arrest and bail of a vessel was involved, and three National Court judges in three separate cases had recently come to different conclusions as to whether or not the National Court retained an Admiralty jurisdiction.

To recover assets, the liquidator may bring legal proceedings in the name of the company. Preventing the company, directors or shareholders from bringing proceedings protects the assets of the company from depletion as a result of unwarranted litigation, and preserves the assets of the company for the unsecured creditors.[185]

In *Ace Guard Dog Security Services Ltd and Yama Security Services Ltd v Telikom PNG Ltd*,[186] the Supreme Court found that the appellant was not incorporated as a company and therefore had no legal standing. It was therefore incompetent to institute the appeal. An alternative argument before the court was that the appellant at the time of filing of the Notice of Appeal was in liquidation and the appeal had been commenced by persons other than the liquidator without the liquidator's consent, contrary to ss 298 and 310(2) and Schedule 8 of the Companies Act 1997. The Supreme Court held that the appeal filed on behalf of the applicant was incompetent, as it was filed after the winding up had commenced, and the approval of neither the liquidator nor the court had been obtained. This was in breach of s 298(1)(c)(i) of the Companies Act 1997. One of the arguments rejected by the court was that s 298(1)(c)(i) of the Companies Act 1997 is only applicable to legal proceedings brought against the company and not applicable to commencing proceedings such as an institution of an appeal ("commence or continue legal proceedings *against* the company or in relation to its property"). However, the court summarily dismissed this argument:

> Having regard to s 298 and Schedule 8 of the Companies Act 1997, the powers of liquidator extends not only to proceedings filed against the company but relates also to proceedings that may be commenced by the company. This includes institution of an appeal. There is no merit in this argument and we would dismiss it.[187]

Counsel for the appellant further submitted that in an appeal it was not necessary to obtain the consent of the liquidator or to get an order from the court, as a director of a company in liquidation had residual powers to file an appeal. He relied on *Quan Resources Pty Ltd v ANZ (PNG) Ltd*.[188] That was an appeal against a decision of the National Court which refused

185 See *Bishop Shipping Services Pty Ltd v The MV "Pedro"* for a consideration of reasons why leave to continue legal proceedings against the company in liquidation would be granted by the court.

186 (2004) SC757.

187 It would seem that s 298(1)(b) was a better ground for rejecting this argument, as s 298(1)(c) is aimed at creditors and outsiders bringing court proceedings *against* the company.

188 [1997] PNGLR 687.

to set aside an order for appointment of the liquidator. A director filed an appeal against the decision of the National Court. The Supreme Court held that the directors of a company have residual powers to appeal against a winding up order or for appointment of the liquidator. This argument was also summarily dismissed:

> We consider that [the *Quan* case] is not applicable to the present case. Those residual powers relate to the winding up of the company or to the appointment of the liquidator. The present case deals with dismissal of a cause of action for not complying with notice of discovery. There is no merit in this argument. We would dismiss it.[189]

In *Quan Resources Pty Ltd v ANZ (PNG) Ltd*,[190] the Supreme Court held that under the Companies Act (Ch 146), the power to challenge a winding up order "is a residuary power of the company which in the first place is used through the Board" to instruct lawyers to oppose a petition or winding up order. If a winding up order is made over the opposition, the company is entitled to appeal against that order. It is submitted that this is still the position under the Companies Act 1997.

TRANSFER OF SHARES

Section 298(1)(d) of the Companies Act 1997 provides that unless the court orders otherwise, a share in the company shall not be transferred. The Act does not stipulate what is the effect of a contravention of the section, though it would seem to be that the transfer is void.[191]

EXERCISE OF SHAREHOLDER POWERS

Section 298(1)(f) provides that a shareholder shall not exercise a power under the constitution of the company or the Companies Act 1997 except for the purposes of Part XVIII (which deals with liquidations). The main powers that a shareholder may exercise under Part XVIII are the power to require the liquidator to summon meetings of shareholders (s 308(2)(a) and (c)); apply to the court for a review of the appointment of a successor to a liquidator (s 331(4)); with the leave of the court, apply for the supervision of the liquidation (s 332); apply for an order to enforce the liquidator's duties (s 334(1)(d)) and for an order that certain persons (the promoter,

189 See Companies Act (Ch 146), s 247(3) and *Bishop Shipping Services Pty Ltd v The MV "Pedro"* [1980] PNGLR 247.

190 [1997] PNGLR 687.

191 Under the repealed Companies Act (Ch 146), s 275(2), such a transfer was expressly stated to be void.

director, manager, liquidator, or receiver) repay money or restore property to the company (s 350); request that the liquidator call a meeting of shareholders to appoint a liquidation committee to assist the liquidator (s 362).

EFFECTS ON COMPANY CONTRACTS

With one exception, unless specifically provided for in the contract, winding up does not in itself terminate any general contract and is not of itself a breach of contract to which the company is a party. The effect of winding up depends on the nature and terms of the contract in question.[192] The one exception to this rule is for contracts of service. A compulsory winding up order constitutes a notice of dismissal for employees.[193] In a voluntary winding up, it is less certain that this is the case.[194] It is a question of fact in the particular circumstances, the issue being whether or not the surrounding circumstances indicate that the company intends to dismiss. Employees who are dismissed may have a number of rights under other laws, such as unfair dismissal legislation.

Duties and powers of liquidator

Duties of liquidator

In *Re Patridge*,[195] the court said:[196]

> Speaking generally, the liquidator's principal duties are to take possession of and protect the assets, to make lists of contributories, to have disputed cases adjudicated upon, to realise assets and to apply the proceeds in due course of administration amongst the creditors and contributors.

192 *Re Tru Grain Co* [1921] VLR 653.

193 *Re General Rolling Stock Co* (1866) 1 Eq 346; *Fowler v Commercial Timber Co* [1930] 2 KB 1; *Re Standard Salt and Alkali Ltd* [1934] SASR 168. Although there are no provisions in the Companies Act 1997 expressly dealing with the effect of liquidation on employment contracts, see Schedule 9, which refers to "termination of the employment . . . *by reason of the commencement of the liquidation*" (emphasis added). The dismissal in this way would usually be a breach of contract by the company for which the employee is entitled to claim damages. Cf *Michael Kandiu v ANZ Banking Group (PNG) Ltd* (2002) N2226. Note, however, that the employee would only be able to claim as an unsecured (not as a preferential) creditor: *David Gopalan v Uni Transport Pty Ltd* [1986] PNGLR 101.

194 *Midland Counties Bank v Attwood* [1905] 1 Ch 357.

195 (1961) SR (NSW) 622.

196 This statement was adopted by the Supreme Court in *Quan Resources Pty Ltd v ANZ (PNG) Ltd* [1997] PNGLR 687 as a succinct statement of the principal duties of a liquidator under the under the Companies Act (Ch 146).

Apart from dealing with the assets of the company, a liquidator has a duty to report on the liquidation to various parties, including the shareholders and creditors.

Duty to realise and distribute assets

Section 303(1) of the Companies Act 1997 provides that the principal duty of a liquidator of a company is to take possession of, protect, realise, and distribute the assets, or the proceeds of the realisation of the assets, of the company to its creditors in accordance with the Act, and where there are surplus assets remaining, to distribute them, or the proceeds of the realisation of the surplus assets, in accordance with s 361(4). That subsection provides that, after paying preferential and all other claims, the liquidator is to distribute the company's surplus assets in accordance with the provisions contained in the company's constitution, or where the company's constitution does not contain provisions for the distribution of surplus assets, or where the company does not have a constitution, in accordance with the Companies Act 1997.

In carrying out the above principal duty, the liquidator must act in a reasonable and efficient manner.

Reporting function

The liquidator has several reporting functions during the course of the liquidation. These include:

- give public notice of his or her appointment and notify the Registrar of Companies (s 305(2)(a) and (b));
- prepare a list of every known creditor of the company (s 305(2)(c)(i));
- prepare and submit to the Registrar the liquidator's initial report containing the prescribed details, including a statement of the company's affairs, proposals for conducting the liquidation and, where practicable, the estimated date of its completion (s 305(2)(c)(ii));
- send a copy of the liquidator's initial report and a notice in the prescribed form explaining the right of a creditor or shareholder to require the liquidator to call a meeting of creditors under s 362 (for the appointment of a liquidation committee to assist the liquidator) to every known creditor and every shareholder (s 305(2)(c)(iii));
- prepare and distribute to creditors and shareholders a six-monthly report on the conduct of the liquidation during the preceding six months, and containing the prescribed details and any further proposals which the liquidator has for completing the liquidation (s 305(2)(d));
- prepare and distribute a final report to creditors and shareholders after completion of the liquidation, and submit the report to the Registrar of Companies for registration (s 307(1)).

Duty to have regard to views of creditors and shareholders

During the course of the liquidation, the liquidator must pay regard to the views of creditors and shareholders.[197] However, he or she is not bound to follow these views, and may exercise his or her judgment independently of them.

Duty to notify suspected offences

Under the Companies Act (Ch 146), a liquidator was required to report on whether in his or her opinion further inquiry was desirable as to any matter relating to the promotion, formation or failure of the company or the conduct of the business of the company. A liquidator could also make further reports stating the manner in which the company was formed and whether in his or her opinion any fraud had been committed or any material fact had been concealed by any person in its promotion or formation or by any officer in relation to the company since its formation, and specifying any other matter that in his or her opinion it was desirable to bring to the notice of the court.[198] The Companies Act 1997 does not contain similar provisions, and the liquidator is not seen as having such a duty. This does not mean that they cannot report such matters to the Registrar of Companies. It merely means that they will not be guilty of a breach of duty for not doing so.

Powers of liquidator

General

A liquidator has the powers necessary to carry out the functions and duties of a liquidator under the Companies Act 1997, and the powers expressly conferred on a liquidator by the Act itself.[199] Schedule 8 (Powers of Liquidators) sets out specific powers that the liquidator has. However, the enumeration of these powers does not limit the extent of the powers conferred by s 310(1), so that the liquidator may have powers that are necessary to carry out his or her functions, even though they may not be specified in Schedule 8.[200] Schedule 8 confers on the liquidator power to:

- commence, continue, discontinue, and defend legal proceedings;
- carry on the business of the company, to the extent necessary for the liquidation;[201]

197 Companies Act 1997, s 308. The liquidator need have regard to these views only if expressed formally through the liquidation committee or meetings of creditors and shareholders.
198 See Kimuli, M A, Amankwah, H A and Mugambwa, J T, *Introduction to the Law of Business Associations in Papua New Guinea*, supra,130.
199 Companies Act 1997, s 310(1).
200 Companies Act 1997, s 310(2).
201 This may be necessary in order to sell the business as a going concern.

- appoint a lawyer;
- pay any class of creditors in full;
- make a compromise or an arrangement with creditors or persons claiming to be creditors or who have or allege the existence of a claim against the company, whether present or future, actual or contingent, or ascertained or not;
- compromise calls and liabilities for calls, debts, and liabilities capable of resulting in debts, and claims, present or future, actual or contingent, or ascertained or not, subsisting or supposed to subsist between the company and any person and all questions relating to or affecting the assets or the liquidation of the company, on such terms as may be agreed, and take security for the discharge of any such call, debt, liability, or claim, and give a complete discharge;
- sell or otherwise dispose of the property of the company;
- act in the name and on behalf of the company and enter into deeds, contracts, and arrangements in the name and on behalf of the company;
- prove, rank and claim in the bankruptcy or insolvency of a shareholder for any balance against that person's estate, and receive dividends in the bankruptcy or insolvency, as a separate debt due from the bankrupt or insolvent, and rateably with the other separate creditors;
- draw, accept, make and endorse a bill of exchange or promissory note in the name and on behalf of the company, with the same effect as if the bill or note had been drawn, accepted, made or endorsed by or on behalf of the company in the course of its business;
- borrow money on the security of the company's assets;
- take out, in his name as liquidator, letters of administration to a deceased shareholder, and to do in that name any other act necessary for obtaining payment of money due from a shareholder or his estate which cannot be conveniently done in the name of the company;
- call a meeting of creditors or shareholders for the purpose of informing creditors or shareholders of progress in the liquidation or connected or ascertaining the views of creditors or shareholders on any matter arising in or connected with the liquidation; and
- appoint an agent to do anything which the liquidator is unable to do.

Power to obtain information and documents

Section 311(1) of the Companies Act 1997 authorises a liquidator, by notice in writing, to require a director or shareholder of the company or any other person to give to the liquidator such records or documents of the company in that person's possession or under that person's control as the liquidator requires. Section 311(3) gives the liquidator power to examine (i.e. question) certain persons about the books or affairs of the company and to request them to provide such information about the business, accounts, or affairs of the company as the liquidator requests and to assist in the liquidation to the best of the person's ability. The persons who may be required to give this assistance include:

- a director or former director of the company;
- a shareholder of the company;
- a person who was involved in the promotion or formation of the company;
- a person who is, or has been, an employee of the company;
- a receiver, accountant, auditor, bank officer or other person having knowledge of the affairs of the company; and
- a person who is acting or who has at any time acted as a lawyer for the company.

If a person declines to be examined by the liquidator or refuses to produce the required documents, the liquidator may apply to the National Court for that person to:[202]

- attend before the court and be examined on oath or affirmation by the court or the liquidator or a lawyer acting on behalf of the liquidator on any matter relating to the business, accounts, or affairs of the company; and
- produce any records or documents relating to the business, accounts, or affairs of the company in that person's possession or under that person's control.

Power to disclaim onerous property

A liquidator may disclaim onerous property.[203] This may be done at any time during the liquidation, provided that the liquidator has not failed to disclaim within time, following the service on him by the owner of the onerous property of a notice to elect whether to disclaim the onerous property.[204] It is irrelevant whether the liquidator has dealt with the property, for example by taking possession of it, trying to sell it, or otherwise exercising rights of ownership in relation to it. Even if this is so, the liquidator may still thereafter disclaim the onerous property.

202 Companies Act 1997, s 316(1).
203 Companies Act 1997, s 319(1).
204 See below for notice to elect whether to disclaim onerous property.

The Act defines "onerous property" as:[205]

- an unprofitable contract; or
- property of the company which is unsaleable, or not readily saleable; or
- property of the company which may give rise to a liability to pay money or perform an onerous act.

A disclaimer under this section brings to an end, on and from the date of the disclaimer, the rights, interests, and liabilities of the company in relation to the property disclaimed, but does not, except so far as necessary to release the company from a liability, affect the rights or liabilities of any other person.[206]

A liquidator who disclaims onerous property must, within one month of the disclaimer, give notice in writing of the disclaimer to every person whose rights are, to the knowledge of the liquidator, affected by the disclaimer.[207]

The effect of a disclaimer is to vest whatever interest the company in liquidation had in the disclaimed property in the state. However, where a person applies to the National Court for an order that the disclaimed property be given to or vested in that person, the court may make an order vesting the property in that person where it is satisfied that it is just that the property should be vested in him.[208] If the court does not make such an order or vests only some of the rights in the person suffering loss or damage as a result of a disclaimer, that person may claim as a creditor of the company for the amount of the loss or damage.[209]

A person whose rights are affected by the disclaimer of onerous property may give the liquidator notice in writing requiring the liquidator to elect whether to disclaim. The liquidator has a period of not less than one month after the date on which the notice is received by the liquidator to disclaim the onerous property.[210] If the liquidator does not disclaim within the stipulated time, he or she cannot do so afterwards.

For an example of an application to the Registrar of the National Court for leave to disclaim an unprofitable contract under the repealed *Companies Act* (Ch146), s 314, see *Re Companies Act and Kawa Pty Ltd*.[211]

205 Companies Act 1997, s 319(2).
206 Companies Act 1997, s 319(3).
207 Companies Act 1997, s 319(4).
208 Companies Act 1997, s 319(6).
209 Companies Act 1997, s 319(5).
210 There is nothing to prevent a longer period than one month after receipt being stipulated. All that the section does is to provide that the notice cannot stipulate a shorter period.
211 [1990] PNGLR 523.

Supervision of the liquidator

The liquidator is accountable for his or her administration of the liquidation, and an application may be made to the National Court to review decisions of the liquidator. In such cases:

> . . . the court will not lightly interfere with the exercise of a liquidator's discretion in the winding up of a company . . . it would normally be necessary to show either that the liquidator's decision was based upon some error of principle or that it had brought about some manifest injustice.[212]

The Companies Act 1997 gives the National Court specific powers for the supervision of the liquidator.[213] The court may:

- give directions in relation to any matter arising in connection with the liquidation;
- confirm, reverse, or modify an act or decision of the liquidator;
- order an audit of the accounts of the liquidation;
- order the liquidator to produce the accounts and records of the liquidation for audit and to provide the auditor with such information concerning the conduct of the liquidation as the auditor requests;
- in respect of any period, review or fix the remuneration of the liquidator at a level which is reasonable in the circumstances;
- to the extent that an amount retained by the liquidator as remuneration is found by the court to be unreasonable in the circumstances, order the liquidator to refund the amount;
- declare whether or not the liquidator was validly appointed or validly assumed custody or control of property; and
- make an order concerning the retention or the disposition of the accounts and records of the liquidation or of the company.

The application for any of the above orders may be made:

- without the leave of the court, by the liquidator, a liquidation committee or the Registrar of Companies; or

212 *Re Papua New Guinea Block Co Pty Ltd (in liq)* [1982] PNGLR 28 at 33. This case was decided under the repealed Companies Act (Ch 146) (then referred to as the Companies Act 1963). Despite the repeal and replacement of the Companies Act (Ch 146), this case is still a valuable guide on this area.

213 Companies Act 1997, s 332(1). The powers given by s 332(1) are in addition to any other powers the Court may exercise in its jurisdiction relating to liquidators under Part XVIII (Liquidation), and may be exercised in relation to a matter occurring either before or after the commencement of the liquidation, or the removal of the company from the register, and whether or not the liquidator had ceased to act as liquidator when the application or the order was made: Companies Act 1997, s 332(2).

- with the leave of the court, by a creditor, shareholder, other entitled person, or director of the company in liquidation.

Apart from the Companies Act 1997 giving the National Court a general power to control and supervise liquidators, the Act confers specific powers in regard to the enforcement of the liquidator's duties. Section 334 provides that certain persons may apply to the court for an order where the liquidator has failed to comply with a relevant duty arising under the Companies Act 1997 or any other Act or rule of law or rules of court, or under any order or direction of the National Court.

An application for a s 334 order may be made by:

- a liquidator;
- a person seeking appointment as a liquidator;
- a liquidation committee;
- a creditor, shareholder, other entitled person, or a director of the company in liquidation;
- a receiver appointed in relation to property of the company in liquidation; or
- the Registrar of Companies.

Where the court is satisfied that there is, or has been, a failure to comply, the court may:

- relieve the liquidator of the duty to comply wholly or in part;[214] or
- without prejudice to any other remedy which may be available in relation to a breach of duty by the liquidator,[215] order the liquidator to comply to the extent specified in the order.[216]

Under s 334(4)(a), the court may remove the liquidator from office where he or she fails to comply with an order made under s 334(3). Where it is shown that the liquidator has persistently failed to comply with his or her duties, or that because of the "seriousness of a failure to comply" with his or her duties he or she is unfit to act as a liquidator, the court may make an order prohibiting the liquidator from acting as such for a period not exceeding five years.[217]

Recovery from directors

As noted above, where the company is being wound up the liquidator has the power to bring legal proceedings in the name of and on behalf of the

214 Companies Act 1997, s 334(3)(a).
215 For example, an action for damages in tort.
216 Companies Act 1997, s 334(3)(b).
217 Companies Act 1997, s 334(5).

company. This would include the right to bring an action against the directors for breach of their duty to the company.

Directors' liability for insolvent trading

The separate entity doctrine provides that a company is alone liable for the debts that it incurs. As we have noted earlier,[218] this principle flows from *Salomon v Salomon & Co Ltd*,[219] and states that a company is a legal entity which is separate from its shareholders and directors, and as such, it (and not its directors) is liable, *inter alia*, for its contracts and debts generally. This principle gives rise to the corporate veil behind which the court cannot look to see who is in control of the company. However, as we have already noted,[220] the courts have recognised certain situations according to the underlying law where it will lift the corporate veil. There are also situations where Parliament has decreed that the veil must be lifted to hold those in control of a company responsible for what are, prima facie, the debts or acts of the company.

Section 348 of the Companies Act 1997 is one instance of a statutory lifting of the corporate veil.[221] This section is designed to prevent directors from continuing to trade (and incur debts) when their company is insolvent or almost insolvent, and therefore unlikely to be able to pay the debts that it incurs. Liquidators are given the right to bring an action against the directors personally if they have allowed the company to trade whilst it was insolvent, and recover compensation for the company. This money would increase the funds that would be generally available to the unsecured creditors.[222]

218 See Chapter 8.
219 [1897] AC 22.
220 See Chapter 9.
221 This section was not based on the New Zealand Companies Act 1993. It is closer to the equivalent Australian provisions, though there are significant differences between them. For a consideration of the New Zealand provisions see Goddard, D, "Directors' Liability for Trading While Insolvent: A Critical Review of the New Zealand Regime" in Ramsay, I M (ed), *Company Directors' Liability for Insolvent Trading* (CCH Australia Ltd and Centre for Corporate Law and Securities Regulation, Melbourne, 2000), Ch 7, pp 169–189; and Noonan, C and Watson, S, 'Rethinking the Misunderstood and Much Maligned Remedies for Reckless and Insolvent Trading' (2004) 21 *New Zealand Universities Law Review* 26.
222 Section 348 also allows a creditor who has suffered loss or damage in a similar situation to bring an action against directors. However, the section does not specify the relationship between the creditor's and liquidator's rights. In other jurisdictions, the liquidator has the primary right, with the creditor being able to bring an action only if certain conditions are fulfilled. However, any amounts recovered are held on behalf of all creditors in the insolvency.

Section 348 applies to a person who:

- is a director of a company at a time when the company incurs a debt; and
- the company is insolvent (i.e. it does not satisfy the solvency test) at that time or becomes insolvent by the incurring of that debt (or that debt together with another or other debts); and
- at that time there were reasonable grounds for believing that the company was insolvent or would become insolvent.

By agreeing to the company incurring the debt, or by permitting the company to incur the debt, a director contravenes the section if there were reasonable grounds for the director believing that the company was insolvent or would become insolvent, or a reasonable person in a like position would have been so aware.

The word "reasonable" connotes a state of mind of knowledge of an ordinary person, not necessarily that of the defendant director, and will be based on objective criteria. The meaning of the word "believing" has not yet been considered in any PNG case.[223]

In Australia, the term that was formerly used was "expect", which was later changed to "suspect". The word "suspect" has been considered in *Queensland Bacon Pty Ltd v Rees*,[224] where Kitto J said that it is more than just an idle wondering, "it is a positive feeling of actual apprehension". The word "expect", by comparison, means that there is a strong expectation of events that will, in fact, come to pass.[225] It is suggested that "believing" is closer to the meaning of "expect", than "suspect".

The test to be applied to these matters is an objective one based on how a reasonable person would act, rather than upon the subjective views of the director concerned. It is irrelevant that the director personally believes that the company satisfies the solvency test. If the director is aware of grounds that ought to have led him, as a reasonable person, to believe that the company was insolvent at the time of the transaction or would have become so as a result of it, or if a reasonable person in the position of the director would have realised the same, the director is liable for failing to prevent insolvent trading contrary to s 238 of the Companies Act 1997.

223 Although the equivalent New Zealand provisions dealing with this area are quite different, the Companies Act 1993 (NZ) does refer to "reasonable grounds for believing that the company would satisfy the solvency test": s 56 (recovery of distributions); see also s 365(1)(f). Cases interpreting this provision will provide some assistance to the PNG courts when they come to interpret the meaning of "believing" in ss 348 and 349.

224 (1966) 115 CLR 266 at 303.

225 See *Commonwealth Bank of Australia v Friedrich* (1991) 5 ACSR 115.

Section 348(2) allows a liquidator to take steps to recover from the director, as a debt due to the company, an amount equal to loss or damage for insolvent trading.

Section 348(2) also allows a creditor to recover from the director in the same way as a liquidator. The Section does not provide how the claims of the liquidator and of a creditor are to be coordinated.[226]

Section 349 of the Companies Act 1997 makes a parent or holding company liable in a similar way to s 348 for the losses incurred in respect of insolvent trading by subsidiaries.

Liability of parent company for insolvent trading of subsidiary

As we noted above, the separate entity doctrine provides that a company is alone liable for the debts that it incurs. This means that companies within a corporate group of related companies are each individually liable for their own debts. The corporate veil has been pierced here, like in the case of directors, by making the parent company liable, in certain circumstances, for the debts of its subsidiary. When this is so, it means that the liquidator may be able to bring an action against the parent company to recover funds and thereby increase the fund that will be available to pay unsecured creditors of the insolvent subsidiary.

Section 349 of the Companies Act 1997 provides that a holding or parent company may be held liable for a debt of a subsidiary which is in liquidation. The parent company will be liable where, at the time when the subsidiary incurred the debt(s), it did not satisfy the solvency test, or became unable to satisfy the solvency test as a result of incurring the debt(s). The parent company will be liable:[227]

- if at the time of incurring the debt, there are reasonable grounds for believing that the subsidiary is unable to satisfy the solvency test, or will so become unable to satisfy the solvency test, as the case may be; and
- either the company, or one or more of its directors, is or are aware at the time of incurring the debt that there are reasonable grounds for so believing; or
- having regard to all the relevant circumstances, including the nature and extent of the parent company's control over the affairs of the

226 In Australia, the general rule is that a creditor may sue provided that the consent of the company's liquidator is given. In certain instances, a creditor may sue for compensation without the liquidator's consent: Corporations Act 2001 (Aus), ss 588R(1), 588S, 588T, 588U.

227 Companies Act 1997, s 349(1).

subsidiary, it is reasonable to expect that the company or a director would be aware of such grounds for belief.

The court may declare the parent company liable for an amount equal to the amount of loss or damage. If the liquidator brings the claim, the money will be available generally for distribution among the unsecured creditors.[228]

Voidable transactions

The Companies Act 1997 recognises that certain transactions entered into before the commencement of a liquidation could have the effect of defeating the *pari passu* principle. For example, a creditor, aware that the company is in financial difficulties, could pressure the company for early repayment of its loan or to provide security. The payment or provision of security will mean that the other creditors will be adversely affected, in that they will receive less in the subsequent liquidation than they otherwise would. The pressure is particularly objectionable where the creditor is related to the insolvent company.

The Companies Act 1997 has a number of provisions whereby certain transactions that unfairly advantage one creditor at the expense of another may be set aside. These are called voidable transactions, because they may be voided or set aside by the liquidator.[229]

Transactions having preferential effect

Where a company has insufficient assets to pay all of its creditors, creditors who are paid in full in the months leading up to the liquidation will be better off than if they had been required to claim as unsecured creditors in the liquidation. In effect, the creditors who have received payment are avoiding the *pari passu* rule imposed on those creditors remaining unpaid at the time of liquidation. Section 340 of the Companies Act 1997 sets out when such creditors must account for the advantage they received.

Such a transaction is voidable on the application of the liquidator if it:

- took place at a time when the company was insolvent (i.e. unable to pay its debts as they became due in the ordinary course of business); and
- took place within six months before commencement of a voluntary liquidation, or in the case of a court ordered (i.e. compulsory) liquidation,

228 Companies Act 1997, s 349(2).

229 Strictly speaking, the Companies Act 1997 sets out only one so-called voidable transaction (transactions that breach s 340). However, for the purposes of discussion, we adopt a wider definition of voidable transaction.

six months before the making of the application to the court together with the period commencing on the date of the making of that application and ending on the date on which the order was made; and
- enabled a person to receive more towards satisfaction of a debt than the person would have received in the liquidation,

unless the transaction took place in "good faith in the ordinary course of business" and the person had no reasonable grounds for suspecting that the company was unable to pay its debts as they became due in the ordinary course of business.

Meaning of "transaction"

Section 340(1) of the Companies Act 1997 defines a "transaction", in relation to a company, to mean:

- a conveyance, transfer, or other disposition of property by the company;
- the giving of a security or charge over the property of the company;
- the incurring of an obligation by the company;
- the acceptance by the company of execution under a judicial proceeding;
- the giving of a release or waiver by the company; or
- the payment of money by the company, including the payment of money under a judgment or order of a court.

It also includes a transaction that is entered into, given effect to, or required to be given effect to because of an order of a court.

Good faith in the ordinary course of business

A transaction cannot be set aside if the person entered into the transaction with the company in good faith "in the ordinary course of business" and had no reasonable grounds for suspecting that the company was unable to pay its debts as they became due in the ordinary course of business. The meaning of the phrase "in the ordinary course of business" has caused much difficulty.

The leading Australian decision of *Downs Distributing Co Pty Ltd v Associated Blue Star Stores Pty Ltd (in liq)*[230] stated that the phrase "ordinary course of business":

> means that the transaction must fall into place as part of the undistinguished common flow of business done, that it should form part of the ordinary course of business as carried on, calling for no remark and arising out of no special or particular situation.

230 (1948) 76 CLR 463 at 477, Rich J.

In applying the New Zealand provisions, it should be noted that the corresponding PNG provisions are more expansive than their New Zealand counterparts. In addition to proving that the transaction was entered into in the ordinary course of business, the "creditor" must also prove that it was done "in good faith", and that he had no reasonable grounds for suspecting that the company was unable to pay its debts as they became due in the ordinary course of business. In this respect the former Australian cases may be more relevant than the New Zealand decisions, as the Australian provisions also referred to the bona fides of the "creditor".[231]

The factors that the court will take into account include:[232]

- whether the nature, timing or circumstances of its payment took the payment outside the ordinary course of business;
- the wider context in which it was made, including the nature and purpose of the contract which gave rise to the payment;
- the question whether the payment was made in the ordinary course of business is to be considered objectively, that is to say by a consideration of the way in which the parties acted, and with what consequence, as distinct from their knowledge, intentions and purposes; however, if, to the knowledge of the creditor, the company had the intention or purpose of preferring the creditor or relieving another debtor, that could itself take the payment outside the ordinary course of business;
- the principal criterion is practice in the commercial world in general;
- regard can also be paid to the company's own past practices and dealings with the creditor, for example by recognising that the payment is atypically prompt or large compared with an established pattern of arrears or small payments;
- in comparing the payment with practices in the commercial world in general, the main focus is the ordinary operational activities of businesses as going concerns, not responses which would be normal for companies faced with abnormal financial difficulties or companies intent upon selling or winding down their businesses.

In *Salvatore Algeri v Patrick Leslie*,[233] the National Court found that K50,000 collected from villagers was invested in a Fast Money or "Money Rain" scheme operated by Millenium Corporation Ltd and thus became available

231 For an analysis of the New Zealand cases, see Watson, S, *et al. The Law of Business Organisations*, supra, 429–436.

232 See *Re Modern Terrazzo Ltd (in liq); Bowden v Macdonald* [1998] 1 NZLR 160 at 175, Fisher J. See also *Julius Harper Ltd v FW Hagedorn & Sons Ltd* [1989] 2 NZLR 471; *Countrywide Banking Corporation Ltd v Dean* [1998] AC 338; *Re Anntastic Marketing Ltd (in liq)* [1999] 1 NZLR 615; *Waikato Freight & Storage (1988) Ltd v Meltzer; Re Excel Freight Ltd (in liq)* [2001] NZCA 106 and *Carter Holt Harvey & Anor v Waller* [2003] NZCA 133.

233 (2001) N2119.

as part of the general funds of the company, once the company had been put into liquidation. The money was withdrawn sometime before the winding up order, and put into a trust account with a firm of lawyers, and it was held that this was a "transaction" within the meaning of s 340(1)(a) of the Companies Act 1997. Leslie was, at the time of the transaction, a responsible officer of the company General Manager Public Relations. He occupied an important financial position, similar to a financial controller of a company or chief accounting officer in a public authority or organisation. He was thus fully conversant with the operation and financial status of the company. The judge held that, moreover, the transaction in question took place at a time when the defendant ought to have been fully aware of the financial position of the company, in view of the position he held with its accompanying authority, duties and responsibilities. Despite his disclaimer, the court found that the defendant was fully cognisant of the fact that at the time of the transaction, the company was "unable to pay its debts as they became due in the ordinary course of business". The transaction was therefore "covered by the undue preference doctrine" and the withdrawal of the K50,000 at the relevant time was a voidable transaction capable of being set aside pursuant to s 341 of the Companies Act 1997.

The court concluded that the transaction was not conducted or undertaken in good faith and for valuable consideration as envisaged by ss 341 and 342(1), nor pursuant to s 342(2)(a) and (b). It also came to the conclusion that the transaction took place within the restricted and specified periods as defined under ss 340(3), 340(5) and 340(6) of the Companies Act 1997. "The withdrawal of the K50,000.00 took place after 14 July 1999. The company's petition for winding up was made on 11 November 1999. The winding up order was made 12 and entered 15 November 1999, all of which happened within four (4) months of the transaction in question." The court therefore set aside the "transaction".

Void charges in favour of "relevant persons"

A charge created by an insolvent company may be set aside not only under s 340 (transactions having preferential effect, discussed above) but also under s 345 (void charges) which deals solely with the creation of charges by insolvent companies in favour of certain persons.[234] Under s 345, a company charge is deemed always to have been void if:

- it was created in favour of a "relevant person" (hereafter chargee);
- the chargee purports to take a step in the enforcement of the charge within six months after its creation;[235] and

234 Charge is defined in s 2(1) of the Companies Act 1997.

235 Section 345(2) sets out certain steps that are to be taken as steps in the enforcement of the charge. It is not an exhaustive list: it includes appointing a receiver and entering into possession or assuming control of the charged property for the purpose of enforcing the charge.

- the National Court has not given the chargee permission (leave) to enforce the charge.[236]

The Act defines "relevant person" (i.e. the chargee) as a person who was an officer of the company at the time when the charge was created, or within six months immediately preceding the date of its creation.[237]

Although charges that offend the section are void, the transaction may nevertheless on some occasions lead to the transfer of rights thereunder. A purchaser of property subject to the charge will obtain a good title to it if he purchased it in good faith and for value:

- from a chargee, the chargee's agent, or a receiver appointed by a chargee under the exercise of powers conferred by the charge or implied by law; and
- the purchaser did not have notice that the charge was created in favour of a "relevant person".

Void floating charges[238]

Secured creditors are generally unaffected when a debtor company goes into liquidation. They are entitled to exercise their rights over the secured assets, and will usually be repaid in full, provided that the security was sufficient to cover the debt.

Section 347 of the Companies Act 1997 provides that a charge created by the company within six months before the commencement of the liquidation (i.e. the appointment of the liquidator) is void as against the liquidator, except in certain specified situations. The section aims to prevent companies on the verge of insolvency securing past debts by granting floating charges over their assets in favour of particular creditors, so as to remove those assets from the control of the liquidator, and thereby give some existing creditors an advantage.

A floating charge created within six months before the commencement of the liquidation (i.e. the appointment of a liquidator) will not be void (i.e. it will be valid) where the company was solvent (i.e. able to pay its debts as they became due in the ordinary course of business) immediately after the time of creation of the charge.[239]

236 Section 345(3) sets out when the court may grant leave.

237 Companies Act 1997, s 345(7).

238 This section seems to have been based on the predecessor section to s 588FJ of the Corporations Act 2001 (Aus).

239 Companies Act 1997, s 347(3).

The charge will also not be void if it secures consideration given to the company or at its direction at or after the time of creation of the charge. The consideration may be in the form of a contemporaneous or future advance, guarantee or supply of property or services to the company, and interest on any of these amounts.[240] This exemption does not apply in two situations. First, it will be void if it secures an advance to the company which is then applied to discharge, directly or indirectly, an unsecured debt owed by the company to the chargee, or if the chargee is a body corporate, a related entity.[241] Secondly, it does not apply to a charge securing payment for property or services to the extent that the amount secured exceeds the market value of the property or services when supplied to the company.[242]

Setting aside voidable transactions and charges

Only a liquidator has the power to apply to the National Court to set aside a voidable transaction.[243] If the court holds that a transaction is voidable, it has a wide range of remedies to choose from in deciding how best to remedy the situation. These include:

- an order requiring a person to pay to the liquidator, in respect of benefits received by that person as a result of the transaction, such sums as fairly represent those benefits;
- an order requiring a person to pay to the company an amount equal to some or all of the money that the company has paid under the transaction;
- an order requiring property transferred as part of the transaction to be restored to the company;
- an order requiring property to be vested in the company where it represents in a person's hands the application, either of the proceeds of sale of property, or of money, so transferred;
- an order releasing or discharging, in whole or in part, a debt incurred or a charge, security, or guarantee given by the company;
- an order declaring an agreement constituting, forming part of, or relating to the transaction or specified provisions of such an agreement, to have been void at and after the time when the agreement was made, or at and after a specified later time;

240 Companies Act 1997, s 347(2).

241 Companies Act 1997, s 347(4). See Companies Act 1997, s 346(5) for definition of related entity, which is applied to this section by s 347(7).

242 Companies Act 1997, s 347(5).

243 Companies Act 1997, s 341.

- an order varying such an agreement in the manner specified in the order and, where the court thinks fit, declaring the agreement to have had effect as so varied at and after the time when the agreement was made, or at and after a specified later time;
- an order declaring such an agreement, or specified provisions of such an agreement, to be unenforceable;
- an order requiring security to be given for the discharge of an order made under this section; and
- an order specifying the extent to which a person affected by the setting aside of a transaction or by an order made under this section is entitled to claim as a creditor in the liquidation.

If the property transferred by the company is land, the court may order that the land be transferred to the liquidator. In this respect, ss 340 and 341 act like an exception to indefeasibility, allowing a Torrens title transaction to be upset and the name of the registered owner to be removed from the Torrens register.[244]

Restrictions on recovery (defences)

There are certain defences available to persons whom it is claimed benefited from voidable preferential transactions. The availability of the defences depend on whether the person transacted directly with the company, or received the benefits of the transactions indirectly from another person who so transacted, i.e. third parties.

Even though the court may hold that a voidable transaction has taken place, the Act does not allow recovery of property or compensation from recipients in certain situations. If the person who holds the money or property at the time that the liquidator brings the setting aside action is not the person with whom the company entered into the transaction in the first place, that person may be able to resist the claims of the liquidator.

The s 342(1) defence allows the setting aside of a transaction or the making of an order under s 341 not to affect the title or interest in property which that person has acquired from a person other than the company and for valuable consideration and in good faith.[245]

Whereas the s 342(1) good faith defence is available only to third parties, the defence of change of position is available both to those with whom the

244 Companies Act 1997, s 342(3).

245 The term "good faith" is not defined; however it may be equivalent to "without knowledge of the circumstances under which the property was acquired from the company", which words instead of bona fide appear in the equivalent New Zealand provision.

company transacted, and third parties to whom the property or gain obtained from the company was passed on. It should also be noted that, whereas the s 342(2) defence is available only in respect of voidable transactions, the change of position defence (set out in s 342(2)) goes much further and applies to any claim for recovery of property or its equivalent value by the liquidator.[246] Section 342(2) provides that recovery by the liquidator of property or its equivalent value, whether under s 341 or any other section, or under any other law, or in equity or otherwise, may be denied wholly or in part where:

- the person from whom recovery is sought received the property[247] in good faith and has altered his position in the reasonably held belief[248] that the transfer to that person was validly made and would not be set aside; and
- in the opinion of the court, it is inequitable to order any recovery or recovery in full.

Referring to the element of bona fides (good faith) in the s 341(2) defence, Beck and Borrowdale state:[249]

> In the case of a voidable transaction under sec 340 of the 1997 Act, it is likely that an honest negative belief must be shown in relation to each of the elements of insolvency, advantage and ordinary course of business. If the recipient cannot show an honest belief that the company was solvent, that no undue advantage would accrue and that the transaction was unremarkable, it may be difficult to persuade a court that recovery should be denied.
>
> "Good faith" . . . must at least require that the recipient of the property or money be shown to have honestly believed that the transaction would not involve any element of undue preference either of himself or of any guarantor.[250]

246 It is suggested that the section is not a code, and that the underlying law change of position defence also applies to recovery of property by a liquidator: cf *National Bank of New Zealand Ltd v Waitaki International Processing (NI) Ltd* [1999] 2 NZLR 211.

247 It is suggested that the term "property" includes a payment of money by the company.

248 *MacMillan Builders Ltd (in liq) v Morningside Industries Ltd* [1986] 2 NZLR 12 at 17.

249 Beck, A and Borrowdale, A, *Papua New Guinea Companies and Securities Law Guide*, supra, para 1437.

250 *Re Orbit Electronics Auckland Ltd (in liq)* (1988) 4 NZCLC 64,237 at 64,244, Thorp J, expressly approved by the Court of Appeal in *Re Orbit Electronics Auckland Ltd (in liq); WH Jones & Co (London) Ltd v Rea* (1989) 4 NZCLC 65,170, based on predecessor provisions in the New Zealand Companies Act 1955 which are not exactly the same as the new provision.

It is suggested that these requirements go too far and that in order to prove good faith, the recipient merely needs to prove that it was not aware of any reason to doubt its entitlement to receive the benefit in question.

In *Westpac Banking Corporation v Nangeela Properties Ltd (in liq)*[251] the majority of the New Zealand Court of Appeal held that the mere receipt of payment or property does not constitute a change position. For the change of position defence to arise there must be some act done after receipt of the money or property.[252] Also expenditure on items which the recipient would have had to pay for in any event does not constitute a change of position. However, to cancel a guarantee after receipt of payment would amount to a change of position. In addition to proving change of position, the recipient must show that it would be inequitable for the court to order that the liquidator recover all or some of the money. "Inequitable" means that it would be unfair or unjust, and in the context of repayment, it means that the recipient would be in a worse position than if he had never received the money or other property at all.

Uncommercial transactions[253]

Section 343(1) of the Companies Act 1997 allows the liquidator to apply to set aside an "uncommercial transaction" which is made with "the specified period", provided that certain conditions apply. The section defines "specified period" as (i) the period of a year before the commencement of the liquidation, or (ii) in the case of a company that was put into liquidation by the court, the period of a year before the making of the application to the court together with the period commencing on the date of the making of that application and ending on the date on which the order of the court was made.[254]

An "uncommercial transaction" is defined as a transaction[255] "where, and only where, a reasonable person in the company's circumstances would not have entered into the transaction".[256] In deciding on this matter, the court may take any "relevant matters" into account, including (i) the benefits (if any) to the company of entering into the transaction, (ii) the detriment

251 [1986] 2 NZLR 1.

252 Cf *MacMillan Builders Ltd (in liq) v Morningside Industries Ltd* [1986] 2 NZLR 12.

253 The New Zealand Companies Act 1993 does not have a corresponding provision. It does, however, have a section dealing with transactions at undervalue (Companies Act 1993, s 297), which is not replicated in the Companies Act 1997. See Companies Act 2001 (Aus), s 588FB(1) for the Australian provision, which has an identical definition of "uncommercial transaction". It seems that this provision was the model for the PNG provision, and as such, Australian cases interpreting s 588FB(1) will be highly persuasive.

254 Companies Act 1997, s 343(2)(b).

255 "Transaction" has the meaning set out in s 340(1): Companies Act 1997, s 343(2)(c).

256 Companies Act 1997, s 343(2)(a).

to the company of entering into the transaction, and (iii) the respective benefits to other parties to the transaction of entering into the transaction. This is an objective standard. The liquidator does not have to prove that the directors intended to defraud or injure the company or its creditors. The test is whether a reasonable person would view the transactions as uncommercial.[257]

The other conditions that must apply before the court will set aside an uncommercial transaction are that, when the transaction took place, the company:

- was unable to pay its debts as they became due in the ordinary course of business; or
- was engaged, or about to engage, in business for which its financial resources were unreasonably small; or
- incurred an obligation knowing that the company would not be able to perform the obligation when required to do so.

It should be noted that the transaction need not be an insolvent transaction, though it is almost certain that in most cases where the liquidator is bringing a claim under this section, it would be.

Unlike the provisions dealing with unfair preferences (transactions having preferential effect) that are designed to prevent equal benefits being distributed to different members of the general body of creditors, the uncommercial transaction provisions seek mainly to redress debtor behaviour, that is, to stop the debtor company unjustly enriching a particular party, often an associated person or entity or related party, at the expense of the general body of creditors. This type of provision was developed to discourage those in control of a company from transferring assets or opportunities to associates or related parties so that they benefit and the creditors lose out. Specifically, the section aims to prevent companies from disposing of assets through transactions which result in the recipient receiving a gift or obtaining a bargain of such magnitude that it could not be explained by normal commercial practice,[258] and to prevent "a depletion of the assets of a company which is being wound up by, relevantly, 'transactions as an under-value' entered into within the specified limited time prior to the commencement of the winding up".[259]

257 The reasonable person "in the company's circumstances" would need to take into account the state of knowledge of the company, and this would include consideration of the knowledge of the directing mind of the company: *Tosich Construction Pty Ltd (in liq) v Tosich* (1997) 15 ACLC 1,402 at 1,406.

258 See Parliament of Australia, Explanatory Memorandum to Corporate Law Reform Bill 1992 (Aus), para 1044.

259 *Demondrille Nominees Pty Ltd v Shirlaw* (1997) 15 ACLC 1716. See Keay, A R, *McPherson: The Law of Company Liquidation* (4th edn, LBC Information Services, Sydney, 1999), p 460.

A liquidator can challenge many transactions under s 343 of the Companies Act 1997. Among the transactions likely to be successfully challenged are those where the company:[260]

- makes gifts;
- agrees to perform tasks for no consideration;
- purchases property that has a market value less than the price paid;
- leases an asset over its rental value;
- disposes of property for a price less than its market value;
- supplies an asset on lease below its rental value;
- agrees to pay for services a sum that exceeds their value;
- agrees to provide services for a sum less than their value;
- provide a guarantee for no benefit or a benefit less than the value of the benefit conferred by the guarantee;
- provides security for a previously unsecured loan.

Transactions for inadequate or excessive consideration

Section 344 of the Companies Act 1997 applies where a director or a person who controlled the company in liquidation or a person or company closely associated with either, or a related company, purchased property or services from the company in liquidation at an undervalue or sold property or services to the company at an overvalue. Where such a transaction took place within the five years preceding the liquidation,[261] the liquidator can recover from the director, controller or related party, as compensation, an amount by which the company has overpaid or was underpaid.

Recovery may be sought from the following:

- a person who was, at the time of the transaction (i.e. acquisition or disposition, provision, or issue), a director of the company, or a nominee or relative of or a trustee for, or a trustee for a relative of, a director of the company; or
- a person, or a relative of a person, who, at the time of the transaction, had control of the company; or
- another company that was, at the time of the transaction, controlled by a director of the company, or a nominee or relative of or a trustee for, or a trustee for a relative of, a director of the company; or

260 Transactions based on Goode, R M, *Principles of Corporate Insolvency Law* (2nd edn, Sweet & Maxwell, London, 1997), pp 356–357 and Australian Law Reform Commission *General Insolvency Inquiry*, Report 45 (ALRC, Sydney, 1988) (Harmer Report), para 668.

261 For a court ordered liquidation, the period is extended by the time taken by the court proceedings: Companies Act 1997, s 344(4)(b).

- another company that was, at the time of the acquisition, a related company.

Payment of creditors

Once the liquidator has collected all the assets of the company, he must then pay the debts of the company. All legally enforceable claims may be admitted.[262] Section 351 provides that a debt or liability, present or future, certain or contingent, whether it is an ascertained debt or liability or a liability for damages, may be admitted as a claim against a company in liquidation.

Creditors fall into three general categories: (i) secured creditors; (ii) preferential creditors and (iii) unsecured creditors.

Secured creditors

Secured creditors are entitled to look to their security for repayment. The usual type of secured creditor would hold a mortgage or debenture over company property. For example, a bank may have loaned money to the company and in return obtained a mortgage over the buildings and land owned by the company. If the bank decides to realise the property (i.e. exercise its power of sale), it will usually recover more money from the sale than is necessary to meet the expenses (e.g., employment of an auctioneer or real estate agent) and the amount owed (both principal and interest). In such a case, the excess must be transferred to the liquidator for addition to the fund due to be distributed to the unsecured creditors.[263] If the sale is insufficient to cover the expenses and loan repayment, the bank may prove in the liquidation as a creditor for the shortfall.[264] A secured creditor may also decide, instead of selling the property, to value the property subject to the charge and claim in the liquidation as an unsecured creditor for the balance due, if any, or surrender the charge to the liquidator for the general benefit of creditors and claim in the liquidation as an unsecured creditor for the whole debt.[265]

Preferential creditors

Preferential creditors are so called because they are paid in preference to unsecured creditors, i.e. before unsecured creditors. The liquidator is

262 For a case where the claim was not legally enforceable, and the claim to admit was lawfully refused, see *Johns v Thomason* [1976] PNGLR 15.

263 Companies Act 1997, s 353(3)(b).

264 Companies Act 1997, s 353(3)(a).

265 Companies Act 1997, ss 353(1)(b) and (c). See *Re Civic Constructions Pty Ltd* [1971–72] PNGLR 414, where it was argued, unsuccessfully, that a secured creditor had surrendered its charge.

required to pay out of the assets of the company the expenses, fees, and claims set out in Schedule 9 to the extent and in the order of priority specified in that Schedule.[266] Preferential creditors rank behind secured creditors,[267] but ahead of unsecured creditors. Preferential claims are listed below in order of priority:[268]

1. Fees, expenses and costs.
    - the fees and expenses properly incurred by the liquidator in carrying out the duties and exercising the powers of the liquidator and the remuneration of the liquidator; and
    - the reasonable costs of a person who applied to the Court for an order that the company be put into liquidation, including the reasonable costs of a person appearing on the application whose costs are allowed by the Court; and
    - the actual out-of-pocket expenses necessarily incurred by a liquidation committee.
2. Employee entitlements.
    - all wages and salaries of any employee, for the four months preceding the commencement of the liquidation, but not exceeding K20,000 (or such greater amount as may be prescribed at the commencement of the liquidation);[269]
    - all amounts due in respect of workers' compensation that accrued before the commencement of the liquidation, but not exceeding K20,000 (or such greater amount as may be prescribed at the commencement of the liquidation);
    - all remuneration becoming payable to an employee in respect of annual leave or long service leave (or where the employee has died, to any other person in the employee's right) on the termination of the employment before or by reason of the commencement

266 Companies Act 1997, s 360(1).

267 There is one exception, in the case of a loan by a secured creditor secured by a floating charge being deferred to certain preferential creditors: Schedule 9, s 7.

268 Note that a creditor may contract out of the *pari passu* rule by entering into a debt subordination agreement. Section 361(3) of the Companies Act 1997 provides that a creditor may agree, "before the commencement of a liquidation", to accept a lower priority in respect of a debt.

269 In *David Gopalan v Uni Transport Pty Ltd* [1986] PNGLR 101, the National Court (Cory J) held that "all wages or salary of an employee . . . in respect of services rendered by him to the company" in s 310(1)(d) of the repealed Companies Act (Ch 146) did not include damages for wrongful dismissal. This case is dealt with in more detail in Chapter 13 (Receivership).

of the liquidation, but not exceeding K20,000 (or such greater amount as may be prescribed at the commencement of the liquidation);
- amounts deducted by the company from the wages or salary of an employee in order to satisfy obligations of the employee, but not exceeding K20,000 (or such greater amount as may be prescribed at the commencement of the liquidation);
- amounts that are preferential claims under s 313(2) (i.e. where the lien arises in relation to a debt for the provision of services to the company before the commencement of the liquidation, the debt is a preferential claim against the company to the extent of K500, or such other amount that may be prescribed at the commencement of the liquidation);
- all mandatory and voluntary employee and employer contributions made, or which should have been made, in accordance with the provisions of the Superannuation (General Provisions) Act 2000, but not exceeding K20,000 (or such greater amount as may be prescribed at the commencement of the liquidation).

3. Costs of compromise.
   - the amount of any costs referred to in s 248(c) (i.e. the costs incurred in organising and conducting a meeting of creditors for the purpose of voting on a proposed compromise).
4. Government charges etc.
   - municipal or other local rates, due from the company at the date of the commencement of the liquidation and having become due and payable within the one year before that date; and
   - assessed income tax, or income tax and social services contribution, being tax or tax and contribution assessed under any Act before the date of commencement of the liquidation and not exceeding in the whole one year's assessment; and
   - any amount due and payable by way of repayment of any advance made to the company, or in payment of any amount owing by the company for goods supplied or services rendered to it, under any Act, relating to or providing for the improvement, development, or settlement of land or the aid, development, or encouragement of mining.

Once preferential creditors have been paid, any remaining assets must be used to pay off all other claims. Unsecured creditors rank equally, and if there are insufficient assets to meet their claims in full, they abate ratably: so each might get 50 toea for every kina that they are owed.

Removal from the register (deregistration)

Once a company has been liquidated, the final step in bringing its existence to an end is deregistration: liquidation does not, therefore, end the life of a company, deregistration does.[270] A company may be deregistered:[271]

- where it amalgamates with another company; or
- where the company has ceased to carry on business and there are no other reasons for the company to continue in existence; or
- where the liquidation of the company has lapsed; or
- where the shareholders or the board of the company requests its deregistration on specific grounds; or
- on the completion of liquidation by the delivery to the Registrar of the liquidator's final reporting documents; or
- where the company's annual return is at least six months late; or
- where the company has failed to submit to the Registrar any document required to be submitted under the Companies Act 1997, within 18 months of the time required for submission.
- When a company is deregistered, the company ceases to exist and any property in the company vests in the Registrar.[272]

270 Cf Companies Act 1997, s 16. Deregistration is carried out by the Registrar of Companies. A company is removed from the register when a notice signed by the Registrar stating that the company is removed from the register is registered: Companies Act 1997, s 365. It is not unknown for a company that has been put into liquidation to be "revived" by a court order terminating the liquidation. Companies Act 1997, s 300. Indeed, it is possible for a company that is dead (deregistered) to be brought back to life, by having its registration reinstated. See Beck, A and Borrowdale, A, *Papua New Guinea Companies and Securities Law Guide*, supra, para 1444.

271 Companies Act 1997, s 366(1). For a brief overview of the deregistration procedure, see Beck, A and Borrowdale, A, *Papua New Guinea Companies and Securities Law Guide*, supra, para 1443.

272 Companies Act 1997, s 373.

Part V

Law of Other Business Organisations

By Alex Amankwah and John Mugambwa

Chapter 15

Partnerships Law in Papua New Guinea

Introduction

A person intending to go into business may want to do so as a sole proprietor or in association with other people, by forming a company or partnership. A partnership is ideal for business ventures that require a limited number of participants, operators or executors.

Whether one adopts an incorporated entity or partnership as the means for accomplishing a business venture, it is important to appreciate those myriads of rules and principles governing the situation, beginning from the establishment, through the continuance and demise of the business. Most of these rules and principles evolved from the common law and equity initially, and have been supplemented by statutory law.

The nature of partnership

Today partnerships in PNG are governed by the Partnership Act (PA),[1] which is substantially based on the English Partnership Act.[2] It is necessary to observe however that the PA does not represent a codification of the law of partnership but a mere delineation of the contours of partnership law: were it a code, Lord Herschell's observation in *Bank of England v Vagliano Bros Ltd*[3] would have been pertinent to its interpretation. However, because it is not, relevant rules and principles of the common law and equity must be read into the statute to fill in the gaps to make the provisions meaningful. Indeed, the PA itself provides:

> The rules of the underlying law applicable to partnership continue in force except so far as they are inconsistent with the express provisions of this Act.[4]

1 Ch 148.
2 (1890) 53 & 54 Vict, c 39.
3 [1891] AC 107 at 144–145.
4 PA, s 2.

Explaining the scope and meaning of a similar provision in the English Partnership Act, the Judicial Committee of the Privy Council said:

> [The] section is in the nature of a sweeping-up provision designed to ensure that the rules of equity and common law applicable to partnership, which were in existence at the time that the Act was passed, should remain in force except in so far as they might be inconsistent with the express provisions of the Act. It is to be stressed that the rules of equity and common law so preserved are the rules of equity and common law relating to partnership, and to partnership only. The result of these matters is, in their Lordships' view, that, when a question of partnership arises, it is the express provisions of the Act to which regard should be first had, and that it is only after such regard has been had that consideration should be given to the effect, if any, of the sweeping up provision . . .[5]

It may therefore be concluded that the law of partnership in PNG is an amalgam of statutory law and relevant common law and equitable principles in force in PNG at Independence and which are consistent with the partnership legislation.

Contract as basis of partnership

A fundamental doctrine of the law of partnership is that partnership is essentially a matter of contract. This means that the rights and obligations of the partners and the *modus operandi* of the business are based on a negotiated agreement. The intention of the partners is of the utmost consequence in the relationship of the partners.[6] The PA implicitly upholds the primacy of agreement in its constant reference to it in specific provisions of the legislation.[7]

Thus, where a business partner brought an action seeking a statutory order for the partition of the real property of the business, the order sought was refused. The court expressed the view that such matters as entitlement to partnership assets are governed by the partnership agreement thus upholding the primacy of contract in a partnership relationship.[8]

5 *Cameron v Murdoch* (1986) 63 ALR 575 at 586.

6 See *Walker v Hirsch* (1884) 27 Ch D 460; *Cox v Hickman* (1860) 8 HL Cas 268; *Re Fisher & Sons* [1912] 2 KB 491.

7 See PA, ss 1, 19, 22, 25, 26, 44. See also Peden, E and Carter, J W "The Bonds of Partnership", (2000) 16 *Journ of Contract Law* 27515; and Bonollo, F, "The Nexus of Contracts and Close Corporation Appraisal" (2000) *Australian Journal of Corporate Law* 96; (2001) 12:3 *Australian Journal of Corporate Law* 165.

8 *Re Bolous* [1985] 2 Qd R 165.

A contract of partnership, as is the case with all contracts, can come into existence in several ways:

(i) express (written);
(ii) implied;
(iii) parol or oral;
(iv) Partly express and oral.

As a contract, a partnership agreement is subject also to all the doctrines and principles of contract especially privity of contract and agency, especially, the principle of ostensible or apparent authority.[9]

Definition of partnership

The PA defines a partnership as "the relationship that subsists between persons carrying on a business in common with a view to profit".[10] Since this definition is consistent with that of a corporation also,[11] for the avoidance of doubt s 3(2) provides:

The relation between members of a company or association that is –

(a) registered as a company under any Act for the time being in force and relating to the registration of joint stock companies; or
(b) formed or incorporated by or under any other Act, letters patent or Royal Charter, is not a partnership within the meaning of this Act.

In order to arrive at a comprehensible meaning of the word partnership, the definition provided in s 1(1) requires a detailed analysis.

Carrying on business

First, the word "business" must be defined. The PA provides a definition for the term. It says "business includes every trade, occupation or profession".[12] The word "includes" suggests that it is not possible to provide an exhaustive

9 PA, s 6.
10 PA, s 3(1).
11 For a comparative analysis of partnership and a corporation see Ivamy, E R H, *Underhill's Principles of the Law of Partnership* (Butterworths, London, 1981), pp 31 *et seq*; Schmitthoff, C M (ed), *Charlesworth's Mercantile Law* (11th edn, Stevens & Sons, London, 1979), pp 144 *et seq*; Morse, G, *An Introduction to Partnership Law* (Butterworths, London, 1986); Towmey, M, *Partnership Law* (Butterworths, Dublin, 2001); and Blackett-Ord, M, London, *The Modern Law of Partnership* (2nd edn, Butterworths, London, 2002).
12 PA, s 1(1).

list of all business pursuits which may conceivably be encompassed by the expression. The legislation therefore provides a few examples of life's pursuits which may be regarded as such. In an Australian tax case, Hill J said:

> The question of whether a particular activity constitutes a business is often a difficult one involving as it does questions of fact and degree . . . There is no one factor that is decisive of whether a particular activity constitutes a business . . . Profit motive, scale of activity, whether ordinary commercial principles are applied characteristic of the line of business in which the venture is carried on, repetition and a permanent character, continuity and system are all indicia to be considered as a whole, although the absence of any one will not necessarily result in the conclusion that no business is being carried on.[13]

Whatever the nature of the business in issue, it must be one that is ongoing in terms of regularity and continuity. As Brett LJ observed:

> The expression "carrying on" implies a repetition of acts, and excludes the case of an association formed for doing one particular act which is never to be repeated. That series of acts is to be a series of acts which constitute a business.[14]

It is possible, however, for a partnership to be formed for the execution of a single venture, for example, for the purchase and disposition by sale of a commercial item if the intention of the parties indicates this clearly.[15]

The effect of such transactions in law is the whittling down of the centrality of continuity, repetition and regularity in the definition of the term "partnership". In this regard, the observation of Dawson J in *United Dominions Corporations Ltd v Brian Pty Ltd* is instructive:

> A single adventure under our law may or may not, depending upon its scope, amount to the carrying on of a business . . . Whilst the phrase "carrying on a business" contains an element of continuity or repetition in contrast with an isolated transaction which is not to be repeated the decision of the court in *Canny Gabriel Castle Jackson Advertising Pty Ltd v Volume Sales (Finance) Pty Ltd* suggests that the emphasis which will be placed upon continuity may not be heavy.[16]

13 *Evans v FCT* (1989) 89 ATC 4450 at 4454–4455.

14 *Smith v Anderson* (1880) 15 Ch D 247 at 277–278.

15 See *Mann v D'Arcy* [1968] 2 All ER 172; *Canny Gabriel Castle Jackson Advertising Pty Ltd v Volume Sales (Finance) Pty Ltd* (1974) 131 CLR 321.

16 (1985) 157 CLR 1 at 15. See also *Chan v Zacharia* (1984) 154 CLR 178 at 196, per Deane J.

Again, it is possible that in some partnership situations continuity may take on a different meaning and may be construed to cover wider terrain than under the PA, for example, for the purposes of taxation.[17]

Carrying on a business in common

The crux of the matter here is communality of interest in the business and actions taken in furtherance of this. In this regard, a partner is an agent of the partnership acting for and on behalf of the partnership.[18] The issue whether a partner has acted in an agency capacity or not is a question of fact.[19]

With a view to profit

It is axiomatic that profit is the motivation for doing business. This distinguishes clubs and other such social aggregations of people from partnerships because although these are also formed for a common purpose, profit is not the main purpose and, in so far as profit accrues from their operations, this is ancillary to their main objectives.[20]

To sum up, an association of people therefore constitute a partnership if they:

(i) carry on a business;
(ii) in common; and do so
(iii) with a view to profit.

In *Cribb v Korn*[21] Barton J echoed the essential legal requirements of a partnership:

> To be partners, they must be shown to have agreed to carry on some business . . . in common with a view to making profits and afterwards of dividing them, or of applying them to some agreed object.[22]

Partnerships and corporations distinguished

It has been observed that the statutory definition of the term partnership could fit a corporation also. However, the two are not one and the same thing and their distinctive characteristics may be summarised as follows:

17 See Income Tax Assessment Act 1959 and *Tikva Investments Pty Ltd v FCT* (1972) 128 CLR 158 at 165, per Stephen J.
18 See PA, s 6.
19 *Lang v James Morrison & Co Ltd* (1911) 13 CLR 1.
20 See *Wise v Perpetual Trustees Co* [1903] AC 139; *Stekel v Ellice* [1973] 1 All ER 465.
21 (1911) 12 CLR 205.
22 Ibid at 216.

(i) While an incorporated company is a legal entity distinct from the membership, a partnership has no legal existence apart from the individual members who form it. Although it is relatively easy to form a partnership, and make it a going concern, the formation of a company is cumbersome, requiring the observance of several procedures and the lodgement of a number of documents with the Register of Companies.[23] Additionally, there is no need to disclose the accounts of a partnership, while disclosure is a matter of concern to the public in the case of a company.

(ii) One of the attractions for forming a company is the possibility of having a limitation on members' liability by members paying fully for their shares. In a partnership, on the other hand, a partner remains liable for the debts of the firm.

(iii) A partnership may engage in an unlimited number range of business, whereas a company's business is limited by its "objects" clause.

(iv) The partnership property belongs to all the partners in common, whereas Fora Company, being a legal entity possessing a separate legal personality distinct from the members, its property belongs exclusively to it and not to the members.

(v) Subject to agreement, a partner may not transfer his share to another so as to make him a member of the firm, whereas the shares of a company are freely transferable like any other chose in action.

(vi) While a partner to all intents and purposes is an agent of his firm, as a general rule a shareholder is not an agent of his company.

(vii) A partnership capital is freely alterable, not so in the case of company capital.

(viii) Finally, in the absence of an agreement to the contrary, the death or bankruptcy of a partner has the consequence of dissolution of the partnership whereas a company has perpetual succession; members come and go and it may go on forever.[24]

James LJ put the matter thus:

> An ordinary partnership is a partnership composed of definite individuals bound together by contract between themselves to continue combined for some joint object, either during pleasure or during a limited time, and is essentially composed of the persons originally entering into the contract with one another. A company . . . is the result of an arrangement by which parties intend to form [an association] which is con-

23 See Chapter 7.

24 See Ivamy, E R H, *Underhill's Principles of the Law of Partnership*, supra, at p 31.

> stantly changing, [an association] today consisting of certain members along with others who have come in, so that there will be a constant shifting of the [association], a determination of the old and a creation of a new . . . with the intention that . . . the new...shall succeed to the assets and liabilities of the old.[25]

Determining the existence of a partnership

The existence of a partnership agreement usually evidences the intention of the parties to establish a partnership. Where there is no written agreement, the conduct of the parties will be scrutinised with reference to relevant contractual principles to establish that intention. The PA itself provides sufficient guidance in this regard in its provision of the rules set out in s 4.

Concurrent interest in property

Co-ownership or community of interest in any property "does not of itself create a partnership".[26] Thus, where two brothers inherited the manufacturing business of their deceased father as tenants in common which they maintained as a going concern with three houses adjoining the factory, it was held that in respect of the business they were partners, as they shared the profits during the period relevant to the case, but that in respect of the land and houses – the building which housed the factory and the three adjoining houses – they were not partners.[27] As North J observed:

> It is not the law that partners in business, who are the owners of the property by means of which the business is carried on are necessarily partners as regards that property.[28]

The following differences must also be noted:

(a) whereas partnership is the result of consensus or agreement, co-ownership is the consequence of the exercise of the will of a grantor or devisor or the course of the law;
(b) whereas partnership gives rise to agency, co-ownership does not;[29]
(c) whereas partnership necessitates the carrying on of a business, that is not the case with co-ownership;[30]

25 *Smith v Anderson* (1880) Ch D 247, at pp 273–274.
26 PA, s 4(a).
27 *Davis v Davis* [1984] 1 Ch 393.
28 Ibid at 401.
29 See PA, s 6.
30 See PA, s 3(1).

(d) whereas a partner who intends to transfer his or her interest to others must obtain consent of the other partners in order to do so, co-ownership may be unilaterally severed;[31] and
(e) whereas in a partnership, profits and losses are shared, that is not necessarily the case in the co-ownership situation.[32]

The sharing of "gross returns"

The sharing of gross returns "does not of itself create a partnership".[33] Gross returns are the composite net receipt or revenue accruing from the operations of a business before any offset of expenses. Thus, an agreement under which a lessee of premises on which a theatrical performance took place was entitled to 60 per cent of the net take while the management of the performing group took 40 per cent was held not to create a partnership between the parties.[34] Swinfen Eady LJ expatiated on the principle thus:

> Although the gross takings were divided between them, there was not any partnership; each had to discharge his own separate liabilities in respect of the venture. The travelling expenses, the remuneration of the actors, the cost of the appliances had to be borne entirely by Mill. The theatre rent and outgoings, the cost of lighting, and the cost of playbills were wholly to be borne by the defendant. One of them may have made a profit out of the venture, and the other might have made a loss. Neither of them had authority to bind the other in any way; there was no agency between them. The sharing of gross returns does not of itself create a partnership.[35]

Receipt of a share of profits

Where a person receives a share of the profits of a business, such receipt is "prima facie evidence only that he is a partner in the business".[36] The phrase "prima facie evidence" suggests that a presumption in favour of the existence of a partnership is created by the fact of a person's receipt of a share of profits. However, that presumption may be rebutted or negatived by other factors and considerations.[37]

31 See PA, s 18(3).
32 See PA, s 3(1).
33 See PA, s 4(b).
34 *Cox v Coulson* [1916] 2 KB 177.
35 Ibid at 181; see also *Cribb v Korn* (1911) 12 CLR 205, supra.
36 PA, s 4(c).
37 PA, s 4(c)(i)–(v).

In *Badeley v Consolidated Bank*,[38] Lindley LJ, quoting from the dicta of Sir Montague Smith in *Mollwo March & Co v The Court of Wards*,[39] said:

> It was contended at the Bar, that whatever may have been the intention, a participation in the net profits of the business was, in contemplation of law, such cogent evidence of partnership that a presumption arose sufficient to establish, as regards third parties, that relation, unless rebutted by other circumstances. It appears to their Lordships that the rule of construction involved in this contention is too artificial for it takes one term only of the contract and at once raises a presumption upon it. Whereas the whole scope of the agreement, and all its terms, ought to be looked at before any presumption of intention can properly be made at all.[40]

Factors which negative the presumption in favour of partnership

PAYMENT OF DEBTS

Payment of debts out of business profits does not of itself constitute the recipient of the amount involved into a partner of the payor. This is in fact a common law principle stamped with statutory imprimatur. Thus, in *Cox v Hickman*,[41] where trustees to whom the management of a partnership was assigned were sued on bills of exchange which were subsequently dishonoured, the fact that the bills were accepted by the trustees in the name of the partnership which was then a going concern was held not to constitute the trustees into partners and therefore liable for the debts and liabilities of the partnership. This is because the trusteeship arose in circumstances entirely different (i.e. a debtor–creditor situation) from a partnership setting.[42]

PAYMENT TO EMPLOYEES OR AGENTS

Payments out of business profits to employees or agents under contracts of employment do not make the recipients partners in the business. Such payments are in the nature of emoluments or remunerations for services rendered the partnership.[43]

38 (1888) 38 Ch D 238.
39 (1872) LR 4 PC 419 at 433.
40 Ibid at 258–259. *Badeley v Consolidated Bank* (1888) 38 Ch D 238 at 258–259.
41 (1860) 8 HL Cas 268.
42 See also *John Bridge & Co v Magrath* (1904) 4 SR (NSW) 441.
43 *Beckingham v Port Jackson & Manly Steamship Company* (1957) SR (NSW) 403; *Re Buchanan & Co* (1876) 4 QSCR 202.

PAYMENT TO DECEASED PARTNER'S SPOUSE OR CHILD

Payments to the widow or child of a deceased partner in the nature of an annuity out of business profits do not of themselves constitute such recipient into a partner in the business. Such payments are considered a form of superannuation and arise out of an agreement creating the obligation to make such payments prior to the demise of the deceased partner.[44]

INTEREST PAYMENTS

Credit and loans are the lifeblood of business and those who provide credit for business may agree to take a certain proportion of the profits accruing from the operations of business debtor. Such payments do not of themselves constitute a creditor into a partner in the business in question. The agreement merely secures the creditor the right to repayment of the amount lent,[45] just as other rights under a loan contract, for example, the right to inspect the records of the business. However, where a loan is a mere ploy or pretence and designed to secure the creditor control of a partnership, there is no right of repayment.[46]

Payments in respect of goodwill

Goodwill is an invaluable and intangible business asset. It is the idea that "old customers will resort to the old place". On the acquisition of a business by a new proprietor, this ensures continuity of profits in undiminished volumes.

Payments representing a proportion of goodwill out of business profits to a previous owner of the business do not of themselves reconstitute such erstwhile owner a partner in the existing business.[47]

The foregoing makes it clear that the recipients of payments of sums of money out of the profits of business do not automatically become partners in the business in question. Being a partner in a business carries with it the implication of or assumption of the onerous burden of liability for the debts of the business. Such liability can only be assumed when a person consciously, that is intentionally, does so. It has been said, correctly, that liabilities should not be imposed on people behind their backs.[48]

44 *Commissioner of Inland Revenue v Lebus* [1946] 1 All ER 476.
45 *Badeley v Consolidated Bank* (1888) 38 Ch D 238.
46 *Re Megevand, ex parte Delhasse* (1878) 7 Ch D 511.
47 See *Hawksley v Outram* [1892] 3 Ch 359, at 372–373, per Lindley LJ.
48 See *Keith Spicer Ltd v Mansell* [1970] 1 WLR 333.

Conduct as evidence of partnership

Conduct – statements and actions – may on occasions provide a clue as to whether an intention to form a partnership does exist.

STATEMENTS

The designation which people attribute to a relationship may or may not in law support a finding that such relationship has in fact materialised. Sometimes statements made are designed to disguise or negate reality.[49]

The task of the courts in such cases, therefore, is to arrive at the objective intention of the parties by minute and critical examination of the statements made by them. Such exercise may result on occasions in the courts' jettisoning the parties' express stipulations. Cozen-Hardy MR graphically put the matter thus:

> It is quite plain that by the mere use of a well-known legal phrase you cannot constitute a transaction that which you attempt to describe by that phrase. Perhaps the commonest instance of all . . . is this: Two parties enter into a transaction and say "It is hereby declared that there is no partnership between us". The court pays no regard to that. The court looks at the transaction and says "Is this, in point of law, really a partnership?" It is not in the least conclusive that the parties have used the term or language intended to indicate that the transaction is not that which in law it is.[50]

Thus, in the Australian case, *Canny Gabriel Jackson Advertising v Volume Sales (Finance) Pty* Ltd,[51] where the parties labelled their business arrangement a "joint venture", the High Court held that that designation notwithstanding, the arrangement was in fact, applying the relevant legal tests, a partnership.

The opposite side of the coin is that merely because the parties call their business arrangement a partnership does not necessarily stamp it with the quality of a partnership. Thus, in *Commissions of Inland Revenue v Williamson*,[52] where a father and his two sons leased a farm as joint tenants and operated it for several years without entering into a formal partnership

49 *Pooley v Driver* (1876) 5 Ch D 458 at 483–484, where Jessel MR opined that parties who made a statement denying that they ever intended to be partners were in reality attempting to avoid assuming responsibility for the liabilities of the partnership.

50 *Weiner v Harris* [1910] 1 KB 285 at 290.

51 (1974) 131 CLR 321.

52 (1928) 14 TC 335.

agreement, the CIR taxed the business on the basis of sole proprietorship, which was disadvantageous rather than as a partnership which was more favourable in terms of the assessment for taxation. In the view of the Lord President:

> [Y]ou do not constitute or create or prove a partnership by saying that there is one. The only proof that a partnership exists is proof of the relations of agency and of community in losses and profits and of the sharing in one form or another of the capital of the concern.[53]

EFFECT OF HOLDING OUT

Holding out is tantamount to a representation in respect of a factual situation which may be true or false. The existence of a partnership may be the consequence of a representation that a person is a partner in a business. The person being held out would clearly be disadvantaged for liabilities he or she might not wish to assume. Thus, where a young architect was taken into practice as an associate but was in fact designated on the firm's business letterhead and advertisements as a partner without more, the court expressed great doubt that a partnership existed, and concluded that merely holding out a person as a partner was not conclusive of the fact that that person had indeed become a partner.[54]

It is possible that a "salaried partner" is indeed a partner, if that person is held out by the other(s) as a partner. In *Stekel v Ellice*,[55] Megarry J remarked:

> It seems to me impossible to say that as a matter of law a salaried partner is or is not necessarily a partner in the true sense. He may or may not be a partner, depending on the facts. What must be done, I think, is to look at the substance of the relationship between the parties; and there is ample authority for saying that the question whether or not there is a partnership depends on what the true relationship is and not on any mere label attached to that relationship.[56]

Formation of partnership and legal formalities

It is ironical that the Partnership Act contains nothing on the formalities that must be observed in the creation of a partnership.[57] A written agreement will

53 Ibid at 340.
54 *Floydd v Cheney* [1990] 1 All ER 446.
55 [1973] 1 All ER 465.
56 Ibid at 473.
57 Section 16 of the repealed Companies Act (Ch 146), provided that the maximum number of partner was 20. There is no corresponding provision in the Companies Act 1997. See also above, p 181.

suffice and can save the parties many legal headaches in the future rather than reliance on verbal or gentleman's agreement.

Where a partnership is formed for an illegal purpose, no action will be entertained by a court of law for the breach of the partnership agreement and no accounts will be ordered; and there can be no question of sharing of profits.[58]

The question of capacity is governed by the same rules as contract generally.[59] However, non-members who had no notice of the illegal status of the partnership when they transacted business with it have the right of indemnity against the members.[60]

The firm name

Section 1(2) of the PA provides:

> Persons who have entered into partnership with one another are, for the purposes of this Act, *called collectively a firm*, and the name under which their business is carried on is called the *firm-name*. (Emphasis added.)

Since a partnership has no independent existence – a legal personality – apart from the individual partners who comprise it, a firm is a legal device to clothe it with an identity for the purposes of legal proceedings and other legal consequences, such as the firm's liabilities. It may sue and may be sued. The implications of a firm name are dealt with in detail under the Business Names Act (BNA).[61] The name of the firm must be registered and must include the following particulars: name of the firm, general nature of the business, the principal place of business, the names of each partner, the nationality of each partner and other occupations of each of the partners. Non-registration of a firm name is an offence punishable by a fine not exceeding K200.[62]

The PNG National Court Rules Act provides:

> *Proceedings in business names.*
> Where a claim for relief is made against any person in respect of anything done or omitted or suffered in the course of, or otherwise relating to,

58 *Foster v Driscoll* [1929] 1 KB 470.
59 *Goode v Harrison* (1821) 5 B & Ald 147.
60 *Smith v Anderson* (1880) 15 Ch D 247 at 273.
61 Ch 145, ss 3, 4, and 8.
62 BNA, s 3; see also *Re Shearer Shaer* [1927] 1 Ch 355.

> a business carried on within Papua New Guinea by that person under a business name and that business name is not, on the date on which proceedings in the Court for that relief are commenced, registered under and for the purposes of the Act, in relation to that person, then, subject to this Division –
> (a) the proceedings may be commenced and prosecuted against that person in that business name; and
> (b) that business name shall, for the purpose of the proceedings, be a sufficient designation of that person in any process or other legal document or instrument; and
> (c) any judgment given or order made in the proceedings may be enforced against that person or, where there are two or more such persons, against any of them.[63]

To conclude, it must be emphasised that the absence of a written partnership agreement is not conclusive of non-existence of a partnership, for that fact notwithstanding, a partnership may be implied by law in the relationship of the parties, if their conduct evinces the necessary intention on their part, as people dealing with each other at arm's length, to become business partners.

Partners' relationship with people dealing with the firm

Partners are regarded at common law as principals and agents of their firm. They have the authority of the firm to act on its behalf and so bind the firm in their undertaking. The authority to bind the firm may be actual as where authority given relates to a specific undertaking, or ostensible where there is in no authority to do a specific thing, but what was done, falls within the scope of the type of business that the firm ordinarily engages in. The agency relationship between partners in a firm and the firm is given statutory backing by the PA. It provides in s 6:

> Each partner *is an agent of the firm* and of his other partners for the purpose of the business of the partnership, and the act of any partner who does any act for carrying on in the usual way business of the kind carried on by the firm of which he is a member binds the firm and his partners, unless –

63 Ch 38, Order 5, 34; see *Re Wenkam, ex parte Battams* [1900] 2 QB 699 for an interpretation of this provision. Also the Queensland (Australia) decision in *Madden v Kirkegard Ellwood and Partners* [1983] 1 Qd R 649.

(a) the partner so acting has in fact no authority to act for the firm in the particular matter; and
(b) the person with whom he is dealing knows that he has no authority or does not know, or does not believe, him to be a partner.[64]

An identical Australian provision was construed by the High Court of Australia in *Construction Engineering (Aust) Pty Ltd v Hexyl Pty Ltd*.[65] In that case the court said:

> [The section] comprises two distinct limbs. The first deals with actual authority. It provides not that every partner is *deemed to be* an agent of the firm for the purposes of the partnership business but that every partner *is* an agent of the firm . . . for that purpose . . . In substance, that first limb states the common law . . . The second limb of [the section] deals with ostensible authority. Even though actual authority be lacking, the act of every partner who does any act for carrying on in the usual way business of the kind carried on by the firm . . . binds the firm and his partners unless the other party either knows that he has no authority, or does not know or believe him to be a partner. Again, this limb effectively states the common law.[66]

Where the authority of the partner is actual, there would appear to be a minuscule of or no doubt about the binding effect of the transaction on the firm except where the authority is further actually limited by the partners. However, where the authority is ostensible, the *Construction Engineering* case appears to stipulate four rigorous conditions for the transaction to be binding on the firm:

(i) the transaction in question must be within the scope of the partnership business;
(ii) the transaction must be effected in the usual way;
(iii) the outsider must not know or suspect that the partner was acting beyond his or her actual authority; and
(iv) the outsider must have known or, at least, must have formed the belief that the person with whom he or she was dealing was a partner.

The two phrases "business of the kind" and "in the usual way" in both s 6 of the PA and the *Construction Engineering* case do not lend themselves to easy interpretation. Case law, however, provides some assistance.

64 Emphasis added.
65 (1985) 155 CLR 541.
66 Ibid at 547–548.

"Business of a kind"

In *Mercantile Credit Co Ltd v Garrod*,[67] where two partners operated a garage and one fraudulently sold a motor vehicle to the plaintiff in clear breach of the prohibition in the partnership agreement against the purchasing and selling of motor vehicles, it was held that the test for determining the issue was not the kind of business carried on in the defendants' particular garage, but rather, what type of business "the outside world" and the plaintiff would associate with or expect to see done in garages anywhere within the court's jurisdiction.[68]

"In the usual way"

Here a partner has brought the transaction in question within the scope of the firm's business. However, if a reasonably minded outsider ought to or should have had notice of some form of irregularity in the way the transaction was being carried out, the outsider has only himself or herself to blame for concluding the transaction in spite of his or her uneasiness with the conduct of the transaction. Thus, in *Golberg v Jenkins*,[69] where a partner purported to borrow money on behalf of his firm at the inordinate rate of 60 per cent, an action by the lender against the firm to recover the loan and interest failed. In that case Hodges J stated:

> A person conducting his transactions in the ordinary way during the year 1888, would have been able to obtain all the advances which he could reasonably require at rates varying from 6 to 10 per cent; but in this case, referring to the last transaction, the interest was something over 60 per cent, and that, in my opinion, is not conducting business at all; and the person lending the money on those terms knows that the person borrowing is not conducting an ordinary business transaction, and that, therefore, the partner borrowing would have no power to bind his co-partners.[70]

Implied powers

Even where a partner has no express or ostensible authority to engage in particular business activities, he or she would be endowed in law with

67 [1962] 3 All ER 1103.
68 Ibid at 1104, per Mocatta J.
69 (1889) 15 VLR 36.
70 Ibid at 88–89.

implied powers if the transactions in issue are those that are necessary and incidental to the achievement of the firm's business objective or purpose. The powers are spelt out in *Bank of Australiasia v Breillat*,[71] and include the power to borrow money, pledge or sell the firm's property, hire workers, receive payments due the firm, and issue and accept negotiable instruments for and on behalf of the firm, if the firm is one that engages in trading.

Ratification

An obviously unauthorised transaction may become binding on the firm if the firm decides to adopt it as its own deeds. This is the effect of the principle of adoption. It has to be observed however that not every transaction is adoptable. An illegality, for example, cannot be clothed with legality by ratification.

Holding out

The doctrine of holding out is an aspect of the principle of ostensible authority and is based on the representation of a person, whether a partner or non-partner, as vested with the powers of the firm to affect relationship with outsiders that binds the firm. The consequence of outsiders' reliance on the representation which works to their detriment or prejudice is that the firm is saddled with legal liability for the loss suffered by the outsiders provided that the real partner(s) acquiesce in the representation. This result is given statutory recognition by the PA. It provides in s 4:

> (1) Subject to Subsection (2), a person who, by word or conduct, represents himself, or who knowingly permits himself to be represented, as a partner in a firm, is liable as a partner to any one who has on the faith of any such representation given credit to the firm, whether or not the representation was made or communicated to the person giving credit by or with the knowledge of the apparent partner making the representation or permitting it to be made.

The basis of liability is the equitable principle of estoppel by conduct which precludes those making the representation from controverting or denying the set of facts represented. Equity has an aversion for people "blowing hot and cold".[72]

71 (1847) 6 Moore Moo PC152, 13 ER 642.
72 *Inwards v Baker* [1965] 2 QB 29, [1965] 1 All ER 446.

Applying the premise of the doctrine Eyre LC said:

> [If a person] will lend his name as a partner, he becomes, as against all the rest of the world, a partner, not upon the ground of the real transaction between them, but upon principles of general policy, to prevent the frauds to which creditors would be liable, if they were to suppose that they lend their money upon the apparent credit of three or four persons, when in fact they lent it only to two of them, to whom, without the others, they would have lent nothing.[73]

Implicit in the Lord Chief Justice's dictum are three ingredients in the establishment of the firm's liability:

(i) the making of a representation by either the person held out or by someone else acting with his or her knowledge that that person is, in fact, a partner in a particular firm;
(ii) the advancement of credit to the firm; and
(iii) the credit so given was made on the faith of or reliance on the representation;
(iv) whether a conduct amounts to a representation or not is a question of fact and depends on the circumstances of each case.[74]

The term "credit" connotes property real or personal and includes a chose in action given to the person represented as a partner of a firm by an outsider.[75] The phrase "on the face of the representation" implies that the act of giving credit was influenced and induced by the representation, and resulted in a loss or harm. In *Lynch v Stiff*,[76] the High Court of Australia said:

> In our opinion there is no justification for making any addition to the requirements of the section by holding that the person who has given credit must show that, apart from the holding out, he would not have given credit . . . it is sufficient if that party acts to his prejudice upon a representation made with the intention that it should be so acted upon, though it is not proved that in the absence of the representation he would have so acted.[77]

It must be observed that estoppel operates generally as a shield not a sword; it affords a defence and not a cause of action.[78]

73 *Waugh v Carver* (1793) 2 Hy BL 235 at 246, 126 ER 525 at 532.
74 *Martyn v Gray* (1863) 14 CB (NS) 823, 143 ER 667.
75 *Re Harvey, ex parte Chapman* (1964) 11 FLR 485.
76 (1943) 68 CLR 428.
77 Ibid at 434, per Latham CJ, Rich, McTiernan, and Williams JJ.
78 *Willmott v Barber* (1880) 15 Ch D 96 at 105–106.

The liability of the firm

As a general legal proposition, the liability of a firm to outsiders is unlimited. The parties are liable for the debts and other obligations of the partnership to the extent of their individual or personal fortunes.

The firm's liability may arise *ex contractu* or in tort. The general principle of law is that the firm's liability in contract is joint[79] while it is joint and several in tort.[80]

Debts and obligations

Debts and obligations arise mostly out of a contractual setting and are subsumed under s 10, which provides:

> Each partner in a firm is liable jointly with the other partners for all debts and obligations of the firm incurred while he is a partner, and after his death his estate is, subject to the prior payment of his separate debts, liable in due course of administration for any of the debts and obligations that remain unsatisfied.

While a partner's liability is "joint" after such a partner's death, his or her estate is "severally" liable for the firm's debts and obligations. The distinction between "joint" and "several" liability is brought out in *Kendall v Hamilton*,[81] where Lord Cairns LC enunciated the following principle:

> It is the right of persons jointly liable to pay a debt to insist on being sued together. If then there are three persons so liable, and the creditor sues two of them, and those two make no objection, the creditor may recover judgment against those two. But should he afterwards bring a farther action against the third, that third may justly contend that the three should be sued together . . . If, therefore, when the third is sued, and requires that the other two should be joined as parties, the creditor has to admit that he cannot join the other two because she has already received judgment against them in the same cause of action, this is equivalent to saying that he has disabled himself from suing the third in the way in which the third has a right to be sued.[82]

A plaintiff must choose carefully whether to sue the partners as a firm or the partners as individuals because of the Rule of Procedure on Third

79 PA, s 10.

80 PA ss 11, 12, 13; see also *Hamlyn v Houston* [1903] 1 KB 81; *Kendall v Hamilton* (1879) 4 App Cas 504; *Beavan v Webb* [1901] 2 Ch 735; *Bagel v MillenMiller* [1903] 2 KB 212.

81 (1879) 4 App Cas 504.

82 Ibid at 517.

Party Election. There is only one cause of action and therefore only one remedy.[83] Lord Cairns also expatiated on the position of a deceased partner. He said:

> Where a member of the partnership died, the debts became in the eye of a Court of Law the debts of the survivors; but the survivors, on the other hand, in a Court of Equity, had the right, as against the estate of a deceased partner, to say that his representatives should not withdraw any part of the partnership property until all the debts were paid or provided for. If, therefore, a Court of Equity was administrating the assets of a deceased partner, it would, in order to clear his estate, ascertain his liabilities to the partnership, and for this purpose would ascertain the debts due from the co-partnership at his death. From this the transition was easy to giving the creditors of the partnership a direct right, and not merely an indirect right, through the surviving partners, to come for payment against the assets of the deceased partner; and from this again the transition was easy to the expression which said that partnership debts, in the eye of a Court of Equity, were joint and several – not thereby meaning that a Court of Equity altered or changed a legal contract, but merely that the court, in order, before distributing assets, to administer all the equities existing with regard to them, would go behind the legal doctrine that a partnership debt survived as a claim against the surviving partners only, and would give the creditor the benefit of the equity which the surviving partners might have insisted on.[84]

Needless to say that debts and obligations incurred by the firm *after* the death of a partner would not bind the deceased partner or have any effect on his or her estate because those debts and obligations would not have been incurred "while the (deceased) is a partner".[85]

Torts and civil causes

These are covered by s 11 of the PA, which states:

> Where, by any wrongful act of any partner acting in the ordinary course of the business of the firm, or with the authority of his co-partners, loss or injury is caused to a person who is not a partner in the firm, or a penalty is incurred, the firm is liable to the same extent as the partner.

As with most tortious acts and omissions, a nexus has to be established between the plaintiff's injury or loss and the defendant's (firm or partner's)

83 See National Court Rules (Ch 38), Order 5, r 34.
84 *Kendall v Hamilton* (1879) 4 App Cas 504 at 517.
85 See *Bagel v Miller* [1903] 2 KB 212.

conduct. Importantly, the conduct must be something that takes place "in the ordinary course of the business of the firm".[86]

Criminal wrongs

"Wrongful act" includes criminal wrongs. Case law would suggest that the liability of a firm arises only in cases involving breach of the provisions of a regulatory statute that does not require proof of *mens rea* or "intent" as an ingredient of the offence.[87]

Misapplication of money or property

Section 12 of the PA provides:

> Where -
> (a) a partner, acting within the scope of his apparent authority, receives money or property of another person and misapplies it; or
> (a) a firm in the course of its business receives money or property of another person, and the money or property so received is misapplied by one or more of the partners while it is in the custody of the firm,
> the firm is liable to make good the loss.

This covers fraud and other acts of conversion committed by a partner as an agent of the firm.[88] The agent's authority of course may be actual, apparent or may arise from the fact of holding out some one as clothed with the firm's authority.[89]

The money or property in issue must be *received* by the agent "in the course of (the firm's) business". Therefore, if the money or property did not get into the custody of the firm, nor property in it pass to the firm, there will be no basis for affixing the firm with liability.[90]

Improper use of trust property

Section 14 of the PA provides:

> (1) Subject to subsections (2) and (3), if a partner who is a trustee improperly uses trust property in the business or on the account of the

86 See *National Commercial Banking Corporation of Australia Ltd v Batty* (1986) 160 CLR 251 at 260; *Polkinghorne v Holland* (1934) 51 CLR 143; *Walker v European Electronics Pty Ltd (In Liq)* (1990) 23 NSWLR 1.
87 See *Clode v Barnes* [1974] 1 All ER 1169; *Bishop v Chung Bros* (1907) 4 CLR 1262.
88 See *Lloyd v Grace and Smith & Co* [1912] AC 716 at 725, per Earl Loreburn LC.
89 *Rhodes v Moules* (1895) 1 Ch 236; *Mann v Hulme* (1961) 106 CLR 136.
90 *Tendring Hundred Waterworks Co v Jones* [1903] 2 Ch 615.

partnership, no other partner is liable for the property to the persons beneficially interested in it.

(2) This section does not affect any liability incurred by a partner by reason of his having notice of a breach of trust.

(3) This section does not prevent trust money from being followed and recovered from the firm if it is still in its possession or under its control.

This section deals with trusteeship situations involving partners in their individual or personal capacity and outside the firm's business. The law does not impose a fiduciary relationship between the beneficiaries and the firm as such in those circumstances. The principle is subject to the imperatives of the doctrines of notice and tracing.

Partners, the firm and property

Fiduciary relationships

As agents of the firm, the law imposes a fiduciary relationship between them. This arises from the mutuality of confidence or trust each reposes in the other. In *Helmore v* Smith,[91] Bacon CJ said:

> [The] mutual confidence [of the partners] is the life-blood of the concern. It is because they trust one another that they are partners in the first instance; it is because they continue to trust each other that the business goes on.

Their position is no different from that of trustees of property; and as such, they must pursue only that which is mutually beneficial as agreed between them. The common good dictates that partners should place the firm's interest over and above their individual and personal interests and avoid any conflict of interest situations in their dealing with partnership matters. The inception of the partners' fiduciary relationship with the firm is governed by equitable principles of justice and fairness and will depend on the circumstances of each case. For instance, it could come into existence prior to the formalisation of the partnership agreement, as where some property is acquired in anticipation of the finalisation of a partnership deed. In *United Dominions Corporations Ltd v Brian*,[92] the High Court of Australia said:

> A fiduciary relationship can arise and fiduciary duties can exist between parties who have not reached, and who may never reach, agreement . . .

91 (1886) 35 Ch D 436. See also Peden, E and Carter, J W, "The Bonds of Partnership" (2000) 16 *Journal of Contract Law* 45.

92 (1985) 157 CLR 1.

> In particular, a fiduciary relationship with attendant fiduciary obligations may, and ordinarily will, exist between prospective partners who have embarked upon the conduct of the partnership business or venture before the precise terms of the partnership agreement have been settled . . . [In the present case] in particular, each participant was under a fiduciary duty to refrain from pursuing, obtaining or retaining for itself or himself any collateral advantage in relation to the proposed project without the knowledge and informed assent of the other participants.[93]

On the basis of similar logic, the trusteeship could continue well after the dissolution of the partnership.[94] In the PNG case of *Canisius Karingu v Papua New Guinea Law Society*,[95] the plaintiff, a partner in a law firm, was suspended by the defendant from practice. He applied for a new practice certificate at the end of his suspension period, and was requested by the defendant, under the relevant regulations, to provide a report on his firm's trust account. Because the firm operated two accounts, one by the plaintiff and the other by the other partner in the firm, the plaintiff submitted a report on the account operated by himself only. The plaintiff's application was rejected because the defendant ruled that the report was incomplete as it contained nothing on the second account operated by the other partner in the firm. The plaintiff appealed that ruling to the National Court. Kidu DCJ said in his judgment dismissing the plaintiff's appeal:

> Clearly, where the partnership is receiving money from clients *in the name of the firm, all partners must be responsible for keeping the records of the account* in accordance with the law.[96]

This case illustrates that suspension does not spell the end of a partnership and the partners' fiduciary relationship subsists throughout that period as well.

Variation of partnership agreement

A partnership relationship may be changed by the partners anyhow and at anytime. Section 20 of the PA provides:

> The mutual rights and duties of partners, *whether ascertained by agreement or defined by this Act*, may be varied by the consent of all the partners, and such a consent may be express or may be inferred from a course of dealing.[97]

93 Ibid at 12–13, per Mason, Brennan and Deane JJ.
94 See *Chan v Zacharia* (1984) 154 CLR 178.
95 Unreported N1842, Case OS No162, 1996, April 15 & 23 1996.
96 Ibid (Emphasis added).
97 (Emphasis added.)

This renders inapplicable to the variation of partnership agreement the common law principle of contract that a written agreement can only be varied expressly and not by parol.

Partnership property

Any property considered in law to be the property of the firm ceases to retain its previous status as individual property and thereafter assumes the character of a common property of all the partners. Thus, where fixtures initially invested in a partnership subsequently appreciated in value at the time of the dissolution of the partnership, the increase in the value of the fixtures was held to become partnership profit to which the original owner of the fixtures was not entitled.[98]

It is possible, however, that property used in a partnership business remains individual property, as where a partner contributed property towards the operations of a partnership on the terms that it remained his or her individual property.[99]

Whether such property retains its character as individual property or has been integrated into partnership property is a matter of fact. The courts would favour integration where property was actually used in partnership business until a contrary intention is proven.[100]

Partnership property must be applied exclusively for the purposes of the firm and in accordance with the partnership agreement.[101] There are several categories of partnership property:

(a) property originally acquired or brought into the partnership business;
(b) property bought on account of the partnership; and
(c) property bought with the firm's money.[102]

In relation to the third category, s 22 provides that this is the position "unless the contrary intention appears". Thus, where the security for a partnership loan included an insurance policy on the life of a partner, the premiums of which were paid out of partnership funds, the presumption will operate in favour of the proceeds accruing on that life policy being considered partnership money.[103]

98 *Robinson v Ashton* (1875) LR 20 Eq 25.
99 *Harvey v Harvey* (1970) 120 CLR 529.
100 See *Waterer v Waterer* (1873) LR 15 Eq 402; *Davis v Games* (1879) 12 Ch D 813.
101 PA, s 21.
102 PA, s 22.
103 See *Carter Bros v Renouf* (1962) 111 CLR 140; *Kelly v Kelly* (1990) 64 ALJR 234.

Land acquired with partnership money

It is pertinent to mention that land acquired with partnership money is converted into personality.[104] This is in keeping with the principle in co-ownership, where equity prefers tenancy in common to joint tenancy especially where partnership money is used in the acquisition of realty. Each person must bring his own money and should be at liberty to take it away. Alternatively, this may be regarded as an aspect of the equitable doctrine of conversion by which land may be converted into personality upon sale.

Rights and duties of partners

The rights and duties of the partners, *inter se*, and the interests they have in the partnership property depend on the partnership agreement express or implied. Subject to any such agreement, s 25 sets out the following rules:

(a) all the partners are entitled to share equally in the capital and profits of the business, and shall contribute equally towards the losses, whether of capital or otherwise, sustained by the firm;
(b) the firm shall indemnify every partner in respect of payments made and personal liabilities incurred by him –
  (i) in the *ordinary and proper* conduct of the business of the firm; or
  (ii) in or about *anything necessarily* done for the *preservation* of the business or property of the firm;
(c) a partner who makes, for the purpose of the partnership, any actual payment or advance beyond the amount of capital that he has agreed to subscribe is entitled to interest at the rate of 6 per cent per annum from the date of the payment or advance;
(d) a partner is not entitled, before the ascertainment of profits, to interest on the capital subscribed by him;
(e) every partner may take part in the management of the partnership business;
(f) no partner is entitled to remuneration for acting in the partnership business;
(g) no person shall be introduced as a partner without the consent of all existing partners;
(h) any difference arising as to ordinary matters connected with the partnership may be decided by a majority of the partners, but no change may be made in the nature of the partnership business without the consent of all existing partners;

104 PA, s 23.

(i) the partnership books shall be kept at the place of business of the partnership (or at the principal place of business, if there is more than one), and every partner may when he thinks fit, have access to, and may inspect and copy any of them. (Emphasis added.)

These provisions will be considered *seriatim.*

(a) Equal sharing of capital, profits and losses

There is a presumption in law that a partnership involves contribution of resources by all the partners. The outcomes, whether they be in the form of profits or losses, must however be apportioned equally among the partners. This is based on the equitable principle that to enjoy profits is to accept losses as well. This presumption may be rebutted by adducing a contrary intention on the part of the partners.

The capital of a business is property and other assets brought into the business by the partners as their contribution to the partnership property and other such assets and property acquired for the business with partners' money. The case of *Kilpatrick v Mackay*[105] illustrates how equal sharing works out here. M bought a hotel for £400 and invited his friend K to contribute £200 towards the operation of the hotel. The hotel was subsequently sold at a profit. It was held that both men were equally entitled to the sharing of the proceeds as capital profits of the partnership.

(b) Entitlements to indemnity

A partner who incurs personal expenses or other liabilities in the ordinary course and conduct of the firm's business or does so in order to protect the firm or preserve the firm's property as a matter of necessity has the right to be indemnified by the firm. The doctrine of "agency of necessity" is a well recognised doctrine of law and provides leeway for doing something which ordinarily would be considered unlawful. Whatever the conduct in issue, it ought to be carried out in good faith, for the act has to be consistent with the fiduciary duty of an agent to a principal.

(c) Advances attract interest payment

Apart from the partners' contribution to business capital, partners may also agree to advance money to the partnership. An advance given to the

105 (1878) 4 VLR 28.

partnership by a partner is not a loan. People cannot grant themselves loans. In *Kilgariff v Morris*,[106] the High Court of Australia observed:

> A contribution by a partner to the funds of the partnership is not a loan to any or all of the partners. It creates no debt payable by the partners to the person standing in the situation otherwise occupied by the lender. The partners are not in a proper sense borrowers who immediately incur a debt which is repayable by them to a creditor ... The result of such contributions is to create the rights and duties which are specified in . . . the Partnership Act.[107]

Thus, by providing for 6 per cent interest charge on advances made by partners to the firm, the Act expressly allows such advances to be treated as loans. Interest may be levied on partners' withdrawals from partnership current accounts; and to overdraw from partnership account unless done fraudulently or improperly does not attract interest payment.[108]

(d) Interest on capital

If a partner's contribution may be viewed as giving that partner entitlement to a share of the profits, then it is clear that a share of the profits does not equate with interest, much in the same way as shares in a company entitles shareholders to dividends only in the company's profits.

(e) Participation in firm management

This provision does not equate anything like the right of equal participation in the management of the business. The word "may" in this subsection is significant as indicating that some members may not be bothered by management issues because of the mutuality of confidence and trust each partner reposes in the others. In reality, however, only active members according to some partnership agreements are saddled with firm management responsibilities.

(f) Entitlement to remuneration

A fiduciary is duty bound to carry out his or her functions as best as he or she could in the circumstances. People are not expected to be paid for carrying out what they are under a legal obligation to perform. A partnership agreement may, however, provide for payment of salary in addition to

106 (1955) 91 CLR 524.
107 Ibid at 528.
108 *Wilks v Howey* [1954] VLR 22.

entitlement to a share of the profits. Additionally, it is customary for partners in anticipation of a share of the profits to be allowed to take out or withdraw periodic (weekly or fortnightly) amounts. These do not constitute remuneration.

(g) Introduction of new partners

Again, this subsection rests on the basic premise of the mutuality of trust and confidence which partners repose in each other. Thus, there should be no change in the composition of membership unless agreed to by all the partners.[109] On the question of consent, there is no indication as to when it must be manifested. In *Lovegrove v Nelson*,[110] however, Lord Brougham LC stated:

> To make a person a partner with two others, their consent must clearly be had, *but there is no particular mode or time required of giving that consent*; and if three enter into partnership by a contract which provides that, on one retiring, one of the remaining two, or even a fourth person who is no partner at all, shall name the successor to take the share of the one retiring, it is clear that this would be a valid contract which the court must enforce, and that the new partner would come in as entirely by the consent of the other two, as if they had adopted him by name.[111] (Emphasis added.)

The phrase "be introduced as a partner" means that measures taken by partners short of an induction process are perfectly legal. Such measures could include assignments[112] and sub-partnerships[113] (partnership within a partnership).

(h) Mechanism for resolving differences

Two concepts emerge from the wording of this subsection, viz differences involving decisions on:

(i) ordinary matters; and
(ii) the nature of the partnership business.

109 See *Byrne v Reid* [1902] 2 Ch 735. The principle in this case is based on the doctrine of privity of contract. But see *Franklin v Swethling's Arbitration* [1921] 1 Ch 238.
110 (1834) 3 My & K 1, 40 ER 1.
111 Ibid at 8.
112 *Re Garwood's Trusts; Garwood v Paynter* [1903] 1 Ch 236. Section 32 codifies the common law to the effect that an assignee must not "interfere in the management or administration of the partnership business or affairs . . ."
113 *ANZ Banking Group Ltd v Richardson* [1980] Qd R 321.

There is no guidance in the provisions as to how these matters should be approached. It is clear, however, that "ordinary matters" are mundane while "the nature of the business" would seem to go to the issue of matters of fundamental importance to the firm such as its purpose or objective.

In decision-making matters the cardinal principle of natural justice is "*audi alteram partem*". The right to be heard and consulted in a partnership setting was enunciated in *Const v Harris*.[114] Lord Eldon V C said in that case:

> [The plaintiff] had a right to be consulted; his opinion might be overruled, and honestly overruled, but he ought to have had the question put to him and discussed. In all partnerships, whether it is expressed in the deed or not, the partners are bound to be true and faithful to each other. They are to act upon the joint opinion of all, and the discretion and judgment of any one cannot be excluded. What weight is to be given to it is another question.[115]

(i) Access to books and records

The implications of profits and losses sharing mandate that partners be constantly appraised of the full fact of the state of affairs of the business, especially, the state of partnership finances. Without access to the books and records it would be difficult for a partner to know such matters. The partners may examine the books and records personally or employ agents to do so on their behalf.[116]

Other additional rights and duties of partners

The PA makes provision for some other rights and duties that are not covered by s 25. The provision includes rendering of accounts,[117] making of private profits,[118] partners in competition with the firm[119] and expulsion.[120] These also will be considered *seriatim*.

114 (1824) Turn & R 496, 37 ER 1191.
115 Ibid at 506; 1191.
116 *Bevan v Webb* [1901] 2 Ch 59 at 68, per Collins LJ.
117 PA, s 29.
118 PA, s 30.
119 PA, s 31.
120 PA, s 26.

Rendering of accounts

Section 29 of the PA provides:

> Partners are bound to give true accounts and full information of all things affecting the partnership to any partner or the legal representatives of a partner.

These provisions merely reinforce those of s 25(i) which emphasise the importance of transparency in the maintenance of the books and records of a partnership. "Full information" connotes full disclosure of facts and matters within the knowledge of a partner to the others; and "firm accounts" connotes accurate accounts, not just accessibility of the account books. The duty subsists even beyond the dissolution of the partnership when facts are learnt which could affect significantly the outcome of negotiations to buy out a partner.[121]

Accountability for private profits

Since the common good is the driving force behind a partnership, whatever advantage accrues from a partner's undertakings in the course of partnership business must benefit all the partners. The relevant provisions are contained in s 30 of the PA. It states:

> (1) Each partner shall account to the firm for any benefit derived by him, without the consent of the other partners, from any transaction concerning the partnership, or from any use by him of the partnership property, name or business connection.
> (2) Subsection (1) applies to transactions undertaken, by a surviving partner or by the representatives of the deceased partner, after a partnership has been dissolved by the death of a partner, and *before the affairs of the partnership have been completely wound up.* (Emphasis added.)

James LJ stated the principle thus:

> No agent in the course of his agency, in the matter of his agency, can be allowed to make any profit without the knowledge and consent of his principal.[122]

121 *Law v Law* [1905] 1 Ch 140.
122 *Parker v McKenna* (1874) LR 10 Ch 96 at 124.

That principle was applied in the Australian case of *Birtchnell v Equity Trustees, Executors and Agency Co Ltd*[123] in which Dixon J accepted the "joint advantage" premise of partnership business as the basis for the principle.[124] The rule applies also to both pre-partnership[125] and post-partnership[126] conduct of the partners which has direct correlation with the partnership.

Competition with firm

Section 31 provides:

> If a partner, without the consent of the other partners, carries on any business of the same nature as and competing with that of the firm, he shall account for and pay over to the firm all profits made by him in that business.

The purview of this section is limited to engagement in *business of the same character or nature*,[127] *which results in rivalry with the business of the firm of the partner.*[128]

Expulsion of a partner

This will be considered under *Termination of Partnership*, below.

Termination of partnership

Termination connotes the dissolution of the partnership. As a creature of contract or agreement, a partnership existence can be brought to an end by consensus, that is, by the conscious decision of the partners to end their relationship. However, as a consequence of the doctrine of privity of contract any change in the composition of membership could have the same effect. A change in composition could be the result of death, expulsion or retirement of a partner or the induction of a new partner.

123 (1929) 42 CLR 384.
124 Ibid at 407–408.
125 See *United Dominions Corp Ltd v Brian Pty Ltd* (1985) 157 CLR1; *Fraser Edmiston Pty Ltd v AGT (Qld) Ltd* [1988] 2 Qd R 1.
126 *Chan v Zacharia* (1984) 154 CLR 178.
127 See *Glassington v Thwaites* (1882) 1 Sim & St 124, 57 ER 50; *Aes v Benham* [1891] 2 Ch 244; and *Dean v MacDowell* (1878) 8 Ch D 345.
128 *Trimble v Golberg* [1906] AC 494. See also *Jenkins v Bennett* (1965) WAR 42, where the issue was whether a husband's "advice" to the wife who engaged in competition with the firm of the husband came within ambit of the rule. It was held that it did not.

Technically, a partnership is not extinct until it is wound up and its assets sold and the proceeds distributed among its creditors and the residue to the partners. Thus dissolution *per se* does not spell the demise of the partnership, because the old firm could be reorganised bringing a new one into existence in the place of the previous or old entity.

Change brought about by expulsion, retirement or introduction of a new partner

Expulsion

Expulsion as a sanction against a member flies in the face of the mutuality of trust and confidence which underwrites a partnership business. Section 26 provides:

> A majority of the partners have no power to expel a partner *unless a power to* do so has been conferred *by express agreement between* the partners. (Emphasis added.)

The power to expel is thus circumscribed, the section stipulating an express agreement between the partners as a condition precedent to its exercise. The courts construe the agreement strictly.[129] Additionally, due to the fiduciary nature of the relationship of partners, there is the equitable requirement that the power be exercised in good faith.[130]

Retirement

Here a member decides of his or her own volition to exit or withdraw from the partnership. Section 27 provides:

> (1) Where no fixed term has been agreed on for the duration of the partnership, any partner may determine the partnership on giving notice of his intention to do so to all the other partners.
> (2) Where the partnership was originally constituted by deed, a written notice signed by the partner giving it, is sufficient notice for the purposes of Subsection (1).

The firm, however, remains a going concern of the remaining partners subject to the payment of appropriate compensation by them to the retiree for

129 *Bond v Hale* (1969) 72 SR (NSW) 201.
130 *Blisset v Daniel* (1853) 10 Hare 493, 68 ER 1022.

his or her share of the old partnership asset and goodwill which they would continue to use in the partnership business.[131]

Introduction of a new partner

The introduction of a new member brings a new partnership into existence, superseding the old. In *Income Tax Commissioner for City of London v Gibbs*,[132] Lord Wright provided an analysis of the resultant legal position of the introduction of a new partnership member:

> The old business is superseded by a new business, with a different division of property ownership, of powers of agency and representative capacity, of rights on dissolution and of all the incidents of partnership, including joint liability . . . A joint business carried on by four is different from a joint business carried on by five, even if the five include the original four. The addition of the new partner changes the constitution of the firm.[133]

The statutory régime of termination

The PA enumerates the following ways of termination of partnership:

(i) dissolution by expiration or notice;[134]
(ii) dissolution by insolvency, death or charge;[135]
(iii) dissolution by illegality;[136]
(iv) dissolution by court.[137]

Dissolution by expiry or notice (s 33)

The section begins: "subject to any agreement between the parties . . ." The intention of the parties therefore takes precedence over the specifics of the statutory prescription. The agreement may provide, for example, that upon the retirement of a partner, the partnership may "buy out" the retiring partner's share of the business. If a member retires, therefore, no dissolution takes place, as the old partnership will continue to function until the parties

131 *Sobell v Boston* [1975] 2 All ER 282.
132 [1942] AC 402.
133 Ibid at 430.
134 PA, s 33.
135 PA, s 34.
136 PA, s 35.
137 PA, s 36.

enter into a fresh partnership agreement. However, the section provides for the automatic dissolution of a partnership where:

(i) if entered into for a fixed term, by the expiration of the term; or
(ii) if entered into for a single adventure or undertaking, by the termination of the adventure or undertaking; or
(iii) if entered into for an *undefined time*, by any partner giving *notice* to the other of his intention to dissolve the partnership.[138]

The only problem here relates to the requirement of notice where the life-span of the partnership is not spelt out (an undefined time) in the partnership agreement. However, duration can be inferred from an agreement even though the agreement does not indicate a time period with specificity. Thus, where a partnership agreement provided: "This agreement shall be terminated by mutual agreement only", the court interpreted that provision to imply continuity of the partnership for the period of the joint lives of the partners.[139]

The notice must be given in good faith and "not for the purpose of deriving an undue advantage from the state of the firm's engagements".[140]

Dissolution by insolvency, death or charge (s 34)

Section 34 provides:

> (1) Subject to any agreement between the partners, a partnership is dissolved as regards all the partners by the death or insolvency of a partner.
> (2) A partnership may, at the option of the other partners, be dissolved if any partner permits his share of the partnership property to be charged under this Act for his separate debt.

DEATH

This section provides for the automatic dissolution of a partnership on the death of a partner and thus affords the estate of a deceased partner legal protection in respect of the deceased's share in the partnership assets which undoubtedly is of a proprietary nature.[141]

138 PA, s 33(1).
139 *Moss v Elphick* [1910] 1 KB 846.
140 *Neilson v Mossend Iron Co* (1886) 11 App Cas 298 at 308, per Lord Watson LJ.
141 See *Sharp v Union Trustee Co of Australia Ltd* (1944) 69 CLR 539 at 551, per Rich J. The cases are not always clear-cut as in *McLloyd v Dowling* (1927) 43 TLR 655, where a partner sent notice of dissolution to another partner and died before the other partner received the notice. It was held that the partnership was dissolved by death and not by notice.

INSOLVENCY

Though the bankruptcy of a partner creates a social disability, that is, disqualification from engaging in the management of business enterprises, it does not take away the partner's entitlement to his or her share in the partnership assets and goodwill.

CREATING A CHARGE

Here, a partner uses his or her separate interest in the partnership to secure a personal debt obligation. The bankrupt partner's disability merely triggers the option to expel such a partner, for until then, no one can physically, without risking breach of the peace, prevent him or her from coming onto the partnership premises.

Dissolution by illegality (s 35)

Section 35 provides as follows:

> A partnership is dissolved by the happening of any event that makes it unlawful for the business of the firm to be carried on, or for the members of the firm to carry it on in partnership.

This section appears to make provision for an extended application of the principle of the common law which makes contracts entered into in pursuance of illegal purposes void. Such contracts are unenforceable since they will be void *ab initio* as contrary to public policy. There are several examples of this, such as a contract, which promotes immorality in public life. The situations covered by s 35, however, are those in which the illegality is *subsequent* to the inception of the partnership. The illegality must impeach the competence of the partnership as a whole to do business, not just an incident of its operations. Thus, where a solicitor inadvertently failed to maintain the currency of his practice certificate which consequently disqualified him under the English Solicitors Act 1957 to practise as a solicitor, it was held that, although the disqualification operated to dissolve the law firm of which he was a member, yet, a new partnership came into existence comprising the remaining members of the firm, which engaged in lawful legal practice.[142]

142 *Hudgell Yeates & Co v Watson* [1978] QB 451. See also *Theunissen v Filippini* (1967) VR 7.

Dissolution by the court (s 36)

Section 36 states:

> (1) On application in accordance with Subsection (2), a court may order a dissolution of a partnership where –
>
> (a) a partner is shown to the satisfaction of the court to be of *permanently unsound mind*; or
>
> (b) a partner, other than the partner applying for dissolution –
>
> (i) becomes in any other way *permanently incapable* of performing his part of the partnership contract; or
>
> (ii) has been *guilty of such conduct* as, in the opinion of the court, regard being had to the nature of the business, is *calculated* to affect prejudicially the carrying on of the business; or
>
> (iii) *wilfully or persistently* commits *a breach* of the partnership agreement, or otherwise so conducts himself in matters relating to the partnership business that it is not reasonably practicable for the other partner or partners to carry on the business in partnership with him; or
>
> (c) the business of the partnership can only be *carried on at a loss*; or
>
> (d) circumstances have arisen that, in the opinion of the court, make it *just and equitable* that the partnership be dissolved.
>
> (2) Application for dissolution may be made –
>
> (a) on the ground set out in subsection (1)(a), by the committee or next friend, or a person having title to intervene, on behalf of the partner who is allegedly of unsound mind, or by any other partner; or
>
> (b) on any other ground set out in subsection (1), by any partner. (Emphasis added.)

This section delineates the circumstances in which an application to dissolve a partnership can be entertained by the courts. These are:

(i) permanent unsoundness of the mind;
(ii) permanent incapacity to perform partnership responsibilities;
(iii) conviction for conduct calculated to prejudice business operations;
(iv) wilful or persistent breaches of the partnership agreement;
(v) business operation can be conducted only at a loss; and
(vi) the exercise of the courts' equitable jurisdiction of justice and fairness.

These will be discussed *seriatim* below.

PERMANENT UNSOUNDNESS OF THE MIND

This situation again exemplifies an extended application of the principle of the common law in relation to capacity to enter into contractual relationships. Unsoundness of mind may affect a party's discernment capability to the point that such a party would not be in a position to appreciate the nature of a transaction in which he or she is involved. The general principle is that a contract relating to such a transaction is voidable at the insistence of the person with an unsound mind. However, such a contract will not be voided by the courts if it is shown that the contract was not prejudicial to the interest of the complainant. Thus, in *Gibbons v Wright*,[143] where two deluded sisters (out of three) transferred their interests in property they held jointly with the third sister, the validity of the transfer was upheld.[144]

Under the provisions of s 36, the law recognises that most partnership business involves the entering into contracts by partners with outsiders, hence the provision on unsoundness of mind. The partner prejudiced by such transactions must, however, take steps, by bringing an action for dissolution, for as Sir John Leach pointed out in *Jones v Moy*:[145]

> If [the interested partner] does not apply to the court for a decree of dissolution, it is to be considered that he is willing to wait to see whether the incapacity of his partner may not prove merely temporary.[146]

PERMANENT INCAPACITY TO PERFORM PARTNERSHIP RESPONSIBILITIES

The concern here, incapacity, is that, apart from a partner's unsoundness of mind a partner is incapacitated in some other way ("in any other way"). The right to apply for dissolution is that of a partner "other than the partner applying for dissolution".

The incapacity alleged must leave such partner permanently disabled. Thus, a stroke which rendered a partner bed-ridden for over nine months was held to be within the ambit of the rule. However, where evidence shows that a disabled partner was showing signs of recovery from his ailment, an application to dissolve the partnership will not be entertained by the courts.[147]

143 (1954) 91 CLR 423.
144 See also the earlier case *Wright v Gibbons* (1949) 78 CLR 313, [1949] ALR 287.
145 (1833) 2 M & K 125, 39 ER 892.
146 Ibid at 130, 895.
147 *Whitewell v Arthur* (1865) 35 Beav 140, 55 ER 848.

CALCULATED PREJUDICIAL CONDUCT

This is the right of a "partner, other than the partner applying for dissolution", to make an application for the dissolution of a partnership – a cross- or counterclaim situation. The phrase "has been guilty of such conduct" would suggest conviction for a criminal offence rather than imposition of liability in a civil action.[148]

The words "conduct calculated" mean conduct "conducive" to loss or injury, not necessarily one designed or wilfully engaged in to harm or cause injury to the firm. Thus, the conviction of a partner for constant and persistent evasion of railway fares was held not to be sufficient to satisfy the legal requirement of this subsection. The test is as formulated in *Pearce v Foster*[149] by Lindley LJ:

> [I]f this kind of conduct had been known to the persons who were accustomed to deal with this firm, that very knowledge would damage the firm.[150]

WILFUL OR PERSISTENT BREACHES OF PARTNERSHIP AGREEMENT

This subsection stands on two pedals:.

(i) wilful or persistent breach of the partnership agreement; and
(ii) the near impossibility of carrying on business as a consequence of the former.

Examples of the first abound and include persistent failure to maintain correct account books.[151] Examples of the second pedal include a complete breakdown in the confidential relation of partners which leads to mistrust and lack of confidence in each other.[152] The extreme type of that situation will include mutual animosity which leads to a situation where the parties no longer communicate with each other, or just plain incompatibility of personalities.[153]

CONDUCTING BUSINESS AT A LOSS

This situation is the antithesis of the main purpose of partnership, that is the making of profits. It is axiomatic that people do not get into business to

148 *Snow v Milford* (1868) 18 LT 142.
149 (1886) 17 QBD 536.
150 Ibid at 542.
151 *Cheeseman v Price* (1865) 35 Beav 142, 55 ER 849.
152 *Baxter v West* (1860) 1 Drew & Sim Sm 173; 62 ER 344; *Jenkins v Bennett* (1965) WAR 42.
153 *Knight v Bell* (1887) 13 VLR; *Cayron v Russell* (1897) 3 ALR 137.

make losses.[154] It is not the point that the firm is making losses at the present time if profits are likely to be made later.[155]

The same holds good for situations where, without the partners' injection of fresh capital into the business, the prospect of profits would be negative.[156]

The courts' equitable jurisdiction

It is not possible to provide an exhaustive list of all the situations and circumstances which may conceivably fall within the omnibus provision of this subsection. A few examples will suffice:

(i) an overbearing majority of partners pressuring the minority to toe their line of action;[157]
(ii) loss of mutual trust and confidence between the partners;[158]
(iii) perpetual deadlock in the firm's decision-making processes;[159]
(iv) perpetual state of disagreement between the partners;[160] and
(v) the necessity of preventing business not mandated by the partnership[161] agreement.

The legal consequence of dissolution

It has been pointed out above that the dissolution of a partnership does not necessarily signal the demise of the partnership. Two scenarios are possible upon dissolution, viz:

1. winding up the affairs of the business; or
2. the remaining partners forming a new partnership in place of the old and continuing business from where the old partners left it.

Only in scenario 1 is the partnership truly extinct and, even then, only after the partnership assets have been realised, creditors of the partnership paid off and any residue divided among the surviving partners and the estate of deceased partners, if any.

Many issues come to the fore upon the dissolution of a partnership. These include:

1. the position of clients and outstanding contracts;

154 *Handyside v Campbell* (1901) 17 TLR 623.
155 Ibid.
156 *Jennings v Baddeley* (1856) 3 K & J 78, 69 ER 1029.
157 *Ebrahimi v Westbourne Galleries Ltd* [1973] AC 360.
158 *Knight v Bell* (1887) 13 VLR.
159 *Re Yenidje Tobacco Co Ltd* [1916] 2 Ch 426.
160 *Cayron v Russell* (1897) 3 ALR 137.
161 *Bricar Nominees Pty Ltd v Rowella Pty Ltd* [1986] 1 Qd R 362.

2. the nature of the authority of the remaining partners to continue to represent the firm; and
3. the distribution of the firm's assets.

These will be discussed *seriatim*.

New partnership in place of old

This implies a change in the membership of the firm. However, retiring partners remain liable for all debts and obligations of the firm contracted before their retirement unless properly discharged from liability.[162] By the same token, an incoming partner is not liable "to the creditors of the firm for anything done before he became a partner".[163]

A retiring partner may however absolve himself or herself from liability by release. Section 17(3) provides:

> A retiring partner may be discharged from existing liabilities by agreement between himself and the members of the firm as newly constituted and the creditors, and such an agreement may be express or may be inferred as a fact from the course of dealing between the creditors and the firm as newly constituted.

Notice of change

In respect of outsiders, especially clients and creditors, it is important that they be informed of any change in the composition of the firm so that they can advise themselves as to what course to take in their relationship with the firm.[164]

It is a right any partner may exercise. Notification puts such people on notice of the change and assists also a retiring partner to avoid liability for the consequences of business transacted by the firm after his or her departure or retirement.

Authority of remaining partners to represent the firm

It is important for outsiders who deal with the firm to know the state of affairs of the firm in order to be apprised of the status of their investment and the wisdom in continuing to deal with the firm. Such knowledge can be gained only from possession of information about the firm. Herein lies the

162 PA, s 18(2) and (3).
163 PA, s 18(1).
164 PA, s 38.

importance of notifying the public about change in the composition of the firm, which is mandated by s 38. The consequences of such notice are set out in s 37, which provides:

> (1) Where a person deals with a firm after a change in its composition, he is entitled, until he has notice of the change, to treat all *apparent members* of the old firm as still being members of the firm.
> (2) For the purposes of Subsection (1), an advertisement in the National Gazette is notice to persons who had dealings with the firm before the date of the dissolution or change so advertised.
> (3) The estate of a partner who dies or who becomes insolvent, or of a partner who, not having been known to the person dealing with the firm to be a partner, retires from the firm, is not liable for partnership debts contracted after the date of the death, insolvency or retirement, as the case may be. (Emphasis added.)

The phrase "apparent members of the old firm" poses a problem of interpretation, for it could mean a "known" member of the firm, whether active or passive, and it is of no consequence whether a claimant had dealt with such a partner of the firm or not. It could also be interpreted to imply a former partner who was known to a claimant when that member was factually still a member of the firm. In *Tower Cabinet Co Ltd v Ingram,*[165] Lord Goddard CJ offered the following interpretation of a similar provision in the English Partnership Act. He said:

> [The] true construction to be put on this section is that there must be actual knowledge, which may be acquired either because of the fact that it is notorious or because it has been directly communicated. It is not sufficient to say that other people knew . . . it does not follow that because other people knew it, he knew it.[166]

In respect of persons who have not previously dealt with the firm, the notice, if published in the National Gazette, binds them as from the date of publication.[167]

Buying out a retiring partner

Most of the concerns here lie in the realms of insolvency and accounting practices.[168] Thus, only the legal issues will be treated and very briefly.

165 [1949] 2 KB 396.
166 Ibid at 405.
167 *Scarfe v Jardine* (1882) 7 App Cas 345 at 355, per Lord Blackburn LJ.
168 See *Sobell v Boston* [1975] 2 All ER 282.

The partnership agreement may expressly provide for the transitional matters such as buying out a departing partner, or this could be covered under a new agreement when dissolution of the partnership is contemplated. The remaining partners could do any number of things under their "apparent authority" under s 39 of the PA. Section 39 provides as follows:

> (1) Subject to Subsection (2), after the dissolution of a partnership the authority of each partner to bind the firm, and the other rights and obligations of the partners, continue, notwithstanding the dissolution, *as far as is necessary to wind up the affairs of the partnership and to complete transactions begun but unfinished at the time of the dissolution.*
>
> (2) The firm is not bound by the acts of a partner who has become insolvent, but this subsection does not affect the liability of a person who has, after the insolvency, represented himself or knowingly suffered himself to be represented as a partner of the insolvent.[169]

The amount payable is often the subject of controversy because of the complex accounting and valuation principles which govern the issue. For example, should "goodwill", which undoubtedly is part of the partnership assets, be included in the calculation? So what is goodwill? One may ponder.

There is no provision on this in the PA; however, simply put, it is the benefit arising from a firm's business connection or reputation. In *Cuttwell v Lye*,[170] Lord Elton defined it as "the probability that the old customers will resort to the old place". Wood V-C supplements this definition in *Charton v Douglas*.[171] He says:

> Goodwill must mean every advantage, every positive advantage, if I may so express it, as contrasted with the negative advantage of the late partner not carrying on the business himself – that has been acquired by the old firm, or with any other matter carrying with it the benefit of the business.

On the purchase of goodwill, the purchaser usually acquires the premises of the old firm and the right to use the name of the old firm, and also the right to represent himself as the successor of the old firm. Goodwill is a partnership asset[172] and, on the death or retirement of a partner, does not devolve on the surviving partners but must be acquired or bought by them.[173]

169 (Emphasis added.)
170 (1810) 17 Ves 335.
171 (1859) Johns 174.
172 *Jennings v Jennings* [1898] 1 Ch 378.
173 *Public Trustee v Schultz* (1964) 111 CLR 482.

If a partnership is dissolved, the goodwill is not sold or bought; each partner is free to carry on business under the old firm's name provided he or she does not thereby incur liability for the others.[174] Thus, whenever there is an agreement to the effect that on dissolution the partnership assets including goodwill shall be taken by one of them at valuation, this must be valued on the basis that the outgoing partner has the right to carry on a similar business.

The rights and duties of the parties include the following:

(i) The vendor may carry on a similar business as the old one which had been sold, but he or she must not use the old firm's name or represent himself or herself as carrying on the business. This is to protect the business of the purchaser.

(ii) The vendor may not canvass the customers of the old firm or solicit any customer of the old firm to deal with him.[175]

(iii) The vendor may advertise that he or she is still in business provided the advertisement does not go against the first two matters stated above.[176] The case of *Charton v Douglas*[177] is instructive in this regard. B, C and JD carried on business as JD Co. JD retired; B and C then carried on business under a new name, viz B and C and added "late JD & Co". JD also carried on business in adjoining premises after forming a new firm, which he named JD & Co. In an action by B and C to restrain JD, it was held that although his name was JD he could not use it, though he was entitled to practise in the vicinity; he could also be restrained from canvassing old customers of the old firm.

(iv) unless the right to the use of the old firm name is expressly assigned, the purchaser of the goodwill must not use that name so as to expose any of the partners in the old firm to liability.[178]

Where a partnership deed provides that, on the death of a partner, the surviving partner shall acquire the deceased partner's share of the assets, the executor(s) of the deceased partner would not be allowed to solicit customers of the firm.[179]

Sometimes the assignment of the firm's goodwill is not the voluntary act of the partners, e.g. on the sale by the trustee in bankruptcy of business carried on by the bankrupt; where this is the case, the purchaser cannot restrain the bankrupt from canvassing his old customers.[180] Similarly, if a

174 *Burchell v Wilde* [1900] 1 Ch 551.
175 *Trego v Hunt* [1896] AC 7.
176 *Labouchere v Dawson* (1872) LR 13 Exq 322.
177 (1859) Johns 174.
178 *Townsend v Jarman* [1900] 2 Ch 698.
179 *Boorne v Wicker* [1927] 1 Ch 667.
180 *Walker v Mothram* (1881) 19 Ch D 355.

debtor assigns all his property to a trustee for the benefit of his creditors he cannot be restrained by the trustee from canvassing his old customers.[181]

The amount due payable to the outgoing partner becomes a debt[182] and could be subject to a limitation statute. And, if payment is further delayed for any reason, s 43 comes into play. It provides:

> (1) Subject to Subsection (2), where –
> (a) a member of a firm dies or otherwise ceases to be a partner; and
> (b) the surviving or continuing partners carry on the business of the firm with its capital or assets without any final settlement of accounts as between the firm and the outgoing partner or his estate, in the absence of any agreement to the contrary the outgoing partner or his estate is entitled, at the option of himself or his representatives, to such share of the profits made after the dissolution as the court finds to be attributable to the use of his share of the partnership assets, or to interest at the rate of 5 per cent per annum on the amount of his share of the partnership assets.
>
> (2) Where by the agreement for partnership an option is given to the surviving or continuing partners to purchase the interest of a deceased or outgoing partner, and the option is duly exercised, the estate of the deceased partner, or the outgoing partner or his estate, as the case may be, is not entitled to any further or other share of profits.
>
> (3) If a partner assuming to act in the exercise of an option referred to in Subsection (2) does not in all material respects comply with the terms of the option, he is liable to account under Subsection (1).

The importance of s 43 lies in the fact that partners do not reap any benefit from their improper misapplication of partnership assets after dissolution but before accounts are finally and completely settled.[183]

Return of premium payment

Often, a new partner who lacks experience, knowledge or clout is admitted on condition that he or she compensates the firm for accepting him or her with all

181 *Fahey v Cooper* [1927] 2 KB 384.

182 Section 44 reads: "Subject to any agreement between the partners, the amount due from surviving or continuing partners to an outgoing partner, or to the representatives of a deceased partner, in respect of the outgoing or deceased partner's share, is a debt accruing at the date of the dissolution or death."

183 See *Powell v Powell* (1932) 32 SR (NSW) 407; also *Manley v Sartori* (1927)[1927] 1 Ch 157; *Barclays Bank v Bluff* [1982] 1 Ch 172; *Cameron v Murdoch* (1986) 63 ALR 575; and *Pathirana v Pathirana* [1967] AC 233.

the known disabilities. Such compensation is usually in the nature of a "premium" (an inducement in effect), and is in addition to any capital contribution, and is not refundable. Where premium is paid for a fixed term and the partnership is dissolved prematurely, that is, before the expiration of the full term, it is only fair and equitable that a refund commensurate with the unexpired term be given to the payer. Section 41 provides for this eventuality. It states:

> Where one partner has paid a premium to another on entering into a partnership for a fixed term, and the partnership is dissolved, otherwise than by the death of a partner, before the expiration of the term, the court may order the repayment of the premium, or of such part of the premium as, having regard to the terms of the partnership contract and to the length of time during which the partnership has continued, it thinks just, unless –
> (a) the dissolution is, in the opinion of the court, wholly or chiefly due to the misconduct of the partner who paid the premium; or
> (b) the partnership has been dissolved by an agreement containing no provision for a return of any part of the premium.

Partnership resulting from fraud or misrepresentation

Where a partnership was induced through fraud or misrepresentation, again by application of ordinary doctrines of contract, the party misled or deceived may rescind the partnership agreement. The relevant provisions read:

> Where an agreement for a partnership is rescinded on the ground of fraud or misrepresentation of one of the parties to it, the party entitled to rescind is, without prejudice to any other right, entitled –
> (a) to a lien on, or a right of retention of, the surplus of the partnership assets, after satisfying the partnership liabilities, for any sum of money paid by him for the purchase of a share in the partnership and for any capital contributed by him; and
> (b) to stand in the place of the creditors of the firm for any payments made by him in respect of the partnership liabilities; and
> (c) to be indemnified by the person guilty of the fraud or making the misrepresentation against all the debts and liabilities of the firm.[184]

In the celebrated case of *Senanayake v Cheng*,[185] the respondent sued for the recovery of her capital contribution to the firm of stockbrokers which was represented to her by the appellants as a "gold mine". She was not allowed to exercise her right to inspect the firm's account books initially.

184 PA, s 42.
185 [1966] AC 63.

Subsequently, however, when she inspected the books she discovered that the firm was actually in dire financial straits. Within 24 hours of discovering the true financial status of the firm, she called for a meeting of the partners to be summoned and demanded the return of her capital contribution. The appellants refused, whereupon she brought an action in court for the amount. The Court of Appeal granted the relief sought under the equivalent English provisions.

Winding up the partnership altogether

Rather than keeping the business afloat with a new membership, the partners may opt to wind it up and thereby bring its existence finally and truly to an end. As indicated above, the partners (that is, those who are solvent) may complete outstanding contracts and commitments in order to finalise all partnership business.[186]

Section 40 sets out the rights of the parties in those circumstances. It states:

> (1) On the dissolution of a partnership, each partner is entitled, as against the other partners in the firm and all persons claiming through them in respect of their interests as partners –
> (a) to have the property of the partnership applied in payment of the debts and liabilities of the firm; and
> (b) to have the surplus assets after payment of those debts and liabilities applied in payment of what is due to the partners respectively after deducting what is due from them, as partners, to the firm.
>
> (2) For the purposes of Subsection (1), a partner or his representative may, on the termination of the partnership, apply to the court to wind up the business and affairs of the firm.

This can be done only after valuation and realisation of the partnership assets which, as pointed out earlier, involve more valuers and accountants than lawyers.[187]

Section 45(b) sets out clearly the order of priority of distribution of assets: first, the creditors of the firm who are owed debts and other liabilities; secondly, advances of partners; thirdly, capital of the partners; and finally the residue as profits due the partners. Conversely, if there are losses rather than profits, these are to be equitably shared among the partners. Section 45 states expressly:

186 See *Re Bourne* [1906] 2 Ch 427; *Davis v Firman* (1902) 28 VLR 53; and *Re McMaster Construction Pty Ltd* [1902] 9 Qd R 628.

187 See, however, *Public Trustee v Schultz* (1964) 111 CLR 482.

In settling accounts between the partners after dissolution of partnership, the following rules shall, subject to any agreement, be observed –
(a) losses, including losses and deficiencies of capital, shall be paid first out of profits, next out of capital, and lastly, if necessary, by the partners individually in the proportions in which they were entitled to share profits;
(b) the assets of the firm, including the sums (if any) contributed by the partners to make up losses or deficiencies of capital, shall be applied in the following order –
(i) in paying the debts and liabilities of the firm to persons who are not partners;
(ii) in paying to each partner rateably what is due from the firm to him for advances as distinguished from capital;
(iii) in paying to each partner rateably what is due from the firm to him in respect of capital,
and the ultimate residue (if any) shall be divided among the partners in the proportion in which profits are divisible.

Where a partner is insolvent, the rule in *Garner v Murray*[188] applies. The rule is to the effect that solvent partners are not obligated to assume more than their own share of the losses of the partnership. However, if the losses are so enormous as to consume the firm's capital as well, they become liable for the debts to the extent of their individual and personal fortunes, that is, an unlimited liability situation.

Limited partnership

In the UK, there is the phenomenon of a hybrid of an incorporated entity and a partnership, which is governed by the Limited Partnership Act 1907. PNG does not have the equivalent of the UK legislation.[189] The most that can be said is that a partnership can be converted into an incorporated association by the mere act of incorporation.

Conclusion

The dearth of decided cases on partnership in PNG is indicative of the limited use to which the device is being put. It is conjectured that, apart

188 [1904] 1 Ch 57.
189 This is in vogue in five Australian states and New Zealand also: see Partnership (Limited Liability) Act 1988 (Qld); Part 3 of the Partnership Act 1892 (NSW); Part 3 of the Partnership Act 1958 (Vic); the Limited Partnerships Act 1909 (WA); the Limited Partnerships Act 1908 (Tas); and Part II of the Partnership Act 1908 (NZ). On the problems associated with limited partnership, see Blackett-Ord, M, "Limited Liability Partnerships and the Problem with Legal Uncertainty" (2000) *New Law Journal* 1590.

from persons engaging in professions, trades and occupations such as accounting, law, medicine and the like, ordinary people do not, it would seem, find the need to employ it in the pursuit of their business ventures. That notwithstanding, there is the need for a reappraisal of the entire régime of partnership law to make it more relevant to modern business needs. There is no reason that an entity endowed with all the paraphernalia of a corporation should be denied the attributes of a corporation, that is, legal personality.[190]

190 See a recent discussion on the issue: Bradley, C, "Partnership: Twenty-First Century Anglo-American Partnership Law?" (2001) 30 *Common Law World Review* 330.

Chapter 16

Law of Co-operatives

Introduction

The International Co-operative Alliance (ICA) defines a co-operative as "an autonomous association of persons united to meet their common economic, social and cultural needs and aspirations through a jointly owned and democratically controlled enterprise".[1] The co-operative movement had a fairly long and chequered history in PNG. It thrived during the colonial period, but declined to oblivion post-Independence. Indeed, but for recent developments, one would be tempted to leave the study of the law of co-operatives in PNG to legal historians. The most important of these developments include the creation in 2000 of the Office of Cooperative Societies Unit, within the Department of Trade and Industry, with a mandate to revitalise the co-operative sector; and, in 2003, the promulgation of a new set of Co-operative Regulations. In addition, official rhetoric suggests that the government is beginning to give priority or at least some impetus to revitalising the co-operative movement in PNG. Before we focus on the co-operative movement in PNG, it is important for readers to understand the nature of the co-operative form of business organisation and the difference between it and other business organisations.

Nature of co-operatives

Co-operation has always been a feature of humankind. As a modern phenomenon, the co-operative form of business organisation originated in England amongst the industrial workers in the mid nineteenth century, shortly after the introduction of the modern joint stock companies and as a reaction to it. Co-operatives started as an urban consumer retail enterprise but soon

1 Quoted in Sharma, G K, *Co-operative Laws in Asia and the Pacific: Part III – Present Situation and Future Trends* (1997) (electronic format made available by the International Co-operative Alliance http://www.wisc.edu/uwcc/icic/issues/leg-tax/Co-operative-Law-in-Asia-and-the-Pacific1/Part-III—Present-Situation-and-Future-1.html, para 1 under the heading "Statement on the Co-operative Identity".)

spread to rural areas amongst farmers. During the latter part of the nineteenth century, the concept engulfed several parts of Europe and North America. Early in the twentieth century, the co-operative movement spread to India and gradually to other Asian and African countries, mainly courtesy of the colonial administrators.[2] Today, the co-operative form of business organisation is an international movement. Though some associate it with socialist or communist countries, the co-operative movement also operates in capitalist countries such as the US, Canada, Israel and Australia. An Indian Registrar of Co-operatives appropriately described the co-operative movement as representing:

> . . . a happy mean between the forces of extreme individualism on the one hand and socialism and communism on the other. It stands for individual rights tempered by considerations of justice, equity and fair dealing as between man and man, and its one great aim is to prevent the exploitation of the weaker by the stronger party.[3]

In addition, it is inaccurate to equate co-operatives with the traditional co-operation amongst indigenous communities. "Co-operation" or co-operative, as used here in a technical sense, is different from the indigenous kind of co-operation.[4] The main features that distinguish co-operatives from other forms of business organisations are the co-operative values and principles.

Co-operative values and principles

At the 1995 Manchester Congress of the International Co-operative Alliance, the Congress adopted an "Identity Statement on Co-operatives", which includes the definition of "co-operative", "co-operative values" and "principles", for the guidance of the co-operative form of business organisations.[5]

The identity statement defines a "co-operative" as "an autonomous association of persons united voluntarily to meet their common economic, social, and cultural needs and aspirations through a jointly owned and

2 For a historical account of the evolution of co-operatives, see the University of Wisconsin Center For Co-operatives website: www.wisc.edu/uwcc/icic/def-hist/history/index.html.

3 Quoted in Hough, E M, *The Co-operative Movement in India* (OUP, Bombay, 1966), p 741.

4 Asante, S K, *Property Law and Social Goals in Ghana* (Ghana University Press, Accra, 1976), p 283.

5 *International Co-operative Alliance Statement on Co-operative Identity: Background Paper to the Statement on identity* (8 January 1996); and *ICA Statement on Co-operative Identity* (8 January 1996). See the University of Wisconsin Center for Co-operatives website: www.wisc.edu/uwcc/icic/issues/prin/21-cent/background.html.

democratically controlled enterprise".[6] Co-operatives are based on certain values: self-help; self-responsibility; democracy; equality; equity; and solidarity. In addition, co-operatives, irrespective of the nature of their business or area of operation, should conduct their affairs in accordance with the "co-operative principles". The ICA, however, makes it clear that the seven co-operative principles are not dogma. Rather they are guidelines (or best practice) for co-operatives that want to put co-operative values into practice.[7] The co-operative principles are as follows:

Voluntary and open membership

This principle means that membership of co-operatives should be voluntary and available, without artificial restrictions or any social, religious or political discrimination, to all persons who wish to benefit from co-operative membership and are willing to accept the corresponding responsibilities. Conversely, voluntary membership also means that members who wish to resign from a co-operative society should be free to do so without any hindrance. The moral of the principle is that co-operative societies must justify their existence to the people. If the people feel that membership does not serve their interests they will stay away.[8]

Democratic control

The control of the organisation must be based on democratic principles. Thus, in all matters that entail voting in the management of co-operatives, the principle is one member one vote irrespective of the number of shares held by a member. This is in recognition of the fact that people working together to achieve a common objective should have equal say in the joint enterprise.[9] This is in direct contrast to the situation with ordinary corporations where control of the enterprise usually depends on the amount of capital contributed by a shareholder: one share one vote, or the type of share held, which may give preferential voting power.

Member economic participation

The principle of member economic participation entails limited return on share capital. This principle is related to the second principle, above. Its basis is that, whilst co-operatives acknowledge capital as an important

6 Ibid.
7 Münkner, H-H, "Co-operative Principles and Values – Developing Co-operative Societies in a Globalised Economy", paper presented at the second Asia-Pacific Regional Research Conference, Cebu, Philippines, 18–19 February 2003.
8 Ibid.
9 Ibid.

factor of production that should be rewarded, they reject the notion that it should be a means of exploiting other members as patrons of the association. In conformity with this principle, co-operatives place a limit on the rate of interest that is paid on share capital. Any profit or surplus (as it is usually called by co-operatives) arising out of the society's operations must be distributed to members in such a way as to avoid one or some members gaining at the expense of other members. This is usually achieved by refunding to the members at the end of the financial year a share of the net surplus, if any, in proportion to patronage or use of the society's services. For example, a retail shop co-operative society pays rebates to members in proportion to the amount of business a member conducts with the shop in the financial year. In other words, the more a member purchases from the co-operative shop the higher is his or her share of its net surplus.

Autonomy and independence

This means that co-operatives should enjoy a certain degree of autonomy and a right to run their organisation as they see fit. Accordingly, as long as co-operatives act within the scope of the legal framework, they should not be subjected to greater outside supervision or interference than other business organisations.[10]

Education, training and information

The fifth principle is the commitment to education. Co-operatives must strive to promote education amongst their members, officers, employees and the general public in the co-operative values and principles and the laws, which govern co-operatives. This, in a sense, is intended as a mass campaign to spread the co-operative gospel. Success or failure of the co-operative movement largely depends upon the conviction of the members and the public about the operation and advantages of conducting business through co-operatives. However, the principle goes further. It demands that co-operatives should aim at educating their members to improve their economic production, for example, by teaching them the best farming methods, modern business management, marketing, and the impact of globalisation on socio-economic conditions. One writer has observed that education of members and employees "is one of the goals of the co-operative society to make its members fit for survival under changing conditions and accordingly has to be treated as a necessary investment in human resources development and as a cost factor".[11]

10 Paz, Y, "Towards the Future: Co-operatives in the Coming Years", paper presented at the Second Co-operative Forum, February 2003 (ICA Conference papers).

11 Münkner, H-H, "Co-operative Principles and Values in Developing Co-operative Societies in a Globalised Economy", supra note 7.

Co-operation amongst co-operatives

All co-operatives must endeavour to collaborate in every practical way with other co-operatives at local, national and international levels. The co-operative is a movement, hence, the need to assist and work with other co-operatives to improve the quality of life of members wherever they may be. Networking of co-operatives, whether at provincial, national or international level, strengthens co-operatives in competition with multinationals.

Concern for the community

Co-operatives are part of the community in which they operate. This principle calls for social responsibility on the part of co-operatives and their members. This entails, amongst other things, working towards improvement of the community in the area they operate, showing concern for neighbours, participating in development activities, and showing concern for the environment. In short, co-operatives and their members should be good citizens.

Advantages and disadvantages of co-operatives

Advantages

In developing countries, co-operatives are particularly suited to rural people with low income. By forming co-operatives, people can contribute funds to provide themselves with facilities, which as individuals they could not afford. For example, they could purchase a truck to transport their produce; build storage for their produce prior to marketing them; employ experts to assist them in their work, and so on. Farmers marketing their produce through co-operatives have a greater bargaining power than if they did so individually, in competition against each other. By handling members' produce in bulk, co-operatives may reap some economies of scale. For example, reduction of middle-men, staff expenditure and marketing costs would result into more income to the members. From the buyers' point of view, co-operatives bring together a large number of small producers into a unit that buyers of that produce could deal with.[12]

At a national level, several advantages may accrue from using a co-operative form of business organisation. The co-operative values and principles foster unity and co-operation amongst the grassroots in their struggle to improve their economic situation. It is a convenient means of encouraging the common people to participate in the economic development of their local area and country. Because of the nature of the composition of their

12 "Five Good Reasons for Co-operatives" (Oct–Dec 2003) 10(4) *Asia Pacific Coop News*.

membership and the distribution of surplus income earned by the association, co-operatives ultimately facilitate a wider distribution of wealth to the population than ordinary companies whose shareholders are, usually, an exclusive class of relatively rich people. Unlike company shareholders, who tend to live in urban areas, co-operative members are local people. Whatever income they earn is spent locally, which boosts the local economy and development. Moreover, co-operatives are rooted in local areas irrespective of their economic fortunes. Ordinary companies, on the other hand, operate in an area for as long as there is profit to be made. If they can make a better profit elsewhere, they just wind up and leave.[13]

Disadvantages

Co-operatives have several drawbacks. Perhaps the most important drawback is their inability to attract large capital investment. Co-operatives do not appeal to large capital investors because co-operatives do not recognise capital as the key factor of production. As we have seen, co-operative principles and values preclude the distribution of profits, and control of the enterprise based on capital, which is the antithesis of most corporations. For this reason, co-operatives tend to suffer from lack of private capital investment. Co-operatives are also subject to more control and supervision than ordinary corporations in their management and activities. Many business people resent officious civil servants, let alone politicians, telling them how to run their business. Indeed, in many countries government interference in the running of co-operatives is often cited as one of the main reasons for the failure of the co-operative movement.[14]

Organisation of co-operatives

Co-operative societies

Traditionally, the co-operative movement is organised in tiers, which form a pyramid-shaped structure. At the bottom of the structure are primary co-operative societies, whose membership consists of individuals. The primary societies serve their members directly. Their size may vary from small village societies to large societies serving several villages. The range of business of primary societies also varies from single-purpose co-operative societies engaging in, for example, retail trading, to multiple-purpose societies combining, for instance, retailing and product marketing. Primary societies form the foundation of the co-operative movement. Success of the movement invariably hinges on grass root support.

13 Paz, Y, "Towards the Future: Co-operatives in the Coming Years", supra note 10.

14 Sharma, G K, *Co-operative Laws in Asia and the Pacific, Part III – Present Situation and Future Trends*, supra note 1.

Co-operative societies' association

A number of primary societies may unite to form a "co-operative societies' association", or a "secondary society" as it is sometimes known. Associations or secondary societies operate on the same basis as primary societies, except that their membership is limited to primary societies. Through these associations, primary societies can combine their resources to purchase in bulk or acquire major capital assets that as individual societies they would not afford. For example, primary retail societies could combine to form a wholesale co-operative societies' association, which serves the member primary societies.

Co-operative union

Secondary societies may further federate to form a union at a regional or provincial level. For example, wholesale co-operative associations in a particular province could combine to form a provincial wholesale co-operative union, which serves the member associations. At the top of the pyramid, there is a nationwide federation: the "apex" union composed of the unions.[15] At the international level co-operatives are united under one umbrella of the International Co-operative Alliance.

It should be stressed that it is not mandatory for co-operatives to follow the traditional structure. Circumstances in a particular country or region might dictate a different structure. Indeed, as will be seen, the Papua New Guinea Co-operative Societies Revitalisation and Development Project creates a new co-operative structure for PNG.[16]

The co-operative movement in Papua New Guinea

Officially, the co-operative movement started in PNG in 1947, when the Australian Colonial Administration established a "Co-operative Section" within the Department of District Services and Native Affairs.[17] Officers were assigned the task of encouraging the indigenous people to form co-operatives. The Administration's motive was partly to stimulate economic activity amongst Papua New Guineans and partly as a tactical move to guide potential "political forms of resistance into proper channels".[18] As was the case in other colonies, one of the results of the Second World

15 For example, s 106 of the Co-operative Societies Act 1982 makes provision for the registration of three or more primary societies as an "association of societies"; at least three associations as a "federation of associations"; and at least three federal organisations as a "composite society".

16 See *The Co-operative Societies Revitalization and Development Project and its Management* (unpublished PNG Government Paper, 2003).

17 Singh, S, "Co-operatives in Papua New Guinea" (1974) 58 *New Research Bulletin* 1–2.

18 Fitzpatrick, P and Southwood, J, "The Community Corporation in Papua New Guinea" (IASER seminar paper, Port Moresby, 14 October 1976), p 14.

War was that the natives acquired political awareness, which the Administration feared might be used against it if not controlled. The Administration identified the co-operative movement as one of the channels to divert the attention of would-be political agitators.

During its initial stages, the co-operative movement consisted mainly of simple village trade stores. Under the Administration's encouragement and guidance, the movement quickly spread. The area of activity also became more diversified, from consumer societies to marketing of primary produce, especially coffee, cocoa and copra. The number of primary co-operative societies rose from 98 in 1950 to 316 by 1958, with membership of 8,556 in 1950 and 109,175 by 1968.[19] There was also an upsurge of secondary associations during the same period: 11 in 1955 and 14 by 1968.

In the 1960s, the Administration stepped up its commitment to the promotion of the co-operative form of business organisation as a means of promoting the indigenous peoples' socio-economic development. More administrative officials were assigned to assist co-operative societies in managing their affairs, preparing budgets and accounts, and generally policy formulation. A co-operative education centre was also established to provide training in the various elements of business and management of co-operatives in accordance with the co-operative principles. In 1970, the Laloki Co-operative College was established with the assistance of the United Nations Development Programme. The object of the college was to expand co-operative education both in terms of numbers of trainees and in terms of the quality of the programme. In the same year, the office of the Registry of Co-operatives was upgraded to a Division of Co-operative Extension within the newly created Department of Trade and Industry. Several positions in the department were upgraded to senior levels with a view to attracting persons of a higher calibre.[20]

Unfortunately, the steps taken by the Administration were rather late. In spite of the steady increase of the number and membership of co-operatives in the 1950s and the 1960s, by the end of the 1960s signs of failure of the movement in the colony were evident. Several primary societies had returned losses for at least three consecutive financial years; many were either in the process of liquidation or were not trading at all. Most of the large co-operative unions that were established to service primary societies were also in serious financial difficulties.[21] The people's faith in the co-operative movement was rapidly declining.

19 Singh, S,"Co-operatives in Papua New Guinea", supra note 17, pp 3, 5 and 11. Another source estimates that by the late 1960s there were 455 co-operatives in the country (see LaMotte, J D, *Revitalizing the Co-operative Sector in Papua New Guinea* (International Labor Organization working paper, 2002).

20 Singh, S, "Co-operatives in Papua New Guinea", supra note 17.

21 See *Committee of Inquiry into Co-operative Societies in Papua New Guinea Report* (Port Moresby, September, 1972), p 6.

Some placed the blame on the Colonial Administration for not doing enough to assist co-operatives, whilst others thought that the failure of the movement was due to over-enthusiastic bureaucratic interference in the management of co-operative affairs, which was resented by the members.[22] Others theorised that the co-operative principle of open membership that coerced people of different clans or tribes (some traditional enemies) to carry on business together, was unworkable in many areas of the country. Constant factional infighting from the directors' level to the regular members, which made it impossible for most co-operatives to function efficiently, strengthened this assertion. Others thought that Australian entrepreneurs instigated the failure of the co-operative movement in order to thwart competition. Most likely, however, the decline of the co-operative movement was due to a combination of several factors. In fact, at around the same period worldwide co-operatives were fighting with their backs to the wall.

Committee of inquiry

On 20 November 1970, the House of Assembly resolved to establish a committee of inquiry to examine the achievements and problems of the co-operative movement in the territory, and the role of the Administration. The committee was also to make recommendations as to the future of the co-operative movement in the country. The committee was appointed in August 1971, and it reported in September of the following year.[23] Its findings confirmed that the co-operative movement was collapsing. It attributed this to several reasons. The committee found that many co-operatives were making losses because of mismanagement and/or incompetence of their managers and directors. Some co-operative officers were embezzling funds, whilst others had private business in direct competition with the co-operatives they were managing. The committee also found that the Administration, in its enthusiasm to encourage ordinary Papua New Guineans to form co-operatives, unduly raised their expectations. Many people were disillusioned when the promised high yields from their investment in co-operatives did not materialise.

Competition from private companies, mainly expatriate owned, was, according to the committee, another key factor for the failure of the movement. Being better organised and having easier access to finance, private companies were able to offer more attractive terms for goods and services than those offered by the co-operative societies. For instance, they paid farmers higher prices and in cash for their produce; and the goods sold in their shops tended to be cheaper than those in the co-operative shops. As a result, many members of co-operative societies became "disloyal" to their societies.

22 Ibid. See also, Singh, S, "Co-operatives in Papua New Guinea", supra note 17.
23 *Committee of Inquiry into Co-operative Societies in Papua New Guinea Report*, supra note 21.

The committee also found the policies and actions of the Administration partly responsible for the demise of the co-operative movement. It criticised the Administration's lack of a definite and rational policy towards co-operatives. Officials of the Division of Co-operative Extension were too few and many of them were incompetent or insufficiently trained to fulfil the role of advising co-operatives in financial and managerial matters. Moreover, the committee noted that the co-operative education was inadequate, in particular, because it did not provide for the training of the ordinary members who formed the foundation of the movement.

In spite of these criticisms, the committee generally commended the role of the co-operative movement in social and economic development of the indigenous peoples. It felt confident that that role would continue in the future. The committee made several proposals for improvement. Its main recommendations included a re-organisation of the relevant administrative division responsible for co-operatives, re-structuring the co-operative education, encouragement of the people to form co-operatives and provision of assistance to those in operation. The committee, nevertheless, warned the administration to be more vigilant in identifying co-operatives that were not economically viable and to wind them up before they incurred further losses. The committee also recommended the repeal and replacement of the Co-operative Societies Act 1965, by a much simpler legislation that the ordinary people would understand.[24]

The demise of the co-operative movement

The committee's report perhaps confirmed rather than allayed the Independent Government's misgivings of the future role of the co-operative movement in the socio-economic development of ordinary Papua New Guineans. Instead of reforming the co-operative movement, the government actively moved to abolish it. It sought to promote the incorporated business group, which was a new form of business organisation unique to PNG, as the key vehicle for engaging ordinary people in economic activities.[25] The Co-operative Societies Act 1965 was repealed by the Companies (Co-operative Companies) Act 1975.[26] The latter Act made provision for the incorporation of a "co-operative company",[27] which was a halfway house between an ordinary company and a co-operative society registered under the repealed Act.

24 Ibid, pp 16–23 and generally.
25 See Chapter 17, Business Group Incorporation.
26 Section 6, Act 106 of 1975.
27 Section 361H, Companies Act 1963 (c 146), s 361H as amended by s 3 of the Companies (Co-operative Companies) Act 1975. The latter Act inserted a new Division 5 into the Companies Act 1963, to govern co-operative companies. Reference hereafter is to the relevant provisions of the Companies Act as amended.

Section 373 of the Companies Act defined a "co-operative company" as one limited by shares and by guarantee, and whose articles of association complied with the requirements of s 377, of the Act, and the word "co-operative" formed part of its name. Under s 377, a co-operative company was required to include in its articles of association: that its membership was open to all individuals and business groups incorporated under the Business Groups Incorporation Act; that all members with the same number of shares had equal voting rights; that payment of dividends was restricted; that shares of members who resigned or were expelled from the company were redeemable; and that all directors had to be members of the company. Section 378 restricted the manner of distribution of profits amongst the members. It provided that after payment of dividends on shares and payment to the Co-operative Education Trust (and any other payment to charitable organisations or community welfare as approved in a general meeting) any remaining surplus had to be distributed to the members in accordance with the business they conducted with the company. Clearly, the intention of the legislation was to give legislative effect to some of the co-operative principles discussed above. Otherwise, co-operative companies were subject to the same provisions of the Companies Act, just like any other incorporated company.

The underlying policy was to phase out co-operative societies and replace them with co-operative companies under the administration of the Registrar of Companies. As a transitional measure, all co-operative societies registered under the Co-operative Societies Act 1965, were deemed to be registered under the Companies Act as "co-operative companies".[28] Under the Act, the converted societies had a grace period of nine months to amend their rules in line with the prescribed requirements of co-operative companies. Any converted co-operative company that failed to comply with these requirements within the specified period became a public company by default.[29]

At about the same time, the Companies Act 1963,[30] was amended to make a special dispensation for companies whose membership comprised of indigenous Papua New Guineans from complying with some of its provisions. The main effect of the exemption was to make it cheaper to incorporate and manage the companies that qualified. The government hoped that this would encourage more Papua New Guineans to take advantage of carrying on their business through a business association incorporated under the Companies Act.

28 Companies (Co-operative Companies) Act 1975, s 4.
29 Companies (Co-operative Companies) Act 1975, s 4(3) and (4).
30 Chapter 146 was repealed and replaced by the Companies Act 1997.

In practice, many co-operative societies were dissolved, mostly unofficially, while some converted themselves into incorporated business groups. Some continued to appear in the register of companies as "co-operative companies" mainly due to the statutory conversion, but the official suspicion was that most never got off the ground. There is no evidence of any new co-operative company formed and incorporated under the Companies Act. Recent estimates of the number of co-operative companies which are still operative vary between 20 and 30.[31]

Attempts to resuscitate the co-operative movement

By the early 1980s, some national leaders had second thoughts about the abolition of co-operative societies. Amongst those was Sir John Guise, the first Governor-General of PNG, who was an ardent supporter of the co-operative movement in its heyday. When Sir John re-entered politics, he moved a Private Member's Bill to reinstate the co-operative movement. The Bill made provision for the registration of co-operative societies and co-operative companies and management. Sir John had the backing of the then Prime Minister, Sir Julius Chan, a former co-operative officer and a strong supporter of the co-operative movement. Subsequently, Parliament enacted the Bill as the Co-operative Societies Act 1982, and the Act commenced in April of the same year.[32] Despite the support of the two prominent politicians, however, the idea did not find favour with many in the government, and the enactment of the Bill did not lead to any increase in the number of co-operatives or the revival of those that were already registered. Any pretence of official assistance of co-operatives gradually ceased, and the office of the Registrar of Co-operatives, provided for in the Act, existed only in name. The co-operative system in PNG seemed to be dead and buried.

Nevertheless, the Co-operative Societies Act remained, and remains, a valid law. Before we consider its provisions, we should review the recent developments (referred to in the introduction to this chapter) in the PNG co-operative movement saga.

Revitalisation of the co-operative movement

Background

The proposal to revitalise the co-operative movement in PNG was first floated by the Department of Trade and Industry in 1995. Due to several

31 LaMotte, J D, *Revitalizing the Co-operative Sector in Papua New Guinea* (International Labor Organization working paper, 2002).
32 Ch 389.

factors, including lack of funds, continuous departmental changes and apathy of some government officials, no positive action was taken.[33] It was not until 2000 that the government took a decisive action to revive the co-operative movement. In that year, the then Minister of Trade and Industry, Honourable Michael Nali, announced the establishment within the Department the Office of the Co-operative Societies Unit (CSU). The CSU was established pursuant to the Co-operative Societies Act 1982. Finance was not made available until the following financial year when the government made a budgetary commitment of K400,000 a year for five years towards the running of the newly established office. At the time of writing, the CSU is fully operational. The Registrar of Co-operatives heads the office, supported by two assistant registrars, a legal adviser and a small team of other support staff.

Revitalisation plan

The CSU has the task to spearhead the revitalisation of the co-operative movement in the country. Its mission statement is:

> To encourage effective meaningful participation of ordinary people in the rural communities and villages in the national development process to perpetuate economic prosperity, enhance progress on communal welfare and to restore dignity to individuals through the Co-operative Society Movement.[34]

To that end, the CSU has the responsibility to review the co-operative societies' law and to adopt strategies conducive to the revival of the co-operative movement. It must also provide support and co-ordinate the activities of all co-operative organisations. Such support would include assisting co-operative societies with feasibility studies of a proposed economic activity, and identifying government programmes and policies that could be linked with or conducted through the co-operative network, for example, rural development, micro-financing, and national food strategy programmes.[35] The CSU is aware that success of the revitalisation project will very much depend on ordinary Papua New Guineans being convinced that forming or joining co-operative societies is a viable proposition. Therefore, vital to the CSU's strategy is to conduct extensive awareness campaigns throughout the country of the value of carrying on business through the co-operative movement.

33 *Report on the Co-operative Society Movement in Papua New Guinea and Its Status and the Revival Strategy* (unpublished Government paper, Port Moresby, April 2001).
34 Ibid.
35 Ibid.

Why co-operatives?

The government sees the co-operative movement as the best vehicle through which to implement its "rural development, people's empowerment and poverty eradication" strategy.[36] The reason is co-operative societies are based on the "values of self-help, democracy, equality, and solidarity and co-operative members believe in the ethical values of honesty, openness, and social responsibility and caring for others . . .". Moreover, according to the government:

> Co-operative societies do not only create a conducive environment to do business in the spirit of competition but also stimulate economic activities in the rural areas and which programmes will be geared towards effective participation of rural people in business activities in the villages.[37]

Some may dismiss the above as a rhetorical endeavour to revive a business structure that had its heyday during the colonial period, which subsequently proved unworkable. However, the government claims that the object of the revitalisation project is not to revive completely the pre-independence co-operatives system, but rather to start a new structure for co-operative societies that has been designed taking into account the economic, political and social conditions of PNG.[38] Unlike the pre-Independence co-operative movement structure, the new organisational structure has two tier levels: primary co-operative societies and secondary co-operative societies.[39]

Primary co-operative societies are village-based societies whose membership consists of village groups and individual farmers or producers. The revitalisation project identifies particular commodities or resources in each province that farmers or producers can develop through co-operative societies. For example, in the Highlands region, the target resource is coffee and livestock; in Momase it is coffee, copra, cocoa and rice; in the Southern region, it is mainly copra and marine products; and in New Guinea Islands it is copra, cocoa and vanilla.[40] It is the CSU's task to encourage producers to form or join co-operative societies for their respective resource. The members themselves will be responsible for the management of their

36 *The Co-operative Societies Revitalisation and Development Project and Its Management* (unpublished PNG Government Paper, 2003).

37 Ibid.

38 Ibid. See also LaMotte, J D, *Revitalizing the Co-operative Sector in Papua New Guinea*, supra note 31.

39 Compare with the pre-independence four-tier structure discussed above.

40 CSU, Sectorial Target For Development (information provided to the authors by the Registrar of Co-operatives, Port Moresby, July 2004).

societies, with the support and assistance of the co-operative association to which they are affiliated.

There is a "co-operative association" for each province. These are the "secondary" societies in the new co-operative movement structure. Membership of co-operative associations consists of primary co-operative societies. All primary co-operative societies must be affiliated to the co-operative association in their province. The main task of the co-operative associations is to unify primary co-operatives in the respective province. The association is supposed to provide management and logistic support to its member societies. Such support may include transporting produce, marketing, purchasing goods from wholesale dealers and distributing them to the societies. Unlike primary co-operative societies, whose members are responsible for their management, the management of co-operative associations is the sole responsibility of the relevant Provincial Commerce Division. The provinces are also supposed to meet the cost of management of the associations, though societies may be required to contribute. The government hopes that eventually co-operative associations will become financially viable and able to operate autonomously. At that stage, the provincial authorities will withdraw and let private bodies take over the management of co-operative associations.

Future of the co-operative movement

The revitalisation of the co-operative movement project, at least on paper, looks very promising. The government hopes that, if the revival is successful, co-operative societies could well become the biggest employer in the country and will create new employment opportunities for the people, especially in rural areas. In this regard, the revitalisation has the backing of the International Labour Organization. Success in the end will very much depend on the government's resolve to support the co-operative movement and the conviction of ordinary Papua New Guineans of the benefit of forming and/or joining co-operative societies. Reportedly, since the CSU became functional, many ordinary people have expressed interest in forming or joining co-operative societies. At the time of writing, the CSU has received 839 applications to form co-operative societies, 362 of which were registered.[41]

Obviously, if co-operative societies perform, people will join them; if they do not get tangible results within a relatively short period, the people will desert them in droves, perhaps forever.[42] The future of the co-operative movement at this stage is unpredictable.

41 Information provided by the Office of Co-operative Societies, Port Moresby December 2006.

42 LaMotte, J D, *Revitalizing the Co-operative Sector in Papua New Guinea*, supra, cautions the Government in its campaign for co-operative societies not to over promote the concept otherwise it might create unrealistic expectations.

Co-operative societies law

The 1982 Co-operative Societies Act[43] is still current law. Its preamble declares that the object of the Act is to provide for the establishment of co-operative societies and for related purposes. As earlier stated, until recently the Co-operative Societies Act was a dead letter in the statutory books for almost 20 years. The co-operatives revitalisation scheme discussed above has obviously breathed new life in the Act. If the scheme is successful, the Act will most likely be drastically amended or even repealed and replaced with another piece of legislation, which provides for the "new look" co-operative movement in PNG. If the scheme fails to materialise, the Act is likely to remain idle on the statutory books. Because of the prevailing uncertain circumstances, we shall limit our discussion of the Act to key general provisions. We hope this will give readers sufficient insight into the law of co-operatives and be able to compare and contrast it with the legal régime, which governs other business organisations.

Registration procedure

The Act makes provision for the registration and incorporation of co-operative societies. Section 21 of the Act stipulates that a minimum of seven "eligible" persons who desire to "promote common economic and social interest in accordance with co-operative principles" may apply for registration under the Act as a "society".[44] The application must be in the prescribed format: Form 1 of Schedule 2 of the Co-operative Societies Regulation 2003.[45]

There is no definition in the Act of the term "co-operative principles", but quite clearly, reference must be to the traditional co-operative principles discussed above.[46] "Eligible persons" mean "automatic citizens"[47] of PNG

43 Ch 389. The only new legislation is the Co-operative Societies Regulation 2003, made by the Head of State under this Act (SI No 1 of 2003).

44 Under s 1, the interpretation provision of the Act, the term "society" means "a society, association, federation or composite society registered under this Act".

45 See r 3 of the Co-operative Societies Regulation 2003. The Regulations prescribe diverse forms for various applications and other actions under the Act. The format appears to be mandatory.

46 It has been suggested that "to bring clarity and thought about co-operatives", the co-operative values and principles, as recently adopted by the ICA, should be incorporated in the relevant legislation. See Sharma, *Co-operative Laws in Asia and the Pacific*, supra.

47 An "automatic citizen" is a person born in PNG before Independence Day both of whose grandparents were born in PNG (Article 65(1) of the Constitution). Under Article 68(5), an Act of Parliament made in the period of ten years after Independence Day (16 September 1975) could confer "a benefit, right or privilege" to automatic citizens for the purpose of giving them advantage or assistance. The Co-operative Societies Act was enacted within this period. The parliamentary power to confer special statutory rights to automatic citizens has long expired. In any case, limiting membership of co-operatives to a particular citizen group would be counterproductive.

who, at least, must be 18 years old.[48] The applicants must further comply with the pre-registration requirements prescribed in s 22 of the Act. Broadly, prior to their application they must hold a meeting attended by at least seven eligible persons. At that meeting, they must agree in writing on the objects of the proposed society and the reasons for believing that the society will achieve these objectives.[49] Moreover, they must propose rules of the society which, as a minimum, comply with s 51 of the Act. At least seven eligible persons present at the said meeting must sign an application form for membership of the proposed society.[50] Section 22 provides that those persons "may" appoint a board of directors and such other officers as are provided for in the rules of their proposed society.[51]

Upon satisfaction of the foregoing requirements, the proposed board of directors must, within a period of two months of its nomination, submit to the Registrar of Co-operatives the application form duly signed by at least seven eligible persons. The form must include the society's proposed name, two sets of names and addresses of the members of the board, and two copies each of the statement of the agreement and of the rules of the proposed society.[52] Unlike an application for the incorporation of a company, compliance with the registration requirements does not automatically guarantee incorporation. Section 26 states that the Registrar "may" register the proposed society; or in writing, request the applicants to amend their application to conform to the Act and re-submit it as a fresh application; or decline to register a proposed society. It is submitted that the use of the term "may" suggests that the legislature intended to give the Registrar discretion to refuse to register a proposed society if he or she was satisfied that registration was, in the circumstances, inappropriate or that the society was unlikely to achieve its objectives as a co-operative society. Where the Registrar declines to register a proposed society, he or she must inform the applicants in writing the reasons for the refusal.[53]

Once a society is registered and a certificate of incorporation is issued, it becomes a corporation by the name under which it is registered, which must include the word "co-operative" and end with "limited". The society thereafter acquires the usual attributes of a body corporate and has the power to do all things necessary for the furtherance of its objects as set out in its rules.[54]

48 Section 20.
49 The statement must be in "Form 4 of Schedule 2 of the Co-operative Societies Regulation 2003: see r 5 thereof.
50 Section 23(b).
51 Though s 223(b) uses the permissive word "may", in the overall context of the provision the appointment of a board of directors is required for registration of a proposed society.
52 Sections 24 and 25. The list of eligible persons and of the directors of the proposed society must be in Form 3 and Form 5, respectively, of Schedule 2 of the Co-operative Societies Regulation 2003: see r 4 and 5 thereof.
53 Section 26(c).
54 Section 30–32.

Membership rights and liabilities

A person becomes a member of a co-operative society either by being one of the signatories to the application for the registration of the society, or by subsequent admission to the society in accordance with its rules.[55] Since societies registered under the Act are subject to co-operative principles, they must maintain an open membership policy to all persons wishing to become members, if they are prepared to accept the responsibility membership entails. All members must purchase the minimum number of shares, if any, prescribed in the rules. However, the Co-operative Societies Act limits the maximum number of shares that any single member may purchase. Section 60 of the Act provides that, except with the Registrar's consent, no member may acquire more than one fifth of a society's issued shares or such lesser number of shares as the rules of the society might from time to time provide.

Section 31 of the Act states that, subject to the provisions of the Act,[56] the liability of individual members of the society is limited to the nominal value of the issued shares he or she holds, if not already paid for, and to any charges or fees due to the society. Members, on the other hand, enjoy several rights. They are entitled to share in the accumulated net surplus, if any, distributed by way of dividends on shares; or as bonus or rebate in cash or shares in proportion to the amount of business conducted with the society in the relevant financial year; or in any other manner approved by the Registrar.[57] Upon a member's death, the co-operative society must pay the nominal or net value of his or her shares (as certified by the Registrar, whichever is the lesser) to the administrator of the deceased's estate within a period of twelve months of the date of death.[58] Other membership statutory entitlements include a right to vote at the society's meetings; and a right to inspect the society's books such as rules, balance sheet, registers, and profit and loss accounts.[59] The rules of the society may also provide additional rights to the members.

Management of co-operatives

Like ordinary companies, co-operative societies have two main organs, namely, the general meeting of members and the board of directors. Subject to the Act, the society's rules determines the distribution of power between these organs.

55 Section 64.
56 Presumably, this refers to provisions of the Act that impose liability upon members who hold a position of office in the society, see e.g., ss 27 and 69.
57 Section 95.
58 Section 62.
59 Sections 75–83 and 85.

General meeting

A general meeting of members of the society must be held within three months (or such longer period as the Registrar may permit) after the end of the society's financial year.[60] All members have a right to attend, deliberate and vote at the general meeting, except members who are disqualified from voting because of default in the payment of moneys due to the society from them.[61] In accordance with the co-operative principles, the will of the majority prevails on a basis of one member one vote irrespective of the number of shares held. Generally, voting on any resolution is by show of hands, unless at least five members present demand a poll.[62] Voting at a poll may be by proxy if the rules of the society allow it.[63]

The main business of the general meeting is to appoint and remove directors of the society,[64] and it has the power to wind-up the society by a special resolution.[65] In addition, subject to the Act, the general meeting may exercise any other business as may be provided in the rules.

Board of directors

All co-operatives societies must have a board of directors constituted by at least three directors elected by the members or nominated in the original application for the registration of the society.[66] Section 67(3) of the Act prohibits co-operative societies to appoint or retain non-members as directors of the society. Otherwise, members are free to elect any member as a director in accordance with the rules of the society. The directors' tenures of office depend on the rules of the society. However, under s 72 of the Act, the office of a director is deemed to be vacated (in addition to any grounds stated in the rules) if the incumbent is convicted of a criminal offence; or bankrupt; or absent from three consecutive meetings of the board without the board's consent; or ceases to be a member of the society. By s 70, the board must meet to conduct the society's business as often as the rules of the society prescribe or the board thinks necessary. However, it must meet at least once every three months.

The management and control of a co-operative society lies largely with its board of directors. Section 66 of the Co-operative Societies Act provides

60 Section 76.
61 Section 79.
62 Section 77. A poll vote usually entails voting on the basis of one share one vote. It is submitted that if a society's rules allow members to vote according to the number of shares held that would be inconsistent with the co-operative democratic principle of equal control of the society.
63 Section 81.
64 Sections 67(1), 72(g).
65 Sections 82 and 127.
66 Sections 66 and 67.

that, subject to the Act and the society's rules, the board of directors may exercise all the powers of the society as if they had been expressly conferred upon it by the society. Apart from their other duties, the directors have to see to it that the society discharges all its obligations under the Act and the rules of the society. Section 152 imposes criminal liability on any director or officer of a society who knowingly authorises or negligently allows a society to act in breach of the Act.[67] However, the Act absolves directors from personal liability for loss to the society for any act or omission of the board, except acts or omissions resulting from their gross negligence, wilful misconduct or failure to comply with the provisions of the Act or the society's rules.[68]

Government control of co-operatives

Co-operatives societies are subject to greater control by the government than ordinary companies are. Government control touches almost all aspects of co-operative societies' management. For example, unlike ordinary companies, co-operative societies do not have the freedom to distribute their annual accumulated surplus as their directors see fit. Under s 92 of the Co-operative Societies Act, all societies must contribute 20 per cent of their annual net profits to a "Statutory Reserve Fund" until the amount in the reserve is equal to 50 per cent of the aggregate amount of the paid up capital and moneys raised on loan or received on deposit and which remains unpaid. Section 95 provides that, subject to the Act and the society's rules, the directors may distribute the remainder of the accumulated surplus to the members by way of dividend on any share of the society or by way of bonus or rebate (in cash or shares), in proportion to the amount of business conducted with the society in the relevant financial period. The section limits to 6 per cent (or such amount as may be prescribed) of the total annual dividend that may be awarded based on shares held.[69] The Act prohibits co-operative societies to distribute their accumulated surplus in any other manner except with the consent of the Registrar. In any case, the co-operative societies must seek the Registrar's written consent prior to the distribution of dividend or bonus or rebate.[70]

Other powers of the Registrar

The Registrar of Co-operatives is the main arm of the government for the control and supervision of co-operatives under the Act. As discussed earlier,

67 Section 152.
68 Section 69.
69 This provision mirrors the third co-operative principle earlier discussed: limited return should be paid on share capital.
70 Section 95(2).

the Registrar's role starts from the time an application is made to register a proposed society. He or she determines whether a proposed co-operative society ought to be registered. We have seen above the Registrar's powers with regard to the distribution of accumulated surplus. He or she maintains a general supervisory role over the societies' accounts books. Societies must submit to the Registrar annually a list of members, a statement of assets and liabilities, a copy of the auditors' report, if any, and any other returns as may be prescribed.[71] Under s 12 of the Act, the Registrar has the power to demand and examine any document kept or used by the society in relation to its business affairs.

Moreover, the Registrar has the power in certain cases to intervene directly in a society's management. For instance, he or she may impose a limitation on the aggregate amount of undischarged liability that a society may incur;[72] this prevents the society from borrowing money over the limit set. Under s 43 of the Co-operatives Societies Act, the Registrar has the power to restrict a society from entering into an agreement or class of agreements the value of which exceeds an amount specified by him or her. By s 16(1), the Registrar has the power to sack by written notice any director, officer or employee of a society. The section does not specify the ground upon which the Registrar could exercise these powers, other than a requirement that the notice must state the reasons for sacking the person concerned. In appropriate cases, the Registrar may appoint an official manager to manage the society.[73] Finally, subject to s 128 of the Co-operative Societies Act, the Registrar may order a society to be wound up and may strike off the register any society that is defunct.[74]

There is provision for appeal to the Minister against any decision of the Registrar. Section 18 of the Act provides that any person aggrieved by the Registrar's decision may appeal to the Minister. The later at his or her discretion confirm, annul, vary or substitute the Registrar's decision.[75]

Co-operative companies

As already pointed out, all co-operative societies that were originally registered under the repealed Co-operative Societies Act 1965, were deemed to be registered under the Companies Act 1963 as "co operative companies", and administered under a new Division 5 of the Act. The legal position of

71 Section 88.
72 Section 39.
73 Section 111.
74 Section 148.
75 Although the section says that the Minister's decision is final, it does not oust the courts' inherent and constitutional power of review of the Minister or Registrar's decision in an appropriate case. See generally *Kekedo v Burns Philp (PNG) Ltd* [1988–89] PNGLR 122.

co-operative companies was unclear after the enactment of the Co-operative Societies Act 1982. Section 170 of the latter Act provides that a "former society" (which is defined in the Act as a company incorporated under the Companies Act 1963 as a co-operative company)[76] shall be deemed to be registered under the Co-operative Societies Act and subject to its provisions. Section 171 gave the Registrar of Co-operatives the power to order a former society to take the necessary steps to comply with the provisions of the Act. The Act did not state anywhere whether co-operative companies otherwise remained subject to the provisions of the Companies Act. Some suggested that the Co-operative Societies Act by implication repealed Division 5 of the Companies Act, with the effect that such companies ceased to be subject to the latter Act.[77] It would seem, however, that in practice the Registrar of Companies (presumably also because there was no Registrar of Co-operatives) continued to administer under the Companies Act the very few co-operative companies that survived.[78] Interestingly, the current Companies Act 1997 does not refer to "co-operative companies". This suggests that the Registrar of Companies has no jurisdiction over co-operative companies. In the circumstances, we submit that the Registrar of Co-operatives is the one to administer the surviving co-operative companies, if any, under the Co-operatives Societies Act.

76 Co-operative Societies Act 1982, s 169.

77 Tashjian, P, *Business Organizations in Papua New Guinea* (Lawbook Co, North Ryde, NSW, 1989), pp 62, 205.

78 As already seen, estimates vary between 20 and 30 of the number of former co-operative societies that converted to companies and were still operative by 2000. (See LaMotte, *Revitalizing the Co-operative Sector in Papua New Guinea*, supra.) However, the source does not say whether any of these companies was operating as a "co-operatives company".

Chapter 17

Business Group Incorporation

"Business group incorporation" is a customary group incorporated under the Business Groups Incorporation Act,[1] for carrying on business and other economic activities. It is a unique form of business organisation whose membership is restricted to persons of the same customary group and is mainly regulated by the customary law of the members of the group. This chapter examines the main features of incorporated business groups and the future operation of these groups. To appreciate the subject, a brief background review of the Act is necessary

Origin of the Act

The Business Groups Incorporation Act, was enacted in 1974. During the second reading of the Bill in the House of Assembly, Honourable Ebia Olewale, then Minister of Commerce, explained that the legislation was necessary to provide:

> ...a simple and flexible form of incorporation for Papua New Guineans to enable all manner of business enterprise to be commenced without most of the restrictions which are present in other existing corporate legislation [2]

The overall objective was to achieve a greater participation by ordinary Papua New Guineans in the national economy by establishing group enterprises, which were soundly managed. This was consistent with the proposed future economic development strategy of the newly proclaimed self-government of Papua New Guinea. Hitherto, expatriates and expatriate owned firms almost exclusively dominated the economy of the country. The Independent Government sought to facilitate the country's economic development by redirecting economic activities from the urban centres to

1 Chapter No 144 (Consolidated to No 14 of 1994).
2 House of Assembly Debates, 28 June 1994, Vol 3, no 32, p 3869.

rural areas and promoting small-scale businesses, artisans and services relying, wherever possible, on Papua New Guinean forms of economic activities.

Already in some parts of the country, there were a growing number of groups of people pooling their resources to engage in business or other economic activities, for example, retail, public motor vehicles (PMV) or truck operators, plantation ownership, and sale of primary produce such as coffee and cocoa. The sizes of the groups ranged from a handful to several dozens of people. Their methods of operation and organisation also varied. A study conducted in the 1960s of the money-pooling groups in the Goroka area revealed that most of these groups were clustered around a local entrepreneur or "big man" who collected contributions from, normally, his close relatives (members of his family or clan) for a specific or unspecified business venture. Under most arrangements, the contributors usually left the entrepreneur free to manage the business as he saw fit. Moreover, there was no strict accountability to the contributors for the use of the funds. Dividends, if any, were rarely paid; very often payment to contributors was in kind, for example, by gifts of goods from the shop and free rides in the business vehicle. Evidence also suggested that some contributors were satisfied by merely being members of a successful enterprise.[3]

Technically, all those groups whose membership exceeded 20 were illegal. Section 16(3)(b) of the Companies Act (Cap 146)[4] prohibited the formation of an association or partnership consisting of more than 20 people from carrying on business with a view to gain by the association or partnership or individual members unless it was incorporated under the Companies Act or some other law. Whether a particular money-pooling group was illegal under this provision was, of course, a question of fact. In practice, no group was ever prosecuted for contravention of this law. Interestingly, however, government extension officers employed to develop indigenous enterprises, were, reportedly, discouraged from assisting "illegal" business organisations. Their superiors warned them that by working with unregistered organisations they risked prosecution for the "serious" offence of conspiracy under the Criminal Code.[5]

Customary groups wishing to carry on business had a choice of three business forms: partnership, cooperative society and registered company. For various reasons, none of the three was considered suitable in this regard. Of the three, a partnership was the easiest and cheapest business

3 Finney, B R, *New Guinea Entrepreneurs – Indigenous Cash Cropping, Capital Formation and Investment in the New Guinea Highlands* (New Guinea Research Bulletin No 27, 1969, The Australian National University).

4 This Act was repealed and replaced by the Companies Act 1997. The current Act has no equivalent provision.

5 Fitzpatrick, P and Southwood, J, *The Community Corporation in Papua New Guinea* (IASER seminar paper, Port Moresby, 14 October 1976), p 17.

organisation to form and run. There were no legal requirements for its formation or management. However, carrying on business as a partnership exposed the members to unlimited liability. In any case, many money-pooling groups had more than 20 members, so they could not legally form partnerships.

Co-operative societies were once upon time regarded as the key factor for the economic development of the indigenes. The Australian colonial administration introduced the co-operative movement in Papua New Guinea shortly after the Second World War, specifically to promote the indigenes' business organisations. Although several societies were registered, and for almost two decades the movement enjoyed some prosperity in the colony, by the early 1970s it was on the decline. A committee of inquiry set up by the administration to investigate the affairs of the co-operative movement identified several causes of its failure and recommended some remedies. In spite of the committee's expressed optimism about the future role of co-operatives in developing and promoting the ordinary Papua New Guineans' business activities, the administration thought otherwise. It was convinced after the inquiry that the cooperative movement was a spent force and unlikely to achieve these objectives.[6]

Incorporation of a company under the Companies Act was for various reasons considered inappropriate for indigenous people's business organisations.[7] The procedure for incorporation of a company was relatively expensive, which made it feasible only for large and potentially more successful business. For the ordinary people the pre-incorporation expenses were bound to consume the little capital they had for starting their business. Secondly, management of a company was complicated by excessive formalities and regulations under the 400-odd sections of the Companies Act and the common law requirements. Without skilled management, accountants and constant legal advice (services which were scarce and very expensive), it was impossible for the ordinary people to comply with, let alone comprehend, the requirements of company law. A proposal to amend the Companies Act to remove some of the complex provisions was rejected by the government because it did not provide a total solution to the problem of devising a suitable business organisation for the indigenous entrepreneurs. Besides, the government feared that tinkering with the Companies Act could lead to many administrative problems for the office of the Registrar of Companies.[8]

6 See Law of Co-operatives, Ch 16.

7 For a detailed discussion of the background to the business groups, see Goldring, J, *Business and the Law in PNG* (1974) 2 MLJ 224; Nash, G, *The Territory's Legal Structure and Indigenous Business Enterprise – the Need for Change* (unpublished, Waigani Seminar, 1969). For opposing view, see Healey, F, *Companies in P and NG – The Legal Framework* (unpublished, UPNG Waigani Seminars, 1969).

8 Subsequently, the Companies Act was amended to make provision for the exemption of companies composed of local persons from some of the sections of the Act, see ss 368–372.

In the event, the government decided that the best solution was to create a new type of business organisation, designed specifically to accommodate ordinary Papua New Guineans and their lifestyle. The outcome was the Business Groups Incorporation Act. Part of the aim of this Act was to supplement the Land Groups Act,[9] which made provision for the incorporation of customary groups for purposes of owning and dealing with customary land. Thus, instead of the land groups just owning and working on their land, they could, in addition, incorporate their land group under the Business Groups Incorporation Act and carry on business together as a group.

The Business Groups Incorporation Act

The Act was a compromise between the complex provisions of the Companies Act (Ch 146), the over-regulated co-operative societies and the informal money-pooling business groups. Section 1 of the Act declares that the purposes of the Act are to provide:

(a) greater participation by local people in the national economy by their establishing of group business and other economic enterprise;
(b) for the use of sound principles in the management of business;
(c) some formal structure of business groups for the basic protection of the members of business groups and persons dealing with those groups;
(d) for the use of simple rules for the regulation and control of business groups; and
(e) for the better and more effective settlement of certain disputes.

The Act aims to achieve these objectives by incorporating customary and similar groups and conferring upon them power to carry on business and auxiliary functions and secondly, by allowing a wide scope for self-regulation and settlement of the groups' disputes without recourse to the ordinary courts.

The Act provides simple machinery for incorporation of business groups. A minimum of three persons, being members of the proposed management committee of the business group, may apply in writing or verbally to a Deputy Registrar for incorporation of the group.[10] In practice, an official form must be completed by all applicants (in the case of oral applications the form has to be filled in by the Deputy Registrar) detailing certain information required under the Act. Two other forms completed by the relevant

9 Chapter 147.
10 Section 11.

Business Development Officer (BDB) and the group's proposed dispute-settlement authority must accompany the application. The contents of these forms are outlined below.

Qualification for incorporation

A business group is not registrable under the Business Groups Incorporation Act, unless it is a "customary group". There is no express definition of a customary group in the Act. The omission was deliberate to allow some degree of flexibility in the interpretation of a customary group. Thus, a customary group may consist of a family, clan (or possibly a combination of families or clans) or tribe as long as the group is bound by the same custom. Section 11(3) of the Act specifically precludes the Registrar from rejecting applications merely because the group comprises part only of a customary group, or that the group consists of members or part of a landowners' group. Nor could the Registrar decline to register a group simply on the ground that it includes persons who are not members of the primary group, provided that he or she is satisfied that those persons regard themselves, and the others in the group regard them, as bound by the relevant custom of the primary group. For example, customary groups usually regard outsiders who marry within their group as part of the group by virtue of marriage.

The Act prohibits the Registrar to incorporate a group in certain circumstances. First, under s 11(4) the Registrar must not incorporate a group if he or she is satisfied that its characteristics are so "temporary, evanescent or doubtful" that the group has no corporate nature. Secondly, under s 11(6), except with the Minister's consent, the Registrar must not incorporate a group by a name which, in the Minister's opinion, is undesirable or which the Minister has directed the Registrar not to accept. Undesirable names include names that are obscene, offensive, deceptive of the group's character or business, or similar to already existing names.

Under s 11(5) the Registrar "may" refuse to incorporate a group if he or she is satisfied that the group is not a customary group or has no real connection with a particular customary group, or that it comprises of persons who are not members of the customary group. Although the provision appears to give the Registrar discretion to incorporate a group that may not necessarily satisfy these requirements, in practice it seems that the Registrar does not exercise this power. For instance, if it appears to the Registrar that a group's constitution has some scope for membership of persons outside the customary group (except as indicated above) invariably the Registrar will decline to incorporate the group. The main reason for this is the fear that non-traditional members of a group might not totally accept the group's customary law, which might later cause friction within the group.

The Registrar may also refuse to incorporate a customary group where he or she is of the opinion that some other form of incorporation or organisation under some other law would be more appropriate and effective.[11] For example, the Registrar may advise a group whose objectives are essentially social to incorporate itself under the Associations Incorporation Act (Ch 142). In other cases, the Registrar may feel that because of the nature of a group's intended objects and the level of sophistication of the members, incorporation under the Companies Act might be a better proposition than under the Business Groups Incorporation Act.[12]

Constitution of the group

The application for incorporation must include the group's proposed constitution. Section 14 of the Business Groups Incorporation Act, prescribes the minimum content of the constitution. The information includes the group's name; qualification for membership; composition and manner of appointment of the management committee; quorum for committee meetings, which must not be less than three members; manner in which the group's acts are evidenced; customary law applicable to the group; and its proposed dispute-settlement authority. The constitution may also include any other matters that the group, with the approval of the Registrar, desires to include. Usually, the applicants simply write their proposed constitution in the application form. Upon incorporation, the information is transcribed in the certificate of incorporation as the group's constitution.[13] Some groups have bound constitutions (sometimes specially prepared by lawyers), but it is not necessary. What matters is certification by the Registrar of the content of the group's constitution.[14]

Dispute-settlement authority

Before incorporating a group, the Registrar may demand and consider comments from the group's proposed dispute-settlement authority,[15] and any other information that he or she thinks relevant.[16] For this purpose, official forms completed by the proposed dispute-settlement authority and the relevant Business Development Officer normally accompany applications for incorporation. The proposed dispute-settlement authority must declare in the form its ability and willingness to adjudicate in the group's disputes and its assessment of the adequacy or otherwise of the group's proposed constitution and the arrangements for settling disputes. In addition, it must affirm whether

11 Section 11(5)(d).

12 Information gathered though discussion with the Deputy Registrar of Business Groups.

13 See ss 11(9) and 16(1).

14 Section 16(2)(b).

15 A "dispute-settlement" authority could be a village court; or a "customary authority" having customary jurisdiction over the members of the group, see s 2(2).

16 See s 12.

or not the applicants constitute a customary group which complies with the requirements of s 11(3), (4) and (5) of the Business Groups Incorporation Act. The Business Development Officer must comment on whether incorporation of the group is the most appropriate form of organisation for the subject group. He or she advises the Registrar of any accounts records that the group should be required to keep, the nature of the group's proposed business and any other matter that he or she thinks should be brought to the Registrar's attention.

Effect of incorporation

Based on the information in the application and the foregoing forms, the Registrar decides whether to incorporate a group. If the Registrar declines to incorporate any group, he or she must give the applicants a written statement of the reasons for the decision.[17] On the other hand, if the Registrar is satisfied that the applicants have complied with all the requirements of the Business Groups Incorporation Act, and subject to payment of the prescribed fee (presently K100),[18] he or she "may" incorporate the business group by issuing to it a certificate of incorporation.[19] Thereafter, the business group's name must end with the words "Business (Inc.)" or "Business Group (Inc.)".[20]

An incorporated business group enjoys most of the usual attributes of a body corporate. It has perpetual succession and may sue and be sued in its corporate name.[21] Subject to its constitution and the relevant customary law, the group may exercise any powers that may lawfully be exercised by any other body corporate.[22] It may acquire and dispose of land (except customary land), invest its money in or on any security, and borrow money on security over its real or personal property. However, the Act precludes a business group to borrow money from the public or to invite the public to deposit money with the group or lend it money.[23]

Membership rights and liabilities

Membership of a business group is determined as specified by the group's constitution. Section 14(1)(b) of the Business Groups Incorporation Act, provides that the constitution of a business group incorporation must set

17 Section 11(8).
18 See Business Groups Incorporation Regulations, reg 6, Schedule 2.
19 Section 11(1). The use of the permissive word "may" in s 11(1) suggests that the Registrar has the power to refuse to register a group even if it satisfies the requirements of the Act. Compare that provision with s 14 of the Companies Act 1997, which provides that after the Registrar receives a properly completed application for registration of a company, the Registrar "shall" incorporate the company.
20 Section 11(7).
21 Section 17(1).
22 Sections 17(1)(d) and 18(1).
23 Section 18(3).

out the qualifications and disqualifications, if any, for membership of the group. However, as we have seen, this is subject to the statutory requirement that membership of a business group is open only to people from the same "customary group" as defined in the Act.[24]

Generally, members' rights and liabilities are matters for the group to decide in accordance with their customary practice. With reference to members' liabilities, s 34(1) of the Business Groups Incorporation Act adds that, subject to the group's constitution or any relevant customary law, liability of members on the winding up of the group is limited to the amount of each member's interest in the property of the group, plus any money owed to the group. Essentially, this means that members' liability is limited to their investment in the business group incorporation. However, s 34(2) of the Act specifically states that, notwithstanding the group's constitution and customary law, a member of the management committee is liable beyond his or her liability as a member of the group, for any debts of the group incurred during the period of his or her membership of the committee. Evidently, the object of making the committee members personally liable for the group's debts is to generate from them maximum performance. It is submitted that a blanket application of the provision could lead to unfair results, especially, in those situations where the committee incurred the debts in good faith pursuant to the group's business and the committee's mandate. Perhaps, a fairer approach would be to give the Registrar or the court the power to determine whether in the circumstances of each case the committee members or any of them should be personally accountable for the group's debts and the extent of the liability. There may even be circumstances where members or some of them ought to be accountable for the group's debts beyond their ordinary liability.

Management of a business group

Unlike ordinary companies, which are managed by a board of directors,[25] business groups have no board of directors. Instead, the management of business groups is vested with management committees consisting of at least three members. Subject to the business group's constitution, the nature and extent of the committees' powers is determined in accordance with the members' customary law or practice. However, the Business Groups Incorporation Act imposes certain obligations upon the management committee. We discuss these obligations below.

Duties of the management committee

Section 23 of the Business Groups Act imposes a duty on the committee every 12 months to prepare in a format approved by the Registrar, a statement of

24 Section 11(5).
25 Section 109, Companies Act 1997.

the group's assets and liabilities and to lodge the same with the Registrar within three months of the expiration of the period. By s 24, the Registrar has the power to order a committee of business group incorporation to keep and maintain the accounts and records of some or all of the group's affairs in a manner the Registrar specifies. For example, the Registrar usually require business groups, especially those engaged in buying and selling of goods, to keep a main cashbook and petty cashbook. Section 21 requires the committee to open and maintain a bank account for the group. The committee must pay into that account all moneys it receives in connection with the group's business; and it must make payments on behalf of the group out of that account. Section 22 requires the management committee to give receipts for all capital monies collected by or on behalf of the group. The object of these requirements is to ensure that the committee of business group incorporation conforms to the minimum requirements for a sound management of the group's affairs and to protect the members by ensuring that the group's money and other assets are properly accounted for. Failure to comply in some instances renders each of the members of the committee liable to a criminal offence,[26] and may be a ground for winding up the group.[27]

Distribution of dividends

Section 26(2) of the Business Groups Incorporation Act prohibits the committee to give out to the members of the business group "distributable profits" (defined as the sum of the group's assets less after tax liabilities)[28] until after the committee has lodged with the Registrar the group's statement of assets and liabilities during the period to which the statement relates. Section 26(3) also prohibits the committee to distribute any profits of the business group to a person whether a member or not of the group who is not a native of PNG, as defined by the pre-Independence Ordinances Interpretation Act 1949–1973.[29] Contravention of this provision is an offence punishable by a fine not exceeding K2,000.[30] Receipt of dividends by a non-native calls for a more hefty penalty of up to K5,000 or imprisonment for a term of up to two years. In addition, the court may order such a person to refund the money to the group.[31] Evidently, the object of the provision was to deter

26 Section 21 imposes a fine of up to K2,000 for failure to open or use the group's bank account as stated in the section. Section 49 imposes a similar penalty for contravention of other provisions of the Act, see s 49.

27 Section 28(2)(f)

28 Section 26(1).

29 The term 'native" means an "automatic citizen" of PNG: see s 98 of the Interpretation Act (Ch 2). An "automatic citizen" is a person who is a citizen by virtue of s 65 (automatic citizen on Independence Day) or s 66 (citizen by descent) of the Constitution: see s 3(1) of the Interpretation Act.

30 Section 26(3).

31 Section 26(4) and (5).

non-natives from using business group incorporation as fronts for their economic pursuits.

Within the above limits, the committee has the power to distribute profits in such a manner as it sees fit.[32] Some business groups' constitutions provide for distribution of profits to the members in accordance with the members' capital investment. However, such provisions are rare. Most constitutions are silent or simply state that the committee shall distribute profits as it determines subject to customary law.

Settlement of disputes

One of the unique features of the Business Groups Incorporation Act is the provision for resolving internal disputes. It has been seen that all business groups seeking incorporation must nominate a dispute-settlement authority.[33] Such authority may constitute of a person or persons specified by name, office or position, or determined in the manner prescribed in the group's constitution.[34] The Act also empowers members, who are parties to a particular dispute, to appoint (with the approval of the management committee) an *ad hoc* dispute-settlement authority to deal with their disputes.[35]

The power of a dispute-settlement authority is limited to resolving disputes between the business group and a member or between members concerning the property or affairs of the group. Section 43 of the Act provides that in exercising its power, the dispute-settlement authority is not bound by any rules of law or evidence. Nevertheless, it must exercise its discretion fairly and in accordance with the Act, the group's constitution and the relevant customary law. Regular courts have limited jurisdiction over the business groups' internal disputes. Section 42(1) states that the courts have no power to deal with business groups' internal disputes unless all the parties to the dispute agree to refer the matter to a court, or the group's constitution so provides, or the dispute-settlement authority feels that only a court is best placed to resolve the matter.[36] The dispute-settlement authority determines whether conditions exist to refer a dispute to a court. Section 42(2) provides that the dispute-settlement's decision in this regard is final and not subject to challenge in any court.[37]

Where a dispute-settlement authority decides to refer a dispute to a court, it must do so in a prescribed form and to a court, which ordinarily has

32 Section 26(2).
33 Section 40.
34 Section 40(2).
35 Section 40(3).
36 For discussion, see Mcllwraith, D, *Business Development in Papua New Guinea* (unpublished MLitt Thesis, University of New England, 1983), pp 59–62.
37 Nevertheless, an aggrieved party may seek a judicial review of the dispute-settlement authority: see s 44(2).

jurisdiction over the matter.[38] In all court proceedings, the dispute-settlement authority is entitled to act (and must so act if instructed by a court or by an interested party) as assessor on matters of customary law and matters of common knowledge within the group.[39]

There is no right of appeal against the decision of the dispute-settlement authority or that of the court. However, an aggrieved party may demand for a review or reopening of the decision of a dispute-settlement authority or that of a court (other than the National Court). In the event of a review, in the first instance it must be by way of a fresh hearing by an *ad hoc* dispute-settlement authority nominated by the parties to the dispute with the approval of the group.[40] If any of the parties is dissatisfied with the review, he or she may demand a further review of the decision by a village court. Such court shall consist of at least three village court magistrates (in their absence a customary authority) having jurisdiction over members of the group, the dispute-settlement authority which originally dealt with the matter, and such other customary authorities having jurisdiction over the members of the group as the village court think appropriate.[41] If there is no relevant village court, its jurisdiction in this regard shall be exercised by a customary authority having jurisdiction over members of the business group nominated by the Registrar after due inquiry and consultation with members of the group concerned.[42]

The provision for settling internal disputes is designed to ensure that as much as possible disputes-settlement is kept at the village level. Its advantage is that not only does it save on costs of resolving disputes, but also, more importantly ensures that disputes are settled in a manner and atmosphere that is congenial to the members' way of life. Hence, the decisions are more likely to be accepted by all concerned than decisions of the regular courts, which are foreign to them.

Winding up

The Business Groups Incorporation Act stipulates three methods for the winding up of a business group by the Registrar. First, the Registrar may wind up a business group at the request of the group or its creditor or creditors.[43] Before winding up a group, the Registrar may demand that the group or the petitioning creditor(s), respectively, submit a certified statement of the group's financial affairs.[44] Secondly, the Registrar may wind up a group on

38 Section 42(3)(b).
39 Section 42(3)(c).
40 Section 44(2) and (3).
41 Section 44(4).
42 Section 44(5).
43 Section 28(1)(a) and (b).
44 Section 28(3).

the basis of a report of the dispute-settlement authority (or a village court with competent jurisdiction or any other court dealing with the group's disputes under the Act) to the effect that the affairs of the group are such that its continued incorporation is undesirable.[45] The Registrar must give a fair hearing to all interested parties before he or she makes the order to wind up the group.[46] Thirdly, the Registrar acting on his or her own motion may wind up a business group on any of the following grounds:[47]

- cessation of function by the group;
- change in the group's composition so that it no longer satisfies the requirements of the Act, stipulated in s 11;
- inability and unlikelihood within a reasonable time to pay debts;
- failure to keep records of accounts as required under s 38;
- subject to customary law, if the group conducts its business in a manner that is unfair and oppressive to any member of the group; and
- failure to submit to the Registrar for two consecutive years the group's statement of assets and liabilities.

There is a provision for appeal to the Minister by any interested person aggrieved by the Registrar's decision to wind up a business group or refusal to do so.[48] In addition, the National Court may in certain circumstances order the Registrar to wind up a business group. Section 29(1) provides that a creditor of a business group may petition the National Court for the winding up of a business group where the Registrar refuses to make the order and the Minister dismisses an appeal against the Registrar's decision. Alternatively, a creditor may petition the National Court directly for an order to wind up a business group, without prior reference to the Registrar, on any of the grounds stipulated in s 28(2).[49]

The commonest formal ground for winding up business groups is the failure to submit to the Registrar the group's statement of assets and liabilities for two consecutive years (though normally it takes at least four years before the Registrar commences steps to wind up the defaulting group). In practice, however, most groups simply stop functioning without any formal winding up.

The future of business groups

The object of the Business Groups Incorporation Act was to provide a simple legal framework by which ordinary people with limited education and knowledge of modern business could conduct business for their

45 Section 28(1)(c).
46 Section 28(6)(a).
47 Section 28(2).
48 Section 45.
49 See s 29(2). For other rules relating to winding up a business group: see ss 30–36.

socio-economic development and participation in the economic development of their country. Since its enactment, hundreds of groups have been incorporated,[50] though relatively a small number of them are actually functioning. Many business groups wind up soon after their incorporation. Usually, this is due to the failure of the business to pick up early as anticipated, leading to disillusionment among the members. Others fail because the members had no serious intention to carry on business as a group in the first place. Their motive for incorporation might have been for a specific purpose; for example, to obtain financial assistance from non-government organisations, many of which are not normally extended to individuals or unincorporated bodies. In addition, it is common for a group to incorporate for the sole purpose of receiving money from a local politician who insists on incorporation as a condition for his or her generosity. Such groups disband once they receive the money.

In late 1980s, the then Deputy Registrar of Business Groups Incorporation, informed the authors that in spite of the relatively small number of groups that survived after incorporation, the Act had a measure of success. He said that several business groups, especially in Enga Province, were performing quite well. The number of applications for incorporation of business groups was on the rise throughout the country, which indicated the increasing popularity of the business groups as a tool for the promotion of ordinary Papua New Guineans' business activities. However, our recent discussion with a number of government officers in the Department of Trade and Industry, paint a very different picture. Applications for incorporation of new groups are drastically down, as are the number of business groups that are still active, though no one knows the exact number.

The future of business groups, according to one official, is bleak. Why is that so? Part of the blame for the decline of business group incorporation is the government's lack of commitment and failure to assist the groups. Business groups were never intended to stand on their own without substantial government help, especially, in providing advice in the proper business management practices. Due to inadequate funds, there are not enough properly trained business development officers, especially in the provinces, to advise business groups. Left on their own without government assistance and/or encouragement, many business groups gradually cease to operate. The recent revitalisation of co-operative societies, if successful, will further contribute to the decline of business groups. In some sense, this would be an ironic turnabout, since, as we saw earlier, the concept of business group incorporation was introduced to replace the co-operative movement. The decline of business group incorporation has also come about because many enterprising Papua New Guineans are moving away from family- or clan-based business enterprise to sole entrepreneurship under the Companies Act.

50 Unofficial estimate is at least 10,000 groups.

The trend is facilitated by the Companies Act 1997, which makes it easier for individuals to incorporate themselves and run their business as a limited liability company.

According to some government officials, the concept of business group incorporation has outlived its usefulness and they do not envisage its role in the socio-economic development of ordinary Papua New Guineans and the country as a whole. Some see the revitalised co-operative movement as the way forward in this regard. With respect, in our view, getting rid of business group incorporation would be too drastic a decision, considering that the concept is well established in the country. The revitalisation of co-operative societies may well lead to the further decline in and need for business group incorporation. However, there is no guarantee that the revitalisation programme will succeed. Moreover, business group incorporation provides an alternative business organisation to ordinary people, especially in rural areas, who wish to conduct business with their family or clan members in accordance with their customary practice. The main attribute of business group incorporation is that the members generally manage their business organisation in accordance with their customary law. It is a form of business organisation that is designed to suit PNG's unique social circumstances. Moreover, business group incorporation act as training ground for those at grassroots level who might later wish to conduct business as sole entrepreneurs or in association with other business people outside their local area.

Accordingly, in our view, instead of allowing business groups to die a natural death, their attributes should be promoted side by side with the advantages of conducting business through the revitalised co-operative movement or sole entrepreneurship under the Companies Act. Let the people decide the best form of business organisation for their particular circumstances. However, business groups, like co-operative societies, need to be assisted by the government to establish themselves and function properly. We are not suggesting that the government should make day-to-day investment decisions for them or hand them money; rather it should advise them on sound management practices. For this purpose there is a need for more and better trained business development officers to teach and advise the management committees the best management practices. General education of the management committees in the basics of business management and book-keeping is imperative. The Registry, which is responsible for business groups, should have adequate staff to process applications for incorporation and to police all business groups to ensure that they comply with the minimum statutory requirements, especially, with regard to the keeping of financial records and submitting annual statements of assets and liabilities. The importance of keeping proper records cannot be emphasized enough. For instance, as we have seen, business groups are prohibited from distributing dividends to members until after the management committee lodges with the Registrar a statement of the group's assets and liabilities. However, in practice, few business groups comply with this requirement. Because of shortage of investigating officers, it may take the Registrar several years before catching up with the defaulting business groups by which time in most cases it is too late to prevent the group (if it is still operative) from distributing non-existent profits.

Finally, we propose a review of the business groups incorporation, to bring it in line with modern circumstances. One particular aspect of the Act that may need reconsideration is the provision that members of a business group must be from the same customary group.[51] There is nothing wrong with this; if that is what the members want. However, in our view, where a particular business group wishes to adopt an open-door policy the law should not stand in its way. Whilst restricting membership of a business group to persons from the same customary group has the potential to eliminate areas of possible misunderstanding and factional fights, it is submitted that a strict application of the rule may be counter-productive and an unnecessary deprivation of many ordinary people of the benefits of incorporating their business groups under the Business Groups Incorporation Act. Thus, for example, settlers in Morata who happen to come from different customary groups cannot incorporate their business group under the Act. If they wish to incorporate their business they have either to form a limited liability company or a co-operative society neither of which may be suitable for their business. It is submitted that for the future development of the business group incorporation, the restriction of groups to customary membership needs to be relaxed. It should not be assumed in all cases that ordinary Papua New Guineans from different customary groups are incapable of carrying on business together as a group. The Registrar should exercise his or her discretion to incorporate business groups even if the members are not from the same customary group, provided that the Registrar is reasonably satisfied that the group is viable and can function as a business group.

51 Section 11.

Index

absolute liability 389–91
abuse of process 601
acceptance of delivery of goods 60–3, 72–3
accountability, agents' duty of 108
acquiescence in implied authority 420
actual authority 410–11; *see also* implied actual authority
"affairs of a company" 349–51
agency cheques 151–2
agency law 87–119, 392, 436
agency relationships 104–5
  formation of 93–4
  termination of 116–19
agents
  authority of 92–101
  breaches of faith by 108–9
  characteristics of 88–92
  dismissal of 109
  duties of 105–6, 115
  for infants 132
  liability of 113
  remuneration of 109–10
  rights of 109, 115–16
  sale of goods by 45–6
alienated land 189
Aliens (Property) Act 272
allotment of shares 482–3
alternate directors 278
Amet CJ 298, 333
Andrew AJ 532
apparent authority *see* ostensible authority
articles of association 219, 407, 496
"ascertained goods" 34–9
Asprey JA 400
Associations Incorporation Act 193–5, 710
Atkin LJ 4, 141, 144, 164, 389
Atkinson J 251
Attorney-General 583
attornment 56
attribution of fault 387–91
auction sales 37
Audit Act 270
audit committees 293
Australia 4, 123, 130, 142, 146–9, 169, 240–1, 318, 320, 322, 332, 336, 358, 367–8, 409, 416, 443–4, 560, 596, 616, 620; *see also* High Court of Australia
"available market" criterion 68–70, 75–8

Bacon CJ 656
bailment 10–11, 43, 50, 65, 71, 89–90, 108, 140
bank customers 128–33, 140–59
  banks' duties to 144–7
  changes in contractual terms applying to 148–9
  duties owed to bankers by 147–8
  termination of relationship by 148–9
bank drafts 151
Bank of Papua New Guinea 124–5, 582
bank references 145–6
Bankes LJ 130, 145
bankruptcy 63, 137, 180, 283
banks
  functions of 123–4
  liabilities of 159–69
Banks and Financial Institutions Act 582–3

Barton J 639
Barwick CJ 146
Beck, Andrew 218–19, 368, 465, 485, 512–13, 587, 590, 596–9, 601, 625
beneficial ownership of property 183
bills of exchange 137–9, 149–50
bills of lading 41, 139–40
bills of sale 520
Blanchard J 217
blank cheques 152–3
boards of directors
  of companies 184, 285–9, 294–7, 356–7, 392, 399, 410–13
  of co-operatives 701–2
bona fide actions of directors 300, 310–11, 318
book value 521–2
Borrowdale, A. 218–19, 368, 465, 485, 512–13, 625
borrowing by companies 498
Bowen LJ 105, 140
breach of contract 66, 74, 81, 163–4, 259
breach of duty (by directors) 302–7, 342, 370–1, 340, 614–15
breach of faith 108–9
breach of warranty 71, 74–5
Bredmeyer J 419–20
Brett LJ 119, 153, 638
bribery 306
Brown J 548
Buckley LJ 47–8
Burt CJ 6
business, definition of 637–8
business development officers 710–11
business groups, incorporated
  future prospects for 716–19
  management of 712–13
  membership rights and liabilities 711–12
  winding-up of 715–17
Business Groups Incorporation Act 185–7, 202, 705–19
"business judgement" rule for company directors 333–4
Business Names Act 179–80, 647
business structure, types of 174
buyers of goods
  duties of 62–3
  remedies for breach of contract available to 70–80
buybacks and buyouts *see* shares
Cairns LJ 110–11, 653–4
Canada 464
Cannings J 267, 431–3
capacity of companies 226–8, 231–2, 394–9
capital of companies 474
carriers of goods 57–8
caveat emptor 18, 25
CCH Reporter 427
certificates of incorporation 212
chairpersons of company boards 278–9, 413
Chan, Sir Julius 694
charges on goods being sold 32
charges over company assets 502–22
  assignment and variation of 526
  categories of 519–22
  definition of 507–8
  priority of 524–6
  registration of 507–12
  release of property from 526
  time for 512–14
  see also fixed charges; floating charges
cheques 137–59
  crossing of 157–8, 162
  endorsement of 152–6
  holders of 154
  negotiation of 158–9
  presentation of 156–7
  types 151–2
  validity, regularity and liability 142–4, 155–6
Chesterman J 349
chief executive officers (CEOs) 279, 411–13, 416
  of regulatory statutory authorities 287–8
Chorley, Lord 128, 139
circular resolutions of company boards 286
citizenship of companies 233
civil wrongs, corporate liability for 380–4
Claims By and Against the State Act 264–70
Clarke JA 461–2
"closely held" companies 205–6
Cockburn CJ 135–6
cohabitation 105
commercial bills 138
commercial transactions, protection of 43, 46, 53

commission payable to agents 109–10, 117
common law
  on agency 46, 87–8, 91, 105–6, 112, 118
  on banking 128–36
  on companies 240–3, 262, 298, 305, 310–17, 372, 390, 545
  on partnerships 635–6
  on sale of goods 3, 5, 8, 11, 43, 45, 59, 61, 71, 78, 81
common seal of a company, use of 234, 392, 399–402, 407–8, 438–9, 458
companies 197–206
  limited by guarantee 476
  structure of 227–36
  types 203–6
  see also capacity; constitutions; incorporation; overseas companies; registration; separate legal entities
Companies (Co-operative Companies) Act 692
Companies Act (1997) 181–2, 191–4, 198–225, 273–5, 288–91, 296, 310, 316, 321, 330, 341, 380, 393, 396–7, 402, 406–7, 448, 458, 460, 485, 522, 528–9, 534–6, 562–3, 567, 571–5, 618, 707, 718
  directors' compliance with 322–5, 567–8
  mandatory provisions of 222
  Part XIII 517
  provisions for lifting of corporate "veil" 243, 261–4
  Schedule 3 293
  Schedule 4 285–6
  Schedule 8 605, 609–10
  Schedule 15 524–5
  Section 2 484, 500–2, 507–8
  Section 3 552
  Section 11 210, 568
  Section 12 210
  Section 16 229, 239, 476, 647, 706
  Section 17 226, 228, 397, 498
  Section 18 397
  Section 19 397–8, 406, 410, 449, 452–67
  Section 20 466
  Section 22 214, 519
  Section 32 405
  Section 37 475–80
  Section 38 408, 477
  Section 41 484
  Section 42 481–3
  Section 43 311, 480–1
  Section 45 483
  Section 47 482
  Section 49 483
  Section 50 486, 490
  Section 51 488
  Section 54 489
  Section 57 492, 497
  Section 59 493
  Section 60 492
  Section 63 495
  Section 75 234, 399–401
  Section 78 580
  Section 79 235
  Section 91 496
  Section 107 275–80
  Section 108 228
  Section 109 297, 399, 411
  Section 111 292–4
  Section 112 325–6
  Section 114 322–5
  Section 115 331–4
  Section 116 294
  Section 118 302
  Section 119 328
  Section 123 328–9
  Section 128 228–9
  Section 129 229, 276–7, 283
  Section 134 282
  Section 138 410
  Section 142 362–5
  Section 143 372–7
  Section 144 377
  Section 145 376
  Section 146 376–7
  Section 147 342–3, 370–1
  Section 148 371
  Section 149 342, 370
  Section 151 313
  Section 152 223, 263, 282–3, 347–54, 358, 361, 370–4
  Section 154 473
  Section 155 399–401, 458
  Section 157 224, 262
  Section 159 225
  Section 160 262
  Section 164 360
  Section 169 418

Companies Act (1997) (*continued*)
Section 219 366
Section 220 367
Section 221 518
Section 222 511–12, 517–18, 522–3
Section 224 506, 526
Section 225 507, 513, 515
Section 226 501, 511
Section 228 513–14
Section 229 514
Section 231 524
Section 238 616
Section 254 530
Section 256 537
Section 257 530, 538
Section 264 541–3
Section 268 543–4
Section 269 544–5
Section 279 559
Section 280 561
Section 281 556–8
Section 282 558
Section 283 558
Section 286 559
Section 290 581
Section 291 564–5, 579–85, 600
Section 298 604–6
Section 299 575
Section 303 608
Section 310 609
Section 311 610–11
Section 328 576–7
Section 329 577
Section 330 566
Section 333 213
Section 334 614
Section 335 586–7
Section 337 588, 591
Section 338 591–4, 599–600
Section 339 600
Section 340 618–19
Section 342 624–5
Section 343 628
Section 344 628
Section 347 526–7, 622
Section 348 322, 334–9, 615–17
Section 349 617
Section 360 560
Section 361 608
Section 373 693
Section 377 693
Section 382 207–8
Section 385 208
Section 393 209
Section 396 516
Section 412 261
Section 421 258–9
Section 426 283–4
Section 428 284
Section 439 213
Section 453 502
company names 213–19
company property, ownership of 232–3
company secretaries 289–92, 418–20
compensation for oppressive treatment 359
compensatory damages 340
compromise between companies and their creditors 602
conditions in contracts 14–15
conflict rule for company directors 303–5
conflicts of interest 107, 300–3, 327–8
Conrick, Brian 149
consent to possession of goods 47, 51–2
consequential losses 66
consideration, monetary 9–10, 30
Constitution of Papua New Guinea 87, 92, 240–1
Schedule 2 258
Section 41 247, 546–50, 560
Section 53 549
Section 56 233
constitutions of business groups 710–12
constitutions of companies 219–23, 226, 359–60, 369–70, 380, 394, 397, 402
alteration of 222–3
rights and obligations conferred by 221–2
short and *long* forms 221–2
constructive authority 422
constructive delivery of goods 56
constructive knowledge 460–7
constructive notice 48, 444–6, 467
contempt of court 256, 259–60
contracts
corporate liability for 392–416
effect of liquidation on 607
effect of receivership on 540–1

made directly with companies 399–410
made indirectly through companies' agents 410–16
for sale of goods 5–9, 13–54
of service 10–11
contributory negligence 168–9
control of companies, legal interest in 254–7, 380
conversion, tort of 164–5
convertible notes 501
co-operative associations 697
co-operative companies 703–4
definition of 693
co-operative movement in Papua New Guinea
demise of 692–4
future for 697
historical development of 689–91, 707
resuscitation of 694
revitalisation of 694–7
Co-operative Societies Act 694, 698–704
Co-operative Societies Unit 695–7
co-operatives 190–1, 683–704
advantages and disadvantages of 687–8
autonomy and independence of 686
co-operation between 687
definition of 683
government control of 702
management of 700–2
member participation in 685–6
membership rights and liabilities 700
nature of 683
organisation of 688–9
values and principles of 684–7, 696–8
corporate "veil" 234–5
lifting of 237–59, 265–6, 269–72, 615
corporate liability 379–473
for civil wrongs 380–4
for contracts 392–416
for crimes 384–91
"corporate opportunity" concept 305–8
corporate personality 226
corporation, types of 201–2
corporations sole 196–7
counterclaims against creditors 597–8
Court of Appeal, District of Columbia 139
Court of Appeal, English 30, 52–3, 72, 103–4, 165, 230, 259, 296, 382, 419, 545, 680
Court of Appeal, New South Wales 42–3, 320, 336
Court of Appeal, New Zealand 351–3, 372, 387, 556–7, 596, 626
court orders for sale of goods 45
Cozen-Hardy MR 645
Cranworth, Lord 93–4
creditors 499, 522, 602
contingent or *prospective* 581–2
definition of 581
meetings of 566
offsetting claims against 597–8
payment of 629–31
preferential 559–60
priority between 559
see also secured creditors
crimes, corporate liability for 384–91
Criminal Code 390–1, 706
cross-demands in liquidation 598–9
cross-shareholding 227
crossed cheques 157–8, 162
"crystallisation" of charges 504–5, 539
Cussen ACJ 406–7
Custodian for Trust Land 197
custom 14, 54, 186
customary authority 456–7; *see also* "usual" authority
customary groups 707–9, 712, 719
customary land 187–90, 233, 708
customary law 5, 185, 201, 714, 718

Dal Pont, G E 434–5
damaged goods 15
damages 66–80, 163–4, 225, 232, 340, 364–5, 529, 558, 588
assessment of 68, 80–1
for breach of warranty 74–5
mitigation of 70
for wrongful non delivery of goods 75
Davani J 286, 288
Davies, P L 392–3
Dawson J 638
de facto directors 277–80
de minimis maxim 61
deadlock in a company's affairs 572–3
Deane J 80–1
debentures 500–1, 506–8, 519

debt
  definition for purposes of solvency test 487
  disputed 595–7
  incurring of 335–8
  of partnerships 643
debt capital 498–9
deceit as a tort 115
defamation 165
defects in goods, curing of 30
deferred shares 481
Deklin, A 199–204
delay in delivery of goods 42, 59
delegation
  authority for 106–7
  by company boards 292–7, 392, 411–13
  by liquidators 575
deliverable state, goods in 37, 42, 58
delivery of goods 42, 52, 55–9
  acceptance of 60–3, 72–3
  failure of 75–6
  refusal of 67–8, 80
democratic processes 685
Denning, Lord 43, 131–2, 155–6, 167, 239, 382
deregistration of companies 632
derivative actions 232, 236, 341–5, 371–8
  leave required for 373–6
descriptions of goods being sold 16–21, 25
diligence, exercise of 106
Diplock LJ 99–101, 411, 455
directors of companies
  appointment and removal of 276–7, 281–5
  authority as individuals 416
  bringing about liquidation by acting in their own interests 573–4
  definition of 275–80, 296
  disqualification of 283–5
  duties of 273–340; of care, diligence and skill 319–20, 331–4, 489; categories of 275; codification of 297–9; on conflict of interest 300–3; fiduciary 300–4; of loyalty and good faith 299–303; owed to creditors 322, 326; owed to shareholders 321–2, 342–3; remedies for breach of 340; statutory 322–40; to use powers for proper purposes 308–10
  fettering of discretion 317–19
  powers in liquidation 604
  right to information 292
  use of company information by 328–9
  see also boards of directors
directors of co-operatives 701–2
disclaiming of onerous property 611–12
disclosure
  of information to shareholders 365–7
  of share dealings by company directors 329–31
discounts on shares 490
discretion granted to company directors 317–19
disposition of goods
  by buyers in possession 51
  by mercantile agents 46
  by sellers in possession 49–50
dispute-settlement authorities 710–11, 714–16
distributions by companies 484–91
diversion of business 354–5
dividends 474–5, 488–9
  as debt 491
  of incorporated business groups 713–14, 718
  restriction of 355–6
  "Division 4" status 203–4, 209–10
Dixon J 24, 476, 665
Doherty J 35
Dorwick, F E 88
due care, exercise of 106
Dunedin, Lord 129
duty of care 108, 133, 146

Eldon, Lord 663
election, right of 113
emblements 8–9
employees of trading companies, authority of 420
Employment Act 175
employment contracts 540–1, 556–7, 607, 643
endorsement of cheques 152–6
"entitled persons" 369, 492, 580
equitable duties 107
equity capital 474–5, 498–9
  uncalled 519, 521
equity principles 3–4, 88, 107, 241, 651

essential terms in contracts 59–63
estate agents 110
estoppel 44–5, 93, 99, 108, 162, 410, 422, 435, 457, 651–2
examination of goods being bought 25–7, 73–4
exclusion causes 33
execution (of debt) returned unsatisfied 602
executive directors 278, 416
exempt companies 206, 209–10
express authority 95, 410–11
express terms in contracts 13
external administrators 535
Eyre CJ 134, 652

façades, companies used as 245–6, 255
failure to act, liability for 323–4, 357–8
fairness of transactions 82–4
Fairness of Transactions Act 33
fiduciary duties and relationships 90, 107–8, 224, 300–4, 656–7, 661
finance, corporate
  debentures and charges used for 500–22
  other sources of 236, 497–8
Finkelstein J 540
fitness of goods for purpose 18–24
fixed charges over company assets 236, 502–5
floating charges over company assets 236, 502–6, 519–21, 526, 559
  liquidation of 526–7
  problems with 505
  voiding of 622
FOB ('free on board') terms 41, 67
Ford, H A J 427
foreign companies *see* overseas companies
forest management agreements 190
forgery 103, 160–2, 459–60, 463–8
founders' shares 481
fraud 7, 47–8, 52, 54, 245–6, 255, 258, 302–3, 379, 381, 459, 463–8, 570–1, 679
  use of companies for purposes of 259–61
Frauds and Limitations Acts 146, 407–8
freedom of contract 33
Fridman, G H L 412
Frost CJ 75–8, 82, 389–91, 440–2, 471
Full Court of Victoria 534
"future goods" 34, 36, 39–40

Gavara-Nanu J 429–30, 470–1
"general property" 8, 10
German New Guinea, former territory of 197
gifts 9–10
Gleeson CJ 337
Goddard, Lord 675
good faith 48–53, 107, 167, 325–6, 619, 625, 712
goods
  classification of 34–5
  definition of 8–9
Goods Act 3–5, 9–16, 23, 33, 64, 71, 111
  Section 1 8
  Section 3 8
  Section 6 5–7
  Section 11 46, 62
  Section 12 71–2
  Section 13 29, 32
  Section 14 18
  Section 15 18, 22
  Section 17 34, 39
  Section 18 35–6, 39, 58
  Section 20 41–3
  Section 21 43–4
  Section 22 49
  Section 24 54
  Section 25 49–53
  Section 27 55
  Section 28 56
  Section 29 41, 56, 58
  Section 30 60
  Section 32 57–8
  Section 34 73
  Section 35 72–3
  Section 37 63, 67–8
  Section 43 65
  Section 48 65
  Section 49 66–7
  Section 50 67–9, 75
  Section 51 77
  Section 52 81
  Section 53 74
  Section 54 78
  Section 58 5, 45

goodwill of a business 180–1, 217, 521, 644, 676–8
"governing directors" 279
Gowans J 325
Grantham, R B 398–9
Greene, Lord 299–300
Greig J 584–5
guarantors of a company's obligations 409–10
Guise, Sir John 694

Haldane, Viscount 382
Halsbury, Lord 238–9, 440
"harsh or oppressive" conduct 247, 546, 560
Herschell, Lord 127, 136–7, 635
hidden defects in goods 28–9
High Court of Australia 52, 81, 110, 127–30, 147–9, 168, 241, 256, 415–16, 435, 443, 581–2, 649, 652, 656–7, 661
High Court of New Zealand 375
Hill J 638
Hinchcliffe J 547–8
hire purchase 11–12, 522
Hodges J 650
holding companies 238, 250–1, 255, 262, 319, 617
"holding out" doctrine 646, 651–2
Holt CJ 135
House of Lords 4, 10, 17, 21, 23, 59, 102, 141, 230–3, 256, 272, 306–7, 319, 343, 570

implied actual authority 409–22, 433, 442, 458
implied authority for agents 95–7
implied conditions in contracts 18–29
implied terms in contracts 13–16, 140
implied undertakings on title to goods being sold 29–31
implied warranties 31–2
Income Tax Act 270–1
incorporated associations 193–5
incorporated business groups 185–7, 705–19
incorporated land groups 187–90
incorporation of companies 173, 184, 210–13, 228, 237
  refusal of 186
incumbrances on goods being sold 32
indemnities 117, 554, 557–8, 660
Independent Consumer and Competition Commission Act 217, 387–8
independent contractors 89–90
"indoor management" rule 436–68
Industrial Safety, Health and Welfare Act 175
infants 91, 132
Informal Sector Development and Control Act 176–9, 182, 187
injunctions 226–7, 259, 362–5
innominate contract terms 15
inside information 370
insolvency 56, 64–5, 180, 238, 326, 337, 416, 528, 562, 566
  commercial 585–6
  liquidation on grounds of 585–6
  of partners 669
Insolvency Act 536
insolvent trading 262, 334–9, 370
  directors' responsibility for 615–17
  parent companies' liability for 617–19
inspection of company records by shareholders 367–8
instalment delivery of goods 61
Instruments Act 118
insurance agents 89, 114
insurance brokers 114
interest payments 79, 644, 660–1
interim injunctions 364–5
International Co-operative Alliance 683–5, 689
International Labour Organization 697
Interpretation Act 384–5, 591–2
investment advice 147
Investment Promotion Act 208, 271
Isaacs J 127, 314

James LJ 640–1, 664
Jervis CJ 437–8
joint liability 653
joint ventures 182–3, 319, 645
Judicial Proceedings (Interest on Debts and Damages) Act 79

Kandakasi J 98, 160, 227–52, 256–61, 265, 269–70, 298–302, 317, 549–50, 592
Kapi DCJ 68–70, 254–5, 298, 333, 547

Kaputin J 547
Keith LJ 435
Kelly J 578
Kidu DCJ 547, 657
Kimuli, M 447–8
King J 325–6
Kirby P 238, 461
Kitto J 616

Land Groups Act 187–90, 202, 708
Land (Ownership of Freeholds) Act 233
Land Registration Act 519, 546–51
Land Tenure Conversion Act 190
land transactions 94, 271–2, 659
Lawrence J 163–4
Laws Adoption and Adaptation Act 530
Lawyers Act 536
Lay J 244, 246, 253–5, 267–9
leases 539, 555–6
"legal personality" concept 173, 229, 231, 239, 242, 257, 647, 682
Lenalia J 594
lex mercatoria 135–6
"liabilities" defined for purposes of solvency test 487
libel 165
lien, right of 64–6, 110, 116
Lightman J 545
limited liability 186, 189, 192, 195, 204–5, 229, 234–8, 712
"Limited" or "Ltd", use of 216, 219, 235
limited partnerships 681
Lindley LJ 104, 111–12, 643, 672
liquidation of companies 235, 263, 360, 528, 559, 632
  court-ordered 567
  duration of 564
  effect of commencement of 603–7
  following breakdown of "mutual trust and confidence" 569–71
  following deadlock 572–3
  following directors' acting in their own interests 573–4
  following failure of substratum 571–2
  following fraud or misconduct 570–1
  on grounds of insolvency 585–6
  "just and equitable" grounds for 263, 361–2, 568–72
  objectives and principles of 562–3
  prohibition of legal proceedings during 604–6
  in the public interest 574
  as a shareholder remedy 360–8
  voluntary 361, 564–7, 607
liquidators 574–85
  appointment of 576–85
  duties of 607–9
  interim or *provisional* 578–9
  powers of 609–16
  registration of 576
  reporting function of 608
  supervision of 613–15
livestock trade 63
loan capital 474–5
Lopes LJ 132
Los J 298, 333

Macnaghten LJ 102, 237, 503
Malynes, Gerard de 135
management committees of business groups 712–13
managers of companies, authority of 418
managing directors (MDs) 279, 412, 416–18
mandates for banking services 159–62
Manning Committee (1962–64) 149–50
Mansfield CJ 135
Manuhu J 112, 533–4
market overt doctrine on sale of goods 53–4
Married Women's Property Act 535
Mason CJ 399–400
Matthew J 161
mediation, use of 84
memoranda of association 219, 230, 396
mens rea offences 386, 655
mental disorder 131–2; *see also* unsoundness of mind
mercantile agents 46–8, 52–3
merchantable quality 18, 22–7
Mining Development Act 535
minority shareholders 569
  exclusion from management 355
  remedies for 345–6, 361
minors 131–2; *see also* infants
misapplication of money and property 655
misappropriation rule for company directors 305–8

misrepresentation 679
missionary organisations 197
mitigation of loss 70, 80
Mocatta J 142
money laundering 145
mortgages and mortgaged property 140, 502, 545–50
motor vehicle drivers 115
Murphy J 148

Nali, Michael 695
"national companies" 271
National Court of Papua New Guinea
  and agency law 96
  and company capacity 241, 258, 260, 265
  and company financing 497, 514
  and corporate liability 402, 470–1
  and directors' duties 281–4
  and incorporated business groups 715–16
  and liquidation 564–7, 575–8, 581–4, 587, 591–2, 599–605, 611–14, 620–3
  and receivership 529–33, 548, 550, 554, 558–9
  and sale of goods 76, 82
  and shareholder remedies 347, 350, 361–3, 366–7, 374–6
  "national enterprises" 271
National Housing Corporation 267, 269
natural justice 242–3, 258
negative pledges 506, 526
negligence 166–8, 550, 557–8
  contributory 168–9
negotiable financial instruments 133–40
  history of 134–7
  nature of 137–40
nemo dat principle 43–4, 134
  exceptions to 43–54
New Zealand 217–18, 240–1, 244, 273, 297–8, 301, 323, 332, 345, 358, 362–4, 375, 398–401, 473, 536, 593–4, 620
  Law Commission 199, 308, 317, 486
  see also High Court of New Zealand
Nicholson J 461
nominee directors 276, 280–1, 318–19, 329
non-delivery of goods 75–6
non-executive directors 278
North J 641

obedience, agents' duty of 106
O'Donovan, J 534
offsetting claims against creditors 597
Olewale, Ebia 705
Ollerenshaw J 584
onerous property, disclaiming of 611–12
oppressive conduct by companies 343–58, 368–61; *see also* "harsh or oppressive acts"
oral contracts 7
order cheques 152
"ordinary course of business" 47–8, 53, 619–21
ordinary shares 478–9
Organic Law on the Integrity of Political Parties and Candidates 202, 535
Organic Law on Provincial Governments and Local-level Governments 198
"organic" theory of liability 379–81, 384
ostensible (or apparent) authority 97–101, 409–11, 421–42, 458, 649–51
overseas companies 206–8, 372, 516, 588
  legal status of 233
  liquidation of 209–10
  registration of 208–9

Papua New Guinea Banking Corporation (PNGBC) 247–50, 269
parent companies 227, 243, 253–5, 262, 617
pari passu principle of liquidation 563, 618
participating preference shares 481
partners
  calculated prejudicial conduct by 672
  deceased 644, 654, 668–9, 677
  expulsion of 665–6
  implied powers of 650–1
  insolvency of 669
  introduction of 662, 667
  permanent incapacity of 671
  relationships with firm's clients 648–52
  retirement of 666–7
  rights and duties of 659–65
partnership 181–2, 234, 635–82, 706–7

asset distributions 680–1
business accounts 664
business conducted at a loss 672–3
contract basis of 636–7
definition of 637–46
as distinct from corporate status 639–40
formation of 646–8
liabilities of firms 653
property of firms 658
termination of 665–81
partnership agreements 641, 648, 676
persistent breaches of 672
variation of 657–8
Partnerships Act 535, 635–41, 646–59, 663–81
passing off, tort of 214, 217
patents 521
payment orders 152
Pearson, LJ 100–1, 434
Pennycuick J 581–2
perpetual succession 188, 192, 195, 234, 236
personal actions against companies or their directors 341–3, 346–7, 368–71, 615
personal liability
of business group committee members 712
for company debts 243
of directors for improper share issues 489
of receivers 556–8
petitions 194
plantation redistribution scheme 189
Police Offences (Rubbish Dumping) Act (1969) 390–1
Port Moresby Stock Exchange 184, 205, 236, 282
possession of goods
by buyers 51
consent to 51–2
delivery of 55–6
by sellers 50
power of attorney 95, 111
irrevocable 118–19
Pratt J 403, 405
pre-emptive rights of shareholders 483
preference shares 479–81, 499
preferential creditors 505, 559–60, 629–31
preferential transactions 618
pre-incorporation contracts 224–5, 262
pre-receivership contracts 555–6
presumption of inability to pay debts 586
rebuttal of 602–4
presumptive intentions of contracting parties 36
price reductions 24
Prices Regulation Act 388
Priestley JA 461–2
principals
consent to be bound by agents' acts 93
legal capacity to act 91–2, 103
named and disclosed 111
remedies for agents' breaches of faith 108–9, 113
undisclosed 111–14
Pritchard J 96, 242, 388–9, 415
private companies 205
Privatization Act 269–70
Privatization Commission 247–50, 269–70
privity of contract 134
Privy Council 13–16, 20, 129, 168, 231, 312, 571, 636
profit rule for company directors 305
profits of partnerships
accountability for 664
sharing of 642–3, 660
promissory notes 138
promoters of companies 262–3
proper purposes
common law doctrine of 310–17
as possible part of underlying law 315–17
use of company directors' powers for 308–10
proprietary companies 203–6
public companies 205
Public Curator 197
"public" documents 466
"public interest" liquidations 574

quality of goods being sold 17–18, 75
quantum meruit 109
qui facit per alium per se 91
quiet enjoyment of goods 31–2

Raine J 295
ratification 93, 101–4, 469–73, 651

Reading, Lord 165
receivers
  appointment of 529–37, 554–5, 602
  disqualification of 536–7
  duties of 543–52
  liabilities of 554–8
  notification and reporting functions of 552–4
  powers of 541–3, 546–51
  status of 537–9
receivership 360, 528–61
  and contracts 557
  court supervision of 558–9
  effect on debtor companies 539–41
  general and *particular* 543
  types of 528–9
rectification of company records 360
redemption of shares 493–5
refunding of purchase price of goods 80
Register of Charges 507–10, 515–17, 526
Registrar of Associations 195
Registrar of Business Groups 185–6, 712–19
Registrar of Companies 204, 208–17, 220, 261, 284–5, 290, 450, 453, 455, 483, 503, 507–19, 526, 554, 558–9, 564, 567, 575, 582, 693, 704, 707–10
Registrar of Co-operatives 694–5, 699–704
Registrar of Incorporated Land Groups 189
registration of companies 210–12, 228
Regulatory Statutory Authorities (Appointment to Certain Offices) Act 287–8
Reid, Lord 23, 385
rejection of goods 18, 70–4
reliance on sellers' descriptions of goods 20–1
remuneration committees 293
repossession of goods 32
representations in relation to contracts 13
representative actions against companies or their directors 341–3
repudiation of contracts 68
repurchase of shares 492
re-registration of existing companies 212–13
reselling of goods 78
"responsible officers" of companies 427–9
"retention of title" clauses 523
Reynolds, F M B 421
Richardson J 351–3
Richmond J 161
Rickett, C E F 398–9
risks
  to goods themselves 58
  in sale of goods 40–2
Rogers AJA 240, 244
"Romalpa" clauses 523
Romer LJ 319–20, 504
Russell, Lord 110

Sakora AJ 380, 383, 395, 425–8, 439, 444–5
sale of goods
  by agents 45–6
  law of 3–12
  in a *market overt* 53–4
  performance of contracts for 55–63
  "sale or return" contracts 39, 41
Salika J 244, 256–9, 266–7, 407–9, 430–1
Salmon LJ 291
samples as basis for sales 27–9
savings and loans societies 191–3
savings banks 126
Scarman LJ 148–9
Scrutton LJ 165
secrecy in banking 144–6
secured creditors 497, 501–2, 528–9, 538, 559–61, 563, 629
Securities Act 535
sellers of goods
  duties of 55–61
  remedies for breach of contract 63–70
separate legal entities, doctrine of
  companies as 227–33, 237–9
  disregard of 243–72
  exceptions to 243
servants, employment of 89–90
services, provision of 10–11
set-off
  between creditors 598
  for third parties to contracts 114
setting aside

of uncommercial transactions 626–8
of voidable transactions and charges 623–4
several liability 653
"shadow" directors 277, 280
share capital *see* equity capital
share dealings by company directors, disclosure of 329–31
share options 484
share transfers, voiding of 606
shareholders 183–4, 220, 231–4, 474, 499, 565
definition of 580
discount schemes for 490
powers of 281–2, 294–7, 606–7
protection of minorities 222
remedies available to 341–78; statutory 347–60; through liquidation 361–8
rights of 365–8, 483; infringement of 341–2
shares 474–5
allotment of 482–3
buybacks 220
buyouts 223, 358–9, 492, 496–7
classes of 477–61
financial assistance for purchase of 495–6
issue of 311–13, 357–8, 476, 481–3
issued instead of dividends 490–1
nature of 476–7
redemption of 493–5
repurchase of 492
rights attaching to 477
shelf-companies 210
single shareholder-director companies 228–9, 255, 417–18
Slade LJ 99, 442
small businesses 175–6, 180–2, 277–8
Smith, Sir Montague 643
sole agents 88–9
sole proprietorship 174–81, 184
solvency test 486–9, 494
special damages 78
special property 8, 10
"specific goods" 34–9, 58, 71–2
"specific performance" remedy 81–2
spot contracts 63
stale cheques 159
stale statutory demands 601
state, the, definition of 265–7, 270
statutory authorities, regulatory 287–8
statutory bodies 195–6, 267
statutory demands
abuse of 601
failure to comply with 586–7
issuing of 587–90
responding to 590–1
setting aside of 592–600
stale 601
statutory injunctions 362–5
statutory managers 535
stolen goods 54
stoppage of goods in transit 65–6, 110–11
Street J 395–6
subordination of a debt 525–6
subsidiary companies 227, 238, 251–5, 319
"substantive" as distinct from "formal" authority 458
substratum, failure of 571–2
Supreme Court of New South Wales 129, 147–8
Supreme Court of Papua New Guinea 41–2, 57–8, 65, 98, 241–4, 261, 265, 269–71, 298–9, 316, 320, 333, 352, 424, 440, 444, 530, 547, 605–6
Supreme Court of Queensland 37, 349
Supreme Court of Victoria 338
Supreme Court of Western Australia 6, 360
suspected offences, notification of 609
Swinfen Eady LJ 642

Tadgell J 320
Tashjian, P C 192–3
tax avoidance 270
terrorism 145
third parties to contracts, remedies for 116
third party election 113
time, lapse of 74
time as an essential item in a contract 59–60
Tomlin J 162
tort 108, 115–16, 164, 381, 393, 654–5
trade marks 521
trading banks 125–6
trading solvency 486

transactions
  definition of 619
  for inadequate or excessive consideration 628–9
  uncommercial 263, 626–8
transfer of property 7–8, 34–43, 133–4, 224
  consequences of 40
transfer of title to goods 43–55
travellers' cheques 138–9
trespass 557–8
tribes 201, 709
trusts and trusteeship 90, 111, 183, 506–7, 655–6
Turquand's case, rule of *see* "indoor management" rule

ultra vires acts 103, 226, 394, 396
"unascertained goods" 34–6, 39–40
uncommercial transactions 263, 626–8
unconditional appropriation of goods 40
unconditional contracts 36–7, 72
unconditional sale of goods 42
underlying law
  on duties of directors 299–310, 319–20
  on priority of charges 524–6
  on receivership 528, 536, 538, 556–7, 560
Underlying Law Act 240–1
unincorporated businesses 174–82
  advantages and disadvantages of 184
unpaid sellers 64, 66
unsoundness of mind 92, 283, 671; *see also* mental disorder
Upjohn J 68–9
"usual" authority 97, 415, 421, 433; *see also* customary authority

vertically-integrated companies 227
vested rights 104, 117–19
vicarious liability 89, 381–6, 389–93
void or voidable contracts 47–8, 119
void or voidable transactions 131–2, 618–26
voluntary liquidation 361, 564–7, 607

wages, receivers' liability for payment of 556–7
waiving of rights 59–60
warranties 14–15
  implied 31–2
  see also breach of warranty
Watson, Lord 114
Watson, S M 296
Wespac Bank 123, 125
Wilberforce, Lord 19, 22
Williams J 163
Wilson J 76
winding-up
  of companies *see* liquidation
  of incorporated business groups 715–17
Wood V-C 676
Woods J 25, 83, 252–3
Workers' Compensation Act 175
Wright LJ 164, 470

Yeats J 26

For Product Safety Concerns and Information please contact our EU
representative GPSR@taylorandfrancis.com
Taylor & Francis Verlag GmbH, Kaufingerstraße 24, 80331 München, Germany

www.ingramcontent.com/pod-product-compliance
Ingram Content Group UK Ltd.
Pitfield, Milton Keynes, MK11 3LW, UK
UKHW022211190926
475702UK00003B/311

* 9 7 8 0 4 1 5 4 2 5 3 2 2 *